THE HISTORY AND THEORY
OF INTERNATIONAL LAW

The Law of Nations
in Global History

THE HISTORY AND THEORY OF INTERNATIONAL LAW

General Editors

Nehal Bhuta
Professor of Public International Law, European University Institute

Anthony Pagden
Distinguished Professor, University of California Los Angeles

Benjamin Straumann
Alberico Gentili Senior Fellow, New York University School of Law

In the past few decades the understanding of the relationship between nations has undergone a radical transformation. The role of the traditional nation state is diminishing, along with many of the traditional vocabularies which were once used to describe what has been called, ever since Jeremy Bentham coined the phrase in 1780, 'international law'. The older boundaries between states are growing ever more fluid, new conceptions and new languages have emerged which are slowly coming to replace the image of a world of sovereign independent nation states which has dominated the study of international relations since the early nineteenth century. This redefinition of the international arena demands a new understanding of classical and contemporary questions in international and legal theory. It is the editors' conviction that the best way to achieve this is by bridging the traditional divide between international legal theory, intellectual history, and legal and political history. The aim of the series, therefore, is to provide a forum for historical studies, from classical antiquity to the twenty-first century, that are theoretically informed and for philosophical work that is historically conscious, in the hope that a new vision of the rapidly evolving international world, its past and its possible future, may emerge.

PREVIOUSLY PUBLISHED IN THIS SERIES

International Law and Empire
Historical Explanations
Edited by Martti Koskenniemi, Walter Rech, and Manuel Jiménez Fonseca

Formalizing Displacement
International Law and Population Transfers
Umut Özsu

C. H. Alexandrowicz, Madras, November 1960

Reproduced with the kind permission of the University of Sydney Archives (G3/187)

C. H. ALEXANDROWICZ

The Law of Nations in Global History

Edited by
DAVID ARMITAGE
and
JENNIFER PITTS

OXFORD
UNIVERSITY PRESS

OXFORD
UNIVERSITY PRESS

Great Clarendon Street, Oxford, OX2 6DP,
United Kingdom

Oxford University Press is a department of the University of Oxford.
It furthers the University's objective of excellence in research, scholarship,
and education by publishing worldwide. Oxford is a registered trade mark of
Oxford University Press in the UK and in certain other countries

First Edition published in 2017

Published in the United States of America by Oxford University Press
198 Madison Avenue, New York, NY 10016, United States of America

British Library Cataloguing in Publication Data
Data available

Library of Congress Control Number: 2017930520

ISBN 978–0–19–876607–0

Series Editors' Preface

The historian of international law Charles Henry Alexandrowicz (1902–75) is today largely forgotten, but, as the present volume shows, his scholarship was in many ways prescient and offers a refreshing view with a deep historical perspective. The underlying picture of world history in many ways anticipates more recent scholarship in world and economic history. The weight Alexandrowicz attributes to Asian and African polities in their political, legal, and commercial relations with early modern Europe contradicts earlier, more Eurocentric, accounts, but it resonates very well with the work of the late Christopher Bayly, or Kenneth Pomeranz, or John Darwin, to name but a few prominent examples. Indeed, Alexandrowicz might be said to have pioneered, from the angle of the history of what he called the 'classic law of nations,' much that is being written under the label of global history today.

The following elements of Alexandrowicz's underlying picture of world history deserve mention. Alexandrowicz wrote many of his most original essays and articles during his tenure at the University of Madras in newly independent India. For him, historical study was emphatically neither antiquarian nor historicist, but assumed political and normative urgency. As a result of his historical scholarship he thought that he was in a position to claim that there had existed, before 1800, a long-standing universal international order that had included as a matter of course non-European empires and states, among them newly independent states such as India. It followed for Alexandrowicz that world-historically speaking colonialism was but a blip—'ideological cataclysm' in the early nineteenth century had introduced a parochial period of European colonial states that acknowledged only each other as sovereigns. In the bigger historical picture, however, this was the exception rather than the rule, Alexandrowicz thought. Nineteenth- and twentieth-century colonialism emerges in Alexandrowicz's thought in lockstep with what he considered a pernicious jurisprudential doctrine, positivism. Interestingly, it might even be said that colonialism for him appeared more intimately connected with this jurisprudential outlook than with either empire or even Eurocentrism. As David Armitage and Jennifer Pitts point out in their learned introduction, Alexandrowicz did not conceive of colonialism in terms of empire, and he did not think colonialism was exclusive to non-European continents. An Austro-Hungarian citizen by birth and of Polish background, Alexandrowicz saw the partitions of Poland in a similar light as European colonialism in Asia and Africa. There was continuity to Poland's statehood from the partitions in the eighteenth century to 1918 (whether conceived along Roman lines in terms of *postliminium* or simply as reversion to sovereignty) as there was continuity to Ceylon's or Madagascar's statehood during colonial rule, and there were important parallels between the normative orders associated with the Holy Roman Empire and the Mughal Empire.

While Alexandrowicz was almost certainly wrong to claim that Asian state practice had shaped the early modern law of nations in any direct way (his example was Grotius, whose early work he thought was influenced by what he knew of East Indian norms and practice, but we now know that Grotius was not in fact so influenced), he was certainly correct in the overall picture he drew of Asian and African empires and states interacting as sovereigns with European empires and states. He was also right in giving the appropriate weight to the commercial character of these relationships, and their normative consequences. The contribution of East Indian trade and the treaty-regimes with various Asian commercial states to the development of an early modern international order was crucial to Alexandrowicz not least because of its universalist implications. What he termed the classic law of nations, that is to say the global normative order that prevailed in the centuries before the Congress of Vienna (1815), was in his view based on universal natural law, while the parochial, Eurocentric order afterward was governed by a normatively arbitrary positivism based exclusively on power politics.

Alexandrowicz's assessment of the earlier law of nations was overly nostalgic and represented the projection of a normative ideal. What he perceived as a system of reciprocity and equal sovereignty of states constrained and held together by a classic law of nations was in reality no such thing. Rather, to the extent that European states accepted reciprocity and equality in their dealings with extra-European polities they did so because they were simply not in a position to subdue these polities. They accepted reciprocity, in other words, simply because they had to, lacking the power for legal or informal subordination. Sometimes, as was the case for the Dutch in Japan from the seventeenth century deep into the nineteenth, Europeans had to accept humiliating terms simply to maintain trading relationships. Whenever there was equality and reciprocity it existed as the outcome of equilibrium or, at best, as the result of commercial sociability and enlightened self-interest. Nor was there of course ever a perfectly reciprocal 'Westphalian' *ius publicum Europaeum* even in Europe, as Alexandrowicz would have been the first to admit.

When Alexandrowicz's vision of a universal law of nations did at last become a reality of sorts, after decolonization, this universalization of international law paradoxically came about, as Jörg Fisch has pointed out, as the result of European weakness, not strength. According to Fisch, the decline of European power brought about a normative system of universal sovereign equality and reciprocity which, albeit—*pace* Alexandrowicz—recognizably European in origin, had even in Europe only ever been accepted reluctantly, if that. While European states had power, they prevented this normative order from having any force in their dealings with the outside world, but once they were sufficiently weakened, it was a normative order that seemed very attractive to the newly decolonized states. 'International society has become a worldwide system not due to European power, but in consequence of European decline', according to Fisch. To the extent that this system represents a universal ideal of inherent normative attraction that is not inherently or specifically European it is very much congenial to the universal order at once described and aimed at by Alexandrowicz: his classic law of nations. The present collection of Alexandrowicz's little known essays and articles complete with a scholarly introduction will undermine our deeply ingrained positivist myopia and will make us see the very category of Eurocentrism from a fresh, cosmopolitan Central European angle.

Benjamin Straumann

New York City
August 2016

Preface

In recent years there has been a growing awareness of the need to write a global history of law of nations that disengages from parochial national and regional histories. It is hoped that these developments will bring centre-stage the work of Charles Henry Alexandrowicz, a scholar who was among the first to conceptualize the history of international law as that of intersecting histories of different regions of the world. Alexandrowicz was aware that, while the idea of writing a global history of law of nations is liberating, there is no guarantee that it will not become the handmaiden of contemporary and future imperial projects. What were needed were critical global histories that provincialize established Eurocentric historiographies and read them alongside other regional histories.

Alexandrowicz began writing on the history of law of nations in Asia during a decade-long stay in India (1951–61). He arrived there a mere four years after India had attained independence from British rule. These were early and crucial years in the life of the nation. At the time, there was some churning going on in the infant Indian discipline of international law. While there were only a handful of 'international lawyers' it was felt there was a need to decolonize the history of international law through writing about the prevalence of rules of international law in pre-colonial India. The move was important in three different contexts. First, by describing a common corpus of inter-state rules of conduct in pre-colonial India, international law scholars could affirm the civilizational unity of India. Second, such an effort helped demonstrate that pre-colonial Indian states dealt with European nations on an equal footing, thereby sustaining the growing view that independent India and other Asian states should play a central role in world affairs. (This sentiment received a fillip when India, along with Indonesia, played a leadership role in the 1955 Bandung Conference.) Third, there was the ongoing debate as to whether newly independent states should subscribe to an international law that was colonial in origin. In this respect the claim that Asian states contributed to the development of international law lent coherence to the proposed dualistic approach—accepting international law but simultaneously striving to transform it for the benefit of peoples of third world nations. It also gelled with the view that the problem with modern international law was its colonial content and not its inherent nature and character. The significance of the work of Alexandrowicz lies in the fact that he addressed all these issues through his pioneering scholarship.

Alexandrowicz was sensitive not only to the postcolonial context in which he found himself but more generally to the fate of weak nations derived from the history of his native country of Poland. The combination of parallel situations and converging biography gave him a unique vantage point from which to offer a distinctive history of international law. By the time he started working on the history of the law of nations, the standard narrative of international law as a product of

European Christian civilization had long been part of western textbooks such as Lassa Oppenheim's *International Law* (1905, and later editions). The first edition of Arthur Nussbaum's well known but Eurocentric *A Concise History of the Law of Nations* (1947) had also just been published. These texts contained what may be called monologic histories of international law, which continue to be written even today, underline the continuing significance of his work.

Against such unilateral histories, Alexandrowicz proceeded to write a dialogic history of international law. He spent time researching unpublished archives of the Record Office in Madras, where he resided, and in other cities, to understand the engagement of India and Asia with international law and the role it had played in the relationship with European nations. In the years that Alexandrowicz was writing, contributions were being made by Indian researchers such as K. A. N. Shastri, Hiralal Chatterjee, M. K. Nawaz, and C. J. Chacko, the last of whom delivered the Hague Academy lectures in 1958 on the subject of 'India's Contribution to the Field of International Law Concepts'. His own theses were validated during his lifetime by the International Court of Justice in the *Right of Passage over Indian Territory* case (Portugal–India) (1960) which *inter alia* treated as valid a treaty concluded in 1779 between Portugal and Maratha rulers.

Alexandrowicz distinctively recognized that colonialism did not influence the evolution and development of international law in a singular way. The colonizers encountered different situations in different regions and responded to them accordingly. While colonialism and imperialism are necessarily central to all accounts of histories of modern international law written from a non-western perspective, these often conflate different encounters that have distinct trajectories. It is however important not to flatten out what is a rugged field. For instance, the history of the law of nations in what Alexandrowicz called the 'East Indies' assumed a different course from that in sixteenth-century Spanish America. In the circumstances, he was not interested in fashioning a general theory but narrated a regional history of international law that needed to be taken into account in telling the global history of the law of nations. He documented and evidenced the view that Asian states were active participants in the shaping of the law of nations in the pre-colonial period. This claim was not about Asia having international law in the manner of Europe, as it is sometimes interpreted; it was instead a necessary corrective to narrow and apologist histories.

The historian Eric Hobsbawm observed that in the non-western world academic history was either absent or did not come of age till the last quarter of the twentieth century. Today, as non-western histories mark their presence, there is for the first time the possibility of writing an authentic global history of law of nations as these histories address crucial absences and silences in the official history written in the western world. It is therefore ironic that just as the turn to history has come about in the field of international law the interest in it has waned in Asia and Africa. The perception is that while attempts to retrieve pre-colonial history had a certain role to play in the initial years after independence there are more urgent issues to attend to today. Such a view is myopic as the need for retrieving pre-colonial histories is necessary in order to shape a transcivilizational approach to international law. For this we need to undertake detailed excavation of the culture, practices, and rules which over the centuries constituted law of nations in different civilizations of the world. The recovery of regional histories of international law must therefore be an ongoing exercise as professional historians make new materials available on the pre-colonial history of African and Asian nations. It hardly needs to be added that a transcivilizational approach will greatly strengthen the fabric of contemporary international law. A glimpse of such an effort can be seen in Sri Lankan Judge Christopher Weeramantry's opinions on the International Court of Justice in the *Legality of Nuclear Weapons* (1996) and the *Gabčíkovo-Nagymaros Project* (1997) cases.

Alexandrowicz's work profoundly complements new non-western histories of international law that reveal continuity in the conceptual and doctrinal apparatus of the discipline in the colonial and postcolonial worlds. The two histories—of the existence of international legal practices in the pre-colonial world and the continuing reproduction of imperial doctrines and concepts in the present—have the common objective of displacing a provincial history of international law, the one through recording past practices in the non-western world and the other by examining how European international law came to be constituted through its engagement with the colonial project. Alexandrowicz's history provides an important corrective to an over-elaborated thesis about imperialism that denies agency to both the pre-colonial and postcolonial states. In short, anyone interested in the history of international law, or in understanding how contemporary international law can play a progressive role, cannot afford to neglect his writings. Any history of the writing of a dialogic, plural, and democratic history of international law must give Alexandrowicz pride of place. It is worth recalling here that his work had a profound impact on Indian scholars like R. P. Anand who carried forward his legacy even as he made his own distinctive contribution to the telling of the story of international law.

It is hoped that this collection will make Alexandrowicz's writings more widely available and read. David Armitage and Jennifer Pitts have rendered a great service to the community of historians and international lawyers by reprinting his seminal essays. Their perceptive introduction succinctly sums up the context, issues, problems, and questions that engaged Alexandrowicz, as well as some of his central theses. His writings are a gold mine waiting to be explored: it is surprising that this work has not received, from international lawyers, the kind of attention that the writings of other distinguished European scholars, Hersch Lauterpacht or Hans Kelsen for instance, have gained for their reflections on the function of law in the international community. Alexandrowicz contributed to the effort of promoting the idea of international rule of law by rejecting a Eurocentric history and theory of international law. It is particularly disappointing that the non-western world has not yet paid the tribute it should have to this extraordinary scholar who inspired so many Asians and Africans to write the history of international law in their respective regions. We cannot afford to forget his trailblazing contributions.

B. S. Chimni

Acknowledgements

Tracking C. H. Alexandrowicz's fugitive articles and farflung life has been a labour of the left hand for many years. For help and encouragement along the way, we are indebted to Tony Anghie, Renu Barrett, Upendra Baxi, the late Chris Bayly, Arnulf Becker Lorca, Lauren Benton, Eyal Benvenisti, Nehal Bhuta, Tony Blackshield, B. S. Chimni, Mark Curthoys, Richard Davies, Rohit De, Anna di Robilant (and the Elizabeth Battelle Clark Legal History Series at the Boston University School of Law), Joanna Epstein, Andrew Fitzmaurice, Marc Galanter, James Gathii, Stella Ghervas, Afroditi Giovanopoulou, Magdalena Głogowska, Pierre-Emmanuel Jacob, Alison Johnson, Ashraf Khan, Sunil Khilnani, Madhav Khosla, Klaudia Kierepka, Benedict Kingsbury, Harshan Kumarasingham, James Loeffler, Emma Mackinnon, Malgorzata Mazurek, Darrin McMahon, Ilana Miller, Denise Monbarren, Jacqueline Mowbray, S. Muthiah, Monika Nalepa, Anthony Pagden, Vengrai Parthasarathy, Lyndel Prott, Vikram Raghavan, H. S. Gururaja Rao, N. Ravi, Katharina Rietzler, Joan-Pau Rubiés, Philippe Sands, Roma Sendyka, Mira Siegelberg, Nyree Simpson, Paulina Starski, Tristan Stein, Andrzej Suchcitz, Michael Tworek, Natasha Wheatley, Jacobine Wieringa, and Tara Zahra. Warmest thanks also go to the University of Chicago's Neubauer Collegium for Culture and Society for supporting our collaboration.

For permission to reproduce Alexandrowicz's works, we are grateful to these organizations and their representatives:

The American Society for International Law (chs. 16, 22, and 25);

Annales. Histoire, Sciences sociales (ch. 6);

Cambridge University Press (chs. 17, 26);

Elsevier (ch. 19);

Oxford University Press (chs. 1, 2, 8, 11, 13, 23, and 24);

The Royal Institute of International Affairs (ch. 27);

Sage Publications (chs. 28, 29);

The United Nations Institute for Training and Research (ch. 20).

We owe special thanks to Kenny Chumbley for his tireless help in securing permissions.

The essays and articles collected here first appeared in the following publications; in line with Press policy, their original house styles have been retained:

1. 'Kautilyan Principles and the Law of Nations', *British Year Book of International Law*, 41 (1965–66), 301–20.

2. 'Paulus Vladimiri and the Development of the Doctrine of the Coexistence of Christian and Non-Christian Countries', *British Year Book of International Law*, 39 (1963), 441–48.
3. 'Mogul Sovereignty and the Law of Nations', *The Indian Year Book of International Affairs*, 4 (1955), 316–24.
4. '"Jus Gentium" and the Law of Nature in Asia', *The Aryan Path*, 27 (1956), 13–19.
5. 'Some Problems in the History of the Law of Nations in Asia', *The Indian Year Book of International Affairs*, 12 (1963), 3–11.
6. 'Le Droit des Nations aux Indes Orientales: Aux XVIe, XVIIe, XVIIIe siècles', *Annales. Histoire, Sciences Sociales*, 19 (1964), 869–84, 1066–84.
7. 'Grotius and India', *The Indian Year Book of International Affairs*, 3 (1954), 357–67.
8. 'Freitas *Versus* Grotius', *British Year Book of International Law*, 35 (1959), 162–82.
9. 'The Discriminatory Clause in South Asian Treaties in the Seventeenth and Eighteenth Centuries', *The Indian Year Book of International Affairs*, 6 (1957), 126–42.
10. 'A Persian-Dutch Treaty in the Seventeenth Century', *The Indian Year Book of International Affairs*, 7 (1958), 201–06.
11. 'Puffendorf-Crull and the Afro-Asian World', *British Year Book of International Law*, 43 (1968–69), 205–08.
12. 'A Treatise by J. H. G. Justi on Asian Government', *The Indian Year Book of International Affairs*, 9–10 (1960), 136–42.
13. 'Doctrinal Aspects of the Universality of the Law of Nations', *British Year Book of International Law*, 37 (1961), 506–15.
14. 'G. F. de Martens on Asian Treaty Practice', *The Indian Year Book of International Affairs*, 13, pt. II (1964), 59–77.
15. 'The Continuity of the Sovereign Status of China in International Law', *The Indian Year Book of International Affairs*, 5 (1956), 84–94.
16. 'The Legal Position of Tibet', *American Journal of International Law*, 48 (1954), 265–74.
17. 'Is India a Federation?', *The International and Comparative Law Quarterly*, 3 (1954), 393–403.
18. 'Le rôle des traités dans les relations entre les puissances européennes et les souverains africains (Aspects historiques)', *Revue internationale du droit comparé*, 22 (1970), 703–09.
19. 'The Partition of Africa by Treaty', in Kenneth Ingham, ed., *Foreign Relations of African States: Proceedings of the Twentyfifth Symposium of the*

Colston Research Society Held in the University of Bristol, April 4th to 7th, 1973 (London, 1974), pp. 129–57.

20. 'The Role of Treaties in the European-African Confrontation in the Nineteenth Century', in A. K. Mensah-Brown, ed., *African International Legal History* (New York, 1975), pp. 27–68, 191–99.
21. 'The Role of German Treaty Making in the Partition of Africa', *The Indian Year Book of International Affairs*, 18, pt. II (1980), 161–203.
22. 'The Juridical Expression of the Sacred Trust of Civilization', *American Journal of International Law*, 65 (1971), 149–59.
23. 'Empirical and Doctrinal Positivism in International Law', *British Year Book of International Law*, 47 (1974–75), 286–89.
24. 'The Theory of Recognition *in Fieri*', *British Year Book of International Law*, 34 (1958), 176–98.
25. 'The Quasi-Judicial Function in the Recognition of States and Governments', *American Journal of International Law*, 46 (1952), 631–40.
26. 'Israel *in Fieri*', *International Law Quarterly*, 4 (1951), 423–30.
27. 'New and Original States: The Issue of Reversion to Sovereignty', *International Affairs*, 45 (1969), 465–80.
28. 'The New States and International Law', *Millennium*, 3 (1974), 226–33.
29. 'The Charter of Economic Rights and Duties of States', *Millennium*, 4 (1975), 72–74.

Every effort has been made to trace copyright holders. Any outstanding claims to copyright may be addressed to the publisher.

All URLs were current as of 1 November 2016.

David Armitage and Jennifer Pitts

Cambridge, Mass., and Chicago
November 2016

Contents

‘THIS MODERN GROTIUS’

AN INTRODUCTION TO THE LIFE AND THOUGHT OF C. H. ALEXANDROWICZ

We may be able to learn from the past what the present is unable to teach us.
(C. H. Alexandrowicz)[1]

Since the late nineteenth century, international law has taken something of a roller-coaster ride. The most influential account of its trajectory has argued for a slow, painful ‘rise’ beginning in the 1870s, followed by a swiftly accelerating ‘fall’ to its nadir in the 1960s.[2] Yet, as so often happens, anxieties about irrelevance inspired resurgence. In the closing years of the twentieth century, the fortunes of international law started to climb again, beyond the academy as well as within it. As two of its leading practitioners (including the one who had earlier pronounced its obsequies) recently remarked, ‘From an exotic specialisation on the fringes of the law school, international law has turned during the twentieth century into a ubiquitous presence in global policy-making as well as in academic and journalistic commentary.’[3] This move from the margins foreshadowed a remarkable renaissance in the twenty-first century, when international law has become more ever-present in international relations, political theory, and history. Two factors stand out in explaining the latest ascent of international law: the impact of globalization and the return of history. These motives are novel but not unprecedented: as this introduction will show, they had converged productively before, starting in Madras in the 1950s, with consequences that have both lessons and cautions for the new history of international law in our own globalizing, historicist moment.

Globalization—the acceleration and thickening of transnational and interregional connections—exposed the limitations of ‘classic’ international law inherited

[1] C. H. Alexandrowicz (hereafter, CHA), ‘Introduction’, in Gesina H. J. van der Molen, ed., *Alberico Gentili and the Development of International Law: His Life, Work and Times*, 2nd revised edn (Leiden, 1968), p. ix.

[2] Martti Koskenniemi, *The Gentle Civilizer of Nations: The Rise and Fall of International Law, 1870–1960* (Cambridge, 2001).

[3] James Crawford and Martti Koskenniemi, ‘Introduction’, in Crawford and Koskenniemi, eds., *The Cambridge Companion to International Law* (Cambridge, 2012), p. 1.

from the nineteenth century. In particular, decolonization and post-colonial reconstruction revealed how reigning legal norms and established international institutions were dominated by the heirs of colonial empires and their hand-picked allies. The former objects of imperial subjection and control accordingly asserted their rights as subjects within a greatly expanded and fundamentally transformed international society. This led to a series of challenges to an international legal order that had been centred first on Europe, then on the Atlantic world, and finally in the organs of international and global governance that perpetuated structural inequality in all its forms. Following the Second World War, international lawyers from beyond the West—especially in Asia (South, East, and Southeast) and Africa—joined later proponents of 'Third-World Approaches to International Law' (TWAIL) and then self-critical international lawyers across the world in their efforts to provincialize Eurocentric international law and to propose robust alternative frameworks for regulating transnational relations.[4] As we shall see, one major taproot of this tendency can be traced to an unexpected origin in Central Europe between the wars, amid an earlier moment of imperial collapse and post-imperial reconstruction.

History became central to the late twentieth-century enterprise of globalizing international law. Uncovering the processes by which the international order had been formed in the past became an indispensable tool for reforming it in the future. Suppressed sovereignties could be reinstated and alternative distributions of power restored, not least by laying bare the machinations of the mighty over those whom they deliberately marginalized. The critical use of history reinforced a broader turn to the past which has been one of the most remarked-upon features of recent scholarship on international law.[5] The history of international law had a distinguished pre-history, of course, which stretched back to the earliest disciplinary accounts of the law of nations in the late eighteenth and nineteenth centuries by D. H. L. von Ompteda, G. F. von Martens, Robert Ward, Henry Wheaton, and others, and then forward to mid-twentieth-century works by Wilhelm Grewe, Arthur Nussbaum, and (more idiosyncratically) Carl Schmitt.[6] However, the history of international law had been mostly marginal to the discipline as a whole except when it could provide affirmatory just-so stories. Only when conjoined with postcolonial approaches could it become an effective vehicle of critique.

[4] Upendra Baxi, 'Some Remarks on Eurocentrism and the Law of Nations', in R. P. Anand, ed., *Asian States and the Development of International Law* (Delhi, 1972), pp. 3–9; Martti Koskenniemi, 'Histories of International Law: Dealing with Eurocentrism', *Zeitschrift des Max-Planck-Instituts für europäische Rechtsgeschichte*, 19 (2011), 152–76; Arnulf Becker Lorca, 'Eurocentrism in the History of International Law', in Bardo Fassbinder and Anne Peters, eds., *The Oxford Handbook of the History of International Law* (Oxford, 2012), pp. 1034–57.

[5] Philip Allott, 'International Law and the Idea of History', *Journal of the History of International Law*, 1 (1999), 1–21; George Rodrigo Bandeira Galindo, 'Martti Koskenniemi and the Historiographical Turn in International Law', *European Journal of International Law*, 16 (2005): 539–59; Alexander Orakhelashvili, 'The Relevance of Theory and History—The Essence and Origins of International Law', in Orakhelashvili, ed., *Research Handbook on the Theory and History of International Law* (Cheltenham, 2011), pp. 3–22; Matthew Craven, 'Theorising the Turn to History in International Law', in Anne Orford, Florian Hoffmann, and Martin Clark, eds., *The Oxford Handbook of the Theory of International Law* (Oxford, 2016), pp. 21–37.

[6] Martti Koskenniemi, 'A History of International Law Histories', in Fassbinder and Peters, eds., *The Oxford Handbook of the History of International Law*, pp. 943–71.

The origins of that critical rapprochement between the history of international law and criticism of the impact of empire lie in the work of the remarkable Polish–British scholar and lawyer, Charles Henry Alexandrowicz (1902–75).[7] Alexandrowicz pioneered historical study of international law in its extra-European contexts, a vein of research that is now fundamental to the history of international law and to global history more generally. Unlike contemporary scholars who assume that international law was an exclusively European phenomenon, or those who find only Eurocentrism in various forms in the history of European thought on international and global affairs,[8] Alexandrowicz recognized international law's complicity with European imperial expansion and sought in history resources for a more egalitarian and less Eurocentric international order. In the era of decolonization, he used history to unsettle the 'orthodox view' that 'New States are faced with the *fait accompli* of the existing international legal order and must accept its principles as they find them.'[9] This critical historicist approach to the law of nations arose from interests in empire, statehood, and the continuity of legal identity that had begun in Poland in the inter-War period.

Alexandrowicz's beginnings in Austrian Galicia inspired questions that would animate his scholarship across a career spanning from the First World War to the zenith of decolonization, and from Kraków to Cambridge via London, Madras, and Sydney.[10] He was born Karol Aleksandrowicz in October 1902 in Lemberg (Lviv/Lwów), the son of Franciszek Aleksandrowicz (1856–1927), a major general in the Austro-Hungarian army who ended his career at the same rank in the Polish army after the First World War.[11] His mother, Maria Gregorowicz, claimed Scottish Jacobite descent: Karol's early education at Vienna's prestigious Catholic *Schottengymnasium*, at a time when few non-Viennese pupils attended the school, may thus have been somewhat overdetermined.[12] After the First World War, and

[7] Alexandrowicz published his work under various versions of his name: Karol Aleksandrowicz, Carolus Alexandrowicz, Karol Alexandrowicz, Charles Henry Alexander, C. H. Alexander, Charles Henry Alexandrowicz-Alexander, C. H. Alexandrowicz-Alexander, Charles Henry Alexandrowicz, and C. H. Alexandrowicz (the version by which he was and is best known). This diversity of spellings, along with the fact that many of the journals in which many of his early articles appeared have not been digitized, has occluded large parts of his oeuvre. With only a handful of exceptions, all the pieces collected here are being reprinted for the first time since their original publication: see the 'Bibliography of the Writings of C. H. Alexandrowicz', below.

[8] For example, John M. Hobson, *The Eurocentric Conception of World Politics: Western International Theory, 1760–2010* (Cambridge, 2012).

[9] CHA, 'The New States and International Law', *Millennium* 3 (1974), 226 (p. 404 below).

[10] Unless otherwise specified, biographical information in this and following paragraphs comes from CHA, 'Biographical Note', *Recueil des Cours*, 100 (1960), 205; T. S. Rama Rao, 'Introduction', *The Indian Year Book of International Affairs*, 11 (1962), vii–ix; *Who's Who* (London, 1974), p. 40; W. A. Steiner, 'Charles Henry Alexandrowicz (1902–1975)', *British Year Book of International Law*, 47 (1974–75), 269–71; Clive Parry, 'Obituary: Professor Charles Alexandrowicz', *The Australian Law Journal*, 49 (1975), 644; Rama Rao, 'Prof. C. H. Alexandrowicz: A Tribute', *The Indian Year Book of International Affairs*, 18, pt. II (1980), viii–xii.

[11] Piotr Stawecki, *Słownik biograficzny generałów Wojska Polskiego* (Warsaw, 1994), pp. 67–8; Henryk Piotr Kosk, *Generalicja polska: popularny słownik biograficzny* (Pruszków, 1998), p. 44.

[12] Marsha L. Rozenblit, *The Jews of Vienna, 1867–1914: Assimilation and Identity* (Albany, NY, 1983), p. 116.

the restoration of Polish statehood in 1919, he studied law at the Jagiellonian University in Kraków, where he took his doctorate in 1926, and published widely in the field of canon law. This might explain Alexandrowicz's later interest in what he called the 'Jagiellonian school of the law of nations' in the Middle Ages.[13] It certainly accounts for his lifelong interest in legal pluralism and the history of comparative law.

Alexandrowicz had emerged from the same milieu in Habsburg Galicia that produced two of the greatest legal theorists of the mid-twentieth century, Hersch Lauterpacht (1897–1960) and Raphael Lemkin (1900–59), both of whom were also brought up in Lemberg. If that city has an 'unexpected place' in the history of international law, then Alexandrowicz deserves consideration alongside his better known Jewish contemporaries there. Lauterpacht and Lemkin were both educated at the Jan Kazimierz University in Lemberg but Lemkin had previously spent a year in the Jagiellonian law faculty in 1919–20, just before Alexandrowicz studied there.[14] Unlike Lauterpacht—the Whewell Professor of International Law at Cambridge, QC, FBA, and Judge of the International Court of Justice (ICJ)—Alexandrowicz never scaled the peaks of academic and institutional eminence; nor did he help to shape international institutions or their emergent norms, unlike Lemkin, the only begetter of the Genocide Convention.[15] He held no permanent position in Britain; the United States was not on his intellectual trajectory, except for a year as a visiting professor in Ohio after retirement;[16] and unlike another contemporary, the Cambridge public lawyer Sir Ivor Jennings (1903–65), he never became an itinerant constitution-maker for new countries in the British Commonwealth.[17] He spent the bulk of his career on what might be called the intellectual semi-periphery, first in India (1951–61) and then in Australia (1961–67).[18] It was there, in the

[13] CHA, 'Paulus Vladimiri and the Development of the Doctrine of the Coexistence of Christian and Non-Christian Countries', *British Year Book of International Law*, 39 (1963), 448 n. 1 (p. 61 n. 28 below). See also the near-contemporary *magnum opus* on Vladimiri and his school: Stanislas F. Belch, *Paulus Vladimiri and his Doctrine Concerning International Law and Politics*, 2 vols. (The Hague, 1964).

[14] Philippe Sands, 'A Memory of Justice: The Unexpected Place of Lviv in International Law: A Personal History', *Case Western Reserve Journal of International Law*, 43 (2011), 739–58; Sands, *East West Street: On the Origins of 'Genocide' and 'Crimes Against Humanity'* (New York, 2016), p. 143.

[15] Raphael Lemkin, *Totally Unofficial: The Autobiography of Raphael Lemkin*, Donna-Lee Frieze, ed. (New Haven, 2013); Elihu Lauterpacht, *The Life of Sir Hersch Lauterpacht, QC, FBA, LLD* (Cambridge, 2010). More generally, see James Loeffler and Moria Paz, eds., *The Law of Strangers: Critical Perspectives on Jewish Lawyering and International Legal Thought* (Cambridge, forthcoming). Alexandrowicz contributed Indian and later Burmese case-notes to the *International Law Reports* for 1953–58 edited by Lauterpacht and, after his death in 1960, by his son, Elihu Lauterpacht: Hersch Lauterpacht, 'Preface', in Lauterpacht, ed., *International Law Reports*, 23 (London, 1960), p. v.

[16] Alexandrowicz held the Gillespie Visiting Professorship at the College of Wooster in 1969–70: 'Wooster Today', *Wooster Alumni Magazine*, 84, 1 (November–December 1969), 24.

[17] *Constitution-Maker: Selected Writings of Sir Ivor Jennings*, ed. Harshan Kumarasingham, *Camden Fifth Series*, 46 (Cambridge, 2014); Kumarasingham, 'Eastminster—Decolonisation and State-Building in British Asia', in Kumarasingham, ed., *Constitution Making in Asia: Decolonisation and State-Building in the Aftermath of the British Empire* (London, 2016), p. 28 n. 4, draws the connection with Alexandrowicz.

[18] The non-evaluative term 'semi-periphery' is borrowed from Arnulf Becker Lorca, *Mestizo International Law: A Global Intellectual History, 1842–1933* (Cambridge, 2014), pp. 18–19.

Indo-Pacific region, that 'this modern Grotius' broke new ground, in ways that he might not have done had he followed a more conventional path for one of his early formation and intellectual gifts, to a chair at Columbia or Cambridge, for instance.[19]

Alexandrowicz's first scholarly specialism was Polish marital law and its history, on which he received his doctorate from the Jagiellonian University in 1926.[20] This was, of course, a central concern of canon law; it may have become personally relevant to Alexandrowicz, who was married twice in Poland before the war.[21] The law of marriage was also a particularly pressing problem in Polish history. Due to Poland's history of partition and extinction in the eighteenth century, its partial reconstruction after the Congress of Vienna, and its subsumption into the Austro-Hungarian Empire, Polish marriage law was divided regionally and between canon and civil law, central and eastern Poland observing canon law alone but western and southern Poland following civil marriage. The resulting confusions and collisions about such matters as marital consent, dissolution and divorce, and remarriage (or the prohibition against it) generated contentious case law and fertile ground for work on conflict of laws and the enduring effects of historic legal pluralism.[22] Alexandrowicz himself saw this as a richly fertile 'problem of comparative law':[23] the matrix of many of his leading concerns as an historian of the intertemporal and transnational law of nations can be found here. After his years at the Jagiellonian and three years working at the Bank of Poland, he practised law in Kraków and Katowice (1930–39) before being appointed to a lectureship at the Higher School of Social Sciences in Katowice on the eve of the Second World War.[24] In 1934,

[19] 'Afro-Asia cannot afford to forget the juristic contribution of this modern Grotius who showed it its rightful place in the panorama of International Law': Rama Rao, 'Prof. C. H. Alexandrowicz', xii.

[20] Karol Aleksandrowicz, *Konsens małżeński w nowym kodeksie prawa kanonicznego i w dawnem prawie kanonicznem* [*Marital Consent in the New and Old Code of Canon Law*] (Włocławek, 1927); Aleksandrowicz, 'Błąd, przymus i bojaźń przy zawieraniu małżeństw według nowego i dawnego prawa kościelnego' ['Error, Coercion, and Fear in Contracting Marriages according to New and Old Church Law'], *Ateneum Kapłańskie*, 19 (1927), 468–81; Aleksandrowicz, *Zezwolenie na małżeństwo w prawie kanonicznem i w prawie polskiem* [*Marital Permission in Canon and Polish Law*] (Włocławek, 1931); Carolus Alexandrowicz, *De primis vinculi matrimonii in judicio episcoporum cracoviensium defensoribus (saec. XVIII)* (Rome, 1933); Aleksandrowicz, *Brachium saeculare według obecnie obowiązujących i dawniejszych konkordatów* [*Brachium Saeculare according to Current and Past Legally Binding Concordats*] (Kraków, 1934); Aleksandrowicz, *Małżeństwa domniemane w prawie kanonicznym* [*The Presumption of Marriage in Canon Law*] (Kraków, 1934); Aleksandrowicz, *Prawo małżeńskie* [*Marriage Law*] (London, 1943); Aleksandrowicz, *Prawo osobowe, według kodeksu cywilnego b. Królestwa Polskiego (przy uwzględnieniu prawa cywilnego francuskiego)* [*Personal Law according to the Civil Code of the Former Kingdom of Poland (as Compared to French Civil Law)*] (London, 1944).

[21] Franciszek Moskal, *The Passions of an Optimist: My Life as an Emissary with the Polish Government-in-Exile in World War II, as a Productivity and Management Counsellor with Canadian Manufacturers and as a Consultant in Post-Soviet Poland* (Rawdon, 2005), pp. 91–2.

[22] Ulrike Harmat, *Ehe auf Widerruf?: der Konflikt um das Eherecht in Österreich 1918–1938* (Frankfurt am Main, 1999); Harmat, 'Divorce and Remarriage in Austria-Hungary: The Second Marriage of Franz Conrad von Hötzendorf', *Austrian History Yearbook*, 32 (2001), 70–90.

[23] Karol Alexandrowicz, 'Marriage Law in Poland: A Problem of Comparative Law', in *Studies in Polish and Comparative Law: A Symposium of Twelve Articles* (London, 1945), pp. 156–67.

[24] CHA, 'Curriculum Vitae' (23 May 1943), Polish Institute and Sikorski Museum, London (hereafter, PISM), A.48.2.IX/12.

he had also undertaken legal research in Paris, where he was elected to the Société d'histoire du droit.[25] Religion was also evidently important to him in this period, as in 1931–32 he published a conservative Catholic socio-political journal, *The Living Word of Father Oraczewski*.[26] To the end of his life, he would identify as Roman Catholic.[27]

As a Pole by descent but an Austrian by citizenship until 1919, Alexandrowicz was a member of a suppressed nationality, part of a nation without a state who claimed continuity and identity under the integument of a multiethnic empire. This history of empire and of multiple claims to jurisdiction inflected his concerns long after he had moved from Galicia to Tamil Nadu. The defining question of his career, at least for other international lawyers—the suppression and recovery of sovereignty within and after empire—first arose not in post-imperial India but in Central Europe and then in exile in Paris and London. It opened Alexandrowicz's eyes to illuminating parallels—for example, between the Holy Roman Empire and the Mughal Empire—but it also left him with a consistent equation in his work between sovereignty and statehood and a general aversion to conceiving of empire, even in India, within the categories of colonialism.

At the start of the Second World War, Alexandrowicz joined the Polish Army as an officer and took part in the defence of Lviv against attack by the Wehrmacht and the Red Army.[28] After the collapse of Poland in September 1939, he fled to Romania with the historian, politician, and former Jagiellonian professor Stanisław Kot and his family.[29] A member of a 'pro-government, pro-British, sharply anti-German' faction of the Polish exile community in Bucharest in 1939–40 that was committed to combating the authoritarian Sanacja ('Sanitation') movement,[30] he chaired the Army's research commission, which was, among other duties, tasked with maintaining the continuity of the Polish state, including its legal code.[31] After

[25] Académie des sciences d'outre-mer, 'Alexandrowicz, Charles Henri': <http://www.academieoutremer.fr/academiciens/fiche.php?aId=849> last accessed 1 November 2016.

[26] Karol Aleksandrowicz, ed., *Żywe Słowo Księdza Oraczewskiego: tygodniowe pytania i odpowiedzi o sprawach bieżącego życia* [*The Living Word of Father Oraczewski: Weekly Questions and Answers about Everyday Life*] (Warsaw, 1931–32). Czesław Oraczewski was a priest, political activist, and Polish patriot with right-wing, anti-secularist, monarchist views: Jerzy Pietrzak, 'Oraczewski, Czesław, pseud. Agnis Arman (1891–1965)', in Władysław Konopczyński, et al., eds., *Polski slownik biograficzny*, 50 vols. to date (Kraków, 1935–), XXIV, pp. 151–3.

[27] CHA, 'Application Form' (27 July 1968), The College of Wooster Faculty, Archives Collection (The College of Wooster), Box 10 (Alexandrowicz, Charles H.).

[28] CHA, 'Curriculum Vitae', PISM.

[29] Tadeusz Paweł Rutkowski, *Stanisław Kot 1885–1975: Biografia Polityczna* (Warsaw, 2000), p. 163.

[30] Władysław Kański, 'Bukareszt, 30 sierpnia 1940r.' (30 August 1940), PISM, KOL 25/41 (Kolekcja 25, Stanisław Kot collection). Kański was Polish vice consul in Bucharest: Wolfgang Jacobmeyer, *Heimat und Exil: die Anfänge der polnischen Untergrundbewegung im Zweiten Weltkrieg* (Hamburg, 1973), pp. 131, 305.

[31] CHA, 'Sprawozdanie. Komisji Badawczej przy Ambasadzie R.P. w Bukaresczcie [Report: Research Commission of the Polish Embassy in Bucharest]' (29 June 1940), PISM, A/26/V/1; see also Tadeusz Dubicki and Stanisław Jan Rostworowski, *Sanatorzy kontra Sikorszczycy, czyli, Walka o władzę na uchodźstwie w Rumunii 1939–1940* (Warsaw, 1993), pp. 72, 84; Władysław Horst, 'Józef Kordian Zamorski przed Komisją Rejestracyjną w Bukareszcie', *Teki Archiwalne*, 27 (2000), 129–30.

a brief arrest by the right-wing Romanian Iron Guard, he evacuated to Istanbul with other members of the Polish government, where he continued to combat the Sanacja faction.[32] By May 1941, he had reached London, by way of Cairo and Freetown, to join the Polish government in exile under Władysław Sikorski. The provisions of the Polish Constitution, under which the President could appoint his own successor, who in turn created his own government far beyond Polish soil, ensured that the Polish government had a special status among the exile governments. 'This internationally recognised continuity was a valuable asset for a state which had emerged into independence only 20 years before after more than a century of non-existence,' one historian has noted.[33] It must also have strengthened Alexandrowicz's convictions about the need to protect continuity of sovereignty and legitimacy, especially as one of his tasks as a member of the Polish committee on legislative work was to restore pre-war legal codes on the return of the government.[34]

In London between 1941 and 1946, Alexandrowicz was a financial counsellor to the Polish Embassy and then acting governor of the Bank Gospodarstwa Krajowego, the Polish state development bank (1943–46); he also served in the Home Guard (1942–45).[35] During this period, his second marriage, to Irena Thetschel-Aleksandrowiczowa, collapsed: Irena had moved to New York in 1941; on returning to London in August 1943, she discovered her husband was having an affair and filed for divorce.[36] In late 1945, Alexandrowicz married Marguerite Gabrielle ('Gaby') Drabble (1908–96), an Englishwoman of partly French descent whose mother had been born in the British community in pre-Revolutionary Russia; Irena returned to New York a few months later.[37] After the war, he chaired the European Central Inland Transport Organization (ECITO), an Allied reconstruction agency designed to restore mobility in Europe, for a year before it was wound up in 1947.[38] He continued to write and lecture on Polish,

[32] CHA, 'Do Pana Ministra Sprawiedliwości R.P. w Londynie' [To the Polish Minister of Justice in London] (late 1940), PISM, KOL 25/41; Report from [Jozef Jordan?] Rozwadowski, Istanbul (11 December 1940), PISM, KOL 25/37A.

[33] Dariusz Stola, 'The Polish Government-in-Exile: National Unity and Weakness', in Jan Láníček and James Jordan, eds., *Governments-in-Exile and the Jews during the Second World War* (London, 2013), p. 93.

[34] Grzegorz Kulka, *Komisje prawno-ustrojowe Rady Narodowej RP na emigracji w latach 1939–1991* (Warsaw, 2009), pp. 80–2.

[35] CHA, curriculum vitae (3 November 1960), Personnel (Staff) Files [Registrar], University of Sydney Archives (University of Sydney), Series 136, Container 171 (Alexandrowicz, Charles Henry). In a letter of December 1943, Alexandrowicz mentioned his research on German banks in Europe: CHA to Stanisław Kot, 4 December 1943, PISM, KOL 25/25/1, Folder: Grudzien [December] 1943.

[36] Moskal, *The Passions of an Optimist*, p. 139; Passenger and crew lists of vessels arriving at New York (3 October 1941), National Archives and Records Administration, Immigration and Naturalization Service Record Group 85, Film T715, roll 6583; Gaby Alexandrowicz to Richard Davies (24 July 1995), Drabble and Stock Family Papers, Leeds Russian Archive (University of Leeds), LRA/MS 1379. A son remained in Poland: CHA, 'Curriculum Vitae', PISM.

[37] CHA and Marguerite Gabrielle Drabble, marriage certificate (6 November 1945), General Register Office (England and Wales) (hereafter, GRO), December 1945, Paddington, 1a, p. 137; Gdynia America Shipping Line, outwards passenger list, Cardiff–New York (6 March 1946), The National Archives (UK) (hereafter, TNA), BT 27/1580/39.

[38] On the ECITO, see CHA, 'The European Economic Institutions', *The Year Book of World Affairs*, 2 (1948), 185–90; CHA, *International Economic Organisations* (London, 1952), pp 199–201; Frank

European, and economic affairs in these years but his career soon returned to the law, presumably with the aim of settling down and beginning a new life in London after his third marriage. Alexandrowicz was called to the bar at Lincoln's Inn in January 1948 and took British citizenship in January 1950.[39] While in practice as a barrister, he lectured part time on law and international relations at the University of London (1948–51) but a new opportunity soon appeared that would decisively reorient his intellectual trajectory towards South Asia and the post-colonial world.

When in 1951 the Vice-Chancellor of the University of Madras decided to set up a new Department of International and Constitutional Law (the first such research department in India), Alexandrowicz was chosen to lead it, on the recommendation of his former teacher David Hughes Parry, director of the University of London's Institute for Advanced Legal Studies.[40] Alexandrowicz soon became a pivotal figure in the rapidly growing world of Indian legal education and scholarship. This was a moment, just after independence in 1947 and soon after the new Indian Constitution had come into effect in 1950, when the Indian legal academy was in need of reform and when the expertise of European and American lawyers who were not indelibly associated with the former colonial power was in particular demand.[41] Alexandrowicz, only recently naturalized and with his Polish background, would not have been identified as British: indeed, when the Alliance Française was inaugurated in Madras in 1953, he was elected its first president.[42] Another of his contemporaries, the denazified German lawyer Friedrich Berber (1898–1984), also arrived in India in 1951. He advised Jawaharlal Nehru's government on matters such as water rights before returning to a chair in Munich in 1954.[43] Berber must have become acquainted with Alexandrowicz in these years, though Alexandrowicz himself would remain in India until 1961.

Schipper, *Driving Europe: Building Europe on Roads in the Twentieth Century* (Amsterdam, 2008), pp. 165–6.

39 CHA, call to the bar (26 January 1948), in *The Records of the Honourable Society of Lincoln's Inn: The Black Books*, VI: *A.D. 1914–A.D. 1965*, ed. P. V. Baker (London, 2001), p. 768; CHA, naturalization certificate (31 January 1950), TNA, HO 334/336/10553; CHA, oath of allegiance (3 February 1950), *The London Gazette*, Supplement 38862 (14 March 1950), 1285.

40 D. Hughes Parry to the Registrar, University of Sydney (10 December 1960), Personnel (Staff) Files [Registrar], University of Sydney Archives; A. L. Mudaliar, 'Prof. C. H. Alexandrowicz: A Tribute', *The Indian Year Book of International Affairs*, 11 (1962), [xi].

41 Jayanth K. Krishnan, 'Professor Kingsfield Goes to Delhi: American Academics, the Ford Foundation, and the Development of Legal Education in India', *American Journal of Legal History*, 46 (2004), 447–99.

42 'Cultural Relations with France', *The Hindu* (14 August 1953), 6; S. Muthiah, *A Madras Miscellany: A Decade of People, Places and Potpourri* (Chennai, 2011), p. 671.

43 Katharina Rietzler, 'Counter-imperial Orientalism: Friedrich Berber and the Politics of International Law in Germany and India, 1920s–1960s', *Journal of Global History*, 11 (2016), 127–33. Berber published two essays under Alexandrowicz's editorship: F. J. Berber, 'The Indus Water Dispute', *The Indian Year Book of International Affairs*, 6 (1957), 46–62; Berber, 'International Aspects of the Holy Roman Empire after the Treaty of Westphalia', in CHA, ed., *Studies in the History of the Law of Nations (Grotian Society Papers), The Indian Year Book of International Affairs*, 13, pt. II (1964), 174–83.

Plate 1 Farewell party for Dr Suri Bhagavantam, Osmania University, 8 March 1957. Gaby Alexandrowicz is first on the left, C. H. Alexandrowicz third from the left. Reproduced with the kind permission of H. S. Gururaja Rao

Over the course of a decade, Alexandrowicz created a 'Madras School of Law' which trained leading scholars of the field in India as well as major Indian jurists and advocates.[44] As one of his former students recalled, 'His knowledge was phenomenal and his lectures were brief but salient.'[45] He wrote widely on Indian law and constitutionalism and acted as honorary legal adviser to the Government of India and to Prime Minister Nehru.[46] He associated with two of the authors of the Indian Constitution, B. R. Ambedkar and Alladi Krishnaswamy Iyer, and

[44] [CHA,] 'Department of International and Constitutional Law', *Journal of the Madras University. Section A. Humanities*, 28 (1957), 361–62. Alexandrowicz's contribution is still often overlooked: for example, he and the University of Madras are absent from the account of Indian legal history in the 1960s in Mitra Sharafi, 'South Asian Legal History', *The Annual Review of Law and Social Science*, 11 (2015), 312–13. For his retrospective reflections on legal education in India, see CHA, 'Legal Education', in Humayun Kabir, ed., *The Teaching of Social Sciences in India, 1947–67* (Delhi, 1968), pp. 191–200; CHA, 'The Dichotomy in Control of Legal Education (Academic and Professional)', in S. K. Agrawala, ed., *Legal Education in India: Problems and Perspectives* (Bombay, 1973), pp. 48A–51.

[45] Vengrai Parthasarathy, 'My Professor—A Great Guy', *Vengrai.com* (24 November 2014): <http://www.vengrai.com/?p=114> last accessed 1 November 2016.

[46] For Alexandrowicz's writings on Indian history, jurisprudence, and international relations from these years (not collected here), see CHA, 'The Supreme Court of India as a Habeas Corpus Bench', *Journal of the Madras University. Section A. Humanities*, 22 (1951), 71–81; CHA, 'American Influence in Indian Constitution Making', *Journal of the Madras University. Section A. Humanities*, 23 (1952), 78–87; CHA, 'International Law in India', *International and Comparative Law Quarterly*, 1 (1952), 289–300; CHA, 'The Indian Constitution', *The Year Book of World Affairs*, 7 (1953), 258–82; CHA, 'Common Law Prerogative Writs in India', *Indian Year Book of International Affairs*, 2 (1953), 199–213; CHA, 'The Kashmir Deadlock', *Political Quarterly*, 25 (1954), 236–45; CHA, 'Delegation of Legislative Power in India', *American Journal of Comparative Law*, 3 (1954), 72–9; CHA, 'American Influence on Constitutional Interpretation in India', *American Journal of Comparative Law*, 5 (1956), 98–105; CHA, 'Le Cachemire: aspect juridique

with Radhabinod Pal, the dissenting Indian judge on the Tokyo war crimes tribunal, all of whom were members of the Indian Committee of Comparative Law Alexandrowicz had initiated in 1953.[47] Around the same time, he founded and edited *The Indian Year Book of International Affairs* (1952–86), modelled on the British *Year Book of World Affairs* to which he had been a frequent contributor. Alexandrowicz produced an essay for almost every early issue of the *Indian Year Book*; as editor, he solicited contributions from leading thinkers within India as well as major figures from beyond, among them Berber, Bertrand Russell, Georg Schwarzenberger, and Quincy Wright;[48] and he promoted some of the key figures in India, such as M. K. Nawaz and R. P. Anand, who were then theorizing international law in the New States, at the beginning of the first wave of the TWAIL movement in the global South.[49]

Alexandrowicz's paradoxical combination of distance from the ostensible centres of learned life and proximity to new scholarly materials decisively redirected the course of his work. As his student and then successor at the University of Madras, the Indian jurist T. S. Rama Rao recalled, Alexandrowicz responded creatively to the wealth of material available in Indian archives as well as to the relative absence of the standard works in contemporary European international law with which he had been accustomed to work. As a result, he began an intensive study of the practices of international law in Asia, especially those between Indian and European actors.[50] The East India trade, he argued, had contributed fundamentally to the development of the law of nations. Nineteenth-century European jurists erased this contribution from the legal and historical record and

du conflit Indo-Pakistanais', *Österreichische Zeitschrift für Öffentliches Recht*, 7 (1956), 296–308; CHA, 'India's Himalayan Dependencies', *The Year Book of World Affairs*, 10 (1956), 128–43; CHA, *Constitutional Developments in India* (Bombay, 1957); [CHA,] 'L'influence française sur la Constitution de l'Inde', *The Indian Year Book of International Affairs*, 6 (1957), 376–85; CHA, ed., *A Bibliography of Indian Law* (Madras, 1958); CHA, 'India Before and After Reorganisation', *The Year Book of World Affairs*, 12 (1958), 133–55; CHA, 'Föderalismus in Indien', *Schweizer Monatshefte*, 39 (1959), 754–64; CHA, 'The Secular State in India and in the United States', *Journal of the Indian Law Institute*, 2 (1960), 273–96; CHA, 'Personal Liberty and Preventive Detention', *Journal of the Indian Law Institute*, 3 (1961), 445–58.

47 Alva Myrdal, 'Report on Mission to India and Egypt' (4 February 1953), 3–4, UNESCO Archives, Paris, X07.83 (Missions of Myrdal); [CHA,] 'The Indian Committee of Comparative Law', *International and Comparative Law Quarterly*, 3 (1954), 101–2. Iyer was chair, Ambedkar and Pal vice-chairs, and Alexandrowicz secretary-general of the Committee, which was the Indian branch of the UNESCO International Committee of Comparative Law.

48 For example, see CHA to Bertrand Russell (26 March 1958), Bertrand Russell Archive Collection (McMaster University), RA1, Class 410, Box 1.23 (though Russell never contributed to the journal).

49 M. K. Nawaz, 'The Law of Nations in Ancient India', *The Indian Year Book of International Affairs*, 6 (1952), 172–88; Nawaz, 'International Law in the Contemporary Practice of India: Some Perspectives', *Proceedings of the American Society of International Law*, 57 (1963), 275–90; Nawaz, *The Changing Law of Nations: An Indian Focus* (Calcutta, 2000); R. P. Anand, 'Asian States and the Development of a Universal International Law: Report of a Seminar', *International Studies*, 11 (1969), 167–84; Anand, ed., *Asian States and the Development of International Law*; review by CHA, *International and Comparative Law Quarterly*, 21 (1972), 812–13. B. S. Chimni has identified Alexandrowicz as one of the crucial precursors of TWAIL: Chimni, 'The World of TWAIL: Introduction to the Special Issue', *Trade, Law and Development*, 3 (2011), 16; see also Chimni, '10 x 10', *International Journal of Constitutional Law*, 8 (2010), 44.

50 Rama Rao, 'Prof. C. H. Alexandrowicz', x–xi.

insisted that international law was an exclusively European product, but one that thanks to the achievements of European civilization had a moral claim to govern the entire world.

Alexandrowicz first presented his findings at length in 1960 when, on Hersch Lauterpacht's recommendation, he lectured at the Hague Academy of International Law for the first time.[51] This material later formed the substance of his most enduringly influential book, *An Introduction to the History of the Law of Nations in the East Indies (16th, 17th and 18th Centuries)* (1967).[52] In the same year, he founded the Grotian Society for the study of the history of international law and remained its president and research director until his death in 1975.[53] Such was the esteem in which Alexandrowicz was held by his Indian colleagues that, when he retired from the University of Madras in 1961, two of them nominated him for the Nobel Peace Prize, 'in recognition of his historical researches on the treaty and diplomatic relations between European and Asian powers'.[54] Alexandrowicz himself nominated Grenville Clark and Louis B. Sohn, American authors of the best-selling book *World Peace through World Law* (1958), that same year.[55] No one could begrudge the Nobel Committee's award of Peace Prizes in 1961 and 1962 to Dag Hammarskjöld and Linus Pauling respectively, though a third Madras colleague did nominate Alexandrowicz in 1964 (again without success) 'for strengthening the bonds between the nations of the world, especially those of Asia and the West'.[56]

After a decade teaching in India, Alexandrowicz left Madras in May 1961.[57] In August that year, he moved to Australia and to a post as Associate Professor of International Legal Organization at the University of Sydney. Although this was nominally a demotion from his full professorship at the University of Madras, he soon found himself amid an intellectual ferment in the School of Law at Sydney and in the newly created Australian Society of Legal Philosophy (ASLP). The

[51] Arnold, 1st Baron McNair to the Registrar, University of Sydney (2 December 1960), Personnel (Staff) Files [Registrar], University of Sydney Archives.

[52] CHA, 'Treaty and Diplomatic Relations between European and South Asian Powers in the Seventeenth and Eighteenth Centuries', *Recueil des Cours*, 100 (1960), 203–320; revised and expanded as CHA, *An Introduction to the History of the Law of Nations in the East Indies (16th, 17th and 18th Centuries)* (Oxford, 1967).

[53] CHA, 'The Grotian Society', *American Journal of International Law*, 61 (1967), 1058; CHA, ed., *Studies in the History of the Law of Nations (Grotian Society Papers)*; CHA, ed., *Grotian Society Papers: Studies in the History of the Law of Nations*, 2 vols. (The Hague, 1970–72). The Society was wound up in 2001.

[54] Nobel Prize, 'Nomination Database', T. M. P. Mahadevan (1961): <http://www.nobelprize.org/nomination/archive/show.php?id=15805> last accessed 1 November 2016; T. S. Rama Rao (1962): <http://www.nobelprize.org/nomination/archive/show.php?id=16981> last accessed 1 November 2016.

[55] Nobel Prize, 'Nomination Database', CHA (1961): <http://www.nobelprize.org/nomination/archive/show.php?id=15829> last accessed 1 November 2016; CHA to Harry B. Hollins (20 January 1961) and CHA to Nobel Committee (20 January 1961), Grenville Clark Papers (Dartmouth College), Series 22, Box 264 (Nobel Peace Prize, 1958–61), Folder 35; Grenville Clark and Louis B. Sohn, *World Peace through World Law* (Cambridge, Mass., 1958). Like Alexandrowicz, Lauterpacht, and Lemkin, Louis B. Sohn (1914–2006) was born in Lemberg: Sands, 'A Memory of Justice', 746–8.

[56] Nobel Prize, 'Nomination Database', Rama Ras (1964): <http://www.nobelprize.org/nomination/archive/show.php?id=18445> last accessed 1 November 2016.

[57] 'Prof. C. H. Alexandrowicz', *The Hindu* (9 May 1961), 7.

moving spirit behind both was another emigré, the British-Jewish legal scholar Julius Stone (1907–85), who developed strong contacts in India, made imaginative—often international—appointments as Challis Professor of Jurisprudence and International Law at Sydney, and attempted to bring law into closer dialogue with philosophy and history in the Australian legal academy.[58] During these Sydney years, Alexandrowicz extended his historical studies deeper in time, to Kauṭilya's *Arthaśāstra*, originally from the first or second century CE, and to the reflections of Paulus Vladimiri/Paweł Włodkowic (1370–1435) on Christian-infidel relations: his later articles on Kauṭilya and on Vladimiri, as well as a key article on 'Doctrinal Aspects of the Universality of the Law of Nations', were all presented as working papers to the ASLP between 1962 and 1967.[59] He also completed research for his masterwork on the law of nations in the East Indies, which he later submitted for the Sydney degree of Doctor of Laws. 'Our author is a specimen of Marco Polo', one of his examiners wrote of the book. 'One can, as it were, scarcely credit some of his traveller's tales. But he alone has made the journey and . . . his will always remain the distinction of being first in the field.'[60]

When Alexandrowicz retired from Sydney in 1967, he returned to London where he died from cancer on 26 September 1975.[61] In his remaining years, he was attached to the British Institute of International and Comparative Law (1968–69) and latterly to the Centre of International Studies at Cambridge (1969–75). He acted as a 'poor man's lawyer' at the South London Christian Mission in Bermondsey and taught European Community law for the University of Notre Dame in London (1973–75).[62] He also gathered research material on the evolution of Australia's external sovereignty before the First World War but never published on the subject.[63] His interest in treaty relations between European and non-European peoples

[58] Leonie Star, *Julius Stone: An Intellectual Life* (South Melbourne, 1992), pp. 119–20, 123–4, 130; Ivan A. Shearer, 'The Teaching of International Law in Australian Law Schools', *Adelaide Law Review*, 9 (1983), 76, 77; Upendra Baxi, email communication (22 March 2012). Stone inspired and led the seminar, 'Indian Traditions and the Rule of Law Among Nations' in Delhi (9–11 March 1960): *Indian Traditions and the Rule of Law Among Nations: Report of the All-India Seminar, 1960* ([n.p., n.d. [Delhi, 1960]). (Alexandrowicz did not attend.)

[59] Australian Society for Legal Philosophy, [Proceedings and Papers, 1960–1975,] 3 vols. (Sydney, 1960–75); CHA, 'Doctrinal Aspects of the Universality of the Law of Nations', *British Year Book of International Law*, 37 (1961), 506–15 (ASLP.11) (pp. 168–79 below); CHA, 'Paulus Vladimiri' (ASLP.20); CHA, 'Kautilyan Principles and the Law of Nations', *British Year Book of International Law*, 41 (1965–66), 301–20 (ASLP/IVR/35) (pp. 35–52 below). On Alexandrowicz's reading of Kauṭilya, see also Upendra Baxi, 'Kautilyan Principles and the Law of Nations: A Comment' (1967) (ASLP/IVR/35a): <https://www.academia.edu/8133285/KAUTILYAN_PRINCIPLES_AND_THE_LAW_OF_NATIONS_A_COMMENT> last accessed 1 November 2016.

[60] Clive Parry, 'Report on two works entitled "An introduction to the history of the Law of Nations in the East Indies" (1967) and "World Economic Agencies, Law and Practice" (1962) submitted by Professor C. H. Alexandrowicz for the degree of LL.D. of the University of Sydney' (24 February 1969), Personnel (Staff) Files [Registrar], University of Sydney Archives.

[61] CHA, death certificate (26 September 1975), GRO, September 1975, Croydon, 11, p. 1580.

[62] CHA, 'Application Form', College of Wooster Archives; Thomas L. Shaffer, 'Report of the Dean, 1973–74', *Notre Dame Lawyer*, 50 (1974), 177 n. 38; *Notre Dame Report '73–'74*, 3, 4 (26 October 1973), 70; *Notre Dame Report '74–'75*, 4, 4 (25 October 1974), 98.

[63] CHA to Hedley Bull (22 October 1971) and Bull to CHA (28 January 1972), Records of the Australian Institute of International Affairs (National Library of Australia), MS 2821, Box 93: Series

also continued but its main focus shifted from Asia to Africa. In 1968, he gave another course of lectures at the Hague Academy on 'The Afro-Asian World and the Law of Nations,' which was later revised as his second major historical work, *The European-African Confrontation: A Study in Treaty Making* (1973).[64] Aside from other essays on treaty relations in Africa, many of Alexandrowicz's late publications spoke to pressing international concerns in these years: the expansion of the 'Family of Nations'; 'the appearance or re-appearance of Afro-Asian states'; the attitude of these 'new' states to existing international law; the need to welcome them into international society, unencumbered by the prejudices of positivism; and the revisions to international law demanded by the 'state explosion' of the period—from 51 states in 1945, to 125 in 1968, and *c.* 140 by 1974.[65]

Equally striking in retrospect are some of the absences from Alexandrowicz's thought in this period. For example, he paid little attention to contemporary discussions of self-determination and first-generation human rights; he always avoided the still-novel terms 'Third World' (coined in 1952) and 'Non-Aligned Movement' (from 1961) to describe the blocs of states that most captured his attention, and he never discussed the Bandung Conference of Asian and African nations that met in Indonesia in April 1955.[66] His body of writing bears at best only an oblique relation to perhaps the major axis of global political division at the height of his career, the Cold War: only rarely did he admit that that the 'two Great Powers in the world today . . . had two different ideologies which found expression in their different conceptions of international law'.[67]

Alexandrowicz focused his attention on law, not politics. He remained deeply interested in procedural questions of the formation of international law,[68] and the

3—Research Committee Chairmen's Correspondence Files, 1969–82 (Prof. C. H. Alexandrowicz, 1972–73).

[64] CHA, 'The Afro-Asian World and the Law of Nations (Historical Aspects)', *Recueil des Cours*, 123 (1968), 121–210; CHA, *The European-African Confrontation: A Study in Treaty Making* (Leiden, 1973). 'Le cours de M. Alexandrowicz ... a beaucoup séduit ses auditeurs', reported the Secretary General of the Academy. 'Aussi savant historien et juriste que brillant professeur, M. Alexandrowicz a remporté un réel succès': 'Rapport du Secrétaire général sur les activités de l'Académie durant l'été 1968' (1968), Records of the Hague Academy of International Law (The Peace Palace, The Hague), uncatalogued.

[65] CHA, 'Introduction', in van der Molen, *Alberico Gentili and the Development of International Law*, p. viii (125 states); CHA, 'The New States and International Law', 226 (*c.* 140 states—in fact, there were 138 UN member states by 1974); CHA, 'Empirical and Doctrinal Positivism in International Law', *British Year Book of International Law*, 47 (1974–75), 286–9 (pp. 404, 349–53 below). There are currently (2016) 193 UN member states.

[66] Though other international lawyers at the time did, of course: Luis Eslava, Michael Fakhri and Vasuki Nesiah, eds., *Bandung, Global History and International Law: Critical Pasts and Pending Futures* (Cambridge, forthcoming).

[67] 'International Law: Need for Clarifying Rules Stressed', *The Hindu* (13 February 1952), 7 (quoting CHA, 'International Law and the Use of Force in International Relations', British Council lecture, Madras, 12 February 1952); see also CHA, 'Comecon: The Soviet Retort to the Marshall Plan', *World Affairs*, 4 (1950), 35–47; CHA, 'The Soviet Conception of International Law and the Doctrine of Positivism' (12 December 1963), Australian Society for Legal Philosophy (ASLP 18a).

[68] See, for example, CHA, 'The Voting Procedure in the Security Council', *Justitia* (Hyderabad), 4 (1958), 21–5; CHA, *The Law-Making Functions of the Specialised Agencies of the United Nations* (Sydney, 1973).

ways in which it would have to be radically reconsidered in light of the proliferation of states. For example, he noted that the 'weighted' system of international law-making by which the major powers had a 'decisive voice', however acceptable in the homogeneous nineteenth-century context in which powerful and weak states had similar social and economic structures, was no longer appropriate given the diversity of participating states, particularly in their economic organization (free-market, communist, and the 'compromise solution' settled on by most developing states).[69] He celebrated the New States' use of UN General Assembly procedures to challenge the body of nineteenth-century customary law, such as special protections for foreign investors, that the European powers had been using in the wake of decolonization to maintain their dominance and limit the economic autonomy of the New States. Yet his genius for perceiving analogy and continuity did not blind him to the differences between phases in the life of the family of nations. He was fully aware how the grip of the past might paralyse the present: history could confine as well as liberate.[70]

As a scholar with a long-standing interest in international organizations and communication,[71] Alexandrowicz had repeatedly stressed the importance of history for contemporary international problems: 'Any current international issue may call for a thorough knowledge of international antecedents and legal precedent.'[72] Central to his work across almost a quarter of a century were questions of continuity and discontinuity in international law that went back to his Polish roots and to his formative interest in canon law and its history. Were the so-called 'new' states of the post-War world in fact new or 'old'—that is, restored or revenant—members of international society? Could sovereignty have endured under colonialism, to be recovered after it ended? Was it possible to go back behind a hierarchical and discriminatory positivist international legal order to return to 'the vital foundations of the law of nations' beneath 'Bentham's international law which continues to bear the seeds of its own crisis'?[73] To answer such questions, Alexandrowicz relied on the fundamentally historicist principle of intertemporal law (*lex retro non agit*): 'the past deserves to be viewed in light of the law as it stood at the particular period under consideration. The law which matters for its proper understanding cannot be *ex post facto* law.'[74] Historical research was essential to establish a universal and non-discriminatory international law in his own time.

It was therefore fitting that some of Alexandrowicz's very last publications addressed that ambivalent dialogue between history and the present. In two brief articles published in the British journal *Millennium* just before his death in 1975,

[69] CHA, 'The New States and International Law', 229–30 (pp. 408–9 below).

[70] CHA, 'Paralysis Symptoms of the Treaty of Rome of 1958', *Co-Existence*, 12 (1975), 13–19.

[71] CHA, *International Economic Organisations*; CHA, *World Economic Agencies: Law and Practice* (London, 1962); CHA, *The Law of Global Communications* (New York, 1971).

[72] CHA, 'Introduction', in CHA, ed., *Grotian Society Papers 1972: Studies in the History of the Law of Nations* (The Hague, 1972), p. vii.

[73] CHA, 'Some Problems in the History of the Law of Nations in Asia', *The Indian Year Book of International Affairs*, 12 (1963), 3 (p. 76 below).

[74] CHA, 'G. F. de Martens on Asian Treaty Practice', *The Indian Year Book of International Affairs*, 13, pt. II (1964), 77 (p. 193 below).

he voiced emphatic support for the political-legal strategy of using the New States' numerical majority in the UN General Assembly to revise international law. Declaring the early 1970s 'a turning point in the history of international law,' he perhaps over-optimistically looked forward to the prospect of the New States using their 'overwhelming majority' as a legal counterweight against the economic and political strength of the older powers in the context of the emergent (but ultimately short-lived) New International Economic Order.[75] In these articles, he was more explicit about the politics of international law than he had ever been; he more openly acknowledged the fault lines of international politics between capitalism and communism; he looked to the Latin American countries as having '[led] the way' in responding to European economic domination and legal manoeuvering.[76] These terse pieces suggest subtle but significant new directions that his thought might have taken had he lived longer. The principled commitment to intertemporal and transnational equity visible in these late essays, as throughout his wide-ranging oeuvre, makes Alexandrowicz the forgotten founder of the current critical movement to historicize international law.

Alexandrowicz believed that history was the cure for the oppressive weight of the past. From the early 1950s to the mid-1970s, he elaborated and refined a picture of world history since the fifteenth century in which, starting in the late eighteenth century but becoming definitive in the period after 1815, a universal, naturalist law of nations had given way to a distinctly 'un-universal positivism' in international law.[77] The major axes of difference between the two frameworks, in Alexandrowicz's account, were: the scope of the family of nations (universal *versus* European); the approach to civilizational, religious, and racial difference (non-discriminatory and multi-ideological *versus* arrogant and intolerant); and the theory of recognition of states each presupposed (declaratory *versus* constitutive). Here is perhaps his most succinct statement of what Alexandrowicz believed was lost in the transition from 'naturalism' to 'positivism' and from the law of nations to international law:

> The universality of the Family of Nations, the multi-ideological character of the Law of Nations (its attitude towards ideological struggles such as the Christian-Islamic or the Catholic-Protestant conflicts), its non-discriminatory approach to civilisation, religion or race, declaratorism in respect of recognition as well as the doctrine of *bellum justum* were all functional qualities peculiar to the 'natural law' system within the classic law of nations.

The 'elimination' of naturalism and the triumph of positivism 'contributed to a system of international law which accepted colonial expansion and the institution

[75] CHA, 'The New States and International Law'; CHA, 'The Charter of Economic Rights and Duties of States', *Millennium*, 4 (1975), 72–4 (pp. 404–10, 411–13 below); Nils Gilman, 'The New International Economic Order: A Reintroduction', *Humanity*, 6 (2015), 1–15.

[76] CHA, 'The New States and International Law', 228 (p. 407 below).

[77] CHA, 'Some Problems in the History of the Law of Nations in Asia', 8 (p. 79 below). For an overview of Alexandrowicz's historical writings, see Mohammed Ashraf Ali Khan, 'The History of International Law: As Interpreted by Alexandrowicz' (M.Phil. thesis, Jawaharlal Nehru University, 2001).

of war as a mode of settlement of international conflicts.'[78] That described the world in which Alexandrowicz had grown up as well as the one where he found himself in the 1960s and to which 'new' states claimed entry on their own terms.

International law's indifference to its own history, he charged, had cut the field off from its universalist roots in transregional exchanges in the early modern period. Such willed ignorance prevented any passage across the great barrier of the nineteenth century when 'the law of nations by some ideological cataclysm had ceased to be the universal law of all nations under which all States in all Continents could enjoy equal rights with other nations provided they had achieved Statehood and the necessary degree of civilisation.'[79] Alexandrowicz never explained the causes of that 'cataclysm': only towards the end of his life, when pressed at a seminar, did he suggest that the Industrial Revolution may have been to blame, as it changed the criteria of 'civilization' from cultural achievement to technological superiority.[80] Archival and textual research, arrayed against the fallacies of anachronism, presentism, and Eurocentrism, and conducted over a much longer *durée* than international lawyers' usual myopic perspective of a century or less, would be the means to bridge the abyss. Only then could the consequences of cataclysm be reversed for large parts of the world's population, particularly in Asia and Africa.[81]

Alexandrowicz's own turn to the history of the law of nations occurred in the context of debates around so-called 'New States'. That term most often referred to the post-colonial polities that emerged in the course of decolonization in the 1950s and 1960s and it appeared prominently in discussions among social scientists and lawyers of the time.[82] In this respect, it is striking that Alexandrowicz's earliest direct engagement with the urgent contemporary questions raised by emergent statehood, as well as his first tentative use of history to justify the emergence of a new state as the bearer of continuous sovereignty, was not in relation to an Asian or African entity but rather with regard to the State of Israel. In a short article published in 1951, Alexandrowicz confronted the dilemma posed by the fact that the newly established State of Israel (1948) could apparently not claim sovereignty by either of the established routes for its acquisition, original title by occupation or derivative title

[78] CHA, 'New and Original States', 469 (p. 394 below). On the links among natural law, universalism, and 'declaratorism' (or the absence of constitutivism), see also CHA, *An Introduction to the Law of Nations in the East Indies*, p. 9.

[79] CHA, 'A Persian-Dutch Treaty in the Seventeenth Century', *The Indian Year Book of International Affairs*, 7 (1958), 206 (p. 156 below).

[80] CHA, 'The Partition of Africa by Treaty', in Kenneth Ingham, ed., *Foreign Relations of African States: Proceedings of the Twentyfifth Symposium of the Colston Research Society held in the University of Bristol, April 4th to 7th, 1973* (London, 1974), p. 156 (report on 'Discussion').

[81] '[I]nternational lawyers would be well advised to look at their discipline not only in legal terms prevailing in the last fifty or a hundred years but with a readiness to go back to its roots and to contemplate the lessons of the past which often offer suitable patterns of solution for ever recurring situations': CHA, 'G. F. de Martens on Asian Treaty Practice', 76 (p. 193 below).

[82] For example, see K. M. Panikkar, *The Afro-Asian States and their Problems* (London, 1959); Rupert Emerson, *From Empire to Nation: The Rise of Self-assertion of Asian and African Peoples* (Cambridge, Mass., 1960); J. J. G. Syatauw, *Some Newly Established Asian States and the Development of International Law* (The Hague, 1961); Michael Brecher, *The New States of Asia, a Political Analysis* (London, 1963); CHA, 'New and Original States: The Issue of Reversion to Sovereignty', *International Affairs*, 45 (1969), 465–80 (pp. 390–403 below); Hanna Bokor-Szegö, *New States and International Law*, trans.

transferred by another state. Meticulously tracing the post-Ottoman legal history of the Mandate of Palestine, he argued that although Israel's sovereignty was *sui generis*, it should be understood as continuous, as having passed from the Ottoman Empire to the Principal Allied Powers after the First World War, to the new State of Israel as the final legatee. The 'Family of Nations', represented by the United Nations, then recognized Israel's membership and thereby affirmed its sovereignty.[83] Significant here is his espousal of what he would later call the 'constitutive' theory of state recognition, as opposed to the earlier 'declaratory' procedure which acknowledges the identity of *de facto* and *de jure* statehood.[84]

Because there had never been a 'legal vacuum' in the territory, Alexandrowicz argued, Israel could not claim rights through occupation. This meant that while Israel's effective control over the territory assigned to it by the United Nations General Assembly in November 1947 established its sovereignty there, there was doubt about its sovereignty over the land that the UN had designated for an independent Arab state. It also meant that while Israel was right to deny that it was a successor of the Mandatory Power's rights and duties in the former Palestine, since Britain as Mandatory Power had never held sovereignty, Israel had inherited other rights and duties under customary international law (including duties under private law to indemnify holders of certain concessions). He saw it as being in the interest of the new state that its 'present rights and duties should as far as possible be linked with the past.'[85] While Alexandrowicz's commitment to tracing continuities of sovereignty remained a central theme throughout his career, his use of history, his theory of recognition, and his belief in the obligation of new states to accept the duties prescribed by conventional international law all changed after his translation to Madras. From that post-colonial and semi-peripheral perspective, his historicism became more radical and thoroughgoing.

Throughout the rest of his career, Alexandrowicz would use historical argument to establish the legal equality of states that had been denied both under colonialism and under the post-colonial legal order. He saw the universality of the law of nations, repudiated by the European-dominated legal order, as a peremptory norm (*jus cogens*) of fundamental moral status, akin to the prohibitions on genocide and crimes against humanity.[86] To support that strong claim for equality, he set out to provide historical evidence that decolonizing societies, particularly the 'new Asian democracies,' were not in fact new to international society but were being restored after a colonial period that was not 'a starting point but ... an interlude only,' and a 'period ... of negligible duration.'[87]

Sándor Simon (Budapest, 1970); R. P. Anand, *New States and International Law* (Delhi, 1972); F. C. Okoye, *International Law and the New African States* (London, 1972); CHA, 'The New States and International Law' (pp. 404–10 below).

[83] CHA, 'Israel *in Fieri*', *International Law Quarterly*, 4 (1951), 423–30 (pp. 384–9 below).

[84] CHA, 'The Theory of Recognition *in Fieri*', *British Year Book of International Law*, 34 (1958), 176–98 (pp. 354–74 below).

[85] CHA, 'Israel *in Fieri*', 426 (p. 387 below).

[86] CHA, 'New and Original States', 479; CHA, 'The New States and International Law', 226 (pp. 402, 409 below).

[87] CHA, 'Introduction', *The Indian Year Book of International Affairs*, 3 (1954), viii; CHA, 'Introduction', in Molen, *Alberico Gentili and the Development of International Law*, p. ix; CHA,

In Alexandrowicz's longer historical narrative, early ideological prohibitions on relations with infidels in medieval theology had relaxed under the pressures of European commercial expansion, beginning in the fourteenth century.[88] He regarded legal theory and treaty practice in the early modern period as mutually reinforcing: on his account, naturalist legal theorists took for granted that the law of nations was universally applicable and that treaty relations and a shared legal framework between European states and others were unproblematic. He saw the profusion of treaties between European states and others, especially Asian commercial states, as the most persuasive evidence for the force of this universalist conception. He then identified a radical shift at the end of the eighteenth century, in which ideological transformations in Europe preceded changes in state practice, and European writers declared the obsolescence of universalism even as European state agents continued to recognize Asian states as treaty partners. He maintained that 'limitations imposed on [the Asian states'] legal capacity by ideological change (without their participation in such change) could not produce such far reaching results as their reduction to a sort of extraneity—a status which implied a serious restriction of their position in international law.'[89] That is, their exclusion from the family of nations by the bulk of nineteenth-century legal treatises was illegitimate in legal as well as moral terms, because the Europeans did not possess the legal capacity unilaterally to expel states whose legal status they had once recognized in theory and in practice.[90]

Alexandrowicz's key conceptual, historical, and normative arguments all turned on this distinction between a pre-nineteenth-century law of nations based on natural law and therefore universal, and the positivist, and exclusively European, conception of international law that originated around the turn of the nineteenth century. (It is notable in this regard that he persistently distinguished the 'law of nations' from 'international law' on normative rather than merely descriptive grounds.) That nineteenth-century view was the primary target of his criticism, both historical and normative. Although he was never quite precise about when the

The European-African Confrontation, p. 127. He considered the distinctive legal questions faced by states such as Ceylon, Madagascar, and Algeria that could lay claim to a 'reversion to sovereignty' on the grounds that they had once existed as independent states in CHA, 'New and Original States' (pp. 405–6 below); CHA, 'Les pays afro-asiatiques et le droit des nations: le problème du retour à la souveraineté', *Comptes rendus trimestriels des séances de l'Académie des sciences d'outre-mer*, 34 (1974), 629–37.

[88] CHA, *An Introduction to the Law of Nations in the East Indies*, pp. 83–96. For more recent accounts of treaty relations between Europeans and 'infidels', see Noel Malcolm, 'Alberico Gentili and the Ottomans', in Benedict Kingsbury and Benjamin Straumann, eds., *The Roman Foundations of the Law of Nations: Alberico Gentili and the Justice of Empire* (Oxford, 2010), pp. 127–45; Richard Tuck, 'Alliances with Infidels in the European Imperial Expansion', in Sankar Muthu, ed., *Empire and Modern Political Thought* (Cambridge, 2012), pp. 61–83.

[89] CHA, 'Some Problems of the History of the Law of Nations in Asia', 9 (p. 80 below).

[90] Alexandrowicz describes colonialism as 'certainly not of a legal nature': CHA, 'Some Problems of the History of the Law of Nations in Asia', 9 (p. 80 below); compare CHA, *An Introduction to the Law of Nations in the East Indies*, pp. 234–5. This is a claim directed at the jurists of his own day, who were deciding cases in part based on the treaty practices of European colonial powers, considering such questions as whether the British in India recognized Portugal's right to pass over their territory to reach its landlocked enclaves.

ideological cataclysm had first begun, whether in the late eighteenth century or the early nineteenth century, his often-repeated narrative was notable for failing ever to invoke 1648 as the starting point for an alleged 'Westphalian' international order based on mutually recognizing statehood.[91] This aversion to the myth of 1648 was strategic rather than accidental. The irredeemably Eurocentric Westphalian story was irrelevant to his more radical counter-narrative of interpolity relations in global history as the encounter between regimes of sovereignty—Asian and European—rather than as the export or diffusion of a European model.[92]

For Alexandrowicz, 1815 and not 1648 was the pivot around which world history turned, for it was from the Congress of Vienna and its aftermath that he dated the emergence of the arrogantly positivist vision of legal order Europe imposed on the rest of the world over the course of the nineteenth century.[93] 1815 also marked the moment when the last artificial vestige of Polish autonomy, the Kingdom of Poland, was created by the Congress of Vienna and then gradually subsumed into the Russian Empire. He was well aware of the homology between the two processes. He frequently compared the Mahratta Confederation with the Kingdom of Poland and the collapse of the Mughal Empire with the decline of the Holy Roman Empire, as the 'disappearance of the two most powerful empires of the world had a decisive impact on the law of nations.'[94] The collapse of the Mughal Empire, in rendering China vulnerable to European force, ultimately led to the collapse of the Asian inter-state legal order that had 'been part and parcel of a world-wide international structure.'[95] In Europe the declining entity was replaced by a group of independent powers, the Concert of Europe, that declared themselves bound by the 'public law of Europe,' thus establishing a new and fairly stable interpolity legal order and simultaneously declaring that law to have global validity. India and Poland were both victims of this aggressively self-centred *ius publicum Europaeum* in the nineteenth century.[96]

[91] The *locus classicus* is Leo Gross, 'The Peace of *Westphalia*, 1648–1948', *American Journal of International Law*, 42 (1948), 20–41.

[92] Martti Koskenniemi, 'Expanding Histories of International Law', *American Journal of Legal History*, 56 (2016), 106.

[93] CHA, 'Mogul Sovereignty and the Law of Nations', *The Indian Year Book of International Affairs*, 4 (1955), 317–18 (p. 63 below); CHA, *An Introduction to the Law of Nations in the East Indies*, p. 11.

[94] CHA, '"Jus Gentium" and the Law of Nature in Asia', *The Aryan Path*, 27 (1956), 19 (quoted); CHA, 'Mogul Sovereignty and the Law of Nations', 320–1, 323–4; CHA, 'The Discriminatory Clause in South Asian Treaties in the Seventeenth and Eighteenth Centuries', *The Indian Year Book of International Affairs*, 6 (1957), 141–2; CHA, 'Paulus Vladimiri and the Development of the Coexistence of Christian and Non-Christian Countries', 447 (pp. 75, 65–6, 67–8, 152, 60 below). Alexandrowicz frequently cited John Westlake, *Chapters on the Principles of International Law* (Cambridge, 1894), pp. 193–4, on this analogy.

[95] CHA, 'Mogul Sovereignty and the Law of Nations', 323–4 (p. 68 below).

[96] He also occasionally added Italy; for example, 'Poland's and Italy's political agony hardly disturbed the peace of mind of any of the leading European statesmen, and the Asian powers were relegated to a vacuum from which (they were told) they could be readmitted to legal existence as candidates for membership in the family of nations': CHA, 'Some Problems in the History of the Law of Nations in Asia', 7 (p. 79 below); CHA, *An Introduction to the Law of Nations in the East Indies*, p. 234.

Alexandrowicz's Polish background also explains why he sometimes antedated the beginnings of European positivism to the late eighteenth century: not because of events in Asia, but because this was the moment of the Polish partitions, when a once-proud state was dismembered as evidence of a 'European egocentric attitude' that began with policing the boundaries of Europe and found its most violent expression in South Asia and later in Africa.[97] Yet he found the period also to be pivotal because it was then that the evolution of a theory of recognition, which constituted an important aspect of the emergence of international law, occurred in the crucible of the struggles between the ideologies of legitimism and popular sovereignty around and following the French Revolution. He argued that before the late eighteenth century there was essentially no theory of state recognition, and therefore nothing approximating to modern international law. There was instead an 'inter-dynastic system' that was deferential to hereditary rulers but permitted some interference by outsiders in the internal affairs of a state, such as meddling in the selection of an elective monarch. His reconstruction of the emergence of a theory of recognition and its transformation from an implicitly declaratory theory to an explicitly constitutive one, from the early positivists of the eighteenth century through the invention of a constitutive theory of recognition by Henry Wheaton in the 1840s, is a *tour de force* of historical legal analysis. It exemplifies Alexandrowicz's instinct for significant conceptual puzzles as well as his skill at tracing lines of argument among once significant but later forgotten thinkers.[98]

Alexandrowicz traced the ideological and doctrinal developments that led first to the development of an implicit declaratory theory of recognition, according to which it was argued that all existing states, whatever their regime, had a right under the law of nature to be treated as legal equals. The question of when and how third parties should recognize a rebelling province prompted an evolving response, whereby an initial belief in the importance of recognition by the mother country before others could recognize the rebels as a new state gradually gave way to a 'defactoist' view that third parties could, and should, recognize the new state when the mother country had definitively lost control over it but that their recognition was merely declaratory. The last decisive development came with Wheaton's claim, under the influence of Hegel, that a new state's *de facto* control did not alone confer perfect external sovereignty, which depended instead on its recognition by foreign powers. Unlike the majority of his historical work, his key essay on 'The Theory of Recognition *in Fieri*' (1959) traced developments within Europe and its settler colonies rather than relations with Asian or African states. As he would argue

[97] CHA, 'Doctrinal Aspects of the Universality of the Law of Nations', 510; compare CHA, 'G. F. de Martens on Asian Treaty Practice', 74 ('European egocentricism') (pp. 173, 191 below); CHA, *An Introduction to the Law of Nations in the East Indies*, p. 2 ('European egocentricity'). On the Polish partitions more generally, see Victor Kattan, 'To Consent or Revolt? European Public Law, the Three Partitions of Poland (1772, 1793, and 1795) and the Birth of National Self-Determination', *Journal of the History of International Law*, 17 (2015), 247–81.

[98] CHA, 'The Theory of Recognition *in Fieri*' (pp. 354–74 below).

elsewhere, however, the constitutive theory of sovereignty was a linchpin of the exclusivity and Eurocentrism of nineteenth-century international law.[99]

What difference would it make that many Asian and African states could be shown to be successors to states whose sovereignty was once recognized by European powers? Alexandrowicz's strategy had the advantage of showing something like the hypocrisy or self-contradiction of European states in withholding a recognition they had once granted: the argument entailed an internal critique in which he showed that European states' policy of legal recognition fell short of their own erstwhile standards. At the same time, in setting out to make this case, Alexandrowicz arguably was entering the terms of debate set by the positivism whose agenda he was so eager to expose and refute. His argument, for instance, seems to concede something to the constitutive theory of recognition, in placing such weight on the recognition by other states of a state's sovereignty, despite his explicit avowal of the declaratory theory of sovereignty.

At stake in these debates were legal and political as well as broadly cultural judgements: about which treaties governed contested territorial and other state claims and how such treaties, sometimes centuries old, should be interpreted; about what was necessary to make good on the promise that all states had equal sovereignty; about whether decolonized states were obliged to accept a legal order dictated by Western powers as a condition for recognition; and more fundamentally about whether the nations of Asia and Africa were, as Leopold von Ranke along with many nineteenth-century European thinkers had claimed, 'without history'.[100] Alexandrowicz's claim that non-European states before the colonial 'interlude' had been active makers of international law defied the mainstream European view that the new states were gaining (even earning) admittance to an existing system to which they had always been outsiders and whose terms they were in no position to question or alter. This led to the charge that his desire to justify universalism and sovereign equality in the present had caused him to overstate reciprocity and mutual recognition in the past. As the British theorist of international relations Martin Wight noted in 1971, 'in order to correct an interpretation of the history of the states-system that was exaggerated (as well as being today politically unfashionable), [Alexandrowicz] exaggerates upon the other side.'[101]

Alexandrowicz's view may have been exaggerated, even utopian, but it was not historically or legally unfounded. For him, a signal moment in contemporary international law occurred in the 1960 decision of the ICJ in a dispute between India and Portugal over the territorial enclaves of Dadra and Nagar-Aveli, which had been ruled by Portugal until achieving *de facto* independence in 1954.[102] Although the

[99] For example, CHA, 'The Partition of Africa by Treaty', in Ingham, ed., *Foreign Relations of African States*, p. 129 (p. 230 below).

[100] CHA, 'Empirical and Doctrinal Positivism in International Law', 286 (p. 349 below).

[101] Martin Wight, 'The Origins of Our States-System: Geographical Limits' (1971), in Wight, *Systems of States*, ed. Hedley Bull (Leicester, 1977), pp. 117–28 (p. 118 quoted); Edward Keene, *Beyond the Anarchical Society: Grotius, Colonialism and Order in World Politics* (Cambridge, 2002), pp. 26–8.

[102] ICJ, 'Case concerning Right of Passage over Indian Territory (Merits), Judgment of 12 April 1960', *ICJ Reports* 1960: <http://www.icj-cij.org/docket/files/32/4521.pdf> last accessed 1 November 2016.

Court gave limited recognition to Portugal's claim to sovereignty over the enclaves, and although he favoured the dissenting opinion by the Argentinian Judge Lucio Moreno Quintana, Alexandrowicz regarded the opinion as a salutary legal development and as evidence of the contemporary legal validity of several of his most important historical claims. At stake for him in the ICJ judges' interpretation of the 1779 Maratha-Portuguese treaty that had granted title to the Portuguese were two points above all: first, the eighteenth-century Maratha state's international personality and membership in the Family of Nations; and second, the importance of interpreting treaties according to the legal standards the treaties themselves presupposed, rather than according to later principles of international law. The *Right of Passage* case affirmed the validity of early treaties between Europeans and Asian powers, the recognition of such treaties as binding by Europeans, their recognition of the sovereignty of their Asian treaty-partners, and the significance of attending to diverse perspectives in the determination of the meaning of a treaty. Alexandrowicz cited the case repeatedly in his historical essays as evidence of the contemporary legal significance of pre-positivist legal norms, and of an older 'universal' family of nations.[103]

It was another major ICJ judgment that turned Alexandrowicz to the history of what he called the 'European-African confrontation'. In 1966, the Court decided in the *South West Africa Cases* that Ethiopia and Liberia did not have legal standing to challenge the conduct of South Africa, the mandatory power, in South West Africa (Namibia), including its policy of apartheid. At issue in the cases was the legal nature of the duty of governing countries in the Mandate system, according to Article 22 of the Covenant of the League of Nations, to govern in accordance with the 'sacred trust of civilization' to promote the wellbeing and development of the people under their 'tutelage'. Because the Court was evenly divided, the decision to dismiss the claims of Liberia and Ethiopia was made on the basis of the casting vote by the ICJ President, the Australian Sir Percy Spender; the seven dissenters wrote unusually extensive and wide-ranging dissents protesting that the Court's interpretation deprived the international community of any recourse against abuses of power by Mandatory states.[104] Alexandrowicz's own distinctively historical response to the cases was to challenge the Court's judgment that the 'sacred trust of

[103] CHA, *An Introduction to the History of the Law of Nations in the East Indies*, pp. 3–11; CHA, 'Doctrinal Aspects of the Universality of the Law of Nations', 512; CHA, 'G. F. de Martens on Asian Treaty Practice', 76; CHA, 'Le Droit des Nations aux Indes Orientales', *Annales. Histoire, Sciences Sociales*, 19 (1964), 872–3; CHA, 'New and Original States', 467–8; CHA, 'The Partition of Africa by Treaty', in Ingham, ed., *Foreign Relations of African States*, p. 130 (pp. 176, 192, 86–7, 392, 231 below). For a more recent assessment of the case and its significance, see Prabakhar Singh, 'India Before and After the *Right of Passage* Case', *Asian Journal of International Law*, 5 (2015), 176–208.

[104] ICJ, 'South West Africa (Liberia v. South Africa and Ethiopia v. South Africa), judgment of 18 July 1966', *ICJ Reports* 1966: <http://www.icj-cij.org/docket/index.php?p1=3&p2=3&k=f2&case=47&code=lsa&p3=4> last accessed 1 November 2016.

civilization' had no legal content outside the League of Nations Mandate system, by tracing the prominent place, in both nineteenth-century European treaties with Africans and multilateral European agreements about Africa, of claims about the duties of European states to use the powers they acquired for the benefit of the indigenous populations.[105]

The implication of this longer history was that Europeans had assiduously relied on legal instruments to validate their territorial claims.[106] Alexandrowicz thus went to some lengths to show in his writings on Africa of the early 1970s not only that, before the nineteenth century, Europeans had concluded treaties with Africans, especially North Africans, on terms of equality and reciprocity (as he earlier argued they had in Asia), but also, and more importantly for the disputes of his day, that the nineteenth-century treaties by which African leaders ceded their rights over territory were bilateral instruments in which the Europeans recognized African rulers' sovereignty and international legal standing, and which they saw as constituting 'valid title in international law.' He read the partition of Africa as taking place first with a stage of protection treaties. He insisted on the 'legally binding form' of the treaties, the European states' recognition of the international legal standing of the African rulers with whom they concluded treaties, and even the basis of 'perfect reciprocity' on which some treaties were concluded (with Zanzibar and Uganda, for instance).[107]

Although Alexandrowicz conceded that the protectorate stage was a 'transitory phase leading sooner or later to absorption,' and although his many examples make clear that the Europeans recognized African leaders' sovereignty only to enable them to cede sovereign rights to Europeans, it was important to him to show that 'Africa's entry into the Family of Nations' could be read as taking place not in a 'legal vacuum' but under conditions of legal recognition. He did not consider the objection that, as Antony Anghie has put it, the sovereignty of the African powers was 'artificially created' precisely so that it could then be ceded to Europeans: that

[105] Alexandrowicz saw his historical argument as a purely legal one that avoided the 'political point of view' so he did not, for instance, point out that the court was divided largely along geographical lines: CHA, 'The Juridical Expression of the Sacred Trust of Civilization', *American Journal of International Law*, 65 (1971), 159 (p. 346 below); CHA, *The European-African Confrontation*, pp. 113–15.

[106] CHA, 'The Juridical Expression of the Sacred Trust of Civilization', (p. 342 below).

[107] CHA, 'The Partition of Africa by Treaty', in Ingham, ed., *Foreign Relations of African States*, pp. 139–40, 156; CHA, 'The Role of German Treaty Making in the Partition of Africa', *The Indian Year Book of International Affairs*, 18, pt. II (1980), 188, 195 (pp. 243, 324, 329 below). See also Jörg Fisch, 'Africa as *Terra Nullius*: The Berlin Conference and International Law', in Stig Förster, Wolfgang J. Mommsen, and Ronald Robinson, eds., *Bismarck, Europe and Africa: The Berlin Africa Conference 1884–1885 and the Onset of Partition* (Oxford, 1988), pp. 347–75; Isabelle Surun, 'Une souveraineté à l'encre sympathique? Souveraineté autochtone et appropriations territoriales dans les traités franco-africains au XIXe siècle', *Annales. Histoire, Sciences Sociales*, 69 (2014), 313–48; Mieke van der Linden, *The Acquisition of Africa (1870–1914): The Nature of Nineteenth-Century International Law* (Oisterwijk, 2014); Mamadou Hébié, *Souveraineté territoriale par traité: Une étude des accords entre puissances coloniales et entités politiques locales* (Geneva, 2015).

'sovereignty is a flexible instrument which readily lends itself to the powerful imperatives of the civilizing mission.'[108] In reply to concerns that the coercive nature of such treaties vitiated their status as bilateral or as legally valid, or that international law served as a mere handmaid of colonization, he insisted on their legal significance: 'In most cases,' he argued, 'the scramble [for Africa] was one for legal titles in international law.'[109]

The political stakes of Alexandrowicz's intervention are complex. He aimed to restore to Africa a history of 'civilisation and political organisation' against those who would reduce nineteenth-century African history to a story of exclusively European agency.[110] He sought to demonstrate to contemporary jurists that colonial-era agreements should not be considered binding on postcolonial successor states and to recover an emancipatory role for international law. He maintained that the colonial protectorate was 'at best a political device', since the European powers' mutual agreement to accept one another's outright annexation of their protectorates could not affect the validity of their prior treaties with African rulers. Thus, the 'attempt to draw international law into the orbit of colonialism was ultimately not successful.'[111] But in arguing in this way that colonialism was a relatively brief 'interlude' without legal validity, he arguably drew an untenably sharp distinction between the legal and the political, one that stood in tension with his general indictment of nineteenth-century positivist international law as complicit with the European domination of Asia and Africa.[112]

The stark divide that Alexandrowicz drew between the nineteenth century and the earlier period gives a powerful shape to his narrative that served his project to recreate a non-discriminatory legal order but is also the source of some weaknesses of interpretation. For example, he did not acknowledge the degree to which a sense of moral superiority (partly religious and partly civilizational) already permeated much European thought on other parts of the world before 1800. He often cited Edmund Burke as exemplary of the inclusive posture he associated with

[108] Antony Anghie, *Imperialism, Sovereignty and the Making of International Law* (Cambridge, 2005), pp. 104, 114.

[109] CHA, *The European-African Confrontation*, pp. 5, 12 (quoted), 62–83.

[110] CHA, 'The Role of German Treaty Making in the Partition of Africa', *The Indian Year Book of International Affairs*, 18, pt. II (1980), 197 (p. 331 below). Similarly, his early call to combat the 'vivisection of Asian reality' by integrating historical scholarship with the study of contemporary political and economic problems was intended to restore a recognition of Asians' agency in the past and of their traditions as political resources 'independent of Western materialism and agnosticism': CHA, 'Introduction', *Indian Year Book of International Affairs*, 3 (1954), vii.

[111] CHA, 'The Partition of Africa by Treaty', in Ingham, ed., *Foreign Relations of African States*, p. 154 (p. 257 below).

[112] Helen Kinsella, *The Image Before the Weapon: A Critical History of the Distinction Between Combatant and Civilian* (Ithaca, NY, 2011), pp. 55–6; compare CHA, 'The New States and International Law', 233 n. 16, on 'the type of positivism which was running on parallel lines with colonialism in the nineteenth century' (p. 410 n. 16 below).

pre-nineteenth-century naturalism, as one among 'a number of leading British statesmen' who believed the law of nations governed European relations with Asian states.[113] However, Burke arguably was not representative of his age but rather highly unusual in both his explicit engagement with the question whether Asian states were members of the community governed by the law of nations and his emphatically affirmative answer.[114]

Likewise, Alexandrowicz admired the German legal and political theorist J. H. G. von Justi (perhaps now best known for his influence on Kant), for his critique of European abuses of the customary law of nations. Justi had argued that European traders exploited privileges granted to foreign merchants by Indian Ocean legal custom to establish military outposts and ultimately political supremacy in the region.[115] But rather than recognizing the rarity of this view in European discourse, he cited corroborating passages from the abbé de Raynal's *Histoire des deux Indes* to claim that Justi's views were 'not isolated as far as public opinion in Europe was concerned.'[116] While a number of eloquent and prominent writers in the eighteenth century did indeed voice powerful criticisms of European abuses of law and moral principle in commercial and imperial expansion, they cannot be said to have represented anything like the pre-nineteenth-century consensus Alexandrowicz's narrative suggests.

In this way, Alexandrowicz's narrative invoked a set of heroes and of villains: among his heroes are Vladimiri and Justi, who challenged European prejudices against Asian and other 'supposedly barbarous' governments and who wrote admiringly of Asian laws of warfare that he believed made it possible to conduct hostilities in a relatively humanitarian manner. Alexandrowicz proposed Vladimiri as an early exponent of 'progressive doctrine' on relations between Christians and non-Christians, one who stressed that the dominant European position refusing to recognize legal relations with infidels posed dangers of 'international lawlessness, anarchy and even genocide which might follow from an aggressive Christian power disregarding the factual statehood and rights of non-Christian communities.'[117] Such a judgement, based on careful consideration of the historical context while also frankly anachronistic in its use of categories

[113] CHA, 'The Discriminatory Clause in South Asian Treaties in the Seventeenth and Eighteenth Centuries', 142; see also CHA, 'Mogul Sovereignty and the Law of Nations', 323; CHA, 'G. F. de Martens on Asian Treaty Practice', 72 (pp. 152, 167, 189 below); CHA, *An Introduction to the Law of Nations in the East Indies*, pp. 21–3, 231.

[114] See, for example, Burke's speech of 30 May 1794 in the closing of the impeachment trial of Warren Hastings: Edmund Burke, *The Writings and Speeches of Edmund Burke*, gen. ed. Paul Langford, 9 vols. (Oxford, 1981–97), VII, pp. 282–302. For discussion, see Jennifer Pitts, 'Empire and Legal Universalisms in the Eighteenth Century', *American Historical Review*, 117 (2012), 92–121.

[115] Ulrich Adam, *The Political Economy of J. H. G. von Justi* (Bern, 2006).

[116] CHA, 'A Treatise by J. H. G. Justi on Asian Government', *The Indian Year Book of International Affairs*, 9–10 (1960–61), 139 (p. 165 below).

[117] CHA, 'Paulus Vladimiri and the Development of the Doctrine of the Coexistence of Christian and Non-Christian Countries', 443 (p. 55 below).

like genocide, is characteristic of Alexandrowicz's approach, as is his cautious speculation about the possible influence of the ideas he traces on later doctrinal developments.

Alexandrowicz's essay on Kautilyan principles is, similarly, at once historicizing and driven by a set of enduring normative commitments to a religiously ecumenical legal framework and respect for the sovereignty of weaker powers. He set out in this essay to show with some precision how East Asian principles of inter-state conduct may have influenced modern international law by shaping early modern treaty relations and customs between Indian states and European states and commercial agents. He concluded that the principles of Kauṭilya's *Arthaśāstra* had become merely customary in relations among Indian states, and that it was the encounter with Europeans that drove Indian statesmen to articulate them as explicit principles. He speculated that Indian states' 'multi-ideological' legal framework (particularly pronounced in the Mughal empire after the reign of Akbar), their commitment to 'ties of solidarity' among polities, and their principle of respect for dependent states' sovereignty may have influenced the development of a secularized conception of the family of nations.[118] He also sought evidence of influence of South Asian principles on Europeans in the writings of authors including Raynal and Justi who he argued seem to have been aware of Indian ideas about the separation of political and religious functions and about the rules for conduct in war.

By focusing on the doctrinal universalism of thinkers such as Grotius, Freitas, Wolff, and Vattel, Alexandrowicz overlooked or downplayed the features in their work, and in that of a broader tradition of European writing on relations with Asian states, that called into question their inclusion as full members in the community governed by the law of nations. Although he noted the ideological diversity of the earlier period, he was scouring that period for evidence for his claim of a non-discriminatory legal universalism and so overlooked differences of opinion among Europeans: particularly the belief, widespread though by no means universal at that time, in Europeans' civilizational superiority over Asians, Africans, and native Americans. Accounts of 'oriental despotism' make little appearance in his narrative.[119] And he failed to see that what historians now call 'interpolity law' could generate conflict as well as cooperation.[120] Such shortcomings may be forgivable if we recall the prevailing assessment of the exoticism, inferiority, and normative irrelevance of extra-European legal orders by Alexandrowicz's contemporaries among historians of international law, most notably Wilhelm Grewe who strongly

[118] CHA, 'Kautilyan Principles and the Law of Nations', 312, 318–19 (pp. 45, 51 below); Kauṭilya, *King, Governance, and Law in Ancient India: Kauṭilya's Arthaśāstra*, trans. Patrick Olivelle (Oxford, 2013).

[119] On which see Jennifer Pitts, *Boundaries of the International* (forthcoming), ch. 2.

[120] Lauren Benton and Adam Clulow, 'Legal Encounters and the Origins of Global Law', in Jerry H. Bentley, Sanjay Subrahmanyam, and Merry E. Wiesner-Hanks, eds., *The Cambridge World History*, VI, 2: *The Construction of a Global World, 1400–1800 CE: Patterns of Change* (Cambridge, 2015), pp. 80–100.

contested Alexandrowicz's account of the universalism of the pre-positivist law of nations.[121]

Equally striking is the absence of Latin America from Alexandrowicz's historical narratives. Beginning in the 1810s, the various Latin American polities were the first new or post-colonial states to be recognized as entering the international system in the nineteenth century, in the wake of the successful assertion of anti-colonial independence by the United States. (The independence of Haïti, declared in 1804, was much more hard-fought.)[122] Latin America supplied the earliest challenges to the Eurocentrism and hierarchy of nineteenth-century international law, by lawyers such as the Argentinians Carlos Calvo and Luis Drago and the Brazilian Ruy Barbosa.[123] Latin American jurists continued up to the heyday of decolonization to intervene innovatively in debates over the legal implications of colonialism and its aftermath, as Alexandrowicz's own admiration for the dissenting opinion of the Argentinian jurist Lucio Moreno Quintana in the ICJ suggests. It is accordingly somewhat surprising that he seems to have had so little contact with or interest in historical or contemporary Latin American contributions to his subject except at the very end of his career.

The trajectory of the Iberian empires in the New World departed in some key respects from the central themes and narratives that Alexandrowicz developed in his work on Asia and Africa. Empires of territorial conquest from the start, they could not be said to have followed the path that he attributed to Europeans in Asia, in which they began as commercial agents fully prepared to recognize extra-European polities as legal counterparts and only later excluded non-Europeans from international law as their aspirations turned territorial. The new Latin American states could not be seen as returning to an international system of which they had once been members, as Asian and North African states could. And however subordinate their place in international politics and even, at times, under international law, these states had not been excluded in principle from the community of international law by nineteenth-century jurists but as European settler colonies were considered, as the major mid-nineteenth-century treatise by Henry Wheaton put it, participants in the 'public law of Europe, and of the American nations which have sprung from the European stock.'[124] Moreover, the Latin American states gained independence during exactly the period that Alexandrowicz considered international law's darkest

[121] Wilhelm G. Grewe, 'Vom europäischen zum universellen Völkerrecht: Zur Frage der Revision des "europazentrischen" Bildes der Völkerrechtsgeschichte', *Zeitschrift für ausländisches öffentliches Recht und Völkerrecht*, 42 (1982), 449–79; Grewe, *The Epochs of International Law* (1984), trans. Michael Byers (Berlin, 2000), pp. 152, 465–6; Becker Lorca, *Mestizo International Law*, pp. 32–4; Jörn Axel Kämmerer and Paulina Starski, 'Imperial Colonialism in the Genesis of International Law—Anomaly or Time of Transition', *Journal of the History of International Law*, 19 (2017).

[122] David Armitage, *The Declaration of Independence: A Global History* (Cambridge, Mass., 2007); Julia Gaffield, *Haitian Connections in the Atlantic World: Recognition after Revolution* (Chapel Hill, NC, 2015).

[123] Becker Lorca, *Mestizo International Law*, pp. 103–6, 152–60.

[124] Henry Wheaton, *Elements of International Law: With a Sketch of the History of the Science*, 2 vols. (London, 1836), I, p. 51.

time, when it was narrowing from a universal to a purely European enterprise under the influence of positivism.[125]

Alexandrowicz's commitment to discovering a multi-ideological legal framework for transnational relations occasionally led him into overstatement. One of his claims in particular has not stood the test of time: that Asian norms had not merely intersected with those of European sovereigns but had also fundamentally shaped the development of the law of nations as Europeans conceived it. Alexandrowicz acknowledged the difficulty of tracing causation but pointed to the influence of Indian Ocean maritime traditions on Grotius's conception of *mare liberum* and on the law of fishing rights as candidates.[126] He anticipated by decades the recent burst of interest in Grotius's early writings on the affairs of the Dutch East India Company (VOC),[127] and his essay 'Freitas *Versus* Grotius' (1959) remains a rare and authoritative account of the Portuguese jurist Serafim de Freitas's official response on behalf of the Spanish crown to Grotius's *Mare Liberum* (1609).[128] For Alexandrowicz the key question raised by that controversy was whether these treatises were produced in a 'legal vacuum,' or whether there instead existed a legal framework, informed by regional state practice and 'express or implied legal traditions,' recognized by the participants in the Indian Ocean trade, European and Asian alike. He maintained that Grotius must have researched regional practices in the VOC archives and that his legal arguments were informed by local principles, and that on the key question of the sovereignty and legal equality of the Asian sovereigns, Grotius and Freitas were in agreement, though he attributed to Freitas a more robust, and legally justified, conception of their sovereign right to refrain from trade with Europeans or withdraw access to their territories.[129]

More recent scholars have severely questioned this aspect of the 'Alexandrowicz thesis' on the grounds that Grotius himself knew little about the actual practices in the Indian Ocean arena and that he had his own domestic reasons, springing from the ideological needs of the VOC and from the circumstances of Dutch

[125] Mikulas Fabry, *Recognizing States: International Society and the Establishment of New States since 1776* (Oxford, 2010), stresses the importance of Latin American independence for the formation of modern theories of recognition and statehood.

[126] CHA, 'Grotius and India' (pp. 113–20 below); see also R. P. Anand, 'Maritime Practice in South-East Asia until 1600 A.D. and the Modern Law of the Sea', *International and Comparative Law Quarterly*, 30 (1981), 440–54; Anand, *Origin and Development of the Law of the Sea: History of International Law Revisited* (The Hague, 1983).

[127] Hugo Grotius, *Commentary on the Law of Prize and Booty* (1604), ed. Martine Julia van Ittersum (Indianapolis, 2006); Grotius, *The Free Sea* (1609), ed. David Armitage (Indianapolis, 2004); van Ittersum, *Profit and Principle: Hugo Grotius, Natural Rights Theories and the Rise of Dutch Power in the East Indies, 1595–1615* (Leiden, 2006); Eric Wilson, *The Savage Republic: De Indis of Hugo Grotius, Republicanism, and Dutch Hegemony within the Early Modern World-System (c. 1600–1619)* (Leiden, 2008); Peter Borschberg, *Hugo Grotius, the Portuguese and Free Trade in the East Indies* (Singapore, 2011).

[128] Serafim de Freitas, *De iusto imperio Lusitanorum asiatico* (Valladolid, 1625); on Freitas, see now Mónica Brito Vieira, '*Mare Liberum* vs. *Mare Clausum*: Grotius, Freitas, and Selden's Debate on Dominion over the Seas', *Journal of the History of Ideas*, 64 (2003), 361–77; Anthony Pagden, *The Burdens of Empire: 1539 to the Present* (Cambridge, 2015), pp. 130–47.

[129] CHA, 'Freitas *Versus* Grotius', *British Year Book of International Law*, 35 (1959), 164–5 (pp. 123–4 below); CHA, *An Introduction to the Law of Nations in the East Indies*, pp. 41–82.

republicanism after the revolt from Spain, for promoting the freedom of the seas and espousing theories of divisible sovereignty.[130] It is less clear that Alexandrowicz thought that European treaties recognized Asian states as possessing equal sovereignty and sharing membership in a law-of-nations community or that practices in South and Southeast Asia were not derogatory to the sovereignty of non-European states. He also insisted, against nineteenth-century views and those of more recent scholars, that the so-called capitulations, agreements granting legal privileges to European merchant communities in the Ottoman Empire and elsewhere, did not establish the legal inferiority or compromise the sovereignty of the states granting such privileges.[131] However, recent scholarship on early modern Eurasia has affirmed at least some 'clear parallels with political practices across the region,' in the process of re-examining questions Alexandrowicz had first raised regarding indigenous treaty-making, diplomacy, and legal consciousness.[132]

Alexandrowicz was engaged in a fundamentally recuperative project. His aim was to loosen the conceptual and ideological grip of what he called positivism but could more broadly be called the nineteenth-century understanding of international law.[133] He deplored its 'fallacy of projecting the present onto the past,' particularly the error of assuming that nineteenth-century Europe's economic and military supremacy, and consequent posture of cultural and legal superiority, had characterized their earlier relations with Asian states. He saw his own expansive vision for a more just, inclusive, and egalitarian international order presaged by

[130] C. G. Roelofsen, 'The Sources of *Mare Liberum*: Contested Origins of the Doctrine of the Freedom of the Seas', in W. P. Heere, ed., *International Law and its Sources: Liber Amicorum Maarten Bos* (Deventer, 1988), pp. 93–124; Borschberg, *Hugo Grotius, the Portuguese and Free Trade in the East Indies*, pp. 80–81, 109, 145 ('The "Alexandrowicz thesis" ... cannot be sustained by any stretch of the imagination'); Eric Wilson, 'The "Alexandrowicz Thesis" Revisited: Hugo Grotius, Divisible Sovereignty, and Private Avengers within the Indian Ocean World System', in Ooi Keat Gin and Hoang Anh Tuan, eds., *Early Modern Southeast Asia, 1350–1800* (London, 2015), pp. 28–54.

[131] CHA, *An Introduction to the Law of Nations in the East Indies*, pp. 97–128; CHA, 'Some Problems of the History of the Law of Nations in Asia', 10–11; CHA, 'G. F. de Martens on Asian Treaty Practice', 67; CHA, 'A Treatise by J. H. G. Justi on Asian Government', 137 (pp. 81–2, 186, 164 below). For more recent assessments of the capitulations see, for example, Feroz Ahmad, 'Ottoman Perceptions of the Capitulations, 1800–1914', *Journal of Islamic Studies*, 11 (2000), 1–20; Maurits H. van den Boogert, *The Capitulations and the Ottoman Legal System: Qadis, Consuls, and Beraths in the 18th Century* (Leiden, 2005); Turan Kayaoğlu, *Legal Imperialism: Sovereignty and Extraterritoriality in Japan, the Ottoman Empire, and China* (Cambridge, 2010), pp. 104–48.

[132] Adam Clulow, 'The Art of Claiming: Possession and Resistance in Early Modern Asia', *American Historical Review*, 121 (2016), 29; more generally, see Sanjay Subrahmanyam, *Courtly Encounters: Translating Courtliness and Violence in Early Modern Eurasia* (Cambridge, Mass., 2012); Saliha Belmessous, ed., *Native Claims: Indigenous Law Against Empire, 1500–1920* (Oxford, 2012); Belmessous, ed., *Empire by Treaty: Negotiating European Expansion, 1600–1900* (Oxford, 2014); Joan-Pau Rubiés, 'Political Rationality and Cultural Distance in the European Embassies to Shah Abbas', *Journal of Early Modern History*, 20 (2016), 351–89.

[133] Nineteenth-century proponents of natural law, or of a fusion of natural and positive law, such as Travers Twiss or James Lorimer, shared their contemporaries' Eurocentrism and their exclusion of extra-European states from the 'family of nations': Twiss, *Two Introductory Lectures on the Science of International Law* (London, 1856), p. 49; Lorimer, *Institutes of the Law of Nations* (Edinburgh, 1884), pp. 98, 123; Andrew Fitzmaurice, *Sovereignty, Property and Empire, 1500–2000* (Cambridge, 2014), pp. 232, 276–84.

the naturalist and universalist conception of the law of nations he believed had distinguished the modern period through the end of the eighteenth century. This classical law of nations 'was in essence not a mono-ideological system';[134] instead, it 'promoted universal intercourse in response to a social reality extending to the whole world,' a process that accelerated in the nineteenth and twentieth centuries with the proliferation of new forms of interconnection and communication, in posts, telecommunications, and aviation. The advent of satellite technology in outer space even allowed an extraterrestrial escape from the constraints of merely 'geocentric law'.[135]

Alexandrowicz's desire to establish equality in the present may have coloured his assumptions about equality in the past. His egalitarian project was progressive and redressive, premised on the creation, or the *re*-creation, of 'horizontal' transnational solidarities to combat the 'vertical' divisions fracturing international society.[136] Yet his vision was also somewhat utopian, based on the belief that international lawyers in particular could refine the norms that would restrain 'power politicians' and force them to 'choose the path of peace'.[137] This antipathy to 'power politics,' his preference for 'international society' in the relations between states, and his scepticism that colonialism was a useful category of historical analysis, may have blinded him to the ways that power saturates law.[138] Alexandrowicz's concern was more to expose the 'fallacy' of Eurocentric positivism as a legal doctrine—and thus to reveal its failure as law—than to explore how it operated as ideology.[139] He argued that positivists' move to condemn the extra-European world to a legal vacuum 'could hardly be considered realistic': it represented a capitulation to 'doctrinal trends' rather than a sound legal argument, and the alternative account he proposed was both legally superior and 'objective'.[140] He tended, in short, to suggest that his work could be

[134] CHA, *An Introduction to the Law of Nations in the East Indies*, p. 237.

[135] CHA, *The Law of Global Communications*, pp. 132, 25, 142 ('The legal status of outer space is not geocentric').

[136] CHA, 'Vertical and Horizontal Divisions of the International Society', *The Indian Year Book of International Affairs*, 1 (1952), 88–96.

[137] 'International Law: The Need for Clarifying Rules Stressed', *The Hindu* (13 February 1952), 7. Alexandrowicz's rejection at this moment of 'power politics' and his faith in the restraining force of international law likely represent an implied critique of Georg Schwarzenberger's pessimistically realist *Power Politics* (1941), which had just been reissued in a much expanded 2nd edition: Schwarzenberger, *Power Politics: A Study of International Society* (London, 1951).

[138] CHA, review of Robert Redslob, *Traité de Droit des Gens* (1950), *International Law Quarterly*, 4 (1951), 437 (on 'Power Politics' *versus* international integration); CHA, 'The Quasi-Judicial Function in Recognition of States and Governments', *American Journal of International Law*, 46 (1952), 631–40 (on 'power politics' *versus* 'international society'); CHA, 'Le Droit des Nations aux Indes Orientales: Aux XVIe, XVIIe, XVIIIe siècles', *Annales. Histoire, Sciences Sociales*, 19 (1964), 1084 (scepticism about 'colonialism') (pp. 375–84, 112 below).

[139] For example, 'the proclamation of [the European positive law of nations] as universal without universal participation was bound to result in a *pars pro toto* fallacy': CHA, 'G. F. de Martens on Asian Treaty Practice', 75 n. 27 (p. 191 n. 37 below).

[140] CHA, 'Doctrinal Aspects of the Universality of the Law of Nations', 515 (p. 178 below); 'If the connections between the West and Asia are to be conceived *in objective terms* ...': [CHA,] 'Introduction', *The Indian Year Book of International Affairs*, 3 (1954), viii (our emphasis).

historical and juridical without being political.[141] Nonetheless, his consistent use of history as a critical solvent of prejudice, his commitment to a cosmopolitan law of nations, and his determination to provincialize Europe long before that move became reflexive still have the capacity to unsettle and inspire. As Alexandrowicz pointedly asked in a posthumously published essay: 'are we to carry on with the outdated axioms of historians of international law still basing the *universal* international law, valid for all continents, on nothing but Western history?'[142]

[141] Contemporary proponents of critical legal studies, in contrast, stress law's inextricability from politics; as Martti Koskenniemi writes, '[t]here is no space in international law that would … not involve a "choice"—that would not be, in this sense, a politics of international law': Koskenniemi, *From Apology to Utopia: The Structure of International Legal Argument. Reissue with New Epilogue* (Cambridge, 2005), pp. 589–96 (p. 596 quoted).

[142] CHA, 'The Role of German Treaty Making in the Partition of Africa', 203 (Alexandrowicz's emphasis) (p. 353 below).

PART I

THE EARLY HISTORY OF THE LAW OF NATIONS

1

KAUTILYAN PRINCIPLES AND THE LAW OF NATIONS (1965–66)

I. Introduction

The historian of the law of nations who intends to ascertain the totality of factors which contributed to the development of our system of international law cannot confine his inquiry to pre-nineteenth-century Europe only. The orthodox view expressed in some of our treatises that the present-day system of international law is exclusively a product of Christian civilization and had been established by the European Family of Nations only is not tenable in the light of historical reality.[1] This view ignores *inter alia* the significance of treaty and diplomatic relations between Europe and a number of Asian sovereigns[2] which accompanied the spectacular growth of East Indian trade during the sixteenth, seventeenth and eighteenth centuries.[3] During that period trade between the two continents had become an important element in the development of European economy and there is no reason to doubt that all the agencies participating in this trade, i.e. the Portuguese and the Dutch, English and French East India Companies (endowed with delegated sovereign powers) on the one hand, and the East Indian sovereigns on the other, applied and generated in their mutual transactions legal principles and usages which ultimately became part and parcel of our generally accepted code of inter-State conduct. The influence exercised by the European agencies on the formulation of East Indian treaties or diplomatic transactions can be studied by an analysis of our classical treatises and the source material contained in European collections of treaties[4] and other documents available in East India Company or other archives. It is, however, much more difficult to ascertain the impact of inter-sovereign usage as observed by East Indian rulers *inter se* on the formulation of treaties and transactions concluded with European entities, for such usage was rarely defined by writers and the meaning of the relevant rules can only be gathered from historical records part of which are not even translated into European languages. But some of these rules had been sorted out and classified much earlier in the systematic expositions

[1] Nussbaum, *A Concise History of the Law of Nations* (1954).
[2] Not including China and Japan which remained in isolation prior to the nineteenth century.
[3] Van Leur, *Indonesian Trade and Society* (1960).
[4] Collections of treaties by Bicker, Heeres, Aitchison, Hertslet, etc.

of statecraft written in the classical period of Hindu literature. Among the works of this period Kautilya's *Arthasastra* (fourth century B.C.)[5] is one of the most significant sources indicating the principles of inter-sovereign conduct in India and Further India.[6] Whether the rules defined in this work have been fully observed by the sovereigns in the post-classical period up to the advent of the European agencies in the East Indies must remain an open question. But it is nevertheless possible to conceive the existence of a Kautilyan tradition even at that period and, to the extent to which its survival (subject to modifications) can be assumed, it is also possible to see the attitude of East Indian sovereigns towards the European newcomer in the East Indies in a better perspective. This would also allow historians to interpret some of the characteristic features of the approach of these sovereigns to negotiations with European agencies. If such an interpretation is possible, in the light of a tradition which evolved from a well-known classical treatise, an examination of the impact of its principles on the general development of the law of nations could also be attempted.

In 1960 an All-India Seminar was held at the University of Delhi which concerned itself with the possible contribution of Indian traditions to the development of international law.[7] The reading of the Report of the Seminar (which is not commercially available, but can now be found in a few libraries) deserves the attention of historians of the law of nations.

Dr. Rao, Vice-Chancellor of Delhi University, who inaugurated the Seminar, expressed in his opening address the view that the origin of Indian traditions of international law should be sought in *dharma*, the law of righteousness. Indian traditions (he said) are remarkable for their actual or possible reliance on dharmic rules regulating relations between the individual, the family, the community and the State. This system tried to circumscribe the anarchic freedom of the individual and to convert it into a disciplined one. In the inter-State field it found its expression in the habit of discussing conflicting views and interests, arguing and negotiating 'to the limit' in order to preserve peace.[8] The Seminar concentrated on a number

[5] See translations from Sanskrit by R. P. Kangle (1963) and by Shamasastry (1951). Among the post-Vedic sources containing rules of inter-sovereign conduct are the Ramayana, the Mahabharata, the codes of Manu and Yajnavalkya, Kamanadaka's Nitisara, Kalidasa and the works of the Jaina writers (Somadeva and Hemachandra); see U. N. Ghoshal, *History of Indian Political Ideas* (1959). But Kautilya's *Arthasastra* gives the most systematic and complete code of rules dealing with inter-sovereign conduct. As to the meaning of classical or post-classical period, see Ghoshal, op. cit., and Altekar, *State and Government in Ancient India* (1958).

[6] For the purpose of this study, Further India is an area beyond the Indian sub-continent covering Ceylon, Burma, Siam and the Indonesian Islands (also Indo-China).

[7] *Indian Traditions and the Rule of Law among Nations: Report of the All-India Seminar* (1960). A number of well-defined questions were put to its participants by Professor Julius Stone.

[8] Dr. V. K. R. V. Rao's view was *mutatis mutandis* reiterated by Professor J. D. M. Derrett in his critical comment on the Report of the Seminar (*International and Comparative Law Quarterly* 11 (1962), p. 266) in which he considers the question what the world could learn from India's cultural heritage. In an answer to this question he refers to the Gandhian theory of life and its dharmic aspects and he points to the ancient Indian experience of relying on an inter-group public opinion and its pacifying influence in the past. See also Professor Derrett's views in the 'Maintenance of Peace in the Hindu World: Practice and Theory', *Indian Year Book of International Affairs* 7 (1958), pp. 361–87.

of problems such as the significance of *pacta sunt servanda* in *dharmasastra* and *arthasastra*; the importance of *mandala* (circle of States) as the expression of balance of power; the role of the principle of nonviolence (*ahimsa*); the settlement of conflicts by third-party judgment;[9] and the record of diplomacy and negotiation 'to the limit'. The Seminar also compared some of the Hindu traditions with Islamic traditions in India and it examined the question of the extent to which the Indian foreign policy makers at present have tended to act on these ancient traditions.

Before some of these problems are considered it would be relevant to state that it serves no purpose to examine the direct and immediate impact of ancient Indian traditions of inter-State conduct on present-day Indian foreign policy or on our system of international law. The Government of India, as well as the governments of other newly independent States, apply the principles of international law as they find them in the existing treaty and customary law observed by the Family of Nations. The Indian Government may claim to have followed a *sui generis* ideology in international politics, but this ideology is certainly not the direct outcome of the ancient inter-State law of India.[10] What the participants of the Seminar failed to consider is the point in time at which Indian traditions of inter-State conduct were still capable of exercising a direct influence on our system of the law of nations. It must be recalled that these traditions came to an end with the collapse of the independent State system in India and Further India at the end of the eighteenth century and the beginning of the nineteenth century. The possibility of such influence simply vanished at a later date when the Indian sub-continent was either under British administration or under the paramountcy of the Crown, and when the various States of Further India came either under British or Dutch rule or remained semi-independent only and ceased to act on their ancient traditions of inter-State conduct. The only point in time at which a direct influence of such traditions on our law of nations was possible was the period of the sixteenth, seventeenth and eighteenth centuries: at that time many of the sovereigns of India and Further India still enjoyed genuine independence and maintained treaty and diplomatic relations with the European agencies in the East Indies (exercising direct or delegated sovereign powers) to which they tended to apply some of their own notions and usages of inter-State conduct. It is in the framework of these treaties and diplomatic relations that the confrontation of European and Asian legal concepts took place, exercising a measure of influence on the general development of the law of nations. With these considerations in mind an attempt will be made to discuss some of the ancient Indian traditions of inter-State conduct, particularly those evolved from Kautilyan principles, and to recall a few instances in which their application in the sixteenth, seventeenth and eighteenth centuries can be traced in treaties or other transactions concluded with European agencies.

[9] The Seminar expressed the view that such third-party judgment did not exist in ancient India.

[10] The view was expressed at the Seminar that non-violence (*ahimsa*) was quite alien to Indian tradition and practice in inter-State relations. See Derrett, *International and Comparative Law Quarterly* 11 (1962), p. 266. But the doctrine of *ahimsa* tended to be respected in Jainist and Buddhist practice.

Arthasastra

One of the remarkable features of Kautilya's *Arthasastra* lies in the fact that it is a work containing not only rules of government and administration but also a systematic exposition of principles of inter-sovereign relations.[11] Until Kautilya, Chandragupta Maurya's Chancellor, completed his treatise in the fourth century B.C., politics had not been an independent science in India but remained largely a branch of social ethics.[12] *Arthasastra* constitutes a divorce of politics (internal and external) from moral philosophy and creates a dichotomy typical of brahmin learning which contrasted sharply with the Buddhist concept of the supremacy of moral law over and above politics.[13] In terms of European philosophy it might be comparable with the efforts of those theologians and lawyers who tried to extricate the *jus gentium* from the grip of theology. St. Thomas Aquinas was no doubt aware of the need for some separation of the two disciplines, but it was Grotius who made the first decisive effort to conceive the law of nations as a discipline with an existence independent from theology or metaphysics. Comparisons of works so remote in space and time are usually precarious, but there is no risk in emphasizing the trend towards the emancipation of rules of inter-State conduct from religion at different periods in Europe and in the East, though the process of secularization took place in different ways and circumstances. We shall revert to this problem later.

A brief summary of Kautilya's work is bound to start with the fundamental notions of the State on which the further structure of inter-State conduct is superimposed. Unlike the Buddhist doctrine which tends to see the foundations of the State in a quasi contractual relationship between ruler and people,[14] Kautilya—in a truly brahmanist (or Hobbesian) way—is a pessimist and sees government as a remedy to the universal anarchy, or 'the law of the fish' according to which the stronger swallows up the weaker (*matsyanyaya*) (I. 4). The answer to anarchy is *danda* which may *inter alia* mean punishment or sanction. If the sovereign does not use the rod, it gives rise to the law of the fish. He is honoured if he uses it in a just way, he is despised if he is mild, and hated if he is too severe (I. 4).

[11] Ghoshal, op. cit., discusses the gradual development of the literature on politics beginning with the vedic literature, the brahmanical law books (*smritis* and *puranas*) and the works of the Buddhist and Jaina writers. Among the Buddhist writers he refers particularly to Aryadeva, representing the unitary moral standard characteristic to Buddhist doctrine (different from the dual standards of brahmanism).

[12] In the *dharmasastras* the theory of kingship, sovereignty and inter-sovereign conduct was not yet conceived by itself but only as an *incident* of the comprehensive scheme of the social structure. Kautilya perfected the theory and it was then incorporated in the later works written between 200 B.C. and A.D. 300. See Ghoshal, op. cit.

[13] Buddhist theory considered the science of politics as morally questionable. See C. Drekmayer, *Kautilya and Community in Early India* (1962), p. 221.

[14] Buddhist theory contemplates an ideal state of nature which makes it possible for the sovereign and his people to enter into a pact. It rejects the divine origin of classes, but tends to view the sovereign as a religious figure. If so, the sovereign is involved in the propagation of his religion and he cannot be secular. On the other hand, the Kautilyan system separates the ruler's caste from the priestly caste, and allows him to pursue a non-discriminatory policy as far as religion or civilization is concerned. Under this system there is no conflict between temporal and spiritual power. See Ghoshal, op. cit., chs. XXVI–XXVII.

Sovereignty is vested in the ruler (dynasty);[15] but his position within the State is of a peculiar nature, for he is part and parcel of the caste system (*varna*), a social structure of divine origin based on a hereditary division of social functions. The remarkable feature of this system is the separation of the religious function from political power. The first is exercised by the brahmans, the highest caste, while the second is vested in the rulers' or warriors' caste (*ksatryas*).[16] A logical consequence of this separation of power was the secularization of the royal function in the hands of the *ksatryas*[17] and this led further to a secular concept of the law of inter-sovereign conduct, a development quite different from that in Europe at a much later date (Middle Ages). Moreover, the existence of the same caste system across the vertical boundaries of hundreds of States in India and Further India created a horizontal social stratum (whether rulers by birth or by legitimation) with its own bonds of solidarity. Thus dynastic legitimism[18] and to some extent inter-dynastic solidarity are two of the elements which gave some coherence to the otherwise heterogeneous network of States in the Indian sub-continent. Heterogeneity was first and foremost linguistic (as it is today), but also racial or ethnical, if we consider the differences between the Aryan North and the Dravidian South.

An important consequence of inter-dynastic cohesion or solidarity was the principle of respect shown by the victorious ruler to the sovereignty of the defeated ruler. In order to understand this principle which was so essential in the history of Indian States, a brief analysis of the pattern of the network of States has first to be attempted. The classic model of this network is based on the concept of the circle of States (*mandala*), that is to say a group of States linked together by their common affairs of peace and war which found expression in bonds of alliance and neutrality, or in hostility. In the centre of the circle is a hypothetical ruler (*vijigishu*),

[15] Hinsley in his recent work on *Sovereignty* (1966) draws our attention to the gradual evolution of the concept of sovereignty. The theory that sovereignty in the Hindu State was vested in the people seems doubtful. See H. Chatterjee, *International Law and Inter-State Relations in Ancient India* (1958); and J. W. Spellman, *Political Theory of Ancient India* (1964). The sovereign was probably the ultimate proprietary lord of the land and *ryots* (small farmers) received from him small holdings as lease-holders. The *zamindars* (and those assimilated to them) had no proprietary rights, but were revenue collectors only. It was in the absence of great landowners (hereditary) in India that the sovereign's power became absolute. See R. Patton, *The Principles of Asiatic Monarchies* (1801). For a different view according to which territory was not vested in the sovereign but belonged to the State (*rajya*), see Ghoshal, op. cit., p. 213, 370.

[16] Rulers had the title of *rajas* even if they were not *ksatryas*. On the other hand, *ksatryas* were *rajas* even if they were not rulers; see Ghoshal, ibid.

[17] L. Dumont, 'Conception of Kingship in Ancient India', *Contributions to Indian Sociology* (1962).

[18] As to the merits of the hereditary monarchy and dynastic legitimism, Kautilya in his definition of the seven constituent elements of the State (king, minister, country, fortified city, treasury, army and allies) refers to the king as one born in high family (VI. 1), and elsewhere he says that in the people's conviction a weak king of noble birth is preferable to a strong but low-born king (VIII. 2). He also pronounces himself against the foundation of new dynasties, for the king of an established dynasty remains faithful to the traditional concept of royalty. It would follow that in case of war the victorious ruler must abstain from *debellatio* of a defeated ruler, particularly when the latter is of noble birth (principle of inter-dynastic solidarity); see pp. 40–1 below. The theory of the seven elements of the State appears also in *Manu, Yajnavalkya* and in the *Mahabharata*. See Kalidas Nag, *Les Théories diplomatiques de l'Inde ancienne et l'Arthacâstra* (1923). As to the doctrine of the Sovereign and inter-Sovereign relations in *Manu*, see *The Laws of Manu* (transl. by G. Bühler, 1886).

an egocentric sovereign and 'would-be' conqueror, who envisages the world round him as an area of expansion. He considers his immediate neighbours as enemies (*ari*) and the neighbours of his neighbours as friends (*mitra*). In the periphery of the circle are the friends of his enemies, the friends of his friends, and the friends of the friends of his enemies.[19] This obviously seems to be a post-Vedic chessboard concept which is not to be taken literally, but it symbolizes, in the absence of an organization of States, the idea of balance of power.[20] The *vijigishu* in each circle acts in principle according to *dharma* (law of righteousness) but in practice according to expediency (*artha*), and conducts his policy according to requirements of security.[21] But there was not much security in this dynamic arrangement as the Indian sub-continent was covered by a multitude of circles, the centre of each constituting a source of aggression. Prima facie no concept of coexistence seems to be implied in the whole system, but if its deeper motives are explored, some purpose and order tends to emerge out of the chaos. For the final aim of this dynamic policy was the unification of the sub-continent under the most successful *vijigishu*, who would replace decentralization by a universal empire. The sovereign who, through political manœuvring or conquest[22] would gain control over other sovereigns, would become the supreme suzerain or emperor (*cacravartin* or *sarvabhauma*),[23] an ideal rarely realized in Indian history and if it was achieved it usually only lasted for a short period. The Mauryan dynasty unified India during one century and the next effective unification covering the whole sub-continent (or the greater part of it) lasted barely three centuries (Moghul India).[24] In the interminable process of unification, oscillating between centralization and decentralization, a network of suzerains and vassals established itself gradually and some dynasties rose to the level of major powers while others became dependent on one or another overlord. But whatever their position in the network, they remained in principle on the political map of India even if subjected to the control of an actual or potential suzerain or unifier of the sub-continent. Contrary to European practice in the past, *debellatio* was rarely applied here to a defeated ruler. This rule would seem to reveal the consciousness of some inter-dynastic solidarity which prevailed throughout the rulers' stratum (caste). Though it was not an integrative force unifying the Indian sub-continent, it was certainly a social force modifying the harshness of power politics and wars. The European agencies in the East Indies had found their place in the local network of suzerain–vassal relations whether

[19] The circle should be established by the *vijigishu* in front and in his rear (VII. 13).

[20] The concept proposed by Kautilya proves that he conceived *Arthasastra* in the light of pre-Mauryan experience, i.e. before the establishment of the centralised Mauryan Empire.

[21] In spite of the fact that *dharma* prevails in case of conflict over *artha*.

[22] Kautilya advocates political persuasion in preference to war. He states that the powerful sovereign 'should subjugate the weak by means of conciliation' (VII. 16); R. Bhaskaran, 'The Four Upayas of Hindu Diplomacy', *Indian Year Book of International Affairs*, 3, (1954) p. 126.

[23] The *sarvabhauma* is the performer of a sacrifice reserved to suzerains (*asvamedha*).

[24] The period of the Mauryan Empire and its succession States lasted from 325 B.C. to the fourth century A.D. The latter were followed by the Imperial Guptas. But neither the Guptas nor their successors, nor the pre-Moghul Islamic dynasties unified the whole of India.

as suzerains or vassals (real or nominal). Whenever they tried to do away with the rights of their subordinate vassals, they became involved in serious conflicts; and there is no reason to doubt that some of the European writers (Vattel, Justi, de Martens)[25] who became familiar with Eastern State practice formulated their views on sovereignty *inter alia* under the impact of that practice.[26]

The most important part of *Arthasastra* as far as the rules of inter-State conduct are concerned is Book VII relating to the so-called six measures of foreign policy. The first two of these measures are peace (*sandhi*) and war (*vigraha*), the latter being a legitimate institution of the Indian State system in the past.[27] They are followed by neutrality (*asana*), the preparative stage of entry into action (marching—*yana*), alliance (*samsraya*) and dual policy.[28] Peace can, according to Kautilya, be maintained by the conclusion of a treaty with a more powerful sovereign, while war is waged against the weaker one. The idea of neutrality is not comparable to our concept of neutrality but indicates an intermediary stage (neither peace nor war). Alliances are concluded to obtain the protection of a powerful ruler. Kautilya states that the purpose of the sixfold policy is to make a sovereign advance from the stage of decline to the stage of balance, and further to the stage of progress (VIII. 1). He explains in VII. 1 what he means by advancement, i.e. the promotion of one's own 'undertakings concerning forts, water works, trade routes, settling waste land, mines … forests … If there is equal advancement in peace or war, he [the ruler] should resort to peace. For in war there are losses …'.

The system of political expediency shows the true nature of treaty-making in India. Sovereigns are in principle reluctant to conclude a treaty as this involves a limitation of sovereignty and reveals a position of weakness. If the conclusion of a treaty was absolutely necessary, a personal treaty was preferable to a real treaty which would bind the heirs and successors of the contracting sovereigns.[29] But in spite of the disadvantages which may follow from treaty-making, Kautilya emphasizes strongly the principles *pacta sunt servanda* and *bona fides*. Once a treaty is concluded, it is absolutely binding, irrespective of the sanctions attached to it. He states in VII. 17: 'Pledging one's faith or taking an oath is a pact stable in the next world as well as here, a surety or a hostage is of use only in this world, depending on strength. "We have made a pact": thus Kings of old, faithful to their word, made pacts by pledging their faith'.

[25] See Justi, *Les gouvernements de l'Europe comparés à ceux de l'Asie* (1762) [*Vergleichungen der europäischen mit den asiatischen und andern vermeintlich barbarischen Regierungen* (Berlin; Stettin; Leipzig, 1762)]. As to Vattel and G. F. de Martens, see pp. 51–2 below.

[26] As to instances of legal protection of vassal rulers, see this writer's, 'Treaty and Diplomatic Relations between European and South Asian Powers', *Recueil des cours* (1960), pp. 207–320. See particularly the case of the Raja of Benares (p. 216). On the problem of inter-dynastic solidarity see the critical comment by Upendra Baxi, *Kautilyan Principles* (Grotian Society Papers, 1967).

[27] Wars were often connected with frontier disputes, sharing of river waters, dynastic feuds, etc. See M. V. Krishna Rao, *Studies in Kautilya* (1958).

[28] I.e. peace with one ruler while war is waged with another (*dvaidhibhavah*).

[29] As to various types of treaties, see VII. 3.

The pressure within the circle of States made the ruler advance from the state of decline to that of balance and progress, but the circle was, in spite of its dynamism and its relations with other circles, governed by principles which assured a measure of external stability and public order. No sovereign could afford to violate these principles without the risk of losing the confidence of other sovereigns in the circle. Thus each sovereign had the sacred duty to respect the right of other dynasties to continuous existence. *Debellatio* in case of defeat would have been a provocation of the circle, which would have risen against the violator of this right. Kautilya states that the just conqueror is satisfied with the obeisance of the defeated ruler (XII. 1).[30] A weak ruler may be compelled to cede part of his territory but he should retain the capital of his country (XII. 1). He advises the strong sovereign that 'if the weaker [ruler] were to remain submissive in all respects, he should make peace with him. For heroism born of grief and resentment make one fight bravely like a forest fire. And he [the weaker ruler] becomes the object of favour of the circle [of kings]' (VII. 3). And, further, he speaks about the (middle) king grown very powerful, who 'has risen for the destruction of all of us'. The circle should rise against him (VII. 18). In the same way advantages gained by the breach of a treaty are detestable to the circle of States. Kautilya states: 'A gain repugnant to the circle [of Kings] because of the extermination of an ally or the violation of a treaty is an advantage that is dangerous' (IX. 7). Thus the circle is, on the one hand, a dynamic vehicle for the unification of the sub-continent and, on the other, a guarantee of restraint on the part of the rulers and a means for the preservation of the balance of power. The next stage (failing unification) would be the establishment of an international organization, a step which was taken neither in Europe nor in Asia prior to the twentieth century.[31] But confederations of States appeared in the Indian sub-continent in the eighteenth century, to mention only the Maratha State, an association of rulers under the supreme government of the Peshwa at Poona. Moreover, the Moghul Empire at the stage of its decentralization in the eighteenth century became a composite entity similar to the Holy Roman Empire.[32]

Kautilya underlines the importance of negotiations between sovereigns which played a considerable role in the conclusion of alliances and in affairs of war and peace (I. 16). Negotiation 'to the limit' was the principal medium of finding a solution of conflicts before resorting to war. Instead of turning to hostilities, rulers—in

[30] Kautilya contrasts the righteous conqueror with the 'greedy' and 'demoniac' conquerors (XII. 1). The righteous conqueror would obviously respect the caste structure of the people of the defeated country, including its Ruler and dynasty. This is *ksatrya* tradition (W. Ruben, 'Inter-State Relations in Ancient India and Kautilya's Arthasastra', *Indian Year Book of International Affairs*, 4 (1955), p. 141). In this way the *vijigishu* respecting the continuity of the monarchy of his neighbours safeguards the continuity of the monarchical institutions in his own country.

[31] Emeric Crucé in his Project of a Universal Union of States (*Nouveau cynée*, 1623) included not only European powers but also a number of Asian sovereigns, such as the Ottoman Emperor, the King of Persia, the Moghul Emperor and other sovereigns; see E. Nys, *Les origines du droit international* (1894).

[32] As to the similarity between the two empires in the eighteenth century, see Westlake, *Collected Papers on Public International Law* (1914) p. 197; see also F. J. Berber, 'International Aspects of the Holy Roman Empire', *Grotian Society Papers* (1964), vol. 1, p. 174.

a truly Kautilyan spirit—tried to gain the desired advantages in the 'battle of wits' (*mantra-yuddha*). Negotiations were conducted either by sovereigns or by their envoys (*dutas*). What Kautilya writes about *dutas* finds its confirmation in the *Memoir* of Megasthenes, Greek ambassador to the court of the Mauryan Emperor. Megasthenes was sent in the fourth century B.C. by Seleucus Nicator with an embassy to Chandragupta Maurya. He wrote four books of *Indica*, of which only fragments remain. These have been translated into English[33] and contain information about the emperor, his court, the civil service and the caste system as well as other details.[34]

On envoys Kautilya writes (in I. 16) that 'when consultation had led to a choice of decision, the employment of the envoy [should follow]. One endowed with the excellence of a minister is the plenipotentiary'.[35] He is a *nisrstartha* if the matter has been entrusted to him with full power of negotiation; otherwise he is a messenger only.[36] The functions of envoys are: 'Sending communications, recording the terms of a treaty, [upholding his King's] majesty, acquisition of allies ...' (I. 16). As to diplomatic privileges and immunities, Kautilya reserves even to 'the lowest born' *dutas* personal inviolability: 'If not permitted to depart [home], he should stay on'. He may be detained by a variety of reasons. It is remarkable that European ambassadors (whether royal or East India Company envoys), who visited the courts of East Indian sovereigns in the sixteenth, seventeenth and eighteenth centuries, found everywhere the same pattern of diplomatic ceremonial and etiquette which reflected diplomatic usages described in the classical literature. They often complained about restrictions imposed on their freedom of movement by the receiving courts, which gave the impression of detention but were in principle measures directed against espionage about which Kautilya had so much to say (VII. 13, XIII. 1). Finally it has to be noted that the *duta* was always an *ad hoc*, not a permanent, envoy.

This brief account of the provisions of *Arthasastra* relating to rules of inter-State conduct would not be complete without reference to some of the administrative departments in a Hindu sovereign's government which carried out external functions. Significant among them was the Controller of Shipping (II. 28), whose duty it was to 'rescue boats that have gone out of their course or are tossed about on the sea, when they come within the domain [of the State],' and 'he should destroy [boats] that cause harm, also those coming over from the enemy's territory[37] and those

[33] By J. H. McCrindle in 1877.

[34] O. Stein, *Megasthenes and Kautilya* (1921). The author attempts a comparison between *Indica* and *Arthasastra*. Megasthenes draws attention *inter alia* to the respect for the rights of non-combatants in India.

[35] As to a discussion of the qualities of an ambassador in classical European literature see Dr. K. R. Simmonds, 'Gentili on the Qualities of the Ideal Ambassador', *Grotian Society Papers* (1964), vol. 1, pp. 47–58.

[36] *Arthasastra* distinguishes 3 types of *dutas*: (1) The envoy expounding his ruler's affairs and adapting his words to circumstances; (2) the envoy communicating only what he has been told; and (3), the envoy carrying a royal decree. See L. Rocher, 'The Ambassador in Ancient India', *Indian Year Book of International Affairs* 7 (1958), pp. 344–60.

[37] The question may arise whether Kautilya deals here with contraband. See R. P. Kangle, *The Kautilya Arthasastra* (1963), commentary to II. 28. As to meaning of the 'domain', see Meyer's translation (1923), p. 198: 'Von Meerschiffen die in sein Gebiet kommen, soll er den Zoll verlangen'. As to

violating the regulations of the port'. One of the functions was also the destruction of piratical ships (*himsrika*) (II. 28). Kautilya had no doubt an approximately correct appreciation of the difference between the legal status of inland or territorial waters (within his domain) and the high seas (beyond his domain). He considered (mainly for economic reasons) coastal shipping as preferable to mid-ocean navigation (VII. 12), a notion later abandoned by the Southern Indian maritime powers.[38] Among other administrative departments exercising external functions Kautilya lists the Director of Trade, who 'should encourage the import of goods produced in foreign lands by [allowing] concessions ... to those [who bring such goods] in ships or caravans' (II. 16); the Superintendent of Mines, who is *inter alia* concerned with the control of pearl fisheries (II. 28), a significant anticipation of administrative regulation of affairs relating to the continental shelf; and the Superintendent of Passports (II. 34).[39] References to the position of foreigners in Hindu States indicate the spirit of tolerance and non-discrimination with which they were treated. Though the foreigner was in principle outside the social structure of society, he was able to find his proper place under the protection and control of the ruler. Xenophobia was in principle alien to Indian society (particularly in Further India where the caste system was rejected). It tolerated settlements of foreign traders who were allowed to govern themselves by their own law. The establishment of these settlements later led to the adoption of the régime of capitulations.

It has been emphasized above that one of the salient features of the social structure of India (based on the caste system) was the separation of the functions of the two upper strata of society, i.e. the brahmans and the *ksatryas*. While the first was superior to the second and exercised religious functions and expounded the divine law (*dharma*), the *ksatryas* monopolized the task of governing the State, which was essentially of a secular character. The secularization of the royal function was a phenomenon which revealed itself in the domain of internal as well as external affairs. While the sovereign ensured internal public order within his realm with the ultimate help of sanctions (*danda*),[40] external relations were at the mercy of anarchy. Kautilya's objective was to propose a minimum of principles which could diminish the threat of anarchy (*arajaka* and *matsyanyaya* or the law of the fish, II. 13). These principles were at first of a political nature but they were the outcome of past experience, derived from the period before the foundation of the centralized Mauryan Empire, and they stimulated the gradual establishment of a code of usages and customary rules which was similar to our law of nations in its earlier stages. This code, based on the Kautilyan and post-Kautilyan tradition,

pearl fisheries: 'Die Muschel- und Perlen Fischer sollen Schiffszins bezahlen oder auf ihren eigenen Schiffen kreuzen. Ihr Aufseher hat ähnliche Pflichten wie der über die Edelsteinfundgruben'. This is a reference to the similarity of functions of the controller of pearl fisheries and the controller of mines of precious stones.

[38] As to the impact of Kautilyan ideas on maritime practice in the Indian Ocean and indirectly on Grotius, see C. H. Alexandrowicz in *Recueil des cours* (1961), p. 240.

[39] G. J. N. Ramaswamy, *Essentials of Indian Statecraft: Kautilya's Arthasastra* (1962).

[40] The ruler was never a legislator. His task was to implement the law (*dharma*). But according to Kautilya, the royal edict (*rajasasana*) had the force of law.

was in principle secular and allowed the sovereigns in India and Further India to maintain regular relations *inter se* and later with Islamic rulers, as well as with the European agencies which first appeared in the East in the beginning of the sixteenth century.[41] In this way Kautilyan principles, whether in their original formulation or reproduced in the later classic works,[42] exercised a definite influence on our system of the law of nations which the European agencies were compelled to apply in a non-discriminatory manner, irrespective of race, colour or creed. Without such non-discriminatory application the law would have been in the way of the growth of the much desired East Indian trade, and it had therefore to be stripped of all its original prohibitions of an ecclesiastical nature directed against 'infidels' and applied in a spirit of universality which, incidentally, was not alien to the natural law doctrine as already formulated by St. Thomas Aquinas. This development promoted the establishment of a multi-ideological law of nations, that is to say a law not exclusively allied to any ideology, creed or civilization, but a framework of coexistence of various creeds and ways of life. The European agencies in the East learned the lesson of coexistence of Hinduism, Islam and Christianity in India (particularly on the west coast)[43] and transplanted their experience to the West, which had been so long incapable of extricating itself from the obsession of religious wars.

Throughout this section reference has been made to 'Further India'. This region extends to countries which, having escaped various forms of distant Chinese suzerainty, had come under the influence of Hindu civilization and played, together with India, a prominent role in the development of the East Indian trade. The model of the Hindu State and administration had been introduced in these countries through the intermediary of brahmans,[44] without ever reducing them to the role of dependencies of a possible metropolis in India.[45] While India ultimately discarded buddhism and reverted to brahmanism, most of the countries of Further India remained permanently buddhist (Burma, Ceylon, Siam, etc.).[46] On top of the two layers of hinduism and buddhism, Islam started superimposing itself in

[41] Unlike the Chinese sphere of influence in which inter-State relations on a footing of equality were in principle not possible.

[42] See p. 36 above.

[43] Swanston, 'A Memoir of the Primitive Church of Malayala', *Journal of the Royal Asiatic Society*, 2 (1835).

[44] Brahmins were called from India to the Indonesian Islands for the sacral legitimation of dynastic interests and the organization of the State combined with the brahman–*ksatrya* relationship; Van Leur, op. cit., pp. 79–81.

[45] As to the influence of Hindu polity in Further India, Professor G. Coedes writes as follows: 'De leur coté, les arthasastras ou traités de politique ont contribué à façonner l'administration hierarchisée des états de l'Inde Extérieure ...' , *Les états hindouisés de l'Indochine et d'Indonésie* (1948), p. 422. The Hindu Kingdoms in Sumatra, Java and Cambodia were never controlled from India. Professor K. K. Pillay compares in this respect Further India with the cultural expansion of Greater Hellas; see 'Early Indian Imperialism in the Far East', *Indian Year Book of International Affairs*, 3 (1954), p. 144.

[46] Buddhism came from India to Burma in the fifth century A.D. But the idea of kingship remained associated with the Code of Manu and brahmans continued to play an important role at the court; see D. G. E. Hall, *History of South Asia* (1955).

India and Further India in course of time, until it gained absolute control over the major part of India (under the Moghul dynasty) and the Indonesian Islands.[47] The ideology of the Moghuls deviated significantly from that of the Ottoman Empire, as well as from the traditions of pre-Moghul Islamic rulers in India who had been under the political or religious overlordship of the Caliphs (at first effective, then nominal). The reign of the Moghul Emperors Akbar, Jehangir and Shajahan witnessed the victory of a secular policy in inter-group relations in India, no doubt under Hindu influence and in conditions of decline of the *jihad* ideology[48] which, even within the Ottoman Empire, later gave way to treaty and diplomatic relations with European powers and with dissident Persia (sixteenth-century).

In this summary of Kautilyan principles reference has not been made to principles relating to the law of war (*vigraha*) (VII. 1), particularly to the prohibition of the use of poisonous and other objectionable weapons, the distinction between combatants and non-combatants and their treatment (X. 4), and to principles concerning *temperamenta belli* (X. 3, 4). The examination of these provisions would require extensive research into the norms of *yuddha-dharma*.

Vijayanagar and the Marathas

It is not possible, in the limits of this inquiry, to discuss in detail the Kautilyan tradition as followed in India or Further India during the sixteenth, seventeenth and eighteenth centuries. But a few instances in which it revealed itself more clearly may be examined. They are drawn from the history of the last two great Hindu powers in India, i.e. Vijayanagar and the Marathas. Reference may be made to two early Portuguese sources relating to the Kingdom of Vijayanagar, namely the *Book of Duarte Barbosa*[49] and the *Chronicle of Fernao Nuniz* (1535–7).[50] Barbosa gives an excellent description of Vijayanagar, its position in South India and its political significance. Encircled by a number of Islamic States, it took advantage of the advent of the Portuguese in the beginning of the sixteenth century and increased, with their help, its military potential and resistance to Islamic pressure. In 1520 Krishna Raja, king of Vijayanagar, defeated the Adil Shah of Bijapur at the battle of Rajchur and after the termination of hostilities an embassy from the defeated Muslim ruler came to the Vijayanagar court. Fernao Nuniz gives a vivid account of the embassy, and particularly of the speech of the ambassador (*matucotam*) addressed to Krishna Raja. The following are extracts from the speech:[51]

[47] Islam destroyed the central power of the Majapahit Empire on the Island of Java. Van Leur, op. cit., p. 172.

[48] Maclagan, *The Jesuits and the Great Mogul* (1932); P. Spear, *Twilight of the Moghuls* (1951); M. K. Nawaz, 'Jihad', *Indian Year Book of International Affairs* 8 (1959). Emperor Akbar (1542–1605) abolished *jizyah*, a capital tax imposed on non-Muslim citizens (*dhimmis*).

[49] Translated in 1918 by M. L. Dames.

[50] Reproduced in R. Sewell's *A Forgotten Empire: Vijayanagar* (1924), which also comprises fragments of *The Narrative* of Domingos Paes (1520–2).

[51] See translation by Sewell, op. cit., p. 352.

Sire, the Ydallcao [King of Bijapur] my Master, sends me to you; and . . requests you to do him justice. He bids me to say that he bears very good will towards you as a real, powerful, just and sincere Prince; that you have *without reason* violated the friendship and the peace observed and respected by *all Rulers* … [52] that he does not understand why you had come from your kingdom to attack him; that he had been without suspicion when he learned that you besieged the City of Rachol [Rajchur] and that you ravaged and destroyed his country which made him come to its rescue; that all members of his court have been killed by you and his camp invaded and devastated; that you are witness to all these happenings and that he requests you to … return to him his artillery, tents, horses and elephants and all the rest taken from him and to hand back to him the City of Rachol; that if you will give him satisfaction and make restitution of what belongs to him, you can count on him as your loyal friend; but if you refuse to do so, your action will be evil even if it pleases you.

Nuniz writes that after the speech the ambassador received a silk dress and the customary gifts. At the next audience the king gave him his reply, 'that he is ready to make all restitution asked by the Ydallcao but under one essential condition, that the Ydallcao would come and render him homage and obeisance'. This embassy has been chosen among other events as typical of inter-sovereign relations in the sixteenth century. It gives us a description of diplomatic usage observed at that period. The ambassador's argumentation follows the classic tradition, for he accuses the king of having broken 'without reason' the peace respected by 'all rulers' in the regional circle of States. On the other hand, the Hindu sovereign applies to the defeated ruler the classic principle of vassalization. He asks him to recognize him as his suzerain.[53]

Nuniz and Barbosa give us a description of the particular network of suzerain–vassal relations in this part of India. Both also write about the Vijayanagar administration (the king's officers), which comprised the Minister, the treasurer, the master of the horse, the various superintendents, the provincial governors and others. The whole account is reminiscent of the Kautilyan administrative pattern which has just been described. The kingdom of Vijayanagar, which originally extended to Telengana, Tamilnad, Kanara and Carnatica, declined after the battle of Talicot (1565) and was finally stripped of its last possessions by the Marathas (1677). Professor Nilakanta Sastri describes it as 'the last refuge of the traditional culture and institutions of the country'.[54] But in fact these institutions, and some of the Kautilyan tradition, survived among the Marathas until the beginning of the nineteenth century.

The Maratha State had been founded by Shivaji[55] in the seventeenth century, but the sovereignty over the State passed later from his descendants to the Peshwa,

[52] Italics are mine. It is notable that the ambassador (*matucotam*) argued in terms of Hindu tradition.

[53] The embassy also referred to the custom of restitution of war material and prisoners of war after the battle (subject to compensation). Attention may be drawn to the Vijayanagar embassy to the Bahmani Court (1367), which pressed for the conclusion of an agreement by which the contracting parties would renounce the barbarous habit of killing prisoners of war; see Farishta's *Chronicle* (transl. by Briggs), p. 170.

[54] K. A. Nilakanta Sastri, *A History of South India* (1955), p. 293.

[55] Before his coronation (1674), Shivaji had been initiated by brahmans in the rules of the *ksatrya* caste; Bal Krishna, *Shivaji the Great* (1932), vol. 1, pp. 1–2.

who became the hereditary head of the Confederacy of the Maratha Chiefs with its capital in Poona. The Confederacy comprised Baroda, Indore, Gwalior, Nagpur and other States.[56] The Peshwa governed the Confederacy with the assistance of the *mandala*, the supreme council of the circle of associated States, composed of eight members. The administration extended to authorities in charge of the army, public works, postal services, finance, trade and other departments. One of the officers, the *dabir* or *sumant*, was concerned with foreign affairs.[57] The whole organization, which was under the predominant influence of brahmans, reflected the Kautilyan administrative system (II. 5, 6, 16, 18, 19, 21, 28), though modified by Islamic influence which gradually reduced the importance of the *mandala* in favour of the autocratic rule of the sovereign.[58]

The *Transactions of the Royal Asiatic Society*[59] contain the translation of the correspondence of the Peshwa's court (1761–72) prepared by J. Briggs who, in his commentary on the text, draws attention to the fact that some of the authors of the letters were his contemporaries and that events described in them were still vivid in the memory of his generation. At the period covered by the correspondence the relations of the court at Poona with European agencies were still very limited. And, as the translator points out, the correspondence is therefore an example of source material which reflects the activities of an Indian court not being under any external influence, but acting on its own traditions. In conclusion, he underlines the importance of the correspondence as an historical document and praises the high qualities of the Marathas, particularly the religious tolerance of the Hindus.

The correspondence contains the text of a number of Maratha treaties, such as the treaties of 1767–9 between Peshwa Madha Rao and Raghunad Rao (*Ragoba*). According to these treaties, the Maratha Chiefs Sindia, Holkar, Nara Sankar and others undertook to render the 'customary services' to the Peshwa (their overlord) and to abstain from direct communications with other States. It was stipulated in the treaty of 1767 that external communications would take place only through the intermediary of the government of the Peshwa (Article 6). These stipulations reflect *mutatis mutandis* Kautilyan principles relating to suzerain–vassal relations.[60] In the same way the Maratha administration (central and local) reflected to some extent the Kautilyan tradition. The Peshwa's secretariat at Poona (brahman) was composed of several departments and bureaux (revenue, expenditure, accounts, land revenues, public service, etc.). The daily registers of the departments (*roz kird*) recorded all transactions, grants and payments. The Maratha local administration was headed by the *mamlatdar* who was in charge of the various divisions (*sarkar, subha*), or by his subordinates in charge of smaller territorial units (*parganas*). In his account

[56] 'The Maratha Government in many instances resembles the feudal system in Europe; the great chieftains, like the ancient barons, hold their lands by military tenure'; J. Forbes, *Oriental Memoir* (1834), vol. 1, p. 338.

[57] M. G. Ranade, 'Introduction to the Peshwa's Diaries', *Journal of the Bombay Branch of the Royal Asiatic Society* 20 (1902), pp. 450 et seq.

[58] Ranade, ibid. [59] (1830), vol. 2.

[60] According to which the vassal should not undertake diplomatic negotiations without the permission of the suzerain (XIII. 5).

of the Maratha administration S. M. Edwardes states that the whole scheme of government was based on Kautilyan principles. He describes it as a combination of rules derived from the ancient works of Hindu polity, such as *Arthasastra*, and the customs and usages evolved out of the Maratha practice, which modified the former. Kautilyan principles revealed themselves in the internal government of the Maratha State as well as in its external relations.[61]

To these few instances collected from Vijayanagar and Maratha history other examples can be added, such as those drawn from the history of the Rajputs and the west coast of India, where the majority of States were governed by Hindu rulers (Cochin, Travancore, Quilon, Calicut and other minor States).[62] The Rajput princes, who preserved in their dealings *inter se* and in their external relations the customs of ancient Hindu polity, exercised considerable influence on the Moghul emperors, who acknowledged their separate existence as vassals of the Empire. The history of the west coast of India is also illustrative of the kaleidoscope of suzerain–vassal relations, which were later recorded by Jean Bodin in his classic *De la république*.[63] A vivid account of the administration of the Hindu States in this part of India given by François Pyrard de Laval and recording details relating to its civil service, registers of foreign trade, movement of foreigners and other events, cannot fail to remind the reader of the ancient Hindu pattern of administration.

The precise notions of sovereignty which the East Indian sovereigns inherited from their ancient traditions conceived the sovereign as the only agency capable of conducting external affairs. When the Dutch, English and French East India Companies appeared in the East and not only engaged in commercial activities but also acted on their delegated sovereign powers, the question arose whether the East Indian sovereigns would be able to fit them (as commercial companies) into their concept of sovereignty. In practice a satisfactory answer to this question was found only in course of time, when the East India Company governors assumed the status of quasi-sovereigns and set up court in the Asian fashion. Even when all obstacles to co-operation were overcome under the pressure of the growing volume of trade, there remained the traditional reluctance of East Indian rulers to conclude treaties, which had its roots in ancient traditions of Hindu polity. For example, De la Loubère, French ambassador to the Court of Siam (seventeenth century), states that everywhere in the East Indies it is easier to obtain a unilateral grant than to receive any concessions by treaty, which is considered a limitation to the sovereignty of the conceding ruler.[64]

The accounts of English ambassadors to the Court of Ava in the early nineteenth century testify to the reluctance of the latter to enter into treaty negotiations as incompatible with their concept of sovereignty.[65] The European negotiator rarely

61 *Cambridge History of India* (1929), vol. 5, p. 384.

62 K. P. Padmanabha Menon, *History of Kerala* (1929).

63 *Les six livres de la république* (1577), VI. 2 (630).

64 De la Loubère, *Description du royaume de Siam* (1714).

65 D. G. E. Hall, *Michael Symes: Journal of his Second Embassy to the Court of Ava in 1802* (1955); J. Crawfurd, *Journal of the Embassy from the Governor-General of India to the Court of Ava* (1829).

failed to produce a draft agreement in conclusion of the bargaining process, and in the course of time a number of East Indian courts took advantage of the procedure of treaty-making. The Courts of Kandy and Poona were among the first to engage in extensive treaty-making and the former, faced with a succession of European agencies in Ceylon (the Portuguese, the Dutch and the English), knew how to negotiate with one against the other and thus to maintain and strengthen its own sovereign status.[66]

II. Conclusion

The above analysis of the Kautilyan tradition could be summed up in the following way: Kautilya conceives as his point of departure the resistance against internal and external anarchy (our present-day problems relating to external anarchy are *mutatis mutandis* the same). A community protects itself against the consequences of anarchy by the establishment of a supreme authority—the king (III. 13). The king exercises executive and judicial functions and applies the law within the boundaries of the State (III. 1).[67] Though we cannot find in the classical law a clear distinction between public and private law (personal law), there was a certain juridical area which could be classified as one of public law, such as the organization of the government and the administration (I. 3, 4; II, 3, 6, 16, 18) and the direction of the national economy (public works, industry, mining) (II. 1). The functions of the king in the sphere of his internal sovereignty are intimately connected with his task of protecting the community against the hazards of external anarchy (I. 17). The king exercises all prerogatives of external sovereignty in the sphere of inter-State relations, which is beyond the pale of the law. Kautilya concerns himself systematically with external anarchy; he tries to formulate the customs and usages of State practice in the past, and suggests at the same time principles which could form the basis of customs and usages in the future. Among these principles some of the most significant are the following:

The principle of individual responsibility of each sovereign within the collectivity or concert of all sovereigns in the circle of States (*mandala*) for the maintenance of a measure of inter-State public order which is essential to diminish the consequences of anarchy; the principle of balance of power within the circle, modified by the evolution towards centralization of power and potential unification of States under a supreme authority (*kakravartin*, suzerain); the principle of respect for the sovereignty of the dependent or subordinate (vassal) rulers, and the rejection of *debellatio*, which follows to some extent from inter-dynastic *ksatrya* cohesion or solidarity (as rooted in the social structure of society beyond political frontiers); the secular character of inter-State customs and usages (resulting from the separation of royal

[66] See Alexandrowicz in *Recueil des cours* (1960), cited at p. 41 above.

[67] As to the King's legislative function and the role of *rajasasana*, see N. C. Sengupta, *Evolution of Ancient Indian Law* (1954).

and religious functions) which leads to the establishment of a multi-ideological framework, that is to say a system which is not allied exclusively to any particular ideology, creed or civilization, but constitutes a régime of coexistence (Hindu, Buddhist, Islamic and Christian States); the principles relating to the treatment of foreign settlements, which later led to the régime of capitulations; the principle of negotiation to the limit before resort is made to sanctions or force (or even voting) for the solution of conflicts; the employment of diplomacy for carrying out negotiations and the protection of the envoy (*duta*) by diplomatic privileges; finally, the preference given to customary law and usages (para-legal solutions) over treaties, which are a limitation to sovereignty and reveal the initial reluctance of States to submit to treaty sanctions.

To what extent have some of these principles had an impact on the development of our system of international law? Some of them were similar to those applied by the European agencies, but some were different and called for mutual adjustment to make commercial co-operation a workable proposition. Perhaps the strongest influence of the Kautilyan tradition revealed itself in the trend towards the secularization of the law of nations in the Hindu sphere of influence in the East Indies.[68] This trend, supported by the mutuality of interests arising out of the East Indian trade, precipitated the breaking down of barriers and counteracted the prohibition of dealings with 'infidels', which resulted from the protracted religious conflicts in the Christian and Islamic worlds. The principle of responsibility of individual State entities within the concert of States (circle),[69] corroborated by ties of solidarity (beyond political frontiers), may be considered an intermediary stage in the progress towards unification of the family of nations. It constitutes a pattern of parallel development in the East and in the West, but in the process of concentration of power respect for the sovereignty of dependent States was more pronounced in the Kautilyan than in the European tradition (absence of *debellatio*).[70] Burke's pleadings in the trial of Warren Hastings at Westminster, in which the rights of the Raja of Benares (a vassal of the English East India Company) were supported by simultaneous reference to Vattel's *Droit des gens* and to classical Indian traditions, deserves special attention of the historian of the law of nations.[71]

It may also be noted that some of the Kautilyan principles had an indirect impact on a number of European writers in the eighteenth century.[72] Thus the principle of the balance of power in the East Indies (Asia) is discussed by Raynal and Justi.[73] The latter, in his work on comparative government in Europe and Asia,[74] refers

[68] Which differed so much from the position in the Chinese sphere of influence; p. 35 above.

[69] Which found its expression in the respect for the sovereignty of other rulers, the observance of *pacta sunt servanda*, etc.

[70] The attitude of the Great Powers towards the partitions of Poland and the settlement of Italian affairs (beginning of the 19th century) may be mentioned as examples.

[71] Burke, *Works* (1812), vols. 4 and 13.

[72] Though of course they could not be familiar with Kautilya's work, the full text of which was discovered much later by Shamasastry.

[73] Abbé G. T. F. Raynal, *Histoire philosophique et politique des établissements et de commerce des européens dans les deux Indes*, (1770), vol. 2.

[74] Cited above, n. 25.

also to the merits of the separation of the royal and the priestly functions (*ksatrya* and brahman) and its influence on the legal system. Moreover, in his *Historical and Juridical Essays*,[75] Justi seems perfectly aware of the concept of *mandala*, whether in its Kautilyan or Machiavellian version.[76] He also gives a special account of the law of warfare in the East Indies, particularly that relating to *temperamenta belli*.[77]

In conclusion we may state that it is in the process of confrontation of East Indian and European rules of inter-State conduct that the Kautilyan tradition manifested itself in a more definite manner. For while Kautilya had centuries earlier systematically written down the tenets of Hindu government and the customs and usages of inter-State conduct, and while *Arthasastra* had exercised an influence on actual inter-sovereign relations in India and Further India, the ensuing tradition, which had followed State practice, became in the course of centuries more and more circumscribed by modifications and deviations dictated by various factors which shaped the progress of history in the East Indies. But it had survived in largely undefined customs and usages (generally known to brahmans or *ksatryas* only) until the advent of the Europeans in this part of the world. In the course of relations with European agencies, East Indian sovereigns were more than ever before compelled to consider the proposition of negotiation and to define in a more precise manner their proposals or objections, so as to gain the desired advantages in the inter-State 'battle of wits'.[78] It was perhaps then that the undefined tradition took once more a tangible form, before it ultimately disappeared at the end of the eighteenth and the beginning of the nineteenth century. The tentative reformulation of some of its principles in the course of three centuries exercised a measure of influence on the European negotiator and can be traced in the vast number of transactions from which some of our rules of international law were ultimately drawn.[79]

[75] *Historische und Juristische Schriften* (1760), pp. 186–99.

[76] See *Indian Year Book of International Affairs*, 6 (1957), p. 177.

[77] *Historische und Juristische Schriften* (1760), vol. 2 (*Von der Kriegesverfassung*).

[78] K. V. Rangaswami Ayangar, *Indian Cameralism: A Survey of some Aspects of Arthasastra* (1949), p. 116 (*mantra-yuddha*).

[79] An extensive number of East Indian treaties has been systematically recorded by G. F. de Martens in his *Cours diplomatique* (1801); *The Compendium of the Law of Nations* (1789, transl. by W. Cobbett, 1802); and in the *Recueil des traités* (1791). Among these treaties a special section is reserved in the *Cours diplomatique* to the treaties concluded by the Marathas, the last great Hindu power in India. One of the Maratha treaties (the treaty of 1779 concluded with the Portuguese) has been the object of interpretation by the International Court of Justice in the *Right of Passage over Indian Territory* case (Portugal–India), *I.C.J. Reports*, 1960, p. 6.

2

PAULUS VLADIMIRI AND THE DEVELOPMENT OF THE DOCTRINE OF COEXISTENCE OF CHRISTIAN AND NON-CHRISTIAN COUNTRIES (1963)

I.

The first classic writers of the law of nations who concerned themselves with the general legal aspects of relations between Christian and non-Christian communities were Franciscus de Vitoria and Seraphin de Freitas.[1] While Vitoria in his lectures *De Indis* (1532) referred to the Spanish conquest of America, Freitas in his *De Justo Imperio Lusitanorum Asiatico* (1625) discussed the legal problems which arose out of the advent of the Europeans in the East Indies, particularly in reply to the arguments of Grotius, stated in his *Mare Liberum*. However, the actual problem of relations between Christian and non-Christian countries had earlier been the subject of a protracted public controversy at the Council of Constance (1414–18), when the conflict between the Kingdom of Poland and the Teutonic Order (*Ordo Cruciferorum*) over Poland's relations with the pagan communities of Lithuania came up for consideration. This conflict would not by itself justify the special attention of historians of the law of nations were it not for the defence of Polish–Lithuanian co-operation by a prominent Polish theologian and lawyer who may be considered one of the forerunners of a progressive doctrine on the fundamental legal issue of the coexistence of the Christian world with non-Christian countries. The Polish delegation at the Council of Constance included among its members a scholar from the University of Cracow, Paulus Vladimiri, and his submissions to the Council as well as his writings deserve to be recalled. For, unlike the case of the Christian–Islamic struggle which remained ideologically in the strait-jacket of religious fanaticism, the Polish–Teutonic conflict over pagan communities allowed a more dispassionate examination of the issues involved and provided a useful though hitherto unexplored antecedent of events and problems which arose a hundred years later in connexion with European penetration in the East and West Indies.

[1] Apart from theologians who dealt with the particular aspects of the Christian–Islamic conflagration.

II.

Before an analysis of the legal issues at the Council of Constance is attempted, a few remarks about the historical background of the Polish–Teutonic conflict would be relevant. The peaceful conversion by Poland of the greater part of Lithuania to Christianity had taken the wind out of the sails of the Teutonic crusade engaged in the conversion of north-east Europe by military force. The dynastic union between Poland and Lithuania, cemented by the marriage of the Lithuanian sovereign Jagiello with Jadwiga, Queen of Poland, constituted, in Professor Bruce Boswell's words, 'a political revolution of sinister import for the [Teutonic] Order'.[2] It marked the end of its Baltic drive and led in 1410 to its defeat by the combined forces of Poland and Lithuania. The Union between the two countries was sealed by the Pact of Horodło in 1413. In 1415 Polish–Lithuanian co-operation was attacked by the Teutonic Order at the Council of Constance on the ground that Poland had employed an alliance with a non-Christian or virtually non-Christian country to fight against a Christian Order enjoying sovereign status. In order to defend the Polish case, King Jagiełło sent to Constance a delegation under the archbishop of Gniezno, which included Paulus Vladimiri, the Rector of the Jagiellonian University in Cracow.[3] Paulus Vladimiri, born in 1370, had been a student at the Universities of Prague and Padua and one of his professors at Padua had been Franciscus Zabarella, later cardinal and supporter of the Polish cause at Constance.[4] Paulus Vladimiri appeared at the Council as 'Ambassador Regni Poloniae' and his views in response to the Teutonic indictment were stated in a treatise entitled *De Potestate Papae et Imperatoris Respectu Infidelium*.[5] It is this work which deserves the attention of historians of the law of nations.

The author divides his treatise into two main parts, one concerned with the discussion of papal power *vis-à-vis* non-Christian communities and the other relating to the corresponding power of the Holy Roman Emperors in respect of these communities. From the point of view of the law of nations, he submits the following initial question: 'Si infideles habent regna et provincias separatas a nostris et ibidem jurisdictionem exercent et omnia tenent, utrum licet Christianis illis in pace viventibus bellum movere et eorum bona occupare?'[6] As can be seen from this passage, the author concentrated on the problem of existence outside the Christian world of organized political entities governed by their own sovereign authority and endowed with jurisdiction for the implementation of law. Two hundred years later Grotius, in his *Mare Liberum* (Ch. II), considered the same problem in relation to the East

[2] Boswell, 'The Teutonic Order', *Cambridge Medieval History* (1932), vol. 7, p. 259.

[3] Morawski, *Histoire de l'université de Cracovie* (1900); Boswell, 'Poland and Lithuania in the Fourteenth and Fifteenth Centuries', *Cambridge Medieval History* (1936), vol. 8, p. 574.

[4] Brzostowski, *Pawel Wlodkowic* (1954); Paweł Włodkowic is the Polish equivalent for Paulus Vladimiri, i.e. Paul, the son of Vladimir.

[5] *Monuments du droit polonais* (*Starodawne Prawa Polskiego Pomniki*, ed. by Bobrzyński, 1878), vol. 5, pp. 145 et seq. Paulus was assisted at the Council by Caspar of Perugia.

[6] Ibid., p. 162.

Indian communities and his answer was that they had their own sovereigns (*reges*), their own State organization (*res-publica*) and their own laws (*leges et jura*).[7] Paulus Vladimiri arrives at the obvious conclusion that where there is no territorial or power vacuum in the eyes of the law of nations, occupation of non-Christian lands by Christian sovereigns is out of the question. Neither can war against peace-loving States be justified by the fact that they are non-Christian. This again is an anticipation of Grotian doctrine.

The authorities on which Paulus Vladimiri relies are first of all St. Thomas Aquinas and Sinibaldo Fiesco (later Pope Innocent IV). According to the doctrine of St. Thomas Aquinas, the political organization of a community and its sovereignty are, from the legal point of view, a matter of *jus humanum*. The fact that such a community is non-Christian is within the realm of classification of human beings into faithful and infidels, which is the concern of *jus divinum*. But the latter does not annul *jus humanum*, which is based on natural reason, and thus Christian powers have no legal claim to any action against non-Christian entities which are politically organized and have their proper place within the natural family of nations. This excludes the lawfulness of such titles (claimed by some of the European powers) as occupation, discovery or papal concession as well as conversion by force and conquest.[8] An elaboration of this reasoning and its more precise legal formulation is, at a later period, the work of Vitoria[9] and Grotius.

The main authority quoted at the Council of Constance in support of the contrary view was Hostiensis (Henry de Susa, Cardinal of Ostia), who had exercised a predominant influence on the canon law literature of the thirteenth and fourteenth centuries. According to his view, pagan communities could not, since the inception of the Christian era, exist as sovereign States within the family of nations, and the war of Christian powers against them was always lawful. This is what Paulus Vladimiri has to say about the above view in his conclusions submitted to the Council: 'Impium est asserere et absurdum quod infideles alicuius jurisdictionis, honoris, potestatis et dominii essent hodie penitus incapaces, quia haec seditiosa assertio viam praestat in hoc homicidiis et rapinis, quia si non sunt istorum domini, licebit cuilibet ea rapere vel etiam occupare … Non etiam negandum est infidelibus generaliter quod eis humanae societatis jus concedit' (52nd conclusion). Paulus Vladimiri relies here again on St. Thomas Aquinas. The essence of this statement lies in the emphasis on the danger of international lawlessness, anarchy, and even genocide which might follow from an aggressive Christian power disregarding the factual statehood and rights of non-Christian communities. To deny them membership in the family of nations (*humana societas*) means a licence to perpetrate crimes of disastrous dimensions, such as those

[7] See also Vitoria, 'De Indis', *Classics of International Law* (ed. by Nys), pp. 333–4.

[8] The same view had been expressed in the fourteenth century by Bartolus de Saxoferrato, Professor at the University of Perugia; see Fijalek, *Dominus Bartolus de Saxoferrato eiusque in Polonos Auctoritas* (1914).

[9] Winiarski, 'Vitoria et Wlodkowic', *Bulletin international de l'Académie Polonaise des Sciences et des lettres* (1936), pp. 242–7.

which a crusading power might inflict on peace-loving people. The attack of Paulus Vladimiri is expressly directed against Hostiensis when he states: 'Opinio Hostiensis est quod in adventu Christi omnis jurisdictio, principatus, honor et dominium translata fuerunt ab infidelibus ad fideles'. He condemns the cardinal's view that war against infidels who do not recognize the overall sovereignty of the Holy Roman Empire is always just ('bellum semper justum et licitum'), and he refers *inter alia* to Petrus de Ancorano who, against the opinion of the Council of Pisa, opposed the possibility of invasion and occupation by Christian powers of lands of infidels.[10]

In 1416 a new memorandum was submitted by the Polish delegation to the Council of Constance and it is highly probable that it was drafted by Paulus Vladimiri.[11] This memorandum questions the validity of papal and imperial privileges granted to the Teutonic Order—privileges which authorized the Order to invade and occupy non-Christian lands in the Baltic area and to convert their inhabitants to the Christian faith. Two hundred years later Grotius questioned in the same way the validity of the bull 'Inter Caetera' of Alexander VI relating to the East and West Indies. It is hardly conceivable that the attitude of the Polish delegation to fundamental questions of the organizing of the family of nations and of the operation of the law of nations was popular at the Council of Constance. Jacques Lenfant, in his history of the Council published in 1727,[12] refers to this dramatic issue, particularly at the ninth session of the Council at which the Holy Roman Emperor (Sigismund of Luxemburg) and a number of European sovereigns and princes were present. The session was presided over by the Cardinal of Ostia and the participation of the Bishop of Salisbury is particularly mentioned. Lenfant recalls that the Polish delegation branded conquest under the pretext of conversion to Christianity as unlawful and demanded that papal and imperial decrees authorizing the Teutonic Order to invade pagan lands should be considered null and void. This is what he has to say about the pleadings of Paulus Vladimiri: 'C'est là en gros la pièce de Paul Vladimir qui par parenthèse mériterait bien de trouver place entre les auteurs ecclésiastiques. Elle fut lue dans cette Assemblée des Nations, on y agita la matière, mais on n'y termina rien …'.[13] The Council was ultimately unwilling to subscribe to the Polish cause, which had been stated with ability and courage by a scholar who deserves to be ranked among the great writers of the law of nations. The assembly at Constance feared to offend imperial policy which gave support to the Teutonic Order. The submissions and writings of Paulus Vladimiri did not receive due publicity and this no doubt is the reason why the classic writers of the sixteenth and seventeenth centuries did not make express reference to them, though in the process of defending the statehood and rights of

[10] See *Monuments du droit polonais* (1878), vol 5, pp. 162–86 (conclusions follow at p. 186).

[11] Brzostowski, op. cit., p. 98.

[12] *Histoire du Concile de Constance*, vol. 1, p. 238.

[13] *Histoire du Concile de Constance*, vol. 1, p. 393. For other accounts of the activities of the Council see *Ulrichs von Richental Chronik des Constanzer Concils 1414–18* (ed. by Buek, 1882), references to Poland at pp. 37, 44, 49, 50, 88, 91, 100, 136, 150, 154, 159, 162, 202, 207; and von der Hardt, *Corpus Actorum et Decretorum Magni Constantiensis Concilii* (1699), vols. 3–4; *Acta Concilii Constantiensis* (ed. by Finke, 1928), vol. 4.

East Indian powers[14] they employed the same arguments as those proposed by the Jagiellonian scholar at Constance.

III.

There is another aspect of the Polish–Teutonic conflict which came under consideration at Constance, the right of the Christian world to claim admission of missionaries to pagan lands. Paulus Vladimiri relies in his *De Potestate Papae* on the authority of Sinibaldo Fiesco who stated that no non-Christian community could close its doors to the preaching of the Christian faith. The admission of missionaries was, however, one thing, the requirement of the voluntary character of conversion was another. Paulus Vladimiri emphasizes that no change of religion can be imposed on individuals or communities by force. He writes in his conclusions submitted to the Council (17th conclusion): 'Licet infideles ad fidem cogi non debeant.... Potest tamen papa mandare infidelibus quod admittant praedicationem evangelii in terris suis ...'.[15] The problem of the right to missionary activities (*propagatio fidei*) was taken up in 1625 by Seraphin de Freitas[16] who conceived it as the ways and means of opening the doors to the East Indies. Freitas, unlike Grotius, rejected the right of any country to commercial intercourse with other countries, whether in Europe or in Asia, but he insisted on the right of Christians to the propagation of their faith and civilization and linked it with the anti-Islamic crusade in Asia which was no doubt conceived in response to 'Jihad', the just war of Islam against Christians. In this respect the principles of canon law and coranic law came to mortal grips, but the conflict never extended in practice to Hindu and Buddhist communities and the principle of *propagatio fidei* never became a pretext of waging wars against them. The Polish–Teutonic conflict was outside the Christian–Islamic conflagration, and moreover the peaceful conversion by the Poles of Lithuania to the Christian faith rendered the Teutonic crusade meaningless and deprived the Order of its primary objectives in the East European region.

Many of the issues argued at Constance were of a theological nature and they are not of primary interest to the historian of the law of nations. However, at least one more problem deserves our attention, i.e. that of the validity of an alliance (treaty) between a Christian and a non-Christian sovereign directed against a Christian power. The Teutonic Order had suffered a disastrous defeat owing to the Polish–Lithuanian alliance (Union), the combined forces of which won the victory of

[14] While the resistance of the West Indian communities to the Spanish invasion was no more than a short episode, the relations between the European powers and the sovereigns of the East Indies during a period of three centuries were of considerable significance to world trade and even exercised a certain influence on the development of the law of nations; see Alexandrowicz, 'Treaty and Diplomatic Relations between European and South-Asian Powers in the Seventeenth and Eighteenth Centuries', *Recueil des cours*, 100 (1960).

[15] See *Monuments du droit polonais* (1878), vol. 5, p. 186.

[16] *De Justo Imperio Lusitanorum Asiatico* (transl. by Guichon de Grandpont, 1882).

Tannenberg (Grunwald) in 1410. The question arose whether this alliance had been unlawful. Paulus Vladimiri formulates the problem in the following way: 'An Christianus sine peccato potest ad sui defensionem et suae terrae uti auxilio infidelium'. After making reference to Joannis Andreae and to precedents connected with the war against Islam, he states in his 51st conclusion: 'Princeps Christianus *necessitate imminente* ... ad sui defensionem et suae terrae uti potest auxilio infidelium, non solum sibi subiectorum sed etiam aliorum ...'. The assertion of the lawfulness of the alliance in the 51st conclusion is immediately followed by the emphasis in the next conclusion (52nd) on the sovereignty of the ally (Lithuania) in the eyes of the law of nations and reference is made to St. Thomas Aquinas.[17]

It would be difficult to say whether and to what extent the pleadings of Paulus Vladimiri at Constance exercised an influence on the shaping of the European doctrine relating to treaties between Christians and infidels. The classic literature on the subject occasionally reveals joint treatment of the Polish alliances with non-Christian countries and the general problem of treaties between Christians and infidels as such, as for example Bodin who referred to Polish–Ottoman treaties and to treaties between Venice, Genoa and Ragusa on the one hand and Turkey on the other.[18] In 1566 the Ottoman Emperor offered to Emanuel Philibert, Duke of Savoy, the kingdom of Cyprus under the condition of an alliance against Venice. Among the legal advisers in the Duke's council were Pierino Belli[19] and Octavianus Cacheranus. The latter wrote on this occasion his famous treatise *Disputatio an Principi Christiano fas sit pro sui suorumque bonorum tutella foedus inire, ac amicitia infidelibus iungi, ab eisque auxilium adversus alios Principes Christianos petere* (Taurini, 1566). The author condemns an alliance concluded by a Christian prince with Turkey and directed against another Christian prince. Reference is made to Hostiensis, whose views had been relied on by the supporters of the Teutonic cause at Constance. But Cacheranus introduces a new classification of infidels, no doubt connected with European penetration in the East Indies. He distinguishes India and the Tartars from the Islamic world and says that no state of war exists with them so that the anti-Islamic criteria and the ensuing canon law prohibitions cannot be entirely applied to them. Equally the conclusion of an alliance with the King of Persia is considered lawful. This classification is further elaborated by John Henry Pott in his *De Foederibus Fidelium cum Infidelibus* (1686). The author adopts a more liberal attitude towards treaties with infidels and refers several times to Polish precedents. He mentions for instance the negotiations between the King of Poland and the Tartars aiming at the conclusion of an alliance against Turkey. On the other hand he refers to the 'foedus (illud) perpetuum seu reale quod Turcae cum Polonis sub Solymanno fecerunt', and quotes Bodin in support.[20] Reference is also made to

[17] See p. 55 above.

[18] See *Six livres de la république* (1577), Book I, Ch. VIII, p. 106.

[19] Pierino Belli, who had joined Savoyan service in 1561, is the author of *De Re Militari et Bello Tractatus* (1558).

[20] Lenfant, in his *Histoire du Concile de Constance* (vol. 1, p. 405), refers to Polish–Ottoman diplomatic relations which enabled Poland to offer her mediation in the Ottoman–Hungarian war in the fifteenth century.

the anti-Ottoman alliances concluded with Persia. The treatise of Pott reflects the advanced process of secularization of treaty law and the eclipse of the canon law prohibitions against treaty-making with infidels dating back to the reign of Pope Nicholas IV.[21] The author has this to say about treaties with infidels: 'Non pugnant cum jure naturae, sicque omnibus hominibus commune est, ut religionis discrimen non attendat neque differentiam fidelium et infidelium'.

The liberal and secular trend in treaty law, which gathered momentum in the seventeenth century, is also reflected in the work of Fridericus Guilielmus Lyserus, *Disputatio Politica de Foederibus cum Infidelibus* (1676). Lyserus considers all commercial treaties with non-Christians as lawful (*foedus commerciorum cum infidelibus sunt licita*); also non-aggression pacts and treaties with infidels against infidels (e.g. with Persia against Turkey) are valid. Treaties with infidels against Christians are possible *in extremo necessitatis casu*.[22] Von Ompteda, in his work on the literature of the law of nations published in 1785, includes a special chapter in which he gives an extensive list of seventeenth and eighteenth-century writers on the subject.[23] The fact that many of these writers make references to Polish State practice and to Poland's liberal attitude towards relations with non-Christian powers, testifies, at least indirectly, to the influence on doctrinal developments in Europe of that climate of scholarly opinion to which Paulus Vladimiri had given forceful expression at the Council of Constance.

At the beginning of the eighteenth century the author of *Schedulae Gallicae* (1711) writes in answer to a question originating from a Polish correspondent that 'a Christian Prince is allowed to conclude treaties with infidels even against Christians'. No reservations are attached to this answer. The question had been asked in connexion with an alliance between the King of Sweden and Turkey and the author states that 'all Christian doctors ... express the same view and even the most renowned and strict scholars maintain that a Christian Prince could support a non-Christian power in a war against another Christian Prince.... The Popes Paul III, Alexander IV and Julius II made no difficulties in the matter of assistance to infidels whenever they believed that this was dictated by necessity'. The author then adds: 'If I had the good fortune to be the Emperor of the Musulmans, I would

21 Nys, *Les Origines du droit international* (1894), p. 159.

22 This statement is similar to that made by Paulus Vladimiri in the 51st conclusion of *De Potestate Papae*; cited on p. 58 above.

23 In *Literatur des Völkerrechts* (1785), p. 592, Ompteda refers to the works of Schaller (1672), Roehrense (1687), Calanus (1687), Gerber (1711), Hasse (1711), Roeser (1713), Dithmarus (1716), Osiandrus (1736) and Bring (1744), as well as to those of Cacheranus, Pott and Lyserus. However, Ompteda's list is far from being exhaustive. We may refer to *Oldradi Pontani Laudensis Consilia* (1550); *Respons. Clarissimi D. Tiberii Deciani* (1602); and *Christophori Besoldi Dissertatio Politico-Juridica de Foederum Jure* (1622), where the author states: 'The oriental Antichrist, the Turk, is always in the mind of the Calvinists' (our translation). The Council of Constance condemned Wycliffe's principles implying that infidels have no status in the law of nations. It also condemned the doctrines of Jan Huss. But many of the Czech Hussites had fought on the side of the Poles and Lithuanians against the Teutonic Order and a number of fellow professors of Paulus Vladimiri at the Jagiellonian University were sympathizers of Wycliffe and Huss. See Kot, *Five Centuries of Polish Learning* (1941), p. 4. Awkward and complicated situations arose at the Council of Constance when the ecclesiastical members of the Polish delegation ceased to see eye to eye with its lay members; Boswell, op. cit., p. 54 above, n. 3, at p. 573.

think more than four times before concluding alliances with Christian Princes. For we see today that the majority of them don't know what it means to keep faith'. Finally, a reference follows to the East Indies: 'Les Hollandais ont fait assez souvent des alliances avec des Roys Payens aux Indes Orientales pour se défendre contre ceux qui voulaient s'opposer sans raison à leurs établissements'. The author here puts European and Asian precedents in juxtaposition and we may assume that the Polish precedent had not been in vain, for the legal arguments which emerged out of it were widely employed by all those writers who concerned themselves with the relations between Europe and the East Indies since the beginning of the sixteenth century, particularly Grotius and Freitas. On the other hand, the period of the collapse of the independent Asian State system in the East Indies at the end of the eighteenth century witnessed also the collapse of Poland, to a great extent under the pressure of those intransigent dynastic forces which stood in the way of a liberal and non-discriminatory conception of the family of nations.

IV.

Before concluding this brief study of Paulus Vladimiri, it may be relevant to mention that the Council of Constance had also to deal with the so-called 'Falkenberg' incident, which had been intimately connected with the main issues before its members. John Falkenberg, a Dominican friar, had written on behalf of the Teutonic Order a satire against Poland in which he argued that the war of the Order against Poland was just, since its king had virtually reverted to paganism. In his fanaticism he went so far as to recommend the extermination of the Poles: 'Pro exterminio Polonorum et eorum Regis Jagyel[lo]'. Falkenberg, who concerned himself particularly with the contribution of the Polish–Lithuanian alliance to the defeat of the Order at Tannenberg (Grunwald), supported the right of the Emperor and the Order to the conversion of the Lithuanian pagans by force, a task which had been rendered superfluous by their peaceful conversion by the Poles.[24] Paulus Vladimiri joined issue with Falkenberg and his reply to the satire was presented to the Council in 1417.[25] He underlines the natural right of all people (irrespective of religion) to live unmolested within the framework of their State organizations. The Poles defended their Christian and non-Christian neighbours who were threatened with extermination. Paulus Vladimiri, calling the disregard of human rights *haeresis prussiana*, concludes: 'Quod haec doctrina non solum est falsa et erronea, sed

[24] See Brzostowski, op. cit., p. 54 above, n. 4, at p. 105. The original manuscript of the satire has not been discovered; ibid., p. 107.

[25] *Magistri Pauli Vladimiri Decretorum Doctoris Scriptum Denunciatorium Errorum Satyrae Joannis Falkenberg O.P. Concilio Constantiensi Datum* (ed. by Belch, 1955). It may also be mentioned that treatises in defence of the Teutonic Order were written by Bishop Jacob of Lodi (*Tractatus Episcopi Laudensis contra Polonos*), by Ardicinus (Königsberg) and by John Vrebach of Bamberg. Vladimiri wrote in reply to John of Bamberg a new treatise, *Tractatus de Ordine Cruciferorum et de Bello Polonorum contra Dictos Fratres*; see Brzostowski, op. cit., pp. 116, 127, and *Monuments du droit polonais* (1878), vol. 5, pp. 233–96.

inquantum divinae legi repugnat, est haeretica, impia et insana; inquantum suadet homicidia iniusta et iniuste fieri est periculosa, scandalosa, temeraria et crudelis; inquantum tollit Polonis legitimam defensionem contra ius naturale, est seditiosa, iniuriosa et politiae turbativa, et, per consequens, piarum aurium offensiva et pro tali condemnanda'.[26] Paulus Vladimiri fought not so much against Falkenberg as for the condemnation of his publicly expressed doctrines which in his view were leading to the commission of international crimes. The Council was neither willing to take sides in the Polish–Teutonic dispute nor to take steps in the collateral 'Falkenberg' affair. But the latter had proved too much for the Poles and on their appeal to Pope Martin V a commission of cardinals was appointed which condemned Falkenberg's work. Martin V confirmed the verdict in 1424.[27]

After this no historical data of any importance are available about the activities of Paulus Vladimiri and he seems to have retired into private life. His work has been completely forgotten but deserves to be recalled as it anticipates significant doctrinal developments in the law of nations (particularly connected with European–Asian relations). Moreover, his ideas germinated in a milieu of prominent scholars to which, at a later period, Copernicus belonged and to the high standing of which Leonard Coxe of Thame (Principal of the Abbey School at Reading) testified in 1518 in his *De laudibus celeberrimae Cracoviensis Academiae*.[28]

[26] *Magistri Pauli Vladimiri Decretorum* … (ed. by Belch, 1955). Apart from the satire, Falkenberg also wrote the *Liber de Doctrina Potestatis Papae et Imperatoris*, in which he attacked Paulus Vladimiri; Brzostowski, op. cit., p. 118.

[27] Ibid., pp. 136, 150.

[28] Kot, op. cit., p. 59 above, n. 23, at p. 5. It might perhaps be permissible to speak about a Jagiellonian school of the law of nations, since the views propounded by Paulus Vladimiri were also expressed by other prominent scholars at the University of Cracow (founded in 1364 and reorganized in 1400), e.g. Stanislaw of Skarbomierz (the first Rector of the University), who in his sermon on just war defended the position of non-Christian countries in natural law: see Ehrlich and Langrod, *Zarys Historii Prawa Narodów* (1949). See also Ehrlich, *Pawel Wlodkowic i Stanislaw ze Skarbomierza* (1954).

3

MOGUL SOVEREIGNTY AND THE LAW OF NATIONS (1955)

I.

The historian of the law of nations, when considering Mogul sovereignty, external and internal, is concerned with two main problems: first the legal status of the Mogul Empire within the family of nations and the type of law applicable to interstate relations at that time, and second, the internal structure of the Empire which was essentially based on a network of suzerain–vassal relationships. It would be impossible within the scope of a brief analysis to examine all the relevant State practice but the discussion of a few characteristic events might be helpful to throw more light on these problems. Such events may be chosen from Anglo–Mogul relations in the sixteenth, seventeenth and eighteenth centuries. The period between the reign of Emperor Akbar and Emperor Aurangzeb saw the greatest expansion of the Empire and one of the most remarkable episodes during this period, an episode which helps to illustrate the legal nature of relations between India and the West, was the embassy of Sir Thomas Roe to the Court of Agra.

When Sir Thomas Roe, endowed with letters of credence from King James I to Emperor Jehangir, the successor of Akbar, left England in 1615, Alberico Gentili, a Professor at Oxford University and one of the greatest international lawyers of all time, had already published his treatise on 'The Law of War' and his monograph 'On Embassies'.[1] According to Gentili the law of nations applied to all independent nations of the world, whether they were Christian or not.[2] Non-Christian States enjoyed full sovereignty and exercised the right of sending and receiving ambassadors, and in this respect Gentili quoted instances from Asian State practice, referring particularly to Islamic powers and to Persia.[3] These views had earlier been expressed by Jean Bodin,[4] the classic writer on sovereignty and they were later

[1] *A Concise History of the Law of Nations* by A. Nussbaum, 1950, p. 75.
[2] *Les Fondations de Droit International* (Introd. by A. Pillet), Paris, 1904.
[3] *De Legationibus Libri Tres* by Alberico Gentili (Transl. by G. J. Laing) ed. by J. B. Scott, 1924.
[4] *Six Books of a Commonweale* by J. Bodin (Transl. by R. Knolles), London, 1606 (Lib. I, Ch. VIII, p. 89).

shared by Hugo Grotius.[5] Complete de facto independence of a State meant at the same time de jure sovereignty irrespective of any formal act of recognition. Our present-day system of international law has radically deviated from this naturalist conception of sovereignty and it may be useful to consider briefly the differences between the two systems so as to avoid the fallacy of judging State practice in past centuries by ex post facto notions of international law.

According to present-day international law which is largely the product of European State practice in the last 150 years, no State can enter the family of nations and acquire international personality unless it is recognised by the existing powers. The school of law which considers recognition as an act constitutive of statehood, leaves unrecognised States to a great extent outside the orbit of international law. This theory is intimately connected with the birth of the positivist conception of international law which disregards the law of nature.[6] However, it would be difficult for positivists and constitutivists to deny that no *theory of recognition* existed before the nineteenth century in the law of nations, though acts of recognition, declaratory in their nature, had been known in earlier State practice. The de facto birth of a State had meant its legal birth in the eyes of the universalist law of nations, and had implied membership of the family of nations irrespective of religion or civilisation. The same legal principle was professed by eighteenth century international lawyers and found its full expression in the 'Droit des Gens' of Emerich Vattel.[7] After the Congress of Vienna in 1815 a restricted number of European Powers proclaimed themselves as the founder group of the modern international society and assumed authority to admit new member States or to readmit old members who did not participate in the foundation of the group. All Asian States who for centuries had been considered members of the family of nations found themselves in an ad hoc created legal vacuum which reduced them from the status of international personality to the status of candidates competing for such personality. Such a change in the law which was supposed to be based on the consent of Powers in disregard of the universalist conception of natural law, was hardly supported by the consent of all the nations of the world, particularly in Asia. It seemed as if a restricted group of States identifying themselves with the rest of the world proposed to the unrecognised Powers a pars pro toto fallacy. One of the greatest paradoxes connected with this change was the so-called admission of the centuries-old Turkish Empire in 1856 to the family of nations (Concert of Europe)[7a] and a number of international lawyers have not hesitated to expose its absurdity.[8]

[5] Grotius appeared in 'Mare Liberum' as the classic advocate of the sovereignty of Indian and Asian Rulers against Portuguese claims (See: 'Grotius and India' by C. Alexandrowicz, *Indian Year Book of International Affairs*, 1954 (ch. 7 below)).

[6] *The International Law of Recognition* by Ti-Chiang Chen, 1951, p. 26.

[7] *The Law of Nations by Monsieur de Vattel* (Ed. by J. Chitty), 1834 (Book I, Ch. I, §4).

[7a] *International Law* by L. Oppenheim (6th ed.), Vol. I, p. 46.

[8] 'The Treaty of Paris and Turkey's Status in International Law' by H. McKinnon Wood (1943 *American Journal of International Law* p. 26 seq.); *Great Britain and the Law of Nations* by H. A. Smith, 1932, Vol. I, p. 17.

We have engaged in the above digression to make it clear that the legal position of Asian Powers before the nineteenth century and their vested rights must be judged on the basis of pre-positivist law which knew nothing of recognition as a condition of sovereignty within the family of nations. It seems probable that Sir Thomas Roe went to India with Gentilian notions of the law of nations and that diplomatic intercourse between England and the Mogul Empire was established on the assumption that both Powers were members of the family of nations and that there was no need of mutual formal recognition.

Sir Thomas Roe on arriving in India found himself in a part of the world in which the exchange of ambassadors between rulers was based on a tradition as old as that in Europe. In spite of the difference between European and Asian habits and usages, the English ambassador had no difficulty in speaking a common language of diplomatic custom with the Emperor and the authorities of the Empire. He emphasised in the account of his embassy that he asserted his right to diplomatic privileges not on the basis of the custom of England, but of 'the consent of the whole world'.[9] Neither had he any difficulty in securing for himself and his retinue treatment in accordance with the law of nations which the authorities of the receiving Empire accorded to him with all customary courtesy. Moreover, the negotiations between him and the Imperial court for a treaty which was intended to normalise the position of the English East India Company in India, showed that procedures of treaty making as known to the law of nations of that period were observed by both sides. Though the treaty was not signed by the Emperor who was not interested in receiving reciprocal advantages in Europe, its essential provisions were embodied in his firman (letters patent) which enabled the East India Company to develop trade under more favourable conditions. This type of diplomatic exchange and treaty making between European Powers and Asian rulers spread at that time all over South East Asia and it was obvious that mutual dealings took place on a basis of reciprocal acknowledgment of sovereignty and of the principles of the law of nations. The position remained the same up to the beginning of the nineteenth century.[10]

II.

In dealing with problems of internal sovereignty of the Mogul Empire the most important question is that of the suzerain–vassal relationship between the Emperor and the dependent rulers and powers in India which remained at the basis of its constitutional structure up to the end of the eighteenth century. The Emperor's

[9] *The Embasy of Sir Thomas Roe to India, 1615-19* (ed. by Sir W. Foster 1926). The expression 'the consent of the whole world' shows the importance of State practice emphasised by Gentili (*op. cit.*, p. 90).

[10] *Collection of Treaties and Engagements with the Native Princes and States of Asia* (publ. by the British Gov. in India), 1812. See also: *The Acquisition and Government of Backward Territory in International Law* by M. F. Lindley, 1926, pp. 12–19.

overlordship in relation to his vassals constituted a legitimate institution and was enforced by effective sanctions throughout the sixteenth and seventeenth centuries. With the gradual decline of Imperial authority in the eighteenth century this institution was deprived of political substance and effectiveness but though the Emperor lost his grip on unruly dependencies, he was still acknowledged by all subordinate Powers as the originator and grantor of legal titles to local territories all over India. An interesting analogy presents itself in this respect between two declining Empires in two different continents: the Mogul Empire and the Holy Roman Empire.[11] The disintegration of the latter after the treaty of Westphalia in 1648 resulted from and intensified the growing sovereignty of its vassal rulers who, after their emancipation from Imperial control, established among themselves a network of independent international relations. The rapid development of international law in this period was certainly connected with the fundamental changes in the suzerain–vassal relationship within the Empire. The progress of this evolution depended on the possibility of superseding the former unity of the Empire by a new balance of power. Such a balance extending to the whole of Europe was finally achieved after the Napoleonic wars and found its expression in the establishment of the 'Concert of Europe' governed by its own law, the Public Law of Europe. As we have seen the whole change was at the same time accompanied by an ideological change from the naturalist conception of the law of nations to a system of positivist international law. However, before the final stage of this evolution was reached at the beginning of the nineteenth century, an interim stage appeared between the period of full suzerainty of the Holy Roman Emperor over his dependencies, and the period of final disintegration. In this stage suzerainty survived as a formal institution devoid of political substance. But though it remained for the next hundred and fifty years after the Westphalian treaty merely a symbol of unity, it was not deprived of legal significance.

The same evolution took place, mutatis mutandis, within the Mogul Empire. After Emperor Aurangzeb's death a gradual process of emancipation of local rulers, viceroys and governors was set into motion by the force of events, and the Emperor's suzerainty declined throughout the eighteenth century. Nevertheless it subsisted as a formal institution of legal significance. Here lies the analogy between the Imperial institutions in Europe and in India.[12] Throughout the eighteenth century both were deprived of effectiveness while remaining legal symbols. Historians who consider them empty shells over-simplify the position and ignore the fact that the Mogul Emperor participated in the struggle for the balance of power as the agency distributing legal titles. In this capacity he represented also the formal unity of India in its last phase. No ruler or other power ignored the importance of a Mogul grant which formalised their power positions. Even the Mahrattas who initiated a vigorous movement for national unity relied on Mogul titles for the formalisation of their conquests.

[11] *Chapters on the Principles of International Law* by John Westlake, 1894, p. 194 seq.
[12] Westlake, *op. cit.*, p. 194.

This conviction about the value of the surviving Mogul legalistic principle also prevailed among European Powers who had joined in the local game of power politics. All East India Companies, whether English, Dutch or French, had established their first territorial possessions on the basis of firmans received directly or indirectly from the Emperor. The Imperial grant remained for all European statesmen and generals, not excluding Robert Clive, a sort of charter by which a legal seal was put on new power positions. An outstanding example in this respect is the grant of the Diwanee of Bengal, Bihar and Orissa to the English East India Company in 1765.[13] The Emperor conceded this title to the Company following Clive's military achievements, thus legalising its de facto position in these provinces. Prof. John Westlake compares this grant with a transaction effected by Francis II, the last Holy Roman Emperor, i.e. the cession of territory to France at Luneville in 1801 though the territory had been obtained earlier from Prussia by the treaty of Basle in 1795. Similar analogies existed, in Prof. Westlake's view, between the position of Mogul provincial governors, such as the Nizam of the Deccan or the Nawab Vazir of Oudh, and the German Vassal States.[14] While in both cases de facto independence was established by the vassals in the eighteenth century, the formal suzerainty of the Holy Roman Emperor and the Mogul Emperor was not ignored.

The English East India Company had included itself earlier into the network of vassal–suzerain relations within the Mogul Empire and had become part of its constitutional structure. Its relations as an Indian power with other Indian powers and rulers were subject to the law of nations as applied in the subcontinent. It made treaties, alliances, wars and peace with them and like them it finally 'bowed in compliment only to Mogul supremacy'.[15] However the struggle for the balance of power in which it participated, never gave the same results as the analogous struggle in Europe; whereas Europe finally witnessed the establishment of a Concert of Powers with its own Public law, no such Concert of Indian Powers or any Public Law of India or Asia ever emerged out of the turmoil of events. The last vestiges of Mogul suzerainty as a formal legal institution disappeared at the close of the eighteenth century and with the disintegration of the Empire from within, its sovereignty in the framework of the family of nations was lost.

III.

At the time when the disintegration of the Mogul Empire became apparent, two solutions of Indian problems in their entirety were contemplated by the East India Company. One school of thought mainly represented by Robert Clive and Warren Hastings advocated the ultimate establishment of English rule by title of conquest.[15a] This policy in spite of treaty making brushed aside all idea of restoring

[13] *Collection of Treaties and Engagements with the Native Princes and States of Asia* (publ. by the British Gov. in India), 1812, No. XVI, p. 43.

[14] Westlake, *op. cit.*, p. 194.

[15] Westlake, *op. cit.*, p. 194.

[15a] As to the policy of the French East India Company, see: *La Politique Indienne ou Considérations sur les Colonies des Indes Orientales*, Amsterdam, 1768.

the balance of power by supporting the Emperor against his rebellious vassals. The adherents to the second school of thought favoured a policy of strengthening the Emperor in relation to his vassals and in this way of terminating the prevailing lawlessness. Vansittart, governor of Bengal in succession to Robert Clive, planned the restoration of Oudh to the direct rule of the Emperor and the latter's return to Delhi.[16] Anglo–Mogul friendship found an even more outspoken advocate in Major Morrison who claimed to have secured for his policy the support of Col. Dow, and Mr. Nathaniel Smith, a Director of the East India Company.[17] Morrison, opposing Hastings' plans, suggested a direct alliance between Great Britain and Emperor Shah Allum who seems to have been prepared to transfer sovereignty over Bengal, Bihar and Orissa direct to 'His Britannick Majesty' King George III. Under the proposed treaty the Emperor would have received military assistance as well as the payment of 26 lakhs of rupees stipulated to him in 1765 which Hastings had meanwhile stopped. Morrison called Hastings' move 'a dishonourable blow to the law of nations'. Criticising the Company's policy in this respect he wrote: 'A charter granted to a commercial company must virtually lose its being, when that company, having become sovereigns, are found unequal in the weight of government'. His idea was the appointment by the Crown of a viceroy who would be assisted by a council and would co-operate with the Emperor in strengthening peace in India. In Morrison's view such an arrangement could have brought all the unruly vassals back to their proper place and would have normalised trade and helped to extend it to China. He wrote in conclusion that 'the stability and solid dignity of regal government must have infinitely greater weight with Asiatick Princes than the fluctuating unsteady resolves of a company of private men ...'.[18] Whether Morrison's proposals were practicable remains an open question but they certainly suggested a *solution by law* which later found an enthusiastic supporter in the Rt. Hon. Edmund Burke who opposed the Company's policy during the trial of Warren Hastings.[19]

IV.

In his work on the Indian Protectorates, C. L. Tupper made the following comment on the simultaneous disappearance of the Mogul Empire and the Holy

[16] *The Men who Ruled India (The Founders)* by P. Woodruff, 1954, p. 118.

[17] *The Advantages of an Alliance with the Great Mogul* by John Morrison, London, 1774.

[18] It may be interest to note that Major Morrison was appointed Mogul Ambassador to the Court of St. James, but the details of his mission to London are scarcely known. As to his appointment as a British subject, Morrison pointed to the precedent of Sir Robert Shirley who acted in the seventeenth century as ambassador of the King of Persia at the time when Persia sought alliances with European Powers against Turkey, then fully engaged in her attack against the Holy Roman Empire.

[19] *Works of the Rt. Hon. Edmund Burke*, 1826, Vol. XV, p. 109 seq. Warren Hastings admitted in his 'Free Inquiry into the various causes of the alarming state of our affairs in the East Indies' (London 1783) that the Emperor's 'name and family subsist with all the latent rights inherent in them'.—In fact 'the current coin of every established power was struck in the name of (Emperor) Shah Allum' (See: *Our Indian Protectorates* by C. L. Tupper, 1893, pp. 37–8).

Roman Empire from the international scene: 'It is perhaps interesting but it is a mere accidental coincidence that the pacification of India ... followed closely upon the pacification of Europe at the Congress of Vienna in 1815'.[20] We may ask ourselves whether the coincidence was really accidental. The sequence of events showed remarkably similar developments in the suzerain–vassal relations within both Empires. Had it also proved possible to achieve a balance of power between the emancipated rulers of India (for instance under Mahratta leadership) India could have witnessed the establishment of its own Concert of Powers and its own Public Law in the same way as Europe. The collapse of the Mogul Empire made the position of China highly vulnerable and ultimately resulted in the break-down of independent inter-State relations in Asia which, until the decline of the naturalist conception of a universal law of nations, had been part and parcel of a world-wide international structure. The Mogul Emperor remained in the nineteenth century a shadow of the past only. But 'homage continued to be offered on the part of the British Government to the Great Mogul till the cold season of 1842-3 when it was prohibited by Lord Ellenbrough'.[21] Until then British rule had still formally acknowledged Mogul suzerainty. During the Mutiny the last successor of the Mogul dynasty was proclaimed Emperor by the independence movement but he was tried in 1857 after the failure of the rising. 'It might have been pleaded, at least in mitigation that only some fifteen years before, his dynasty had been still led to believe that England was its tributory'.[22] This is what Professor John Westlake, one of the greatest English authorities on international law, remarked about the trial. It testifies to the survival, until the middle of the nineteenth century, of the legal status of a dynasty which had more than a century earlier lost its grip on Indian and Asian politics.

[20] Tupper, *op. cit.*, p. 53.

[21] Tupper, *op. cit.*, p. 80.

[22] Westlake, *op. cit.*, p. 197.

PART II

ASIA AND THE LAW OF NATIONS

4

'JUS GENTIUM' AND THE LAW OF NATURE IN ASIA (1956)

The two most significant developments of contemporary international law are its universal extension to all nations capable of independent political organization and its endeavour to enforce the prohibition of aggressive wars. The principle of universality of the 'family of nations' and the doctrine of 'just war' were already an integral part of the classic law of nations (*jus gentium*), conceived on the basis of the law of nature, but at the end of the eighteenth century they were lost in the process of the law's conversion into a positivist system, based only on the consent of states and state practice.

The conception of the law of nature found its way into the Greek system of inter-city relations; it existed also in ancient Rome and was later developed by the Roman Catholic Church in its framework of canon law. The mediæval structure of Europe was based on the existence of the two correlated centres of power: the Holy Roman Empire, which represented secular authority and the Church of Rome, which was the repository of ecclesiastical jurisdiction. Under this system of unified power there was at first little room for the development of the law of nations. The gradual emergence of autonomous political units, however, such as the Italian city-states and the kingdoms of England and France, promoted treaty-making and an increasing number of inter-state relations. As the Holy Roman Empire approached its period of disintegration, particularly after the Peace Treaty of Westphalia in 1648, there was more opportunity for the growth of the law of nations as a separate discipline.[1]

Similar developments took place at various periods in the history of Asia. China early developed her own notions of inter-state law and practice with a strong emphasis on the institution of vassal states who acknowledged the supreme authority of the imperial suzerain. There seems to have been legal equality among these mutually independent states in the Chinese Commonwealth. Diplomatic intercourse was well known and envoys enjoyed immunity though to a lesser degree than in the West. The distinction between combatants and non-combatants during warfare came to be acknowledged and humanitarian principles were observed to a substantial degree. Confucius planned the establishment of a great union of Chinese States, but imperial power prevailed over this conception. The same institutions developed

[1] *A Concise History of the Law of Nations*, by A. Nussbaum, 1950.

in Japan where, according to historians, treaty-making was known as early as in the third century A.D.

India's contribution to the development of the law of nations in Asia was equally remarkable. As a unified imperial power appeared only at intervals and for comparatively short periods in the history of the subcontinent, the relations between the many Indian rulers resulted in the development of principles of an international or quasi-international character. Kautilya's *Arthashastra* bears witness to the existence of a well-defined set of rules which prevailed in the various 'circles' of states. Interstate law in India knew humanitarian rules of warfare, the inviolability of envoys (*dutas*), the vassal–suzerain relationship and principles relating to maritime intercourse.[2]

It is also noteworthy that since the Middle Ages the treatment of foreign merchants became the object of treaty stipulations. In Asia, as in Europe, foreign trading communities fought for the relaxation of the practice of seizure of ships and the confiscation of the property of deceased foreigners by the local sovereign (*jus albinagii*). The law of nations developed by Muslim states witnessed even speedier development resulting from the close contacts of the Islamic powers with Europe. The fight between Islam and the Christian world created a centuries-long tension, the consequences of which were strongly felt in India and Asia since the end of the fifteenth century.

There is no risk in saying that the conception of natural law was not alien to these systems of interstate law in Asia. It may be that canon law in Europe helped to make it more precise there because it distinguished clearly between positive divine law (*jus divinum positivum*), *i.e.*, revealed law; the law of nature (*jus divinum naturale*), *i.e.*, law based on reason and human nature; and, finally, man-made law (*jus humanum*). These three categories of law were known in Asia, though the more intimate interconnection between natural law and revealed law made a clear distinction between the two more difficult and perhaps sometimes impossible. But this is a problem of philosophy rather than one of jurisprudence. The fact remains that the notion of natural law existed in Asia, that it conceived human nature in its ideal and moral sense, as in Europe, and that it was ready to be extended to the whole of mankind. It was based on the broad principle of non-discrimination between nations and implied generally the idea of just war. The idea of a law of nature in the sense of self-preservation, strongly emphasized by Emeric de Vattel, the Swiss jurist and writer, in the eighteenth century, found its early expression also in Kautilya's *Arthashastra*, though not necessarily as an overriding device (see Book VII).

It is often thought that no law of nations had been applied to intercontinental intercourse between European and Asian powers during the period of political equality between them in the sixteenth, seventeenth and eighteenth centuries. This, however, is hardly warranted by facts.[3] Among the European powers who entered the Asian game of power politics, the Portuguese were first; then came the Dutch,

[2] *International Law in Ancient India*, by S. V. Viswanatha, 1925.
[3] *Asia and Western Dominance*, by K. M. Panikker, 1954.

the English and the French. Vasco da Gama, who landed in 1498 on the west coast of India, brought a queer mixture of notions to the Asian scene. He came to discover and occupy new lands, to buy spices, to undercut the trade of the Arab merchants and Venice, and last but not least to make converts to Christianity. He felt legally entitled to act on the commands of his king, who believed he had been authorized in 1502 by Pope Alexander VI to start conquests in non-Christian lands. The world had been, according to the papal bull, *'Inter Cætera'* of 1492, divided between the two great sea powers, Spain and Portugal, one with the mission to sail westwards, the other eastwards. The line of demarcation, drawn in the bull, was later adjusted in the treaty of Tordesillas of 1494, concluded between Spain and Portugal.

As soon as Spanish rule in America made itself brutally felt on the ruins of the Aztec and Inca empires, a powerful reaction appeared among Roman Catholic writers in Spain who endeavoured to clarify the prevailing confusion of ideas. Conquest, they said, was a political affair, a matter of *jus humanum*. Conversion, on the other hand, was a matter of *jus divinum*, but it should not disturb the peaceful existence of organized political communities in non-Christian lands. So argued Franciscus de Vitoria (1480–1546), Professor at the University of Salamanca, Spain, and his school, and it goes to the credit of Spain that he was allowed to attack the policy of his own king and country. But Vasco da Gama, like Cortez, was no follower of Vitoria but an empire builder and so were the Portuguese viceroys who followed him and who seized Goa. The prestige of international lawyers (theologians) was not yet powerful enough to influence decisively public opinion and political decision.

The Portuguese who, thanks to the support of the Raja of Cochin and the Vijayanagar rulers, were able to destroy the maritime trade monopoly of Arab merchants in India and Asia and to shatter the sea power of the Zamorin of Calicut, had soon to face the competition of the Dutch who brought, apart from naval power and a trading spirit, an aggressive challenge to the legal notions of the Catholic monarchs. The Dutch were Protestants and so was their greatest lawyer, Hugo Grotius, usually considered the father of the law of nations. The construction put by the Catholic sea powers on the papal title of discovery and the conversion of non-Christian lands became a matter of doubt. Historians often tend to identify papal policy with the policy of Catholic monarchs, though what the Church of Rome conceived as a religious device was often distorted by secular authority for purposes of power politics. The responsibility for excessive zeal rested with the monarchs, who, whenever it suited them, became, '*plus Pape que le Pape*' (more popish than the Pope). Be that as it may, the prestige of Grotius overshadowed world opinion from the beginning of the seventeenth century. In his *Mare Liberum* (Freedom of the Seas), published in 1609, he made it clear that the Portuguese in India and Asia established relations and made arrangements with Asian rulers on a footing of equality and that any other European power could do the same. Whatever Grotius intended primarily to show by his arguments, particularly to prove the right of the Dutch to sail freely across the oceans and to participate in Asian trade, he gave at the same time to Asian rulers the status of sovereigns in his law of nations. He could not have done otherwise, as his legal notions were based on a system of natural law which implied the equality of organized political communities all over the world. Otherwise the law of nature could not have been what it was meant to be. Moreover, Grotius relied in *Mare Liberum* on all the arguments of Franciscus de Vitoria and proved that the conceptions of the Protestant and the Salamanca schools of the law of nations were not divergent in the above field.

Whereas the Dutch arrived in the East to challenge Portuguese vested interests by physical force, the English came with a policy of negotiation. In 1615 Sir Thomas Roe, an English ambassador, set foot on Indian soil and travelled from Surat to Agra to present letters from King James to Jehangir, the Moghul Emperor. His task was to open negotiations and to obtain a treaty securing trading rights to English merchants.[4] Seventeen years earlier, one of the greatest international lawyers of all times, Alberico Gentili (1552–1608), an Italian Protestant who had become a professor of law at Oxford, had published his famous works on the law of war. Gentili's law of nations based on the law of nature was universal law relating to the whole of mankind and he could not have given any sovereign ruler in Asia a position inferior to that of sovereign monarchs in Europe. The embassy of Sir Thomas Roe fully testifies to the English notions of the law of nations at this period. They were not different from those formulated later by Grotius and the motive behind them was certainly more selfless.

A battle of wits took place at the court in Agra, where Sir Thomas Roe had to face the Portuguese Jesuit mission which had come much earlier from Goa.[5] The Moghul court became clouded with intrigues, but it would be an over-simplification to blame one or the other side for excessive zeal. Diplomatists tend to criticize on the part of their adversaries what they consider justified in the implementation of their own mission. In spite of English–Portuguese tension, Father Corsi, S.J., offered to Sir Thomas Roe to mediate between the English and the Portuguese, so as not to expose Christian agencies in India to the disgrace of disunity. Sir Thomas Roe was certainly the last to betray his Christian ideals. But, whereas he and those who came after him from England enjoyed the unfailing support of their king, the King of Portugal undercut, about the middle of the eighteenth century, the existence of the Jesuit mission at the Moghul court by banishing all Jesuits from Portuguese dominions. The provincial centre of the *Societas Jesu* in Goa disappeared (1759) and their greatest scholar, Father Joseph Tieffenthaler, appealed to the English for protection.

It seems fair to assume that a three-cornered game of power politics between the Moghuls, the English and the Portuguese, without Dutch and French intervention, would probably have been distinguished by less violence and by more compromise and treaty-making. The fact that Dutch intervention came in the seventeenth century intensified the fight against the Portuguese in Asia and made Grotius formulate his case on behalf of the Dutch East India Company in a truly dramatic way. Side by side with the Dutch, the rulers of Asia became the *dramatis personæ*. Their policy was not to limit intercourse and trade to the Portuguese but to establish relations

[4] *The Men who Ruled India: The Founders*, Vol. I, by Philip Woodruff, 1953.
[5] *The Jesuits and the Great Mogul*, by Sir Edward Maclagan, 1932.

with other European powers. In order to enable them to pursue this policy, Grotius endowed them in *Mare Liberum* with full independence and sovereign status in a *chef-d'œuvre* of the classic law of nations.[6]

After the death of Aurangzeb the disintegration of the Moghul Empire together with the ascendency of the English East India Company put things in a different light. The unifying power of the Moghuls had disappeared and neither the Marathas nor any of the other Indian or European powers were able to restore the balance. A similar development had taken place in Europe where, after the Treaty of Westphalia in 1648, the unifying power of the Holy Roman Empire had ceased to be effective and where the balance was temporarily at the mercy of ruthless power politics. The disappearance of the two most powerful empires of the world had a decisive impact on the law of nations. The ideal of the law of nature with its underlying conceptions gave way to the law of survival from which a positivist system of international law emerged. At the time of the Congress of Vienna in 1815 the family of nations was restricted to those represented at the Conference table. The Asian powers, paradoxically including even Turkey, did not find their proper place under the new system. Whereas it proved ultimately possible to establish in place of the Holy Roman Empire a more or less predictable balance of power which resulted in the creation of the Concert of Europe with its own public law, there was no Concert of rulers in India to supersede the Moghul Empire. International law conceived as the public law of Europe excluded the whole world (except the American continent) and covered Asia in the status of colonial possessions only. The Chinese Empire, whose future, in spite of isolation, was doomed after the downfall of the Moghuls, was equally outside the family of nations which followed for nearly 150 years the positivist conception of international law. Today international lawyers have started revising the notions of international law and a revival of certain ideas of the law of nature seems to be in sight. Two of its most fundamental conceptions have again found their proper place: the universality of the 'family of nations' which covers all continents, and the concept of 'just war' by which we endeavour to ban aggressive war from the international scene.

[6] 'Grotius and India', by C. H. Alexandrowicz-Alexander. (*The Indian Year Book of International Affairs*, Vol. III, 1954 (ch. 7 below)).

5

SOME PROBLEMS IN THE HISTORY OF THE LAW OF NATIONS IN ASIA* (1963)

Why study the History of the Law of Nations in Asia if there is no longer much interest in the History of International Law as such? The attention of international lawyers is more and more concentrating on legal aspects of contemporary problems of international relations and politics and on the operation of tribunals and quasi-tribunals and the case law produced by them. This, however, rarely saves them from being peripheral in their activities and rather distant from the centre of the great questions of juridical significance. One of the reasons of this deplorable state of affairs is the divorce of international law from its vital historical sources and the general disinterest in the study of its history. The writers of present day treatises of international law usually devote a few introductory pages to the history of the subject but these short chapters are mostly based on similar introductions in 19th century treatises and one often wonders who was the last international lawyer in the past who saw with his own eyes the works of Vitoria, Gentili, Grotius or Vattel. A lifeless repetition of historical slogans about the development of the law of nations is, however, not only useless to the reader but definitely does harm to the standing of international law within the family of legal subjects. One can still find on the shelves of law libraries the 'Classics of International Law' published by the Carnegie Foundation but they usually rest under a heavy layer of dust. The time has come to shake it off and to return to some of the vital foundations of the law of nations, a term which is so much more meaningful than Bentham's international law which continues to bear the seeds of its own crisis.

One of the first tasks of historians of the law of nations would be the rewriting of the historical introductions in new editions of generally recognised treatises. Without pointing to any one of them individually, it would be fair to state that some of the historical notions conveyed to students have become untenable. The development of the family of nations has often been described in the following

* This article is based on the factual material contained in 'Treaty and Diplomatic Relations between European and South Asian Powers in the 17th and 18th centuries' (*Recueil des Cours*, Vol. 100, 1960) but a number of further conclusions are drawn to provide guidance for students of the history of the law of nations in Asia (East Indies).

way: The law of nations apparently grew up among the Christian nations of Europe only. It extended to the American continent at the end of the 18th century and at the beginning of the 19th century. Then came the Christian Negro Republics of Haiti and Liberia. But it was only in 1856 that the Ottoman Empire (a non-Christian State) was admitted to the Concert of Europe (a pars pro toto expression for the leading members of the family of nations). Other Asian States came much later, the capitulations being in the way to their unquestioned status within the family of nations.[1] Without engaging in undue criticism of this sort of historical picture, it seems useful to recall that the Ottoman Empire concluded as early as 1535 a significant treaty with Francis I of France and this treaty was followed by agreements concluded with almost all the major European powers which maintained, long before the 19th century, permanent embassies in Constantinople. Francis I who risked the sanction of invalidity of a treaty concluded with a non-Christian power (and directed against the Holy Roman Empire) addressed the following apology to Pope Paul III: 'The Turks … are not outside human society in such a way that we would have more intimate relations with barbarians[2] than with infidels. It would mean that we ignore the links which nature established among human beings; but they all have the same origin; whatever relates to human beings cannot be strange to other human beings. If nations are divided among themselves, it is not nature which separates them but tradition and usages; it follows that relations between members of the same community are more intimate than those among different States, but the separation does not affect the brotherly union among all members of humanity. It would have evil effects if the ties of blood and nationhood would estrange particular societies from the universal society of nations …. differences of religion and cultural tradition cannot destroy the natural association of mankind'.[3] What is remarkable in this statement, is the emphasis on the universality of the family of nations as based on the natural law ideology which rose above differences of religion and civilisation. The treaty of 1535 constituted a turning point in the field of treaty law which had been for centuries under the impact of the struggle between Christian Europe and Islam. Let us consider briefly some of the elements of legal change in which European–Asian relations played a significant role.

Long before the arrival of the Portuguese in the East Indies, commercial interests started making inroads in the intransigent attitude of Canon law towards relations with the non-Christian East. The European market being badly in need of East Indian spices and other Asian merchandise, sought co-operation with Islamic traders who held the monopoly of navigation and trade between the Indonesian Islands, India and the Red Sea. The Republic of Venice took the initiative of importing and distributing spices and obtained in 1345 an ecclesiastical licence for maintaining relations with Islamic trade centres, the licence being an exception to the general prohibition of co-operation with 'infidels'. When the Portuguese destroyed the Venetian–Islamic monopoly and carried spices by direct sea route round the Cape of Good Hope

[1] *Concise History of the Law of Nations* by A. Nussbaum.

[2] (Titian left the portrait of one of them!)

[3] *Les Origines du Droit International* by E. Nys, 1894, p. 162.

(which they sold in Europe at competitive prices), the objection to Christian–Islamic co-operation lost more of its significance. Anti-infidel ideology was hardly followed up in practice as the Portuguese concluded treaties with East-Indian powers, whether Muslim or Hindu. In fact the Portuguese allied themselves politically with a number of Hindu Sovereigns, to mention only those of Vijayanagar, Cochin, Quilon and Travancore, who welcomed them as natural allies against the pressure of Islam in the East. This no doubt is the reason why in the works of European writers the category of 'infidels' did not really extend to Hindu (or Buddhist) powers. In this respect Seraphin de Freitas in his 'De Justo Imperio Lusitanorum Asiatico' (1625) states that the Portuguese came into conflict with non-Islamic powers in the East Indies only in exceptional circumstances e.g., with Calicut which had become a centre of Islamic traders. But the Portuguese concluded treaties even with Islamic powers as can be seen from a survey of treaties in Judice Biker's *Collecção de Tratados*.[4]

Treaty making also gathered momentum in the relations between the Dutch East India Company and Asian countries in the 17th century. The student of the history of the law of nations in the East Indies would be well advised to consult some of these treaties as contained in the collection 'Corpus Diplomaticum Neerlando-Indicum' published by Heeres. As far as the English Company is concerned, the collections by Aitcheson, Chalmers and Logan and other minor collections are available. No collection of treaties concluded by the French Company has been completed with the exception of the Recueil des Traités by Reinach which does not, however, contain the important Indian treaties. There are references to various treaties in the works of Martineau and Kaeppelin but few texts of treaties can be found in them. But though no collection is yet available, it is notorious that the French Company concluded numerous treaties and other transactions (contained for instance in firmans and other decrees) with Indian Rulers and with the Rulers of Siam, Indo-China and Burma.

It follows from these observations that no legal or theological theory was able to stand in the way of the natural expansion of European–Asian relations, mainly dictated by the increasing demand for Asian merchandise in Europe. The growth of these relations was also accompanied by political considerations as for instance the tendency of certain European powers (e.g., German Sovereigns) to seek an alliance with Persia against the Ottoman. Empire.[5] If this was the position, the question may be asked, why did 19th and 20th writers of international law reverse the picture and, after dismissing European–Asian relations prior to the 19th century from the history of international law, introduce independent Asian countries such as Siam, Persia, China and others as newcomers to the family of nations in the 19th century. The reasons for this volte-face in the literature of international law must be sought in the great ideological changes which took place at the end of the 18th and at the beginning of the 19th century.[6] Even if these changes were not accompanied

[4] This collection contains Portuguese treaties concluded in the East Indies since the beginning of the 16th century.

[5] See also the French-Siam alliance in the 17th century directed against the Dutch.

[6] See 'Doctrinal Aspects of the Universality of the Law of Nations' by C. H. Alexandrowicz, published in 1961, *British Year Book of International Law*, p. 506 (p. 168 below).

by actual State practice, they had a vital impact on some of the 19th century writers who divorced themselves more and more from the historical roots of the jus gentium and its centuries old reality.

The divorce from the past led to the gradual elimination of the natural law outlook by the growing European positivism. Two elements had been inter alia essential in the above outlook, the principle of universality of the law of nations and the principle of identity of de facto and de jure State sovereignty. The principle of universality of the law of nations was and is inherent in a law derived from reason and not based on human will alone. Natural law (common to all mankind) is reasoned and objective law which is not at the mercy of the discretionary consent of States. But once the deification of the State and of national sovereignty reached dimensions such as those envisaged by Hegel, there was no room for any other law than that made by sovereign States as unlimited law makers. At the same time positivism became intimately connected with all the trends of European self-centredness which was so characteristic for the period following the Congress of Vienna. What mattered in the process of law making, was the consent of the powers sitting round the European conference table which considered themselves the spokesmen of the family of nations. The Concert of Europe and the Family of Nations became identical terms and the minor European powers had to be content with the passive role assigned to them by the great powers. Poland's and Italy's political agony hardly disturbed the peace of mind of any of the leading European statesmen, and the Asian powers were relegated to a vacuum from which (they were told) they could be readmitted to legal existence as candidates for membership in the family of nations.

In the same way as universality, the principle of identity of de facto and de jure sovereignty had also been connected with the natural law ideology. It is precisely the collapse of this principle under the impact of positivism which made it possible for the great powers to transform the status of the sovereign Asian countries from that of international persons into that of candidates for international personality and membership of the family of nations. It may be briefly recalled that the fact that prior to the 19th century de facto sovereignty of a State meant automatically its de jure sovereignty, was intimately connected with the absence of any theory of recognition. If acts of recognition occurred in practice they were declaratory in nature. No constitutive theory of recognition ever made its appearance in any of the classics of the law of nations up to the end of the 18th century. It did not exist in the works of the Spanish writers nor did Bodin, Gentili, Grotius (and the Grotians) or even Moser and Martens ever conceive such a theory. The last two writers, in spite of being positivists, still retained a minimum of principles of natural law which they allowed to coexist with their new European-centred outlook. However, the positivists of the early 19th century destroyed this coexistence and started combining their un-universal positivism with constitutivism. Henry Wheaton was among the prominent writers of this period, one of the first to split sovereignty into internal and external sovereignty, and he maintained that a State may acquire by its de facto independent existence internal sovereignty but that its external sovereignty would be dependent on the recognition of the powers constituting the family of nations.[7] The later writers of the positivist school then defined the new international 'caste system'. As stated above, they considered the old Christian powers of Europe as the nucleus of the family of nations. They admitted extensions of this family to North and South America and some of them singled out Haiti and Liberia as the first sovereign countries with a Christian but non-European population. We have already seen that the Ottoman Empire had been considered the first non-Christian candidate State. All countries east of Turkey found themselves in the same boat and this extended not only to those which survived the collapse of the Asian state system such as for instance Siam or Persia but also to those countries which in the 19th century disappeared from the political map of the world such as Burma, Ceylon, the Marattas, the Mogul Empire and the independent Kingdoms of Indonesia. Those which vanished into oblivion had to wait for their re-birth in one or another form until the end of the second world war. But those which survived had to submit to the consequences of the ideological changes conceived in Europe. It is the task of the student of the history of the law of nations in Asia to look back on these changes and to ascertain and measure the degree of artificiality with which they were brought about. Though in the absence of sufficient factual material it is not yet possible to pass judgment on the past, it would not be premature to question the positivist view on the development of the family of nations and the law of nations. For, if the Asian States which existed prior to the 19th century were generally acknowledged as capable of concluding treaties, maintaining diplomatic relations, waging war, making peace and participating in a spectacularly expanding world trade, limitations imposed on their legal capacity by ideological change (without their participation in such change) could not produce such far reaching results as their reduction to a sort of extraneity—a status which implied a serious restriction of their position in international law.

Would students of the history of the law of nations be able to ascertain some inter-connexion between these legal developments and the idea of colonialism which is certainly not of a legal nature? A further consideration of the problem may enable them to provide an answer to a question which is not only the concern of historians but also has some relevancy to contemporary issues. The point is that the elimination of the natural law principles of universality of the family of nations and of declaratory recognition and their replacement by a European Club of States endowed with power of constitutive recognition of non-members of the club outside Europe, provided a new legal pressure mechanism in the hands of the great powers. Again it would be interesting to explore whether the use of this mechanism intensified the burden of colonial pressure as experienced not only by tribal communities in various continents but also by the politically organised Asian entities with an age long cultural tradition. The International Court of Justice (in the Indo–Portuguese dispute over the right of passage to the Portuguese enclaves)[8] recognised a treaty

[7] See 'The Theory of Recognition in Fieri' by C. H. Alexandrowicz, published in 1958, *British Year Book of International Law* (ch. 24 below).

[8] I. C. J. Reports, 1960, p. 6.

concluded between the Maratta Empire and the Portuguese (1779) as a valid transaction in the law of nations. If so, the Maratta Empire must have been in the sphere of international existence (as expressly stated by the judges) and thus the same must be said about other Asian State entities in the 18th century such as Ceylon, Burma, the Mogul Empire, the States of the Deccan and Mysore, not to mention Persia, Siam or the Ottoman Empire.[9] Those which survived in the 19th century, could not have been reduced to the status of candidates for admission to the family of nations and for recognition. If in fact they were re-admitted or recognised (always with emphasis on the problem of capitulations as raised by the European powers) these acts of re-admission or recognition were in so far meaningless that they were simply inter-temporal adjustments caused by ideological changes.[10] Students of the history of international relations could throw more light on the political aspect of these quasi-legal acts, for if their juridical significance was negligible, they may have been rather acts of political pressure under the cloak of law.

The above problems have been tentatively formulated as a starting point for further research. No definite answer to them is yet available. Before concluding our considerations, one or two final observations would be relevant. 19th and 20th century writers have devoted much attention to capitulations as an element of delaying the 'entry' of Asian States into the family of nations. In this connexion it may be recalled that the foundation of European settlements in the East Indies had been possible only thanks to the age long Asian tradition which allowed merchants to establish themselves by their own laws. The existence of such communities enjoying a fair measure of autonomy in foreign territory had never been derogatory to the sovereignty of the territorial power which granted concessions to foreign merchants. Let us mention only one or two examples such as the concessions accorded to Muslim traders in the Hindu States on the West coast of India or those accorded to Chinese traders in the Indonesian Islands.[11] The conversion of these 'capitulations' (sensu lato) into instruments of exploitation of the territorial sovereign took place much later at the initiative of the Europeans in Asia. Once the latter managed to treat their concessions as irrevocable, the position of the conceding territorial sovereign became precarious. But this legal development can hardly testify to the inferiority of civilisation within the countries whose hospitality the Europeans enjoyed. The exposition of the law of capitulations by 19th century international lawyers in Europe which (according to them) placed the Asian powers to a great extent outside the family of nations is hardly tenable and calls for reconsideration.

Apart from the questions considered above in a summary way, there are further problems which deserve the attention of the student of the history of the law of nations in Asia such as those of maritime law (Grotius wrote his 'Mare Liberum' entirely with reference to navigation and trade in the Indian Ocean, and Seraphin de Freitas joined issue with him against the background of the Asian scene), those

[9] China and Japan (unlike the East Indies) are outside these considerations as they did not (with a few exceptions) maintain intercourse with European powers prior to the 19th century.

[10] *Recueil des Cours*, ut supra.

[11] *Indonesian Trade and Society* by J. C. Van Leur, 1955, and *Recueil des Cours*, ut supra.

of the law of war (relating to prisoners of war, non-combatants and temperamenta belli), of Suzerain–Vassal relations and diplomacy. None of these problems with reference to the 16th, 17th and 18th centuries have been hitherto sufficiently explored from the European or Asian point of view. The East Indies constituted the meeting ground of the Portuguese and the Dutch, English and French East India Companies on the one hand, and a number of Asian Sovereigns on the other. The more their contacts became intensified, the more a mutual classification of legal status took place within the framework of diplomatic exchanges and treaty making. The question arises what were the criteria of statehood and sovereignty which determined the attitude of the Europeans towards their Asian counterparts and vice versa. The East Indies had a code of principles of inter-State relations but it constituted entirely customary law. The exploration of these inter-State customs is a task fraught with considerable technical difficulties. But it may be useful to undertake it in order to appreciate the contribution of three centuries of European–Asian relations (on a footing of equality) to the development of the law of nations. A proper understanding of this contribution may serve to remove some of the doubts and ambiguities relating to the past which cannot be explained away by those superficial statements which can still be found in the historical introductions to some of our present day treatises of international law.

6

LE DROIT DES NATIONS AUX INDES ORIENTALES

AUX XVIE, XVIIE, XVIIIE SIÈCLES (1964)

L'UNIVERSALITÉ DE LA FAMILLE DES NATIONS

Examinant, dans ses études sur l'histoire sociale et économique de l'Asie, le problème de l'équilibre entre l'Europe et l'Asie au XVIIIe siècle, J. C. van Leur écrit: 'L'immense progrès technique du XIXe siècle a introduit l'élément exotique dans la littérature concernant l'Asie et a imposé en même temps une image d'états orientaux tombés en décadence et de despotismes anarchiques, mis en opposition avec la force motrice, la perfection et le libéralisme des états chrétiens de l'Occident. La littérature missionnaire et politique a appliqué cette image à tous les états, à commencer par la Turquie et la Perse jusqu'à la Chine et au Japon… Il y a lieu de se méfier de cette image de décadence projetée en arrière, du XIXe siècle vers le passé. Ceci est particulièrement évident si l'on considère le XVIIIe siècle… La Perse était au XVIIIe siècle un pays encore intact. En Inde, l'établissement du pouvoir local et même régional par la France et l'Angleterre ne troublait la puissance de l'Empire Mogol que superficiellement. Les états de la Birmanie et de l'Inde extérieure restaient intacts également…'. Van Leur se demande enfin si l'équilibre entre l'Europe et l'Asie fut renversé au XVIIIe siècle et il donne une réponse catégoriquement négative.[1]

Le procédé abusif qui consiste à projeter vers le passé un état de choses vrai seulement pour le XIXe siècle, et qui a abouti à une déformation de la réalité historique des XVIe, XVIIe et XVIIIe siècles en Asie, existe également dans la littérature de droit international.[2] Si nous consultons les principaux ouvrages consacrés au développement de la famille des nations, l'extension de cette famille s'y trouve habituellement expliquée de la façon suivante: l'Europe chrétienne est conçue comme étant le noyau de la famille des nations et de la civilisation chrétienne. Les premiers pays non-européens à être admis dans cette famille furent les États-Unis, certains pays

[1] *Indonesian Trade and Society*, par J. C. van Leur, 1955, p. 271.

[2] Notre discussion se limite à ces trois siècles, car c'est pendant cette période (commençant avec l'arrivée de Vasco da Gama en Inde) que plusieurs puissances européennes ont maintenu des relations sur un pied d'égalité avec un grand nombre de souverains aux Indes Orientales. Voir: *Traités et Relations diplomatiques entre les pays d'Europe et de l'Asie du sud*, par C. Alexandrowicz (Recueil des Cours de l'Académie de Droit International), 1961, t. 100; trad. par M. Lévy; cité ci-après: *Recueil des Cours*.

d'Amérique latine et les républiques chrétiennes de Haïti et du Liberia. Ce n'est que postérieurement, en 1856, qu'un premier état non-chrétien, la Turquie, fut admis dans ce que l'on appelait 'le concert européen'. Le Japon, la Chine, la Perse et le Siam y furent admis bien plus tard.[3]

Une telle conception de la naissance de la famille des nations est-elle conciliable avec le droit et les faits du passé? Est-il possible de considérer que la Turquie et les autres puissances asiatiques ne sont devenus membres de la famille des nations que postérieurement à Haïti et au Liberia? Pour la Turquie par exemple, les relations diplomatiques qu'elle a eues, depuis le XVIe siècle, avec la plupart des grandes puissances d'Europe, les nombreux traités conclus, ses diverses relations commerciales avec les pays européens, montrent clairement qu'elle faisait partie de la famille des nations antérieurement au XIXe siècle. La position des autres puissances asiatiques était pratiquement identique. L'Empire Mogol en Inde, la Perse, le Siam et les puissances indonésiennes ont exercé le droit de légation actif et passif et ont conclu de nombreux traités avec des puissances européennes. Ces diverses transactions ont eu lieu dans le cadre du droit classique des nations. Le commerce entre l'Europe et les Indes Orientales était d'une importance primordiale pour l'économie européenne. Afin d'obtenir des privilèges commerciaux, les compagnies des Indes Orientales (partiellement souveraines) se sont insérées dans le réseau des relations suzerain-vassal aux Indes Orientales et elles ont quelquefois accepté d'être dans une position juridiquement subordonnée à l'égard d'un souverain local.[4] Elles ont commencé leur carrière commerciale et politique grâce à l'attitude des souverains asiatiques envers la position juridique des communautés étrangères en général. Les coutumes maritimes en vigueur aux Indes Orientales permettaient une communication régulière transocéanique. En cas de guerre, on observait certains principes, traditionnellement acceptés par les pays asiatiques, comme ceux relatifs aux 'temperamenta belli'. Aussi les auteurs européens classiques (Grotius, Freitas, Wolff, Martens et Vattel) ne mettent-ils pas en doute, à l'époque, la valeur des anciennes civilisations asiatiques. Et même s'ils les apprécient avec certaines réserves, ils considèrent la famille des nations comme une communauté universelle s'étendant non seulement à l'Europe mais encore à l'Asie, sans tenir compte des différences de religion ou de civilisation.

Le point de vue des auteurs classiques était évidemment fondé sur le droit naturel, que celui-ci fût de nature religieuse ou séculière. Le trait essentiel de ce droit était son universalité.[5] On doit aussi souligner que l'école classique, telle qu'elle est mise en évidence par l'œuvre de Grotius, n'a jamais considéré les pays asiatiques comme

[3] Voir *International Law*, par Oppenheim, 1958, I, 48; *Traité de Droit International Public* par P. Fauchille, 1922, I, 1 (28, 31, 72); *Traité de Droit International Public*, par M. Sibert, 1951, I, 22.

[4] Au XVIIIe siècle, le gouverneur de Pondichéry accepta la dignité de Nawab de l'Empire Mogol, et la compagnie des Indes Orientales anglaise reçut la diwanie de Bengale, Bihar et Orissa ('Lord Clive,' par Macaulay, *Critical and Historical Essays*, 1883).

[5] Il y avait différentes conceptions du droit naturel: celle de l'école espagnole, la conception plus séculière de Grotius et celle des Grotiens, basée sur les Droits Fondamentaux des Nations. Mais toutes ces conceptions reconnaissaient l'universalité de la famille des nations (*Natural Law*, par A. P. d'Entrèves, 1952; 'Contribution à l'Histoire des Sources de Droit des Gens,' par P. Guggenheim, *Recueil des Cours de l'Académie de Droit International*, 1958, t. II); *Recueil des Cours, op. cit.*, ch. VI.

terrae nullius ou comme susceptibles de découverte ou d'occupation à la suite d'une donation papale. Chaque fois que les puissances européennes ont acquis des droits territoriaux aux Indes Orientales, elles l'ont fait par un traité de cession ou par la conquête, conformément aux principes du droit européen des nations et aux coutumes alors en vigueur dans les pays asiatiques.[6]

En outre, selon le droit classique depuis Bodin,[7] la souveraineté *de facto* de n'importe quel monarque indépendant, en Europe ou en Asie, signifiait automatiquement une souveraineté *de jure*. Aucune théorie de la reconnaissance des états n'existait dans le droit des nations antérieurement au XIXe siècle. (Si des actes de reconnaissance à l'égard d'un état souverain étaient effectués, ils avaient un effet déclaratif et non constitutif.) Tout souverain admis à conclure un traité, ou à nouer des relations diplomatiques, avait automatiquement sa place dans le domaine du droit des nations. Comment se fait-il alors que l'Empire Ottoman et d'autres puissances asiatiques, qui avaient leur place dans la famille des nations avant le XIXe siècle, aient pu être soudain relégués à la position de candidats à l'admission dans la famille des nations au XIXe siècle? L'explication se trouve dans l'extinction graduelle de la conception 'naturaliste' du droit international, et dans la croissance du positivisme au XIXe siècle (faisant appel au consentement des états européens). Mais ce changement n'a eu lieu que graduellement.[8] A mesure que se développait le commerce entre l'Europe et l'Asie, le droit (qui était au début universel) commençait à se rétrécir et se contracter.[9] Avec le déclin de la doctrine du droit naturel, l'Europe se mit à chercher un droit positif et régional, fondé sur les traités et usages exclusivement européens. Ce droit 'positif' se proclamait valable (sur la base d'un faux raisonnement de *pars pro toto*) pour le monde entier sans la participation des états asiatiques, qui se trouvèrent alors candidats à l'admission dans cette famille des nations tout à fait réorientée.

Pendant une période transitoire, de la fin du XVIIIe siècle au début du XIXe siècle, les idées positivistes et les idées naturalistes ont encore coexisté. Mais ce modus vivendi s'est détérioré au début du XIXe siècle. Après les guerres napoléoniennes et le Congrès de Vienne, le climat juridique s'est modifié en Europe et il est devenu peu à peu exclusivement positiviste.[10]

Quels que soient les changements intervenus, il est évident qu'on ne doit juger les relations internationales au cours des XVIe, XVIIe et XVIIIe siècles qu'en fonction

[6] Voir les traités conclus par les Portugais depuis le début du XVIe siècle (*Collecção de Tratados*, par J. Biker, 1881); les traités conclus par les Hollandais depuis le XVIIe siècle (*Corpus Diplomaticum Neerlando-Indicum*, par J. E. Heeres, 1907-31); les traités conclus par les Anglais depuis la moitié du XVIIe siècle (*Collections des traités*, par Aitcheson, 1909; G. Chalmers, 1790; W. Bolts, 1772; W. Logan, 1906); et les traités conclus par les Français depuis la seconde moitié du XVIIe siècle (*Recueil des traités*, par L. Reinach, 1902; cette collection ne contient pas les traités conclus en Inde).

[7] *Les Six Livres de la République*, Livre sixième, ch. II.

[8] C. H. Alexandrowicz, 'The Theory of Recognition *in Fieri*' (*British Year Book of International Law*, 1958) (ch. 24 below).

[9] C. H. Alexandrowicz, 'Doctrinal Aspects of the Universality of the Law of Nations' (*British Year Book of International Law*, 1961) (ch. 13 below).

[10] Le droit international est aujourd'hui redevenu universel, non pas en fonction du droit naturel, mais sur la base de la conception des Nations Unies comme organisation universelle.

du droit alors en vigueur, et non pas en fonction d'une doctrine créée post facto. De nombreux auteurs de droit international aux XIXe et XXe siècles ont eu tendance à commettre cette erreur et à projeter sur le passé les principes du droit contemporain. La même erreur a été commise par un grand nombre d'historiens qui ont ignoré la réalité de la scène asiatique dans le passé.[11] Le fait que le XIXe siècle ait créé sa propre conception d'une famille des nations plus restreinte, ne signifie nullement qu'une famille des nations universelle n'ait pas existé antérieurement. En tout état de cause on ne peut considérer les puissances asiatiques qui ont disparu des cartes politiques du globe, ou qui ont survécu au déclin des états asiatiques au XIXe siècle, comme n'ayant jamais eu aucune existence au sein de cette famille dans le passé.

A la lumière de ces considérations, l'entrée de la Turquie, de la Perse, du Siam, de la Chine et du Japon dans la famille des nations aux XIXe et XXe siècles ne peut signifier admission (reconnaissance) *sensu stricto*; elle constitue tout au plus un ajustement, rendu nécessaire par les changements de la doctrine juridique au cours du XIXe siècle.

Il est intéressant de noter que la Cour Internationale de Justice, dans son récent arrêt sur le différend entre l'Inde et le Portugal au sujet des enclaves, a exprimé l'opinion que le traité de 1779 conclu entre les Portugais et les Mahrattes devait être interprété sur la base de la loi du XVIIIe siècle. Les Portugais prétendaient devant la Cour qu'ils avaient acquis, en vertu de ce traité, un droit de souveraineté sur les enclaves qui leur avaient été cédées par l'Empire des Mahrattes, l'une des principales puissances de l'Inde au XVIIIe siècle, et qu'ils avaient donc droit au libre passage vers ces enclaves à travers le territoire des Mahrattes (appartenant maintenant à l'Inde). Le gouvernement de l'Inde alléguait que le traité n'avait pas transféré la souveraineté et qu'il n'existait aucun droit de passage; que les successeurs territoriaux des Mahrattes, c'est-à-dire les Anglais, et, postérieurement à 1947, la République de l'Inde, n'étaient donc liés par aucun droit de passage, contrairement à ce que prétendaient les Portugais. L'avis de la Cour fut que le traité de 1779 n'avait pas transféré la souveraineté des enclaves aux Portugais et ne leur avait conféré qu'un titre féodal mineur (un jagir,[12] c'est-à-dire le droit de lever l'impôt dans les enclaves), que les Portugais n'avaient acquis leur souveraineté que plus tard, à la suite de négociations avec l'administration britannique en Inde. La Cour insistait sur une interprétation de l'institution de jagir selon le droit en vigueur en Inde au XVIIIe siècle.

Mais le gouvernement indien contestait en outre la validité même du traité de 1779, comme n'ayant pas été conclu en conformité avec les principes du droit des traités admis de nos jours. C'était là, manifestement, apprécier une transaction entre deux états sur la base du droit *ex post facto*. A cet égard, la Cour Internationale

[11] Van Leur, *op. cit.*, p. 271.

[12] Voir matériaux concernant le jugement du 12 avril 1960, Affaire du droit de passage sur territoire indien, Portugal c. Inde, t. II, p. 581: Le terme mogol 'jagir' (*saranjam* en Mahratte) s'entend d'une concession, ou octroi gratuit fait en considération d'objectifs politiques ou militaires. Il était classé par la chancellerie mahratte comme 'Dumala,' c'est-à-dire concession réversible. Les Portugais prétendaient que son caractère réversible était modifié par le fait que la concession était garantie dans une transaction bilatérale (le traité de 1779).

déclara que la validité du traité devait être jugée exclusivement sur la base du droit des nations et des coutumes valables en Inde au XVIIIe siècle, et non en fonction du droit des XIXe et XXe siècles. Elle constata que 'les Mahrattes considéraient eux-mêmes le traité de 1779 comme valable et obligatoire à leur égard et qu'ils ont accordé effet à toutes ses dispositions. Il n'ont émis à aucun moment un doute quelconque sur la validité ou le caractère obligatoire du traité'. Le juge Moreno Quintana, dans son opinion séparée, se référa aux deux textes du traité (mahratte et portugais) échangés d'une façon coutumière en Asie,[13] et déclara valable le traité, comme étant fondé sur une volonté commune de créer des droits et des obligations réciproques entre *deux personnes juridiques* reconnues comme telles dans les relations internationales.

Cet avis ne nous laisse aucun doute en ce qui concerne l'application des principes généraux du droit des nations à la souveraineté des Mahrattes et autres pays asiatiques et à leur statut juridique dans la famille universelle des nations. L'arrêt de la Cour Internationale constitue un point de vue stimulant pour une étude nouvelle de certains problèmes de l'histoire de droit des nations, particulièrement aux Indes Orientales. Prétendre que les relations entre l'Europe et les Indes Orientales, pendant la période qui suivit l'arrivée de Vasco de Gama en Inde, n'étaient pas régies par le droit des nations, ou encore que les souverains asiatiques n'appartenaient pas à la famille des nations, est une position tout à fait insoutenable.[14]

Les XVIe, XVIIe et XVIIIe siècles constituent la période de formation de notre droit des nations. Mais quelle était la contribution des puissances des Indes Orientales au développement de ce droit? Une réponse satisfaisante à cette question ne serait possible que si les recherches historiques nous apportaient des renseignements exacts sur le droit développé dans la pratique entre les états des Indes Orientales dans leurs relations réciproques. Or il est difficile de se faire une idée précise là-dessus, car ce droit n'était pas écrit mais plutôt implicite dans les coutumes du monde hindou,

[13] Les matériaux sur lesquels la Cour basa son jugement (voir t. II, p. 425) montrent que le traité de 1779 s'était conclu par l'échange de deux textes: la communication faite par le vice-roi portugais de Goa au Peshwa (chef du gouvernement Mahratte) d'un texte portugais (4 mai 1779), et la confirmation de ce texte par le Peshwa sous forme d'un texte en langue mahratte (17 décembre 1779). Quoiqu'il y eût des différences de mots dans ces deux textes, ils constituaient ensemble 'un véritable accord entre les deux parties contractantes'. Donc 'la concession faite (par les Mahrattes) à l'État portugais a pour base un traité conclu entre deux états souverains' (p. 441). Nous lisons aussi dans la réplique du Portugal: 'Il faut tenir compte du fait que l'établissement de traités par échange de textes authentiques entre les gouvernements intéressés était d'usage courant à cette époque chez les peuples d'Asie' (p. 425). Ce point de vue a été entièrement admis par la Cour.—Let. II des 'Transactions of the Royal Asiatic Society' (1830) contient une traduction (par J. Briggs) de la correspondance secrète de la Cour du Peshwa Madha Rao (1761-1772) et des traités conclus par le Peshwa; on y voit la procédure suivie pour conclure ces traités: la préparation d'un texte par une des parties contractantes et son acceptation de la part de l'autre.—L'usage des traités bilingues était appliqué dans divers pays asiatiques et c'était fréquemment la langue perse (le français de la diplomatie asiatique) qui était employée (*Recueil des Cours*, p. 291).

[14] Dans l'affaire de l'île Palmas (1928) (2 United Nations, Reports of International Arbitral Awards, 1948, p. 829) l'arbitre-juge constata que le droit international ne pouvait pas être appliqué aux traités conclus entre la Compagnie hollandaise des Indes Orientales et les princes indigènes ou communautés non reconnues comme membres de la famille des nations. Cette conclusion trop générale n'est pas conciliable avec l'opinion exprimée par la Cour internationale dans l'affaire du droit de passage (Portugal, c. l'Inde).

bouddhiste et islamique. Les principes relatifs aux relations entre états que l'on peut relever dans la littérature classique de l'Asie ne sont pas toujours applicables à la période des XVIe, XVIIe et XVIIIe siècles. Étant donné cela, l'unique solution est une analyse des sources historiques de cette période, particulièrement des traités et transactions diplomatiques. Mais celles-ci sont si abondantes qu'elles nécessiteraient l'étude des archives et des bibliothèques de différents centres d'Europe et d'Asie, ce qui supposerait, en outre, la connaissance de nombreuses langues européennes et asiatiques. Une recherche aussi intensive ne nous était pas possible actuellement. Nous avons donc dû effectuer une sélection parmi les traités et autres documents qui étaient à notre disposition. Nous nous sommes référés à un certain nombre de traités et de transactions diplomatiques considérés comme les plus importants, ainsi qu'à l'œuvre des auteurs classiques européens sur le droit des nations, particulièrement à l'ouvrage peu connu de Séraphin de Freitas, *De Justo Imperio Lusitanorum Asiatico* (1625) qui fournit des renseignements significatifs sur la scène asiatique aux XVIe et XVIIe siècles.[15]

I. Classifications de la souveraineté et des titres territoriaux

1.—Parmi les problèmes du droit des nations qui se posaient dans les relations entre les Européens et les souverains des Indes Orientales, l'un des plus importants, surtout aux XVIe et XVIIe siècles, était le problème de la classification mutuelle du point de vue de la souveraineté et de la personnalité juridique. A cet égard rappelons que, sous réserve de quelques exceptions, le droit des nations est un droit public en vigueur exclusivement entre les états souverains et ne s'étend pas aux communautés sans organisation politique perfectionnée—même si elles possèdent un droit privé et une organisation sociale. Une classification positive signifiait donc l'acceptation réciproque d'une personnalité internationale et d'une capacité de conclure des traités, et autres transactions bilatérales, sur un pied d'égalité. Elle exprimait la reconnaissance mutuelle de l'ordre territorial, administratif, maritime et commercial et, dans une certaine mesure, de la civilisation des parties contractantes. Elle stimulait la transformation graduelle du droit des nations vers un système *séculier*, indépendant de telle ou telle forme de civilisation ou de religion.

Comme nous le verrons, Grotius donna expression à cette transformation et distingua plusieurs aspects de cette classification. Si nous considérons celle-ci du point de vue européen, nous voyons qu'elle ne présentait pas en pratique de difficultés insurmontables. Les Européens se voyaient amenés à adopter la classification coutumière que les souverains asiatiques pratiquaient entre eux. Cette classification intra-asiatique se manifestait principalement de deux façons: 1° la façon dont ces souverains traitaient mutuellement leurs envoyés et ambassadeurs,[16] que l'on peut

[15] Traduction par A. Guichon de Grandpont (1882); *Do Justo Imperio Asiatico dos Portugueses*, Introdução do Marcello Caetano, 1960, t. I.

[16] L'ambassadeur (Duta) était, selon la doctrine classique hindoue, un messager *ad hoc* de son souverain. Mais les Dutas d'un rang plus élevé pouvaient aussi négocier. Indépendamment du rang, chaque

constater à travers les privilèges et immunités accordés aux envoyés et le cérémonial observé au cours de leur réception;[17] 2° la façon dont un souverain était intégré dans le réseau des relations suzerain-vassal en Asie—cadre légal dans lequel les états aux Indes Orientales avaient tous leur place, à un rang plus ou moins haut ou bas.[18]

En ce qui concerne les différents souverains asiatiques, l'empereur mogol et l'empereur ottoman étaient des suzerains par excellence. Eux seuls ne furent jamais vassaux.[19] Ils envoyaient rarement des missions diplomatiques en pays étranger, et jamais en Europe.[20] L'unique exception importante furent les ambassades turques, sous Selim III.[21] Mais ils recevaient des ambassades des autres souverains sur un pied d'égalité.[22] Les documents et sources concernant les missions diplomatiques aux Indes Orientales aux XVIe, XVIIe et XVIIIe siècles, nous apprennent que les ambassadeurs des empereurs mogol et ottoman et des autres grandes puissances asiatiques, comme la Perse, le Siam, la Birmanie et Ceylan, jouissaient toujours de privilèges et d'immunités spéciales grâce à la haute position des souverains qu'ils représentaient.[23] Mais les rois du Siam, de la Birmanie et de l'Indonésie se trouvaient, à certaines époques, vassaux de la Chine, bien qu'étant eux-mêmes suzerains d'autres états d'une position inférieure. Les rois de Ceylan reconnaissaient, au XVIe siècle et

Duta jouissant de certains privilèges et immunités. C'était un crime d'ordre très grave de tuer un Duta. Voir: *The Ambassador in Ancient India*, par L. Rocher, Indian Year Book of International Affairs, 1958. Voir aussi *Description du Royaume de Siam* par M. de La Loubère, 1714, t. I, p. 327

[17] Toutes les ambassades aux XVIe, XVIIe et XVIIIe siècles étaient des missions *ad hoc* (demi-permanentes tout au plus).

[18] Il faut distinguer le terme 'souverain' du terme 'suzerain'. Le vassal (aussi bien que son suzerain) était un souverain mais il exerçait seulement les droits de souveraineté intérieure. Ses droits de souveraineté extérieure étaient limités par les pouvoirs dominants du suzerain (protecteur). Compte tenu de l'existence d'un réseau d'états suzerains et vassaux aux Indes Orientales, l'idée de l'égalité des états n'était pas praticable. La classification des états reflétait des différences considérables de pouvoir et statut juridique (*International Law and Inter-State Relations in Ancient India*, par H. Chatterjee, 1958, pp. 43–44).

[19] *Histoire des Relations internationales*, publié sous la direction de P. Renouvin, t. II, p. 174 sq.—L'empereur de la Chine n'envoyait pas d'ambassadeurs pour établir des relations avec d'autres souverains sur un pied d'égalité, et, quand il en recevait, il traitait chaque ambassade étrangère comme un signe de soumission. Les souverains qui envoyaient des ambassadeurs à Pékin, comme par exemple les souverain-de l'Indonésie ou de l'Indochine, étaient considérés comme des vassaux. En plus, l'empereur n'avait pas l'habitude de conclure des traités avec d'autres souverains, à l'exception des traités conclus avec la Russie: traité de Nerchinsk, 1689 et traité de Kiakhta, 1727. La Chine et le Japon restaient, antérieurement au XIXe siècle, en dehors de la sphère des transactions européennes-asiatiques.—En ce qui concerne l'ambassade de Lord Macartney (1792-94), voir: *An Authentic Account of an Embassy from the King of Great Britain to the Emperor of China* by Sir George Staunton, 1799. Cf. *La Chine et le Droit international*, par J. Escarra, 1931.

[20] En ce qui concerne les échanges d'ambassades entre la Cour de Delhi et la Cour de Constantinople, voir: *Memoir on the Diplomatic Relations between the Courts of Delhi and Constantinople in the 16th and 17th Centuries*, par J. Hammer (Transactions of the Royal Asiatic Society, t. II, 1830).

[21] Ottoman Diplomacy and the European State System',' par J. C. Hurewitz (*Middle East Journal*, printemps 1961).

[22] *Travels of Monsieur de Thévenot*, 1687, I, pp. 25, 63, 84; II, pp. 104, 168; *Voyages du Chevalier Chardin en Perse*, 1735, pp. 367–371.

[23] Ces privilèges s'étendaient à l'inviolabilité personnelle, à l'immunité de juridiction criminelle et civile et à la franchise d'hôtel. *Theatrum Ceremoniale*, par J. C. Luenig, 1713, et mémoires des missions diplomatiques, par exemple: *The Embassy of Sir Thomas Roe to India, 1615-19*, éd. par Sir W. Foster, 1926; *Description du Royaume de Siam*, par M. de La Loubère (ambassadeur français au Siam), 1714.

au début du XVIIe siècle, une suzeraineté purement formelle du roi du Portugal; mais après l'expulsion des Portugais par les Hollandais, ils traitèrent avec ces derniers sur un pied d'égalité. Parmi les puissances de l'Indonésie les états de Mataram (Java), Bantam, Atchen, Macassar et Ternate étaient des centres de suzeraineté.[24] Le continent indien a constitué un réseau de suzerains et vassaux jusqu'à son unification par les Mogols aux XVIe et XVIIe siècles. L'Empire Mogol resta un état centralisé jusqu'au milieu du XVIIIe siècle, où ses principaux gouverneurs provinciaux se déclarèrent demi-indépendants et finalement souverains. La désintégration de l'Empire Mogol ressemble à celle du Saint Empire Romain Germanique au XVIIIe siècle, avec les deux empereurs réduits à une position nominale *(de jure)* et leurs vassaux élevés au rang de souverains *de facto*.[25]

Ainsi la classification des souverains asiatiques révélait un petit groupe de puissances de premier rang et une multitude de vassaux placés sous leur suzeraineté ou protection. Ces derniers étaient fréquemment prêts à transférer leur obédience d'un suzerain à l'autre et même à l'accorder à un protecteur européen. C'est au cours de ces transferts de dépendance que des erreurs de classification ont parfois été commises.

Il est intéressant de noter que le premier gouverneur général de la Compagnie Anglaise en Inde, Warren Hastings, fut inculpé devant le Parlement, à Westminster, d'avoir violé ses obligations (comme pouvoir suzerain) envers le Raja de Benares, un vassal de la Compagnie (auparavant vassal du souverain d'Oudh). Au cours de ce procès (qui révéla des contributions excessives imposées au Raja), E. Burke, le grand écrivain politique anglais,[26] défendit les droits du Raja sur la base des principes du droit des gens énoncés par E. Vattel.[27] Selon Vattel, un vassal a une position bien définie dans le cadre du droit[28] et il peut lui-même renoncer à la protection du suzerain si celui-ci n'honore pas ses obligations envers lui. C'est justement ce que le Raja réclamait d'après les anciennes coutumes entre états en Inde: le respect pour sa souveraineté, une classification au-dessus du niveau d'un *zamindar* (jagirdar) ne jouissant pas de droits souverains. Le procès intenté à W. Hastings reflète sans doute la possibilité d'une co-existence des idées juridiques et politiques occidentales et orientales, divergentes mais conciliables dans le cadre d'un droit des nations universel, auquel Vattel adhérait malgré son attitude 'positiviste' envers l'ordre international.

Voici encore deux autres exemples des problèmes qui se posaient aux souverains classifiants. La Compagnie française avait obtenu du prince de Boyanor certains droits à Mahé (sur la côte occidentale de l'Inde). Boyanor était une dépendance du roi de Colastry qui était un allié de la Compagnie anglaise (installée à Telichery). Pour amoindrir la valeur des titres que Boyanor avait accordés aux Français, les

[24] *Nusantara*, par B. H. M. Vlecke, 1945; Van Leur, *op. cit.*, p. 175.

[25] *Chapters on the Principles of International Law*, par John Westlake, 1894, p. 194 sq.

[26] Burke, *Works*, 1821, vol. IV, XIII.

[27] *Droit des Gens*, t. I, ch. XVI.

[28] J. Chitty dans sa traduction du *Droit des Gens* de Vattel (1834) rappelle l'affaire d'une dette fondée sur un traité entre la compagnie anglaise et le prince d'Arcot (Carnatte) qui était un vassal de la compagnie. Il indique que cette affaire ne pouvait être soumise à la juridiction anglaise, compte tenu du caractère souverain du prince et de la nature internationale du traité.

Anglais prétendaient que le prince de Boyanor n'était pas un souverain et que les concessions accordées par lui pouvaient être mises en question par son suzerain à Colastry. La réponse française à ces doutes d'une nature juridique se trouve dans un Mémoire écrit à Mahé le 30 juillet 1724 et soumis au Conseil Supérieur de Pondichéry. L'auteur de ce mémoire écrit: 'Pour cela j'observeray premièrement que Boyanor est absolument reconnu pour Souverain et Maître absolu du pays où nous sommes établis non seulement de tous les sujets qui y sont sous sa domination mais encore des Princes de cette côte … Boyanor jouit de toutes sortes de droit de souveraineté, il a des Nambiars ou gouverneurs dans les villes et postes; un conseil souverain composé du Prince (ou souverain) qui doit luy succéder et de ses premiers Nambiars ou grands, a droit de vie et de mort sur tous ces sujets…, donne des grâces, gouverne ses états monarchiquement sans prendre ni recevoir de qui ce soit aucun ordre, et c'est une imagination … de la part des anglais de soutenir qu'il n'est que gouverneur … sous Colastry'. La conclusion de cet exposé classifiant, est que Colastry ne peut 'exclure la nation française de Mahé, pays dont il n'est pas le maître'.[29]

Second exemple de ces problèmes de classification: par le traité de 1801, l'état de Nauing (Malaisie) qui avait été sous la dépendance des Hollandais devint vassal britannique. Quand la compagnie anglaise essaya de s'arroger l'exercice de la juridiction criminelle (particulièrement en ce qui concernait la peine de mort), elle rencontra une opposition acharnée du souverain de Nauing et finalement fut obligée de renoncer à usurper cette juridiction. On constata que le souverain, reconnu comme tel par les Hollandais depuis 1765, avait le droit autonome d'exercer les pouvoirs judiciaires (et le pouvoir de lever des impôts) dans son état. Dans un exposé juridique de cette controverse on lit: 'Les gouvernements européens ne concluent pas des traités avec leurs sujets'. Dans le traité de 1801, la compagnie anglaise avait reçu le pouvoir de contrôler les relations extérieures de Nauing (vassal) mais non celui d'exercer la souveraineté dans ce pays. L'usurpation de cette souveraineté s'opposait aux principes du droit des nations et on admettait une erreur de classification.[30]

Ces exemples, ainsi que d'autres,[31] illustrent bien quelle était la position des vassaux dans le cadre des relations suzerain-vassal aux Indes Orientales. Il est évident que c'était une position bien définie et que les droits des vassaux à la souveraineté

[29] Mémoire concernant l'établissement de la Compagnie de France à Mahé, coste Malabare dans les états de Boyanor (1724) (Archives coloniales, Inde 469). En ce qui concerne les titres obtenus par la compagnie française du prince de Boyanor (Bargaret), voir Archives coloniales, Inde 457 (Paravanas, titres, etc.). Voir aussi *Diary and Consultation Book*, 1724 (Fort Saint-George, Madras), p. 46 sq.

[30] 'History of Selangor,' par R. C. Winstedt (*Journal of the Malayan Branch of the Royal Asiatic Society*, vol. XII, Art III, October 1934); *Treaties and Engagements affecting the Malay States and Borneo*, par Maxwell-Gibson, 1924, p. 57.

[31] Par exemple celui des chefs Mahrattes (Briggs, *op. cit.*, p. 140) ou du Zamorin de Calicut qui cherchait à 'se mettre sous la protection de la Couronne de France' (1775) (*Histoire d'Ayder-Ali-Khan*, par Maistre de la Tour, 1783, p. 196). D'autre part, les Rajas de la côte Malabare qui étaient vassaux de Tippou Sultan, cherchaient à se mettre sous la protection de la compagnie anglaise (Fort Saint-George Letters, Polit. Dep., 1790, paragraphe 83).

intérieure et extérieure (bien que limités par les prérogatives du suzerain) étaient généralement reconnus et respectés. Nous reviendrons sur ce problème plus loin.

Si nous passons maintenant à la classification des entités européennes par les souverains asiatiques, un des problèmes les plus difficiles pour ces derniers étaient leurs rapports avec les compagnies des Indes Orientales. Une compagnie de marchands (quoique investie de pouvoirs demi-souverains) était un phénomène peu familier en Asie, avec lequel les princes orientaux se trouvèrent confrontés depuis le commencement du XVIIe siècle. Auparavant, au cours du XVIe siècle, les Portugais occupaient en fait, en l'absence d'autres puissances européennes aux Indes Orientales, une position de monopole. Mais, après l'arrivée des Hollandais, Anglais et Français, la situation devint plus compliquée. Quand on considère l'organisation portugaise d'un côté et celle des trois compagnies de l'autre, on peut constater les différences suivantes:

Les Portugais vinrent en Asie en tant que serviteurs de la Couronne du Portugal. Bien que le vice-roi ait possédé des pouvoirs étendus et une liberté considérable d'action, il était le subordonné direct du roi de Portugal et faisait partie de la hiérarchie du gouvernement royal. Les équipes envoyées de Lisbonne aux Indes Orientales se composaient du vice-roi, accompagné par des personnages du service militaire et mari-time, par des juges, des officiers de douane (contrôlant les 'Alfandicas') et des agents de commerce, tous avec un salaire fixe.[32] Il faut aussi mentionner les missionnaires qui s'efforçaient d'établir des communautés chrétiennes en Asie.

Tout au contraire les compagnies hollandaise, anglaise et française étaient des organisations principalement commerciales, leurs pouvoirs militaires et politiques étaient au début subordonnés à leurs entreprises commerciales. Ces compagnies ne participaient ni à l'action anti-islamique, qui était un des buts principaux des Portugais, ni à des activités missionnaires étendues. Les Hollandais, les Anglais et les Français vinrent aux Indes Orientales non pas comme subordonnés de leurs gouvernements mais comme employés de compagnies créées spécialement comme des associations de marchands. C'est seulement pour appuyer et faciliter ces activités commerciales que les compagnies étaient autorisées par leurs chartes à entretenir avec les souverains asiatiques des relations impliquant la possibilité d'exercer activement et passivement le droit de légation, de conclure des traités, d'acquérir des territoires et même, au besoin, de faire la guerre. Ainsi, ces compagnies apparaissent aux Indes Orientales comme douées d'une double capacité: tout d'abord comme des organisations dont le but primordial est le négoce; et ensuite comme munies de pouvoirs souverains ou demi-souverains; en d'autres termes comme des souverains délégués, sous le contrôle direct ou indirect d'un souverain européen. Ce contrôle était plus direct et plus strict dans le cas de la Compagnie française (souvent appelée 'création ministérielle') que dans celui de la Compagnie hollandaise et de la Compagnie anglaise qui jouissaient d'une plus grande autonomie.[33]

[32] 'Notes on the Portuguese in Malaya,' par I. A. Macgregor (*Journal of the Malayan Branch of the Royal Asiatic Society*, May 1955); *Book of Duarte Barbosa* (trad. par M. D. Dames, 1918); 'Chronicle of Fernao Nuniz, 1535-37,' in *A Forgotten Empire, Vijayanagar*, par R. Sewell, 1924.

[33] *Histoire des Colonies françaises*, par G. Hanotaux et A. Martineau, t. V; *La Compagnie des Indes Orientales et François Martin*, par P. Kaeppelin, 1908. *The Acquisition and Government of Backward*

Une question se pose: quelle était la réaction des souverains asiatiques envers ces organisations européennes si hétérogènes? Tout souverain asiatique avait conscience d'une solidarité inter-dynastique (Ksatriya ou autre); c'est sur cette base que le plus souvent il tentait de trouver un langage commun avec un souverain européen. Du point de vue juridique, il se trouvait dans une position plus normale lorsqu'il traitait avec un vice-roi, représentant directement un monarque européen, que lorsqu'il traitait avec une compagnie commerciale. C'était toujours la personne du roi du Portugal qui, par l'intermédiaire du vice-roi de Goa, paraissait comme partie contractante dans les transactions mutuelles. Ainsi, en 1507, le souverain d'Ormuz consentit à payer tribut au roi du Portugal en tant que vassal personnel. En 1513 le prince de Cochin, qui devint un allié des Portugais dans la lutte contre Calicut (sous la souveraineté d'un prince hindou, le Zamorin, mais en même temps centre de commerce mahométan), écrivit au roi du Portugal en l'assurant 'que Cochin lui appartiendra de la même façon que Lisbonne,' ce qui (en pratique) impliquait la reconnaissance de sa suzeraineté.[34] Il en était de même pour le roi de Ceylan. J. Bodin écrit à ce sujet: 'On sait assez que les rois de Portugal depuis cent ans, ayant fait voile en haute mer, après avoir découvert les richesses d'Orient, et continué la route des Indes, ont si bien trafiqué, qu'ils se sont faits seigneurs des meilleurs ports d'Afrique et occupé à la barbe du roi de Perse l'isle d'Ormuz... et contraint les roys de Cambarre, de Calicut, de Malachie, de Cananor à leur faire la foi et hommage... et si ont arraché aux Turcs... les plus grandes richesses des Indes et rempli l'Europe des trésors d'Orient pénétrant jusqu'aux Moluques'. Il est remarquable de voir Bodin posséder une connaissance parfaite des événements en Asie et apprécier la position des vassaux aux Indes Orientales sur la base d'une analogie avec le statut des vassaux en Europe auxquels il attribuait le caractère de souverains.[35]

Quant à l'attitude des monarques asiatiques envers les compagnies européennes, il faut remarquer qu'ils les considéraient fréquemment (malgré leurs pouvoirs demi-souverains) comme leur étant inférieurs et demandaient souvent à prendre contact avec les souverains qui avaient créé ces compagnies, c'est-à-dire les rois de France et d'Angleterre, ou les États Généraux des Provinces Unies des Pays-Bas. Le gouverneur général de la Compagnie hollandaise réussit à s'imposer comme une sorte de suzerain à certains princes indonésiens, mais cette suzeraineté n'était au début guère plus que l'expression de l'établissement d'un monopole commercial qui laissait toute autonomie gouvernementale et administrative aux vassaux, sous la condition d'effectuer les 'liveringen' ou livraisons d'épices et d'autres marchandises à prix fixe.[36]

Territory in International Law, par M. F. Lindlay, 1926, pp. 94-100; en ce qui concerne le caractère diplomatique des ambassades des compagnies des Indes Orientales, voir: *Quaestionum juris publici libri duo*, par Bynkershoek, 1737, II, 3, 6, 8.

[34] J. Biker, *op. cit.*, t. I; dans le traité de 1547 entre les Portugais et le souverain de Vijayanagar qui constituait la base d'une alliance dirigée contre le Adil Shah de Bijapur, le roi du Portugal apparaît comme partie contractante. Ce traité révèle l'action coordonnée des Portugais et puissances hindoues contre l'Islam en Inde (*The Aravidu Dynasty of Vijayanagar*, par H. Heras, S. J.).

[35] *Les Six Livres de la République*, 1577 (Livre sixième, ch. II). En ce qui concerne les relations entre les Portugais et l'empereur mogol, voir: *Twilight of the Mughals*, par P. Spear, 1951; *The Jesuits and the Great Mogul*, par Sir E. Maclagan, 1932.

[36] Van Leur, *op. cit.*, p. 90: *Vlecke, op. cit.*, p. 140.

Et chaque fois que les Hollandais avaient à traiter avec une des grandes puissances asiatiques, tels l'Empire Mogol, la Perse, Ceylan ou le Siam, la position était différente et les États Généraux (ou le prince d'Orange) étaient obligés d'apparaître comme partie contractante aux transactions.[37] Les plus importants parmi les souverains indonésiens revendiquaient fréquemment leurs droits à cet égard; ainsi le roi de Bantam, qui était prêt à traiter les ambassadeurs du prince Maurice d'Orange comme envoyés sur un pied d'égalité, mais refusa d'envoyer à Batavia ses ambassadeurs au gouverneur général qu'il considérait seulement comme chef des marchands (1624). En 1681 le même roi écrivit à Louis XIV en vue de la fondation d'un établissement français à Bantam.[38] De même le Susuhanan (empereur) de Mataram (qui avait succédé à l'Empire de Majapahit) traitait les Hollandais comme une organisation de marchands. Les Français et les Anglais ont rencontré les mêmes difficultés en ce qui concerne les transactions et relations diplomatiques avec les grandes puissances aux Indes Orientales. Souvent ces difficultés ne pouvaient être résolues que par l'envoi d'un ambassadeur royal dépêché directement d'Europe à la cour d'un monarque asiatique. Telle fut l'ambassade de Sir Thomas Roe, envoyé par le roi James Ier à la Cour mogole au début du XVIIe siècle. L'empereur mogol se refusait absolument à traiter avec la compagnie anglaise sur un pied d'égalité. Pour permettre à la compagnie de développer ses activités commerciales en Inde, le roi d'Angleterre dut agir en dehors de la compagnie et ouvrir des pourparlers directs.[39] Au XVIIIe siècle Lord Cornwallis, gouverneur général de la compagnie anglaise, se plaignait de ce que les ambassadeurs de la compagnie, engagés dans des négociations avec le roi de la Birmanie, ne fussent pas traités sur le même pied que les ambassadeurs d'un roi souverain.[40] Les mêmes considérations s'appliquent aux ambassades envoyées par la compagnie française à Delhi (Agra) et les ambassades royales françaises au Siam au XVIIe siècle.[41]

2.—Abordons maintenant la classification des droits territoriaux et surtout le problème d'acquisition de territoires. Ce problème prend de plus en plus d'importance dans les périodes de grandes découvertes, quand la légalité d'acquisition de nouveaux titres devient une question primordiale. La classification territoriale dépend dans une large

[37] Par exemple: dans les traités avec le roi de Ceylan (1612-1766) et avec le roi de la Perse (1631) (*Recueil des Cours*, p. 292). Voir aussi l'ordonnance du roi du Siam de 1634 qui faisait une distinction entre les ambassadeurs du prince d'Orange et les ambassadeurs du gouverneur général de la Compagnie hollandaise (*Tijdschrift voor Indische taal-, land- en volkenkunde*, deel XIII).

[38] P. Kaeppelin, *op. cit.*, p. 184; le Zamorin de Calicut envoya en 1513 une ambassade à Lisbonne (*Saint Francis Xavier*, par J. Brodrick, 1952); en 1675, le roi de Golconda exprima le désir d'envoyer une ambassade en France (Archives nationales, Colonies (C2, 62, 310); voir aussi les ambassades du roi de Siam et du souverain d'Atohen en Hollande au xviie siècle (*Nusantara*, p. 105).

[39] Sir Thomas Roe écrit dans les Mémoires qu'il avait reçu à la Cour Mogole tous les privilèges et immunités coutumiers (Discours sur les Mémoires de Sir Thomas Roe, 1683; aussi éd. par W. Foster, 1926).

[40] Voir aussi la lettre du roi Alaungpaya à Georges III (1758) (*South-East Asia*, par B. Harrison, 1954, p. 149) (*Burma in the Family of Nations*, par le Dr. Maung Maung, 1956, p. 25).

[41] Voir la mission de M. Bebber, président de la compagnie à la Cour Mogole en 1666 (Archives coloniales, Inde 457). Un échange d'ambassades royales entre la France et le Siam eut lieu dans la période de 1684 jusqu'à 1687 et elle aboutit à la conclusion de plusieurs traités (*Recueil des traités*, par L. Reinach, 1902).—Caron, qui était directeur de la Compagnie française en Inde, attira l'attention de la Compagnie et du Gouvernement français sur l'importance du statut de l'ambassadeur aux yeux des princes orientaux 'qui ont grand égard et examinent la qualité de ceux

mesure de la classification personnelle (comme souverain ou non-souverain) du pouvoir qui s'exerce sur le territoire en question. N'importe quel souverain peut acquérir unilatéralement un territoire classé comme *terra nullius*, par occupation effective ou par découverte. Une telle occupation est possible en cas de l'absence d'un pouvoir souverain sur le territoire. D'autre part, si une communauté est considérée comme souveraine, c'est-à-dire s'il y existe une organisation politique et un souverain qui contrôle cette organisation et exerce une responsabilité internationale sur le territoire de cette communauté, un tel territoire ne peut être acquis par un autre souverain que bilatéralement, c'est-à-dire par un traité de cession (un titre dérivatif), et l'acquisition se fait sous réserve des droits et obligations du prédécesseur. En outre, une acquisition de territoire peut avoir lieu par suite d'une conquête sanctionnée par un traité de paix à la fin des hostilités. Mais si le souverain vaincu disparaît de la scène internationale, il y a une *debellatio* et son territoire est entièrement annexé par le souverain conquérant.

En ce qui concerne le changement territorial par traité de cession, ce processus était bien connu dans le droit coutumier aux Indes Orientales.[42] Mais la doctrine hindoue classique sur la conquête était différente de la doctrine établie en Europe.[43] Ainsi le *dharmavijaya* rejetait l'annexion du territoire conquis et recommandait la transformation du souverain vaincu en vassal; et surtout la conquête n'aboutissait jamais en droit à l'annihilation *(debellatio)* du souverain vaincu, mais plutôt à sa vassalisation. Une doctrine semblable existait aussi dans l'idéologie bouddhiste (dhammavijaya) qui suivait les idées brahmaniques. Cette théorie hindoue se rencontre dans l'*Artashastra* (21-1) ainsi que dans les œuvres de Kalidasa (Raghuvanisa-IV) qui considère la conquête juste comme un moyen pour établir l'Empire universel, avec un Empereur suzerain suprême (çakravartin) et des vassaux (royaumes dépendants) unis dans le cadre de cette organisation décentralisée.[44] Centralisation et décentralisation étaient les traits caractéristiques de toute l'histoire des Indes et de l'Inde extérieure. Quoique l'établissement de l'Empire mogol témoignât des principes islamiques de conquête et de centralisation, la décadence de cet Empire au XVIIIe siècle offre l'exemple le plus significatif de vassaux qui, au cours de sa

qui ont ces commissions…' (*Histoire des Indes Orientales*, par S. de Rennefort, 1688).—Nous lisons dans les observations relatives à l'ambassade de Tippou Sultan en France (1787) que les Asiatiques 'ont toujours la curiosité de s'informer quand quelqu'un est mis en place dans ce pays s'il est d'une grande caste'. L'auteur de ces observations écrit aussi 'qu'une semblable question me fut faite en 1785 à l'occasion de M. le vicomte de Souillac et il ne me fut pas difficile de répondre d'une manière satisfaisante' (Archives nationales, Colonies C2, 179, 106).

[42] *International Law and Inter-State Relations in Ancient India*, par H. Chatterjee, 1958, p. 31; *International Law in Ancient India*, par Viswanatha, 1925, p. 170.

[43] *International Law and Relations in Ancient India*, par N. Sastri (Indian Year Book of International Affairs, 1952; *Inter-State Relations in Asia*, par N. Sastri (Indian Year Book of International Affairs, 1953); voir aussi Chatterjee, *op. cit.*, p. 69 (discussion de Yuddha-dharma). Viswanatha, *op. cit.*, pp. 178, 183; en ce qui concerne la discussion de 'digijaya,' voir p. 46.

[44] La croissance de l'empire Magadha eut lieu graduellement par la conquête et pas l'assimilation des différents états. L'empire des Guptas s'établit de la même façon mais dans la période qui suivit sa consolidation; un développement dans le sens opposé eut lieu quand les gouverneurs de l'empire se proclamèrent demi-souverains et vassaux (samantarajas). Un roi 'samanta' faisait hommage à son suzerain mais en cas d'affaiblissement du pouvoir de celui-ci, il tentait d'obtenir le rang d'un souverain indépendant. Voir: 'Samanta. Its varying significance in Ancient India,' par L. Gopal (*Journal of the*

décentralisation et désintégration, s'émancipaient du pouvoir du suzerain, réduit à un statut juridique purement nominal.

Dans son mémoire sur les établissements français en Asie, P. P. Darrac (capitaine et chef de la loge française à Dacca) écrit: 'A l'époque de 1793 l'Inde ... se trouvait partagée entre six puissances dont les autres petits états étaient ou tributaires ou vassaux; les deux états de Marates, le Nizam, Tippou Sultan, les Anglais et les Siks formaient ces six puisances...'.[45] La compagnie anglaise qui succéda à l'Empire mogol en Inde ne respecta ni le regroupement des vassaux ni la conception coutumière de la conquête aux Indes Orientales; et elle ne toléra l'existence des vassaux indiens (même des principaux d'entre eux) qu'après leur réduction à un niveau qui ne correspondait plus aux idées traditionnelles de la souveraineté. La situation était la même pour les vassaux indonésiens sous la suzeraineté de la compagnie hollandaise au XVIIIe siècle.[46]

II. La controverse Grotius–Freitas

Problèmes de la Souveraineté

Dans son *Mare Liberum*, publié en 1608, Grotius s'occupe surtout du conflit entre les Hollandais et les Portugais aux Indes Orientales.[47] Mais ce sujet l'amène à considérer la position des souverains asiatiques vis-à-vis de ce conflit, ainsi que les problèmes du droit maritime observé dans l'Océan Indien, au XVIe siècle et au début du XVIIe siècle. Grotius souligne que les Portugais étaient pratiquement incapables d'agir conformément aux titres juridiques qu'ils s'étaient arrogés *a priori* avant de s'établir en Inde, c'est-à-dire le titre de donation papale sur les pays des Infidèles,

Royal Asiatic Society, parts I and 2, 1963). Un exemple classique de la procédure de libération d'un vassal du pouvoir du suzerain est discuté par G. Coedes, *Les Etats hindouisés d'Indochine et d'Indonésie*, 1948, p. 167. Cet exemple est pris de l'histoire du Cambodge: le roi Jayavarman II (802-850), le fondateur de la royauté angkorienne, invita un brahmane 'à faire un rituel pour que le pays des Kambujas ne fût plus dépendant de Java et qu'il n'y eût plus qu'un seul souverain qui fût chakravartin (monarque universel)'. 'Les Cailendras de Java paraissent avoir revendiqué pour eux le titre d'empereur universel qui avait appartenu autrefois aux rois du Fou-nam. Ceci est de nature à expliquer la façon dont Jayavarman II, revenu de Java, établit son autorité sur le Cambodge au début du IXe siècle'.

[45] ['Mémoire historique sur les établissements français en Asie et principalement au Bengale par P. Darrac, chef de la loge de Dacca'] Archives nationales, Colonies C2, 115 (166); voir aussi *The French in India (1763-1816)*, par S. P. Sen, 1958, p. 323.

[46] Cette politique (plus proche de la doctrine islamique que de la doctrine hindoue) fut préconisée par Lord Clive dans sa lettre du 27 avril 1764 aux directeurs de la compagnie anglaise; mais elle rencontra opposition du gouverneur du Bengale, Vansittart, qui proposa de respecter la souveraineté de certains états indiens (*Considerations on Indian Affairs*, par W. Bolts, 1772, n° XVI, 146). Au XIXe siècle, les Anglais transformèrent leur suzeraineté en Inde en 'paramountcy'.

[47] Il est possible que Grotius ait écrit son œuvre après avoir fait des recherches dans les archives de la Compagnie hollandaise, qui lui demanda de préparer une opinion juridique sur la saisie, par les Hollandais, d'un vaisseau portugais dans le détroit de Malacca en 1602 et sur le conflit hollandais-portugais dans cette région. L'œuvre écrite par Grotius était le *De Jure Praedae*, dont 'Mare Liberum' est le chapitre XII (voir traduction par R. van Deman Magoffin).

la découverte ou l'occupation. Il était impossible aux Européens d'acquérir aux Indes Orientales des titres territoriaux par occupation car il n'y avait pas de *terra nullius*.[48] Grotius rejette aussi en l'occurrence le droit de découverte, car, écrit-il: 'Quid quod ne reperisse quidem Indiam ullo modo dici possunt Lusitani quae tot a saeculis fuerat celeberrima' ('Les Portugais ne peuvent avoir aucune prétention d'avoir découvert l'Inde qui était si célèbre depuis des siècles'). En ce qui touche au problème des Infidèles, Grotius (conformément à Francisco de Vitoria[49]) ne considère pas les différences de religion et de civilisation comme faisant obstacle à l'existence d'une famille universelle des nations où trouvent place toutes les communautés, chrétiennes et non chrétiennes, possédant une organisation politique et juridique et exerçant des pouvoirs souverains. Dans un passage célèbre sur les communautés des Indes Orientales, Grotius dit qu' 'elles ont actuellement et eurent toujours leurs rois (souverains), leur organisation d'état (res publica) et leurs lois et systèmes juridiques' (ch. II). La conclusion qu'il en tire est que les Européens ne peuvent acquérir de titres aux Indes Orientales que par des transactions conclues conformément au droit des nations.

La classification proposée par Grotius était-elle de nature dogmatique ou plutôt de nature pragmatique? L'œuvre de Grotius est essentiellement le plaidoyer d'un avocat sur des questions de grande importance pour la Compagnie hollandaise, et il recourt à l'argumentation juridique la plus convaincante possible. La négation de la souveraineté des Portugais dans les territoires des Indes Orientales était étroitement liée à l'existence de la souveraineté des princes de ces régions, avec lesquels les Hollandais espéraient entrer en relations et tentaient de conclure des traités en vue de certains privilèges, en particulier des concessions commerciales. Une autre question se posait: quelles devaient être, juridiquement, les conséquences d'un refus des princes orientaux d'entretenir des relations avec les Européens? La conquête était rarement tenue pour une solution acceptable—compte tenu de la doctrine du 'bellum justum' prononcée si catégoriquement par Grotius et partagée mutatis mutandis par les souverains asiatiques.[50] Existait-il d'autres restrictions à la souveraineté? Deux réponses différentes étaient fournies à cette question, l'une admettant des restrictions d'une nature commerciale (Grotius) et l'autre admettant des restrictions d'une nature religieuse (Freitas).

Grotius marque clairement que la souveraineté n'est pas un critère absolu. La liberté du commerce et de la navigation ne peut être refusée à personne sous le prétetxe de la souveraineté d'un pays. S'appuyant sur l'œuvre de Gentili,[51] Grotius déclare qu'aucun état ni aucun souverain 'ne peut interdire aux étrangers d'avoir des relations avec leurs sujets ni de faire du commerce avec eux'.[52] Cette liberté *naturelle* du commerce impose des obligations aux souverains partout au monde, que ce soit

[48] Avec l'exception des Philippines occupées par les Espagnols au XVIe siècle.

[49] *De Indis*, II, 1.

[50] H. Chatterjee, *op. cit.*, p. 69 (discussion de Yuddha-dharma).

[51] Gentili (1552-1608), juriste italien, professeur de droit à l'Université d'Oxford. Il est probable que Sir Thomas Roe, ambassadeur anglais à la Cour Mogole, avait été son étudiant (Foster, *Alumni Oxonienses*, 1891, III, 1272).

[52] *Recueil des Cours*, p. 226.

en Europe ou en Asie. Elle constitue une limitation naturelle de la souveraineté d'un pays.

En ce qui concerne le conflit entre deux aspects du droit naturel (c'est-à-dire le principe de la souveraineté et celui du droit d'accès aux pays étrangers), Freitas se trouve en désaccord avec Grotius et fait remarquer que la liberté naturelle d'accès à un pays étranger n'est pas conciliable avec le principe de la souveraineté territoriale. Dans son en se référant au texte de Grotius d'après lequel 'la navigation et le commerce sont permis à titre *précaire* par les princes d'Orient à ceux qui se rendent dans leurs pays...' (ch. II). Si ce titre (ainsi que l'autorisation qui en découle) est précaire, 'ces princes ont, par cela même, et selon la loi naturelle, le droit de *révoquer* cette autorisation...'. Freitas somme Grotius de se déclarer sur ce problème et dit: 'il serait contradictoire *De Justo Imperio Lusitanorum Asiatico*,[53] Freitas cherche une solution que je puisse, en vertu d'un droit naturel immuable, naviguer et négocier aux Moluques malgré les maîtres du pays; et qu'en vertu du même droit, les rois des Moluques puissent m'interdire la navigation et le commerce. C'est pourtant cette contradiction qu'admet notre Inconnu,[54] en accordant à un prince... cette faculté d'interdiction'. (Ch. I.)

Freitas énonce ici l'un des principes les plus invoqués par les souverains asiatiques aux Indes Orientales, c'est-à-dire le principe de la *révocabilité* du commerce libre et des privilèges concédés aux Européens sous n'importe quelle forme (concessions territoriales, monopoles commerciaux, capitulations, etc.). Il accorde donc (selon le droit naturel des nations) une priorité à la souveraineté sur le droit d'accès et de négoce, qui ne devra jamais être utilisé aux dépens du droit du souverain—droit sacré dans les coutumes juridiques aux Indes Orientales.

L'exposé donné par Freitas explique jusqu'à un certain degré l'attitude des souverains aux Indes Orientales envers la conclusion des traités avec les Européens et envers la validité des transactions intervenues alors. On constate, chez ces souverains, une résistance (sinon une répugnance) à la conclusion d'un traité en forme et la préférence pour une concession unilatérale et révocable accordée à une puissance européenne. Si la conclusion d'un traité était inévitable, un traité personnel paraissait préférable à un traité réel (qui liait les successeurs du souverain contractant). En outre, les princes concédants tenaient beaucoup à la formule 'rebus sic stantibus,' car celle-ci permettait de révoquer une concession en cas d'un changement de circonstances qui n'étaient pas prévisibles au moment de la conclusion du traité.[55] Les Européens, au contraire, insistaient pour obtenir un traité (de préférence aux concessions unilatérales et révocables), et pour qu'y soient introduites des clauses

[53] L'œuvre de Freitas publiée en 1625 (traduction par Guichon de Grandpont, 1882) était une réponse au 'Mare Liberum' de Grotius. Celui-ci déclara que cette œuvre 'méritait une réponse' mais après avoir été exilé de son pays, il ne l'écrivit jamais (Hugonis Grotii, *Epistolae*, 1687, 144 (796) Le portugais Séraphin de Freitas était professeur à l'Université de Valladolid (*Trois Précurseurs portugais*, par M. B. Amzalak, pp. 41-94).

[54] Le 'Mare Liberum' a été publié anonymement en 1608.

[55] *Recueil des Cours*, p. 296. En ce qui concerne la formule de 'rebus sic stantibus,' H. Chatterjee, *op. cit.*, (p. 69) fait référence à *Artashastra* (7-17). Malgré l'emploi de cette formule, le principe '*pacta sunt servanda*' était un des principes fondamentaux dans cette œuvre.—Le serment et les otages étaient fréquemment utilisés pour assurer l'exécution de traités (7-17) et il en était de même dans la pratique des états islamiques (*Recueil des Cours*, p. 294).

discriminatoires; et leur pression aboutissait à l'irrévocabilité expresse des transactions et donc, finalement, à l'inégalité des parties contractantes et à la restriction de la souveraineté des pays asiatiques. Contrairement à la doctrine de Grotius, le point de vue adopté par Freitas détruisit juridiquement *ab initio* la possibilité d'une telle évolution. En opérant ce choix entre le principe de la souveraineté et le principe de la liberté, de négoce et d'accès commercial, Freitas (consciemment ou non) donnait expression au droit coutumier en vigueur aux Indes Orientales: celui-ci, tout en connaissant la liberté de commerce (et en accordant un traitement très libéral aux communautés des marchands étrangers) sauvegardait la juridiction du souverain grâce au principe de la révocabilité des concessions, qui assurait la continuité de sa souveraineté.[56]

Grotius lui-même avait des doutes sérieux sur la supériorité du principe du commerce libre par rapport au principe de la souveraineté. Au cours des négociations entre Hollandais et Anglais à Londres en 1613, auxquelles il participait, Grotius fait soudain volte face et défend les établissements et sphères d'influence hollandais aux Indes Orientales contre l'accès des Anglais, surtout dans la région de l'Indonésie. Les Anglais affirmaient qu'ils avaient un titre valable à faire le commerce avec certaines communautés en Indonésie et qu'ils devaient jouir du droit d'accès libre conformément aux principes du droit des nations. Les Hollandais répliquèrent que la liberté de commerce pouvait être modifiée par les traités obtenus des princes indonésiens qui leur accordaient un monopole du commerce. C'est dans ces circonstances que l'on attira l'attention des Hollandais sur les arguments soutenus par Grotius dans son *Mare Liberum*. La réponse de Grotius fut que les traités 'supprimaient la liberté du droit des gens,' ce qui était difficilement compatible avec l'argumentation qu'il avait suivie dans cette œuvre. On ne doit pourtant pas croire que Grotius avait

[56] Quand Sir James Lancaster proposa en 1602 au souverain d'Atchen la conclusion d'un traité commercial, le souverain répondit qu'il ne pouvait lier ses successeurs et que les concessions accordées aux Anglais devaient être révocables à la seule discrétion du souverain (*The Voyages of Sir James Lancaster*, Hakluyt Society, 1940).—De La Loubère, ambassadeur français au Siam en 1687, écrit sur l'attitude des princes aux Indes Orientales: 'Ils nous recevront plutôt dans un port, ou dans une place (par concession unilatérale) qu'ils ne conviendront avec vous de vous les livrer par un traité…' (*Description du Royaume de Siam* par Mr. de La Loubère, Amsterdam, 1714, t. I, p. 327 sq.). Nous trouvons aussi dans les transactions diplomatiques un modèle de négociations qui mérite notre attention. Les éléments essentiels en étaient les suivants: si un souverain local cherchait un allié européen afin qu'il l'aidât à expulser de son territoire la puissance européenne concessionnaire, le nouvel allié demandait habituellement la souveraineté sur les territoires qu'il aurait conquis. Cette prétention ne pouvait être acceptée par le souverain asiatique qui considérait les concessions accordées aux Européens comme limitées par sa souveraineté et comme *révocables*. Cette argumentation était par exemple employée par le roi de Ceylan dans ses négociations avec les Hollandais pour l'expulsion des Portugais (XVIIe siècle), ou dans les négociations entre le même roi et les Anglais pour l'expulsion des Hollandais (XVIIIe siècle) ou dans les négociations entre le souverain de Johore et les Hollandais pour l'expulsion des Portugais de Malacca (XVIIe siècle) (*Account of Mr. Pybus's Mission to the King of Kandy in 1762*, publ. 1862; *Diary of an Embassy from the Government of Fort St. George to the Court of Candia in 1795*, in Military Sundry Books, serial 4384-86, Madras Record Office. 'Translation of Dutch Documents at the Hague relating to the Capture of Malacca in 1641,' *Journal of the Malayan Branch of the Royal Asiatic Society*, janvier 1936, annexe III. En ce qui concerne les négociations entre la compagnie française et le roi de Ceylan (1672) dirigées contre les Hollandais, voir *Mémoires de François Martin (1665-94)*, éd. par Martineau, t. I, pp. 342-346. Le roi de Ceylan se servait parfois, dans les négociations avec les compagnies européennes, de la réserve '*rebus sic stantibus*' (*Diary of an Embassy*, in *supra*).

fondamentalement changé d'opinion. Il avait seulement, en tant qu'auteur d'un plaidoyer, suivi la voie de la nécessité, et il est à noter que par la suite il a formulé à nouveau sa théorie dans son *De Jure belli ac pacis*.[57]

Quoique Freitas refuse d'accorder aux Européens le droit d'accès aux pays asiatiques en se fondant seulement sur la liberté de commerce, il réclame ce droit d'accès pour les Portugais en faisant appel à un autre principe: la liberté de propager la foi. Ce droit avait un caractère non pas seulement missionnaire, mais essentiellement anti-islamique. Les Portugais en effet étaient engagés dans une guerre totale contre le monde mahométan,—guerre que Freitas nommait 'bellum justissimum' (ch. IX) et qui les forçait à établir des alliances avec les puissances hindoues, comme Vijayanagar, Cochin ou Travancore, soumises à la pression de l'Islam. Tandis que, du point de vue juridique, les Hollandais s'autorisaient de la liberté de commerce pour entrer aux Indes Orientales, les Portugais réclamaient le droit d'accès dans le but de défendre la civilisation chrétienne menacée en Asie par les Musulmans. Le 'bellum justissimum' était d'ailleurs proclamé par Freitas comme une simple réplique au 'Jihad' de l'Islam (la guerre totale contre les 'Infidèles'[58]); et le 'justum imperium Lusitanorum asiaticum' était défendu par lui d'après des principes de droit canon mis en opposition avec les principes du droit coranique.

L'attaque portugaise contre le monde musulman dans son centre asiatique avait réussi à établir des points stratégiques à Ormuz (aux dépens de la Perse), à Goa (aux dépens du royaume musulman de Bijapur) et à Malacca (conquis sur le royaume de Malacca[59]). Ce 'justum imperium,' qui était purement maritime, avait aussi réussi à affaiblir le monopole musulman du commerce des épices dont la république de Venise avait profité jusqu'au XVIe siècle. Mais ajoutons que, du point de vue juridique, l'action portugaise produisait un effet imprévu et contraire aux intentions des belligérants, car la pratique entre-états aux Indes Orientales menait automatiquement à la conclusion de nombreux traités et d'autres arrangements entre les puissances européennes et les pays 'infidèles' et annulait les prohibitions du droit selon lequel ces transactions étaient interdites.[60] Cette évolution aboutissait graduellement à séculariser le droit des nations et à le soustraire aux prohibitions du droit canon et du droit coranique qui étaient incompatibles avec les nécessités du commerce mondial. Les auteurs classiques européens, tels que Gentili, Grotius, Freitas et d'autres, se trouvaient indirectement affectés par ce développement du droit, car, pour que les traités commerciaux entre les pays européens et asiatiques

[57] Voir *Grotius's East Indian Mission in England*, par G. N. Clark (Transactions of the Grotius Society, t. 20, 1935); *The Life and Works of Hugo Grotius*, par W. S. M. Knight, p. 137.

[58] La théorie juridique musulmane divisait le monde en deux grandes régions parfaitement séparées: *Dar-al-Islam*, c'est-à-dire le monde musulman, et *Dar-al-Harb*, le monde extérieur à l'Islam. *Jihad* (c'est-à-dire un état permanent de guerre) prit le sens de *bellum justum* ou de guerre sainte. Mais l'empire Mogol, la plus grande puissance islamique aux Indes Orientales, ne pratiquait pas le Jihad. Tout au contraire (sous l'empereur Akbar) il adopta une politique de tolérance presque séculière.

[59] Grotius, qui ne reconnaissait pas la souveraineté des Portugais dans les territoires des Indes Orientales, admettait leur souveraineté à Goa et Malacca: 'Non enim de Malacca, non de Goa loquimur, coloniis Lusitanorum'. Mais il raya ce texte du manuscrit (voir '*De jure praedae*' ch. XII: a collotype reproduction of the original manuscript,' in *Classics of International Law*, 1950, p. 97).

[60] Voir les traités dans les collections de Biker, *op. cit.*, I et de Heeres, *op. cit.*

eussent les résultats escomptés, il n'était pas possible de permettre que leur application fût entravée par une notion périmée du droit où les motifs religieux l'auraient emporté sur les nécessités des relations mondiales.[61] La coïncidence des intérêts des parties contractantes ne pouvait que stimuler un esprit de coexistence et de tolérance mutuelle.[62]

Problèmes du droit maritime

La seconde partie de la controverse entre Grotius et Freitas, se rapporte principalement au problème de la liberté de la mer. Dans ses études sur l'histoire sociale et économique de l'Asie, J. C. van Leur décrit le port de Malacca au moment de l'arrivée des Portugais et montre l'existence d'un réseau parfaitement organisé de relations commerciales et maritimes, avec la participation de tous les pays d'Asie, à commencer par la Turquie et la Perse jusqu'à la Chine et au Japon. Malacca recevait les vaisseaux de tous ces pays et sur son marché avait lieu un échange de marchandises telles que étoffes de l'Inde, soieries et porcelaine de la Chine, épices de l'Indonésie, bois de Siam, etc.[63] Le fonctionnement de ce réseau commercial, établi au centre des Indes Orientales, était étroitement lié aux conceptions de la communication transocéanique dans l'Océan indien. Quel était donc le régime maritime qui régissait cet état de choses?

Nous trouvons des mentions de règles maritimes dans l'*Artashastra* qui remonte au IVe siècle avant Jésus-Christ. Son auteur (Kautilya) parle de l'existence d'un surintendant des affaires maritimes qui aurait eu juridiction sur les vaisseaux navigant dans l'Océan et dans les eaux territoriales. Sa juridiction se serait étendue, entre autres, à la protection des navires désemparés, à la contrebande et à l'application de mesures contre la piraterie (himsrika, 2-28). La navigation côtière était alors préférée à la navigation transocéanique (samudrasayana, 7-12). Toutefois, cette situation se modifia avec la découverte, par les Grecs et les Romains, de techniques maritimes nouvelles qui permirent d'établir des routes maritimes au travers de l'océan.

Après la chute de l'Empire romain, les relations maritimes entre l'Est et l'Ouest cessèrent; mais la partie orientale de l'Océan indien fut néanmoins un centre de navigation et de commerce intenses entre les pays de la partie sud de l'Inde, l'Indonésie, la Malaisie et la Chine. L'établissement par les Maures d'une route maritime entre l'Indonésie, l'Inde et la mer Rouge et le développement du commerce des épices

[61] Dans le cadre du droit canon l'opinion progressiste de Sinibaldo Fiesco (Pape Innocent IV) avait prévalu graduellement sur l'opinion de Hostiensis exprimée par O. Cacheranus dans la *Disp. an principi christiano fas sit foedus inire cum infidelibus*, 1569 (*Recueil des Cours*, pp. 231-233).

[62] En ce qui concerne la monopolisation du commerce par les compagnies européennes, voir ci-dessous.

[63] Les marchands (essentiellement des milliers de colporteurs réunis en ce que van Leur appelle 'a pedlars trade') se servaient en cas de nécessité des monnaies frappées dans divers pays, liées par un système de taux d'échanges. Du point de vue des gouvernements asiatiques, l'exploitation du commerce était de nature fiscale et ce système fut adopté par les Portugais. Ce n'est que plus tard que les conceptions d'échange développées en Europe au XVIIIe siècle furent graduellement introduites par les compagnies des Indes Orientales. (J. C. van Leur, *op. cit.*, p. 215.)

sur cette route témoignaient de l'existence de techniques de navigation très avancées.[64] Les coutumes maritimes étaient parfois codifiées: ainsi les Codes maritimes de Macassar et de Malacca (xııe siècle).[65] La lecture des divers textes est convaincante: les puissances maritimes aux Indes Orientales observaient, antérieurement à l'arrivée des Européens, un régime coutumier de navigation libre. Ce régime, sans lequel des transactions commerciales auraient été impossibles dans ces régions du monde, tendait plus spécialement à la suppression de l'anarchie et de la piraterie sur les routes maritimes. Les peines sévères contre la piraterie, même hors de la juridiction d'un souverain déterminé, confirment pleinement cette thèse.[66] Bien que les renseignements historiques soient rares sur la matière, il est certain que l'Océan indien, avant le xvıe siècle, n'a jamais constitué un 'mare clausum'.[67] L'arrivée des Portugais et la lutte entre ceux-ci et les Maures pour la domination navale et commerciale de l'Océan indien au xvıe siècle modifia complètement cette situation; et l'établissement des compagnies hollandaise, anglaise et française rendit la situation encore plus complexe. La liberté de la navigation cessa d'être la règle générale et les navires se trouvèrent dans l'obligation d'obtenir des laissez-passer (appelés des 'cartazes' par les Portugais) des puissances maritimes contrôlant les diverses parties de l'océan.

Grotius fut consulté à propos de la capture, dans le détroit de Malacca, d'un bateau portugais par les Hollandais. Il dut rechercher alors quelles étaient les particularités du régime maritime de l'Océan indien, et être frappé par la différence de conceptions entre les coutumes maritimes européennes et celles des Indes Orientales. Alors que les auteurs classiques du xvıe siècle, tels que Gentili, Selden et Welwood, exprimaient des théories reflétant la doctrine du 'mare clausum,'[68] les anciennes pratiques maritimes de l'Océan indien présentaient au contraire l'image d'un 'mare liberum'. Il est donc vraisemblable que Grotius, lorsqu'il a formulé sa théorie de la liberté des mers, se soit trouvé en quelque sorte encouragé par le fait que les anciennes pratiques maritimes de l'Asie concordaient avec sa thèse.

[64] Voir les extraits de *Mahi't*, œuvre turque de 1558, traduite par J. Hammer et publiée en 1832 dans le *Journal de la Société Asiatique du Bengale*, t. I; aussi t. VII (1838).

[65] Une traduction de ces codes de l'arabe se trouve dans la collection de J. M. Pardessus (1845, t. VI). Pardessus offre aussi des extraits du 'Code de Manou' (Manova Dharma Sastra, libre VIII, sloka 156) et du 'Commentaire de Kulbuka'; les références au droit maritime dans l'*Artashastra* se trouvent dans 2-28 et 7-12.—Un texte remarquable concernant le droit maritime en Inde est l'édit du Maharaja Ganapait du xıııe siècle. Ce prince 'assurait la sécurité des commerçants étrangers dont les navires auraient fait naufrage sur les côtes de son état'. Alors qu'antérieurement la cargaison des navires naufragés était confisquée par l'état côtier, ce prince ordonna que désormais seuls les droits d'entrée seraient exigés (*Epigraphia Indica*, XII, p. 188).

[66] *Freitas versus Grotius* (British Year Book of International Law, 1959) (chapter 8 below).

[67] Parmi les témoignages des voyageurs européens aux Indes Orientales, notons 'The Itinerary of Ludovico de Varthema of Bologna, 1502-08' (traduction par J. Winter Jones, 1928). Warthema, qui visita l'Inde, Ceylan, Pegu et l'Indonésie et qui voyagea à bord de différents navires, témoigne de la liberté de navigation dans l'Océan indien. Voir aussi *The Travels of Ibn Batuta* (traduction par S. Lee, 1829); Ibn Batuta qui, au milieu du xıve siècle, se rendait en mission en Chine, nous donne une description des coutumes maritimes chinoises. Voir aussi *Intercourse between India and the Western World* par Rawlinson, 1926; *Description of the Various Classes of Vessels*, par Edye (Journal of the Royal Asiatic Society, t. I, 1834; *Ancient Navigation in the Indian Ocean*, par Edkins (Journal of the Royal Asiatic Society, t. XVIII, 1886); *Le Droit Maritime International*, par Eugène Cauchy, 1862, t. I, p. 383.

[68] *Freitas versus Grotius*, op. cit.

Cette contribution des Indes Orientales au développement de notre droit des nations ne se termine pas ici. Dans le chapitre VII du *Mare Liberum*, Grotius écrit: 'Praeterea accolae totius tractus... asiatici partem maris quisque sibi proximam piscando et navigando perpetuo usurparunt' (ch. VII). Il constate que, malgré incapacité juridique, pour les puissances maritimes asiatiques, d'établir leur souveraineté sur la mer, elles ont néanmoins la coutume d'acquérir des droits de contrôle de navigation et de pêcheries dans les eaux territoriales et les zones adjacentes de leur littoral. Dans son *Droit des Gens* (I, 287), Vattel parle des pêcheries de perles au large de Ceylan et de Bahrein, sur lesquelles les états côtiers avaient acquis des droits d'exploitation dépassant largement la limite normale des eaux territoriales. Freitas va plus loin.[69] Il réclame pour les Portugais le droit de quasi-possession dans l'Océan indien. Il conçoit cette quasi-occupation de la mer comme étant de nature fonctionnelle. Elle n'est pas établie pour elle-même, mais en fonction d'un objectif qui est le maintien de la sécurité sur des routes maritimes bien déterminées, reliant certains territoires entre eux, en somme l'exercice de la responsabilité pour éliminer l'anarchie en haute mer.[70] Au fond Freitas ne se prononçait pas en faveur de la théorie du 'mare clausum'; il étendait seulement la conception de la quasi-possession sur les zones territoriales (implicite dans les coutumes des Indes Orientales) à des zones fortement élargies, c'est-à-dire des zones d'accès et des zones routières qui permettaient aux Portugais de contrôler la communication transocéanique, surtout contre l'agression des Maures. La conception asiatique des zones limitées, à laquelle Grotius donna ainsi expression dans son œuvre, fut adoptée par notre droit international moderne. Au début, on admit sous l'influence de Grotius, une mer libre sans exception en faveur des puissances côtières sauf pour les eaux territoriales (3 milles). Mais graduellement le contrôle des états maritimes sur les eaux côtières s'élargit jusqu'aux limites indiquées dans l'œuvre de Vattel, reflétant les anciennes coutumes asiatiques et assurant un compromis entre l'intérêt collectif des nations *(mare liberum)* et l'intérêt de la puissance maritime individuelle (eaux territoriales et zones).

III. Le principe de la révocabilité des concessions et son déclin

Nous avons vu que Freitas insistait sur le principe de la révocabilité des concessions accordées aux Européens aux Indes Orientales. Ce principe réclamé par les souverains concédants se manifestait aussi dans le domaine des capitulations et des arrangements pré-capitulaires. Les capitulations sont une institution juridique morte, mais comme elle a été enterrée sans diagnostic final, une analyse 'post-mortem' serait utile à la compréhension correcte de sa nature et de son déclin. De nos jours les juristes internationaux prétendent presque tous que l'admission retardée des puissances asiatiques dans la famille des nations aux XIXe et XXe siècles provenait de l'infériorité de leurs civilisations dont ils voient le signe dans l'existence

[69] *Freitas versus Grotius*, op. cit.

[70] Freitas, *op. cit.* (ch. VIII, X, XI, XIV).

des capitulations.[71] Selon le régime des capitulations (abolies au xxe siècle) les puissances européennes exerçaient sur leurs nationaux résidant en Asie une juridiction consulaire. Cette juridiction constituait une limitation imposée à la souveraineté territoriale des états asiatiques, considérés comme incapables de protéger les intérêts des Européens en Asie. Étrange explication: car les capitulations étaient à l'origine une institution juridique asiatique très ancienne qui justement servait à protéger les intérêts des étrangers. C'est grâce à cette institution que les Européens purent fonder leurs premiers établissements de commerce aux Indes Orientales à partir du début du XVIe siècle.

Nous emploierons le terme de 'capitulations' dans deux sens: celui de concessions accordées par le souverain territorial, unilatéralement, à une communauté étrangère (capitulations *sensu lato* ou arrangements pré-capitulaires); et celui de traités entre deux états, l'état concédant et l'état dont les membres (résidant à l'étranger) étaient des nationaux (capitulations *sensu stricto*).

Les arrangements précapitulaires aux Indes Orientales étaient basés sur une ancienne coutume asiatique: le souverain territorial accordait à une communauté d'étrangers, surtout dans les centres de commerce maritime, le privilège de se gouverner selon sa loi personnelle et une certaine mesure d'autonomie juridictionnelle et administrative. Ces privilèges ou concessions étaient unilatéraux et révocables et ne portaient aucunement atteinte à la souveraineté du pays qui les accordait. La communauté étrangère constituait, grâce à ces concessions, une sorte de société miniature à l'intérieur de la communauté plus large qui lui offrait l'hospitalité. Par exemple dès le VIIIe siècle les marchands musulmans avaient reçu de certains états hindous de la côte ouest de l'Inde des immunités et des privilèges substantiels.[72] De même les marchands étrangers en Indonésie (par exemple la communauté chinoise à Java ou les communautés malaisiennes à Amboyne) jouissaient d'une autonomie considérable, y compris de droits juridictionnels qui étaient exercés par les chefs de ces communautés étrangères.[73] Comme le démontre le Professeur R. Lingat, la situation était la même pour les communautés étrangères au Siam.[74] Mais bien que la loi du pays de leur résidence ne fût pas imposée aux étrangers, ils demeuraient néanmoins soumis à son ordre public et les pays dont ils étaient originaires (ressortissants) n'avaient aucun droit d'intervenir dans la souveraineté de l'état de la résidence. En d'autres termes les concessions précapitulaires constituaient fondamentalement un arrangement coutumier entre les marchands étrangers et l'état territorial. Il ne s'agissait ni d'un acte de pure générosité de la part du souverain accueillant, qui tirait ainsi profit d'une extension de son commerce avec l'extérieur, ni d'un arrangement irrévocable impliquant l'idée d'infériorité de civilisation.[75] Tout au contraire, ces coutumes exprimaient une sorte de garantie de niveau minimum de traitement

[71] Oppenheim, *op. cit.*, p. 682; Fauchille, *op. cit.*, p. 144; Sibert (t. II), p. 68.
[72] N. Sastri, *op. cit.* [73] *Nusantara*, p. 131 sq.
[74] *La Condition des Etrangers au Siam au XVIIe siècle.*
[75] Oppenheim, *op. cit.*, I, 682; Fauchille, *op. cit.*, I-1, 144, 147. Une des raisons pour la concession des droits capitulaires ou précapitulaires était aussi la difficulté d'appliquer la loi du pays concédant aux communautés étrangères qui observaient une loi et une tradition religieuse différente.

favorable accordé aux étrangers comme preuve de la coexistence des communautés appartenant aux différents milieux.

Les marchands européens qui arrivaient aux Indes Orientales auraient été dans l'impossibilité de développer leurs activités commerciales si n'avait existé, précisément, la coutume asiatique de permettre l'installation d'unités d'étrangers juridiquement autonomes. C'est grâce à cette ancienne institution, qui reflétait un esprit de tolérance, que les Compagnies des Indes Orientales ont pu obtenir de souverains territoriaux les concessions qu'ils ont transformées plus tard en grandes organisations administratives, politiques et militaires. Graduellement ces concesssions furent incorporées dans des traités conclus entre l'état concédant et l'état dont les nationaux bénéficiaient d'un droit de résidence. A ce stade les arrangements capitulaires devinrent bilatéraux. Les étrangers se trouvaient protégés par leur état national, et l'état concédant était dans l'obligation de respecter les dispositions du traité capitulaire; ainsi le traité capitulaire de 1535 entre François Ier et l'Empire Ottoman, et les traités entre la Turquie et d'autres puissances européennes (l'Angleterre, la Hollande, la Russie, etc.[76]). En ce qui concerne les traités capitulaires aux Indes Orientales, notons comme exemples-types tous les traités entre les compagnies française, anglaise et hollandaise d'une part et les princes de la côte Malabare de l'autre.[77] On trouve aussi des traités qui concédaient dans le territoire d'une compagnie des capitulations à une communauté locale: ainsi le traité de 1766 entre les Anglais et le souverain du Deccan qui installait à Candapille (territoire de la compagnie anglaise) un représentant pour protéger les intérêts de ses sujets.[78] De nombreux traités capitulaires étaient conclus par la Perse, le Siam et les États indonésiens. Tous ces traités contiennent des dispositions hétérogènes mais ils offrent assez de ressemblances pour que l'on puisse les classer dans un même type d'institution juridique.[79]

Dans la majorité des traités, on faisait la distinction entre la juridiction civile et la juridiction criminelle. Lorsque la compétence était réservée au souverain territorial, le représentant européen (chef du comptoir, consul, etc.) devait être informé des mesures prises et avait le droit de participer à la procédure ou de défendre le sujet européen. Autre distinction à faire, fondamentale: il y avait d'une part les différends entre les membres d'une communauté étrangère (qui étaient en principe tranchés par le chef de la communauté); et de l'autre les différends entre les membres de cette communauté et les sujets du souverain concédant, ou des membres d'une autre communauté étrangère. Dans ces deux derniers cas le souverain était compétent (avec certaines restrictions), ou encore la compétence se trouvait partagée de diverses façons, selon la nationalité du plaignant ou selon la nationalité du défendeur *(actor sequitur forum rei)*. Une formule spéciale fut adoptée dans le traité de 1687 entre la France et le Siam;[80] selon l'article 5 de ce traité, en cas de procès

[76] *Cours Diplomatique*, par G. F. de Martens, 1801, tome III.

[77] Archives nationales, Colonies 457 et 459 et *Recueil des Cours*, p. 254.

[78] *Recueil des Cours*, p. 255. Il y avait aussi des traités capitulaires qui concédaient aux sujets d'un souverain asiatique des privilèges en Europe: par exemple le traité de 1631 entre la Perse et la Hollande (l'établissement des Persans à Amsterdam). Voir Martens, *op. cit.* et *Corps Universel*, par J. Dumont, 1731.

[79] *Recueil des Cours*, p. 257.

[80] *Recueil des Traités*, par Reinach.

civil ou criminel intenté par un serviteur de la compagnie française contre tout ressortissant d'une nation qui ne soit point au service de la compagnie, ou en cas d'un tel procès intenté par un ressortissant d'une nation quelconque contre un autre serviteur de la compagnie, la juridiction appartenait au roi de Siam, mais celui-ci s'engageait à admettre un représentant de la compagnie comme membre du tribunal. Cette formule est sans doute une anticipation des tribunaux mixtes tels que ceux qui ont existé jusqu'en 1937 en Égypte.

La révocabilité mutuelle de ces traités et l'égalité entre les parties contractantes céda la place graduellement, sous la pression des Européens, à l'inégalité et à l'irrévocabilité et c'est à ce stade que les capitulations devinrent une véritable restriction dérogatoire à la souveraineté de l'état concédant.[81] C'est aussi à ce stade que les Européens en Asie commencèrent à être exclusivement soumis à la juridiction de leurs agents (consuls) nationaux. Mais cette évolution ne s'acheva qu'après la chute des états asiatiques au XIXe siècle.

Les 'capitulations' ne sont donc pas une institution juridique d'origine européenne; elles ont leur origine dans le droit coutumier en vigueur aux Indes Orientales. Les Européens n'ont joué d'autre rôle dans cette institution que de contribuer à sa déformation, en y introduisant des éléments d'irrévocabilité et d'inégalité.

Une évolution semblable à celle des traités capitulaires s'est produite dans les traités contenant des dispositions de caractère discriminatoire. A partir du XVIIe siècle, chaque puissance européenne aux Indes Orientales ayant obtenu d'un souverain des concessions commerciales (ou autres) a cherché à lui imposer l'obligation de renoncer à toutes relations commerciales (et plus tard politiques) avec d'autres puissances européennes, de façon à être la seule à bénéficier du négoce local et à jouir d'un monopole. L'application des clauses discriminatoires sous diverses formes aboutit peu à peu à isoler chacun des souverains et à diminuer leur position vis-à-vis des puissances européennes. C'est à ce stade d'inégalité que les discriminations devinrent absolues et irrévocables.

Parmi les premiers traités discriminatoires conclus par les Hollandais[82] figurent le traité de 1604 avec le Zamorin de Calicut (dirigé contre les Portugais), le traité de 1638 avec le roi de Ceylan (monopole d'achat de la cannelle et expulsion des Portugais), le traité de 1663 avec le Raja de Cochin (monopole du commerce des épices) et le traité de 1667 avec le roi de Macassar (expulsion des Portugais et des Anglais). La compagnie anglaise réagit au XVIIIe siècle par la conclusion de traités semblables: les traités (ou autres transactions) avec les princes de la côte ouest de l'Inde, c'est-à-dire le raja de Bringab (1758), le prince de Cotiote (1759), le prince de Colastry (1760), le prince de Cartenad (1761), le raja de Travancore (1773), le raja de Cannanore (1784) et d'autres. Tous ces traités établissaient un monopole d'achat du poivre à l'exclusion des Hollandais ou autres nations européennes. Ceux conclus par la compagnie anglaise

[81] C'est aussi à ce stade que les compagnies européennes commencèrent à se servir de la forme du traité tributaire: par exemple le traité (subsidiaire) entre les Anglais et Mysore après la chute de Tippou Sultan qui était allié avec les Français (1799) (*Recueil des Cours*, p. 274).

[82] *Recueil des Cours*, p. 268 sq.

avec les souverains du Bengale contenaient des clauses discriminatoires d'un caractère politique et militaire: citons le traité de 1763 avec Nawab Mir Jafeer et le traité de 1765 avec Najim-ud-Dowla.[83]

En ce qui concerne la compagnie française (établie en 1664) qui trouva à son arrivée aux Indes Orientales un grand nombre d'établissements européens, sa politique fut d'obtenir des souverains locaux le traitement de la nation le plus favorisée, lui permettant (sans l'application de clauses discriminatoires) de jouir des mêmes privilèges que les Hollandais et les Anglais. Elle obtint, en 1666, de l'empereur Aurangzèbe, ses concessions fondamentales en Inde, qui furent confirmées par l'Farokshir, en 1718, et reconfirmées par plusieurs vassaux et gouverneurs de l'empire.[84] La compagnie française a acquis une grande part de ses titres par des firmans et paravanas accordés unilatéralement par les souverains et s'est rarement engagée dans des opérations agressives contre eux.[85]

Si l'on suit l'évolution de la clause discriminatoire depuis son origine, au début du XVIIe siècle, on peut constater qu'elle s'est étendue graduellement du domaine du commerce, où elle contribuait à la consolidation des monopoles, au domaine politique où elle aboutissait à la prohibition, imposée aux souverains asiatiques, de maintenir des relations avec d'autres puissances (surtout européennes). Cette discrimination qui tendait à isoler les souverains et à limiter leur liberté d'action internationale, rencontrait des obstacles dans la notion juridique de l'inviolabilité de la souveraineté qui prévalait depuis des siècles dans les coutumes d'origine classique aux Indes Orientales. Nous avons vu que cette notion n'était pas étrangère aux écrivains classiques en Europe et rappelé que Vattel était encore cité par E. Burke dans le procès contre Warren Hastings porté devant le Parlement à Westminster. G. F. de Martens nous donne une liste des traités conclus. On y constate à cette époque en Inde que, même dans les conditions les plus défavorables, les souverains indiens conservaient une conscience inébranlable de leur souveraineté—ce qui forçait les Européens à normaliser leurs relations avec ces souverains conformément aux principes du droit des nations. Dans son *Cours Diplomatique*, Martens classifie les traités de cette période en ceux conclus avec les souverains du Bengale, du Deccan, Mysore, Carnatte (Arcot), Tanjore, Oudh et les Mahrattes.[86] Même si des éléments de discrimination et d'inégalité étaient compris dans ces traités, Martens

[83] *Recueil des Cours*, p. 272. Voir aussi le traité avec le prince du Deccan (1754) et avec l'état de Mysore (1770).

[84] Voir la collection des titres aux Archives coloniales, Inde, 457. La compagnie française obtint la cession de Pondichéry du raja de Gengee (confirmée par son suzerain, le roi de Viziapur en 1680) (Archives nationales, Colonies C2, 115-12).

[85] *Cours Diplomatique* (Martens), t. III, p. 147.

[86] Voir: *Cours Diplomatique ou Tableau des Relations Extérieures des Puissances de l'Europe tant entre elles qu'avec d'autres Etats dans les diverses parties du Globe*, 1801, t. III, p. 296 (traités conclus par la compagnie anglaise).

Les traités de 1757, 1760, 1763, 1765, 1768, 1770, 1773, 1775 (Bengale); les traités de 1759, 1766, 1768, 1790 (Deccan); les traités de 1769, 1770, 1784, 1792, 1799 (Mysore); les traités de 1763, 1779, 1785, 1787 (Carnatte); les traités de 1771, 1778, 1787 (Tanjore); les traités de 1781, 1788 (Oudh); les traités de 1739, 1756, 1775, 1776, 1778, 1781, 1782, 1789, 1792 (Mahrattes).—Les Français, jusqu'à la capitulation de Pondichéry en 1793, avaient des relations avec les états de Mysore, Tanjore, Madura,

ne les considère pas comme portant atteinte à la souveraineté de la partie contractante indienne.[87] Le déclin du respect pour le principe de la souveraineté aux Indes Orientales devait se manifester plus tard comme conséquence de l'européanisation du droit des nations au XIXe siècle.

IV. Conclusions

Nous nous sommes demandé quelle était la contribution apportée par les Indes Orientales à la formation du droit des nations aux XVIe, XVIIe et XVIIIe siècles. Il ne faut pas oublier que pendant cette période le droit des nations en Europe était *in fieri* et n'avait pas encore revêtu sa forme définitive. Il était donc susceptible de changements dictés par la pratique des états. C'est aussi pendant ces trois siècles que les états des Indes Orientales qui étaient en communication avec plusieurs puissances européennes avaient encore une mesure d'indépendance suffisante pour que leur voix fût entendue. Il ne faut évidemment pas surestimer l'influence qu'ils ont pu exercer, mais il est néanmoins incontestable que certains développements juridiques ont été directement ou indirectement affectés par la pratique des états aux Indes Orientales. Il semble ainsi que Grotius, lorsqu'il a formulé sa théorie de la liberté de la mer, a été influencé par l'ancienne tradition maritime dans l'Océan indien, fondée sur la conception du 'mare liberum'. La tradition asiatique a également joué un rôle dans l'évolution du droit sur les eaux et zones territoriales et sur les droits de pêche. Enfin, cette tradition peut aussi être considérée comme ayant apporté à la jurisprudence des relations entre suzerain et vassal des précisions extrêmement utiles qui ont permis de mieux apprécier les éléments unifiants de la souveraineté, et qui ont rendu possible la définition du rôle de l'état unifiant et protecteur vis-à-vis de l'état protégé.[88]

Ceylan et d'autres. Voir l'exposé de M. Lescalliers, commissaire de la République (S. P. Sen, *op. cit.*, p. 531) et *Mémoire Historique et Politique sur les Indes Orientales présenté à la Convention Nationale*, par P. I. Moline, 1795.—Tippou Sultan envoya en 1798 une ambassade à l'Isle de France pour renouveler l'alliance dirigée contre les Anglais. Ce souverain n'était pas disposé à accepter la suzeraineté de qui que ce soit et jusqu'à sa défaite en 1799 il agit et fut traité comme souverain sur un pied d'égalité. Le Nizam de Hyderabad a conservé son indépendance jusqu'à la conclusion du traité de 1800, où il s'engagea à consulter la compagnie anglaise en ce qui concerne ses relations extérieures (*Recueil des Cours*, p. 284). Les Mahrattes continuèrent leur lutte jusqu'au début du XIXe siècle.—La plupart des états indonésiens avaient été vassalisés et isolés par la compagnie hollandaise dans la seconde moitié du XVIIIe siècle (Martens, *op. cit.*, p. 342). Ceylan était occupé par les Anglais à la fin du XVIIIe siècle. Mais la Birmanie (Ava) et Atchen luttaient encore pour leur indépendance dans la seconde moitié du XIXe siècle. Le Siam et la Perse survécurent à la chute des états aux Indes Orientales.

87 Si nous examinons les traités conclus entre les souverains indiens, nous constatons que les concessions qu'ils s'accordaient l'un à l'autre (de nature fiscale ou juridictionnelle) n'étaient pas en principe irrévocables ou dérogatoires à leur souveraineté territoriale (voir par exemple les traités de 1752, 1762 et 1766 entre le Raja de Cochin et le Raja de Travancore qui se trouvent dans le 'Record Office' à Ernakulam, Kerala). Voir aussi Briggs, *op. cit.*).

88 Ce rôle a sans aucun doute été violé par la Chine envahissant le Tibet en 1950 (*Foreign Affairs*, avril 1953, p. 495).

La pratique des états a également favorisé un traitement très libéral des communautés étrangères et des compagnies européennes. L'introduction postérieure de l'irrévocabilité des monopoles, capitulations et discriminations (appliquées par les compagnies) n'a abouti qu'à déformer cette pratique. Bien des auteurs européens classiques[89] ont souligné l'utilisation regrettable des institutions asiatiques, faite dans des buts qui leur étaient étrangers. Ainsi J. H. G. Justi, dans *Les gouvernements de l'Europe comparés à ceux de l'Asie* (1762), présente une description classique de la transformation des compagnies européennes en agences politiques et militaires.

Nous avons attiré l'attention sur la contribution des nombreux traités et transactions à la sécularisation du droit des nations qui, sous l'influence des contacts bicontinentaux, se libérait des obstacles posés au début par le droit canon et le droit coranique au commerce mondial. Une étude plus étendue de la pratique des états aux Indes Orientales pourrait aussi montrer la coïncidence des usages diplomatiques en Europe et en Asie. En outre, le droit de la guerre,[90] fondé sur d'anciennes traditions, la distinction entre combattants et non-combattants, l'observation des 'temperamenta belli,' l'échange de prisonniers de guerre et de rançons qui ont permis d'humaniser la conduite des guerres aux Indes Orientales, seraient d'autres sujets qui mériteraient l'attention de l'historien du droit des nations,

Un des problèmes les plus remarquables qui se posait au cours des relations entre les puissances européennes et asiatiques était le problème de la classification mutuelle de souveraineté, fonction qui était exercée des deux côtés par les puissances classifiantes dans leur intérêt propre et en leur qualité de gardiens du droit des nations. Chaque classification constituait une appréciation des qualités essentielles de l'organisation de l'état classifié.[91] Une discussion des traits caractéristiques de l'état asiatique dépasse la tâche de l'historien du droit des nations, mais il nous paraît pertinent de présenter les observations qui suivent.

L'organisation de l'état hindou, basé sur le modèle classique, était régie par les principes de Dharma, c'est-à-dire la loi divine et morale, et par les principes d'Artha, c'est-à-dire la convenance politique. Tandis que l'idée de la nature dans Dharma était celle d'une nature idéale, et correspondait en gros au droit de nature envisagé par Grotius et les Grotiens, la conception de la nature dans l'Artha se rapportait à la réalité des conflits humains, et correspondait aux idées proposées en Europe par

[89] Surtout E. Vattel, *Droit des Gens*, trad. par J. Chitty, 1834, pp. 144-147.

[90] Chatterjee, *op. cit.*, p. 90; Justi, *op. cit.*

[91] En ce qui concerne l'administration de l'état hindou, François Pyrard de Laval nous donne dans son *Voyage*, 1619 (I, 414) l'impression suivante: les fonctionnaires du Zamorin de Calicut enregistraient les marchandises importées pour le Zamorin, les impôts et les taxes payés de jour en jour, les dépenses de la cour royale, les événements importants qui se passaient à la cour et dans le royaume, les noms et les affaires des étrangers qui se trouvaient dans le pays. Tous ces fonctionnaires observaient une discipline parfaite. Il y avait aussi des fonctionnaires de la même catégorie dans les autres villes, dans les ports et aux frontières du royaume. Pyrard ajoute que le même système administratif existait dans les autres états de la côte malabare.—Voir aussi Briggs, *op. cit.*; *Introduction to the Peshwa's Diaries*, par M. G. Ranade (Journal of the Bombay Branch of the Royal Asiatic Society, 1902, t. XX). En ce qui concerne l'organisation de l'état islamique, voir *Ayeen Akbery, or the Institutions of Emperor Akbar* (trad. du persan par F. Gladwin, 1800); 'The Nature of the State in Mughal India,' par Ram Sharma (*Islamic Culture*, October 1939).

Hobbes, qui s'orienteront vers le positivisme juridique et la sécularisation des principes du droit entre-états.[92] Kautilya, l'auteur d'*Artashastra*, présente une image des relations entre-états tout à fait séculière et propose certains principes de conduite en vue de diminuer les effets catastrophiques de l'anarchie extérieure. Ces principes n'avaient pas un caractère juridique, mais contribuaient à la formulation de certains usages et coutumes, à observer dans le cercle des états (mandala). Parmi ces principes, ceux qui se rapportent à la souveraineté extérieure du roi et à la conclusion de traités et transactions diplomatiques sont d'une importance particulière.[93]

L'exercice de la souveraineté extérieure était (sans doute sous l'influence de l'action réciproque entre Dharma et Artha) conditionné par le principe de la solidarité inter-dynastique qui reflétait la solidarité Ksatriya. Une des conséquences en était l'absence complète de l'idée de 'debellatio' dans le droit coutumier hindou. Le souverain vainqueur réduisait le souverain vaincu à la condition de vassal; mais il ne supprimait jamais sa souveraineté. La transformation des souverains en vassaux était intimement liée à l'idée de l'établissement de l'empire universel, sous le çakravartin comme suzerain suprême.[94] Cet empire était envisagé comme stade final de l'élimination de l'anarchie extérieure—idéal poursuivi aujourd'hui *mutatis mutandis* par l'établissement d'une autorité internationale…

Les principes régissant les relations diplomatiques créaient une base de négociations entre les nombreux états de l'Inde, tâche dans laquelle le 'duta' jouait un rôle primordial.[95] Nous avons vu que les princes indiens se montraient souvent très réticents pour conclure des traités avec les Européens: la conclusion d'un traité était considérée comme un signe de faiblesse et même de dépendance, et s'il était indispensable, un traité personnel était préféré à un traité réel qui imposait des obligations aux successeurs du prince contractant. En outre, la possibilité d'une défense basée sur la formule 'rebus sic stantibus' n'échappait pas au souverain, car cette formule impliquait le principe de la révocabilité des concessions accordées aux Européens. Cette attitude envers le droit des traités, que l'on trouve même au XVIIIe siècle dans la pratique des états Mahrattes, reflétait vraisemblablement l'esprit Kautilyen.[96]

Nous retrouvons les mêmes principes dans la pratique des états de l'Inde extérieure car ces états adoptèrent les traits caractéristiques du modèle hindou,[97] qui fut

[92] *Recueil des Cours*, p. 311; 'The Conception of Kingship in Ancient India,' par Louis Dumont (*Contributions to Indian Sociology*, n° VI, Décembre 1962); *A History of Indian Political Ideas*, par U. N. Ghoshal, 1959, ch. XXVII (voir la discussion de la littérature jaïne).

[93] La conduite de la guerre était régie par les principes de Yuddha-dharma (Chatterjee, *op. cit.*, pp. 69-94).

[94] *Inter-State Relations in India and Kautalya's Artashastra*, par W. Ruben (Indian Year Book of International Affairs, 1955).

[95] Une description des usages diplomatiques aux Indes Orientales, particulièrement au Siam, se trouve dans l'œuvre de La Loubère, *op. cit.*, III, ch. XV (L'auteur attire l'attention sur l'importance de la lettre de créance dont l'ambassadeur était porteur et sur les privilèges qui étaient attachés à ses fonctions comme messager du souverain et parfois comme son négociateur).

[96] *Cambridge History of India*, V, 384.

[97] '… Les artashastras ou traités de politique ont continué à façonner l'administration hiérarchisée des états de l'Inde extérieure dominée par la personne du roi…' (Coedes, *op. cit.*, p. 422). En ce

transplanté par les brahmanes dans presque tous les pays des Indes Orientales.[98] Les brahmanes assuraient la légitimation sacrale des anciennes et nouvelles dynasties locales et l'organisation de la bureaucratie et de l'administration publique, surtout de la chancellerie royale qui assistait le souverain dans sa politique intérieure et extérieure.[99] Le modèle hindou changea évidemment sous l'influence du bouddhisme (qui insistait sur l'uniformité de la moralité et de la justice dans la vie privée et publique) et plus tard sous l'influence de l'Islam, mais il restait à la base d'une attitude assez homogène des souverains des diverses religions envers les relations entre-états. Un des phénomènes les plus remarquables est l'absence du 'Jihad' dans l'état islamique aux Indes Orientales, en conséquence de l'influence continue des idées hindoues.[100] L'Empire Mogol et les États indonésiens (après leur conversion à l'Islam) n'ont jamais abandonné certaines de ces idées qui survécurent à l'arrière-plan politique aux Indes Orientales.[101]

Ainsi les Européens se trouvaient en face d'états qui n'étaient pas seulement classifiables comme souverains mais qui, eux-mêmes, appliquaient fréquemment une classification assez critique aux Compagnies des Indes Orientales qu'ils considéraient au début comme des organisations de marchands d'un niveau non-souverain. Nous avons discuté les difficultés qui s'en suivirent dans les négociations diplomatiques et dans la conclusion des traités.

Avant de conclure qu'on nous permette encore deux observations: l'expansion de la civilisation hindoue dans l'Inde extérieure était essentiellement pacifique. Elle permettait des relations entre-états sur la base de négociations, de traités et des relations commerciales très étendues. A l'inverse, les méthodes de la colonisation chinoise reposaient sur la conquête, l'annexion des territoires et l'imposition du modèle de l'état par la contrainte.[102] La pénétration européenne aux Indes Orientales était

qui concerne l'influence de la jurisprudence hindoue dans l'empire Majapahit, voir: 'The Astadasa Vyavaliasa in old Javanese,' par Dr. van Naersen (Contributions to Indian Philosophy, Geography and Ethnology, 1941, t. 100); voir aussi: van Leur, *op. cit.*

[98] La Birmanie, qui a reçu le bouddhisme au Ve siècle avant Jésus-Christ, retenait toujours le modèle hindou de la royauté associée au Code de Manou. Dharma était remplacé par Dhammavilasa et le système des castes fut répudié, mais les prêtres brahmanes continuaient à jouer un rôle important à la cour royale. La situation au Siam était la même *mutatis mutandis* (Winstedt, *op. cit.*; N. Sastri, *op. cit.; Ancient Siamese Government and Administration*, par H. S. O. Wales, 1934, p. 17).

[99] Il y avait partout aux Indes Orientales des ministres ou officiers d'état qui s'occupaient des affaires étrangères, de la réception des ambassadeurs, de la conclusion de traités et de la protection des communautés étrangères. Au Siam c'était le Barcalon (Phraclang), à Ceylan l'Adigar, en Birmanie le Wungyi (membre du conseil supérieur ou Hlutdaw), chez les Mahrattes le Dabir (Sumaut), à Delhi (Agra) le Vizier, en Perse le Doulet, et à Constantinople le Grand Vizier (Luenig, *op. cit.*; Wales, *op. cit.*, p. 90).

[100] On trouve peut-être des traces de la politique du Jihad au XVIe siècle dans les états islamiques de l'Inde qui luttaient (avec l'appui de l'empire Ottoman) contre les Portugais (par exemple Bijapur). Voir: *The Doctrine of Jihad*, par M. K. Nawaz (Indian Year Book of International Affairs, 1959). Il faut noter que l'attitude de l'état islamique envers la doctrine de la conquête était toujours différente de celle de l'état hindou.

[101] Voir la politique de l'empereur Akbar en ce qui concerne la non-annexion des états hindous en Inde (*Some Aspects of Muslims Administrations*, par R. P. Tripothi, 1936). Mais malgré l'absence de Jihad, le Jiziah (ou la capitation) était pendant certaines périodes imposé aux 'infidèles'. (Voir Archives coloniales, Inde, n° 458, 1720).

[102] Coedes, *op. cit.*, p. 64 sq.

donc possible seulement jusqu'à la limite géographique de l'influence hindoue, grâce à laquelle existait un type d'états prêts à coopérer sur un pied d'égalité avec d'autres puissances.[103] La sphère d'influence de l'état chinois, par contre, restait dans l'isolement et n'entra pas dans le cadre de la famille des nations que bien plus tard, sous la pression des Européens au XIXe siècle.

Une dernière considération mérite notre attention. Si les principes fondamentaux du droit des nations appliqués aux relations entre-états aux Indes Orientales étaient semblables à ceux de l'Europe, et si les états des deux continents faisaient partie d'une famille des nations, bi-continentale, il n'y avait donc, antérieurement au XIXe siècle, aucune place juridique en Asie pour l'idée de colonialisme. On n'a jamais prétendu que les partages de la Pologne à la fin du XVIIIe siècle aient été une expression du colonialisme, pas plus qu'on ne peut prétendre que les états italiens aient été la victime du quelconque colonialisme autrichien. Les participants au jeu de la politique de force avaient en principe des chances égales de succès ou de défaite et les conséquences d'une guerre perdue se trouvaient simplement mises en forme et légalisées par un traité ou par la conquête, comme une institution normale du droit international. Il est difficile de prétendre que la situation était fondamentalement différente aux Indes Orientales. Les Portugais, les Hollandais, les Anglais et les Français ont tous acquis des territoires ou d'autres droits par traité ou par conquête. Les sens des traités et de la conquête, ainsi que le droit applicable, étaient parfaitement clairs aux deux parties contractantes, l'européenne et l'asiatique. On peut donc peut-être parler de colonialisme en Asie au sens politique ou économique, mais du point de vue du droit des nations, qui régissait les relations bi-continentales antérieurement au XIXe siècle, ce terme n'a aucun sens.

Si l'on considère dans son ensemble l'histoire des grades puissances asiatiques qui faisaient partie de la famille des nations bien avant la naissance de la civilisation européenne et qui en font partie à l'époque, présente, la période du XIXe siècle, qui a vu la chute du système des états asiatiques, constitue un laps de temps très court. Il serait inexact d'affirmer que cet intervalle, qui dura jusqu'à la fin de la deuxième guerre mondiale, a interrompu sérieusement la continuité de la famille universelle des nations, malgré les changements idéologiques intervenus en Europe au XIXe siècle qui ont essayé de couper les anciens liens avec l'Asia et de restreindre la notion de famille des nations à la notion de 'concert européen'.

[103] Il n'y avait ni dans l'idéologie des puissances européennes ni dans celle des états des Indes Orientales des obstacles à une coopération universelle. La conception de l'universalité *naturelle* de la famille des nations (qui fut détruite par le positivisme au XIXe siècle) leur était commune.—François Ier, dans une letter addressée au pape Paul III, justifie les relations entre la Franc et l'empire ottoman, établies par le traité de 1535, en faisant appel a l'universalité de la famille des nations (*Les Origines du Droit International*, par E. Nys, 1894, p. 162).

7

GROTIUS AND INDIA (1954)

The legal nature of relations between sovereign communities within the Family of Nations must be judged by the law in force at the time of its actual application to these relations. If the law changes, questions of intertemporal law may arise as it happened in the Island of Palmas Arbitration[1] but the legal nature of relations at a previous period of history can never be assessed by ex post facto law. However, this is exactly in what many international lawyers tend to indulge in their appreciation of inter-State relations outside the European continent in past centuries. The Family of Nations, governed by its own law, became in the XIX century a closed society which proved unwilling to open its doors to newcomers. Colonial possessions were then considered a fait accompli. The European powers as well as the United States did not need to look to the past to justify their title to these possessions. But writers on international law have to look to the past if only for academic purposes and whenever they reproduce the Law of Nations in its historic aspect, they are confronted with problems of evolution of the law. It often seemed comfortable to consider contemporary and past reality as identical and thus the present-day student of international law believes himself absolved from going into complicated comparisons between past and present. The Family of Nations of the XX century opened its doors to newcomers from the continent of Asia, but their admission has been not infrequently treated as the opening chapter of their international career as if Asia had been a political vacuum in past centuries. The modern democratic organization of Asian countries has no doubt embodied Western patterns of government but this has little bearing on their cultural and even political traditions. To say that their participation in international history had begun with the advent of the European powers in Asia in the XVI and XVII centuries would be equally a gross over-simplification, not only in the light of records of Asian historians but in the very light of the views of classic writers in Europe at that period which have been often forgotten and ignored. Two of them who made the most outstanding contributions to the formation of the Law of Nations may be singled out: Franciscus de Vitoria, professor at the University of Salamanca (1480–1546) and Hugo Grotius (1533–1645), one concerned with Spanish–American relations, the other with Portuguese–Asian relations. Though the first never went into Asian problems, he influenced decisively Grotius and his views are therefore essential for

[1] *International Law through the Cases* by L. C. Green, 1951, pp. 350–69.

a fuller understanding of initial European–Asian relation from the legal point of view. Grotius has been hitherto considered the father of the Law of Nations but this dignity seems to have shifted to Vitoria: pater semper est incertus. The first of his main works which had kept his paternity alive is 'Mare Liberum'. However, 'Mare Liberum', if compared with Vitoria's 'De Indis Noviter Inventis', reveals itself as a transposition of legal arguments of the Spanish school from the case of America versus Spain to the case of Asia versus Portugal. The following were the historical antecedents of this formative period of the Law of Nations.

Forty years after Columbus had landed on American soil, Franciscus de Vitoria defied official Spanish policy and pronounced the principle of extension of the law between nations to the newly discovered continent. Spanish theologians and lawyers introduced the Central American Communities indirectly into the orbit of the existing Family of Nations and made at the same time an attempt to raise the law *between* nations to the level of a more organic law *of* nations.[2] While Columbus set foot on American soil in October 1492, Vasco da Gama cast anchor in May 1498 in the port of Calicut on the West coast of India. The XVI century witnessed the establishment of relations between Spain and America and between Portugal and India. When the Dutch later challenged Portuguese hegemony in India and in the East, Grotius supported in his 'Mare Liberum' the claims of the Dutch East India Company, based on the principles of freedom of trade and of the high seas, and gave literary form to the developing law of nations as conceived by the Spanish school.[3] It is notable that the law of nations became a direct product of the trade connections established by European explorers who were in search of spices in the East and of gold in the West. At first they brought the Christian Faith in exchange and made it a pretext for expansion. The Church of Rome was careful not to subscribe to this policy though it was finally forced to act as an arbiter between the two main sea powers, Spain and Portugal.[4]

The analogy between Spanish–American and Indo–Portuguese relations must have been at the back of Grotius' mind but he hesitated to define it with more precision. The Spanish school had made it clear that relations between nations, whether Christian or non-Christian, must be governed by principles of justice. Franciscus de Vitoria and his successors in Spain expressed the conviction that the Christian Faith cannot be made a pretext for the exploitation of nations with an 'inferior' civilization.[5] Grotius adopted this principle and applied it to Indo–Portuguese relations. He also advocated complete freedom of relations between nations all over the world. In his view they have the right to sail to each other and to trade with each other and no particular power can establish a sailing or trading monopoly. Whether the motives of his reasoning were as ideological as those of the Spanish scholars

[2] *The Spanish Conception of International Law* by James Brown Scott, 1934.

[3] *The Life and Works of Hugo Grotius* by W. S. M. Knight, 1925, pp. 82–112.

[4] Knight, op. cit., p. 98 (Grotius mentions in ch. III of *Mare Liberum* the Papal arbitration relating to discovered territories in the Bull 'Inter Caetera' of 1492. The line of demarcation of Spanish and Portuguese overseas interests had been later modified by the Treaty of Tordesillas of 1494).

[5] J. B. Scott, op. cit., pp. 137–62.

attacking their own King, seems highly doubtful. Grotius had been briefed as a lawyer to defend the claims of the Dutch East India Company against the Portuguese and he did not hesitate to abandon later his own principles (as stated in 'Mare Liberum') when he defended during his visit to London in 1613 the claims of the Dutch East India Company against the English newcomers in India.[6]

Among all arguments brought forward by Vitoria and later borrowed by Grotius, the argument based on the existence of political bodies on American soil which were capable of self-government and entitled to face outside aggression in self-defence, is the most outstanding. Vitoria in his 'Relectiones de Indis Noviter Inventis' states emphatically that the Spaniards may be entitled to travel to the American continent and to establish freely relations with the communities concerned but they have no right to occupy their lands, to disturb their peaceful existence and impose their rule or faith on them. Vitoria makes this momentous statement about the American Indians in saying: 'Quia habent ordinem aliquem in suis rebus, postquam habent civitates, quae ordine constant, et habent matrimonia distincta, dominos, leges, opificia, commutationes, quae omnia requirunt usum rationis: item religionis speciem ...'[7].

This passage shows that Vitoria had enough material to prove that certain Indian communities in America (Aztecs, Incas) had a distinct political organization, rulers, laws, the institution of marriage, an organized industry, a system of exchange and last but not least their own religion. Drawing his conclusions he emphasizes that the above communities have 'true dominium in both public and private matters, just like Christians, and that neither their rulers nor private persons could be despoiled of their property on the ground of their not being true owners'.[8] Vitoria then engages in an interesting comparison by saying: 'It would be harsh to deny to those, who have never done any wrong, what we grant to *Saracens* ... who are the persistent enemies of Christianity. We do not deny that these latter peoples are true owners of their property, if they have not seized lands elsewhere belonging to Christians'.[9] Vitoria had obviously the Arabs in mind, whose rule in Spain had come to an end, and he therefore brings indirectly his views about Asian communities into the picture.

Grotius in his 'Mare Liberum' proceeds exactly on the same lines. He begins chapter II by denying to the Portuguese sovereignty over Java, Ceylon (or Sumatra) and the greater part of the Moluccas. He emphasizes that the communities in these territories have their own kings, state organization (res publica), and laws. The Portuguese may establish relations with them by mutual arrangements only. They are foreigners (externi) there and not sovereigns (domini).[10]

What must be considered essential in the above statements of Grotius, is his emphasis on the existence of organized political bodies in India and Asia which

[6] Knight, op. cit., pp. 140–1.

[7] '*De Indis*' by Franciscus de Vitoria, edited by E. Nys (in the *Classics of International Law* by J. B. Scott, 1917), p. 333 (S.I.).

[8] *De Indis* (S.I.), op. cit., p. 334. [9] *De Indis* (S.I.), op. cit., p. 334.

[10] *The Freedom of the Seas* by Hugo Grotius (edited by James Brown Scott, 1916, p. 11).

make it in his view impossible for the Portuguese to occupy the respective territories as terra nullius. Thus he excludes the acquisition of these territories by discovery or occupation and leaves Portuguese claims to the title of cession or conquest, provided it is effected by a just war. He discards also the title by conversion of Indians to Christianity or the title based on Papal Donation.[11] As to the first it must be made clear that the Portuguese found on the Malabar coast an ancient Christian community which claimed St. Thomas the Apostle as their founder. Whatever the historical basis of this claim, the community had been there long before the advent of the Portuguese.[12] Marco Polo who visited India in the thirteenth century is a classic witness of the existence of this community, predominantly Syrian-Christian.[13] Hindu Rulers had conferred numerous privileges on the Christians raising them to a position of considerable importance. According to three well known Malayali deeds the Head of the Christian community ranked as a hereditary prince (Utayavar) equal to the Utayavars of Mysore and Coorg.[14] When the Portuguese arrived at the Malabar coast, the Christian community sought their protection and recognition of its rights. Moreover there were instances of Christian Rajas in India to mention the case of the pre-Portuguese Raja of Valiar Vattam or the case of the conversion of the Raja of Tanur or Vettat who sought confirmation by the bishop of Goa in 1548.[15] In other words, though the Christian community was a minority group, India could not be considered an entirely non-Christian land and the peaceful co-existence of Christians, Hindus and Mohamedans could certainly be hailed as an example worth-while following.

As to the political organization of India, its high level of development if compared with that prevailing in other extra-European continents, can hardly escape the attention of historians and lawyers. Grotius starts comparing Portuguese–Asian and Spanish–American relations but in doing so he wavers. The attitude of his mind cannot be assessed from the text of 'Mare Liberum' which he cared to leave to posterity but rather from passages which appeared in the original text but which he decided to cross out.

Our attention to the opening words of chapter II had been drawn above. Let us consider the passage: 'Quid quod ne reperisse quidem Indiam ullo modo dici possunt Lusitani quae tot a saeculis fuerat celeberrima?' The translation is: 'The Portuguese cannot by any means claim to have discovered India which had been famous for so many centuries'. Originally Grotius had added: 'Alia enim India, alia Americana ratio est';[16] these words mean: 'The reason being different in the case of

[11] *De Jure Praedae Commentarius* by Hugo Grotius (in the *Classics of International Law*, edited by J. B. Scott, 1950) (*Mare Liberum*, ch. II–IV).

[12] *The Syrian Christians* by L. K. Anantakrishna Ayyar, 1926, pp. 2–25.

[13] *The Life and Time of Marco Polo* by Henry H. Hart, 1941; Marco Polo by M. Collis, 1949; Christians and Christianity in India by P. Thomas, 1954.

[14] *Malabar* by William Logan, 1906, p. 268.

[15] *The Cochin State Manual* by C. Achyuta Menon, 1911, p. 77; *Malabar and the Portuguese* by K. M. Panikkar, 1929, p. 22; P. Thomas, op. cit., p. 37.

[16] *De Jure Praedae Commentarius* by Hugo Grotius, a Collotype Reproduction of the Original Manuscript (in *Classics of International Law* by J. B. Scott, 1950, p. 98). *Mare Liberum* was a publication

India and in the case of America'. Obviously he excluded discovery as a title because of the existence of a highly developed cultural and political tradition in India and Asia and all the ancient ties between Europe and Asia. But then he changed his mind and crossed the words out. The question may be asked, why? He could not have been afraid to draw an analogy which would have only weakened the case of the Portuguese. Or was it foresight not to strengthen the case of the Indian communities and rulers who were already coming under the sway of the Dutch? Did he feel that he was on uncertain ground or was it lack of a more thorough knowledge of Vitoria? The latter may have been probably one of the reasons but the main reason may have been the nature of 'Mare Liberum' itself which was primarily not an academic treatise but the statement of a case written by a lawyer who followed the path of expediency. No doubt material available in Dutch archives could throw more light on this question.

In chapter II Grotius writes: 'Recte igitur dicit Vitoria non magis ista ex causa Hispani ius in Indos quaesitum quam Indis fuisset in Hispanos, si qui illorum priores in Hispaniam venissent. Neque vero sunt Indi Orientis amentes et insensati, sed ingenuosi et solertes....' The translation is: 'Vitoria then is right in saying that the Spaniards have no more legal right over the Indians because of their religion (ista ex causa) than the Indians would have had over the Spaniards if they had happened to be the first to come to Spain. Nor are the East Indians unreasonable or senseless but on the contrary they possess intellectual capacity and shrewdness....'

The words 'Recte igitur dicit Vitoria ... ' were added by Grotius below the text.[17] At the end of the words 'neque vero sunt Indi amentes at insensati', Grotius had added originally 'quo colore in Americanos Hispani utuntur', but crossed these words out.[18] Grotius intended obviously to convey to the reader the argument that the Spaniards arrogated to themselves an apparent or prima facie right (colour of title) to get hold of the possessions of American Indians as the latter could not be considered 'reasonable' human beings. The question may arise whether he understood the expression 'Hispani' as Spanish official circles as opposed to Spanish writers who disapproved of the argument. Possibly the addition of the words 'Recte igitur dicit Vitoria ...' made Grotius cross out the words 'quo colore'. If so, he avoided a comparison which would have been to the credit of Vitoria, who had the courage to oppose the official policy of Spain.

In chapter IV Grotius, summing up, says: 'Quare cum et possessio et titulus deficiat possessionis, neque res dicionesque Indorum pro talibus haberi debeant quasi nullius ante fuissent, neque cum illorum essent, ab aliis recte acquiri potuerint, sequitur Indorum populos, de quibus nos loquimur, Lusitanorum proprios non esse, sed liberos, et sui iuris; de quo ipsi doctores Hispani non dubitant'.[19] The translation is: 'Thus since there is no possession and no title to possession and since

of the twelfth chapter of *De Jure Praedae*. The whole manuscript of *De Jure Praedae* was discovered in 1864 and published in 1868.

[17] *De Jure Praedae*, Manuscript op. cit., p. 98.

[18] *De Jure Praedae*, Manuscript op. cit., p. 98.

[19] *De Jure Praedae*, Manuscript op. cit., p. 100.

the property and the Sovereignty of the East Indies ought not to be considered as if they had been previously res nullius, and since, as they belonged to the East Indians, they could not have been legally acquired by other persons, it follows that the East Indian nations (people) in question do not belong to the Portuguese but are free and sui juris; and this is not denied even by the Spanish doctors'.

At the end of the text Grotius had added the words: 'cum de Americanis disputant',[20] implying that the Spanish writers questioned the liberty and legal position of the American Indians. It seems astonishing that Grotius could have suddenly had any doubt about the opinion of Spanish writers in this respect and thus he did well to cross out these words as the views of Vitoria, Vasquez, and de Castro on the problem were abundantly clear.

Without following up other passages crossed out in other places, it would not be irrelevant to quote a passage in which the change of the text is too significant to be ignored. We have already seen that Grotius begins chapter II with an enumeration of territories in which he denies Sovereignty to the Portuguese: 'Non esse autem Lusitanos earum partium dominos ad quas Batavi accedunt, puta Tavae, Taprobanae, partis maximae Moluccarum, certissimo argumento colligimus, quia dominus nemo est eius rei quam nec ipse umquam nec alter ipsius nomine possedit'.[21] The translation is: 'The Portuguese are not Sovereigns of those parts (of the East Indies) to which the Dutch have access (sail), that is to say Java, Ceylon (or Sumatra), the greatest part of the Moluccas—and this we prove by the most certain argument that nobody is Sovereign of a thing which he himself has never possessed and which no one else has possessed in his name'. Grotius denies here Portuguese Sovereignty over Java, Ceylon (Sumatra) and the greatest part of the Moluccas. However, eliminating from this category of territories Malacca and Goa, he had added originally the following words to the text: 'Non enim de Malacca, non de Goa loquimur, coloniis Lusitanorum' which means 'we do not speak (in this connection) about Malacca and Goa, Portuguese colonies'.[22]

This passage, crossed out by Grotius,[23] calls for some historical explanation. Alfonso de Albuquerque, Vasco da Gama's successor in the East, who became Governor of India in December 1509, conceived the scheme for the conquest of Aden, Ormuz, Malacca and Goa.[24] Goa was needed as a naval base and a colony for the Portuguese who after having established relations with Indian Rulers such as the Rulers of Vijayanagar, Calicut, Cochin, Travancore and Madura, required a permanent stronghold of their own to be on an equal territorial footing with these Rulers. Malacca was important as the headquarters of maritime commerce between the Far East and the Middle East. Aden and Ormuz commanded the entrance to the Red Sea and the Persian Gulf.

[20] *De Jure Praedae*, Manuscript op. cit., p. 100.
[21] *De Jure Praedae*, Manuscript op. cit., p. 97.
[22] *De Jure Praedae*, Manuscript op. cit., p. 97.
[23] *De Jure Praedae*, Manuscript op. cit., p. 97.
[24] *Vasco da Gama and His Successors* by K. G. Jayne, 1910, pp. 78–114.

Albuquerque concentrated first on Goa. The latter, originally a Hindu seaport, had been conquered by the Musulmans in 1469 and became after Calicut their principal harbour on the Malabar coast. The Ruler of Goa was then Yusuf Adil Shah, King of Bijapur, apparently a son of the Ottoman Sultan Murad II who had fought as far as in Hungary. In February 1510 Albuquerque started his attack on Goa in which he was backed by the Hindu population which acclaimed him as their liberator from Islamic domination. The fight for Goa lasted until December when the Portuguese established permanently their rule over the seaport. In April 1511 Albuquerque started his attack on Malacca which was crowned with success in August. After his return, he concentrated on the re-organization of the administration of the Portuguese forts and factories on the Malabar coast. He then secured Portuguese rule in Ormuz in 1515 but died on his return to India on the 16th December on board ship in Goa harbour.[25] Portuguese rule in India was later challenged by the Dutch, French and English East India Companies but though the back of Portugal's sea power in the East was broken in the XVII century,[26] the Portuguese retained after the loss of other possessions, Goa, which constitutes today a major Indo–Portuguese issue. There is no doubt that whereas the Portuguese established only provisional strongholds in various parts of India, they made Goa a regular colony. The passage on Goa which Grotius crossed out of the text, contains two significant words 'Goa—colony'. It seems as if Grotius had become unwittingly the classic witness of Portuguese colonialism on the Malabar coast which independent India claims now to be brought to an end.

There are further passages concerning Goa which Grotius left in the text. They are, however, not directly relevant to the dispute in question. In one of these passages Grotius refers to Manoel, the brother of the governor of Goa who had been 'dispatched with some ships, under instructions to make a warlike attack upon the Hollanders at their very first approach …'.[27] In another passage Grotius refers to the King of Kandy (Ceylon) who 'asked de Waert (Dutch) to stand by with the ships, warding off the forces expected from Goa for the relief of the Portuguese'.[28] These passages refer to the period when the Dutch–Portuguese struggle for hegemony in India and the East was in full swing.[29] The Dutch soon took the place of the Portuguese but had to face the arrival of a new competitor, the English East India Company. As we have seen, Grotius went in 1613 to London to defend the Dutch case against the English Company. In the course of negotiations Grotius argued that the Dutch had been engaged in trade in the East Indies for many years, had sunk much money in it and fought the Portuguese to build up their own trade connections and thus it would be hard upon them that the English East India Company

[25] Jayne, op. cit. [26] *A History of Portugal* by H. V. Livermore, 1947, p. 307.

[27] *De Jure Praedae*, Manuscript op. cit., p. 123; and *De Jure Praedae Commentarius* (Translation by G. L. Williams) 1950, p. 272.

[28] *De Jure Praedae*, Manuscript op. cit., p. 155; and *De Jure Praedae* (Translation), p. 347.

[29] In a letter, dated 27th January 1607, King Philip III urged Alfonso de Castro, Viceroy of the East Indies, to protect on his return to Goa, Portuguese interests against the Dutch (Appendix to the *Freedom of the Seas* ed. by J. B. Scott, 1916, p. 79).

should seek a share in that trade.[30] The Company replied to these arguments that it had a right by the law of nations to sail freely and to trade with all other nations. The Company relied on the same arguments which Grotius had adopted in his Mare Liberum. Though Grotius' work was already known in England, it is not certain whether the Company actually made use of it.[31] But the reasoning was the same and what is more important, there was reliance on both sides on treaties concluded with Indian Rulers[32] which testified once more to the equality of relations between the European Companies and these Rulers.

There is no doubt that the European Powers (Companies), on their arrival in India, had to deal with organized political bodies whose legal conceptions facilitated the immediate establishment of mutual relations. Far from finding themselves in an area of lawlessness, they were confronted with the existence of a sui generis Family of Nations extending all over Asia. Its public and private law might have differed from that prevailing in Europe, but it was based on the same principles of justice. The Law of Nations applied to the relations between East and West in the XVI century and later was law of reciprocity which accepted the Sovereignty of Indian and Asian rulers and communities. Grotius was not the only writer to testify to this state of affairs. Puffendorf, Vattel and other writers expressed later the same views. It is only after the establishment of Western colonial rule in Asia (whether by conquest or treaty) that writers of International Law started denying Sovereignty to these rulers and communities.[33] Their views (if accepted) cannot have any retrospective effect. The classic law on the matter had been clear beyond doubt.

[30] Knight, op. cit., p. 140.
[31] Knight, op. cit., p. 141.
[32] Knight, op. cit., p. 141.
[33] *The Acquisition and Government of Backward Territory in International Law* by M. F. Lindley, 1926, pp. 12–19.

8

FREITAS *VERSUS* GROTIUS (1959)

I.

In 1627, nearly nineteen years after the anonymous publication of his *Mare Liberum*, Hugo Grotius mentioned in one of his letters a work written by Franciscus Seraphin de Freitas in response to his treatise.[1] Freitas was a professor at the University of Valladolid, and the significant title of his work was *De Justo Imperio Lusitanorum Asiatico*. Grotius referred to it in the following words: 'Scriptum est satis diligens et vir dignus cui rescribatur'. But though he considered Freitas 'a man worthy of reply' and though he was urged to answer him he never did so. Instead he suggested in his letter that 'some one of our judges should be sought out and the duty delegated to him', a remark full of irony and perhaps bitterness, written after his trial and imprisonment by his own compatriots whose case he had so ably defended.[2]

Mare Liberum was not an academic treatise in the strict sense of the word but was one of the chapters of *De Jure Praedae* which Grotius produced, probably at the request of the Dutch East India Company and which was in the nature of a lawyer's plea relating to a particular case in which the Company was involved. This case arose out of the seizure of a Portuguese vessel in the Straits of Malacca by a Dutch Admiral in the employment of the Company. Its capture was questioned by some members of the Company who opposed the adjudication of the prize by the Dutch Admiralty Court.[3] In defending the case of the Company Grotius dealt in Chapter XII with the general aspects of the Portuguese–Dutch conflict in the Indian Ocean, and the freedom of the high seas as its central problem.

While Grotius pleaded the case of the Dutch East India Company Freitas was chosen to state a case for the King of Spain who was at that time also the sovereign of Portugal.[4] He fulfilled his task with scholarly care and precision, countering Grotius's reasoning chapter by chapter and pointing out numerous mistakes. Grotius himself admitted in another letter[5] that 'my work about the freedom of the

[1] Hugonis Grotii, *Epistolae* (Amsterdami, 1687), Epistola No. 144, p. 796. Freitas's treatise was published in 1625.

[2] Grotius escaped in 1621 from Holland to France and later became Swedish Ambassador in Paris; see Knight, *The Life and Works of Hugo Grotius*.

[3] Knight, op. cit., p. 81. [4] Amzalak, *Trois Precurseurs Portugais*, pp. 41–94.

[5] See *Recueil de Burman* as quoted by Guichon de Grandpont in his translation of Freitas's *De Justo Imperio Lusitanorum Asiatico* (Preface).

sea was conceived in the best patriotic spirit but it was written "aetate juvenili"'. When it was published he was only twenty-five years old. Indeed, in comparing *Mare Liberum* with *De Justo Imperio Lusitanorum Asiatico* the reader is struck by Freitas's perfect legal erudition and scholastic skill. But while Freitas was an expert in Roman and Canon law and had a profound grasp of the Commentators, Grotius appeared in spite of his young age as a legal reformer of great flexibility and foresight. This is perhaps the reason why Freitas's work, overshadowed by Grotius's spectacular success, has been so utterly forgotten. However, if the history of the classics of the law of nations of the seventeenth century is to be complete, Freitas deserves a proper place among all the other opponents of *Mare Liberum*, particularly Selden and Welwood with whose arguments Grotius dealt in due course.

In considering Freitas's work[6] it is important to remember that it refers to problems arising out of actual State practice in south Asia and the Indian Ocean in the sixteenth and seventeenth centuries. The same is true of *Mare Liberum* which in spite of the generality of its propositions concentrates on the Portuguese–Dutch conflict in the above region and the rôle played in it by the local rulers. Before engaging in a discussion of the legal aspect of this conflict its historical background deserves to be briefly recalled. Vasco da Gama's arrival on the west coast of India marked the opening of a new direct sea route from Europe to Asia, and had in effect a threefold significance—economic, political and religious. It undermined the trade monopoly established by Moorish (Arab) traders, and at the same time attacked the *hinterland* of Islam which drew vital resources from south Asia for carrying out its holy war against Christian Europe. The Moorish trading and navigating community in the East was intimately linked with Venice and with certain Asian ports, particularly the harbour of Calicut on the west coast of India, and it relied on the support of Turkey and Egypt, the latter being the area of transloading of goods shipped from India to European destinations. Spain and Portugal were at that period united under the Spanish Crown and enjoyed in all respects the support of Papal Rome not excluding the conferment on them of a legal title to overseas expansion. The three East India Companies (Dutch, English and French) only gradually came into the picture; the first to appear on the Asian scene in the seventeenth century were the Dutch who were out to break the back of the *Imperium Lusitanorum Asiaticum* irrespective of any ideological conflict. Though these companies were separate legal entities they were endowed by their sovereigns with authority to exercise rights of external sovereignty to the effect that their transactions with other independent powers created rights and duties in the law of nations.[7]

[6] *De Justo Imperio Lusitanorum Asiatico* (1625), and translation into French by Guichon de Grandpont (1882).

[7] See Dr. Kemal, 'The Evolution of British Sovereignty in India', *Indian Year Book of International Affairs* (1957); Hanataux and Martineau, *Histoire des Colonies Françaises*, vol. 5, p. 9; van der Burg and Groot, *The Dutch in Malabar; Selection from the Records of the Madras Government, Dutch Records* (1911).

II.

The first question with which the historian of the law of nations is confronted in assessing the situation in south Asia and in the Indian Ocean from the legal point of view is this: Did the struggle in this region start in a legal vacuum or was it determined by the existence of certain principles which were observed by all the participants in the local game of power politics in accordance with their various express or implied legal traditions? What was the status of the local rulers with whom the European powers exchanged envoys, concluded treaties and waged wars? In the absence of a precise local system of inter-State law, what was the actual contribution of regional State practice to the adaptation of legal notions concerning sovereignty, *bellum justum*, treaty making and maritime custom to new conditions? Grotius was intimately concerned with these questions and he gave in his *Mare Liberum* a tentative answer to each of them. These answers were no doubt based on a thorough study of the relevant factual material which he must have carried out in the archives of the 'United Company' in the Netherlands, and they were formulated in a manner reflecting the typical Grotian blend of the naturalist and positivist conceptions of law.

In Chapter II of *Mare Liberum*[8] Grotius refers to those parts of the East Indies in which the Dutch–Portuguese conflict developed most acutely, i.e. Ceylon, Java and the Moluccas (which is not an exhaustive enumeration), and says that these countries 'always have had their own Kings (*suos reges*), their own government (*suam republicam*), their own laws (*suas leges*) and their own legal systems (*sua jura*). The inhabitants allow the Portuguese to trade with them, just as they concede to other nations the same privilege. Therefore, inasmuch as the Portuguese pay tolls and obtain leave to trade from the Rulers there (*jus mercandi a principibus exorant*), they thereby give sufficient proof that they do not go there as sovereigns but as foreigners. Indeed they only reside there on sufferance (*precario*)'. From this Grotius draws the conclusion that 'the Portuguese have no title at all to sovereignty' (*titulus dominii*). It is quite obvious that he considered the local Asian rulers as sovereigns capable of entering into diplomatic and treaty relations with European powers and in fact a survey of treaties concluded between them and the Portuguese in the sixteenth and seventeenth centuries supplies sufficient proof of actual State practice in this respect.[9] It should be remembered that the Portuguese, unlike the Dutch, English and French, had no real ambition of establishing themselves as a land power in Asia. Their policy first aimed at controlling the sea routes and eliminating Moorish navigation from them, establishing coastal strongholds and trading stations, and securing a monopoly of trade. Later they acquired certain territories under their own sovereignty such as, for instance, Goa and Malacca. Grotius was definitely aware of these exceptions as he added to the above-mentioned text in Chapter

[8] *The Freedom of the Sea* (transl. by Ralph van Daman Magoffin, ed. by J.B. Scott).
[9] Biker, *Collection of Treaties* (*Collecção de Tratados*) (Lisboa, 1881).

II the following words: 'Non enim de Malacca, non de Goa loquimur, coloniis Lusitanorum', but he crossed the words out from the original text which is only too characteristic of a writer engaged in writing a practical advocate's plea.[10] Grotius supports his opening remarks in Chapter II by the concluding text of Chapter IV in which he excludes the possibility of considering the territories of the East India Rulers as *res nullius* and this opinion found its expression in the attitude of the Dutch to these rulers with whom outstanding questions were settled by a long series of treaties.[11]

Freitas hardly disagrees with Grotius as to problems of sovereignty and treaty making, but he adds in all sincerity that some of the possessions which the Portuguese acquired in the East Indies are based on a title of conquest. In this respect he argues in Chapter II that the Portuguese first acquired certain rights by treaties with local rulers, but that in case of breach of treaty on the part of the latter they had to go to war—and their war was *bellum justum*.[12]

Though Grotius accepted the sovereignty of local rulers and stressed the need of a legal title on the part of a European power for the acquisition of rights in their territories, he nevertheless argued in Chapter I that according to the primary (not secondary) law of nations (*jus gentium primarium*) every nation has the right of free access to, and of trade with, every other nation. Freitas rejects this artificial division between a primary and a secondary law of nations. He considers international law a monolithic system though some of its rules are according to the law of nature immutable and some are subject to change. In case of conflict between the right of access to foreign nations and their sovereignty, the latter must prevail. If Asian rulers conceded to European powers access to their territories, such a concession was subject to change and could be withdrawn, otherwise there would be freedom of trade and navigation for the latter at the cost of sovereignty of the former. That Freitas's argument was legally justified follows from the attitude which the Dutch adopted in their conflict with the English over their rights in the East Indies (Indonesian Islands). The argument of the English in the London negotiations for the settlement of the conflict (1613) was that after their arrival in the territories in question they established a good title to trade with local communities as all countries should by the law of nations have equally free access to the East Indies for trading purposes. The Dutch reply to this argument was that this universal freedom of the law of nations may be limited by special arrangements. The Dutch claimed priority on the basis of treaties with local rulers whom they considered as 'bound by their own consent'. To this the English rejoinder was that these treaties were unjust and contrary to the law of nature and that anyhow 'the Dutch would not be unaware of what had been written on this head by the "assertor maris liberi"'.[13] Grotius, who

[10] *De Jure Praedae Commentarius* (a collotype reproduction of the original manuscript, in the *Classics of International Law*, 1950), p. 97.

[11] Heeres, *Corpus Diplomaticum Neerlando-Indicum* (1907).

[12] As to their war against Islam Freitas describes it in a true Crusader's spirit as 'bellum justissimum'; see below.

[13] Clark, 'Grotius's East India Mission in England', *Transactions of the Grotius Society*, 20 (1935), p. 79.

might not have expected to be hoist by his own petard,[14] acknowledged the reliance of the English on the above argument but argued again that the Dutch relied on treaties concluded with local rulers and that the 'contract extinguished the liberty of the law of nations'. The effect of these negotiations on Grotius was that in his later writings the statements about the universal freedom of commerce (as limiting national sovereignty) were restated subject to careful qualifications.[15]

It may be noted, however, that while Freitas argued against the principle of free access to territories under foreign sovereignty for trading purposes, he adopted the same principle for another purpose by advocating free access of Europeans to Asian lands for the purpose of preaching the Christian faith. The consequences of adhering to this doctrine will be discussed below. It is essential to stress that its adoption is a corollary to the ideological conflict between Christianity and Islam which was transplanted by the Portuguese from the European scene to the Asian *hinterland* of Islam in south Asia.

However, in spite of these controversies over limitations of sovereignty, Grotius and Freitas seem to have shared the fundamental view that independent and politically organized societies in Asia were endowed with statehood and sovereignty in the law of nations, and this view was by no means an isolated one. As pointed out by Lindley,[16] the majority of the classic writers followed the opinion of St. Thomas Aquinas (as expressed in his *Summa Theologica*) that dominion was based on *jus humanum* and should not be obscured by the distinction between Christian and non-Christian religion and civilization which was based on *jus divinum* and was irrelevant to sovereignty as a temporal matter. Recognition of sovereignty of Asian or other extra-European States found its expression in the writings of Bodin,[17] Franciscus de Vitoria, Ayala, Gentili, Selden and Puffendorf, and it was later supported by eighteenth-century writers such as Vattel and G. F. de Martens. Vattel dismissing differences of religion as a relevant factor considered any independent State 'which governs itself by its own authority and laws' as sovereign and as a member of the natural society of nations 'subject to the law of nations'.[18] Martens, a writer with a positivist outlook, who relied to a great extent on treaties between European Powers as the basis of the law of nations, also referred to a long series of treaties between European and Asian Powers which obviously appeared as sovereign participants in extra-European treaty arrangements.[19] Thus, there was an overwhelming body of opinion among the classic writers to the effect that diplomatic and treaty relations between European and Asian Powers were based on a footing of

[14] Knight, op. cit., p. 137. [15] See Clark, loc. cit., p. 61.

[16] *The Acquisition and Government of Backward Territory in International Law* (1926), pp. 12 et seq.

[17] *Les Six livres de la republique* (transl. by Richard Knowles, 1606); see L. I, C. VIII where Bodin refers to the sovereignty of the rulers of Turkey, Egypt and Persia and the Caliph (p. 147). Bodin considers 'the Kings of Calicut, of Malachie, of Cambar and of Canor' as vassals of the King of Portugal (p. 147).

[18] *Le Droit des Gens*, L. I, C. I, p. 4.

[19] de Martens, *A Compendium of the Law of Nations* (1789, transl. by Cobbett, 1802); *Cours Diplomatique* (1801); *Recueil de traités* (1817).

equality and that (as stressed by Grotius and Freitas) the former could acquire rights from the latter by legitimate title only such as cession or conquest.

III.

Assuming that a number of Asian communities were endowed with statehood and sovereignty and capable of entering into transactions with the Portuguese and other European powers which produced rights and duties in the law of nations, we have to exclude the possibility of acquisition of their territories by occupation or discovery. Grotius states in Chapter IV that 'the property and the sovereignty of the East Indies ought not to be considered as if they had been previously *res nullius* and as they belonged to the East Indians, they could not have been legally acquired by other persons ...', and he adds that 'this is not denied even by the Spanish doctors'. Indeed, Freitas does not join issue on this point. Neither could the Portuguese according to Grotius have claimed 'to have discovered India which had been famous for so many centuries'. Originally Grotius had added the words: 'Alia enim India, alia Americana ratio est' (Chapter II) but he crossed them out from the text though the remark was, contrary to Vitoria's views, quite feasible.[20] Again it might have been inconvenient in a lawyer's plea. Freitas refers to two meanings of the word 'discovery': the geographical and the legal. He does not maintain that the Portuguese acquired a legal title by discovery but he stresses the fact that they opened the direct sea route to India by circumnavigating the Cape of Good Hope. As will be seen below he attaches legal significance to this fact and considers his Sovereign to have the right on the basis *prior tempore potior jure*.

While Freitas has little to say on occupation and discovery, he engages in a lengthy controversy with Grotius over the title of Papal donation in favour of the Portuguese. In Chapter III of *Mare Liberum* Grotius had referred to 'the partition (of overseas possessions between Spain and Portugal) made by Pope Alexander VI used by the Portuguese as authority for jurisdiction in the East Indies' and had expressed the view that though it had been in the power of the Pope 'to settle the disputes between the Portuguese and the Spaniards' by *arbitration* if asked to do so, the conferment by him of any legal title in the East Indies had no effect in the law of nations. To this Freitas gives a lawyer's as well as a theologian's reply. He admits that the authority of the Pope is spiritual and only indirectly temporal. Thus if he intervenes in the secular sphere, it can only be for religious purposes. He can send missions to non-Christian communities and if they have to go by sea and to engage in trade to keep themselves going ('sub commercii colore') he can confer on them the right of navigation and trade to the exclusion of 'others'. As a theologian Freitas wrote on the assumption of the unity of the Church under the authority of the Pope and he therefore considered the Dutch as being outside this unity and as belonging to the category of 'others'. He also emphasizes in Chapter VIII that the King

[20] 'De Jure Praedae' (Manuscript), op. cit., p. 98.

of Spain had as Count of Flanders acquired sovereignty over the Netherlands and that the Dutch Senate should act in deference to his legal authority. Whatever the objective value of these arguments (which Guichon de Grandpont, the translator of Freitas's work, rightly considers as untenable)[21] it is abundantly clear from the context of Freitas's treatise that the contemplated mission of the Portuguese had, apart from its religious aspect, the undermining of Islam's 'hinterland' in the Indian Ocean as its ultimate purpose.[22] At the back of this political purpose loomed the anxiety of the inhabitants of the Iberian peninsula (who had experienced Islamic domination) to check Islam's progress in Asia.[23] It may be relevant to note that the Islamic power block acted on the doctrine of *Jihad* according to which the world was divided into *Dar-al-Islam* (Islamic sphere) and *Dar-al-Harb* (the rest of the world). *Jihad* implied a state of continuous warfare between the two which could be interrupted by treaties of a temporary character only as if in the nature of a truce.[24] Freitas states that King Emmanuel of Portugal being in charge of the anti-Islamic crusade in Asia had invited other European sovereigns to participate in it, and moreover the promulgation in 1492 of the Bull 'Inter caetera' of Pope Alexander VI *urbi et orbi* constituted a sufficient notification of this policy to all concerned.[25] Freitas notes the complete lack of reaction on the part of other west European powers and this inaction meant in his view their acquiescence in the exclusive mission of the Portuguese in the East Indies.[26]

However, as to the implementation of this mission, Freitas realized that the legal position of the Pope in relation to non-Christians in the East Indies presented

[21] Guichon de Grandpont, op. cit., p. 149; but see Knight, 'Seraphin de Freitas: Critic of *Mare Liberum*', *Transactions of the Grotius Society*, 11 (1926), p. 5.

[22] But it is important to emphasize that the greatest Islamic dynasty in south Asia, i.e. the Moguls, were, at the period of Vasco da Gama's mission and afterwards, ideologically outside the Islamic world in the proper sense of the word. Akbar, the Mogul Emperor of India, had applied a policy of tolerance and religious co-existence throughout his dominions. The position was different on the west coast of India which remained practically outside his Empire. The most powerful among its rulers was the Zamorin of Calicut and he, unlike other Hindu rulers on the west coast, was an intimate ally of the Arab trading community which with the support of Turkey and Egypt tended to dominate the sea routes in the Indian Ocean and the Arabian Sea. This explained *inter alia* the friendly relations and treaties of the Portuguese with other Hindu rulers on the west coast who welcomed the latter as their allies against the menacing pressure of Islam. See *The Book of Duarte Barbossa* (transl. from the Portuguese by Mansel Longworth Dames, 1918), vol. 2, p. 74.

[23] Panikkar, *Asia and Western Dominance* (1954), p. 13.

[24] *Jihad* meant, according to Islamic legal theory, *bellum justum*, but it is doubtful whether it reflected the ideology of the Koran. See Nawaz, 'The Doctrine of Jihad', *Indian Year Book of International Affairs* (1959).

[25] The line of demarcation between Spanish and Portuguese overseas interests had been later modified by the Treaty of Tordesillas in 1494, but it lost much of its significance during the period of temporary unification of Spain and Portugal under the Spanish Crown.

[26] There is also another reason for which Freitas supports the preference given to the Portuguese in the East Indies, i.e. their technical superiority. Since the reign of Henry the Navigator, Portuguese experience in oceanic navigation, including ship building, astronomy, geography, the use of instruments, &c., had reached a level incomparably superior to that of other maritime Powers. The spectacular achievements of Portuguese admirals since Vasco da Gama gave full expression to this technical superiority throughout the sixteenth century, and thus the Portuguese claim to monopoly in navigation and trade in the East Indies was, in Freitas's view, entirely justified by the Papal grant (Chapter VIII).

difficult problems. He agreed with Grotius that the Pope, as head of the Church, could not exercise jurisdiction over non-Christians. Already Vitoria had emphasized, in defiance of Spanish policy, that difference of religion did not justify political and military action.[27] Thus the Pope could not make grants to Christian powers at the expense of non-Christians though he could authorize 'missionary' activities in their territories. In trying to reconcile all controversial factors Freitas says in Chapter IX that three legal points occurred to him: first, non-Christians could not be compelled to accept the Christian faith; second, if they did not accept the Christian faith preached to them, they could not for this reason be deprived of their property rights and this also excluded *debellatio* ('non tamen ex eo eos debellare et bonis spoliare licet'); third, that the Pope could himself, or by the intermediary of Christian Princes, secure freedom of preaching the law of Christ in non-Christian countries.[28] The subjects of such countries who were prevented by their rulers from accepting the Christian faith, or from exercising it, in case of conversion, could be absolved from their allegiance to their rulers. The significant conclusion drawn by Freitas from the last point was that the Portuguese could go to war with a non-Christian ruler who disregarded the freedom of preaching or preserving the Christian faith and thus a war for the purpose of securing such freedom was *bellum justum*,[29] a conclusion with which Grotius utterly disagreed though he accepted the principle of free access of Europeans to the East Indies for trading purposes. However, Freitas emphasized that in practice the Portuguese waged war only exceptionally against non-Moslem countries,[30] as for instance against the rulers of Calicut and Ceylon as to which Freitas remarks in Chapter XVII: 'Constantinus Brigantini filius Indiae Prorex potentissimum Janafatam in Taprobane Tyranum debellavit, coronaeque Lusitanae subegit anno 1560....' But whatever the policy of the Portuguese in this respect, Freitas made it abundantly clear in Chapter IX that they would always avail themselves of the title of conquest against the Turks and Moors: 'Cum tamen contra Turcos et Mauros bellum ex nostra parte semper justissimum sit'.

It may be mentioned here that one of the legal consequences of this uncompromising attitude towards the Islamic world was the condemnation by Freitas (in Chapter XIII) of alliances between Christian and Islamic powers. Such alliances, if offensive, were illicit; if defensive they were tolerable but fraught with evil results. In support of this legal theory Freitas quotes one of the leading authorities on the subject, Octavianus Cacheranus, whose work under the title *Disp. an Principi Christiano fas sit, foedus inire cum infidelibus* (Taurini, 1569) was later mentioned

[27] de Vitoria, *De Indis* (ed. by E. Nys; Classics of International Law).

[28] Which excluded the ancient Christian community of St. Thomas on the west coast of India from Portuguese interference; Brown, *The Indian Christians of St. Thomas* (1956).

[29] This conclusion meant in fact the transplantation by Freitas of Vitoria's views to the Asian political scene.

[30] Their relations with the Hindu world were not dictated by any doctrinal conception, hence their alliances with the Vijayanagar Empire, the Ruler of Cochin, &c., against Muslim powers and their allies.

by Ompteda[31] as an authoritative work on alliances of Christian Princes with infidels.[32]

Thus, while Grotius and Freitas broadly agree as to the application in the East Indies of legal principles relating to acquisition of territory, they disagree fundamentally as to the conception of *bellum justum* and conquest, particularly in relation to the Islamic world.

IV.

Before discussing the Grotius–Freitas controversy over the freedom of the high seas with special reference to the position in the Indian Ocean, the question may arise whether any legal régime existed in the above maritime region before the arrival of the Portuguese at the end of the fifteenth century. Grotius must have concerned himself with the question during the study of the relevant factual material, as he included at the end of Chapter VII of *Mare Liberum* the following passage: 'Praeterae accolae totius tractus Africani et Asiatici partem maris quisque sibi proximam piscando et navigando perpetuo usurparunt, nunquam a Lusitanis prohibiti'. In the light of this statement it seems that the various Asian communities had acquired vested rights of fishing and navigation in certain zones adjacent to their territories (as distinguished from the high seas) and thus Grotius draws from this and other arguments the general conclusion that the Portuguese 'are in possession of no right whereby they may interdict to any nation whatsoever the navigation of the ocean to the East Indies'.

As to sources of maritime law in South Asian countries, it may be noted that the oldest comprehensive treatise on inter-State relations in ancient India, Kautilya's *Artashastra*, which originates in all probability from the early period of the Buddhist Mauryan Empire (fourth century B.C.), makes numerous references to maritime regulations (L. II, C. XXVIII). It speaks about the existence of a superintendent of shipping and his jurisdiction over vessels navigating the ocean close to the shore (*Samudrasanyana*) and inland waters. One of his duties was the care of weather-beaten vessels which arrived at harbours. It is most characteristic of this treatise that it prescribes the application of measures against ships bound for an enemy country and the destruction of all pirate ships (*Himsrika*). It also appears from its text that sea routes along the shore were considered preferable to mid-ocean navigation in the Indian sea (L. VII, C. XII). The turning-point in shipping came with the discovery by the Romans (about A.D. 45) of the navigational use of monsoon

[31] *Litteratur des Völkerrechts* (Regensburg, 1785), p. 592. Ompteda refers also to Pott's work on the subject. Pott enumerates as infidels in the first instance Turks, Saracens and Tartars with whom offensive alliances are forbidden to Christian princes even if such alliances contemplated *bellum justum*. He criticizes particularly the treaty concluded between Francis I of France and Turkey against Emperor Charles V; Pott, *C. D. de Foederibus Fidelium cum Infidelibus* (Jenae, 1686).

[32] In Chapter XVIII Freitas refers to the alliances between the Dutch and infidels in the East Indies directed against the Portuguese and deplores the lack of solidarity of the Dutch in the common cause of Christendom.

winds blowing regularly across the Indian Ocean which made mid-ocean sailing a practicable proposition.[33] After that a regular import of various luxury goods by sea route from the East to the Roman Empire became an important factor in the latter's economy. Moreover, oceanic trade between India and South-East Asia and the Far East experienced a spectacular development following the expansion of maritime activities of south Indian rulers. The sea route between India and China was in common use in the fifth century A.D. Commercial intercourse developed in the ninth century and up to the fifteenth century Chinese junks frequently arrived on the west coast of India.[34] The Indian Ocean became, therefore, much earlier than the Atlantic or the Pacific a maritime centre of far-distant shipping on a big international scale. This tended to lead to the spontaneous growth of a customary régime governing oceanic activities whose primary concern was the fight against maritime anarchy and the suppression of piracy. There were also examples of legislation which regulated controversial problems of maritime law, to mention only the edict of Maharaja Ganapati the purpose of which was to assure 'safety to foreign traders by sea whose vessels might be wrecked on the coast of his territories'.[35] Thus the Indian Ocean could hardly be considered *mare clausum* before the expansion of Moorish navigation and the advent of the European Powers.[36] The situation changed only later with the arrival of the Portuguese in the East Indies who tended throughout the sixteenth century to eliminate Moorish trade and to enforce a régime of far-reaching control of navigation which was *mutatis mutandis* similar to that imposed by the western Powers in various parts of European waters (England, Venice, Genoa, &c.). In the above circumstances it might not be impossible to assume that Grotius in the formulation of his new doctrine found himself to a great extent stimulated by the existence of an ancient maritime tradition in the Indian Ocean which for its vastness and extensive network of sea routes was bound to lend itself to a *mare liberum* outlook. Grotius's distinction between the high seas and territorial zones in which south Asian communities exercised rights of navigation and fishing certainly supports this supposition.

The formulation of this new outlook and its application to the Dutch–Portuguese conflict led Grotius to the denial of all possible titles claimed by the Portuguese in

[33] Rawlinson, *Intercourse between India and the Western World* (1926).

[34] Nilakanta Sastri, *A History of South India* (1955); Panikkar, op. cit., pp. 35–37. Reference may be made to *The Travels of Ibn Batuta* (transl. by S. Lee, 1829) who in the middle of the fourteenth century went on a mission to China and left an account of Chinese shipping regulations relating to the crews of vessels and cargo registers.

[35] While formerly the whole cargo of such ships had been forfeited to the State, the ruler decreed that henceforth nothing but the normal custom duties would be levied on them (*Epigraphia Indica*, vol. xii, 1913–14, p. 188). The appropriation of wrecks and cargoes by rulers was a principle established by immemorial custom but it was gradually modified by legislation and treaty until it disappeared. As to piracy it might have been punishable according to the law or custom of a maritime State (see *Artashastra*) but State practice in the Indian Ocean seems to have evolved a certain identity of customs of oceanic tradition which lifted some principles to the inter-State level. Punishment of piracy as a crime against the safety of traffic and life in the open sea beyond the jurisdiction of any sovereign implied the existence of open oceanic highways.

[36] See Panikkar, op. cit., pp. 35–37. See also Ludovico di Varthemo who, in his *Itinerary from 1502 to 1508* (transl. by J. W. Jones, 1928), testifies to the freedom of navigation in the Indian Ocean.

the Indian Ocean whether by occupation, by prescription or custom or by Papal donation. In support of his basic argument that the sea is *res communis* he refers *inter alia* to Roman law and quotes in Chapter V a reply made by Ulpian in which the latter stated that 'the sea could not be subjected to a servitude because it was by nature open to all persons'. To this argument Freitas replies that Ulpian excludes the imposition of a servitude on the sea only by private law and not by public law. The fact that a servitude cannot be imposed by an individual does not mean that it cannot be imposed by a sovereign. Thus though the sea may be *res communis jure gentium*, it can be charged with a servitude including a prohibition against foreign navigation if it is occupied by a sovereign. In Chapter XIV Freitas reiterates this idea and states that whenever the Roman people asserted their right over a portion of the high seas the latter ceased to be public by the law of nations and became public by the law of the sovereign. Though Grotius advocated a progressive doctrine which in due time proved more convincing than the views of his opponents he seemed to have underestimated the difficulty of transplanting conceptions of Roman law to the public law of nations.[37]

Nevertheless, it would be far from correct to consider Freitas an all-out antagonist of the freedom of the seas. In Chapter X he says: 'Maris ergo elementum commune omnibus est quia infinitum ita ut possideri non queat....' In Chapter XI he discusses the use of the sea and the air and states: 'Haec enim naturaliter propter vastitatem, fluxumque vaguum, *integre* occupari non possunt omnibus hominibus communem decernit Celsus....' The analogy between the high seas and the air space is characteristic. Freitas considers both *res communis* but subject to important limitations obviously dictated by the principle of effectiveness. First of all he emphasizes the existence of maritime zones to which the adjacent territorial State may extend its sovereignty. The question arises what are the limits of these zones. Freitas notes that lawyers found it impossible to agree on this matter—a state of affairs on which we cannot claim to have improved much even today.[38] As it is impossible to find a suitable formula in natural law, the jurisdiction of the territorial sovereign must according to Freitas extend into the high seas according to the possibilities of effective control—a proposition not alien to the tentative policies of some maritime powers today. In Chapter XIV Freitas refers to Grotius's remark about the rights of non-Christian States in Asia whose inhabitants had exercised from time immemorial rights of navigation and fishing in zones adjacent to their

[37] Freitas encountered the same difficulties in his discussion of the Rhodian laws to which he refers in Chapter X. Their interpretation leads him to the conclusion that (1) the law of the sea must be considered as a system requiring the establishment of maritime jurisdiction; (2) the customary *lex maris* does not exclude the jurisdiction of the sovereign of the high seas but includes it; (3) it allows to assume the application of the *actio uti possidetis* to the high seas (a doubtful argument which is denied by Grotius); (4) even if private rights on the sea cannot exist, a sovereign may for their protection impose restrictions including tolls on foreign shipping in harbours as well as beyond them. This interpretation seems doubtful as the Rhodian laws tended to support the conception of the freedom of the sea in the East; see Champagne, *La Mer libre, la mer fermée ou exposition et analyse du traité de Grotius intitulé La Mer Libre et de la replique de Selden ayant pour titre La Mer Fermée*, &c. (Paris 1803); and see below.

[38] Johnson, 'The Geneva Conference on the Law of the Sea', *Year Book of World Affairs* (1959); Waldock, 'International Law and the New Maritime Claims', *International Relations*, vol. 1, April 1956.

territories. He draws from this the logical conclusion that since Grotius admits national jurisdiction in certain portions of the sea, such rights are capable of being exercised not only by the Turks and Moors but also by Christians. He does not limit national jurisdiction only to territorial zones but accepts its extension generally to the vast expanses of the high seas.

In this respect his views are revealing because he operates on the assumption of a possible quasi-occupation of the high seas by a particular sovereign. The rationale of this conception is explained in Chapter IV in the following way: the high seas cannot remain in a state of lawlessness and anarchy. To avoid a legal vacuum the régime of the high seas must be based on some law, whether national law or the law of nations. It must be kept in mind that in the absence of detailed rules supporting the doctrine of the freedom of the high seas as a practical proposition the sea was bound to be open to anarchy and this was evidenced in all periods of history by the concern of the navigating and trading communities with piracy. Asian history in the pre-Vasco da Gama period testifies to the friendly relations between maritime powers such as those between Buddhist India and China, or those developed during the period of the expansion of the maritime empire of Sri Vijaya. The problem of piracy was no doubt tackled in the inter-State practice of those Powers which seem to have treated the high seas as the common concern *generis humani*. To what extent these efforts were successful could only be ascertained by further historical research. As stated above, the Portuguese and other Europeans did not find themselves in the opening stages of their maritime career in the Indian Ocean in a *mare clausum*. But the monopolizing tendency of the Islamic trading community which carried valuable resources by sea to Egypt (already part of the Turkish Empire) and the opposition of the Portuguese to this potential monopoly which they considered a threat to Christian civilization became a highly disturbing factor in this region. In these circumstances the elements of maritime co-existence in the Indian Ocean disintegrated into anarchy[39] and the Portuguese, not without selfish interest, arrogated to themselves the responsibility of converting the anarchy into conditions of security under their own jurisdiction. Freitas emphasizes in Chapter VIII that the Portuguese assumed the exploitation of the new direct sea route between Europe and Asia (which brought Asian merchandise at cheaper prices to the European consumer), and that to this end they diverted from the Arabian Gulf, which was constantly being invaded, the merchandise of India and undermined the uneconomic trade of Turkish merchants in Egypt. In Chapter XII he refers to Portuguese action against piracy in the Indian Ocean, and quotes Seleceus calling it 'ad auxilium purgandi orientis'. Thus the seventeenth century in the Indian Ocean witnessed a state of affairs to which the application of Grotius's doctrine was premature. Its realization proved possible at a later stage at which the European Powers were able effectively to combat anarchy and to co-exist within a *mare liberum* régime. Prior to this period the situation in the Indian Ocean called

[39] See Lacour-Gayet, *La Marine Militaire de la France sous le Regne de Louis XIII et de Louis XIV*, pp. 13 et seq.; Hall, *History of South Asia* (1955), p. 453.

for positive action, and this is exactly the reason why Freitas, far from abandoning entirely the *res communis* conception of the sea, tried to formulate certain principles of national maritime jurisdiction based on quasi-possession of the sea. He states in Chapter XI that in the absence of real occupation of the sea only its quasi-occupation is possible: 'Navigatione et piscatione quasi-occupatur', and he considers such quasi-occupation by the Portuguese as established without interference by the English or the French (Chapter XIV). The Dutch are according to him perfectly capable of establishing a similar right on other sea routes, but they cannot interfere lawfully with those leading to Portuguese trading stations and possessions. It will be seen that the right claimed by the Portuguese emerges as functional in character. In Chapter X Freitas makes it clear that the sea as *res communis* cannot be occupied for the sake of its occupation but rights in it can be acquired in relation to the purpose of their exercise, i.e. the preservation of the security on particular sea routes leading to specified territories. This functional character of quasi-occupation is also true of the maritime zones for, as Freitas states in the same chapter, it can take place only in relation to the land which envelops a particular portion of the sea. It seems that the sovereign asserting the above rights for himself acted in a way also as an agency of the law of nations for the common good of all concerned.

As to the legal title of the Portuguese to maritime jurisdiction, Freitas based it principally on prescription and custom. His main emphasis in Chapter XIV is on the fact that more than one hundred years had elapsed since Vasco da Gama's arrival in India in 1498 and that during this period the Portuguese, without any significant protest on the part of other Powers, asserted and exercised undisturbed control of navigation in the Indian Ocean. In this way they acquired a bona fide right of navigation by immemorial prescription or custom which, with the exception of the Moors, was generally accepted by the free consent of those against whom it was exercised. In this respect Freitas and Grotius differ fundamentally, for though both seem to view the Indian Ocean as practically an open sea before the arrival of the Europeans, Freitas considers it capable of quasi-possession ('mare navigationibus et piscationibus acquisitionis capax esse'—Ch. XIV), whereas Grotius finds any such acquisition of rights irreconcilable with the idea of the high seas conceived as *res communis*.[40]

[40] Under the impact of the opposition to his views Grotius modified to some extent his opinion about the freedom of the seas in his subsequent work *De Jure Belli ac Pacis* (see edition by William Whewell). Grotius says in L. II, C. II (13) that 'the Empire (imperium) of the sea claimed over a portion of it without any other property might easily proceed (from certain claims): Nor do I concede that the law of nations of which I have spoken would stand in the way. It has often been asserted and conceded …'. But Grotius emphasizes at the same time that 'He who holds the sea by occupation cannot prevent an unarmed and harmless navigation upon it' (12). Bynkershoek in his *De Dominio Maris Dissertatio* (ch. ix) refers to the fact that Grotius changed his views after the publication of *Mare Liberum* and expressed his doubts about the limits up to which occupation of the sea is possible (reference to *De Jure Belli ac Pacis*, L. II, C. III. 8).

V.

Before concluding our considerations relating to maritime law it might be interesting to mention briefly the institution of the so-called *cartaz* which was instrumental in the exercise of the control of the seas by the Portuguese. The term 'connotes', according to Portuguese dictionaries, a safe conduct which the Portuguese authorities used to grant in Asia to the friends of Portugal to secure to them safe navigation.[41] The fact that the above term is found in the Arabic vocabulary indicates that the Arabs made early use of *cartazes* for the control of navigation.

Freitas, discussing *cartazes* in Chapter VIII, connects their introduction with the establishment in the East Indies of a Portuguese administration endowed with maritime jurisdiction. They were granted in the name of the King by the Viceroy or by a military or naval commander. Freitas explains the circumstances in which they became necessary and draws our attention to the need of distinguishing friends and allies from enemies on the high seas ('ut foederatos ab hostibus discernarent'). The influence of the Saracens on local rulers in the East Indies increased conditions of anarchy ('dolo ac fraudibus orientis reges in id excitantes') and the situation became even more acute when the Pasha of Egypt and the Emperor of Turkey sent their navies into Indian waters to attack Portuguese ships and possessions ('cum Egypti Campson Turcorumque Imperator ad eandem nostrorum ab India exturbationem classes misissent aliquoties').[42] The *cartaz* appears therefore not only as the means of asserting Portuguese rights but also as an instrument for preserving order and security on international sea routes. Moreover, if we consider the region in question as subject to unlimited maritime warfare (*Jihad*) in which regular naval battles were fought in the sixteenth century, the *cartazes* bear certain similarities to navicerts[43] (see below). The authority issuing the *cartaz* applied a meticulous procedure of search to a foreign ship and ascertained whether its intended voyage was undertaken in good faith ('Fide prius illius qui navem conscendit diligenter explorata'). If the investigation proved satisfactory a safe conduct was issued which protected the ship from interference on her voyage; if the ship sailed without it, she incurred the risk of being stopped and captured with all the consequences ensuing therefrom ('aliter enim a nostris navarchis capi, bonisque omnibus euerti et vita et saltem libertate privari possunt'). Freitas remarks in conclusion that the *cartaz* became part of Asian maritime law by immemorial custom and that the Dutch could not ignore it, the more so that even the author of *Mare Liberum* invokes the same law in relation to the Persians, Chinese, Arabs and others in the above region.[44]

[41] See, for instance, *Dicionario de Lingua Portugueza* (Lisboa, 1844).

[42] Suleiman the Magnificent of Turkey directed the Pasha of Egypt to support actively the Zamorin of Calicut and the Arab trading community. The Egyptian fleet which entered the Indian Ocean was defeated by the Portuguese in 1538 (see Panikkar, op. cit., pp. 51–53).

[43] Smith, *The Law and Custom of the Sea* (1959), p. 155; Colombos, *A Treatise on the Law of Prize*, p. 216; Higgins and Colombos, *The International Law of the Sea* (1951).

[44] The text may be open to doubt, for Freitas says: 'Hinc fit Batavos sine hoc salvo conductu in Indiam navigare non posse, eo maximo quia incognitus [Grotius] idem ius implorat, quo Persae, Sinae,

A number of examples of *cartazes* were included by Judice Biker in his collection of treaties, and it may be of interest to give the content of at least one of them.[45] In a document issued on 9 August 1613 to Idalxa, King of Bijapur, a local Moslem ruler of an Indian State whose territories extended to the west coast, the Portuguese Viceroy in India states as follows:

I, Dom Jeronimo D'Azevedo cause it to be known to all who may see it that in consideration of the ancient amity which El Rey Idalxa has with this State and in view of the treaty concluded with him, a licence and safe conduct are granted to him at the request of his ambassador, to enable six of his ships to sail to Mecca (Arabia), Ormuz (Persian Gulf) and other places. In particular I have the pleasure to issue a licence and safe conduct to his ship 'Mamady' which carries four thousand khandis (of goods), her captain (Nacoda) being Melique Ambar aged thirty years, and which has for its defence twelve iron swivels (guns), twenty muskets and many moorish weapons so that she may start during the present monsoon from the port of Dabul where she is now, for Juda, and return without taking or bringing anything (anybody) prohibited that is to say Greeks, Turks, Abyssinians, cinnamon of Ceylon, pepper, ginger, iron, steel, lead, tin, timber, brass, saltpetre, sulphur, bamboo, and other things prohibited by the Government; neither will she be permitted to carry Portuguese (passengers) nor to bring horses without a licence, and she will be allowed to bring slaves, male and female of her own nationality only: And if there is any suspicion or information that some of these slaves are Christians or children of Christians, an enquiry will be instituted at the provincial council even if some of these children are not yet baptised; and before the ship departs from the port of Dabul she will be visited and searched by the agent of His Majesty who is at the spot and she will receive his certificate on the back of this document; and on these conditions her voyage both outward and homeward will be without any impediment on the part of the captains of the armadas of this State or on the part of other captains and persons, and all persons notified of the above will fulfill and observe these terms without any question; and this shall be sealed with the seal of the royal arms of the Crown of Portugal.

Another *cartaz* quoted by Judice Biker was also granted to the King of Bijapur in the same year and is in identical terms. Portuguese *cartazes* granted at a later period, whether in favour of rulers or private merchants differ little from the established pattern except that a clause was added to the effect that breach of the terms of the *cartaz* on the part of the grantee will render the *cartaz* invalid and that the ship will be seized and forfeited.[46]

The following conclusions may be drawn from the above: The *cartaz* could be viewed in a twofold way, first as an expression of Portuguese jurisdiction assumed in the Indian Ocean under their quasi-occupation, and second as a sort of navicert applied in conditions of continuous warfare against hostile Islamic powers. Navicerts, as is well known, were introduced during the two world wars and involved the submission of a neutral ship and its cargo by the shipper to investigation in advance.

Saraceni et Ethnici in illis partibus utuntur....' Guichon de Grandpont refers in his translation to the Persians, Chinese, &c., as subject to this law, but this may not give the precise meaning of *utuntur*.

[45] Biker, *Collecção de Tratados* (Lisboa, 1881), vol. iv, pp. 181 et seq.

[46] Biker, op. cit.: *cartaz* granted to the King of Canares on 1 March 1714 (vol. iv, p. 183), to Govinda Das Nana on 15 July 1766 (vol. iv, p. 186), &c.

If the latter obtained a navicert from the relevant Allied authority at the point of departure the navicert, although it did not constitute a guarantee against being subjected to visit and search, provided the ship with a passport enabling it to pass easily through Allied maritime controls. Great Britain made navicerts compulsory during the Second World War to the extent that ships not protected by them were deemed to be liable to seizure and condemnation.[47] The *cartaz* covered not only contraband goods but also passengers which was obviously calculated to prevent unneutral service by excluding from the vessel persons liable to be of use to the enemy (Turks, Abyssinians, &c.). The distinction between conditional and unconditional contraband, well known to Grotius,[48] seems not to be reflected in the *cartaz* which enumerates indiscriminately items primarily of use in war as well as merchandise capable of peaceful use only.[49] But merchantmen were entitled to carry guns and weapons for their defence which indicates the existence of conditions of total war. Enemy destination is clearly stated in the *cartaz*, and the mention of Mecca seems to show that ships were also carrying Moslem pilgrims. The exclusion of Christian slaves is a corollary of the Portuguese policy of absolute protection given to their co-religionists. It also follows that the Portuguese exercised the right of search of all vessels on the high seas, a right already implied in the *Consolato del Mare*. But the submission of a ship at the port of departure to Portuguese investigation (which was compulsory) and the issue of the *cartaz* to a bona fide grantee exempted her from interference on the part of Portuguese and other captains and entitled her to their protection. Though some of the *cartazes* do not include a clause referring to sanctions, it is obvious that all ships not carrying a *cartaz* were liable to seizure and condemnation, as expressly confirmed by Freitas.

Thus the *cartaz* appears as an interesting forerunner of the navicert, and testifies to the early development of specific rules of international maritime law in the Indian Ocean. It would be difficult to ascertain to what extent the *cartaz* was a concomitant of maritime warfare on the one hand and the expression of Portuguese general maritime control on the other. The two functions seem intimately interwoven and the case of each *cartaz* must be judged on its own merits, but no doubt the Portuguese–Islamic conflict must have overshadowed maritime practice.

Cartaz arrangements were sometimes made between the Portuguese and Indian rulers by treaty[50]and similar arrangements were also concluded by other maritime powers in the Indian Ocean. State practice on the west coast of India in the seventeenth and eighteenth centuries also affords many interesting examples of maritime custom relating to the identification of ships on the high seas. Diplomatic

[47] See also British practice of issuing ships' warrants (Higgins and Colombos, op. cit.).

[48] *De Jure Belli ac Pacis*, L. III, C. I. 5.

[49] This may imply a policy prohibiting all trading with the enemy, a conception well known to English law at the period in question.

[50] For instance, the treaty of 30 April 1559 concluded by the Portuguese and the ruler of Bakla. In Article V of this treaty the Portuguese Viceroy undertook to give to the ruler four *cartazes* authorizing Bakla ships to navigate freely in the Indian Ocean. Surendranath Sen, 'Historical Records at Goa', *Studies in Indian History* (1930). As to other examples of treaties see Sen, *Military System of Marathas* (1928).

correspondence between the Marathas and European Powers reveals that a vessel in the open sea was liable to capture if it carried neither a *cartaz* nor a passport nor flew the banner of its own State.[51] Frequent references to banners raise the problem whether there existed a proper law of the flag in the meaning of international law. There seems to be no evidence to this effect, but the flag, jointly with the type and name of the ship and the ship's documents, constituted the ways and means of identifying her nationality.[52] A vessel had the nationality of the ruler to which she belonged and if she was a private vessel her nationality was that of the ruler whose subject the owner was. Thus there existed what may be called in contemporary legal language a 'genuine link' between a ship and her home State.[53]

Wherever maritime custom was oppressive (as in the case of shipwreck) it was liable to be modified by treaty and this applied in course of time also to *cartazes*. It is interesting to note that in the Poonem treaty of 4 May 1779 concluded between the Portuguese and the Marathas, which is one of the relevant documents in the present Indo–Portuguese conflict before the International Court of Justice, it was stipulated in Article VIII that 'merchant vessels of both dominions proceeding to any port and encountering the fleets of both parties or any ship of war shall not be taken captive on the ground that they possess no safe conduct (*cartaz*) but shall be allowed to proceed freely'.[54] At that period conditions had radically changed in the Indian Ocean. The Portuguese–Islamic struggle had lost its significance and the prospects of co-existence of the several European East India Companies as well as the Asian Powers in the Indian Ocean warranted the establishment of a régime of freedom of the high seas. Martens gave expression to the impending general acceptance of the new doctrine at the end of the eighteenth century when he referred to the four great seas which compose the ocean and particularly to 'the Indian sea about which the great disputes have arisen' and said: 'The sole dominion (of the sea) may exist in the theory ... the ocean then is free, indeed it ought to be so'.[55]

VI.

Grotius and Freitas were not the only participants in the battle of wits around the freedom of the high seas and the problem of relations between European and Asian Powers. Gentili (1552–1608) concerned himself with these questions earlier and it is interesting to note that his views were in many respects similar to those of Freitas.

51 Sen, op. cit., pp. 178, 246, 250; see also *Dutch Records* (The Hague) (transl. by C. C. Remmerswaal in *Shivaji the Great*, by Bal Krishna, 1932).

52 Edye, 'Description of the Various Classes of Vessels, &c', *Journal of the Royal Asiatic Society*, 1 (1834); Edkins, 'Ancient Navigation in the Indian Ocean', *Journal of the Royal Asiatic Society*, 18 (1886); as to rules of navigation see Mohi't 1558 transl. by Hammer, *Journal of the Asiatic Society of Bengal*, 1 (1832).

53 This may imply a policy prohibiting all trading with the enemy, a conception well known to English law at the period in question.

54 *The Hindu*, 28 March 1956.

55 Martens, *The Law of Nations* (transl. by W. Cobbett, London, 1829), p. 163.

Though he did not accept war 'on account of religion', he nevertheless stated that, with the Saracens (who were part of the Turkish Empire) 'we have an irreconcilable war'.[56] Consequently alliances of Christian States with infidels against other Christian States were according to him unlawful,[57] and Gentili draws our attention to the fact that treaties concluded with Islamic countries used to provide for cessation of hostilities only.[58] Thus similarly to Freitas but unlike Grotius, he envisages a state of affairs between Christian and Islamic Powers which reflected Jihad and the Christian counter-doctrine to a great extent formulated on the basis of Canon law.[59] In the field of maritime law also there are significant similarities between both writers. Gentili considers the sea *res communis*[60] but submits it to far reaching restrictions. He refers to State practice developed by European maritime Powers such as Venice and Genoa which claimed jurisdiction and sovereignty over the sea adjoining their territories up to 'a distance of one hundred miles and even farther'. As to England he says that 'immeasurable is the jurisdiction of our King upon the sea'.[61] Though he denies the claims of these Powers to possession of the sea he nevertheless admits that it is possible for them to exercise jurisdiction and a protectorate over it.[62] Thus he comes near to Freitas's conception of quasi-possession of the sea without attempting a more precise definition.

Welwood, in his *Abridgment of all Sea Laws* published in 1613, also adopts a 100-mile limit of jurisdiction and though he advocates otherwise complete freedom of navigation he concedes to a national sovereign the right to impose restrictions on the freedom of fishing in the high seas. To this Grotius gave a critical reply in which he considered the 100-mile limit as arbitrary and anyhow untenable and rejected the dichotomy of navigation and fishing.[63] Ten years after the publication of Freitas's treatise appeared the most formidable reply to Grotius which came from the pen of Selden in 1635.[64]

[56] *Hispanicae Advocationis libri duo* (Classics of International Law), L. I, C. XX; *De Jure Belli* (Classics of International Law), L. I, C. XII.

[57] *De Jure Belli*, L. III, C. XIX. But commercial treaties with the Turks were not forbidden, see *Hisp. Advoc.*, L. I, C. XXV.

[58] *De Jure Belli*, L. I, C. IX. The state of undefined warfare had its repercussions in the law of contraband. Gentili discusses the case of an English ship loaded with powder and other merchandise which had been captured on its way to Constantinople by the Sardinians and Maltese. He does not consider 'other merchandise' as contral and goods.

[59] *Hisp. Advoc.*, L. I, C. XX.

[60] *De Jure Belli*, L. I, C. IV.

[61] *Hisp. Advoc.*, L. I, C. VIII.

[62] *De Jure Belli*, L. I, C. XIX.

[63] 'Hugonis Grotii Capitis quinti Maris liberi oppugnati a Gulielmo Welwood, etc.', in Muller, *Mare Clausum* (Amsterdam, 1872). Wright, *Some less known Works of Hugo Grotius* (Bibliotheca Visseriana, vol. 7, 1928). Welwood's *Abridgment* was followed up in 1615 by his *De Dominio Maris*.

[64] *Mare Clausum* (transl. by M. Nedham, London 1652; transl. by J. H. Gent, London 1663). Selden divides the British sea into four parts and though he considers the shores and ports of the neighbouring princes as bounds to the south and east, he maintains 'that in the open and vast ocean of the north and west, they [the bounds] are to be placed at the utmost extent of those most spacious seas which are possest by the English, Scots and Irish'. Among the nations claiming dominion of the sea Selden enumerates *inter alia* the Portuguese and the Turks. But his belief that the East had no conception of the freedom of the high seas seems open to doubt as pointed out by Champagne in his comparative study of Grotius and Selden *La Mer libre, la mer fermée* (Paris 1803), in which he discusses the Rhodian laws with special reference to the Byzantine Empire.

Without going into further details which would be beyond the scope of this inquiry it must be stressed that Franciscus Seraphin de Freitas deserves his due place among the writers of the seventeenth century who contributed to the clarification of problems relating to the legal status of the sea[65] and to European–Asian inter-State relations. As the title of his work indicates his main purpose was, apart from replying to Grotius, to justify the 'Justum Imperium Lusitanorum Asiaticum' and to contrast it with another imperium 'justum' as implied in Islamic theory and practice. The fact that many of his views were ultimately overshadowed by Grotius's progressive ideas, does not detract from their significance for the development of certain principles of the law of nations such as those relating to sovereignty, acquisition of territory, just war, maritime jurisdiction, contraband, unneutral service, navicerts and others. The application of these principles in Asian State practice in the sixteenth and seventeenth centuries is bound to disprove the view that the Europeans found themselves in Asia in a legal vacuum. Freitas formulates Portuguese rights in the Indian Ocean on the basis of territorial zones and quasi-possession, functional conceptions which in spite of offering a challenge to lawyers were defined with comparatively more caution than those of other opponents of *Mare Liberum*. All of them gave expression to an interim state of affairs prevailing in the seventeenth century which made it still premature to implement the principles of the freedom of the sea.

[65] Pierre Margry draws our attention to the fact that France was one of the first countries to protest against the Spanish–Portuguese monopoly on the high seas and that she gave support to the conception of *mare liberum* before Grotius; *Les Navigations françaises du XIV*ᵉ *au XVI*ᵉ *siècle* (Paris, 1867). See also *Controversiae Illustres* (1599), by Vasquez, who opposed the claims of Spain, Genoa and Venice.

9

THE DISCRIMINATORY CLAUSE IN SOUTH ASIAN TREATIES IN THE SEVENTEENTH AND EIGHTEENTH CENTURIES (1957)

I.

The study of the history of the law of nations in Asia whether treaty or customary law is still an unexplored field. Treaties concluded by European powers or agencies with the local powers in India and other South Asian countries in the seventeenth and eighteenth centuries are of particular interest to the historian of the law of nations as they date from the period during which the law of nations developed into a coherent legal system.[1] Many of these treaties were recorded by G. F. Martens in his writings and thus became part of the general volume of treaty law which supported the growth of the modern positivist conception of international law. It is noteworthy that these treaties frequently contained discriminatory clauses directed by one European power or agency against another giving full expression to European power politics transplanted from one continent to another. At the time when the Europeans joined the network of inter-state relations in India and elsewhere in South Asia, most of the local rulers were not unwilling to ally themselves with one or the other of the newcomers from the West, whether for the purpose of strengthening their position in relation to other powers, or, in the later stages of the struggle, simply for the purpose of self-preservation. The division of Indian and other South Asian markets among the various European nationalities led gradually to vital changes of territorial sovereignty. The corresponding process of commercial, political and military manoeuvering was accompanied by treaty making which performed the role of formalising the initial power positions and the relevant clauses and stipulations reflect the consecutive stages of the struggle. As soon as some of the European powers or agencies managed to obtain from their Asian counterparts preferential treatment coupled with prohibitions directed against other European

[1] The term 'European agency' applies to the various East-India Companies operating on the basis of charters and exercising extensive rights of internal and external sovereignty.
India being the main region of our inquiry is distinguished from *South Asia* though it is part of it.

nationalities, all of them plunged into retaliatory practices, each attempting to secure the maximum of concessions or the establishment of a monopoly for itself. India and the rest of South Asia was soon covered by a network of monopolies and discriminatory arrangements, a situation which remained in a state of flux until it resulted in a more rigid distribution of possessions which characterised the colonial *fait accompli* in the nineteenth century.

It is impossible within the limits of a short inquiry to refer to all the relevant treaties, the number of which is considerable.[2] Many of them are not easily available and the difficulties in obtaining the original texts or translations from various sources are far from negligible. However, a tentative inquiry into a few treaties selected from older collections, treatises or monographs may enable us to compare the various discriminatory or prohibitory clauses included in them and to see what type or pattern of stipulation used to be adopted by the contracting parties.[3]

II.

The first Europeans to arrive on the South Asian scene were the Portuguese. Vasco da Gama's landing at Calicut on the West coast of India in 1498 opened a significant chapter in the history of European–Asian relations, significant because of the extension of the fight between Christianity and Islam from Europe to the distant East. Portuguese shipping in the Indian Ocean and their trading stations and forts in the East Indies meant the end of 'Moorish' monopoly in trade and navigation on the great sea routes along which Asian spices were shipped and carried to the Mediterranean basin. After the liquidation of 'Moorish' power in the Indian Ocean,[4] the Portuguese were challenged by the Dutch, the Dutch by the English and the English by the French, ultimately all of them challenging each other. Indian and other South Asian rulers played an active part in the game of power politics and treaty making reflected the shifting interests, alliances and enmities.[5] The first of these treaties were concluded in the early sixteenth century between the Portuguese and the rulers of the West coast of India. Some of the most important among them were the Zamorin of Calicut, the closest ally of the Muslim trading community, and further south on the West coast, the rulers of Cochin, Travancore and Quilon who were ready to enter into alliances with the Portuguese in order to escape the overlordship of the suzerain-minded Zamorin.[6] The Portuguese tried to acquire a

[2] Treaties concluded between European powers in Europe and relating to their trade or possessions in South Asia are outside the scope of this paper.

[3] No reference is made in this paper to stipulations relating to most favoured nation treatment.

[4] Barbosa believed that without Portuguese interference on the West coast of India the latter would have come under Muslim domination. See *the Book of Duarte Barbosa*, translated by M. C. Dames, 1918, pp. 74–94.

[5] See: 'Grotius and India' by C. Alexandrowicz, *Indian Year Book of International Affairs*, 1954 (ch. 7 above).

[6] The Portuguese found in the Hindu rulers of Vijayanagar an inland ally against the Muslim ruler of Bijapur. The Vijayanagar rulers acquired a monopoly of horse trade through Goa (*A Forgotten Empire* by Robert Sewell, 1924, p. 186).

lasting monopoly of spices in Calicut but treaty making with the Zamorin finally proved abortive.[7] More successful were the treaties with the Southern rulers which date from the early decades of the sixteenth century and tended towards the establishment of a trade monopoly stipulating that all spices in the land should be sold to the King of Portugal.[8] Vattel referring to the policy of the Portuguese in the East Indies wrote: 'The Portuguese at the time of their great power in the East Indies were for excluding all other European nations from any commerce with the Indians; but such a pretension no less iniquitous than chimerical was treated with contempt; and the other nations agreed to consider any acts of violence in support of it, as just grounds for making war against the Portuguese'.[9] Thus Vattel agreed substantially with Grotius who had branded Portuguese policy in the East Indies as a violation of the law of nations and an infringement of the rights of other powers including those of the independent Asian communities whom he considered as endowed with statehood and sovereignty.[10]

III.

When the Dutch established themselves in the seventeenth century on the West coast of India,[11] leaving the Portuguese to the possession of Goa only, treaty making between them and the local Rajas aimed at the creation of new monopolies in favour of the Dutch East India Company accompanied by discriminatory stipulations against the Portuguese. The treaty between the Dutch and the Zamorin of Calicut of 1604 contained an express anti-Portuguese provision stating in the preamble that it was negotiated 'with a view to the expulsion of the Portuguese'.[12] The treaty of 1663 between the Dutch East India Company and the Raja of Cochin stipulated that all spices would be delivered to the former and that other European nations would be excluded from the trade. This prohibition was obviously directed against the Portuguese and moreover the treaty contained an express provision prohibiting Portuguese ecclesiastics from residing in Cochin without the permission of the Dutch. The treaty was written in duplicate (in Dutch and Malayalam) and signed by the Raja of Cochin and Admiral van Goens on behalf of the Governor-General of the Dutch East India Company in Batavia.[13]

[7] See the Portuguese–Calicut treaty of 1599 (*Asia and Western Dominance* by K. M. Panikkar, 1954, p. 53). See also *History of Kerala* by K. P. P. Menon, 1929, pp. 130–40.

[8] See the Portuguese–Quilon treaty of 1520 which was concluded on the same lines as earlier treaties (1504 and 1516); see K. P. P. Menon, *op. cit.*, pp. 38–48. See also Barbosa, *op. cit.*

[9] Vattel, *Droit des Gens*, transl. by J. Chitty, 1834, p. 144.

[10] See 'Grotius and India', by C. Alexandrowicz, (ch. 7 above).

[11] In the early seventeenth century any extension of the European possessions from coastal trading stations and forts into the interior of India was impossible in the face of consolidated Mogul power. See: *Geschichte des Portugiesischen Kolonialwesens in Ostindien* by Friedrich Saalfeld, Goettingen, 1810 (Saalfeld was one of the leading international lawyers of the early nineteenth century).

[12] K. M. Panikar, *op. cit.*, p.56.

[13] K. P. P. Menon, *op. cit.*, pp. 92-5.

After having eliminated the Portuguese[14] and the English[15] from the Indonesian Islands, the Dutch Company (with its headquarters in Batavia) established its rule in the second half of the seventeenth century within the local State system in the islands.[16] The mutual relations between the Company and the Indonesian rulers took the shape of protectorates or suzerain–vassal relationships and they were embodied in a number of treaties such as those concluded with the rulers of the Molucquas, Java and Macassar.[17] Among the Dutch–Macassar treaties G. F. Martens mentions *inter alia* the treaty of the 18th November 1667 concluded with the Paduca Siri Sultan Hassan-Oudin, King of Macassar. It contains express discriminatory clauses directed against the Portuguese as well as the English, and deserves more detailed consideration.[18]

According to article VI, the King of Macassar and his ministers and counsellors (the Regency) undertook in pursuance of previous obligations, to expel all Portuguese with their families and retinues (without exception) from all parts of the kingdom wherever they happened to be. The same applied to the English who had had their trading stations in these regions since the visit of Sir James Lancaster. It was also stipulated that none of these foreigners would be admitted to trade in the areas of jurisdiction of the above kingdom and that they could stay no longer than the day fixed in the treaty. The authorities of the kingdom undertook not to admit to its territory any other European nation and this was considered a rule without exception.

Article VII gave all concessions of free trade in the kingdom to the Dutch Company to the exclusion of all other European nations as well as other Indian nations through whom the Europeans were likely to act. In article XXIII the Regency of Macassar undertook to close the country to all other nations. In case it had not enough power to enforce the prohibition, the Dutch East India Company would give the necessary assistance. Article XXVII made a concession to English subjects leaving the kingdom in allowing them to take with them their personal belongings.

The above stipulations were the unequivocal expression of the discriminatory policy adopted by the Dutch against other European nations, particularly the Portuguese and the English. The part played in this policy by the local ruler was no doubt of secondary importance; it remained nevertheless a fact that the Dutch were not content to issue unilateral measures but made the local vassal a party to the prohibitions enforced against other Europeans. This transposition of European power politics from Europe to Asia was gradually to gather momentum.

[14] The Portuguese tended to consolidate their local rule in the Indonesian Island: in the sixteenth century by treaties with local rulers (see K. M. Panikar, *op. cit.*, p. 51). Strictly speaking these Islands belong to the *South-East Asian* region.

[15] Sir James Lancaster had reached Achin in 1602 and presented to the local King a letter from Queen Elisabeth. Though he was unable to obtain a commercial treaty, the King granted important concessions to English traders (see: *The Voyages of Sir James Lancaster* 1591–1603, Hakluyt Society, 1940).

[16] K. M. Panikar, *op. cit.*, p. 59.

[17] *Cours Diplomatique* by G. F. Martens, Berlin 1801.

[18] G. F. Martens *op. cit.*; see: *Corpus Diplomaticum Neerlando-Indicum*, edt. by J. E. Heeres (Vols. I–III) which contains treaties from 1596 to 1691.

The seventeenth century witnessed the elimination of Portuguese rule from Ceylon. The Portuguese had arrived in Ceylon in 1505 and entered into treaties with the local rulers on a footing of suzerain–vassal relations. The 'Vasallo d'El Rei' secured the protection of the Portuguese on the condition of granting trade privileges to them and paying a small annual tribute.[19] The Dutch superseding the Portuguese first concluded the treaty of 1638 with Raja Sinha. According to this treaty the Dutch East India Company 'was promised the delivery of all the cinnamon to the exclusion of all other nations in return for our help and protection'. However the treaty not being later renewed, the Dutch relied as to the former Portuguese possessions on the title of conquest and adopted a unilateral policy of keeping away all other European powers from their territories. This is what Governor C. J. Simons wrote in his memoirs and instructions: 'The chief points which demand attention … are the following viz.: (1) friendly relations with the Court or the King of Kandy; (2) prevention of the intrusion of all other European nations into Ceylon; (3) strict observance and watchful guard over the entire navigation of Ceylon'.[20]

Dutch policy, at first based on bilateral arrangements and later pursued on a non-treaty basis, reverted finally to treaty making. The treaty concluded in 1766 between the States General of the United Provinces and the Dutch East India Company on the one hand and the King of Kandy on the other deserves special attention.[21] In this treaty the spheres of sovereignty of the contracting parties on the Island of Ceylon were mutually defined but the King was cut off from the control of the harbours and waterways and thus forced into isolation from the point of view of overseas relations. According to article X of the treaty the Company undertook to pay for the goods acquired in Ceylon, i.e. ivory, pepper, coffee, etc., and its purchases were to take place to the exclusion of all other nations. This clause was followed by the more specific provision in article XXI which forbade the King and the Officers of the Court to maintain any correspondence with other European nations or to conclude treaties with them, a clause which frequently appeared in treaties between the English East India Company and Indian rulers. The King and the Court undertook to deliver to the Company all Europeans (foreigners) who would enter the country unlawfully and not to entertain with Indian Princes any connexions to the prejudice of the Company. On the other hand, the Company undertook according to article XXII not to conclude any treaty with a foreign power against the king of Kandy. Mutual relations were to be maintained according to article XXIII by the exchange of Ambassadors. Dutch rule in Ceylon lasted until the end of the eighteenth century when it was ousted by the English East India Company in 1796.

Vattel commenting in his Droit des Gens on the above type of monopoly treaties considered them just and commendable if they paid respect to the general interest of mankind. If prices stipulated in mutual arrangements were reasonable, they did

[19] *Ceylon and Portugal* by Pieris-Fitzler, 1927, p. 380.

[20] *Memoirs* by Ryclof van Goens, Cornelis Joan Simons and J. C. Pielat, Colombo, 1910, 1914, 1905.

[21] *Recueil de Traités* par G. Martens, Gottingue, 1817.

not violate in his view the law of nature (nations).[22] In Vattel's own words: 'The Dutch by a treaty with the King of Ceylon have wholly engrossed the cinnamon trade; yet, whilst they keep their profits within just limits, other nations have no right to complain'. But when the necessaries of life were involved, other nations could react against the oppressor.[23] As to the validity of treaties concluded with non-Christians, Vattel observed that 'the law of nature (nations) alone regulates the treaties of nations: the difference of religion is a thing absolutely foreign to them. Different people treat with each other in quality of men and not under the character of Christians, or of Mohammetans....'[24] This is obviously a classic opinion of the eighteenth century which was not shared by many international lawyers of the nineteenth century.

IV.

While the Dutch established their undisputed rule in the Indonesian Islands, from which they eliminated all other European powers, the fight in the Indian sub-continent lasted throughout the eighteenth century to result finally in the hegemony of the English East India Company.[25] A long series of treaties concluded by the Company with Indian rulers included a variety of discriminatory stipulations directed against the French,[26] the Dutch and other Europeans. Though the establishment of a trade monopoly enjoyed high priority in these treaties, many stipulations were also of a political and military character. In the seventeenth century the English East India Company had joined the network of suzerain–vassal relations prevailing all over the Mogul Empire and participated in the eighteenth

22 Vattel also observes that the establishment of monopolies was only possible through the creation of powerful Companies carrying on trade with the East. He writes: 'When the subjects of the United Provinces (of the Netherlands) established themselves in the Indies on the ruin of their enemies, the Portuguese, individual merchants would not have dared to think of such an arduous enterprise; and the State itself, wholly taken up with the defence of its liberty against the Spaniards, had not the means of attempting it'. See *op. cit.*, p. 42.

23 Vattel, *op. cit.*, pp. 144–47. Vattel was evidently more sympathetic to the colonial policy of the Dutch than to that of the Portuguese though the same principles of the law of nations must have applied to both.

24 Vattel, *op. cit.*, p. 195.

25 The English East India Company, at first operating at Surat, sought a commercial treaty with the Mogul Emperor through the mission of Sir Thomas Roe, English Ambassador to the Court of Agra. Though the Emperor was unwilling to sign a treaty, he granted by Firman substantial concessions to the Company which strengthened its position in relation to other European powers in India. The Emperor also refused a treaty to the Portuguese who wanted to exclude the English and the Dutch from trade in the Mogul Dominions. (See: 'Mogul Sovereignty and the Law of Nations' by C. Alexandrowicz, *Indian Year Book of International Affairs*, 1955 (ch. 3 above) and *The Jesuits and the Great Mogul* by Sir Edward Maclagan, 1932.) As to treaties between the East India Company and Indian Rulers, see: *A Collection of Treaties etc.* by C. V. Aitchison, Calcutta, 1909.

26 The French secured at first most favoured nation treatment and a factory at Surat granted to them by Firman by Emperor Aurangzeb in 1666. Later they secured further grants and obtained treaties from other Indian rulers. Treaty making was at its height in the eighteenth century. The alliance between the French East India Company and Tippoo Sultan was directed against the English who finally defeated Tippoo. See: G. F. Martens, *op. cit.*, who refers to French–Indian treaties.

century as one of the land powers in the liquidation of the Empire. Treaty making followed events on the various battlefields and negotiations with Indian rulers in the Carnatic, the Deccan, Bengal, the Bombay area and in the North. While these rulers and the European Companies were the direct participants in the struggle, the Mogul Emperor remained in the background, at best legalising power positions by a posteriori grants of titles to sovereignty.[27] Among these grants the most outstanding was the conferment of the divanee of Bengal, Bihar and Orissa on Robert Clive after the battle of Plassey. Similar grants were also made or refused by the Emperor in the Deccan. Thus when Nabob Salabat Jung, the Subadar of the Deccan granted certain territories (the Northern Sircars) to the French Company, the Mogul Emperor, following the expulsion of the French by the English Company, refused to confirm the grant and conferred the title to these Sircars to the English Company. This transaction was embodied in the Imperial Decree (firman) of the 12th August 1765.[28] Six years earlier Nabob Salabat Jung had concluded an agreement with Colonel Forde acting on behalf of the English Company in which he undertook to 'oblige the French troops which are in his country to pass the river Ganges within fifteen days or send them to Pondicherry (the French possession on the East coast of India) or to any other place out of the Deccan country on the other side of the river Kestna....' He had promised at the same time that he would not suffer the French in the future.[29] This agreement deserves special mention as it is listed by G. F. Martens in his *Cours Diplomatique*.[30]

Military or political stipulations of a discriminatory character against the French and other Europeans can also be found in treaties relating to Bengal. G. F. Martens records the treaty between the English East India Company and Meer Jaffier Ally Khan on their reinstating him in the Nabobship of Bengal, dated the 10th July 1763.[31] The treaty was signed on behalf of the Company by Henry Vansittart, John Carnac, William Billiers, Warren Hastings and others. The Nabob stated *inter alia* as follows: 'If the French come into the country, I will not allow them to erect any fortifications, maintain forces, hold lands, zemindaries, etc., but they should pay tribute and carry on their trade as in former times'. G. F. Martens also records the treaty of the 25th February 1765 concluded between the English Company and Najim al Dowlah on their investing him with the Nabobship of Bengal upon the death of his father Meer Jaffier Ally Khan.[32] In this treaty the Nabob undertook new obligations in the following terms: 'I will allow no Europeans whatever to be entertained in my service; and if there already be any, they shall be immediately dismissed.... If the French come into my country, I will not allow them to erect any fortifications, maintain forces....' It is clear from these and other stipulations that

[27] C. Alexandrowicz *ut supra*.

[28] *Treaties and Grants from the Country Powers to the East India Company etc. from* 1756 *to* 1772; printed in 1774; No. IV.

[29] *Treaties and Grants, op. cit.*, No. I.

[30] G. F. Martens, *op. cit.*

[31] G. F. Martens, *op. cit.*, and *Considerations on India Affairs* (Bengal) by William Bolts, London, 1772, No. X.

[32] G. F. Martens, *op. cit.*, and W. Bolts, *op. cit.*, No. XV.

the Anglo–French conflict in Bengal, the Deccan and elsewhere was not confined to military and political manoeuvering but also found expression in treaty provisions of a discriminatory character. As we have seen, these provisions embodied the obligation of the local ruler to expel French military forces from his territory and French nationals from his service. They contained also the particular servitude of not allowing the erection of fortifications by the French and limitations on their trade activities.

Some of the Anglo–Mahratta treaties show the use of similar discriminatory stipulations, particularly directed against the Dutch. In one of these treaties signed at Poona on the 12th October 1756[33] the Mahratta Government undertook never to permit 'the Dutch to settle or come into their Dominions but on the contrary (to) issue express orders to prevent their carrying on any trade therein' (article I). In article XI of the same treaty it was stipulated that 'Dutch goods will not be permitted to be landed at Rajahpore, nor their trade suffered to be carried on there, concerning which the Mahrattas will give proper orders....' This treaty is recorded by G. F. Martens in his *Cours Diplomatique*.

On the 17th May 1782 a treaty of perpetual friendship and alliance was signed between the English East India Company and the Peshwa Madhoo Row Pundit Purdhan.[34] On behalf of the Company acted Mr. David Anderson on the basis of powers delegated by the Governor-General and Council. For the Mahrattas acted Maha Rajah Subadar Madhoo Row Sindia as plenipotentiary of the Peshwa Ballajee Pundit Nana (Furnavese) and the whole of the chiefs of the Mahratta nation binding their heirs and successors. In article XIII of the treaty the Peshwa stated that he 'will not suffer any factories of other European nations to be established ... (except those already established by the Portuguese) ... and he will hold no intercourse of friendship with any other European nations'. According to article XVI Sindia was to guarantee the adherence of both contracting parties to the alliance. The above is a multilateral treaty which differs from the usual type of bilateral treaty discussed above. Apart from discriminatory provisions extending to the commercial, political and military spheres, it contains an exemption from discriminatory treatment on behalf of the Portuguese. This obviously reflected the friendly relations between the English East India Company and the Portuguese who apart from Goa and minor enclaves had meanwhile lost most of their possessions in India and elsewhere in South Asia.

The question arises what is the meaning of the provision of article XIII excluding all friendly intercourse between the Mahrattas and other European nations, a provision similar to that in article XXI of the Dutch–Ceylon treaty of 1766 and in other treaties (see below). If such a provision be viewed in the light of legal classifications as adopted by the classic writers of the eighteenth century, it might be considered as the expression of an unequal alliance impairing the sovereignty of one

[33] *Treaties and Grants*, *op. cit.*, pp. 170 *et seq.* No. I; see also G. F. Martens, *op. cit.*

[34] *Collection* of *Treaties between Great Britain and other Powers* by George Chalmers, London, 1780, Vol. II, pp. 517 *et seq.* See also G. F. Martens, *op. cit.*

of the contracting parties. Vattel distinguishes equal treaties connected with equality of promises and equal alliances with no difference in the dignity of the parties. An unequal treaty, on the other hand, would be one without equivalent promises and an unequal alliance would be concluded by parties with differences in status. According to Vattel unequal alliances could be further divided into those which impair or do not impair the sovereignty of one of the parties. For instance an obligation not to go to war *against a certain nation* would not impair the sovereignty of the party concerned but an obligation not to go to war *against all other nations* would do so as it would stifle the external sovereignty of the particular State.[35] Can the obligation not to maintain intercourse with other European nations, as found in the treaties discussed above, be construed, by analogy, as impairing the sovereignty of the Asian contracting party? The question is of considerable importance, as the answer to it reflects on the legal position of many Asian powers at that period. If Vattel and other authoritative writers are consulted on the point, it does not seem that a stipulation limiting external sovereignty in relation to a specified nation or group of nations only such as 'other' European nations, could reduce a particular treaty or alliance to a level of inequality impairing the sovereign status of one of the parties in the eyes of the law of nations and within the family of nations.[36] At least this is the position if judged by European standards and thus we must come to the conclusion that in spite of all the above treaty limitations the Asian powers in question, who lost their sovereignty in the *nineteenth* century, must in principle be considered sovereign according to the *eighteenth* century rules of the law of nations.

One more problem seems of interest from the legal point of view. The Mahratta rulers made it clear in the treaty under discussion that they were binding their heirs and successors. Had they not done so, the presumption might have been that the treaty was a *personal* one, the prohibiting stipulation being of an odious nature. The express provision binding the heirs and successors of the contracting party allows the classification of the treaty as a *real* one.[37]

As to arrangements between the English East India Company and the rulers of the West coast of India and the neighbouring areas, a number of them contain anti-European discriminatory provisions. In the 'Articles of the Firmaund' granted by the Bringab Rajah in 1758[38] to the Company, the Rajah stated in article II as follows: 'Whatever pepper belongs to me, or is produced in my dominions as Rajah of Bringab, I secure unto you, and will not sell it to any one else, but you shall buy it at the general price settled with the other merchants ...'. The Rajah undertook to oblige the merchants to deliver the pepper at the price settled with them. This type of treaty would according to Vattel's classification establish a monopoly valid in the eyes of the law of nations as it stipulates equitable prices.

[35] Vattel, *op. cit.*, p. 199 seq.

[36] Vattel, *op. cit.* See also Christian Wolff: *Jus Gentium* (transl. by J. Drake) 1934, pp. 395–400 (*Classics of International Law*). See: *Statham v. Statham*, (1912) L. R. 1912 p. 92 at p. 96.

[37] Vattel, *op. cit.*, p. 204. Already A. Gentili considered treaties as binding the heirs and successors of the contracting parties; see: *A Concise History of the Law of Nations*, by A. Nussbaum, 1954, p. 96.

[38] *Treaties and Grants, op. cit.*, No. III seq.

The articles of agreement with the King of Cotiote dated the 23rd August 1759 constitute a commercial as well as a military treaty arrangement.[39] Article IV states that 'for the better preservation of the friendship subsisting between the Company and the King, and for the freedom of their commerce in his dominions, the King promises not to suffer any European nation but them to purchase pepper, cardamoms or sandalwood therein....' So far the commercial provisions. Articles I and VII create a defensive as well as an offensive alliance. According to article I, in case of attack of the French or of any other power on the Company, the King promised to give military assistance to the Company. Article VII states that if the Company proceeds against any of the French fortifications, the King engages not to assist them (the French) in any shape and 'obliges himself to act in conjunction with the Company offensively against them whenever they may think proper'. The lawfulness of an offensive alliance, if not concluded for the purpose of securing peace, may be considered doubtful from the legal point of view.

A royal grant by King Baddacalamcur, regent of Calastria, to the English Company, dated the 9th September 1760,[40] contained a discriminatory provision of a commercial character directed particularly against the Dutch. Article II permitted all pepper to be bought by the Company, stating that 'in order the more firmly to establish this privilege unto them, and especially to prevent the Dutch or any one else purchasing the pepper of Rhandoterrah ...', the above grant was decreed.

The agreement with Sheik Sadoon of Bushire dated 12th April 1763[41] stated in article III that 'no European nation whatever is to be permitted to settle at Bushire so long as the English continue a factory here'. A firman granted by Nabob Hyder Ally Khan Bahauder in 1763 gave the English Company the liberty to build a factory at Quorem (article I) and the sole liberty to purchase all pepper adding: 'Nor shall any European or other nation besides them have leave to purchase pepper within these districts'. These privileges granted to the Company by firman were confirmed in 1770 in a formal treaty of peace between the Hon. Thomas Hodges, President and Governor and the Council of Bombay on behalf of the Company and Nabob Hyder Ally.[42] It was stipulated in article XII of the treaty that no new firman will be granted to any European nation and no new settlement given to any of them. The English Company was to have trade and business preference and the English were to take rank of all other European nations and country powers.

Before concluding the discussion of particular treaties, one more type of stipulation deserves attention. The royal grant from Carem Khan, the Chief Governor of all the Kingdom of Persia, to William Andrew Price, Governor-General for the English nation in 'the gulph of Persia', issued in 1763,[43] contains the following provision: 'No other European nation or other person shall import any woollen goods to any part on the Persian shore in the gulph but the English Company only....' In distinction to the stipulations contained in treaties which are mostly

[39] *Treaties and Grants, op. cit.*, No. VII.

[40] *Treaties and Grants, op. cit.*, No. IX.

[41] *Treaties and Grants, op. cit.*, No. XV.

[42] *Treaties and Grants, op. cit.*, No. XXII. See also G. F. Martens, *op. cit.*

[43] *Treaties and Grants, op. cit.*, No. XVII.

concerned with the purchase and export of spices, this provision secured also an import monopoly to the English Company.

V.

We have seen that the treaties under discussion contained discriminatory provisions of different types.[44] Among them monopolistic provisions relating to the right of exclusive purchase by one European power or agency of spices and other goods at fixed prices to the exclusion of other European powers or agencies, date from the early sixteenth century and can be found in treaties throughout the seventeenth and eighteenth centuries. As long as the prices stipulated by the contracting parties were equitable and the monopoly itself was not odious to other nations, the treaties seemed to have been valid in the eyes of the law of nations. However, Grotius, Vattel and other writers expressed their reservations regarding monopoly techniques adopted by the Portuguese and the same reservations must apply to other powers and agencies using illegal methods.

Indian and other South Asian rulers who appear in these treaties as the sellers or guarantors of sales in the market, also granted to the contracting European power or agency other individual benefits coupled with discriminations against other European nationalities. The relevant discriminatory clauses contain provisions by which the European contracting party secured the expulsion of other European nationals from the territory or service of a particular local ruler. To the same category belong provisions prohibiting foreigners, not being nationals of the contracting European power, from entering the territory of the contracting ruler. These provisions which sometimes extended to the closure of frontiers and harbours to foreigners and to prohibition of free navigation, tended to isolate the ruler and his community from commercial and other intercourse with European countries, each ruler being confined to exclusive relations with one of them, with whom he signed a particular treaty. They also tended to deprive the local ruler of military and other

[44] Discriminatory provisions are also not infrequent in early nineteenth century treaties. See for instance the treaty with the Nizam, Soubadar of the Deccan of the 12th October 1800 in which the Nizam engaged 'neither to commence nor to pursue, in future, any negotiations with any other Power whatever, without giving previous notice, and entering into mutual consultation with the Honourable East India Company's Government....' (article XV). See also treaty with the Peishwah (treaty of Bassein) of the 31st October 1802 in which the Peishwah undertook to expel all Europeans in case of war between the English and any European nation (article XI); this treaty contains also a clause (article XV) similar to article XV of the treaty with the Nizam; a similar clause (article XVII) is also contained in the treaty with the Peishwah of the 31st December 1802; see also treaty with Dowlut Rao Scindia of the 30th December 1803 in which Scindia engaged 'never to take or retain in his service any Frenchman or the subject of any other European or American Power the Government of which may be at war with the British Government.... ' (article XIII); also the treaty with the Raja of Travancore of the 21st January 1805 contains a stipulation limiting his external sovereignty (article VII).

These few instances are taken from a *Collection of Treaties* issued at East India House on the 2nd August 1824 and from *Papers respecting the Pindarry and Mahratta Wars* published on the 3rd March 1824 (London).

technical assistance by which one European power might have supported the ruler against another European rival. Special mention deserve the provisions imposing on a ruler the obligation to remove from his territory troops of foreign European powers or the prohibition to build fortifications. The latter might have contained the elements of an international servitude.[45]

The above limitations imposed on rulers in the Indian subcontinent, Ceylon, the Indonesian Islands or elsewhere obviously reflected on their sovereign status. Most of them sunk gradually to the level of vassals, but the speed of this process was not uniform in all regions. The Dutch reduced the local rulers in the Indonesian Islands from the very beginning to dependence with deprivation of external sovereignty. This development was slower in Ceylon and in the Indian sub-continent.[46] The European Companies in India which exercised extensive rights of sovereignty, were themselves initially in a vassal-like position and it was only after the breakdown of Mogul suzerainty that they started freely to compete with other local powers for hegemony in the sub-continent. The English East India Company tackled one by one the most important local powers such as the Nawabs of Bengal, the rulers of the Deccan and the Carnatic, the rulers of Mysore[47] and the West coast, the Mahrattas and others. Treaty making was part of the perplexing picture of political and military manoeuvering and formalised the consecutive power positions. It is in the process of taking stock after a cease fire or truce that a legal stamp was usually put on a temporary balance of power. Whenever the Company managed to eliminate French or Dutch influence in India and to weaken one or the other of the local powers, it imposed on the latter the obligation to restrict intercourse with other European agencies. Prohibitory provisions directed against them meant abstention from treaty making and external correspondence, and from diplomatic, commercial or military transactions on an independent basis. However, in the light of principles of the law of nations applicable to inter-State intercourse at that period, the severing of relations with a particular power or even group of powers, such as for instance the European powers only, could not yet be considered as the suppression of external sovereignty. We have quoted in this respect the views of Vattel and other writers of the eighteenth century. The views of G. F. Martens, from whose *Cours Diplomatique*[48] a number of Asian treaties have been quoted and who introduced these treaties into the general volume of treaty law supporting

[45] See also the Portuguese–Mahratta treaty of Punem (1779) which gains importance in the recent conflict over Goa.

[46] Other rulers such as the Kings of Burma preserved their independence much longer and avoided the early imposition of a discriminatory policy though they might have granted preferential treatment to one of the European powers or agencies: see *Michael Symes* (*Journal of his second Embassy to the Court of Ava in* 1802) ed. with Introduction and Notes by D. G. E. Hall, 1955.

[47] See for instance Subsidiary Treaty with the Raja of Mysore concluded on the 8th July 1799 for effecting the settlement of the territories of the late Tippoo Sultan. In this treaty the Raja undertook not to communicate or correspond '*with any Foreign State*' without the previous knowledge and sanction of the English East India Company (article VI). This type of provision meant *complete* suppression of external sovereignty characteristic of nineteenth century treaties in India. (See *Treaties and Engagements etc.*, East India House, 1824.)

[48] G. F. Martens *op. cit.*

the positivist conception of the law of nations, may be particularly emphasised.[49] In many instances of State practice in Europe, limitations of sovereignty were imposed by one European power on another without depriving the latter of the legal status of a sovereign State within the universal family of nations. The Mahratta Confederation struggled in the same way as the Kingdom of Poland for the preservation of independence at the end of the eighteenth century. The *de facto* decline of their power of resistance did not mean that they did not fight to the last as bearers of sovereign authority in defence of their national honour. Whether their fate was sealed by conquest, treaty, or otherwise, they could at least, be presumed not to have fought in a legal vacuum[50] if the law of nations was allowed to formalise the multitude of inter-State relations irrespective of religion or civilisation and to preserve in the flow of events the legal continuity of the changing world order.

[49] See also *A Compendium of the Law of Nations founded on Treaties and Customs of the Modern Nations of Europe* by G. F. von Martens (transl. by William Cobbett), London, 1802; see particularly the List of the Principal Treaties and other Public Acts from 1731 to 1832 which contains a number of Asian treaties, pp. 381, 397, 398, 434, 438, 410, 415, 416, 423, 428, 432, 434, etc.

[50] C. L. Tupper (*Our Indian Protectorates* 1893) expressed the isolated view that 'the theory of the Maharattas was as incompatible with the principles of International Law as was the theory of the *First Napoleon*'. But no historian of International Law would agree with his views on Napoleon and the deficiency of the legal analogy must reflect on the status of Asian rulers. Neither was his view shared by a number of leading British statesmen including Burke who regarded the law of nations as the law of India as well as of Europe (see pp. 3 and 37).

10

A PERSIAN–DUTCH TREATY IN THE SEVENTEENTH CENTURY (1958)

It is generally believed that commercial treaties between European and Asian powers prior to the nineteenth century related exclusively to the establishments and the privileges of European traders in Asia. This rule however is not without exception and we find examples of establishments of Asian traders in Europe who significantly enough received the same type of benefits as those enjoyed by European traders in Asia. One of the most characteristic examples is contained in a treaty concluded on the 7th February 1631 at The Hague between the King of Persia and the States General of the United Provinces of the Netherlands in which the latter in return for privileges accorded to the Dutch in Persia conceded reciprocal benefits to Persian traders in the Netherlands.[1]

In this treaty the States General guaranteed safe conduct to Persian nationals who arrived in the Netherlands from Persia, whether in an official or private capacity, which allowed them to enter and leave the country, to move about and to purchase and sell goods and merchandise without exception in all places and towns. This permission also extended to dependent territories.[2]

In terms of International Law the treaty secured national treatment to Persians, granting them the same franchises and rights as those enjoyed by the inhabitants of the Netherlands, even by persons of quality in high positions whenever they engaged in trade.[3]

If Persian nationals carried on small scale transactions (purchases and sales) in their private houses, they were allowed to use their own weights and measures. However, if these transactions were wholesale purchases and sales they had to follow the weights and measures regime of the country so as to protect the purchaser or seller from any possible harm or wrong.[4]

The treaty further stipulated that as soon as there would be a sufficient number of Persian traders in the Netherlands equipped with adequate capital, they would be assigned proper habitations and would enjoy certain exemptions from duties in relation to consumer goods used in their homes.[5] Proper habitations were also to

[1] Dumont: *Corps Universel Diplomatique du Droit des Gens*, Amsterdam—The Hague 1731. This treaty was made at the Assembly of the States General at The Hague by order of the Lords of the States General.

[2] Article I. [3] Article II. [4] Article III. [5] Article V.

be assigned to those commissioned by the King of Persia to represent the Persian nation in the Netherlands and to head the trading community.[6] They were also to enjoy the same exemptions as the traders. The treaty singled out the Agent of H.M. the King of Persia whose house was to enjoy special immunities, particularly the same privileges which were granted to the houses of Agents of European Kings and Princes who resided at the Court of the States General.[7]

The Persian community in the Netherlands was also allowed to establish a bureau (comptoir or factory) staffed by its own people and equipped with funds, and Persian nationals were to enjoy, in respect of trade and administration of justice, the same rights, advantages and prerogatives which were enjoyed by the English (*la Cour Angloise*) who resided in the town of Delft, and by Scottish nationals who resided in the town of Campveere. The treaty stated in connection with the above that the States General had, of old, commercial treaties and intercourse with the Kings of England and Scotland.[8]

The treaty ensured to the Persian Agent jurisdiction over his own nationals (personal jurisdiction) and moreover stated that if any of his nationals should rise against him, oppose him and commit an offence, the Court of the locality where the offence had been committed would give assistance to the Agent and the administration of justice would be assured according to the exigencies of each case.[9]

Further provisions of the treaty related to religious affairs; particularly they guaranteed free exercise of religion to the Persian community in their homes and nobody was allowed to interfere with their religious practices.[10] If a Persian national intended or desired to change his religion, the States General were not to give him encouragement.[11] The adoption of the Christian faith would have certainly meant the abandonment of the community which must have lived a compact and homogeneous life. The above provision tended to ban proselytising and missionary activities which were initiated by European communities in Asia. The treaty provided that in case of change of religion the King of Persia or the person who had in his hands the property of the convert would not deprive him of ownership or possession, but would only take action in respect of the administration of the property.[12]

The treaty also provided for a place of burial for Persian nationals in which they were to bury their dead according to their custom.[13] If a Persian national died without relative or friend near him who could take care of the merchandise, whether his own or belonging to the King of Persia, the local authorities were to see to it that the merchandise would be inventoried and stored until the King or the relatives of the deceased were able to make proper arrangements.[14] The treaty made special provisions for consumable or perishable goods the proceeds of which were to be credited to the account of the King or the successors of the deceased as the case might be.[15]

In summing up the above arrangements it may be relevant to note that they were to some extent similar to arrangements made at that period on behalf of

[6] Article V. [7] Article VI. [8] Article VI. [9] Article X. [10] Article VII.
[11] Article VIII. [12] Article IX. [13] Article VIII. [14] Article VIII.
[15] Article IV.

European traders in Asia. The treaty in question accorded to Asian traders in the Netherlands, particularly in Amsterdam, national treatment in the same way as did some of the Asian rulers to European traders, be it in India, Ceylon, in the Indonesian islands or elsewhere, but of course not in China or Japan whose frontiers remained, with minor exceptions (Canton), closed to foreign traders until they were opened by force in the nineteenth century. Moreover, the treaty of 1631 accorded most-favoured-nation treatment to traders as well as to the official heads of the community and to the Agent of the King of Persia. The above treatment excluded any discrimination between European countries and the Asian contrahent and automatically applied to Persians the benefits given to the English and the Scottish. The Royal Persian Agent enjoyed diplomatic privileges and although he had not the character of a diplomatic envoy in the full sense of the word and was rather a kind of trade commissioner or consul (to use our diplomatic language), he was nevertheless a permanent representative which shows that diplomatic or consular exchanges between Asia and Europe were not confined to *ad hoc* relations.

It would be appropriate to recall that the first and most outstanding example of a fully fledged ambassador sent from Europe to Asia was that of Sir Thomas Roe who represented the English Court at the Imperial Moghul Court in Agra (1615–19). His position was of a dual nature as he was at the same time H.M. Ambassador as well as a servant of the English East India Company. Though he was an ambassador *sensu stricto* his main business as shown by the purpose of his mission was to obtain a commercial treaty for the Company. It would perhaps be fair to say that he was neither a permanent nor a temporary envoy as he was not accredited until revocation but went to the Moghul Court with a specified task; nevertheless his presence in Agra for a prolonged period gave him the status of more than a purely *ad hoc* envoy.[16]

[16] See: 'Mogul Sovereignty and the Law of Nations', by C. H. Alexandrowicz, *India Year Book of International Affairs* 1955 (ch. 3 above). It is also noteworthy that Persian diplomatic practice played at that time the same rôle in certain parts of Asia as French practice played in Europe. When Sir Thomas Roe landed in Surat, he expected to be treated by the Mogul Governor with all the respect due to an Ambassador according to the law of nations; in his own words: 'That I doubted not he, being born a Persian understood the right due unto me ...'. Again, at the Mogul Court the *tertium comparationis* of privileges accorded to the Ambassador was found in Persian diplomatic usages and Persian (similarly to Latin in Europe) was the language of inter-State negotiations. Sir Thomas Roe's mission extended also to Persia and while being in India he wrote to the King of Persia in the matter of Spanish–Persian trade relations and opened negotiations with the Persian Ambassador in Agra. The latter referred *inter alia* to his acquaintance with Sir Robert Shirley, an Englishman who was together with his brother (Sir Anthony Shirley) in the service of the Court of Ispahan and was sent to England as Persian Ambassador in 1624. This Court became, at that time, the centre of diplomatic activity, Persia being in conflict with the Turkish Empire and therefore a potential ally to some of the European Powers. Thevenot who passed at that period through Persia mentions the visits of the Ambassadors of the Duke of Holstein, of Muscovy and of the Mogul Emperor, all testifying to the importance of Ispahan as a centre of negotiations (See: *The Embassy of Sir Thomas Roe to India*. Ed. by Sir W. Foster, 1926, pp. 35, 42, 87, 98, 114, 227; *Travels of Monsieur de Thevenot*, London, 1687, p. 104).

These remarks of a comparative nature may be useful to assess the position of an Asian envoy or agent to a European country in the early seventeenth century. The Royal Persian Agent in the Netherlands seems to have been a fairly permanent official and from the point of view of prestige and immunity his position was comparable to that of certain envoys or agents from England and Scotland, countries endowed at that period with sovereignty as complete as that of France or Spain and certainly with more than any of the countries or dependencies which came under the sway of the Holy Roman Empire.

One more characteristic feature of the Persian community in the Netherlands is the establishment of a bureau which in conjunction with their houses and trading activities presents the same picture as the trading factories of the Europeans in the East. The latter as well as the former were given certain privileges of the type known as capitulations. They allowed the foreign trading community to follow in many respects their own law and gave to their Consul or Agent personal jurisdiction over their nationals which amounted to a significant exception from the jurisdiction of the territorial sovereign. It would perhaps not be unjustified to state that the development of pre-capitulation immunities which were a common feature of foreign trade relations in Asia prior to the arrival of Europeans originated to a great extent from State practice in Asia and constituted a contribution of the customary law of nations as known in Asia to the general law of nations as finally defined in Europe. In this connection mention should also be made of the numerous capitulation treaties made by the Turkish Empire long before its so-called admission to the Concert of Europe in 1856. A survey of ancient treaty stipulations granting privileges to foreign trading communities and exempting them partially from territorial jurisdiction shows none of the flavour of the 'capitulation' which became later derogatory to the prestige of the grantor. It was simply an arrangement between two countries much in the interest of the grantee but accorded by the grantor as a matter of customary privilege which he would expect for his own traders abroad. This was exactly the position in relation to Persian traders in a European country. We have seen from some of the stipulations that the Netherlands which had already at that time a certain experience of dealings with Asian countries, guaranteed capitulations to Persian nationals as a matter of course without considering this privilege as a diminution of their sovereignty. It is quite obvious that the idea of discrimination and of treating capitulations as something damaging to the sovereignty of the grantor State appeared much later when the law of nations by some ideological cataclysm ceased to be the universal law of all nations under which States in all Continents could enjoy equal rights with other nations provided they had achieved Statehood and the necessary degree of civilisation.

Finally it may be noted that the execution of this treaty in practice must have been highly satisfactory as shown by the existence of a flourishing Persian community in Amsterdam at the end of the eighteenth century. To trace its history is not the task of the historian of International Law but we may rely on the testimony of one of the greatest international lawyers of all time, G. F. de Martens, who referred to the Dutch–Persian treaty of 1631 in his *Cours Diplomatique* in which he devoted considerable space to Asian treaties whether concluded with Persia, India, Siam, or other countries. This is what he writes about the treaty, the circumstances of its conclusion and its execution:

La capitulation de 1631 par laquelle en revanche des privileges accordés aux Hollandais en Perse la République accorda aux Persans en Hollande la liberté d'entrer, de commerce, de culte etc. dont ... jusqu'à ce jour les Armeniens et les Persans jouissent à Amsterdam.[17]

[17] Thus Martens testifies at the end of the eighteenth century to the continuous existence of the privileges accorded to Persians and Armenians in Amsterdam. (See: *Cours Diplomatique*, Berlin 1801, Vol. III, p. 342).

11

PUFFENDORF–CRULL AND THE AFRO–ASIAN WORLD (1968–69)

Samuel Puffendorf (1632–94) who, like Grotius, was for some time a member of the Swedish diplomatic service and later became professor at the Universities of Heidelberg and Lund, completed his main work on the *Law of Nature and Nations* in 1672. Ten years later he brought out the first volume of the *Introduction to the History of the Principal States of Europe* and further volumes (II–III) appeared in the next few years.[1] This impressive treatise on European affairs was later extended to other continents constituting an *Introduction to the History of Asia, Africa and America*. The full title of this volume in German is: 'Einleitung zu der Historie der vornehmsten Reiche und Staaten von Asia, Africa und America welche nach dessen Methode ein gelehrter Engelländer kürtzlich abgehandelt und beschrieben. Anjetzo aus dem Englischen ins Hoch-Teutsche übersetzt'.[2]

The title would seem to indicate that the volume on the history of the Afro–Asian world (with an extension to the American continent) was written by an English author and was only later translated into German, becoming Part IV of Puffendorf's world history. The translator states, however, that the author had followed Puffendorf's method of writing history. Puffendorf had treated his subject not only from the point of view of general history but also from the point of view of the theory of the State and inter-State relations. The translator admits that he does not know who wrote the original text of volume IV but he believes that it was Jodocus Crull.[3] National biographical inquiry has in fact referred to the authorship of Crull[4] and a few words about him would be relevant in throwing some light on

[1] *Allgemeine Deutsche Biographie* (1888), vol. 26, p. 705. According to this Biography volumes III and IV are a continuation of the work, added by other authors.

[2] The dates of the various volumes extend from 1730 to 1733 (Brit. Mus. Library).

[3] Preface to vol. IV, p. 173. Another edition of this volume (publ. in Frankfurt in 1706, see National Library in Vienna) contains a preface by the translator who refers to J. Crull in the following words: 'Was das Absehen dieses Werkes sey ... erhellet gleich aus der ersten Seite dieses Buches; Wer aber der Autor welcher es verfertigt kan ich nicht gewiß sagen maßen es demselben nicht gefallen seinen Nahmen beyzufügen; muthmaße aber daß es eben der jenige seyn möchte welcher die Einleitung zu der Historie von Europa so weyland Herr Samuel Freyherr von Puffendorf heraus gegeben in Englischer Sprache continuiret hat und sich J. Crull nennet. Es ist aber selbiges Werck so wohl als dieses erstlich vor einem Jahre oder anderthalb nehmlich zu Ende des 1705ten Jahrs ans Licht gekommen. Den Fleiß welchen der Autor bey demselben angewendet wirstu aus dem Wercke selbst beurtheilen können; die Ordnung aber die er darin gehalten aus beygefügter Vorrede also fort sehen'.

[4] *Dictionary of National Biography* (J. Crull).

this partnership in history writing. This is particularly of interest to historians of the family and law of nations, as we are here faced with the first work on the history of universal inter-State relations covering all continents, civilizations and various types of State formation, making its appearance within the framework of Puffendorf's treatise.

Jodocus Crull was a native of Hamburg. Neither the date of his birth nor the date of his death is exactly known.[5] But it seems certain that he went as a student from Hamburg to the Netherlands and obtained in 1679 a Doctorate of Medicine at the University of Leyden. The *Biographical Dictionary of Hamburg Writers* (edited by Hans Schroeder) refers to his medical dissertation (Theod. Craanen, Lugd. Bat. 1679, 4) and states that he died as a medical student in the Netherlands.[6] However, this information is not correct. We know that he came to England and took in 1681 the degree of Doctor of Medicine at the University of Cambridge.[7] He was elected in the same year a Fellow of the Royal Society and eleven years later became a licentiate of the College of Physicians (1692). His English biographer states, however, that he had little success in medical practice and took to writing in a field remote from medical science, namely history and overseas exploration.[8] Our attention is drawn to translations which he made for some publishers in England. It is here that his interest in Asia appears first. His translation of Dellon's *Voyage to the East Indies* (from the French) appeared in London in 1698.

In the Preface to this work Jodocus Crull addressed the following words to Samuel Sheppard, Sheriff-elect for the City of London and County of Middlesex:

Sir, when I saw so considerable a part of the Nation joined in the design of settling the East India Trade upon a new Foundation, I thought I could scarce pitch upon a more seasonable juncture than this, to make my author(s) appear in England, to give us an account of their ten Years Transactions, among some Nations, where in all probability our Indian Trade is to be carried on to the Honour and Advantage of the English Nation. I will not pretend to enlarge myself here upon the usefulness of Commerce in General, or of that of the Indies in Particular; if the station I am in did not excuse me from undertaking that task, the *universal consent of all civilised Nations*, who look upon traffick as one of the main Pillars of the prosperity of the Common Wealth, is a demonstration sufficient to over-balance any thing that can be said upon so ample a subject by a private hand. And as to what relates to the Indian Trade in particular, our Neighbours the Dutch, who have made it the foundation stone of the present flourishing state of their Common Wealth, are living instances, to convince us what improvements may be made in this kind, if managed by a dextrous hand. I might in this place have made some Reflections, perhaps not altogether useless upon the present condition of some of the Indian Countries, especially upon those on the Coast of Malabar who being divided into so many … Principalities, and for the most part situated very convenient

[5] It is probable that J. Crull died about 1712 or 1713; *Notes and Queries*, 6th series, vol. III, p. 231.

[6] Dr. Hans Schroeder (editor), *Lexikon der Hamburger Schriftsteller bis zur Gegenwart* (1851), No. 688, p. 608. It may be that J. Crull was of Dutch origin.

[7] *Graduati Cantabrigienses* (1823), p. 125 (M.D. *per Literas Regias*, 1681).

[8] *Dictionary of National Biography* (J. Crull).

for Traffick, *seem to invite us to be sharers* with them in the vast advantages the East Indian Trade affords....[9]

Jodocus Crull then speaks about the arrival of the Indian travellers in England and he recommends them to the Sheriff. He makes a reference to the English East-India Company and its activities in the East. This Preface is signed: 'J.C. Med.D'. It is quite clear that Crull had taken an active interest in the East Indies and the idea of continuation (or translation) of Puffendorf's work must have taken shape, leading to arrangements with London publishers.[10]

The author explains in the Preface to volume IV some of the details of his research into Afro–Asian history. Among the sources were not only some of the existing treatises on Asian, African or American history, but also memoirs of travellers and accounts published in newspapers.[11] What strikes the reader above all is the masterly classification of the material and the choice of events which were important to historians and to students of the law of nations. The work is divided into three main parts (Asia, Africa, America),[12] of which the most important is the part devoted to the East Indies. The most interesting section in this part is the description of diplomatic activity and treaty-making which reflected the progress of the Christian–Islamic struggle. Thus the author writes about the sixteenth-century embassies sent by the Shah of Persia to Europe in order to cement an alliance against the Ottoman Empire. In particular the Embassy of Shah Abbas to Emperor Rudolph in Prague is singled out (we know that it was led by an Englishman in Persian service, Sir Anthony Shirley).[13] Other notable diplomatic missions were those sent by Persia to France (e.g. the Embassy of Mehemet Riza Beck in 1715) and the Turkish Embassies to European capitals,[14] sent whenever

[9] Italics are mine. Among other translations by J. Crull are Puffendorf's *Of the Nature and Qualification of Religion in reference to Civil Society* (1698); Puffendorf's *Introduction* (1699, 1702, 1706, 1719); J. Bouvet's *The Present Condition of the Muscovite Empire ... with the Life of the Present Emperour of China* (1699). Crull's other publications include works about Russia and Denmark and Westminster Abbey. See *Dictionary of National Biography and National Library* (Vienna M. 18367, 18374, 18375).

[10] The Cambridge University Library has the sixth edition of the *History of the Kingdom and States of Asia, Africa and America, both Ancient and Modern*. This volume was printed by James, John and Paul Knapton at the Crown in Ludgate St. in 1736. The writer of the Preface to this edition refers to Puffendorf's *History of Europe* and adds: 'The design of the present Undertaking, how far soever it may fall short of the other's excellency, is to do the same in respect to the Histories of Asia, Africa and America so far as the circumstances of things and revolutions of time would possibly allow it'.

[11] Among the works quoted are: *Rerum Persicarum Historia* by Bizarus; *Le Grand théâtre historique ou nouvelle histoire universelle tant sacrée que profane* (Leyden, 1703); and the *Travels of Thevenot and Tavernier as well as the Account of Japan and Formosa* by George Psalmanaazaar who was born in the East 'aber allhier in England sich befindet' (copy in the National Library, Vienna, Preface).

[12] Part I (Asia) contains thirteen chapters: Jewish History (I), the Assyrian Monarchy, Babylon (II), the Empire of the Medes, Cyrus (III), the Persian Empire (IV), China (V), Japan and Formosa (VI), Tartary, Chingis Chan (VII), the Mogul Empire (VIII), the Kingdom of Syria (IX), Troy, Lydia and Pergamos (X), the Turkish Empire, Cyprus (XI), the Kings of Edom (XII), Arabia, the Caliphs (XIII); Part II (Africa) contains six chapters: Egypt (I), the Commonwealth of Carthage (II), the Cheriffs of Africa, Fez, Morocco (III), the Kingdom of Numidia, Lybia, Mauretania (IV), Tunis (V) and Ethiopia, Guinea (VI); Part III (America) contains two chapters: Mexico (I) and the Incas of Peru (II).

[13] *Introduction to the History of Asia, Africa and America*, vol. IV, p. 352.

[14] e.g. to France (1715) or to Vienna (1719/20), ibid., p. 610.

the Court in Constantinople exceptionally decided to make use of the active right of legation which at first was considered irreconcilable with the tradition of the great Asian Empires. The Embassy of Sir William Norris to the Mogul Emperor Aurangzeb (1701) is mentioned and the author emphasizes some of the objectives of this embassy, i.e. to give support to the newly created English East-India Company which was to replace the former Company.[15] The author refers to the isolationist policy of China and Japan but he does not fail to mention the role of the Jesuit-astronomers at the Court of Peking and the mission of St. Francis Xavier, the Apostle of Japan in the sixteenth century.[16]

In the chapter on Africa[17] reference is made to the Barbary States, the commercial treaty-making with Morocco in the eighteenth century, to problems of Turkish suzerainty in North Africa, to Ethiopia and Mauretania.[18] The author also collected information on some of the remote African kingdoms which entered the world political scene only later in the nineteenth century. Thus he speaks about King Monomotapa, Guinea, Sierra Leone and Benin.[19] The activities of the Portuguese, English and French in Africa are referred to. In the last chapter the author concentrates on two American State entities: the Incas (Peru) and Aztecs (Mexico).[20] One of the main sources on the Spanish–American confrontation known to him is the work of Garcilasso de la Vega.

The volume on Asia, Africa and America which after its translation into German was included in Puffendorf's world history,[21] appears as one of the significant works in the series of classic writings which deal with the development of the family and law of nations outside Europe.[22] The first two major works in this group in the seventeenth century were Grotius's *Mare Liberum* and Seraphim de Freitas's *De Justo Imperio Lusitanorum Asiatico*. In the eighteenth century some of the writings of Surland, Justi, Vattel and Martens[23] were further contributions to the classic literature which testify to the interest which many writers showed in the early development of the family and law of nations in all parts of the world. Puffendorf's *Introduction to History* appeared in the second half of the eighteenth century in

[15] Ibid., p. 445. [16] Ibid., pp. 423, 428. [17] Ibid., pp. 754–803.

[18] Ibid., pp. 784, 787, 803. [19] Ibid., pp. 818, 821, 822. [20] Ibid., pp. 823–998.

[21] Puffendorf is one of the classic writers who in spite of his naturalist ideology had a significant appeal in England, for he was one of the first writers of the period of enlightenment who proposed some of the most progressive principles of law and politics (the natural equality of States and the denial of despotism in any form).

[22] The volumes of Puffendorf's *Introduction to the History of Europe* were translated into English by J. Crull; he wrote a Dedication to these volumes which reads as follows: 'To His Excellency Charles Duke of Shrewsbury, H.M. Principal Secretary of State etc.: Sir, I should scarce have had the boldness to prefix your great name to this Book, had I not been fully persuaded that the extraordinary worth of my author would strongly plead for me to your Excellency's generosity. For, since my intention was that the Sieur Puffendorf's Introduction to the History of Europe should appear in no less Lustre in this Kingdom, than it has heretofore done in most Parts of Europe, I could not … submit his Treatise to the Protection of any other Person than your Excellency whose judging power is so universally acknowledged: If it endures this test, it must pass current in this Nation … J. Crull M.D'. The relevant volumes available in the Cambridge University Library bear the dates of 1697, 1706, 1719 and 1729.

[23] C. H. Alexandrowicz, *Introduction to the History of the Law of Nations in the East Indies in the 16th, 17th and 18th Centuries* (1967).

French. An edition in eight volumes was brought out by M. Bruzen de la Martinière under the title *Introduction à l'histoire moderne, générale et politique de l'univers* covering Europe, Asia, Africa and America.[24] The extension of Puffendorf's original European history to other continents and civilizations is a logical expression of his 'natural law' approach to the law of nations which is conceived as an inherently universal and non-discriminatory system of law.[25]

[24] *Introduction to the History* ... begun by Baron Puffendorf, continued by M. de la Martinière, improved by Joseph Sayer, Serjeant at Law, 1764. The dates of the volumes in French are 1753–64. An earlier Amsterdam edition is in the *Bibliothèque Nationale* in Paris, G. 12769–70; see also G. 12691, 12698–9, 12771.

[25] Dr. S. Sieber, *Samuel Puffendorf, Staatsdenker, Bahnbrecher und Kämpfer* (1938). See also L. Krieger, *The Politics of Discretion: Pufendorf and the Acceptance of Natural Law* (1965); but *quere* statement on p. 183.

12

A TREATISE BY J. H. G. JUSTI ON ASIAN GOVERNMENT (1960–61)

I.

It is generally unknown that Johann Heinrich Gottlieb von Justi, one of the greatest German political writers of the eighteenth century, made an inquiry into the organisation of some Asian monarchies and published a treatise under the title 'Vergleichungen der Europäischen mit den Asiatischen und anderen vermeintlich Barbarischen Regierungen'.[1] As the title indicates, the purpose of this work was to compare the system of government as known in Europe with that prevailing in Asia, and the expression 'Vermeintlich Barbarische Regierungen' shows Justi's critical attitude towards a climate of opinion in certain European circles which looked upon Asian civilization as an inferior one. While Justi failed to employ a systematic method in the comparative exposition of European and Asian Government, his views on the development of European-Asian relations are of considerable interest to the historian of the law of nations.

Justi refers to the existence of two categories of source material i.e. accounts of merchants and of missionaries on their activities in the Asian continent.[2] He compares the trustworthiness of both and comes to the conclusion that while the first are biased, the second are fairly objective. He justifies this conclusion by a general analysis of the history of the European East India Companies in Asia with particular reference to the interconnection between their commercial and political interests. The following are some of the characteristic points stressed in the Preface and in Chapter VIII of Volume II of his treatise.

Considering some of the important features of international trade, Justi distinguishes between 'Passivhandel' and 'Activhandel'. If a country's foreign trade is mainly based on dealings resulting from the admission of foreign merchants to its

[1] *Vergleichungen der europäischen mit den asiatischen und andern vermeintlich barbarischen Regierungen* (Berlin; Stettin; Leipzig, 1762). Justi (1703–71) was the author of a number of well known treatises such as *Die Chimare des Gleichgewichts von Europe; Chimare des Gleichgewichts der Handlung und Schiffahrt; Historische und Juristische Schriften* etc. His particular interest was the theory of management of State property (Kameralismus).

[2] Justi relies *inter alia* on Rollins's *Neuere Geschichte des Chineser, Japaner, Indianer etc.* and on the works of Du Halde, Navarette and La Loubère.

harbours and centres of commerce, it may be defined as 'Passivhandel'.[3] If, however, a country's merchants do not deal with foreigners in their own markets, but carry their trade abroad, they engage in what is called 'Activhandel'. Here Justi underlines the fact that Asian countries, in so far as they followed the second type of trade, enjoyed generally a record of carrying out their activities in other Asian countries in accordance with the principles of the law of nations. Their merchants were known to engage in foreign trade without the extension of their dealings from commerce to politics. On the other hand, European traders who came to Asian countries, tended to convert their commercial activities into more ambitious operations of a political nature. To illustrate his point, Justi refers to the various East India Companies and detects in their policy a system of overgrown 'Activhandel' which he subjects to heavy criticism. This system consisted in opening commerce with the simultaneous establishment of settlements in Asia. But we may observe that the foundation of foreign settlements of merchants was one of the characteristic features of inter-Asian trade since time immemorial.[4] Asian countries generally observed the ancient customs of allowing such settlements to govern themselves by their own law and habits. This custom was also extended to the European newcomer in Asia who consequently found it possible to set foot in the territories of one or another local Ruler and to open new trade relations. The privileges granted by the particular ruler to European traders were in course of time converted into 'capitulations' which became ultimately derogatory to his sovereignty. Though Justi does not refer to this development from the point of view of the law of nations, he nevertheless indicates some of its antecedents as revealed in available source material.

In particular Justi draws our attention to the fact that most of the original trade settlements of Europeans in Asia tended to become fortified strongholds. Once the military element superimposed itself on the commercial, power economics were liable to come into the picture. Each European commercial company enforced, if possible, a monopoly of trade in the country in which it had settled. Trade monopolies led from power economics to power politics, and the contracting Asian country tended to be cut off from relations with other countries. Once this point was reached, it was only one step to depriving the particular Asian community of its sovereign status. Justi considers such abuse of the idea of 'Activhandel' as a violation of the law of nations. He then emphasises that the Government of China, fully aware of what had happened in the East Indies, rightly imposed limitations on European merchants in Canton in order to counteract possible developments detrimental to its sovereignty.

It would be interesting to recall that Christian Wolff had earlier referred in his *Jus Gentium*[5] to the foreign trade policy of the Chinese, stating that 'for the purpose of preserving their own interests (they) did not wish to unite in trade with other nations'.

[3] European–Asian trade was from the Asian point of view predominantly 'Passivhandel'.

[4] Inter-State Relations in Asia by Prof. K. A. N. Sastri (*Indian Year Book of International Affairs*, 1953).

[5] Translated by J. H. Drake p. 44 (para 75).

Justi's critical remarks are mainly directed against the policy of Spain, Portugal and the Netherlands. In fact the East Indies witnessed during the sixteenth and seventeenth centuries not only a spectacular development of commercial and political penetration on the part of the Portuguese and the Dutch, but also an acute conflict between the two, to which Hugo Grotius referred in his treatise on the Freedom of the High Sea.[6] He as well as a number of other classic writers did not fail to assess the position of Asian Rulers within the universal law of nations and to throw light on the nature of European–Asian relations.

Approximately at the time of the publication of Justi's treatise, another significant work on the East India Companies (Dutch, English and French) was published. Its author, G. T. F. Raynal,[7] refers to European acquisitions in the East Indies and states as follows: 'Si ces grandes acquisitions sont nuisibles, les traités faits pour se les procurer ne sauroient être raisonnables. Il faudra que nos marchands s'ils sont sages, renoncent en même tems et à la fureur des conquêtes et à l'espoir flatteur de tenir dans leurs mains la balance de l'Asie'. And further: 'Si nous avions porté chez les Indiens des procédés établis sur la bonne foi. Si nous leur avions fait connoître que l'utilité réciproque est la base du commerce. Si nous avions encouragé leur culture et leur industrie par des échanges également avantageux pour eux et pour nous, insensiblement on se seroit concilié l'esprit de ces peuples'. This criticism is similar to that of Justi and shows that the latter's views were not isolated as far as public opinion in Europe was concerned.

II.

The Preamble and Chapters I–III of Volume I as well as Chapters I and II of Volume II of Justi's treatise deal with some of the peculiarities of Asian Government. As stated above, these chapters are far from systematically written but they nevertheless reveal Justi's views on the organisation of public affairs in Asian countries and on the value of their civilisations.

Justi underlines the absence of the republican form of government in Asia and criticises at the same time its functioning in certain European States such as Venice and the Netherlands. He also refers with regret to the chaos which resulted from the conversion of the monarchy in Poland into a 'res publica nobilium' headed by a powerless king. Government in the hands of politicians leads, in Justi's opinion, to corruption and weakness of executive power. There is a golden middle way between monarchical despotism and weak government which Justi sees in effective checks imposed on the prerogatives of the monarch. In this connexion he refers to the traditional limitations which circumscribed imperial power in China. The Emperor was looked upon as the father of the nation, and the welfare of the people

[6] Grotius and India (*Indian Year Book of International Affairs*, 1954) (ch. 7 above).

[7] *Histoire Philosophique et Politique des Etablissements et du Commerce des Européens dans les deux Indes* par l'Abbé G. T. F. Raynal, 1770 (Tome Second).

was his primary concern, a conception generally unknown in Europe. High officers of the State and scholars could make representations to the Emperor and suggest improvements in the system of government. Moreover, the reign of each Emperor was the object of critical accounts left by scholars to posterity. Relying on a number of historical treatises,[8] Justi emphasises that the Government of China was not government by imperial discretion alone;[9] it respected the immutable laws of the realm and was based on what he calls 'Collegiale Verfassung'. Legislative and executive power was never exercised without the *regular* participation of bodies of advisers, an institution often ignored in European monarchies.

Similarly to Justi, Christian Wolff had earlier referred to the peculiarities of government in China and had stated that they 'gave their best efforts to training in morals and to statecraft, and so from the most ancient times they have been prominent among the more civilised nations and are so today....'[10]

Turning to judicial power, Justi singles out the tradition in India according to which the Mogul Emperor always acted personally as the Supreme Judge and never disrespected the law as interpreted by jurists. The power to issue death sentences was reserved to the Emperor and was only in special circumstances delegated to subordinate authorities.

Justi also underlines the remarkable organisation of power within the Hindu State in which the priestly caste (Brahmins) was superior to the Ruler (Ksatriya) and thus assured due observance of the law. In the same way as in China, the Ruler could not afford to ignore the advice of scholars and jurists in matters of justice and administration. Moreover, the courts of Hindu Rulers did not engage in the sort of extravagance which characterised only too often the life of so many royal and princely courts in Europe. The Hindu Ruler had the duty of being an example to his subjects and the latter had access to his person and recourse to his justice.

In Chapters V–VIII of Volume II, Justi makes further references to other details of administration such as the preservation of public order and security, taxation, agriculture, industry and commerce, and underlines the fact that the welfare of the people was a fundamental consideration in the policy of the average Asian Ruler. Justi states that he is aware of the many shortcomings of government in Asian countries but that the balance of power generally prevailing within them allowed to classify them as civilised States, not inferior to European notions of civilisation.

[8] See above footnote 2.

[9] Justi states that he finds it impossible to agree with Montesquieu's view that China is a par excellence despotic power.

[10] See *op. cit.*, p. 35 (para 54). In this connexion reference may be made to the instructions given by the King of Great Britain to Lord Macartney, ambassador to the Imperial Court of Peking (1792–94) in which he refers to the people of China as 'the most singular upon the globe among whom *civilization* had existed'; and to the letter written by the King to the Emperor in which he refers to the 'Intercourse between such great and *civilised* nations as China and Great Britain. (*An authentic account of an Embassy from the King of Great Britain to the Emperor of China* by Sir George Staunton, 1799). The purpose of this Embassy was to induce the Emperor to relax the limitations imposed on the British commercial community in Canton and to expand Anglo–Chinese trade relations.

III.

Before concluding this brief account of Justi's treatise, reference should be made to what he writes about the law of war in Asian countries. The relevant remarks appear in Chapter III of Volume II under the title 'Von der Kriegesverfassung'.

Justi states as follows: 'Nothing is more peculiar than the way in which Asian nations wage war among each other. Their armies tend to avoid each other and both sides aim primarily at making prisoners of war and collecting booty. When the Burmese (Peguaner) invade the lands of the Siamese, the latter reciprocate by invading Burma (Pegu); and each is satisfied to secure his booty and to withdraw'. But if the two armies meet, they do not shoot directly at each other but send their bullets and arrows above the head of the other so as to exercise pressure on the enemy rather than to kill. In this respect Justi remarks significantly: 'Dieses ist eine Art eines *Vertrags*, welchen man ohne Verletzung des Völkerrechts nicht brechen kann'.

Thus Justi considers the prevailing mode of warfare based on the tacit consent of States as amounting to local usage or custom which could not be ignored without breach of the law of nations. It served to mitigate the disastrous consequences of warfare. It also gave expression to the principle that any excess of violence beyond that necessary to overpower the enemy, was unlawful. Thus we are faced, at least in some Asian countries, with the existence in the past of a law of warfare which made it possible to conduct hostilities in a fairly humanitarian manner. What Justi writes in this respect, also finds confirmation in the more ancient laws of warfare which had prevailed in India since time immemorial.[11]

No reference is made in this paper to the discussion of problems in Volume III of Justi's treatise such as those relating to the private life of monarchs or to dynastic succession. Justi admits that his comparison between Asian and European government is often highly critical of European institutions and practice, but, as he underlines in the Preface, he intended to question some of the prejudices about Asian countries prevailing in Europe. Above all his primary motive of writing was 'Menschenliebe'—the love of mankind.

[11] Customs of Warfare in Ancient India by W. S. Armour (*Transactions of the Grotius Society*, Vol. 8, 1923).

13

DOCTRINAL ASPECTS OF THE UNIVERSALITY OF THE LAW OF NATIONS (1961)

I.

The process of European consolidation which has been gathering momentum since the end of the Second World War and now tends to assume various organizational forms can be traced back to the second half of the eighteenth century when some of the classic writers on the law of nations first conceived or pronounced the existence of a legally 'organized' European community of States (*Rechtsgemeinschaft*). Then, as well as now, this process was or is confined to the west European and partly central European region, leaving beyond its scope the countries of eastern Europe and the Balkans, though the boundary line between States which participated in it and those which were outside such participation was far from precise or stable. The gradual disintegration of the Habsburg Empire and the expansion to the west of the Russian Empire (irrespective of its form of government) left the boundary line for a long time in a state of uncertainty. Whatever the fluctuating division of areas on both sides, the early positivist writers of the eighteenth century pointed to the existence of a European tradition and continuity of intercourse which in their view justified the conception of a positive European law of nations based on treaties and custom. This regional conception was contrasted with that of the universal and natural conception of the law of nations which found itself in juxtaposition with new trends, and the ensuing conflict between them revealed a number of problems the significance of which is not yet sufficiently appreciated. The question was whether the positivist European reality was reconcilable with the idea of universalism of the law of nations which drew its legal source from the declining concept of natural law but had a reality of its own. To this question various answers were offered and it is characteristic that some of the leading classical writers showed comparatively less understanding for its solution in the long run than some of the lesser-known writers. It may be that the voice of the more 'fashionable' lawyers and authors who were at the same time counsellors or advisers to some of the European sovereigns at that period made itself more readily heard than that of the writers who, being more detached, showed perhaps more foresight as to the consequences of the prevailing ideological conflict. An attempt will be made to recall their views and to compare them with those expressed in the well-known treatises of the late eighteenth- and early nineteenth-century positivists.

II.

The earliest systematic survey of writers and treatises on the law of nations was made by D. H. L. von Ompteda whose *Literatur des gesammten sowohl natürlichen als positiven Völkerrechts* appeared in Regensburg in 1785. One of Ompteda's personal titles on the front page of his work was that of 'Königlicher Gross-Britanischer Comitial-Gesandte bey der Reichsversammlung zu Regensburg'. Whatever the precise meaning of this honorary function it pointed (similarly as in Justi's or in Martens's case) to Ompteda's connexions with the sovereign of Great Britain and Hanover. Most of the eighteenth-century writers discussed by Ompteda were aware of the problem of the continuity of the universal family of nations in the peculiar circumstances created by positivist trends, and this applies to the Moser–Martens school of thought and its adherents as well as to its opponents. At the time of the appearance of Ompteda's work, J. J. Moser had already published his main treatises, while G. F. de Martens was still in the process of completing his works. Among the lesser-known authors listed by Ompteda the names of a few monographic writers deserve mention such as Justi and Surland, the first writing on questions of balance of power and cameralism, the second a relatively forgotten name but worthy of being recalled for his monographs on the law of the sea and on East India affairs.[1] However, the most significant suggestions on a combined naturalist–positivist approach to the law of nations and on the solution of some of its outstanding problems were made by Ompteda himself in the Introduction to the *Literature of the Law of Nations*.

In order to justify his proposed plan for a reconsidered treatment of the law of nations Ompteda offers the following functional classification of *jus gentium*: the bare natural law of nations (*jus gentium naturale*) covers all nations, civilized or not, and thus operates in the widest circle of communities in the most general way. Among the fundamental principles of the law of nature Ompteda gives prominence to the natural freedom, independence and equality of nations. As the development of inter-State relations brought about an expansion or contraction of the law of nature in its practical application, the requirements of intercourse between civilized nations called for a modified natural law of nations (*jus gentium voluntarium*) based on their *consensus praesumptus*.[2] Ompteda quotes as examples of rules of the

[1] Among the works of other writers Ompteda also quotes Bouchaut's *Théorie des traités de commerce* (1777); various essays by von Steck; and Zschackwitz's *Gründliche Nachricht vom Handlungswesen ... sämmtlicher Völker der Welt* (1736). Among earlier writers Ompteda refers to Groening's *Bibliotheca juris gentium exotica seu de juris naturae et gentium principiis iuxta doctrinam asiaticorum, etc.* (1701) (a work concerned with the civilization and legal institutions of extra-European countries); and to Leibnitz's *Codex juris gentium diplomaticus* (1693).

[2] Ompteda refers in this respect to Wolff's *Civitas Gentium Maxima* and to Vattel's *Droit des gens.*

modified natural law of nations the prohibition of use of poisoned weapons or the systematic application of privileges and immunities to diplomatic envoys. These and other rules tended to appear simultaneously or at different periods in various parts of the world under different circumstances governing inter-State relations.[3] The above *consensus presumptus* is revealed irrespective of agreement or express submission to legal rules. Further modifications of the natural law of nations take place by tacit consent generating customary law (*jus consuetudinarium*) or by the conclusion of treaties which create *jus gentium pactitium*. As stated above, this classification presupposes the existence (apart from *jus gentium naturale et necessarium*) of a *jus gentium voluntarium*, a term already used previously by many classic writers including Grotius. Ompteda then concerns himself with the problem of reconciliation of the *jus gentium voluntarium* which tends to be regional law within a particular group of nations bound by intercourse and the universality of the law of nations and offers the following weighty observation:

> In view of the fact that the civilised nations are mainly to be found in Europe, at least until now, the teachers of the law of nations called the last two categories of the law of nations (i.e. the modified and customary law of nations) the European law of nations. However, as there exist outside Europe since a long time, civilised nations ... to which the law of nations of these two categories applies ... the term European law of nations is much too limited.

Ompteda's concern with the above limitation was highly justified for the ascendancy of the positivist conception at the cost of natural law threatened to affect the universal character of the law of nations. Positive law based entirely on custom and treaty tended to be limited to the European sphere of interests (*Particularrecht*) and could not provide a basis for extra-European intercourse with the possible exception of the U.S.A. which received the European law of nations practically *in toto*.

The question before Ompteda was how to secure the idea of continuity of the universal family of nations which had acquired a reality of its own. It is clear from a survey of works relating to overseas trade with particular reference to the well-established European–Asian commercial relations, and from the comment which Ompteda offers to these works, that he tried to assimilate the so-called modified law of nations to the positive law of nations and thus reconcile universalism with positivism. Insisting on the need for a joint treatment of the law of nations from a positivist as well as naturalist point of view,[4] he criticizes the teachers of the European law of nations in an unambiguous way, saying: 'they ignore the primary and true universal rules of the law of nations'. Ompteda's reasoning implies the fear that many civilized nations outside Europe would, according to positivist views, find themselves in a legal vacuum being neither in the orbit of European positive law (*Particularrecht*) nor even covered by the rules of the declining universal natural law which tended to be displaced by the former. As we shall see later, most of the

[3] See, for instance, the classic Hindu literature on the prohibition of unlawful weapons and on the immunity of envoys (Dutas); Armour, 'Customs of Warfare in Ancient India', *Transactions of the Grotius Society*, 8 (1923).

[4] In this respect Ompteda refers to the plan of a work by Carl Gottlieb Günther.

extreme positivists had no satisfactory solution to offer to this dilemma, thus leaving the extra-European State entities which had enjoyed a legal status in the family of nations in the past to the position of candidates for admission to the European circle of States which assumed the role of recognizing or not recognizing external entities.[5] To understand the significance of this situation reference should be made to some of the writers quoted by Ompteda, in the first instance to Moser.

III.

J. J. Moser's principal works are on *The First Basic Notions of the Present European Law of Nations* (1778) and on *The Most Recent European Law of Nations* (1779). As the titles indicate, he is predominantly concerned with the positive *Particularrecht* in the European area. But characteristically enough he is unable to escape the problem of universality of the law of nations which he has to face in the discussion of problems of overseas trade. In his first work he refers, *inter alia*, to the commercial competition between European States in Asia (or Africa) and states as follows: 'Where European nations have only settlements or comptoirs in Asia (or in African States), they cannot exclude there other nations from trade and commerce; this may happen only on the basis of treaties between European nations *inter se* (e.g. the exclusion of the Austrian Netherlands from East India trade) or on the basis of treaties concluded with Asian and African States'. In his second work Moser returns to the suppression of the Austrian East India Company in Ostende and recalls the renewed efforts of the Government in Vienna to organize East India trade from Trieste. He also refers to the memorandum of the King of Prussia presented in 1752 to the United Provinces of the Netherlands in which the King defends the rights of the Prussian East India Company in Emden. To this memorandum the United Provinces replied that the subjects of the King of Prussia have no doubt a natural right to trade with other nations whose harbours are open to all nations of the earth (*tous les peuples de l'univers*) with the exception of those in which the Dutch East India Company received the privilege of exclusive trade. Great Britain issued a declaration in similar terms pointing to the natural freedom of trade with the exception of trade reserved to the English East India Company. Moser then refers to the peculiar circumstances of trade relations maintained with Asian sovereigns and admits that the European law of nations is not applicable to them and thus they must be governed by the natural and universal law of nations which does not allow European powers to occupy the lands of extra-European nations under the pretext of religion or otherwise. It follows from the above that Moser's exclusive positivist European ideology had to give way to some extent to extra-European considerations of a practical nature. Moser, like all other eighteenth-century positivists, does

[5] See 'The Theory of Recognition in Fieri', by C. H. Alexandrowicz, *Indian Year Book of International Affairs*, 34 (1958) (chapter 24 below). Under the natural law of nations recognition of States and Governments, if necessary at all, was declaratory while positivism supported the constitutive theory.

not ban the natural law of nations from the international scene though he admits it only against his principal train of thought and subject to reservations. The concept of universalism was, nevertheless, capable of holding a qualified position of its own in spite of adverse doctrinal developments.

Among the writers quoted by Ompteda, Joannes Julius Surland deserves particular mention. His monograph *Juris Germanorum Navigandi Indias Prima Fundamenta* appeared in Marburg in 1751.[6] Surland refers to East India trade established by the British, Dutch, French, Danes and Swedes[7] who all shared its riches with Portugal and Spain, and complains: 'Solis germanis harum terrarum litora denegata fuerunt'. The following were the three obstacles to German navigation to the East: 'Eorumque navigationi tria potissimum obstare dicuntur: 1) dominium maris, 2) inventio adque occupatio, 3) leges et pacta'. As to possible difficulties connected with restrictions on the freedom of navigation Surland states rightly: 'Omnem de mari libero … cessare litem statuo'. He refers here to Selden's writings and to Grotius's pioneering work on the freedom of the seas and to the ultimate victory of the concept of *mare liberum* over that of *mare clausum.* As to the invocation of the right of discovery and occupation of overseas lands by European nations Surland mentions the claims of the Spanish–Portuguese school of thought based, *inter alia*, on the Papal title (*Bull 'Inter Caetera'*) and, dismissing the lawfulness of these claims, refers to the right of Asian powers to equality within the family of nations: 'Cum pari in parem non concedatur imperium'. Surland quotes, *inter alia*, the eighteenth-century decrees of the emperors of China regulating trade with foreign nations. Finally, Surland recalls the foundation of the East India companies by several European powers and the treaty relations established through these companies with Indian sovereigns and quotes Barbeyrac saying: 'Les autres états … ont la liberté d'aller et de négocier dans les pays des Indes libres et indépendens qui veulent la leur permettre …'. Thus he concludes: 'Cum igitur nullae Germanis obstent leges, ipsis Batavis confitentibus, jus in Indias navigandi habemus'.[8] Surland's argumentation is, of course, primarily directed towards justifying the establishment of German trade in the East Indies, particularly in view of the abolition of the Ostende Company in 1731; but it is significant that he relies on the natural law of nations which provides a universal framework for intercourse between any European nation (even one which had not yet acquired vested interests in the East India trade) and Asian Powers which he considers as sovereign and equal participants in this intercourse. Surland refers also in his work on maritime law[9] to the need for reliance on the natural law of nations in all cases in which affairs

[6] Surland (1724–58) was Professor at the University of Frankfurt a. d. O. He was the son of J. J. Surland, a German jurist (1657–1748).

[7] Unlike the British, Dutch and French East India companies which extended their activities from trade to politics on a grand scale, the Danish and Swedish East India companies were purely trading agencies. The first was established in 1612 (with a new establishment in Altona founded in 1728). The Swedish Company was established in 1731; Rousset, *Recueil historique d'actes* (1731).

[8] And further: 'Nec tamen animum demittat ac de Indiarum commerci plane desperet moesta Germania …'.

[9] *Grundsätze des europäischen See-Rechts* (1750).

relating to East India trade are not covered by treaties. He draws attention to the view according to which treaties regulating generally trade and navigation cannot be presumed to extend to such trade and navigation in the East Indies which either calls for the inclusion of specific provisions in treaties or must be judged by the principles of natural law as the law held in reserve.

Another writer to whom Ompteda makes reference is J. H. G. von Justi, but Ompteda misses among his works the most important as far as the universality of the law of nations is concerned, i.e. his book on Asian government.[10] In this work, as well as in his *Chimäre des Gleichgewichts der Handlung*, &c. (1759), Justi discusses the difference between what he calls *Aktivhandel* and *Passivhandel*, the first expressing the fact that a country carries its external trade to foreign markets, and the second the policy of a country limiting its foreign trade activities to its own internal markets. While the European powers engaged in *Aktivhandel vis-à-vis* Asian countries, the latter contented themselves with pursuing a *Passivhandel*. However, Justi criticizes heavily the activities of the various East India companies engaged in *Aktivhandel* in Asia, and considers their policy of power economics and of supporting their trade with armed forces as unlawful in the law of nations.[11] With Grotius[12] he considers the Asian countries as sovereign and their cultural tradition and political institutions as equal if not superior to Europe's 'aggressive' civilization. In distinction to other writers who displayed a European egocentric attitude, Justi had a fuller appreciation of the significance of European-Asian commercial intercourse within the framework of the universal family of nations which called for the application of the same legal principles to all its participants.[13]

IV.

Ompteda's work is limited to treatises and works on the law of nations published before 1785, and it is for this reason that he does not list or discuss the writings of Martens. Both Moser and Martens occupied apart from their academic activities political advisory posts, Moser as Councillor of the Wurtemberg Estates, and Martens as Aulic Counsellor (*Hofrat*) of the Hanover Government which brought him into contact with the English legal world. No doubt both had a considerable

[10] *Vergleichungen der europäischen mit den asiatischen und andern vermeintlich barbarischen Regierungen* (Berlin; Stettin; Leipzig, 1762).

[11] Reference may also be made to Abbé G. T. F. Raynal who expressed similar views in his *Histoire philosophique et politique des établissements et du commerce des Européens dans les deux Indes* (1770).

[12] See *The Freedom of the Sea* (transl. by van Deman Magoffin, ed. by Scott, 1916).

[13] Justi also recommends the establishment of a universal monarchy in Europe and states thoughtfully that this would lead to the termination of competing European trade monopolies in the Asian countries and allow prices of Asian export goods to find their natural level; see *Gesammelte politische und Finanzschriften* (1761). In this work Christian Wolff's influence on Justi makes itself felt, though Wolff had advocated a universal *civitas maxima* while Justi finds it not acceptable; see *Die Chimäre des Gleichgewichts der Handlung und Schiffahrt* (1759), p. 70. But Justi similarly to Wolff is an exponent of Chinese institutions of government which he considers in many respects worthy of consideration.

grasp of practical questions confronting the European powers in the second half of the eighteenth century, but as to the formulation of legal problems Martens excels Moser by a more systematic classification and exposition of these problems. Among Martens's works the most prominent are his *Essay on the Positive European Law of Nations* (1787), the *Précis du droit des gens modernes de l'Europe* (1789), translated into English by William Cobbett (1795), the *Recueil des traités* (1791), and his *Cours diplomatique ou tableau des relations extérieures des puissances de l'Europe* (1801). Martens's dilemma of reconciling the particular European positive law of nations with the universal natural law of nations has been discussed by Hubrich in his paper on 'Georg Friedrich von Martens und die moderne Völkerrechtsgemeinschaft',[14] but the author confines himself mainly to the examination of Martens's essay on the existence of a positive European law of nations and to his *Précis du droit des gens*, ignoring the significance of his approach to the problem in the *Recueil des traités* and the *Cours diplomatique*. An attempt will be made to recall Martens's views against the wider background of the latter works and to draw attention not only to opinions expressly stated by him in the *Précis* but also to those implied in his other writings and revealing some of the more deep-seated controversies which arose out of the clash between regional European positivism and the universal ambit of the law of nations.

The idea of supplying courts of European sovereigns, universities and scientific institutions with collections of treaties had been taken up long before Martens by a number of writers. In this respect Ompteda draws our attention particularly to the works of Dumont, Lünig and Rousset. Among these collections Dumont's *Corps universel* (1731) had been of outstanding value, and it is characteristic that the author had not confined himself to giving the texts of European treaties only but quoted a number of treaties concluded between European and Asian powers particularly those entered into by the Dutch East India Company with Indonesian and Malayan rulers and by the United Provinces of the Netherlands with Persia.[15] Lünig's name deserves to be recalled in connexion with his *Theatrum Ceremoniale* (1719), in which he refers, *inter alia*, to the diplomatic ceremonial observed in a number of Asian courts such as in Persia, Siam, Turkey and China. The description of diplomatic usages was combined with an account of negotiations which led to the conclusion of treaties such as the French–Siamese treaties in the seventeenth century, the texts of which are given separately by Dumont. Reference to Asian treaties is also to be found in Rousset's *Recueil historique d'actes* (1731), and in Kluit's *Hist. Foederum* as well as in his *Index Chronologicus Sistens Foedera Pacis, Defensionis, Navigationis, Commerciorum*, &c. (1789). All these and other collections were instrumental in assisting Martens in the preparation of his *Recueil des traités* in which he included a good deal of extra-European treaty material. In this

[14] *Zeitschrift für Politik* (1914), pp. 362–89. See also Habenicht, *Georg Friedrich von Martens* (1934).

[15] See the Dutch–Persian Treaty of 1631 which is of particular significance in that it provides for privileges and immunities for a Persian settlement in Amsterdam in the nature of capitulations; see *Indian Year Book of International Affairs* (1960).

respect it would be relevant to recall what Martens writes in the prefaces to the various volumes of the *Recueil*.

After the publication of the first three volumes Martens had been criticized in the *Nouvelle bibliothèque universelle d'Allemagne* (vol. 104, pp. 34–52) for the omission of various treaties from the above volumes. Martens admits in the preface to Volume IV that he had not included in these volumes the treaties between England and East Indian countries which had been published in England in 1790. Reference is here made to: *The Collection of Treaties between Great Britain and Other Powers*, by G. Chalmers which (it may be noted) had been but one of the English collections, earlier collections being *Treaties and Grants from the Country Powers to the East India Company* (1774), or William Bolt's *Consideration of India Affairs* (Treaties, 1772). In the preface to Volume VI Martens states that he included subsequently a number of English–East India treaties in order to correct the omission, and he emphasizes that if he had to start the collection again he would have provided for a separate volume comprising East India treaties for the benefit of those readers who are interested in them. Finally, in the preface to Volume VII he refers to the search for treaties between Great Britain and the sovereign of Bengal which he was able to find and to include in the *Recueil*. It seems quite clear from these statements that though the general purpose of his collection of treaties was to support the exposition of a positive European law of nations, Martens did not ignore the significance of treaty-making in the wider field of extra-European relations and the legal rules observed in universal inter-State intercourse.

His attitude is the same in the *Cours diplomatique* also called *Tableau des relations extérieures*. Martens examines here, *inter alia*, the treaty and diplomatic relations between European and Asian powers adopting the method of their discussion country by country, i.e. between France and India and Siam; between Great Britain and the various independent rulers of the Indian sub-continent; between the Netherlands and the Indonesian and Malayan rulers as well as Ceylon and Persia; and between Russia and China. Reference is also made to the activities of the Danish, Swedish and Prussian companies in the East, and separate observations are offered in relation to the Ottoman Empire. The picture which emerges from the *Cours diplomatique* is far from being exclusively European. Full cognisance is taken of the development of world trade and of legal transactions which accompanied its expansion within the universal framework of the law of nations.

If the above two works of Martens constitute an integral and significant part of his literary legacy in the field of the law of nations, it is impossible to leave them out of account in considering the views he expresses in the *Précis du droit des gens*, much as these views follow the general trend of limiting the law of nations to the sphere of a positive legal European system. The weakness of giving expression to this trend side by side with the awareness of the requirements of an expanding world trade is obvious in the various chapters of the *Précis*. Thus, while Martens emphasizes the existence of that legal system as serving the purposes of a European *Rechtsgemeinschaft* bound together by common ties of intercourse, tradition and civilization, he tends to be inconsistent with his own views when he proceeds to the examination of the external trade of European powers in the East Indies. The inconsistency is the more significant as he supports his views on the theory of the positive law of nations by extensive treaty material quoted in the annex to the *Précis* of which Asian treaties form a far from insignificant part. It would, of course, be possible to argue that the treaties concluded by European countries with a number of Asian powers are simply part and parcel of the positive treaty-making activity of the former in which the latter played an insignificant role only, but again such an interpretation could hardly accord with reality, as the European–Asian treaties (much as they tended to follow the European pattern of draftsmanship) are only too often the expression of a compromise reached between both parties as to the application of their legal conceptions in mutual transactions. The International Court of Justice has recently confirmed the correctness of this proposition when it examined the Maratha–Portuguese Treaty of 1779 in the dispute between Portugal and India over the alleged Portuguese right of passage to the enclaves of Dadra and Nagar Aveli.[16] An attempt was made in the proceedings to contest the validity of the Treaty if judged by our general notions of treaty law. The Court emphasized in its Judgment that an eighteenth-century treaty must be interpreted on the basis of legal notions peculiar to both parties and in force at the time of its conclusion. It considered the Treaty perfectly valid by eighteenth-century standards and stated that both parties to it recognized themselves, bound by its provisions, though the form of the Treaty complied with local usage of including the agreement between the parties in two separate documents written in the language of each of the parties. Moreover, the Court, in interpreting the legal nature of the cession of the enclaves by the Maratha Empire to the Portuguese, took into consideration the peculiar character of the grant made by the Marathas, i.e. that of a Jagir, and analysing its juridical content on the basis of Maratha or Mogul notions of vassalship or feudal tenure, came to the conclusion that no sovereignty was transferred which could justify a Portuguese right of passage through Maratha territory. Judge Moreno Quintana, in a significant pronouncement, stated that the transaction between the parties created 'mutual rights and obligations between two legal persons recognised as such in their international relationship', a statement which leaves us in no doubt about the views of the learned judge (and a number of other judges) on the status of an independent Asian country in the eighteenth-century law of nations. Thus it would not be impossible to view the numerous Asian treaties quoted by Martens in three of his main works in the light of the above observations and to consider them as an expression of ties of intercourse between European and Asian sovereign powers. They do in fact reflect a network of commercial and political relations which could not remain in a legal vacuum. The juridical status of the parties was conditioned by the universality of the natural law of nations which allowed Asian powers to be normal participants in treaty and diplomatic relations within the orbit of the law.[17] On the other hand, the introduction of some of their

[16] *I.C.J. Reports*, 12 April 1960.

[17] As to the validity of treaties between Christian and non-Christian powers, Ompteda refers to a number of monographs dealing with the subject, such as, for instance: Cacheranus, *Disputatio an Principi Christiano Fas sit pro sui suorumque bonorum tutela foedus inire ac amicitia infidelibus iungi*

legal concepts in treaty provisions made them direct contributors to the development of an initial positive law of civilized nations not limited to European intercourse only. A more detailed survey of these treaties would reveal the influence which Asian powers exercised on their contents, such as, for instance, in respect of vassalship, certain institutions of maritime law, the jurisdiction exercised over merchants in foreign territory containing elements of capitulations, the exchange of prisoners of war, and so on.[18]

However, it is undeniable that while Martens in the handling of the treaty material seems to be implicitly open to the wider conception of the law of nations, he remains in the theoretical exposition of the law, in his *Précis du droit des gens*, a staunch adherent to the positivist doctrine. Particularly, he denies the existence of a universal positive law of nations and points to the differences in habits between European and extra-European nations, stating that even Turkey, in spite of her European possessions and relations, differs from the European approach to the law of nations in many respects. He concedes, therefore, the universal character of the law of nations within the framework of natural law only, and rejects Ompteda's proposition to assimilate the modified natural law of nations to positive law. Thus we read in the *Précis*: 'If from the fact that all states and people inhabit the same globe … and that it will be possible one day to establish between them a positive society, one could draw certain principles distinguishable from those of the law of nations, *jus cosmopoliticum*, those principles must be considered as being of philosophical origin only and not drawn from positive law'. Martens refers here to Kant's doctrine of the *Jus Cosmopoliticum* and to the significance of modern communication (navigation) which makes it possible in Kant's words 'to exploit the right to the earth's surface common to all mankind in the interest of commerce'.[19] Distant continents may come into peaceful relations which are finally publicly legalized, bringing mankind at last nearer to what Kant calls a cosmopolitan (federal) constitution. Emphasizing the rapidly spreading commerce of the peoples of the earth, Kant stresses that, 'the conception of cosmopolitan law is not a fantastic, extravagant idea of morality (only); on the contrary it is a necessary supplement … to the law of nations as well as to the universal rights of mankind in general'.

Martens is well aware of the legal requirements of world commercial intercourse; he speaks in the *Précis* about 'Indian kings (who) concluded treaties with certain European powers' and about the freedom of the latter to trade with the peoples of

(Taurini, 1569); or Pott, *De Foederibus Fidelium cum Infidelibus* (Jena, 1686). While commercial treaties between Christian and non-Christian powers were considered perfectly valid by these authors, political treaties were classified by them to the effect that alliances with Muslim powers were invalid or questionable, while treaties with Hindu (or Buddhist) powers were regarded as not objectionable. See also Ward, *Enquiry into the Foundation and History of the Law of Nations* (1795), vol. 2, pp. 325–6.

[18] Treaty-making between European and Asian Powers contributed to a considerable extent to the secularization of the Law of Nations. See 'Treaty and Diplomatic Relations between European and South-Asian Powers in the seventeenth and eighteenth Centuries', by Alexandrowicz, *Recueil des cours* (1960).

[19] Kant's *Perpetual Peace* (transl. by O'Brien), *Grotius Society Publications*, 7 (1927).

India and of other parts of the globe if the latter *agree* to such trade.[20] But though he admits 'that there are nations outside Europe which cannot be denied the character of civilised nations', he is reluctant to call the law applicable to such relations the law of civilized nations which in his view is undefined if compared with the European law. These statements dismissing the possibility of an extension of the idea of universality from natural to positive law are not quite reconcilable with Martens's wide treatment of extra-European commercial relations, and they lead to the absurd conclusion that while the universality of the law of nations could be legally upheld on the basis of the natural law concept, it was not admissible on the basis of the positive law of nations which tended to assume a monopolistic position with Europe as its centre. The legal principles of universal relations, much as they had a reality of their own, were therefore gradually shifted to a second, more and more insignificant, plane; and this leads to the conclusion that the re-universalization of the law of nations could only have taken place by positivist ways and means, i.e. by the admission of extra-European State entities to the European positive society. However, this view, as proposed by the later positivists (if judged by objective standards), must be considered as offending the idea of the continuity of the family of civilized nations from which the extra-European entities (which had enjoyed an international legal status prior to the nineteenth century) could not be presumed to have disappeared. In this sense Hubrich, in his discussion of Martens's dilemma, speaks about the meaningless admission of Turkey to the European concert (family of nations) in 1856.[21] Its meaninglessness is the more striking if the development of the family of nations (as for instance conceived by Oppenheim)[22] is presented as the gradual enlargement of the circle of Christian States in Europe (including the U.S.A.) to the Christian States outside Europe, e.g. Haiti and Liberia, and much later to non-Christian powers such as Turkey, Persia, Siam, China or Japan. The question may arise whether it is really feasible to consider Haiti and Liberia as older members of the family of nations than the Ottoman Empire, Persia, Siam or China which, as testified by Martens and other classic writers, entertained treaty and diplomatic relations with various European powers since the sixteenth or seventeenth century.[23] Whether the Moser–Martens school of thought is directly responsible for the more or less general acceptance of these views may be doubted, but it had its impact on a number of writers indirectly, particularly through the early nineteenth-century positivists such as Schmalz, Klüber, Wheaton and others who gave to its ideas a more permanent, though legally distorted, shape.[24]

[20] See *Précis* (2nd ed., 1801), p. 235: 'Chaque nation de l'Europe est en droit d'établir un commerce avec tous les peuples des Indes ou d'autres parties du globe *qui sont disposés à y donner les mains* ...'. (italics are mine).

[21] See op. cit.

[22] See *International Law* (8th ed.), vol. 1, pp. 48–9. See also Nussbaum, *A Concise History of the Law of Nations* (1954), p. 190.

[23] As to the status of Turkey in international law see McKinnon Wood, *American Journal of International Law* (1943), pp. 262 et seq.; and Smith, *Great Britain and the Law of Nations*, vol. 1, p. 17.

[24] Hubrich, op. cit. See particularly Schmalz, *Völkerrecht* (1817); Klüber, *Droit des gens modernes de l'Europe* (1819); and Wheaton, *Elements of International Law* (1st ed., 1836 and 3rd ed., 1848).

V.

Before concluding this brief examination the question may be asked whether it would be possible for the historian of the law of nations to suggest a reconsideration of the meaning of the above doctrinal developments in the light of a new tentative analysis of theory and practice of the law of nations in Europe as well as Asia in the past. If it is a feasible proposition at all it must proceed on the lines of assessment of the realities which confronted the family of nations at a period of ideological changes. The eighteenth-century world was at the same time one of expanding world commercial relations and one of contracting international legal conceptions. The conflict between the two tendencies did not allow a proper place to be found for the natural law principle of world intercourse within the positive law of nations which was shrunk to the European area. But whatever the possible way out of this dilemma, a solution which condemned extra-European participants in world intercourse to a legal vacuum could hardly be considered realistic. To say for the convenience of upholding doctrinal trends which tended to be one-sided at the cost of consistency that State entities which had enjoyed legal status within the natural family of nations in the past are in a doubtful legal position if judged by positivist standards is to judge the past by *ex post facto* law and to offend the dogma of continuity of the family of civilized nations. Thus the so-called admission or readmission of extra-European States as found in the treatises of nineteenth-century writers can only mean an inter-temporal re-adjustment of their position caused by doctrinal developments. The family of nations could not have been reduced from universality to a regional framework by a change of doctrine. Admission of new States was and is possible only in relation to entities which came newly into being. It cannot comprise those of them which existed long before and drew their legal status from a law of civilized nations in mutual intercourse whose universality had been an undisputable reality.[25]

It is in the light of these observations that the views of writers such as Ompteda who advocated the assimilation of the modified natural law of nations to the new positive law and the adoption of a law of civilized nations seemed more in consonance with the reality of events than those of some of the well-known positivist writers who allowed themselves to be carried away by the compelling force of doctrinal trends.[26]

[25] As to the fallacy of considering capitulations as an impediment to the acceptance of this view, it would be relevant to state that the origin and development of capitulations calls for a thorough reconsideration; Alexandrowicz, loc. cit., p. 250.

[26] There might also have been other reasons for which the elimination of the natural law concept was not wholly advisable even from the European point of view, to mention the partitions of Poland which by positivist standards were justifiable but were a flagrant violation of the principles of the natural law of nations (see Introduction to Martens's *Précis du droit des gens* (ed. by Vergé, 1864), p. xvi.

14

G. F. DE MARTENS ON ASIAN TREATY PRACTICE (1964)

I.

Georg Friedrich de Martens is the author of the first systematic compendium of the European Law of Nations, perhaps one less extensive than J. J. Moser's treatise[1] and one less popular and imaginative than Vattel's *Droit des Gens*, but certainly a work which excels all contemporary writings on the Law of Nations by its thoughtful lay-out and careful legal formulations. If Martens's significance lies in his positivist European approach to problems of the law of nations, why bother about Asian treaty practice which appears in his work only as a sideline, obviously of secondary importance? The answer to this question must be sought not in Martens's express opinions but in his occasional remarks and references which reveal an undercurrent of thought never brought to the forefront. But though hidden between the lines of the text, it allows us to ascertain the presence of a dilemma which must have confronted the writers of the eighteenth century positivist school and indeed remains a problem even to present day positivists in international law. The point is that at the time when European international lawyers of the non-naturalist brand assumed the monopoly of formulating the principles of the law of nations on the basis of available treaty material and customary law, they could not ignore the existence of a considerable volume of treaties concluded between European and Asian powers. These treaties had been instrumental in legally formalising the operation of world trade which contributed significantly to the expansion of European economy.[2] When Martens displayed in his works the extensive treaty material which was to show that the law of nations in its positivist aspect was to be extracted from inter-European relations, he found European treaties intermingled with European–Asian treaties which could hardly support the idea of an exclusively European-centred positive law of nations. He could have welcomed the availability of this material, for it tended to point to the possibility of conceiving a universal positive law of civilised nations and thus could have helped to salvage the idea of the universality of the law which was rendered precarious by the decline of the naturalist conception. But it

[1] See *Versuch des neuesten Europäischen Völkerrechts* (1770–80).

[2] The importation of merchandise from the East Indies brought in its wake some cultural influence from Asia, a phenomenon which can be traced back to the days of the Roman Empire.

was difficult to expect a writer who set out to compose a treatise on European law to abandon his principal idea and to draw conclusions from Asian treaty material which in a way was outside the scope of his inquiry. Not being able to put to himself clearly the problem of reconciliation of European positivism with the universality of the law of nations, Martens confined himself to quoting, in addition to European treaty material, that relating to Asia and left the drawing of conclusions to the reader.

The significance of Martens's literary legacy is usually connected with his principal treatise, i.e., the *Précis du Droit des Gens Modernes de l'Europe fondé sur les traités et l'usage* (1789), which was translated into English by William Cobbet in 1795. However, for the purpose of our considerations it would be wholly misleading to confine ourselves to the *Précis* (Compendium) for Martens refers to Asian treaty practice also in his *Cours Diplomatique ou Tableau des Relations extérieures des Puissances de l'Europe tant entre elles qu'avec d'autres états dans les diverses parties du globe*; and, in his *Recueil des Traités* he gives the text of many Asian treaties which are listed in the *Précis* or discussed in the *Cours Diplomatique*.[3] The interrelationship between these three works has been largely ignored by historians of the law of nations and deserves careful attention.

II.

The *Précis* contains a systematic exposition of principles of the law of nations and the treaties listed at the end of the work constitute so to say the raw material from which many of these principles are drawn in a truly positivist way. As stated above, we find among these treaties a considerable number of Asian treaties but with a few exceptions no reference is made in the text of the *Précis* to the peculiarities of European–Asian relations. However, in the *Cours Diplomatique* Martens often engages in a discussion of the negotiations preceding the conclusion of treaties and offers his comments on their significance within the general framework of external relations '*dans les diverses parties du globe*'. The treaty material is in both works in chronological order but in the *Cours Diplomatique* Martens attempts its classification on a geographical basis and, moreover, he groups the Asian contracting parties according to certain classes determined by various degrees of sovereignty. Among the leading Asian sovereigns appear the rulers of China, the Moghul Empire, Persia, Siam and Ceylon,[4] not to mention the sovereigns of the Ottoman Empire which

[3] Martens (1756–1821) could be rightly described as a Pan-European, for he served not only his own country (Hanover) but also the kingdom of Westphalia (created by Napoleon) and Great Britain (in the capacity of counsellor). Though a German professor, civil servant and diplomat, he wrote many of his works originally in French and they were only later translated into German or English.

[4] China, Persia and Siam never lost their independence while the Moghul Empire disintegrated in the eighteenth century. Burma disappeared as a sovereign power in the 1880s. The rulers of Ceylon became first dependent on the Portuguese, then on the Dutch and at the end of the eighteenth century their kingdom came under British rule.

is not primarily within the scope of our considerations. A further group comprises all those sovereigns who in the eighteenth century emerged out of the debris of the Moghul Empire such as those of Bengal, the Carnatic, Mysore, the Deccan, Oudh and the Maratha Confederation. Then follows the multitude of heterogeneous vassals of various degrees of dependence who were compelled to submit to different overlords according to changing political circumstances. In this network of power politics appear first the Portuguese and then three East Indian Companies (the Dutch, English and French) who found in it their proper place sometimes as vassal[5] and more often as suzerain or equal in status.[6]

The Portuguese established in the sixteenth century a maritime Empire in Asia with its headquarters in Goa and developed a wide network of treaty relations endowing a number of local rulers with the status of vassals of the Crown of Portugal. Their Empire collapsed in the seventeenth century under the impetus of Dutch expansion and Martens makes no reference to the relevant treaties which were obviously unknown to him.[7] But he has much to say about the Dutch East India Company whose policy in the East Indies he characterises by observing that the Company tended to reduce local princes to vassalship and to obtain delivery of goods at fixed prices, usually unfavourable to them.[8] Among the treaties in support of this observation he quotes those concluded in the seventeenth century with Indonesian rulers, particularly with the Princes of Macassar, Ternate, Tidor, Java and the rulers of the West coast of India such as Calicut, Cochin and Cranganor.[9] On a different footing were the treaties with the King of Ceylon[10] who preserved his independent status. Among the eighteenth century treaties Martens quotes those concluded with the Kings of Salangor and Johore over whom the Dutch established their suzerainty. The text of these treaties as well as of the treaty of 1766 concluded with Ceylon appears in the *Recueil des Traités*. Martens also refers to Dutch–Japanese relations maintained in a limited way through the settlement at Desima. However, the most interesting treaty quoted by Martens is that concluded in 1631 with the King of Persia which established a Persian trade settlement in the Netherlands. This treaty will be discussed in more detail below.

[5] See the conferment in 1765 of the Diwanee of Bengal, Bihar and Orissa on the English East India Company which made the latter a Grand Officer of the Moghul Empire (*Cours Diplomatique*).

[6] The legal position of the East India Companies as semi-sovereign agencies endowed by their sovereigns in Europe with delegated powers made their relations with the leading Asian sovereigns frequently precarious and thus ambassadors had to be despatched direct from Europe to the respective Asian sovereign whenever he was unwilling to treat a trading company on a basis of equality (see the embassy of Sir Thomas Roe to the Moghul court in 1615, or that of Lord Macartney to the Emperor of China in 1792). It may also be noted that some of the Asian sovereigns were reluctant to expand their relations with European powers, a fact which is duly noted by Martens, particularly in relation to China.

[7] These treaties have been later collected by Judice Bicker in his *Collecção de tratados* (1881).

[8] Vattel in his *Droit des Gens* considers Dutch policy reconcilable with principles of the law of nations (transl. by J. Chitty, 1834, p. 144).

[9] See the treaties of 1609, 1611, 1650, 1658, 1667, 1668, 1669, 1784 and the treaties of 1610, 1663, 1674.

[10] See the treaty of 1766.

The two other East India Companies, the English and the French, were involved in the eighteenth century in an acute struggle which ended with the withdrawal of French power from the Indian sub-continent. Martens has therefore little to say about French–Indian treaties except for recording the acquisition by the French of Pondicherry in 1751,[11] and for pointing out the general character of French alliances directed against their English rival including the treaty of friendship with the Sultan of Mysore whom the French assisted until his defeat in 1799. But of much greater interest to the historian of the law of nations are the treaties between France and Siam in the seventeenth century. Martens draws attention to their significance from the missionary point of view but fails to make proper reference to the treaties of 1687 though he enables the reader to trace their text by referring to Dumont's *Corps Universel.*

By far the most extensive treaty material contained in the *Cours Diplomatique* relates to the activities of the English East India Company in India. Martens classifies the treaties concluded with Indian rulers on a geographical basis enabling the reader to reconstitute the political map of India in the eighteenth century and the kaleidoscopic changes on it. The unifying power of India, the Moghul Emperor, had been at that period reduced to a nominal status, but he still retained the prerogative of legalising the *de facto* arrangements imposed on him by his gradually emancipated vassals. The English East India Company had been one of them and participated to the fullest extent in the struggle for overlordship in India. Martens's chronology of treaties contains suggestive indications of the progress of this contest which, as rightly stated by Professor Westlake, revealed striking analogies with the disintegration of the vassal-ridden Holy Roman Empire.[12] The English Company, similarly to the French, occupied for a long time a '*status mixtus*' on the Indian legal scene; it was a semi-sovereign agent of its own sovereign in Europe, a *de jure* vassal of the Moghul Empire, a *de facto* sovereign vis-à-vis other local *de facto* sovereigns and generally speaking a political and commercial power destined to re-unify India, a task which had never been crowned with lasting success in Indian history.

Among the Indian treaty makers, Martens distinguishes roughly speaking six local powers, i.e., the rulers of Bengal,[13] the Deccan,[14] Mysore,[15] the Carnatic,[16] Tanjore,[17] Oudh[18] and the Maratha confederation.[19] The treaty material contained in the *Cours Diplomatique* records the ultimate absorption of Bengal by the Company, the subordination to it of Mysore, the Carnatic and Tanjore, the relations with the sovereigns of the Deccan and Oudh and the competition with the Marathas for succession to Moghul rule in India. While the treaties between

[11] Pondicherry, though under the *de facto* sovereignty of India, is still *de jure* under French sovereignty.

[12] *Collected Papers on Public International Law* (1914).

[13] See the treaties of 1757, 1760, 1763, 1765, 1768, 1770, 1773, 1775.

[14] See the treaties of 1759, 1766, 1768, 1790.

[15] See the treaties of 1769, 1770, 1784, 1792, 1799.

[16] See the treaties of 1763, 1779, 1785, 1787.

[17] See the treaties of 1771, 1778, 1787.

[18] See the treaties of 1781 and 1788.

[19] See the treaties of 1739, 1756, 1775, 1776, 1778, 1781, 1782, 1789 and 1792.

the Dutch East India Company and Indonesian rulers are instruments of suzerain-vassal relations of a stereotype character, the Anglo–Indian treaties are of a great variety and constitute an essential contribution to the clarification of the concept of sovereignty and suzerainty showing some of the dynamic potentialities of protected and vassal states in the framework of the law of nations as later evidenced within the Ottoman Empire. A comparative and more detailed analysis of these treaties (jointly with other European–Asian treaties) would enable historians of the law of nations to reconsider a wide range of problems which in present day treatises are presented in a hardly satisfactory way. These problems extend *inter alia* to the field of capitulations which in the light of Asian tradition reveal different characteristics from those ascribed to them by orthodox writers in Europe; further to international commercial standards (most-favoured-nation and national) which were a corollary to trade expansion in the experimental Asian scene; to the discriminatory clauses in commercial monopoly treaties; to the inter-connection between monopoly and vassalship which was reflected in the theory of equal and unequal treaties; and to the impact of treaty making between Christian and non-Christian powers on the secularisation of treaty law. It should be kept in mind that European–Asian treaty practice preceded the decline of the independent Asian state system in the nineteenth century and thus came in time to exercise some influence on the development of treaty law as such which was still *in fieri* in the eighteenth century.

It has been stated above that treaty relations between European powers and the Ottoman Empire are outside the scope of these considerations. These relations have frequently been discussed by historians of the law of nations within the framework of the European law of nations. Martens considers the Ottoman Empire as being on the European side of the border line dividing the two continents. However, Ottoman treaties deserve to be brought into the picture in so far as they often provide a *tertium comparationis* in European–Asian relations throwing light on problems of capitulations and vassalship. As to Russia, Martens refers to her treaty relations with Persia in the seventeenth and eighteenth centuries and to her success in overcoming in the seventeenth century China's reluctance to deal with European powers on any other than a unilateral basis. He draws our attention to the Russian–Chinese treaty of Nertshinsk of 1689. Finally Martens refers to three minor East India Companies, the Danish, Swedish and Prussian. No treaty-making of any significance evolved out of their operations in Asia.

III.

This brief introduction to Martens's survey of Asian treaties as adopted in the *Cours Diplomatique* may enable the reader to follow some of the details comprised in these treaties. As it is, however, practically impossible to go into all of them, a tentative selection is suggested enabling us to understand the problems most relevant to our main purpose of showing *the inadequacy of the European conception of positivism to respond to the inherent requirement of universality of the family of nations.* To what extent Martens has been unwittingly driven to an implicit admission of this inadequacy, will follow from his occasional statements in the *Précis du Droit des Gens* which will be considered later. Three treaties selected *inter alia* for discussion are the Dutch–Persian treaty of 1631, and the French–Siam treaties of 1685 and 1687.

The first of these treaties, the text of which has been published in Dumont's *Corps Universel* (1731), concedes certain privileges and immunities to a Persian settlement in the Netherlands. Martens remarks about this settlement that it existed still at the end of the eighteenth century in Amsterdam. Why concentrate in the first instance on this generally ignored document? First of all it proves the possibility of application of capitulations in favour of an Asian community in Europe in the past while most of the writers believed them to be an institution connected with the inferiority of Asian civilisation and with the decline of sovereignty of Asian powers. In fact capitulations are the product of Asian civilisation and date back to a period long prior to the arrival of Europeans in Asia. It was ancient customary law in Asia to grant concessions to settlements of foreign merchants who were allowed to govern themselves by their own laws and habits and constituted a sort of miniature society within the larger community whose hospitality they enjoyed.[20] Moslem merchants used to receive such concessions in the Hindu states on the West coast of India in the eighth century and later, and the same applies to other parts of Asia such as for instance the foreign settlements in Siam. These capitulation (or pre-capitulation) arrangements allowed foreigners, apart from following their own personal law, to enjoy a fair measure of administrative autonomy within the general framework of jurisdiction of the territorial sovereign. There was no suggestion in this institution to the effect that the concessions granted by the territorial sovereign were in any way derogatory to his sovereignty. They amounted to a minimum standard of treatment of foreigners on the basis of a generally accepted custom or usage. It is exactly thanks to the existence of this institution that European merchants who settled in Asian countries in the sixteenth, seventeenth and eighteenth centuries were able to make a suitable start. However, they converted in course of time their initial footholds into larger administrative units combining their privileges with commercial and military expansion. It is only at this later stage that these privileges became capable of being derogatory to the Asian territorial sovereign. The same process can be observed in the Ottoman Empire where concessions to European residents were from the beginning embodied in formal capitulation treaties. Martens offers in the *Cours Diplomatique* a list of these early treaties which starts with the French–Ottoman treaty of 1535, decried by early European monographers on treaty law as an alliance of a Christian sovereign with infidels against another Christian sovereign (the Holy Roman Empire).[21]

The first capitulation arrangements between European and Asian powers in the early seventeenth century were in principle revocable and never offended the

[20] C.H. Alexandrowicz, 'Treaty and Diplomatic Relations between European and South Asian Powers in the Seventeenth and Eighteenth Centuries', *Recueil des Cours*, 100 (1960), p. 261

[21] See Cacheranus, Pott and others listed in Ompteda's *Literature of the Law of Nations* (1795).

sovereignty of the local ruler. Such were for instance the concessions obtained in 1602 by Sir James Lancaster from the ruler of Achem (Sumatra) which allowed English merchants to govern themselves by English law. Such were the concessions granted in 1639 by a vassal of the Vijayanagar kingdom to the first English settlement in Madras.[22] Moreover, when these privileges became one of the foundations of the semi-sovereign status of the English and French East India Companies in India, it was still not impossible to apply them reciprocally. Thus, in the treaty of 1770 between the English East India Company and the Moslem ruler of Mysore a high officer of the ruler (Killedar) was established in one of the Company's possessions to perform jurisdictional functions in relation to the ruler's subjects. This treaty is quoted by Martens in his *Cours Diplomatique*.

The various jurisdictional provisions in East Indian treaties can be classified into those relating to civil or criminal jurisdiction. In cases reserved to the jurisdiction of the territorial Asian sovereign, the agent of the European community was usually given an opportunity of participating in proceedings in which one of its nationals was involved. Disputes between members of the particular European community were in principle reserved to the jurisdiction of the head of the community while disputes between members of the community and subjects of the territorial state belonged (subject to limitations) either to the respective local ruler or alternatively to the head of the community. In this respect the nationality of the defendant was usually essential in deciding who was to assume jurisdiction and apply the law.[23] We shall however see that still another formula was adopted in the French–Siam treaties.

These observations have been offered to justify the need for reconsideration of the origin and development of the law of capitulations which is treated by some of the positivist writers (nineteenth century or contemporary) as evidence of the dubious membership of Asian powers in the family of nations. The Dutch–Persian treaty of 1631 is bound to provide further counter-evidence disproving this conception. Martens defines this treaty as *Capitulation des Etats-Généraux des Provinces Unies avec le Roi de Perse Shah Sophi sur les privilèges accordés aux marchands perses et sur un bureau de commerce accordé à eux en Hollande*.[24] The privileges were granted '*en revanche des privilèges accordés aux Hollandais en Perse*'. Article X of the treaty provides for the establishment in the Netherlands of an agent of the King of Persia endowed with jurisdictional powers. If any Persian national under his protection should resist his orders and commit an offence, the local Dutch authorities would extend their assistance to him to secure due administration of justice. The royal agent had according to Article VI a quasi-diplomatic status and enjoyed in his residence the same immunities as those accorded in respect of resident quarters to agents

[22] *Recueil des Cours* (1960), p. 254.

[23] Compare these provisions with similar provisions in the Ottoman capitulation treaties (see Cours Diplomatique); see also *Recueil des Cours* (1960), p. 257.

[24] It is notable that the treaty had been negotiated directly between the King of Persia and the States-General of the United Provinces, over the head of the Dutch East India Company (see T. E. Heeres, *Corpus Diplomaticum Neerland-Indicum* Part I (1596–1650)).

of European sovereigns at the Court of the States-General. Most-favoured-nation treatment was also accorded to Persian nationals who enjoyed in matters of trade and administration of justice the same rights as those granted to English nationals residing in Delft and to Scottish nationals residing in Campveere. Moreover Article II granted to Persian settlers national treatment in respect of freedom of movement and trade. Further privileges relate to exemptions from duties in respect of consumer goods used in settlers' homes (Article V) and freedom of exercising religion in such homes (Article VII). Article VIII abolished the *droit d'aubaine*, a provision which can also be found in other treaties to mention again the arrangement between Sir James Lancaster and the ruler of Achem (1602) which provided that wills of English settlers were to be honoured by the local authorities and that in case of intestacy the English Governor would take charge of the property of the deceased. Similarly Article VIII of the Anglo–Ottoman capitulation treaty of 1641 stated that if an Englishman died in the Sultan's territories his property would go to his testamentary successors and if he died intestate the Consul would look after the property. This treaty is listed by Martens in the *Cours Diplomatique*.

This short survey of the treaty of 1631 would prove the readiness of European powers in the pre-nineteenth century law of nations to grant capitulations to Asian settlements in Europe '*en revanche des privilèges*' granted to Europeans in Asia. The Royal Persian agent in the Netherlands acted no doubt in the capacity of a commercial and judicial consul and it is notable that in the treaty of 1718 between Austria and the Ottoman Empire the latter received the right to appoint consuls in Austrian territory.[25] Moreover Moslem settlements in Poland and in the Balkans governed themselves by their own personal laws and generally possessed autonomy in the management of their internal affairs.[26]

A *sui generis* jurisdictional formula was adopted in one of the Franco–Siam treaties. Diplomatic negotiations between the two countries resulted in 1685 in the conclusion of a treaty which conferred privileges on French missionaries in Siam. Article III of the treaty extended certain rights to subjects of the King of Siam who had embraced the Christian faith, a peculiar arrangement in which one contracting power protects the interests of subjects of the other for reasons of ideological affinity. Article V entrusted high officers of the Kingdom (Mandarins) with the hearing of complaints in case of injustice done to these local Christians but judgment was only to be given after taking the advice of a royal judge in each case. In 1687 two more treaties were concluded, one relating to military co-operation between the contracting countries, and the other to their commercial relations. The commercial treaty granted a concession to the French East India Company to build a factory and allowed the Company to enjoy free trade in the Kingdom of Siam (Articles I and II). Article V relating to jurisdictional questions left disputes between servants of the French Company (French or other nationals) to the competence of the principal officer of the Company, a provision similar to those found in most of the capitulation treaties in the Ottoman Empire and in the East Indies. Any Frenchman in the

[25] Though without jurisdictional powers.

[26] See *Recueil des Cours* (1960), p. 265.

service of the Company who committed homicide or another crime against another Frenchman in the service of the Company was to be arrested by the latter and sent to France for trial. However, civil or criminal proceedings initiated by a servant of the Company against a non-Frenchman (not in the service of the Company) or vice versa were within the competence of the King of Siam but according to Article V the King agreed to invite in each case an officer of the Company (endowed with powers by the King of France) to be a member of the Court and to function in a judicial capacity. Thus we are faced with the existence in the seventeenth century in an Asian country of a mixed tribunal, *mutatis mutandis* of the same type as the mixed Court existing in Egypt up to 1937 or even later. It may also be mentioned that the treaty of military co-operation of 1687 contained the following provision in Article VII: '*La justice militaire des troupes françaises appartiendra aux français*'. Thus French forces in Siam enjoyed jurisdictional immunity, a kind of 'military capitulation' or exemption which appears frequently in our present day inter-allied military arrangements.[27]

IV.

A special group of treaties listed by Martens relates primarily to commercial monopolies and suzerain–vassal relations. The question may arise what is the (*prima facie* irrelevant) interrelationship between the two? In this connection reference may be made to the views of a writer contemporary to G. F. de Martens and often quoted by him i.e., J. H. G. von Justi. They do not appear in any of his well-known publications but in a generally forgotten work under the title '*Les gouvernements de l'Europe comparés à ceux de l'Asie etc*' (1762). Justi, similarly to Abbé Raynal,[28] criticises the policy of the European East India Companies in Asia and particularly their development from trading agencies to powerful political and military units which administered commercial monopolies leading to the reduction of Asian states to the level of dependencies (vassals). Whether this criticism was motivated by objective considerations or whether it was rather the expression of dissatisfaction felt in Germany which had missed the opportunity of competing effectively with Great Britain, the Netherlands and France in the participation in Asian commerce, may be open to doubt.[29] Martens's treaty material in the *Cours Diplomatique* throws some light on the legal aspects of East India Company activities. One of the characteristic features found in treaties concluded between them and Asian rulers is the appearance of the discriminatory clause stipulated by one European country against another. The

[27] *Recueil des Cours* (1960), p. 260; and see *Recueil des Traités* by Reinach (1902), and *La condition des étrangers au Siam au XVIIe siècle* by R. Lingat.

[28] Martens often quotes Raynal's works; see particularly *Histoire philosophique et politique des établissements et du commerce des Européens dans les deux Indes* (1770). See also *Théorie des traités de commerce entre les nations* by M. Bouchaud (1777), p. 189.

[29] In this respect Martens quotes J. J. Surland's *Juris Germanorum Navigandi Indias Prima Fundamenta* (1751).

Asian contrahent concedes in this type of treaty absolute preferential treatment to the contracting European Company which monopolises trade in a particular Asian state to the exclusion of all European rivals. In its most drastic form the discriminatory clause appeared already in the seventeenth century in the Dutch–Indonesian treaties listed by Martens (see above). It imposed on the contracting local ruler the duty to trade exclusively with the Dutch East India Company and to eliminate all other European nations (particularly the Portuguese and the English) from his territories. The English East India Company retaliated against the Dutch in treaties concluded with Indian rulers and extended discrimination also against the French. The relevant treaties with the rulers of Bengal, Mysore, the Carnatic, the Deccan, Oudh and the Marathas (as listed by Martens) all testify to the reality of this development. A survey of these treaties shows that the discriminatory clause, apart from monopolising trade, extended to the expulsion of 'other' European nationals from the territory of the contracting ruler, the closure of frontiers and harbours to foreigners, the prohibition of free navigation, the prohibition of accepting foreign military or technical assistance, the prohibition to build fortifications (which contained the element of an international servitude) and ultimately the prohibition of maintaining external relations with other European powers.[30]

But though the discriminatory treaty clause exercised a significant influence on the balance of power in the East Indies, its legal effects were not in principle allowed to become detrimental to dependent rulers if viewed from the standpoint of legal classification as known to the classic writers. When Grotius, Pufendorf, Wolff and Vattel gradually developed the theory of equal and unequal treaties, they made it clear that unequal treaties such as those of vassalage did not necessarily suppress the sovereignty of the dependent ruler. Martens, following this classification, states expressly in his *Précis* that 'mere alliances of protection, tribute or vassalage which a state may contract with another do not hinder it from continuing perfectly sovereign'. Inequality of treaty was not in itself a reason for disrespecting its sovereignty. It had been emphasised by Vattel that the relationship between a dependent ruler and his suzerain remained the concern of the law of nations and that it was unlawful for the protector (suzerain) to take advantage of inequality of relationship and to exploit his overlordship at the cost of the dependent power. As long as the latter had not transferred its constituent rights to the superior power, or as long as their mutual relations were based on treaty or other mutual arrangement, the inferior party could denounce the overlordship if the superior was guilty of violation of the law. Vattel quotes as an example the resistance of the inhabitants of Lucerne against Hapsburg domination. In the trial of Warren Hastings (the Governor General of the English East India Company) before Parliament at Westminster, E. Burke relied on Vattel in the defence of the Raja of Benares (a subordinate ruler) whose rights had been infringed by the East India Company. Burke referred in this respect to the 'natural equity (and) the law of nations' which authorise a subordinate ruler to resist any violation of his rights by the suzerain or protector. The Raja of Benares

[30] The prohibition of foreign relations with other Asian powers was generally not practicable.

could hardly be presumed to have been aware of his position in the law of nations as stated by the classic writers in Europe, but he relied no doubt on Hindu tradition as evidenced in Kautilya's *Arthashastra* (fourth century B.C.) which prohibited in any case the *debellatio* of the vassal by the suzerain.[31]

Martens in his *Précis* (p. 270) refers to treaties between Indian sovereigns (Kings) and European powers 'in virtue of which those powers enjoy an exclusive trade with them'. He states further that 'those kings are bound not to make any alteration towards favouring or opening commerce with other (European) powers'. However, similar limitations on free trade in the East Indies were also imposed on European powers (see for instance the liquidation of the Austrian Ostende Company in 1731) and moreover any of these limitations were treated as an exception to the generally recognised liberty of treaty making which extended also to Asian nations. Thus in another passage Martens stresses the right of any European nation to engage in trade with Indian nations 'provided the latter are willing to admit it',[32] a statement which leaves us in no doubt about Martens's view on the *universal* application of the fundamental principles of the law of nations in the process of inter-European as well as European–Asian treaty-making. In support of the above statement Martens quotes Kluit's *Historia Foederum*, Surland's *Erläutertes Recht der Deutschen nach Indien zu handeln* (1752) and Moser's *Versuch* (VII, 449, 359).[33] The significance of the influence of the above works on Martens will be briefly considered.

Adrian Kluit, a Dutch historian (1735–89) and professor of the University of Leyden since 1779, wrote apart from the *Historia Foederum* also the *Index Chronologicus Sistens Foedera Pacis, Defensionis, Navigationis, Commerciorum, etc.* (1789). In these works reference is made to treaties between the Dutch East India Company and Asian rulers such as the rulers of Macassar (1604), Ternate and Tidor (1607, 1609, 1613, 1629, 1630), Calicut (1610), Java (1611), Cochin (1663) and to further treaties with Indonesian and Indian rulers (1668, 1674, 1693, etc.) some of which are drawn from Dumont's *Corps Universel.* Kluit's influence on Martens as a collector of treaties is obvious. J. J. Surland's work (quoted in German) is otherwise known under its Latin title *Juris Germanorum Navigandi Indias Prima Fundamenta* (1751). He tends to justify Germany's claim to trade in the East Indies and emphasises the right of any European power (irrespective of monopolies established by others) to engage in independent relations with Asian sovereigns. In this respect Surland quotes Barbeyrac as saying that any power has 'freedom of access and navigation to the free and independent countries of India which allow them to do so'. This is precisely the language used by Martens in his *Précis* and it becomes clear that the emphasis on the sovereignty of Asian rulers as actual or potential contrahents was to a great extent conditioned by the competition between European powers which

[31] *Recueil des Cours* (1960), pp. 215–17. In this connexion it may be noted that the invasion of Tibet by China was a breach of international law.

[32] See *Précis*, second ed. (1801), p. 235.

[33] Martens also refers to Bouchaud's *Théorie des traités de commerce* (1777) and to Rousset's *Recueil Historique d'Actes, Negotiations, Mémoires et Traités* (1731).

were driven to resort to it whenever a particular monopoly imposed by one of them became too oppressive to others. Be that as it may, power politics and economics had their due influence on the extension of the European law of nations to the Asian continent and it was obvious that the intimate inter-connection between world trade and the law of nations made the restriction of the positive law of nations to Europe a doubtful proposition. Even more illuminating is Martens's reference to J. J. Moser's *Versuch des neuesten Europäischen Völker-Rechts* (1779), for Moser in spite of his positivist approach, stresses the freedom of commerce '*pour tous les peuples de l'univers*'. Limitations on this freedom may be imposed by treaty but Moser does not restrict the range of treaties to inter-European relations but refers expressly to treaties with Asian sovereigns though he supports the universality of the law of nations by the natural law ideology which he contrasts with the positive law of nations.[34]

It would be relevant to state that Martens's and Moser's unwillingness to concede an express extension of the positive European law of nations to the Asian continent was by no means shared by other contemporary writers to mention only Ompteda[35] who tried to assimilate the modified natural law of all civilised nations, based on their *consensus praesumptus*, to the positive law of nations, and thus to rescue the idea of universality of the law within the framework of positivism. The success of this attempt, if it had prevailed over the restricted positive European law of nations, could have been gratifying in its consequences, for it would have meant the existence of a measure of common European–Asian legal ideology which would have helped to minimise the negative effects of European egocentricism. Instead, the positive European law of nations which had set itself up as a monopolising system, became not only a school of law but also of egocentricism with the result that the spread of the positivist concept at a later stage from Europe to other parts of the world tended to create new centres of egocentricism in international law and politics. Positivism divorced from the pre-nineteenth century principle of universality of the family of nations was therefore bound to degenerate into a self-defeating system, for though it is obvious today that the law must be universal, its universality cannot be based on a multitude of egocentric positivist schools of thought, be they Asian, African, or East European (Communist). The idea of universality of the law of nations, as proposed in Martens's days by Kant,[36] has therefore to look for another legal formulation which cannot be found elsewhere than in the inherent quality of mankind and the family of nations to be universal, a consideration which Martens as a positivist was unable or reluctant to take into account.[37]

[34] See *Versuch* (1779), Vol. VII, pp. 449–51.

[35] *Literatur des gesammten sowohl natürlichen als positiven Völkerrechts* (1785), pp. 18–20, 31. See: 'Doctrinal Aspects of the Universality of the Law of Nations'. *British Yearbook of International Law* (1961), pp. 506–15 (ch. 13 above).

[36] See *Perpetual Peace*, translated by H. O'Brien, Grotius Society Publications No. 7 (1929).

[37] When the coexistence of the European positive law of nations and the declining natural law universality of the family of nations proved to be a futile proposition, the proclamation of the former as universal without universal participation was bound to result in a pars pro toto fallacy. It may also be noted that the universality of the law of nations was a characteristic feature of the natural law ideology, whether in its scholastic or 'Grotian' version.

V.

While Martens does not draw any specific conclusions from the Asian treaty material which he had collected and included in his works, the material speaks for itself and suggests compelling reasons for conceiving the existence of a fairly wide meeting ground on which European and Asian countries were not only able to engage in trade but also to exchange cultural values and legal ideas. The development of an extensive treaty practice covering both continents reveals the mutual respect for certain fundamental rules such as *bona fides* or *pacta sunt servanda*. Flexible adjustment was made possible by resort to *rebus sic stantibus*.[38] European–Asian treaty making over an uninterrupted period of three centuries helped to overcome the obstacles on the part of Christian writers as to the validity of treaties between Christian and non-Christian powers. Its impact on the secularisation of treaty law as such was remarkable.[39] Various types of treaties show a wide range of legal institutions to the evolution of which the European as well as Asian contracting parties made their proper contribution such as in the field of Suzerain–Vassal relations, commercial standards and capitulations. It has been shown elsewhere that the freedom of the high seas, which is a condition of world commercial expansion, is an idea which Grotius most probably drew from his enquiry into maritime custom prevailing in the Indian Ocean before the arrival of Europeans in Asia. Similarly the respect for the immunity of diplomatic envoys as known in Asia[40] made mutual negotiations a workable proposition, and even the *temperamenta belli*, as particularly stressed by Justi in his work on Asian government, made it possible to wage wars in the East Indies on a fairly humanitarian basis.[41] A further exploration of the sources from which Martens collected his treaty material would no doubt lead to the discovery of other legal institutions which could be included in the record of European–Asian co-operation prior to the nineteenth century.

To conclude our considerations it would be relevant to emphasise that a revival of knowledge of the pre-nineteenth century law of nations seems a proposition worthy of attention. The International Court of Justice considered in 1960 a case in which a grip on historical material would not have detracted from the otherwise excellent quality of the judgment. In the Indo–Portuguese dispute over the enclaves of Dadra and Nagarhaveli the judges had to consider the validity of an eighteenth century treaty (the Maratha–Portuguese treaty of 1779) and of legal institutions instrumental in the transfer of sovereignty of the enclaves from one contracting party to the other. In some of the arguments of the parties before the Court there seemed to have been a tendency to look at an eighteenth-century treaty through 'the eyes' of present day treaty law.[42] Would it not be more in consonance with

[38] *Recueil des Cours* (1960), p. 296.

[39] See Robert Ward's *Enquiry into the Foundation and History of the Law of Nations etc.* (1795), pp. 325–27.

[40] In Turkey subject to limitations in time of war.

[41] *Recueil des Cours* (1960), pp. 313–14.

[42] This argument has been rejected by the judges (ICJ Reports, 1960).

generally accepted principles of law to consider the system of law under which a treaty was concluded as primarily relevant to its interpretation? If so, international lawyers would be well advised to look at their discipline not only in legal terms prevailing in the last fifty or hundred years but with a readiness to go back to its roots and to contemplate the lessons of the past which often offer suitable patterns of solution for ever recurring situations. The nineteenth and twentieth century writers had not infrequently a tendency of promoting some of their 'progressive' views by an escape from pre-positivist law. Even if such an escape helped to pursue with more vigour the building up of a law based on the realities of modern State practice, the severance of links with the past is not a sufficient reason for ignoring it altogether. The continuity of the Family of Nations and its law has a reality of its own which does not permit international lawyers to confine their attention to selected periods and problems but calls for the exploration of all the relevant antecedents of law making, at least in the last five centuries. In any case, the past deserves to be viewed in the light of the law as it stood at the particular period under consideration. The law which matters for its proper understanding cannot be *ex post facto* law.

15

THE CONTINUITY OF THE SOVEREIGN STATUS OF CHINA IN INTERNATIONAL LAW (1956)

Historians of the law of nations agree that China enjoyed the position of a fully sovereign State up to the conclusion of the Sino–British treaty of Nanking in 1842.[1] Likewise, no international lawyer will question the present-day sovereign status of China, present-day meaning the period since the end of the First World War when limitations on Chinese territorial sovereignty imposed by a number of powers, including Japan, tended to be removed one by one. However the peculiar nature of the interim period between 1842 and say, 1918, in which these limitations were in force, led some writers to the conclusion that China's position as a subject of international law was to some extent doubtful. It has also been maintained that her status as a member of the family of *civilised* nations was somewhat questionable.[2] As it is one thing for a State to be sovereign, subject to well-defined limitations, and another to have a doubtful legal position within the society of *civilised* States, the question may be asked whether and to what extent China's status as a civilised nation has been questioned in actual State practice, and whether the continuity of her sovereign position has been affected by events prior to the treaty of 1842 and developments which followed later in the middle and second half of the nineteenth century. We shall not attempt to give an answer to this question in the light of the provisions of the various post-1842 treaties (except perhaps those relating to diplomatic intercourse), as this would be a repetition of what has been sufficiently explored. Our task is rather to throw light on the opening stages of the above interim period, particularly to discuss one of the first diplomatic missions sent to Peking for the purpose of establishing closer relations with the Chinese Empire, and

[1] Professor G. Keeton (*The Development of Extraterritoriality in China*, 1928, I, p. 12) maintains that Vattel in supporting China's right to freedom of foreign trade overlooked the fact that China was not a member of the family of nations which is subject to the rules of international law. This statement is not warranted by Vattel's fundamental views on the society of nations. He states in his *Droit des Gens* (Book I, ch. I, para 4) that all sovereign States—and China was undoubtedly one of them—are members of the natural society of nations 'subject to the law of nations'.

[2] See for instance: *Elements of International Law* by H. Wheaton (Fourth English Ed.) 1904, p. 23; *International Law* by L. Oppenheim, 1952, I, pp. 46–7. For a critical discussion of 'the Standard of Civilisation in International Law', see Dr. G. Schwarzenberger's article in *Current Legal Problems*, 1955.

to enquire into some of the nineteenth century diplomatic correspondence which reveals a number of interesting points to the historian of international law.

It might first be appropriate to recall that China entertained in past centuries extensive political and commercial relations with other nations and was far from pursuing a policy of isolation. In the first centuries of the Christian era Canton appeared already as an 'open port'.[3] Following an ancient Asian tradition China conceded also some measure of extraterritoriality to foreigners and granted concessions to merchants of other nations. These were based on the assumption of equality of nations unlike in the post-1842 treaties which tended to convert them into limitations of sovereignty imposed on the grantor. The Chinese Commonwealth developed also a widespread network of suzerain–vassal relations in which the Emperor of China assumed the position of overlord in relation to a number of countries in the sphere of Chinese civilisation. It is within the outer fringes of this network in South-East Asia that a European power, Portugal, first started to make inroads into the vested rights of China. In the conditions of growing conflict resulting from increasing Portuguese pressure, embassies despatched by the Portuguese to the Court of Peking remained unsuccessful. Imperial China thereafter pursued a policy of distrust and isolation towards all European powers. At the beginning of the eighteenth century Canton was the only port open to overseas trade and direct relations between the Court of Peking and European powers were out of the question. European traders in China had to deal with a special corporation of Chinese merchants called *Kong hang* which was recognised by the Government of China as an official agency holding a monopoly of foreign trade. English merchants enjoyed a limited liberty of action in Canton but this soon proved inadequate to the requirements of expanding commercial intercourse. It is in these circumstances that the Government of Great Britain decided to support the English community in China by sending a special ambassador to the Court of Peking.

It might be interesting to compare the above situation with a similar situation in India at the beginning of the seventeenth century. Here, as there, the English commercial community (East India Company) experienced a deadlock in the development of trade relations. Here as there an ambassador was sent to clear the way. The details of Sir Thomas Roe's embassy to the Mogul Court at Agra (1615–19) are well known.[4] No doubt the embassy helped to improve the position of the East India Company in India and this may have been the reason for the belief of the Court of St. James in the beneficial results of diplomatic negotiation in support of commercial activity. These are some of the antecedents of the embassy of Lord Macartney to China (1792–4) which deserves a more detailed discussion.[5]

The intended embassy was announced to the Chinese authorities by three commissioners of the East India Company who had been selected to regulate affairs

[3] *La Chine et le Droit International* by Professor J. Escarra, 1931, pp. 3–37.

[4] 'Mogul Sovereignty and the Law of Nations' by C. H. Alexandrowicz (*Indian Year Book of International Affairs*, 1955) (chapter 3 above).

[5] *An Authentic Account of an Embassy from the King of Great Britain to the Emperor of China* by Sir George Staunton (Secretary to the Embassy), London, 1779.

in Canton. They were asked to deliver a letter from the Chairman of the Court of Directors (Sir Francis Baring) to the Chinese Viceroy in Canton in which Sir Francis stated that 'His most Gracious Sovereign being desirous of cultivating the friendship of the Emperor of China, and of improving the connection, intercourse and good correspondence between the Courts of London and Pekin, and of increasing and extending the commerce between their respective subjects, had resolved to send his well-beloved cousin and counsellor Lord Macartney ... as his Embassador Extraordinary and Plenipotentiary to the Emperor of China, to represent his person ...' and to establish 'a perpetual harmony and alliance between them'. Sir Francis requested the information to be conveyed to the Court of Peking trusting in the proper reception of the embassy.[6] The initial steps taken show a striking analogy between Sir Thomas Roe's and Lord Macartney's embassies.

More information about the embassy to Peking can be gathered from His Majesty's private instructions to his ambassador, signified to him through one of the Secretaries of State. In these the King stated that 'a greater number of his subjects, than of any other Europeans, had been trading, for a considerable time past, in China; that the commercial intercourse between several other nations and that great Empire (China) had been preceded, accompanied or followed by special communications with its sovereign ...'. The King concerned with the position of his subjects now claimed 'the Emperor of China's protection for them with that weight which is due to the requisition of one great Sovereign from another ...' and stated that 'a free communication with a people, perhaps the most singular upon the globe among whom *civilisation*[7] had existed, and the arts been cultivated, through a long series of ages, with fewer interruptions than elsewhere, was well worthy, also, of being sought by the British nation, which saw with pleasure, and with gratitude applauded, the several voyages undertaken already, by His Majesty's command, and at the public expense, in the pursuit of knowledge, and for the discovery and observation of distant countries and manners' but that 'in seeking to improve a connection with China, no views were entertained except those of the general interest of humanity, the mutual benefit of both nations, and the protection of commerce under the Chinese government'.[8]

The same views were expressed in the letter written by the King to the Emperor of China in which he stated that 'the natural disposition of a great and benevolent sovereign, such as His Imperial Majesty, whom Providence had seated upon the throne for the good of mankind, was to watch over the peace and security of his dominions; and to take pains for disseminating happiness, virtue and knowledge among his subjects; extending the same beneficence, with all the peaceful arts, as far as he was able, to the human race'. Excluding any intention of conquest or territorial aggrandisement the King stated further that he had been anxious 'to enquire into the arts and manners of countries, where *civilisation*[9] had been improved by the wise ordinances and virtuous examples of their sovereigns, through a long series

[6] Staunton, *op. cit.*, I, p. 50. [7] Italics are mine. [8] Staunton, *op. cit.*, I, p. 53.
[9] Italics are mine.

of ages; and felt, above all, an ardent wish to become acquainted with those celebrated institutions of his (Imperial) Majesty's populous and extensive Empire, which had carried its prosperity to such a height, as to be the admiration of all surrounding nations'. And finally that being 'at peace with all the world, no time could be so propitious for extending the bounds of friendship and benevolence, and for proposing to communicate and receive the benefits which must result from an unreserved and amicable intercourse between such great and *civilised*[10] nations as China and Great Britain'.[11]

No official documents originating from a great power could bear better testimony to the position of China within the family of *civilised* nations and to her status in the law of nations at the close of the eighteenth century. It can hardly be assumed that the position was different fifty, or one hundred years later when international lawyers started questioning the test of civilisation in relation to China. The same argument may be applied to Japan and to certain other Asian countries, as Lord Macartney received also 'embassadorial powers addressed to the Emperor of Japan and the King of Cochin-China as well as a general commission to all Princes and States where he might have occasion to touch in the Chinese seas'.[12]

The reception of Lord Macartney by the Emperor took place at Zhe-hol. The ambassador presented the box with the address of His Majesty and the Emperor expressed 'the satisfaction he felt at the testimony which his Britannic Majesty gave to him of his esteem and goodwill, in sending him an embassy, with a letter and rare presents; that he, on his part, entertained sentiments of the same kind towards the sovereign of Great Britain and hoped that harmony should always be maintained among their respective subjects'.[13] In fact the Emperor, in order to help the English trading community, appointed after the audience[14] a new Viceroy in Canton who confirmed the assurances given to the ambassador at the Imperial Court and enquired whether the King of Great Britain would send again a diplomatic mission to China 'as a testimony of the subsisting friendship of His Britannic Majesty'.[15]

It is not our task to discuss in detail further developments in Sino–British relations which were far from satisfactory.[16] However, the attitude of the British Government towards China remained unchanged. In the eighteen-thirties it sent superintendents of trade to Canton to 'maintain a good and friendly understanding both with the officers, civil and military, and with the inhabitants of China'.[17]

[10] Italics are mine.

[11] Staunton, *op. cit.*, I, p. 55. As to the Emperor's reply to the King, see: *Glimpses of World History* by J. Nehru, 1949, p. 332.

[12] Staunton, *op. cit.*, I, 57.

[13] Staunton, *op. cit.*, III, p. 38. It may be mentioned that Lord Macartney was relieved from the ceremony of prostration before the Emperor.

[14] Staunton, (*op. cit.*, III, p. 43) writes about the reception after the audience that 'the commanding feature of the scene was the calm dignity and sober pomp of Asiatic grandeur, which European refinements have not yet attained'.

[15] Staunton, *op. cit.*, III, pp. 259, 319–20.

[16] A second embassy under Lord Amherst in 1816 failed to reach the Emperor (see Wheaton, *op. cit.*, p. 22; Keeton, *op. cit.*, I, p. 25).

[17] *British and Foreign State Papers*, Vol. XXII, p. 1229.

Viscount Palmerston wrote on the 25th January 1834 to Lord Napier, the superintendent, in the following words: 'In addition to the duty of protecting and fostering the trade of H.M. subjects with the port of Canton, it will be one of your principal objects to ascertain whether it may not be practicable to extend that trade to other parts of the Chinese dominions. And for this end you will omit no favourable opportunity of encouraging any disposition which you may discover in the Chinese authorities, to enter into commercial relations with H.M. Government. It is obvious that, with a view to the attainment of this object, the establishment of direct communications with the Imperial Court at Pekin would be desirable; and you will accordingly direct your attention to discover the best means of preparing the way for such communications....' He further instructed the superintendent to 'adopt no proceedings but such as may have a general tendency to convince the Chinese authorities of the sincere desire of the King to cultivate the most friendly relations with the Emperor of China....'[18]

Lord Napier recommended a different policy. In a letter written on the 7th February 1835 to Earl Grey he advised to extort a treaty 'which shall embrace the public and private interests of all civilised nations who may be induced to trade with that people'.[19] In a subsequent letter written to Viscount Palmerston on 14th August 1835 he expressed the absurd view that if the Emperor were opposed to an expansion of trade, we should 'remind him he is only an intruder', alluding to his Tartar descendence. He advised the application of force but stated that should the British Government 'prefer making gradual proposition by an embassy', he would recommend 'none of that ostentation practised in the instances of Macartney and Amherst....'[20] The Duke of Wellington, disagreeing with Napier's policy had written on the 2nd February 1835 that 'it is not by force and violence that His Majesty intends to establish a commercial intercourse between his subjects and China; but by the other conciliatory measures so strongly inculcated in all the instructions which you have received'.[21] Lord Napier's mission failed and after his withdrawal trade relations with China improved temporarily.[22]

It may be interesting to quote here from a memorial of the British merchants in Canton written to Lord Palmerston on the 21st March 1838: 'Respect for European international law as well as common justice may also render it expedient for the British Government to dictate to the Emperor of China, if it have the power, the regulations under which the commerce of his Empire with foreigners will be conducted....'[23] The difference of views between the local British community and the British Government is characteristic, particularly in the reference to international law which seems strange in this sort of memorandum.

In 1839 Sino–British relations deteriorated rapidly resulting in war and in the conclusion of the Treaty of Nanking in 1842. According to this treaty[24] five Chinese

[18] *State Papers*, Vol. XXII, p. 1232.

[19] *State Papers*, Vol. XXII, p. 1258 seq.

[20] *State Papers*, Vol. XXII, p. 1241.

[21] *State Papers, op. cit.*

[22] *State Papers*, Vol. XXII, p. 1295 (see Memorandum by the Duke of Wellington of the 24th March 1835.)

[23] *State Papers*, Vol. XXVII, p. 1334.

[24] *Treaties between the Emperor of China and Foreign Powers* edited by W. F. Mayers, London, 1877.

ports were opened to British trade and the Island of Hong Kong was ceded to Great Britain. But the latter agreed that on the assent of the Emperor to the treaty British forces would be withdrawn from Nanking and the Grand Canal and would 'no longer molest or stop the trade of China' (Article XII). The treaty also contained provisions relating to customs duties on the export and import of goods (Article X). The next treaty concluded in Tientsin in 1858[25] provided that 'all questions in regard to rights, whether of property or person, arising between British subjects shall be subject to the jurisdiction of British authorities' (Article XV) which meant a serious limitation on Chinese sovereignty but, as we have seen, not inconsistent with the ancient tradition of Asian countries.

However, more important from the point of view of China's status in international law is the provision in Article II of the treaty which provides for the exchange of ambassadors, ministers and other diplomatic agents 'in accordance with the universal practice of great and friendly nations'. The legal position implied in this provision seems paradoxical. If it be assumed that China was reluctant to accept it and if it is realised that the exchange of ambassadors must imply mutual recognition, it was a European power which sought the recognition of China and not vice versa. The same seems to be the position in all treaties subsequently concluded between China and other powers such as France, the United States, Russia, Japan, Germany, Holland, Belgium, Denmark, Austria, Portugal and others.[26] In spite of certain limitations imposed on China in these treaties, they all stipulated the exchange of envoys in accordance with the law of nations and for the establishment of mutual diplomatic relations. Whatever the constraints which China had to suffer in connection with all these arrangements, the express treaty provisions relating to diplomatic intercourse testify to China's uninterrupted sovereign status in the law of nations. Moreover, these provisions were in several cases supported by statements which leave us in no doubt as to China's legal position. For instance Article I of the Sino–American treaty of 1858 (Additional Articles)[27] stated that the Emperor of China in making concessions to foreign powers 'has by no means relinquished the right of eminent domain or dominion' over the territories in question. According to Article II 'any privilege or immunity in respect to trade or navigation within the Chinese dominions which may not have been stipulated for by the treaty, shall be subject to discretion of the Chinese Government and may be regulated by it accordingly....' Article V provided for the right of voluntary emigration of citizens of China and the United States from one country to the other. Finally Article VIII stated that 'the United States, always disclaiming and discouraging all practices of unnecessary dictation and intervention by one nation in the affairs or domestic administration of the other do hereby disclaim and disavow any intention or right to intervene in the domestic administration of China....'

More information as to the attitude of the United States to the international status of China can be gathered from the diplomatic correspondence between the Secretaries of State and American envoys to China. Mr. Cushing writing on the

25 Mayers, *op. cit.* 26 Mayers, *op. cit.* 27 Mayers, *op. cit.*

29th September 1844 to Mr. Calhoun about the position of Great Britain which 'had stipulated for the absolute exemption of her subjects from the jurisdiction of the Empire ...' stated that 'this exemption in behalf of citizens of the United States is agreed to in terms by the letter of the treaty of Wang-Hiya. By that treaty the laws of the Union follow its citizens and its banner protects them even within the dominion of the Chinese Empire'.[28] But these limitations of Chinese jurisdiction did not affect her sovereign status for as stated earlier in Mr. Webster's (Secretary of State) letter of 8th May 1843 to Mr. Cushing in China, the United States treated the Emperor of China in the same way as 'the Emperor of Russia or any other of the great powers of the world'.[29]

Mr. Fish (Secretary of State), writing to Mr. Bancroft on the 31st August 1869 stated that 'the great principle which underlies the articles of July 1868 is the recognition of the sovereign authority of the Imperial Government of Pekin ...' Commenting on the procedure of treaty-making between China and the United States he wrote that 'it came voluntarily from China and placed that power in theory on the same diplomatic footing with the nations of the Western world'. The treaty (1858) 'recognises the Imperial Government as the power to withhold or to grant further commercial privileges and also as the power whose duty it is to enforce the peaceful enjoyment of the rights already conferred'. 'While it confirms the international jurisdiction conferred by former treaties upon European and American functionaries over the persons and properties of their countrymen, it recognises at the same time the territorial integrity of China and prevents such a jurisdiction from being stretched beyond the original purpose'.[30] Mr. Fish then touched upon the 'co-operative policy' or uniform action of the great powers in China which dated from about the year 1863 and operated inter alia through the use of the most favoured nation clause. He observed as to this policy that so far as it 'was aggressive and attempted to force upon China measures which could not be enforced upon a European or American State by the rules of the equitable code which regulates the intercourse of civilised nations, that article (eighth article of the July treaty) may, when ratifications are exchanged, prevent the United States from participating in such a policy'.[31] The question was a practical one as the revision of the British treaty of 1858 was under consideration (revision of tariffs).

The policy of the United States as the only Western nation which is 'a commercial power of the Pacific Ocean and a country exporting largely from and importing largely into China' was made clear in subsequent dispatches of the Secretaries of State such as of the 7th June 1880 and the 26th February 1883. In the latter it was observed that 'the attitude of the United States towards China as towards the other countries of Eastern Asia has been consistently a friendly one. We have not attempted to impose our views upon them by force ... we have met in a like

[28] *A Digest of the International Law of the United States taken from documents issued by Presidents and Secretaries of State* etc., ed. by Francis Wharton, vol. I, para 67.

[29] Wharton, *op. cit.* [30] Wharton, *op. cit.* [31] Wharton, *op. cit.*

amicable spirit and it is believed that the result has been for the advantages of both the nations....'[32]

In the light of the above considerations it may be asked again whether the view of some international lawyers as to the doubtful status of China within the family of nations in the interim period between the Nanking treaty and the First World War can be seriously upheld. It has been shown from instances drawn from documents of first rate importance that China's position as a member of the family of *civilised* nations was not questioned by Great Britain at the close of the eighteenth century or even later. The position was the same according to the policy of Russia which before the nineteenth century concluded a number of treaties with China on a footing of equality, to mention only the treaties of Nertschinsk (1689) and Kiakhta (1727) and the second treaty of Kiakhta (1768).[33] All Western powers and Japan who obtained privileges for their nationals and other concessions in China at the cost of the latter's rights of territorial jurisdiction, sought at the same time the establishment of mutual diplomatic relations on a footing of equality. In fact they offered equality against the Emperor's reluctance to grant it in the face of increasing foreign pressure. China had no need to seek anybody's recognition but was rather in a position where her recognition was sought by others. These mutual acts of recognition implied in the stipulated exchange of diplomatic envoys were no more than acknowledgments of facts and can hardly be interpreted as acts of admission to the family of nations of which China was one of the most ancient members.

'From the dawn of her history', writes Professor Escarra, 'China observed international law ... Though convinced of the superiority of her civilisation, she liberally received foreigners to the point of respecting their personal status'. She later closed her frontiers 'jealously to foreign penetration' but her markets being essential to world economy she opened them again.[34] All the limitations imposed on her jurisdictional rights in her own territory were transient—at least not permanent enough to justify the view that her status in international law was not continuous. The signing of the so-called Mackay treaty between Great Britain and China in 1902 marked the beginning of the end of the period of limitations when the former promised the abandonment of the privilege of jurisdictional extraterritoriality. The same promise was repeated by other powers in subsequent years. In 1910 and 1912 China participated in The Hague conferences and she joined, after the First World War, all the great international institutions such as the League of Nations, the Permanent Court of International Justice, the International Labour Office, the International Chamber of Commerce and other agencies. She adhered to the Kellogg Pact in 1929. During the Second World War her status as a great power was finally re-established.

[32] In so far as limitations on China's jurisdictional rights were stipulated, they were not the privilege of Western powers only but had been equally to the benefit of Japan as can be seen from the provisions of the treaty of the 13th September 1871 (Wharton, *op. cit*). Japan imposed the same limitations on Corea in the treaty of the 26th February 1876 (Mayers, *op. cit*).

[33] Escarra, *op. cit.*, pp. 8–10.

[34] Escarra, *op. cit.*, pp. 36–7.

16

THE LEGAL POSITION OF TIBET (1954)

Tibet has recently been invaded by Communist China and deprived of independence. The Mao Tse-Tung Government justifies the invasion by China's claim to suzerainty over Tibet, though the latter, before finally disappearing from the international scene, had again and again denied that she was still a vassal of China. It therefore may be of interest to international lawyers to examine the legality of China's title. No doubt such title existed in the past but it has undergone an evolution characteristic of all suzerain–vassal relationships in the Middle East, Asia, or Africa. The vassal states in the Balkans had gained independence after their liberation from Turkish domination in the nineteenth century. One by one various vassal states tended to acquire a higher status in the family of nations, and there is no risk in saying that with minor exceptions all the major cases of suzerainty now belong to the past. There was no doubt a general tendency for all nations who were still under the guardianship of some overlord state to emancipate themselves and to enter the family of nations as fully fledged international persons. The alternative was absorption by the suzerain, a solution uncommon in present circumstances of disappearance of all types of overlordship in the international field. Notions of national sovereignty are apparently of high importance in Communist international law. It seems therefore astonishing that China, a Communist Power, has flagrantly disregarded the claim of Tibet to attain what all her sister nations in Asia have attained in the last thirty years.

It would be difficult to analyze Sino–Tibetan relations from the legal point of view if the relationship between superior and inferior state as such were indefinable. Suzerainty lacks juristic precision and in principle each case of suzerain–vassal relationship must be considered on its own merits. However, it is possible for international lawyers to detect certain characteristic features which are common to all cases.[1] Suzerainty was originally an institution of feudal law and was used to describe the particular relationship between the feudal lord and his vassal.[2] The latter owed allegiance to the suzerain ruler, he had to pay him tribute, give him his military support and was entitled to his protection. Feudal institutions were characteristic of the period of interdynastic relationships, when the overlord ruler,

[1] L. Oppenheim, *International Law* (1952), Vol. I, pp. 170–178; C. C. Hyde, *International Law* (1945), Vol. I, p. 48 *et seq.*

[2] S. V. Viswanatha, *International Law in Ancient India* (1925), pp. 26–27; P. C. Jessup, 'Palmas Island Arbitration', *American Journal of International Law*, Vol. 22 (1928), p. 745.

and not his people, was endowed with legal as well as political sovereignty, and was capable of receiving allegiance from the subordinate ruler. With the disappearance of feudalism and dynastic policies, this type of suzerainty, which was determined by the constitutional law of the suzerain state, disappeared entirely.

The institution of suzerainty then entered the field of modern international law and became a kind of international guardianship. The vassal state of the nineteenth and twentieth centuries is deprived of external sovereignty though it retains internal sovereignty, which the suzerain state is under a duty to respect. Deprived of external sovereignty, the vassal state has no position of its own in the family of nations. It is essential to remember that it remains a portion of the suzerain state which represents it entirely in relations with other nations. In principle all treaties concluded by the suzerain state are *ipso facto* binding on the vassal; the latter is automatically party to a war in which the suzerain is engaged, and the suzerain state is externally responsible for all actions of the vassal. These are some of the main common features of vassal states in modern international law. The Indian Princely States were, until the independence of India, vassals of the British Crown which exercised the rights of paramountcy in relation to them. As mentioned above, the Balkan states which were vassals of the Ottoman Empire gradually achieved independence in the nineteenth century. Some of them were first allowed to enter into certain non-political treaties with other nations, without participation of the suzerain. Bulgaria, while still a vassal state, fought a war against Serbia which had already ceased to be one. On the other hand, Egypt, while still a vassal of Turkey, was not considered a belligerent when Turkey entered the First World War in 1914. Thus it happened not infrequently that suzerainty, though still continuing on the basis of an historical relationship, became a *nominal* title ripe for elimination or conversion into a title more favorable to the subordinate state. This is of great importance in the consideration of the Tibetan case.

A number of vassal states, in their striving for independence, attained before complete liberation first a higher status of dependence, that of protectorate. Protectorates have this in common with the suzerain–vassal relationship: that they both created a kind of international guardianship. Protected states have, however, not only internal sovereignty, but are able in a number of cases to exercise some of the attributes of external sovereignty, though the latter is in principle vested in the protector state. Not infrequently the relationship between protector and protected was or is of a contractual nature, a feature not inherent in the suzerain–vassal set-up.[3] The basic treaty between protector and protected is of an international character and of interest to third Powers. Thus a protected state has to some extent a position within the family of nations, and therefore enters directly the orbit of international law. In distinction to a vassal state, the protected state is not part of the protecting state; it is not automatically a party in a war in which the latter is engaged, and treaties concluded by the protecting state are not *ipso facto* binding on the protected

[3] Robert Redslob, *Traité de Droit des Gens* (1950), p. 126; Jean Escarra, *La Chine et le Droit International* (1931).

state. These are differences of outstanding importance to international lawyers who analyze a particular relationship between superior and inferior state and may find that what is called suzerainty by name is in fact a protectorate in law or vice versa. Further, it may not be out of place to mention the existence of so-called quasi-protectorates in which the status of the protected state is higher than in a protectorate proper. In this category we may include the former protectorates established by the United States in relation to some of the Latin American Republics such as Cuba, Panama, the Dominican Republic, Haiti, and Nicaragua. Inter-American solidarity which received cordial support from the United States helped to convert these relationships into treaty relations on a basis of perfect equality.[4]

Definition of suzerainty and protectorate as precise as possible in the light of existing precedent might enable us to examine Sino–Tibetan relations in their historical and contemporary aspects. The history of these relations may be divided into several periods. The first period was one of equality and mutual independence; it came to an end at the close of the seventeenth century. At the beginning of the eighteenth century the Dalai Lama, the spiritual and temporal ruler of Tibet, still enjoyed a position of highest prestige in relation to the Chinese Emperor.[5] Dependence of peace-loving Tibet on the military aid of China against Tartar and Goorkha invasions strengthened the position of China. In the second decade of the eighteenth century Chinese suzerainty over Tibet became an established fact. The interest of the Manchu Emperors in their new vassal increased with the growing influence of the Dalai Lama as a spiritual authority over Buddhist communities outside Tibet, in Mongolia, Nepal, Bhutan, Sikkim, and India.[6] As a temporal ruler the Dalai Lama owed personal allegiance to the Manchu Emperors, he recognized their overlordship in the political, military and financial fields, and as their tributary he had to offer them fealty.[7] This suzerainty was obviously one of Chinese feudal law. To preserve their rights in Tibet, the Manchu Emperors maintained their permanent representatives (Ambans) in Lhasa, the capital of Tibet. It was the Amban's task to exercise all rights of external sovereignty over Tibet, and particularly to isolate her from the outside world. Interference of Ambans in the internal affairs of Tibet brought the country more and more into the constitutional framework of the Chinese commonwealth.[8] Thus Tibet was, at this period, entirely outside the family of nations. So was China before the middle of the nineteenth century, and she acquired a fully sovereign status only after the First World War.[9]

The old feudal suzerainty of China over Tibet tended to convert itself into a more modern suzerain–vassal relationship in the second half of the nineteenth century.

[4] C. C. Hyde, *op. cit.*, p. 56 *et seq.*

[5] *An Account of Tibet: The Travels of Ippolito Desideri* (1932), p. 209.

[6] Sven Hedin, 'Tibet', *The New Orient* (published for the New Orient Society of America), Vol. II, p. 89.

[7] L. Austine Waddell, *Lhasa and Its Mysteries* (1905), pp. 18, 27–28; D. K. Sen, 'China, Tibet and India', *India Quarterly*, April–June, 1951, p. 112 *et seq.*

[8] Jean Escarra, *op. cit.*, p. 240; L. A. Waddell, *op. cit.*, p. 166; W. W. Rockhill, 'Tibet', *Journal of the Royal Asiatic Society*, Vol. 22 (1891), pp. 7, 203–205.

[9] G. Keeton, *The Development of Extraterritoriality in China* (1928).

This was a matter of gradual evolution which finally resulted in the emergence of Tibet on the wider international scene. It was precipitated by the conflict between British and Russian interests for influence in Lhasa.[10] The advance of the Tsarist Empire in Asia was in full progress and caused serious anxiety in Whitehall as the British Government felt responsible for the security of her Indian Empire. Russian infiltration into Afghanistan had been successfully checked, and it was essential for British policy not to allow any Russian expansion into Tibet. For this purpose Great Britain, unwilling to infiltrate herself into Tibet, except for commercial relations, supported Chinese suzerainty over Tibet. We shall, however, see that the Tibetan struggle for independence from China reduced the suzerain rights of the latter to a much greater extent than British policy was prepared to admit. The gradual decline of Chinese suzerainty can be understood by recalling some of the major events in the regional game of power polities, and, what is more important, by close examination of some of the provisions of successive treaties in which Great Britain, Russia, China, and Tibet were the contracting parties.[11] It is also essential to be aware of the frequent misapplication of legal terms in these treaties, and to call the particular relationships defined in them by their proper name from the point of view of international law.

In 1890 Great Britain concluded a treaty with China in which the latter recognized the British 'Protectorate' over Sikkim, a small sub-Himalayan state between India and Tibet. According to Article II of the treaty, the contracting parties recognized British control 'over the internal administration and foreign relations' of Sikkim.[12] The fact that Great Britain secured control over external as well as internal sovereignty of Sikkim showed that the latter was a vassal and not a protected state, though it may well be admitted that it is a protected state in relation to India today. This is not the only example of misapplication of a legal term, and we shall see further instances of it later. In Article VI of the treaty the contracting parties reserved for special arrangements methods of direct communication between British India and the Tibetan Government. Thus it was obvious that Tibet had begun to break through the isolation imposed by her Chinese suzerain, and had entered the field of wider international intercourse. The weakening of the influence of the declining Manchu dynasty in Lhasa resembled, *mutatis mutandis*, the gradual liberation of some of the Balkan states from the suzerainty of the declining Ottoman Empire in the second half of the nineteenth century.[13] Chinese suzerainty over Tibet became more and more nominal and the Dalai Lama was able to take advantage of the conflict between the Powers interested in Tibet and assume a bargaining position. What he had to offer was the establishment of a protectorate over his country, and he was inclined at the beginning of the twentieth century to choose as protector Tsarist Russia, which was in the process of establishing a strong grip

[10] Percival Landon, *The Opening of Tibet* (N. Y., 1905), pp. 10–14.
[11] Sir Charles Bell, *Tibet Past and Present* (1924), Appendix V–XIV.
[12] Sir Charles Bell, *op. cit.*, Appendix V, p. 281. [13] P. Landon, *op. cit.*, p. 212.

over Mongolia and was eager to extend it to Tibet.[14] In reaction to these developments Great Britain directed to Lhasa in 1904 a mission escorted by a military force for the purpose of entering into direct negotiations with the Tibetan Government. Negotiations resulted in the conclusion of the British–Tibetan treaty of 1904. Accounts of eyewitnesses in Lhasa testify to the almost total disappearance of the influence of the Chinese Ambans on Tibetan affairs.[15] In concluding the treaty, the head of the British mission announced that 'England is now at peace with Tibet', a significant statement for the status of Tibet at that time. In Article IX of the treaty

> the Government of Tibet engaged that without the previous consent of the British government (a) no portion of Tibetan territory shall be ceded, sold, leased, mortgaged, or otherwise given for occupation, to any foreign power; (b) no such power shall be permitted to intervene in Tibetan affairs; (c) no representatives or agents of any foreign power shall be admitted to Tibet; (d) no concessions for railways, roads, telegraphs, mining or other rights shall be granted to any foreign power or to the subject of any foreign power. In the event of consent to such concessions being granted, similar or equivalent concessions shall be granted to the British government; (e) no Tibetan revenues whether in kind or in cash, shall be pledged or assigned to any foreign power, or to the subject of any foreign power.[16]

This treaty was confirmed two years later in 1906 in a convention between Great Britain and China.[17] It was stated in Article III of this convention that China was not a foreign power in the meaning of Article IX of the treaty of 1904. In Article II of the convention Great Britain undertook not to annex any Tibetan territory or to interfere in the administration of Tibet. One year later in 1907 a new convention was concluded between Great Britain and Russia.[18] Whereas in the two previous treaties no mention had been made of Chinese suzerainty over Tibet, this convention recognized it expressly. Great Britain stated her 'special interest in the maintenance of status quo in the external relations of Tibet'. To this end both contracting parties undertook 'to respect the territorial integrity of Tibet and to abstain from all interference in the internal administration'. Both parties also undertook to negotiate with Tibet through the intermediary of China only, though Great Britain stipulated for herself the right of direct commercial relations with Tibet.

It follows from the above treaties that Chinese suzerainty, which had been reduced to a nominal right in 1904, tended to be revived with the support of Great Britain.[19] However, this revival, promoted by British policy, could not alter the fact that Tibet through new treaty arrangements had left the narrow framework of exclusively bilateral relations with China and entered the orbit of international law and relations. Great Britain had appeared as an additional guarantor of the territorial integrity of Tibet and as her *de facto* co-guardian in the same way as China and

[14] *Ibid.*, p. 214; L. A. Waddell, *op. cit.*, p. 52; Arnold J. Toynbee, *Survey of International Affairs*, 1920–1923, pp. 431–432; T. A. Taracouzio, *The Soviet Union and International Law* (1935), p. 36.

[15] P. Landon, *op. cit.*, pp. 385, 396, 413, 483; Sven Hedin, *Central Asia and Tibet* (1903), p. 456; L. A. Waddell, *op. cit.*, pp. 413, 418.

[16] Bell, *op. cit.*, Appendix VII, pp. 284–286.

[17] Bell, *op. cit.*, Appendix VIII, pp. 287–289.

[18] Bell, *op. cit.*, Appendix IX, pp. 289–291.

[19] Bell, *op. cit.*, p. 61.

Russia became co-guardians in relation to Mongolia.[20] Russia had not been allowed to proceed with the establishment of a protectorate over Tibet, but the multilateral arrangements of the three Powers interested in Tibet, which found their expression in one group of treaties and conventions, had raised Tibet from the status of a vassal to that of a protected state. All the symptoms of a protectorate thus established at the beginning of the twentieth century will clearly appear in the ensuing period. In 1910 Great Britain established a protectorate over the state of Bhutan, and it was obvious that Tibet could not have been considered as having a status inferior to that of Bhutan.[21]

In 1911 the revolution in China banished the Manchu Emperors from Peking and established a new republic.[22] At this time Tibet expelled the Chinese representatives and garrisons from the whole country. It is difficult to consider Tibet now otherwise than in her initial stage of independence. Personal allegiance of the Dalai Lama towards the Manchu Emperor came to an end, and as sovereignty in China now vested in the Chinese people, no new type of allegiance of Tibet towards China could have replaced the one which had been abolished. With the gradual consolidation of the new republic in China the latter tried to re-establish her influence in Lhasa on a new basis. Cultural and commercial relations between China and Tibet had not died out, and continued intercourse again brought Chinese political representatives to the Court of the Dalai Lama. They tried to help China to exercise in relation to Tibet certain rights of which Tibet was not prepared or eager to avail herself. Foremost among them were the wider rights of external sovereignty. Though Tibet had established direct relations with British India and had even negotiated through the famous Lama Dorjeff with the Court and Government in St. Petersburg, it was still possible for China to represent Tibet generally in the family of nations.[23] With the exercise of these rights tendencies to interfere in the internal administration of Tibet appeared again. These new conflicts in British–Sino–Tibetan relations called for a new settlement. This was attempted at the Simla Conference in 1914 in which all three Powers participated.

Though the Simla Agreement was initialed by the three contracting parties, the Chinese Delegation finally refused to sign it, so that it remained a bilateral arrangement between Great Britain and Tibet only.[24] According to this agreement Tibet was divided into two parts, outer Tibet and inner Tibet. The latter was the part nearer India, including Lhasa, the capital. The former was the more remote and primitive part nearer China. In outer Tibet the Dalai Lama was to remain complete sovereign and no Chinese influence was to be admitted. The Tibetan Government was also to retain the administration of inner Tibet, but the Chinese were allowed to maintain their own communities there and protect them by their own officials.

[20] Louis Nemzer, 'The Status of Outer Mongolia in International Law', *American Journal of International Law*, Vol. 33 (1939), p. 452 *et seq.*; H. B. Morse and H. F. MacNair, *Far Eastern International Relations* (1931), p. 567.

[21] Bell, *op. cit.*, Appendix XI, p. 297; see also pp. 246–247.

[22] Chou Hsiang-Kuang, *Modern History of China* (1952).

[23] L. A. Waddell, *op. cit.*, p. 52.

[24] Bell, *op. cit.*, pp. 154–155.

The Chinese representative was to remain in Lhasa and British trade agents were allowed to reside in the country. All these provisions show that Tibet had, subject to certain exceptions, established complete internal sovereignty, and that her external sovereignty was a matter of co-ordinated British and Chinese policy. It is therefore astonishing to find a provision in the agreement according to which Chinese 'suzerainty' over Tibet was again recognized.

From the legal point of view the following observations have to be offered on this provision. First of all, China did not become a party to the agreement from which she withdrew and could not therefore claim rights of suzerainty on its basis. If the legal basis of suzerainty is to be sought in the pre-Simla position, it is beyond doubt that suzerainty had disappeared after the Chinese revolution and had never been re-established in its previous form. We have seen that with the abolition of the Manchu Dynasty there was no longer any case for allegiance, and that the suzerainty after having been transferred from the orbit of Chinese feudal law into the domain of international law, soon converted itself into a protectorate in which China could hardly have been considered the sole protector. Events which followed the Simla Conference in 1914 and later, clearly show that Chinese overlordship over Tibet had been reduced to a nominal title. No historian of this period would deny that Tibet was never a party to all military conflicts during the First and Second World Wars and in the inter-war period in which China was engaged as a belligerent.[25] If Tibet was neutral and not a belligerent in these wars, and, moreover, if treaties concluded by China with other Powers in the above period never extended to Tibet, how could she be considered part of China and its vassal at this time?

Quite to the contrary, apart from treaty relations with British India, she had, according to reliable accounts, concluded in 1913 an independent treaty with Mongolia.[26] The text of this treaty begins with the words 'Whereas Mongolia and Tibet, having freed themselves from the Manchu dynasty and separated themselves from China, have become independent states....' In Article I of the treaty 'the Dalai Lama, sovereign of Tibet approves and acknowledges the formation of an independent Mongolian state ...'; and in Article II the sovereign of the Mongolian people 'approves and acknowledges the formation of an independent state and the proclamation of the Dalai Lama as sovereign of Tibet'. This treaty was said to have been concluded in the same year that Russia, in an agreement with China, had recognized Outer Mongolia as being under Chinese suzerainty.[27] It seems to have been convenient to both Powers (Great Britain and Russia) striving for influence over the Tibetan–Mongolian area, to support the empty legal title of China against each other. This may also be offered as a further comment to the provisions of the Simla Agreement. But as there was discrepancy between *de facto* arrangements and legal title, the first which, after all, matter most, call for legal reformulation by international lawyers who are entitled to disregard a meaningless term repeated in textbooks of international law without any factual basis.

[25] D. K. Sen, *loc. cit.*, p. 112 *et seq.*

[26] Bell, *op. cit.*, Appendix XIII, pp. 304–305.

[27] Bell, *op. cit.*, Appendix XIII, p. 304.

This is not to say that China had given up her aspirations in Tibet. The Dalai Lamas and their government, administering a country practically demilitarized in accordance with a Buddhist-inspired policy, were not eager to be too deeply involved in the wider game of Asian or world politics. All they desired for their people was freedom and reasonable independence from their neighbors. Tibet had for centuries the most intimate cultural relations with China, and she did not oppose the merger of her foreign policy, in relation to the world at large, with China's policy. She was satisfied to exercise certain rights of external sovereignty within a restricted area only, sufficient to maintain her commercial relations with India and close relations with those Buddhist countries which recognize the spiritual supremacy of the Dalai Lama. Instead of recognizing the existing state of affairs after the breakdown of the Manchu Empire, when Tibet rose to the state of a protectorate, or quasi-protectorate, Republican China declared in 1931 Tibet as well as Mongolia to be provinces of China.[28] Needless to say, such a unilateral declaration, unsupported by facts, could have no legal significance. Mao Tse-Tung, some time before he started the civil war in China, made it clear that in case of his success he would promote the establishment of a federation in which Tibet as well as Mongolia would be included. He has kept his promise, though without the realization of a federal plan, in Tibet, and India's attitude in the matter has proved conciliatory. Should Mao Tse-Tung again initiate a Chinese policy in Mongolia, a Sino–Russian conflict is likely to develop, as a conciliatory attitude on the part of Russia in this matter would seem doubtful.

As a result of the complete preoccupation of the Chiang Kai Shek Government with the struggle against Japan, and with its participation in world politics as a major Power, China left Tibet temporarily to her own destiny. It was in this period that Tibet rose from the state of a protectorate to complete independence. We have seen that she was not involved in any of the wars waged by China, and that she started assuming complete responsibility not only for her internal government but also for her foreign policy; in other words, following the logic of events, external sovereignty superimposed itself on internal sovereignty, a development which Tibet shared with her sister nations in Asia. During the Second World War Tibet, in defence of her neutrality, opposed the opening of strategic communications and the transport of goods of a military character through her territory.[29] No longer was there a Chinese representative in Lhasa, and direct communication with India had been established through a permanent diplomatic mission sent from New Delhi to Lhasa. Tibetan diplomatic missions when they later travelled to the West had all the visas required on their Tibetan passports. Moreover, as a fully sovereign nation, Tibet made a tentative approach to the United Nations for admission to membership in the new world organization. In 1950 the invasion of Tibet by Communist China followed, and this brings us to the present period of Sino–Tibetan relations, which can hardly be called bilateral but are dictated by physical compulsion. Independent Tibet suddenly suffers a severe set-back and is reduced to a status of

[28] Jean Escarra, *op. cit.*, p. 463. [29] D. K. Sen, *loc. cit.*, p. 112 *et seq.*

dependency which she had shaken off years ago. Tibet has now become a province of China, and this, at a period of the liberation of nations in Asia, must be considered an anachronism. The question of the aggression of Tibet was proposed as an agenda item for the Fifth Session of the General Assembly of the United Nations, but the Agenda Committee decided not to include it, and the problem has been shelved. Moreover the Government of India has withdrawn its permanent mission in Lhasa, and thus Tibet has lost her last link with the democratic world. The Chinese justify their invasion of Tibet by their claim to suzerainty. If the history of Chinese suzerainty over Tibet is allowed to speak, China has no right and has violated the independence of Tibet. If, on the other hand, China is allowed to rely on treaties, old titles, and legal conceptions which are believed to be dead, such reliance defeats the most sacred notions of international law in Asia, according to which such treaties, titles and conceptions must give way whenever the independence of nations in this and other parts of the world is at stake.

17

IS INDIA A FEDERATION? (1954)

RIGID definitions of law and the impossibility of fitting reality into these definitions caused lawyers to multiply so called quasi-institutions. To quote one or two examples, the controversy over delegation of legislative power caused constitutional lawyers to speak about quasi-legislative power which is power transferred by the legislature to the executive in spite of the principle of separation of powers. To mention another example, lawyers termed functions performed by administrative officers with the application of a judicial procedure, quasi-judicial. International lawyers tend to call the functions of comprehensive international organisations (League of Nations and United Nations), quasi-legislative or quasi-executive. In all these cases the adoption of quasi-institutions helped to by-pass rigid definitions of law and to adapt legal theory to legal reality and practice. Some constitutional lawyers and political scientists have adopted a rigid definition of the federal principle, and as many federations do not correspond in theory or practice to this definition, the institution of quasi-federation, which is said to be midway between a real Federation and a unitary State, was introduced into the picture.[1] The question arises whether the term quasi-federation can serve any practical or academic purpose and if so what is the real meaning of quasi-federation. To answer this question with particular reference to the Federation of India, the definition itself should first be briefly examined.

Sovereign or political power in a federation should be co-ordinated and divided between the centre and the member states in such a way that each of them remains, within its own sphere, independent of the other. In order to apply this definition to a particular federation, the provisions of its constitution as well as constitutional practice must be taken into consideration. Some federations seem to be covered by the above definition, in theory as well as in practice. This is the case of the U.S.A. and of Switzerland. If we consider the Canadian constitution we may come to the conclusion that Canada with her strong federal centre is not really a federation at all. The central government can veto provincial bills or disallow provincial acts and the Lieutenant-Governors of the provinces are appointed by the centre. However, as the veto and the power of disallowance are never abused in practice and as provincial executives are by convention responsible to local legislatures, the existence of a federal government may be assumed. On the other hand there may

[1] *Federal Government*, by K. C. Wheare, 1951.

be federal constitutions which comply with the above definition but in course of time centralisation at the cost of local member states has prevailed. Such is the case of Australia where the original federal balance has been affected by the growing powers of the centre, particularly its financial powers. In other cases centralisation has gone much further. Though an analysis of the constitutions of some of the Latin American Republics, *e.g.*, Brazil, Argentina or Mexico, may justify their classification as federations, it is common knowledge that in practice they are governed in a highly centralised way. It would be justified to include in this category also the U.S.S.R. In the light of the above definition India has been termed a quasi-federation and the question arises whether such classification is justified in theory as well as in practice. The case of Indian federalism is certainly *sui generis* and a brief analysis of its origin may prove helpful to overcome difficulties in defining it.

In the past federations were formed by the union of sovereign states under a new federal government, each retaining control of its own internal affairs. In the process of federating the member states had to surrender their external sovereignty to the central government while retaining their internal sovereignty, or at any rate a substantial part of it. The same applies to colonial federations. Thus federations were formed by arrangements or 'contracts' of public law and we may therefore say that federations proper were originally contractual federations. As to their composition federations may be multi-national or inter-community formations. National heterogeneity played its part in the formation of the Swiss federation composed of French, German and Italian elements, or of the Canadian federation with its French and English regional interests. It was irrelevant in the formation of the U.S.A. or of the Australian Commonwealth where the various founder-states were internally and *inter se* more or less homogeneous from the point of view of national origin of their citizens. It might seem prima facie that multi-national federations should be originally contractual formations, but this is by no means the case. Russia is a typical multi-national State but was not under the Czarist régime a federation. It was gradually transformed after the communist revolution into a federal state when the main Soviet Republics covering various national groups and areas made arrangements for the reorganisation of new Russia. The member Republics of the U.S.S.R. are allowed to preserve their cultural independence and have separate governments. According to the Stalin constitution of 1936 the Union Republics have even the power of secession from the federation. Two of the Republics (Ukraine and Byelo-Russia) exercise certain rights of external sovereignty. But these prerogatives are of theoretical significance only as the U.S.S.R. with complete political and economic centralisation and with a mono-party in the background are in practice reduced to an autocratic State in which the federal structure apart from its cultural aims is tolerated for administrative purposes only. Thus the U.S.S.R. though multi-national are in the same way as some of the uni-national South American Republics not 'contractual' but 'administrative' federations which distinguishes them from the type of contractual federation adopted by the U.S.A., Canada, Australia and Switzerland.

Let us revert again to the case of India. Under British rule India was a combination of two types of units which constituted the component parts of the Indian

Empire. There were about 600 princely states which enjoyed internal autonomy while their external sovereignty was surrendered to the British Crown. The latter exercised the powers of paramountcy in relation to the princely states which meant a *sui generis* relationship of suzerain and vassal. The remainder of India was divided into provinces which constituted altogether British India and were centrally ruled from New Delhi though they acquired gradually more and more autonomy. Neither the provinces (at present states A) nor the princely states (at present states B or C) were homogeneous from the point of view of language and tradition of their inhabitants. The frontiers of princely states were an outcome of historical development and many of these states had inhabitants speaking different languages and belonging to various civilisations though they were and are from an overall point of view Indian nationals. A similar case is that of the provinces of British India the frontiers of which were fixed as a matter of administrative expediency and not by allotment of separate provinces to separate language communities. The present state of Madras which succeeded the former province of Madras is composed of Tamils, Telegus and some Canarese. The state of Mysore is composed of Canarese, Telegus and some Tamils whereas the state of Hyderabad has a Telegu population besides Urdu-speaking Muslims and other minorities. This mixture of languages and civilisations within local states exists throughout the whole of India. In the Constituent Assembly, which was convened to adopt a federal constitution for the new independent state, provinces were represented side by side with princely states and it was prima facie possible for the delegates of various parts of India to enter a 'contractual' arrangement. Possible as it was, it never happened because of the peculiar balance of political power within India in which the Congress Party occupies a monopolistic or nearly monopolistic position. In a way there is some resemblance between the formation of the Indian federation and the U.S.S.R. as in both cases circumstances prevailed which could have favoured the conclusion of contractual arrangements but where owing to a mono-party reality tendencies of centralisation prevailed over those of decentralisation. Of course there is this fundamental difference between India and the U.S.S.R. that the first, though governed by a mono-party, is a real democracy admitting political opposition whereas there is no room for such opposition in the latter which in spite of its federal shape is in practice an administrative federation with 'nominal' federalism only. Therefore in spite of similarity in 'federation making' the U.S.S.R. have in practice no tendencies of political decentralisation which even if existing have no chance of taking any external shape, whereas in India various pressure groups are capable of organisation in conditions of political freedom and personal liberty and are no doubt at work. These tendencies in independent India have resulted in the formation of opposition parties and, what is more important from the point of view of federalism, in the claims of linguistic communities for reorganisation of the federation on linguistic lines. Language means, of course, also a separate local tradition and regional civilisation which gives the impetus to a particular community to have its own political body or state within the framework of the federation. The case of the newly created Andhra state is the most outstanding expression of these tendencies.

Political scientists have expressed the opinion that in the formation of a federation 'not infrequently the real federator of a group of states is the enemy without'.[2] The formation of the Canadian federation in 1867 was apparently fostered by the fear of the Canadian provinces of absorption into their American neighbour. One of the motives of forming the Australian federation was the common purpose of the Australian states to unite against the danger of Japanese aggression in the Pacific. Also in the historically more remote cases of Switzerland and the U.S.A. the common enemy was a powerful promoter of federation. As to Switzerland the purpose of the League of 1291 was to unite the cantons against the Habsburg Empire. The American colonies came together in their struggle against British rule. The unification of India was to a great extent stimulated by the fight of all its component parts for the creation of one independent state. Great Britain is today the friend and ally of India within the Commonwealth on a basis of perfect equality but independence must be preserved against any new common enemy who might happen to threaten from outside or inside the freedom of the new Republic. India has now joined the game of Power Politics in which she has allies and enemies. What has to determine in the first instance her moves including the development of her constitutional structure is consolidation and unity essential for the preservation of independence which by no means preserves itself automatically. The development of Indian federalism is therefore apart from decentralising tendencies likely to take place in the light of this supreme though extraneous factor. The Indian constitution in fact contains a number of emergency provisions which are essential for defining Indian federalism. We shall discuss them below.

Thus the Indian federation is confronted simultaneously with problems of centralisation and of decentralisation and the question arises what role can the constitution play in face of these conflicting tendencies. It is one of the consequences of a 'contractual' federation that its member states have in principle constitutions of their own which co-exist with the constitution of the centre. In India the constitutions of the local states are incorporated into the general constitution. Such merger as we have seen resulted from one of the primary purposes of federating, *i.e.*, from administrative convenience. The attention of the reader of the constitution may be drawn to Article 3 according to which the component parts of the federation may undergo far-reaching changes even without constitutional amendment though the existence of the federation as such enjoys constitutional guarantees. Article 3 reads as follows: 'Parliament may by law—(a) form a new State by separation of territory from any State or by uniting two or more States or parts of States or by uniting any territory to a part of any State; (b) increase the area of any State; (c) diminish the area of any State; (d) alter the boundaries of any State; (e) alter the name of any State. Provided that no Bill for the purpose shall be introduced in either House of Parliament except on the recommendation of the President and unless, where the proposal contained in the Bill affects the boundaries of any State or States specified

[2] 'Introduction to a Study of the Development of Federal Societies', by J. Rivero, *International Social Science Bulletin*, Spring, 1952, p. 32.

in part A or part B of the First Schedule or the name or names of any such State or States, the views of the Legislature of the State or, as the case may be, of each of the States both with respect to the proposal to introduce the Bill and with respect to the provisions thereof have been ascertained by the Parliament'.

It follows from the above provisions that the reorganisation of the federation is a matter of simple Parliamentary majority, that the main states of the federation (A and B) may be vitally affected by the application of Article 3 (states C and D which are of less importance are administered by the centre) and that the process of reshaping the federation depends on the initiative of the President which means the initiative of the central ministry. The provisions of Article 3 show clearly that India is not a contractual federation. A federal contract implies a static status of the member states which are entitled to territorial integrity. States A and B are not parties to any contractual arrangement. They can be unilaterally deprived by the centre of their status. The centre draws no power from the units, it relies on its own power imposed from above. On the other hand as it is extraordinarily easy to carry out any reorganisation in the light of Article 3, the future of the federation depends on what kind of reorganisation is to follow. As we have seen, under the pressure of regional interests the centre may be inclined to yield to the demands of certain linguistic communities and the first case, that of the formation of the Andhra state covering the Telegu-speaking area is already a *fait accompli*. The creation of a new linguistic state must always affect all the surrounding states comprising people speaking the particular language who will tend to be united in the new linguistic state. For instance the creation of the Andhra state threatens to disintegrate the state of Hyderabad. The creation of any new linguistic state is therefore not an isolated problem affecting one particular state only, and besides it constitutes a highly contagious factor as other linguistic communities still without statehood intensify similar *de facto* pressure on the centre. The constitution presents no obstacle to the reorganisation of the federation on linguistic lines, in fact it renders the task extremely easy.

It is obvious that reorganisation on linguistic lines promotes the case of decentralisation as internally homogeneous linguistic states constitute stronger pressure groups in relation to the centre than local states with a mixed population and with the inherent weakness resulting from lack of local unity. However, solidarity based on language and corresponding civilisation is not the only factor which promotes the case of decentralisation. Another factor may be consolidation of regional interests within the framework of the existing organisation. Let us look, for instance, at the case of the state of Mysore. The majority of the people of the state of Mysore is Kannada speaking but there are also other language groups within the state which have owed allegiance to the local ruler (the present Rajpramukh) since a considerable period of time. The state of Mysore is one of these states which by exemplary administration achieved a higher level of civilisation and well-being than many other states in India. Efficient governments and common achievements have created regional solidarity. As one of the major princely states Mysore became a state B after independence and according to Article 371 of the constitution during a period of ten years or longer it remains under the control of the President, that is to say of the centre, which is entitled to give particular directions to states B. It happened recently that the President ordered on the basis of Article 371 a resident of Mysore to be tried for a criminal offence outside the state. The state took strong objection to such restrictions imposed on its jurisdictional rights, and pressure was brought by the legislature of Mysore on its own local government to cause the withdrawal of the order. Regional solidarity backed by the local parliamentary régime prevailed over constitutional centralism and the President had to withdraw the order. This case proves also that genuine parliamentary government within local states is superior to simple provincial status such as prevails in the component parts of the U.S.S.R. or similar federations where local states are reduced to administrative agencies of the centre. Local states A and B exercise real rights of internal sovereignty through their legislatures, executives and judiciaries. Though India is by her origin not a contractual but an administrative federation, federation has a real meaning and is not nominal.

It also follows from the above that whenever the parliamentary régime of a local state tends to break down, such state must become a loss to the cause of federalism. Such a breakdown occurred recently in the Pepsu state[3] which suffered a collapse of the governing coalition. It resulted from the conflict between the Congress Party in opposition and the coalition in power in which inexperienced coalition leaders have not yet the chance of winning their case. As a result the government of the state had to be taken over by the centre. Does it follow that with more successful multi-party governments in local states in the future more decentralisation will take place? The answer seems to be in the affirmative though it would not be advisable to over-generalise from the experience of one state. The formation of multi-party governments was attempted in the states of Madras and of Travancore-Cochin but had to be at first abandoned. It may be attempted again and, if successful as in Travancore-Cochin, it will obviously affect the federal balance in India. The mono-party government of the centre is then likely to be confronted with the problem of coalition governments in local states.

The issue of centralisation versus decentralisation has two other aspects in the Indian constitution, one an emergency and the other a non-emergency aspect. Internal disturbances after independence connected with communal commotion and subversive activities created a temporary state of *de facto* emergency in which Preventive Detention Acts continue to be in force from year to year. This enables the government to detain people without trial for reasons of security. However, these are symptoms of *de facto* and not con-constitutional emergency. Emergency measures *sensu stricto* are provided by the constitution in Articles 352–60. According to these provisions the President may in case of external aggression, of internal disturbances or of the break-down of the machinery of a local state convert the federation or part of it into a unitary state. The centre then exercises extensive powers which encroach on the normal legislative and executive powers of local states. Special provisions are also included in the constitution which provide for the case of financial

[3] Patiala and East Punjab States Union (First Schedule, Part B, Constitution of India).

emergency (Article 360). However, these encroachments should, according to the constitution, always come to an end with the termination of the emergency when the state as a whole is reconverted into its previous federal shape. The members of the Constituent Assembly have shown considerable foresight in including these provisions into the constitution as they may enable the country to face any danger by centralised action without affecting its ultimate federal structure.

Professor Wheare, one of the main exponents of a rigid definition of the federal principle, maintains that India has a quasi-federal constitution, mainly because of the provisions of Articles 249, 352–60 and 371.[4] We have already seen that Article 371 does not justify such a contention. We have also seen that Articles 352–60 are emergency provisions and do not affect the normal structure of the federation. The application of Article 249 may cause a disturbance of the division of legislative powers between centre and local states A and B which is laid down in the three lists of schedule VII of the constitution. The first list includes exclusive powers of the centre, the second exclusive powers of local states and the third list concurrent powers which the centre and local states share. Residuary legislative powers not allocated expressly in schedule VII go to the centre (Article 248). In the U.S.A. and in Australia they go to the local states. The Indian constitution has followed in this respect the Canadian constitutional pattern. According to Article 249 the Council of States, the second chamber of Parliament, can declare 'by resolution supported by not less than two-thirds of the members present and voting that it is necessary or expedient in the national interest that Parliament should make laws with respect to any matter enumerated in the State list specified in the resolution'. In that case the central legislature can make laws for the whole or any part of India with respect to such a matter. The Council of States is not a federal upper house in the meaning of American, Australian or Swiss constitutional law, as states are not represented on the Council by an equal number of representatives. Representation is based on the strength of population in the various states. However, Article 249 may be applied for the furtherance of the national interest only and moreover it contains provisions limiting the period of validity of laws issued on its basis. It does not therefore affect essentially the legislative autonomy of the states and can hardly be quoted in support of quasi-federalism in India.

Interference of the centre into the legislative powers of the states may also take place according to Articles 252 and 253. However, in the first case central Parliament assumes legislative power in relation to local states only on the initiative of a particular state or states and not without its (their) authorisation. In the second case central Parliament can interfere with local powers in any matter connected with the implementation of international treaties, agreements or conventions, bilateral or multilateral. This, however, is an obvious consequence of its powers of external sovereignty which cannot affect the federal status of the country. Adherents of the theory of quasi-federalism may also quote in their support Article 254 of the constitution. According to this article in the case of repugnance of local laws to central

[4] *Federal Government, supra*, p. 28.

laws the latter always prevail over the former. However, according to paragraph 2 of the above article local laws may be reserved for the consideration of the President and may thus keep their validity against central laws. Canada is *inter alia* supposed to be a quasi-federation because local governors are appointed by the centre. This is also the case in India but in both cases local responsible government guarantees full local autonomy. Professor Wheare also supports his contention as to Canada by the fact that local judges are appointed by the centre.[5] So are local High Court judges in India but I fail to see what it has to do with federal status if the judiciary is truly independent. Besides, High Court judges enjoy in the same way as the Supreme Court the power of judicial review and they can declare any law unconstitutional if it is inconsistent with the provisions of the constitution.

Neither can the provisions of the constitution concerning constitutional amendment be quoted in support of quasi-federalism in India. According to Article 368 such amendment 'may be initiated only by the introduction of a Bill for the purpose in either House of Parliament, and when the Bill is passed in each House by a majority of the total membership of that House and by a majority of not less than two-thirds of the members of that House present and voting, it shall be presented to the President for his assent ...'. In certain matters such as the election of the President, the executive power of the Union or of the states, the legislative lists in schedule VII, the representation of states in Parliament, etc., the amendment has also to 'be ratified by the legislatures of not less than one-half of the States specified in Parts A and B of the First Schedule....' Thus the constitution provides for a reasonable balance between centre and states as to the power of amendment with safeguards in favour of the states.

In the distribution of financial resources the Indian states depend to a great extent on the centre which may mean quasi-federal government in practice. The provisions of part XII of the constitution together with the powers of distribution exercised by the centre on the recommendations of the Finance Commission may remind Indian constitutional lawyers of the corresponding position in Australia. But as they are far from destroying the financial autonomy of the local states, there is no reason to suppose that they destroy the federal structure of the whole Union. Other arguments could be brought forward in support of quasi-federalism in India, such as the existence of an all-India civil service, a unified judiciary and single citizenship for all Indian subjects, but they do not change the fact that local states are endowed with sufficient internal sovereignty which after all is the distinguishing feature of a federation proper.

We may now draw a few conclusions from our previous considerations. The application of a rigid definition of the federal principle to various types of existing federations may deprive it of any practical meaning. In its light Canada has a quasi-federal constitution and is federal only in practice. Australia has a federal constitution but is in practice nearly a unitary state. The constitution of the U.S.A. is federal but who can deny that tendencies of centralisation promoted by two world wars

[5] *Modern Constitutions*, by K. C. Wheare, 1951, p. 28.

and by the economic depression in the inter-war period are constantly at work. Switzerland too experiences centralising tendencies. All other federations are quasi-federal or unitary states in the meaning of the definition. Neither has India escaped classification as a quasi-federal state. What then is the purpose of the definition if it leaves no room for federations proper? Such a definition is doomed to remain in a vacuum. We have suggested a distinction between contractual and administrative federations. The distinction refers in the first instance to the origin of various federations but it has also a wider meaning. In contractual federations such as the U.S.A., Australia, Canada and Switzerland, the member states have preserved internal sovereignty or a substantial part of it for themselves. Centralising tendencies have increased the powers of the centre but have not destroyed the powers of the local states. They perform substantial legislative, executive and judicial functions without being reduced to agencies of the centre. In some cases local governments are responsible to local legislatures, in other cases they are responsible to locally elected governors. Local states in some of the administrative federations may irrespective of their non-contractual status possess similar powers of internal sovereignty. If they do, I see no reason why they should be classified as quasi-federations. Neither does it seem expedient to call quasi-federal a federation in which local states have no internal sovereignty at all. They should be called by their proper name as they are unitary states in spite of their federal constitutions. In all cases theory and practice must be considered together in the process of classification. Conventions supplement written law and even if they are *praeter legem* or *contra legem*, they are part of the constitutional law of the particular country. Compared with other federations the case of India is *sui generis*. To promote unity in extremely difficult conditions, she started after gaining independence with a constitution imposed from above. Her central government has considerable powers if compared with the powers of the states, but decentralising tendencies promoted by dynamic linguistic communities as well as by static regional interests and by the appearance of local multi-party governments are continuously at work. The provisions of the constitution are no obstacle in their realisation. They may bring about changes on the political map of India, as linguistic communities tend to get their own political status within the federation. The balance between centralising and decentralising tendencies need not be a matter of uncontrolled fluctuations but can be safeguarded with the help of constitutional devices. Consolidation of local pressure groups and their growing power in relation to the centre gives them the status of *bargaining* communities. Though they have been unable to create initially a contractual formation, they may to some extent give India the appearance of a contractual federation *ex post*.

PART III

AFRICA AND THE LAW OF NATIONS

18

LE RÔLE DES TRAITÉS DANS LES RELATIONS ENTRE LES PUISSANCES EUROPÉENNES ET LES SOUVERAINS AFRICAINS

ASPECTS HISTORIQUES (1970)

L'histoire des traités entre les puissances européennes et les souverains (chefs) africains peut se diviser en trois périodes: la période précoloniale, la période de transition et la période coloniale. La première période coïncide avec la période du droit des nations classiques qui dura jusqu'à la fin du XVIIIe siècle. Dans cette période, les relations entre les puissances européennes et l'Afrique s'établirent principalement avec les pays de l'Afrique du Nord. La seconde période s'étend jusqu'au Congrès de Berlin en 1885 et la troisième période jusqu'à la fin du XIXe siècle. Au cours de ces deux dernières périodes un réseau de traités hétérogènes s'établit dans les régions côtières d'où il s'élargit graduellement vers l'intérieur du continent africain.[1]

Pendant la première période, les traités entre l'Europe et l'Afrique reflétaient les principes classiques d'un système du droit des nations universel et non discriminatoire du point de vue de civilisation, religion et race. Les relations entre les deux continents et particulièrement entre la France d'une part et les souverains africains de l'autre s'établirent sur un pied d'égalité. Un nombre de traités conclus avec le Maroc, l'Algérie, la Tunisie et le Tripoli accordaient aux ambassadeurs ou envoyés de ces Etats africains en France des privilèges juridictionnels qui entraient plus ou moins dans la catégorie des anciennes capitulations.[2] Ainsi le Traité entre la France et le Maroc conclu le 24 septembre 1631 (article IX) déclarait que l'ambassadeur du Maroc en France serait compétent dans les différends entre les sujets du Maroc

[1] Malgré leur hétérogénéité (à cause des différences de pouvoir entre les souverains africains contractants), ces traités étaient néanmoins gouvernés sans distinction par les mêmes principes du droit international. V. «Les Pays Afro-Asiatiques et le Droit des Nations», par C. H. Alexandrowicz dans le *Recueil des Cours de l'Académie de droit international de La Haye*, 1968/I.

[2] E. Rouard de Card, *Traités de la France avec les Pays d'Afrique du Nord*, 1906, pp. 26, 163, 301. Ainsi la théorie positiviste qui parlait de la civilisation supérieure des pays jouissant des privilèges capitulaires, et de la civilisation inférieure des pays concédant ces privilèges n'est fondée sur aucune base historique.

qui résidaient en France. Cette stipulation correspond à la concession accordée dans le même traité au consul français au Maroc qui exerçait la juridiction dans les différends entre les ressortissants français qui résidaient au Maroc.

Le Traité du 17 mai 1666 entre la France et l'Algérie autorisait le souverain d'Algérie à déléguer deux envoyés à Marseille pour examiner toutes les plaintes concernant la violation du traité (article VI). Cet article n'est pas strictement une stipulation juridictionnelle appartenant à la catégorie des capitulations ordinaires mais il est basé sur le principe de la réciprocité entre les parties contractantes et il permettait aux envoyés algériens en France d'exercer des fonctions extra-territoriales y compris la juridiction dans les conflits de compétence.

La même stipulation se trouve dans le Traité du 3 juin 1771 entre la France et la Tunisie. Selon l'article XXI de ce traité le Bey (Dey) de la Tunisie avait le droit de déléguer des envoyés à Marseille pour examiner les plaintes concernant la violation du traité.

Cette situation changea graduellement au XIXe siècle et le principe de la réciprocité et d'égalité des relations disparut des traités africains. C'est à cette période, surtout après la pénétration vers l'intérieur du continent, que les puissances européennes, la France, la Grande-Bretagne, le Portugal, la Belgique, l'Allemagne et l'Italie, s'engagent dans une lutte pour le territoire africain (*scramble for territory*). Cette lutte, ainsi que tous les changements territoriaux, était guidée par les institutions du droit international positiviste du XIXe siècle comme par exemple le « protectorat colonial » et les capitulations appliquées sur un pied d'inégalité. Néanmoins, les souverains africains et leurs gouvernements constituèrent même pendant le XIXe siècle une barrière contre une confrontation unilatérale de la part des Européens. Cette barrière révéla une participation parfois active des Africains dans l'évolution des événements—une personnalité *sui generis*—qui se manifesta de différentes façons.

Notons d'abord que la présence des souverains et d'une organisation politique et gouvernementale exclut définitivement la possibilité de traiter l'Afrique comme *territorium nullius* en droit international. Les recherches historiques démontrent deux grandes influences qui formèrent à une époque reculée, les institutions politiques de la société africaine:[3] l'ancienne influence égyptienne qui s'était infiltrée par la voie de la Nubie (Royaume de Kush) et du Soudan jusqu'à l'Afrique occidentale, et plus tard l'influence islamique qui pénétra du Nord de l'Afrique vers le Sud. Ces deux influences aidèrent la consolidation de l'Etat africain et l'établissement, souvent par conquête, d'un nombre d'empires et de royaumes héréditaires avec un système de pouvoir très centralisé. Il est intéressant de noter que Hugo Grotius se réfère dans son ouvrage classique « *De Jure Belli ac Pacis* » (t. I, Ch. III, s. VIII, 9) à l'Egypte ainsi qu'à l'Ethiopie, et définit ces deux empires comme des Etats gouvernés par des souverains investis d'un pouvoir centralisé. Néanmoins, les cycles de centralisation et de décentralisation qui s'ensuivirent pendant des siècles ne détruisirent jamais la communauté du village autonome qui continua à être le pivot de la tradition

[3] OLIVER et FAGE. *A Short History of Africa*, 1962.

africaine (tribale ou quasi tribale) jusqu'au moment où elle fut prise dans les rouages de l'administration coloniale et tomba sous l'influence du développement social et économique moderne.

La conséquence logique de l'absence de *territorium nullius* en Afrique (excluant toute occupation unilatérale de la part des Européens) fut le traité bilatéral qui avait déjà paru en Afrique du Nord et plus tard dans les pays côtiers du continent africain avant et au cours du XIXe siècle, et qui atteignit son apogée dans les vingt dernières années du XIXe siècle. Pendant que les puissances européennes se livraient à la lutte pour les titres juridiques pour le transfert des droits territoriaux, les souverains africains en tant que possesseurs de ces titres pouvaient dans une certaine mesure influencer les résultats des négociations et même choisir la puissance européenne avec laquelle ils désiraient conclure un traité.

Ainsi dans les négociations entre les Allemands et les souverains et chefs des pays du Sud-Ouest Africain pour la conclusion de traités de protection, ces souverains exigeaient une garantie de la part des Allemands de respecter les traités qu'ils avaient conclus auparavant avec d'autres pays. Parmi des traités de protection, publiés dans le *Nouveau Recueil de Traités* de G.-F. Martens, t. XI, série 2 (1889), citons les traités conclus par l'Allemagne avec Maharero, le chef suprême des Hereros en 1885 (article 2), avec Hermanus Van Wyk, le chef des Rehoboth en 1885 (article 2), avec Manasse, le souverain de la nation rouge à Hoachana, en 1885 (article 2), et avec le capitaine Joseph Fredericks de la Bethanie en 1889 (article 3). La concession accordée par les Allemands dans ces traités garantissait les droits des souverains de l'Afrique du Sud-Ouest de maintenir (au moins temporairement) certaines relations extérieures avec d'autres pays.

En outre, les récits des négociateurs européens, dont celui de Lord Lugard est un exemple typique,[4] sur la conclusion des traités, montrent l'influence considérable des souverains africains dans la rédaction des traités, comme par exemple, à la cour du roi de l'Ouganda. Une des stipulations souvent obtenues concernait le respect de la loi et de la propriété indigène (en tant que privée et individuelle).

En cas de concurrence entre les puissances pour un titre territorial, le souverain africain pouvait parfois choisir la partie contractante européenne, ce qui influença la carte politique de l'Afrique telle qu'elle existe actuellement. Ainsi le Portugal qui avait établi ses premières possessions côtières en Afrique au XVIe siècle, réclama au XIXe siècle de vastes territoires à l'intérieur de l'Afrique qui s'étendaient entre ses colonies de l'Angola et du Mozambique. Le gouvernement du Portugal obtint de l'Allemagne et de la France la reconnaissance provisoire de ses revendications territoriales mais un nombre de souverains africains s'y opposèrent préférant une protection britannique à la protection portugaise. Un cas particulier est celui de Lewanika, le souverain de Barotse. Cette attitude des souverains était essentielle dans cette région de l'Afrique car si le Portugal avait établi le contrôle de la région

[4] Lord LUGARD, *The Rise of an East African Empire*, 1893, II, 23; v. aussi l'expédition de M. de Brazza au Congo et la conclusion du traité Makoko en 1880, H. BRUNSCHWIG, *L'Avènement de l'Afrique Noire*, 1963, p. 146. Le texte de ce traité se trouve dans le *Nouveau Recueil de Traités* de G.F. de MARTENS, t. IX, série 2, 1884, p. 216.

entre l'Angola et le Mozambique, la carte politique de l'Afrique actuelle serait dessinée très différemment.[5]

Les souverains africains influencèrent aussi les événements politiques en ayant recours aux armes pour la défense de leur indépendance et pour obtenir des traités de paix favorables. Certaines batailles dans l'histoire de l'Afrique ont été décisives comme par exemple la bataille d'Alcasar-quivir en 1578 par laquelle le sultan du Maroc décima l'armée portugaise en Afrique. Deux ans plus tard, le Portugal perdit son indépendance et ne reprit sa souveraineté qu'en 1640.[6]

Il est difficile d'estimer jusqu'à quel point les batailles africaines du XIXe siècle influencèrent la destinée du continent. Les Zoulous gagnèrent la bataille de Isandhevana en 1817, les Ashantis celle de Bousasa en 1824, le Mahdi conquit Karthoum et le Soudan égyptien après 1880 et les batailles contre Abd-el-Kader et Abd-el-Krim influencèrent l'histoire de l'Afrique du Nord (voir le traité de paix entre la France et Abd-el-Kader conclu en 1837, et l'établissement par Abd-el-Krim de la République du Rif après la bataille du Mont Anual en 1921).[7] Mais de toutes les guerres suivies de traité de paix en Afrique, la plus spectaculaire fut la guerre entre l'Ethiopie et l'Italie qui résulta en une victoire éthiopienne et dans le Traité de paix de 1896.[8] Ce traité abolit le traité de la prétendue protection italienne de 1889 et fut un tournant d'histoire aussi important peut-être que la défaite de l'armée russe par le Japon en 1904. Il prouva que batailles et traités pouvaient être perdus ou gagnés par les Asiatiques et les Africains et que dans la lutte pour le pouvoir tous les Etats du monde sans exception se trouvaient également vulnérables.

Le droit de guerre en Afrique était jusqu'à un certain point sous l'influence du «*jihad*», institution fondée sur la loi et la tradition islamiques.[9] Le *jihad* convertit les traités de droit international en armistices (d'un caractère temporaire), il élimina presque totalement la possibilité de neutralité des Etats non belligérants et employa le droit de guerre pour ses propres buts (rançon, contrebande, etc.). Le XIXe siècle vit plusieurs cas de *jihad* en Afrique. Mentionnons ici le *jihad* des Foulanis proclamé par Usuman dans Fodio à Socote. Le *jihad* était dirigé contre les dissidents de la foi islamique dans les Etats de Housa. Il fut aussi proclamé par Secou Ahmedou et par Al-haj Umar des Foutadjallan qui vainquit l'empire de Secou en 1862. Ces deux souverains conclurent des traités avec la France qui reconnut leur souveraineté intérieure et extérieure.[10] Tandis que ces cas du *jihad* étaient principalement le résultat des conflits entre-islamiques, le *jihad* du Mahdi au Soudan égyptien aboutit à la fin catastrophique du général Gordon à Karthoum en 1885.[11]

Il était important, dans une opération aussi gigantesque que celle des transferts des droits territoriaux concernant un continent entier, de sauvegarder la légalité

[5] OLIVER et FAGE, *op. cit.*, p. 170; M. GLUCKMAN, *The Ideas in Barotse Jurisprudence*, 1965.

[6] V. Fernand BRAUDEL, *La Méditerranée et le monde méditerranéen à l'époque de Philippe II.*

[7] E. HERTSLET, *The Map of Africa by Treaty*, 1909, II, 643; III, 1149.

[8] HERSTSLET, *op. cit.*, I, pp. 454–458.

[9] Alexandrowicz, *History of the Law of Nations in the East Indies*, 1967, p. 90.

[10] HERTSLET, *op. cit.*, II, p. 628 et s.; E. ROUARD DE CARD, *Les Traités de Protectorat conclus par la France en Afrique*, 1897, p. 120 et s. et *Annales sénégalaises*, 1885, pp. 394-480.

[11] HERTSLET, *op. cit.*, II, 617.

des transactions et d'assurer la validité des titres transférés par les souverains africains. Les éléments essentiels des traités de cession des territoires étaient la capacité juridique du souverain, la liberté de son consentement, la forme et la structure des traités.[12] Dans le texte du traité le souverain faisait fréquemment une déclaration d'indépendance de tout autre souverain présumé (suzerain) et le conseil du souverain (chefs et notables) était en principe associé à la conclusion du traité. La liberté de consentement du souverain dans la conclusion des traités devint l'objet d'une controverse au Congrès de Berlin en 1885. C'est grâce à l'intervention de la délégation des Etats-Unis en faveur de l'application du droit international moderne (qui suivit la doctrine libérale classique plutôt que la doctrine coloniale positiviste du XIXe siècle), que le traité africain fut jusqu'à un certain point protégé par des sauvegardes, comme par exemple par les déclarations des témoins ou interprètes qui témoignaient de la liberté et de la régularité du consentement du souverain africain contractant. A cet égard les compagnies européennes qui opéraient en Afrique (munies de pouvoirs souverains délégués) adoptaient certains modèles de traités qui furent employés dans les négociations avec les souverains africains. Ces modèles établissaient le rôle des témoins et des interprètes dans la conclusion finale des traités.[13]

Le Congrès de Berlin s'occupa aussi de la controverse concernant le protectorat en Afrique qui fut finalement soumis au principe de la notification (article 34) mais pas à la norme de l'occupation effective (article 35). Il est difficile d'imaginer que le Congrès de Berlin ait pu soumettre un Etat protégé (protectorat) à une occupation effective par le protecteur, car en droit international un Etat protégé ne perd jamais sa souveraineté intérieure. Mais la plupart des juristes internationaux de l'école positiviste exprimèrent une opinion contraire. Ils adoptèrent une interprétation des stipulations de l'article 35 « *contra legem* » et favorisèrent la possibilité d'une occupation effective des protectorats africains, contre toutes les règles du droit international traditionnel. La conséquence de la non-observation du texte de l'article 35 fut la nécessité de créer une nouvelle conception du protectorat. Selon cette nouvelle conception (le protectorat colonial), l'Etat protecteur obtint des autres signataires de l'Acte général de Berlin, carte blanche d'occuper et d'annexer le territoire de l'Etat protégé. Une telle conception perdait tout caractère juridique; elle devenait un instrument de la politique de force qui n'avait aucune signification en droit international. En outre, un accord entre les puissances européennes ne pouvait porter atteinte à un traité de protectorat conclu entre l'une de ces puissances en tant qu'Etat protecteur, et un pays africain en tant qu'Etat protégé (« *pacta tertiis nec nocent nec prosunt* »). Un tel accord ne pouvait pas changer les droits et les

[12] *Recueil des Cours, op. cit, supra*, p. 172 et s. Il n'est pas nécessaire de discuter le caractère juridique des traités africains. Ils transféraient sans aucun doute la souveraineté du territoire cédé et non la propriété privée. Ils étaient des traités en droit international public au sens propre du mot. V. H. Hesse, *Les Traités de Protection du Sud-Ouest Africain*, 1906. En ce qui concerne l'importance du principe « *pacta sunt servanda* » dans la tradition africaine, voir Lord Lugard, *op. cit.*

[13] *Recueil des Cours, op. cit., supra*, p. 179; Hertslet, *op. cit.*, I, p. VI; lindley, *The Acquisition and Government of Backward Territory in International Law*, 1926, pp. 172–175.

obligations des parties contractantes d'un traité de protection en Afrique ou ailleurs. Le protectorat colonial était donc une institution politique et non pas juridique.[14]

Les positivistes soutinrent aussi l'opinion que la conception du protectorat colonial était basée sur la pratique uniforme des Etats. Mais il est à noter à ce sujet que la conduite des Etats signataires de l'Acte général du Congrès de Berlin ne fut pas unanime. Les Etats-Unis refusèrent de ratifier l'Acte général, et l'Espagne, bien que le ratifiant, refusa d'appliquer l'article 35 aux protectorats en Afrique.[15] Le cas de l'Ethiopie prouva aussi définitivement que l'établissement du protectorat colonial était fictif même du point de vue politique si l'intention de l'Etat protecteur d'annexer l'Etat protégé était irréalisable.

En ce qui concerne les capitulations, elles reflétaient les changements dans le droit des traités d'une époque à l'autre. Comme nous l'avons vu les Etats de l'Afrique du Nord jouissaient dans la période pré-coloniale, à partir du XVIIe siècle, en France, des mêmes privilèges juridictionnels que ceux dont les envoyés et consuls français jouissaient dans les pays d'Afrique du Nord. La situation changea graduellement au XIXe siècle et les capitulations devinrent onéreuses pour les Etats africains; les positivistes les interprétèrent comme preuve d'une civilisation inférieure, preuve qui ne se basait pas sur la réalité historique soit en Asie, soit en Afrique.[16] Les capitulations en Afrique furent finalement remplacées par les systèmes judiciaires des puissances coloniales qui tolérèrent une autonomie juridictionnelle très limitée en faveur des communautés africaines.

Parmi d'autres stipulations que l'on trouve dans les traités africains mentionnons la clause de la nation la plus favorisée. Son application dans les circonstances spéciales de la coexistence entre les administrations coloniales et les communautés africaines dégénéra souvent en des situations absurdes. Par exemple, selon le Traité entre la Grande-Bretagne et l'Italie de 1905, les ressortissants britanniques ainsi que les sujets du Sultan de Zanzibar sous protection britannique qui résidaient dans le territoire de la côte de Benadir (sous contrôle italien) étaient assurés du traitement de la nation la plus favorisée. Ainsi, les sujets du Sultan de Zanzibar qui résidaient dans ce territoire recevaient un traitement plus favorable que la population permanente de ce territoire. Cette différence de traitement accordé aux personnes de couleur par l'administration italienne, et les difficultés qui s'ensuivirent donnèrent lieu à une démarche diplomatique concernant l'interprétation du traité de 1905. L'ambassadeur d'Italie à Londres soumit une note au Foreign Office dans laquelle il attirait l'attention du gouvernement britannique sur les privilèges accordés aux sujets du Sultan de Zanzibar dans ce traité, et il déclarait que: «Si cette stipulation est considérée comme applicable aux personnes de couleur, le gouvernement italien sera obligé d'accorder un traitement plus favorable aux sujets du Sultan qu'à ses sujets propres de la même catégorie».[17] Notons que les principes du traitement de la nation la plus favorisée auraient pu jouer un rôle positif en contrecarrant

[14] *Recueil des Cours, op. cit., supra*, p. 189 et s.

[15] Lindley, *op. cit.*, p. 149.

[16] *Recueil des Cours, op. cit., supra*, p. 183.

[17] Hertslet, *op. cit.*, III, pp. 956–957.

une politique raciste discriminatoire en Afrique. En fait, ils devinrent une source d'embarras sans contribuer à l'amélioration des relations entre races diverses.

La discussion du rôle des traités dans la confrontation entre l'Europe et l'Afrique pourrait être poussée jusqu'à la période de la domination coloniale pendant laquelle même la souveraineté intérieure des chefs africains fut complètement limitée ou supprimée. Mais une telle discussion serait en dehors du cadre de cette brève étude. Il faut souligner ici que l'établissement des administrations coloniales, souvent sans contrôle effectif sur les territoires de leurs communautés, ne pouvait pas satisfaire aux conditions prescrites par le Congrès de Berlin et particulièrement au principe de l'occupation effective (article 35). Telle était la situation à la fin du XIXe siècle et au commencement du XXe siècle. Dans plusieurs colonies, britanniques, françaises ou autres, un régime de domination indirecte fut imposé aux pays africains (*indirect rule*) en vertu duquel l'ancien souverain africain restait au pouvoir comme quasi-fonctionnaire colonial. Paradoxalement sa présence était toujours nécessaire pour établir un lien réel (*genuine link*) entre les communautés africaines et les administrations coloniales. Ces dernières ne pouvant s'identifier avec des communautés dont la civilisation et les traditions politiques leur étaient étrangères, furent incapables d'établir un lien réel avec les pavs et les peuples qu'elles venaient gouverner. De même que la nationalité d'un individu qui n'a pas de lien réel avec son pays d'adoption, le titre du souverain colonial privé de ce lien n'avait qu'une validité formelle et était juridiquement imparfait (voir l'affaire *Nottebohm* devant la Cour Internationale de Justice, 1955).[18]

[18] Cour Internationale de Justice, Rap. 1955. 4. Selon l'article V, section 13 de la Constitution du Liberia « seules les personnes de couleur seront admises à la nationalité de cette République ». Cette déclaration implique les principes du lieu réel dans la conception de la nationalité libérienne.

19

THE PARTITION OF AFRICA BY TREATY (1974)

I. Introduction

THE ENTRY of the African continent into the orbit of the Family and Law of Nations is part and parcel of the wider process of consolidation of the Family of Nations on a universal scale. This process required negotiation and treaty making between countries belonging to various civilizations, whether in Europe, Asia, Africa or elsewhere. If such countries were considered to be on different (higher or lower) levels of civilization, their confrontation tended to result in the establishment of unequal relations. The question arose as to what were the standards of measuring different levels of civilization. The European Powers in the nineteenth century maintained that they had the right to answer this question unilaterally and they adopted the institution of capitulations and standards of treatment of foreigners as the international legal test of evaluating the comparative value of civilizations. They tended to evaluate foreign civilizations in terms of their own civilization rather than the latter in terms of the former. To understand the reasoning of international lawyers who became the spokesmen of this Euro-centric outlook (differing fundamentally from the views of the pre-nineteenth-century classic writers of the law of nations), some introductory observations would be relevant. The above school of thought conceived the development of the Family and Law of Nations in the following way:[1]

The Christian countries of Europe were considered the original members of the Family of Nations. The Law of Nations was alleged to have grown exclusively through a network of relations between those countries, particularly through treaty, custom and usage. This network originated in Western Europe but gradually extended to the rest of Europe. The European founder club of the Family of Nations assumed the important prerogative of admitting other countries (in Asia and Africa) to the Family of Nations and one of the instrumentalities of admission was the constitutive doctrine of recognition. Under this doctrine existing States, by recognizing new States, conferred on them personality in international law in a constitutive way.[2] The first States outside Europe which were admitted to the Family of Nations were

[1] L. F. L. Oppenheim, *International Law*, Vol. I (The Dominion of the Law of Nations), London, 1920.

[2] To be distinguished from the declaratory theory of recognition which prevailed prior to the nineteenth century.

the Christian States of the American continent (North and South) organized by European settlers. Then followed Christian States with a non-European population *e.g.* Haiti and Liberia (beginning of the nineteenth century). In 1856 the first non-Christian State (the Ottoman Empire) was allowed to join the Family of Nations.[3] But according to the views of international lawyers, its position within the Family of Nations was ambiguous because of the inferiority of its civilization. Evidence of inferiority of civilization was to be found in the regime of capitulations. This regime allowed European residents in Turkey (as well as in some other Asian and African countries) to govern themselves by their own law, under the jurisdiction of their own consuls, a state of affairs which indicated the inferiority of the legal system and status of extra-European countries receiving European residents. The fallacy of this sort of reasoning will deserve special attention (below).

After the Ottoman Empire some other Asian and African States were said to be admitted to the Family of Nations. Here belong, apart from China and Japan, the Kingdoms of Siam and Persia and the Empire of Ethiopia.[4] But their status was still considered ambiguous because of considerations of civilization.

The first and most important gap in this theory of the development of the Family and Law of Nations is shown by the fact that its proponents never asked what the pre-nineteenth-century Family of Nations thought about itself, particularly about the problem of membership of the Family of Nations. Even if it is conceded that the nineteenth-century positivist school of thought reflected nineteenth-century developments and state practice, there was no reason to assume (without the existence of sufficient evidence) that the position was the same prior to the nineteenth-century. Positivism committed the error of projecting its own ideology backwards into the past without taking into consideration the ideology of the classic law of nations and state practice reflected in the works of the classic writers.

The orthodox view of the development of the Family of Nations in Asia has been abandoned by the International Court of Justice which in the Indo–Portuguese case (1960)[5] decided that a treaty concluded in 1779 between Portugal and one of the major Indian Powers (the Marathas) was a transaction which must be governed by the eighteenth-century law of nations and not by nineteenth-century international law. By pronouncing the treaty a valid instrument of transfer of international rights and obligations the Court gave expression to the conviction that the contracting Asian Power was a legal person in the eighteenth-century law of nations (this view was expressly stated by Judge Moreno Quintana). Thus the position of a number of Afro–Asian countries in the pre-nineteenth-century law of nations was far from ambiguous and pointed to an extension of the Family of Nations in parts of Asia and Africa. The whole positivist theory of the development of the Family of Nations calls for revision and is in fact gradually being revised by historians of international

[3] By the treaty of Paris of 1856 Turkey was admitted to the Concert of Europe, an absurd admission if it is recalled that Turkey had treaty and diplomatic relations with the European Powers since the sixteenth century. See J. von Hammer-Purgstall, *Geschichte des Osmanischen Reiches*, Budapest, 1834.

[4] Ethiopia was recognized as a civilized state after the battle of Adowa in 1896.

[5] *International Court of Justice Reports*, 1960, p. 6.

law.[6] The point is that nineteenth-century international law has been formulated as a *universal* system on the basis of *regional* European history only. The facts of Asian and African history were alien to the formulators of nineteenth-century international law. It is therefore essential for historians of international law in Africa to study the available and partly unexplored treaty material concerning European–African relations since the sixteenth century *i.e.* the period of the birth of the classic law of nations. Treaties and negotiations between Europe and Africa prior to the middle of the nineteenth century were governed by the classic (or immediate post-classic) law of nations while African treaties in the second half of the nineteenth century came under the sway of positivist international law which differed from the classic law in a number of essential points. Moreover, an appreciation of the political structure of African countries as revealed by historians of the African continent must throw light on the status of the African contracting party in its relations with one or another colonial power. The partition of Africa can only be properly understood if the status of the territorial sovereign in Africa and the nature of titles conveyed by him is examined on the basis of treaty texts and negotiations surrounding the conclusion of treaties and their implementation or breach. A study of the relevant documents reflecting the 'scramble' for titles to African territory will show to what extent the normal institutions of the law of nations as originally applied to European–African relations degenerated into instruments of colonial penetration in the second half of the nineteenth century, particularly after the Berlin Conference of 1884–1885 which led to a multilaterally conceived plan of partition of the whole continent. Before a discussion of these documents is attempted, an introductory examination of pre-nineteenth-century European–African treaty making and of references of some of the classic writers to Africa may be attempted.

II. Africa and the Classic Law of Nations

Among the great classic writers the first to deal with problems relating to Afro–Asian countries were Hugo Grotius (Dutch) and Seraphim de Freitas (Portuguese). Their primary concern is the East Indies but they also make reference to African problems. Grotius, in his *Mare Liberum* (1609) makes this significant statement: '*Accolae totius tractus Africani aut Asiatici partem maris quisque sibi proximam piscando et navigando perpetuo usurparunt*'. Thus he testifies to the fact that some of the African and Asian maritime countries had the notion of territorial waters or zones adjacent to their shores in which they claimed rights of occupation or quasi-occupation for purposes of fishing and navigation. Such rights were considered as an exception to the freedom of the high seas which these countries seem to have respected. Seraphim de Freitas gave a reply to Grotius in his *De Justo Imperio*

[6] See the contributions of A. Rubin, P. O'Higgins, M. J. Mössner and P. Fischer to the *Grotian Society Papers*, 1968, 1972.

Lusitanorum Asiatico (1625, Chapter X) in which he elaborates the idea of quasi-occupation of certain parts of the sea.

In his *De Jure Belli ac Pacis* Grotius refers to two African empires, Egypt and Ethiopia, and compares their constitutional structure with that of Persia. He emphasizes the absolute power of the King of Persia ('*Apud Persos rex summo cum imperio erat*') and the Kings of Ethiopia and Egypt ('*Idem de Aethiopium regibus tradit D.S. eodem tradente Aegyptorum reges*').[7] This reference might have appeared significant at one time when certain historians maintained that African statehood could to some extent be traced back to the Egyptian pattern and that Egyptian influence came via the Kingdom of Kush (Meroe) to the region of Lake Chad from whence it penetrated westwards resulting in the creation of the Sudanese State model. The latter was characterized by centralized military and bureaucratic power though not of the feudal type[8] and ultimately came under the sway of Islamic law and practice.[9] More recent investigations have, however, cast doubt on this theory.

Another classic writer concerned with Afro-Asian problems is Pufendorf (Crull) who in his *Introduction to the History of Asia, Africa and America* refers *inter alia* to the Barbary States, Ethiopia, Mauritania, the Kingdom of Monomotapa, Sierra Leone and Benin (Part 2, I–VI).[10]

Among the European Powers the first to engage in treaty making on a wider scale was Portugal. The text of the Portuguese–Monomotapa treaty of 1629 is quoted by Judice Biker in his *Collecção de Tratados* which is mainly a collection of Portuguese treaties concluded in the East Indies since the beginning of the sixteenth century. The inclusion of African treaty material in this collection is symptomatic of the approach of the Portuguese to Asian and African countries. The Portuguese attitude to these countries was at first negative since ecclesiastical prohibitions of treaty making with infidels excluded the possibility of bilateral relations on a footing of equality. But these prohibitions (earlier rejected by St. Thomas Aquinas)[11] went overboard when the Portuguese perceived the prospects of the East Indian trade in spices and other goods. They initiated a uniform treaty policy in the East Indies and in Africa (limited to rulers in coastal or near coastal regions). Treaties concluded on this early pattern usually established

[7] *De Jure Belli ac Pacis*, Book I, ch. 3, VIII, 9 and XVI, 3 (*Classics of International Law*, 1925, Latin at vol. 1, pp. 54, 62; translation at vol. 2, pp. 107, 122).

[8] R. Oliver and J. D. Fage, *A Short History of Africa*, London, 1966, pp. 43–7.

[9] Islam brought to Africa an advanced code of conduct of inter-state affairs. It divided the world into two parts i.e. *Dar al Islam* and *Dar al Harb*. A state of war (*jihad*) prevailed between the two but diplomatic and commercial relations between them were possible. If treaties were concluded, they had the character of truce arrangements. Jihad excluded implicitly neutrality but the Islamic law of war generated a number of institutions *e.g.* those relating to Prisoners of War (ransom). 'The Afro-Asian World and the Law of Nations', *Recueil des Cours*, 1968/71.

[10] Pufendorf's authorship of this work seems questionable. In the light of reliable evidence the work may be attributed to Jodocus Crull. See *British Year Book of International Law*, 1968–1969 (ch. 11 above).

[11] See C. H. Alexandrowicz, 'Paulus Vladimiri', *British Yearbook of International Law*, 1963 (ch. 2 above).

suzerain–vassal relations though this was of course not possible with major powers such as the Mogul Empire. Portuguese suzerainty limited the independence of the Asian or African vassal mainly to the extent of establishing a trade monopoly in favour of Portugal. Many of these monopolies led a precarious existence and were successfully contested by the Dutch in the seventeenth century. Grotius and Seraphim de Freitas deal with this contest in detail.

The Monomotapa treaty of 1629[12] stipulates the establishment of vassalship on the cessation of hostilities between the contracting parties. It further guarantees freedom of religion to Christians and it provides for diplomatic relations between the contracting parties including the right of access of high Portuguese officials to the ruler's court.[13] The treaty also contains a jurisdictional clause giving the Captain of Massapa authority to decide civil and criminal cases. Finally there are clauses dealing with trade and mining concessions and the characteristic anti-Islamic discriminatory clause stipulating the expulsion of 'all the Moors from the Kingdom'.

The treaty became a significant piece of evidence in the Delagoa Bay arbitration between Great Britain and Portugal (1875).[14] In this case Great Britain contended 'that the whole country south of the Dundas or Lorenço Marques River and English river, and to seaward, was free and independent: the native inhabitants under their chiefs, retaining absolute dominion (sovereignty) over, and possession of, these territories, over which the Portuguese exercised no jurisdiction. That these Chiefs, with the consent of the natives, and in exercise of their independent rights ceded by treaty, in 1823, the Sovereignty over these territories to the Crown of Great Britain'.

Portugal contended in reply that even 'if Portugal did not acquire sovereignty over the Bay of Lorenço Marques, the territory would still be within the cession made in 1629 by the King of Monomotapa to the Crown of Portugal'. The arguments of the parties to the dispute are interesting from the point of view of acknowledgement by the Colonial power of sovereignty of African Rulers over their territory and the recognition of their capacity of conveying valid territorial titles to territory.

There is no doubt that these early Portuguese treaties in Africa complied with the general rules of the classic law of nations relating to treaty making. The Portuguese spread their network of treaties to various regions of Africa such as the Kingdom of the Congo, Ethiopia and to some countries on the West coast of Africa.[15] Seraphim de Freitas referred to Portuguese treaties as instruments of admission to overseas trade: '*Foedere et amicitia fuimus admissi*'.[16]

[12] J. F. Judice Biker, *Collecção de Tratados*, Vol. I, Lisbon, 1881, p. 234.

[13] As to diplomatic practice in Africa in the past see T. O. Elias, *Africa and the Development of International Law*, New York, 1972, p. 42.

[14] M. F. Lindley, *The Acquisition and Government of Backward Territory in International Law*, London, 1926, p. 40

[15] See for instance the treaty between Portugal and Benin of 1515, Elias, *op. cit.*, p. 6.

[16] *De Justo Imperio Lusitanorum Asiatico*, 1625, ch. II.

III. Pre-Nineteenth-Century Treaties between European Powers and African Countries

European treaty making in North Africa provides valuable evidence of relations (on a footing of equality) between European and African powers under the regime of the classic law of nations.[17] Among the most ancient commercial treaties between North African states and Christian powers is the treaty between Pisa and Tunisia of 1157. Its main concern was the treatment of Christian merchants in North Africa and it allowed Pisans to reside and trade in Tunisia. Arab rule which at first prevailed in North Africa gave way to Turkish domination in the sixteenth century. The Ottoman Empire established its overlordship over all North African communities except Morocco. But in the beginning of the seventeenth century Turkish rule declined and the control of the Ottoman Emperor over the rulers of Tripoli, Tunisia and Algeria became ineffective. The emperor became a nominal suzerain and kept only his religious prerogatives as Caliph.

In the literature of the law of nations the question arose whether the North African (Barbary) States were member states of the Family of Nations capable of contracting or exercising international rights and obligations. Grotius took up the question in his *De Jure Belli ac Pacis* (Book III, 9, XIX, 2). He writes: '... *dum haec scribo,*[18] *judicatum est in summo auditorio Parisiensi, coetus principe Nicolao Verdunio: bona, quae Francorum civium fuerant, ab Algeriensibus, populo praedationibus maritimis in omnes alios grassari solito, capta belli mutasse dominum: ac proinde, cum recepto ab aliis essent, facta eorum qui recepissent*'.

In this passage Grotius refers to a case before a Paris tribunal under the chairmanship of Nicholas of Verdun. The plaintiffs who were French nationals had been deprived of their goods in the course of maritime warfare with Algerians. The defendants maintained that they had acquired the property of the captured goods from the latter and the plaintiffs sued for their recovery. The court refused to give judgment for the plaintiffs and rejected the claim. It referred expressly to '*capta belli mutasse dominum*', in other words the captured goods had changed ownership in the course of war. Thus Grotius implicitly recognised the Algerians as belligerents in the meaning of the law of nations and we may assume that he considered the North African countries and countries in a similar position as having statehood and a *locus standi* in the law of nations. At a later date Sir W. Scott (Lord Stowell) stated in the 'Habana case' that the North African States 'have long acquired the character of established governments with whom we have regular treaties acknowledging and confirming to them the relations of legal status'.[19]

[17] As to French treaties see E. Rouard de Card, *Traités de la France avec les pays de l'Afrique du Nord*, Paris, 1906, pp. 11–376; *Annales Sénégalaises*, Paris, 1885, and M. de Clercq, *Recueil des Traités*, Paris, 1880–1923, Vols. III, IV–X, XII, XIV–XV, XVII–XVIII. As to English treaties, see E. Hertslet, *The Map of Africa by Treaty*, 3 Vols., London, 1909.

[18] Grotius was writing about '*postliminium*'.

[19] Dr. M. J. Mössner, *Die Völkerrechtspersönlichkeit und die Völkerrechtspraxis der Barbaresken Staaten*, Berlin, 1968.

The discussion of treaties concluded by France (and other European powers) with North African States in the period between the seventeenth and nineteenth centuries may help to show how the two sets of powers settled their problems at first on a basis of equality and reciprocity and how with the progress of time and with the change of the law this relationship deteriorated, leading to the collapse of the North African State system in the nineteenth century.[20] The stipulations relating to jurisdiction and to the treatment of foreigners provide a reliable barometer of the political climate and the resulting balance or unbalance of power. It is proposed to examine first treaties concluded by France with Algeria.

In a treaty concluded on 19 September 1628 the Ruler of Algeria and the King of France are styled as emperors and the king addressed the ruler as '*Mon très cher et parfait ami*'. Treaties concluded in 1640 and 1669 between the same contracting parties settled problems relating to the '*Bastion de France*', a stronghold built for the protection of French interests in North Africa. The treaty of 17 May 1666 contains jurisdictional provisions of particular interest to international lawyers. Article VI of the treaty authorizes the contracting Algerian ruler to send two envoys to Marseilles in France to hear complaints in case of violation of the provisions of the treaty. On the other hand French consuls in Algeria had reciprocal jurisdictional rights. Though art. VI is not strictly speaking of a capitulatory nature, it empowered the Algerian envoys in France to perform functions on an extraterritorial level which must have included the right of the envoys to hear complaints arising out of jurisdictional competence conflicts.

The above jurisdictional provisions can also be found in the treaty of 3 June 1711 between France and the ruler of Tunisia. The latter had the right to send envoys to Marseilles to deal with complaints arising out of a possible breach of treaty (art. XXIII). The treaty between France and Morocco of 24 September 1631 goes further. It contains the following provision in art. IX: '*Que s'il arrivent quelque différend entre les Mores Marchands qui seront en France, l'Ambassadeur de l'Empereur de Moroc résidant en France les terminera et le même se fera par l'Ambassadeur ou Consul de France en Affrique*'.[21]

It is noteworthy that in the same year (1631) a treaty had been concluded between the Netherlands and Persia which goes even further than the French–Moroccan treaty. It established a Persian settlement in Amsterdam giving Persian traders the same capitulatory rights which were enjoyed by Dutch traders in the kingdom of Persia.[22]

These are provisions which leave us in no doubt about the law governing in the seventeenth-century treaties between countries belonging to different civilizations.

[20] Rouard de Card, *op. cit.*

[21] 'If disputes arise between Moorish merchants in France, the Ambassador of the Emperor of Morocco in France will exercise jurisdiction in these disputes; the same jurisdiction will pertain to the French Ambassador or Consul in Africa'.

[22] The Dutch obtained a capitulation treaty in 1623. See G. F. de Martens, *Cours Diplomatique*, Berlin, 1801 and J. Dumont, *Corps Universel*, Amsterdam, 1726–31. A special collection of Dutch treaties (East Indies) has been published by J. E. Heeres, *Corpus Diplomaticum Neerlando-Indicum*, The Hague, 1907 (1931).

The French–Moroccan treaty is based on the principle of legal equality of the contracting parties and the reciprocal stipulations in their favour show that capitulations do not reflect the superior or inferior civilization of one or the other contracting party. If so, capitulations were at the time in question no reliable evidence of the legal status of a particular country in the Family of Nations.[23]

As far as Asian tradition is concerned, it had been since time immemorial an established custom to allow settlements of foreign traders to govern themselves by their own law under the jurisdiction of the Head of the Settlement. The receiving territorial ruler never regarded this customary concession as derogatory to his sovereignty.[24] Historical records from the eighth century A.D. onwards show that Muslim merchants received privileges and concessions in the Hindu states on the west coast of India.[25] This custom prevailed at first even in China. Foreign traders were under the protection of the local authorities and governed themselves by their own personal law. The Arabs in Canton were under the jurisdiction of their *kadis* and jurisdictional privileges granted to foreigners were no evidence of the superior civilization of foreign traders which would have been unthinkable in China. However, Chinese policy changed after the arrival of the Portuguese in the sixteenth century and the tendency prevailed to apply Chinese law to foreigners. On the other hand, the treaties concluded between China and Russia (1689, 1727) show that Russian merchants in China were under the jurisdiction of the heads of their settlements. Jean Escarra writing about these treaties classifies extraterritorial (jurisdictional) concessions into *natural* and *artificial* formations.[26] Jurisdictional privileges granted to foreigners (under pre-capitulation arrangements) in China, the East Indies and Africa were an institution of practical significance allowing settlements of foreign traders to follow their own way of life in a country whose hospitality they enjoyed (personal law principle). The European powers in China, the East Indies and Africa incorporated these jurisdictional concessions, granted to their subjects, in treaties which were at first concluded on a footing of equality and degenerated only later into *artificial* instruments of colonial penetration and domination (nineteenth century).

[23] France and the Netherlands were not the only European states to grant jurisdictional privileges to traders from Asian and African countries who resided in Europe. Great Britain and Morocco concluded on 8 April 1791 a treaty according to which disputes arising in England or in English dominions between Moroccan nationals, belonged to the jurisdiction of a mixed court (see art. VIII of the treaty). This court applied English law but it was composed of an equal number of English and Islamic judges. See also British–Moroccan treaty of 28 July 1760 (*Trattati, Convenzione, Accordi Relativi all' Africa*, Vol. I, 1648–1799, published by the Italian Ministry of External Affairs, 1940).

[24] C. Alexandrowicz, *Introduction to the History of the Law of Nations in the East Indies*, London, 1967, p. 98.

[25] Duarte Barbosa, the Portuguese writer, refers to the Moors in Calicut as having a governor of their own who exercised jurisdiction over them without major interference from the rulers of Calicut. Foreign traders in Indonesia (whether Chinese or Arab) had their own quarters and were under the jurisdiction of their own Heads of Settlements who exercised quasi-consular functions. Foreigners in Siam enjoyed internal autonomy in their settlements without interference from local authorities. R. Lingat, 'La Condition des Etrangers en Siam au XVIIe Siècle', *Recueils*, 1958.

[26] J. Escarra, *La Chine et le Droit International*, Paris, 1931.

North African treaties concluded under the regime of the classic law of nations contained a variety of jurisdictional provisions.[27] Subject to exceptions, disputes between nationals of the European contracting party residing in Africa belonged (according to these treaties) to the jurisdiction of the competent European consul.[28] In this respect African custom coincided with Asian tradition. But the question arose under whose jurisdiction were mixed disputes (civil and criminal) *i.e.* disputes between a subject of the receiving African ruler and a European resident. Several solutions were possible. Such disputes were either under the jurisdiction of the ruler's court which decided the case in the presence of the European consul or the disputes went to mixed courts or the principle '*actor sequitur forum rei*' was applied. In the last instance the court of the nationality of the defendant (accused) assumed jurisdiction and applied the law of his nationality.[29]

According to the treaty between France and Tunisia of 30 August 1685, (mixed) disputes between French nationals and Moors or Turks were under Tunisian jurisdiction[30] but they were not in the competence of ordinary courts but reserved to the council of the *dey* and the *divan* (art. XXI). These cases were tried in the presence of the French consul who also participated in trials of Frenchmen who had committed criminal offences against Moors and Turks (art. XXIV). The same solution was applied in mixed disputes according to the French–Tunisian treaties of 16 December 1710 (arts. XVI and XIX), and 3 June 1711 (arts. XVI and XIX), 9 November 1742 (articles XVI and XIX), and the 24 June 1781 (art. V). However, the situation changed in the nineteenth century under post-classic international law. At first, according to the treaty of 15 November 1824, mixed cases were under the jurisdiction of mixed courts composed of an equal number of French and Tunisian judges (art. XIV). If the votes of the judges were equally divided, the case was submitted to the *dey* who took his decision in agreement with the French consul. In 1881 Tunisia became a French Protectorate and the European powers exercised consular jurisdiction on a basis of inequality of relations.[31] The difference between the jurisdictional regime under the classic law of nations and nineteenth century international law is obvious.[32]

The same legal development can be observed in French–Algerian treaties. According to the treaty of 25 April 1684 mixed disputes were under the jurisdiction of the *pasha's* council (art. XVII).[33] Similar jurisdictional stipulations can be

[27] Rouard de Card, *op. cit.*

[28] An exception was the treaty between France and the ruler of Tunisia of 25 November 1665, according to which disputes between French subjects went to the ruler, not to the French consul (art. XXII).

[29] All these solutions can be found in East Indian treaties in the sixteenth, seventeenth and eighteenth centuries. Alexandrowicz, *op. cit.*, pp. 97–119.

[30] See note 28 above.

[31] British consular jurisdiction in Tunisia was abolished in 1883 and so was the consular jurisdiction of other European powers.

[32] The law and the balance of power position reflected each other according to circumstances peculiar to the particular period.

[33] Disputes between French nationals in Algeria were under the jurisdiction of French consuls (art. XVII).

found in treaties concluded between Algeria and other European powers. Thus according to the treaty between Algeria and the City of Hamburg of 22 February 1751 mixed disputes were in the competence of the *pasha* (*dey*).[34] Criminal cases were tried according to local law (arts. XV–XVI). The same solution was adopted in the Danish–Algerian treaty of 16 May 1772. According to the Spanish–Algerian treaty of 14 June 1786 mixed disputes were tried by the ruler in the presence of the Spanish consul (art. XIV). The consul was also to be present in all criminal cases against Spanish subjects. The U.S. treaties concluded with Algeria (1795), Tripoli (1796) and Tunisia (1797) reserved mixed disputes to the ruler, leaving disputes between U.S. citizens to the competence of the U.S. consul.

Analogous jurisdictional solutions were applied in treaties concluded by France or other European powers with Tripoli. Reference may be made to the French–Tripoli treaties of 29 June 1685, 4 July 1720, 9 June 1729 and 18 June 1801, to the Swedish–Tripoli treaty of 15 April 1741 and the Spanish–Tripoli treaty of 10 September 1784.

As to treaties between France and Morocco, emphasis has been put on the treaty of 1631 which gave the Moroccan ambassador in France capitulatory jurisdiction. According to this treaty mixed disputes in Morocco were under the jurisdiction of Moroccan courts and Article XII states that judgments passed by the courts will be carried out in France. The same solution was adopted for judgments in mixed disputes passed in France. French–Moroccan treaties concluded at a later date follow the same formula (*e.g.* the treaty of 29 January 1682 and 28 August 1767) and so do British–Moroccan treaties (1721, 1760). Article IX of the treaty of 1760 assigns jurisdiction in mixed conflicts or disputes to the Emperor of Morocco. On the other hand, disputes between Muslims in England or English dominions were under the jurisdiction of mixed courts (see above).[35]

Jurisdictional provisions are not the only ones to testify to the principle of equality observed in European–African treaty relations under the regime of the classic law of nations. Among other provisions adopted on a basis of reciprocity are those relating to the abolition of the right to shipwreck or the *droit d'aubaine*. According to the French–Tripoli treaty of 29 June 1685 (art. XXI) French consuls in Tripoli had the right to take over the estates of deceased French residents in Tripoli. The ruler could not seize such estates. This principle was equally applied to the estates of African residents who died in France. The treaty of 17 September 1631 stipulated mutual diplomatic privileges for the French ambassador in Morocco and the Moroccan ambassador in France. Even at the beginning of the nineteenth century treaties respect the principle of reciprocity. Thus according to the French–Tripoli treaty of 18 June 1801 the contracting parties guaranteed to each other non-intervention in conflicts with third parties.

[34] Disputes between citizens of Hamburg belonged to the jurisdiction of the consul of Hamburg in Algeria.

[35] See also the British–Moroccan treaty of 8 April 1791.

In the post-classic period of the nineteenth century treaties reveal the change in the law and in the balance of power. Stipulations on a basis of equality give way to discriminatory provisions. This was particularly so in the French–Tunisian treaty of 1881. The British–Moroccan treaty of 9 December 1856 curtailed the rights of the Moroccan government to manage its own regime of customs duties and trade barriers. A hundred years later (1957) the two contracting governments removed this limitation on Moroccan sovereignty as 'inappropriate to existing political and economic conditions'.[36] The period following World War II witnessed a reversion of international law to some of the principles which characterized the regime of the classic law of nations[37] and which were in suspense during the nineteenth and twentieth centuries until the collapse of the colonial regime and the political renaissance of the Afro–Asian world after World War II.[38]

IV. The African Treaties of the Nineteenth Century (The Legal Status of Rulers)

The regime of the classic law of nations was based on State practice (positivist element) as well as on certain principles of natural law from which no derogation was possible.[39] The theological or philosophical background of natural law changed between the fifteenth and eighteenth centuries but some of its principles acquired a functional quality which gave them empirical and practical significance such as the principle of universality of the law of nations irrespective of religion, race, colour, civilization or continent. Positivist law of the nineteenth century became purely law by will (not by reason) based on the consent of the powers and it lent its services to the concept of a Family of Nations divided by tests of higher and lower civilization (above). The will of the States was in fact the will of a few western powers.[40] Before one legal regime gave way to the other, a transitional period marked the gradual replacement of one set of principles by other principles. The transitional period was at first of a static character (ideologically and territorially), at least during the first half of the nineteenth century. European penetration in Africa remained during this period confined to coastal regions. In the second half of the century the 'scramble' for titles to territory set in, to gather momentum after the Berlin Conference in 1885. Hundreds of treaties of cession of territory or protection were then concluded by European colonial powers with African rulers and chiefs and by the end of the century the partition of the continent was a *fait accompli*.[41] It is proposed to

[36] *Cmnd 144*, Treaty Series No. 38 (1957), H.M.S.O.

[37] Here belong *inter alia* the natural law principle of the universality of the law of nations irrespective of religion, race or civilization (principle of non-discrimination).

[38] The restitution of the Afro–Asian world to independence came not as the result of military pressure but as the consequence of the fact that colonialism and its underlying principles became obsolete.

[39] A *quasi-jus cogens*.

[40] A derogation from the tenets of positivism.

[41] Among the inter-European treaties or arrangements relating to the partition of Africa were *inter alia*; the Anglo–French arrangements concerning Egypt (1871–1882); the Anglo-Congolese treaty of 1894; the Anglo–French agreement of 1899 concerning the Nile Basin; the Anglo–French

carry out an examination of some of the nineteenth-century treaties and particularly to show that during this period the ruler or chief was in principle a genuine treaty negotiator capable of transferring to the European contracting party a valid title to territory or other rights and obligations capable of being vested in sovereign entities only. One of the most controversial issues in the literature of international law of the nineteenth century dealing with the partition of Africa was the question of defining the gigantic transfer of the territory of a whole continent from hundreds of African transferors to a few European transferees. Many international lawyers trying to define this operation engaged in *a priori* generalizations without examining in sufficient detail the relevant treaty material and the political and legal structure of the African contracting countries. The present inquiry does not pretend to carry out such detailed examination but it attempts to bring to the reader's attention a number of treaties and other source material from which certain conclusions may tentatively be drawn.

The relevant treaty material can either be found in published collections of treaties, or it is available in archives and remains predominantly unpublished or it can be found in histories of African exploration and memoirs of treaty negotiators. To the first category belong English treaties published in E. Hertslet's *Map of Africa by Treaty*; to the second category belong French African treaties[42] and to the third, German treaties which can also be found in small collections of treaties limited to a particular region *e.g.* the treaties concluded in South West Africa.[43] The contracting parties to these treaties were the African transferors of rights and obligations (often expressly called sovereign rights) and the European transferees, but there are also examples of re-transfer in which the European contracting party acted as transferor and the African contracting party as transferee.[44] In many cases the legal status of the African ruler or chief was defined in the body of the treaty and the relevant clauses indicating his *locus standi* were either of a positive or a negative character. In the first case express reference was made to the legal capacity of the ruler or chief, in the second case the absence of limitations to such capacity was stated in the text.

Thus one of the rulers in the Gambia region completing in 1823 the cession of the Island of Lemain to the British stated: 'Whereas all sovereignty of the said Island at present lies in us and has been handed down to us by our ancestors'.[45] In an earlier treaty of cession relating to the Tombo Island (1821) the ruler is referred to as 'Commonly known by the style and title of Ba Mano, King and Principal Chief of

arrangements of 1889 and 1890 delimiting spheres of influence in Africa; the Anglo–French agreement of 1862 concerning Zanzibar; the Anglo–German agreements of 1886 and 1890 concerning East Africa; the Anglo–German agreement of 1893 concerning West Africa; the Anglo–Italian agreement of 1894 concerning East Africa (Somaliland); the Anglo–Portuguese Convention of 1890–1891; the Anglo–Portuguese treaty of 1882 concerning the Congo (Elias, *op. cit.*, p. 17).

42 Selected treaties are published in the *Annales Sénégalaises* and M. de Clercq's *Recueil des Traités*.

43 H. Hesse, *Die Landfrage und die Frage der Rechtsgültigkeit der Konzessionen in S.W. Afrika*, Jena, 1906 and *Die Schutzverträge in S.W. Africa*, Berlin, 1905.

44 Hertslet, *The Map of Africa by Treaty*, Vol. I, p. 41, Sierra Leone. Territory which was ceded by the ruler of Quiah to Great Britain was retroceded to the ruler in 1872.

45 *Ibid.*, p. 7.

the North Bulloms ...' and he declared that he possessed (together with the chiefs) 'all authority, absolute dominion and undisputed territorial right' in the island.[46] In a treaty of cession concluded by Great Britain in 1840 it is stated that 'Whereas all sovereignty of the ... territory is now vested in the said King of Combo and has descended to him from his ancestors'.[47] The Congo declaration of 1885, exchanged between the Belgian government and the International Association of the Congo (possessing legal status in international law), referred to the treaties 'concluded with the legitimate Sovereigns in the Basin of the Congo'.[48]

British government statements referred to Zululand as 'Zulu Sovereignty'[49] and the judicial committee of the privy council considered Lobengula as independent king and undisputed ruler of Matabeleland and Mashonaland.[50] Even in treaties concluded by European companies with minor African chiefs, cession of territory was effected with all sovereign rights.[51]

The negative clause recording the absence of limitations to the capacity of the transferor of title was often inserted in treaties to make sure that the particular transaction was not subject to approval (or in danger of disapproval) by an overlord exercising control over the transferor. Thus in the treaty of 1888 between Great Britain and the Kingdom of Igbessa it is stated that 'The Kingdom of Igbessa ... is perfectly independent and pays tribute to no other Power'. The clause testified to the absence of any vassalship or dependence.[52] The same formula can be found in other transactions such as the declaration issued in 1888 by the chiefs of Ketu[53] and in the transactions concluded in 1888 with the Ibu towns, the kingdom of Ilaro and the kingdom of Onolo.[54]

The negative clause is frequently found in French African treaties. Thus it is stated in the treaty with the country of Kita (Senegal) of 25 April 1880 in which the latter submitted to French protection: 'The Chief, the Notables and inhabitants of the country of Kita declare that they are independent of any foreign Power'.[55] In a declaration made by the chiefs of the country of Benito of 9 November 1883 in which the latter recognized French suzerainty, the chiefs stated as follows: 'We declare that we are entirely free from any undertaking towards a foreign country other than France and that we are not tributaries to any other nation'.[56]

In another declaration made on the 15 November 1883 the chiefs of Dambbo stated to the French that 'they had never signed or contracted any undertaking towards a foreign country and that they do not depend on any Chief, having not signed or contracted in their name any such undertaking'.[57] Such declarations can

[46] *Ibid.*, p. 8. [47] *Ibid.*, p. 12. [48] *Ibid.*, Vol. II, p. 544.

[49] *Ibid.*, Vol. I, p. 203. [50] *Appeal cases*, 1919, p. 211.

[51] Hertslet, *op. cit.* Vol. I, p. 137. [52] *Ibid.*, p. 105. [53] *Ibid.*, p. 106.

[54] *Ibid.*, pp. 107–8.

[55] Archives Coloniales, Paris, Box doct, 3,340 ('Les Chefs, notables et habitants du pays de Ketu déclarent qu'ils sont indépendents de toute puissance étrangère').

[56] Archives Coloniales 4/490, Gabon ('Nous déclarons etre actuellement libres de tout engagement avec les pays étrangers à la France et à être soumis ou tributaires d'aucune autre nation'.)

[57] Archives Coloniales 4/494, Gabon ('Nous n'avons jamais signé ou contracté aucun engagement avec l'etranger—que nous ne dépendons d'aucun Chef ayant signé ou contracté en notre nom un semblable engagement'.)

also be found in the treaties with the chiefs of Campo of 19 November 1883, the chiefs of Bougié, Igouba and Miongo of the country of Andjé (Gabon) of 6 June 1884, and the Massai of 22 August 1884.[58]

If in fact a contracting chief depended on a paramount ruler (overlord), and if competing European powers tried to obtain territory from him, the scramble for the title was bound to involve not only the chief but also the overlord. Thus Great Britain nearly lost her right of priority to territory on the Niger by concluding a treaty with a subordinate ruler *i.e.* the chief of Bussa. The latter was a vassal of the ruler of Nikki (the suzerain) who was ready to make a treaty of cession with either the British or the French. The British and the French then engaged in a 'race' to Nikki's capital. The British arrived first and secured the territory through a new treaty with him.[59] This and other examples testify to the importance of obtaining a valid title to territory from the holder of the title capable of effecting a valid transfer of territorial rights. The situation in Africa was identical with that in the East Indies.[60]

The problem of clash between two European colonial Powers, one of which had influence on a particular ruler or chief and the other on the latter's overlord, occurred particularly in East Africa. The Sultan of Zanzibar, who gradually submitted to British control (Protection), had sovereignty over the Islands of Zanzibar and Pemba, but also exercised limited control in the nature of 'overlordship' over some of the rulers on the mainland of East Africa (Mrima). A number of these rulers concluded treaties of cession of territory with the Germans who claimed to have obtained valid titles to territory. The Sultan of Zanzibar questioned the validity of these titles and notified the Emperor of Germany to the effect that the ceding ruler had no legal capacity to transfer sovereign rights to the territory without the sultan's approval.[61] The question also arose whether the titles granted by the rulers in East Africa (Usagara, Ukami, Usangu, Uluguru) were not questionable on the ground that territory or territorial rights were allegedly not alienable. P. Reichard (in his work on German East Africa)[62] recalls that land belonged to the community and that the ruler had no right to give more to the European colonial Power than '*usufructus*' in the land (*Mitbenutzungsrecht*). Neither could the ruler cede certain sovereign rights in territory as distinguished from private rights in land. However Europeans acted in principle on the presumption that the transfer of rights by the chief, as the organ authorized to act in the external sphere, constituted a valid title in international law. This presumption was perhaps weaker in the case of village chiefs than in the case of autocratic rulers such as the Zulu king, the King of Uganda or the King of Dahomey.[63] Each case had to be judged on its own merits. In any case the generalizations in which a number of international lawyers tended to engage in

[58] Archives Coloniales 4/495, pp. 506, 515, Gabon.

[59] Lindley, *op. cit.*, p. 170.

[60] Alexandrowicz, *op. cit.*

[61] Hertslet, *op. cit.*, Vol. II, pp. 682–3, 685 and Lindley, *op. cit.*, p. 118. See also the protest of Turkey against the occupation of Tunisia by France, Hertslet, *op. cit.*, Vol. III, p. 1187.

[62] P. Reichard, *Deutsch-Ostafrika*, Leipzig, 1892.

[63] R. Cornevin, *Histoire du Dahomey*, Paris, 1962 and *Histoire de l'Afrique*, Paris, 1966.

relation to a politically and legally heterogeneous continent such as Africa call for re-examination in the light of evidence found in treaties and other source material.

The treaties concluded by the Germans with South West African rulers in the 1880's and 1890's are in a particular category of texts. The most important rulers in this region (Namibia) were Joseph Fredricks of Bethany, Hermanus van Wyk of Rehoboth, Menasse of the Red Nation and Maherero, the paramount chief of the Hereros. Treaties concluded with these rulers (often called captains) in the period of 1884–1885 established protectorates (*Schutzgebiete*) which transferred external sovereignty from the rulers to the Germans but left most of the functions of internal sovereignty to the rulers. Dr. Hermann Hesse in his classic works on South West African Protectorates[64] considers the question of legal capacity of the contracting parties in some of the treaties of protection.[65] He defines the capacity of rulers as '*Aktivlegitimation*' *i.e.* active capacity to transfer rights to territorial sovereignty. The German companies which acted as transferees had (what the author calls) '*Passivlegitimation*' *i.e.* actual or potential capacity to receive (on behalf of the German Reich) the benefit of the transferred titles. Thus, according to Hesse, the treaties are instruments of public international law and what they transferred were not private rights in land but sovereign rights.[66] As these instruments were treaties of protection, they transferred predominantly rights of external sovereignty and certain rights of internal sovereignty *e.g.* jurisdictional rights which created a regime of quasi-capitulations (below).

If the consequences of transfer of rights by treaty are considered, they conveyed in practice what the ruler or chief was able to convey *i.e.* rights of administration, judicial rights and the power to modify or develop the existing customary law. They also gave the transferee the right to represent the country externally. In treaties of protection, the latter right was the main element of the transaction. Reference may be made to a statement of one of the judges in the case of *King v. the Earl of Crewe*,[67] when he said in relation to African protectorates that 'the one common element in Protection is the prohibition of all foreign relations except those permitted by the protecting State'. The measure of statehood which can be found in the structure

[64] Hesse, *op. cit.*

[65] See also K. Stengel, *Die Rechtsverhältnisse der deutschen Schutzgebiete*, Tubingen and Leipzig, 1901.

[66] This view is opposed by some other writers who consider the occupation of African territory by the colonial powers as a unilateral operation. These writers ignore the voluminous treaty material and African political history. As to the political structure of African communities see M. Fortes and E. Evans Pritchard (eds.), *African Political Systems*, London, 1940. African communities can be classified into monarchical and republican entities. The first were based on centralized authority with the Chief as the Head of the community. The chiefless (republican) community which had no centralized government machinery, relied on stronger social cohesion and ties of kinship. In the first group the element of territorial sovereignty was stronger than in the second group which followed the 'personal allegiance' principle. To the first group belonged *inter alia* the Yorubas, Hausa states, the Akan of Ghana, the Zulu state, the Banyankole of Uganda, the Ngwato and Bemba. To the second group belonged *inter alia* the Ibos of Nigeria, the Tallensi of Ghana, the Nuer of the Sudan and the Masai of Kenya (Elias, *op. cit.*, p. 34). Among German writers classifying African treaties as 'treaties of subjection' see the writers quoted by F. Sabersky in his *Der Koloniale Inlands und Auslandsbegriff*, Berlin, 1907. The most reliable analysis of African treaties has been carried out by Lindley, *op cit.* See also footnote 129.

[67] *Appeal Cases*, 1910, p. 588.

of the African transferor varied from case to case. Some African countries had an advanced structure of statehood, other countries, particularly village communities, were on a primitive level of political organization. But in nearly all of them the presence of a transferor capable of conveying a title in international law excluded the possibility of unilateral solutions. Unilateral solutions were possible in Australia where the native (nomadic) population did not form political entities and where the territory remained *territorium nullius* in international law.[68] The situation was different in the Asian and African continents.[69]

V. The Berlin Conference of 1884–85 and the Partition of Africa

The Berlin Conference of 1884–85 has been widely discussed in the literature of international law. However, inadequate attention has been paid to the prominent role played by the United States of America at the conference, in opposition to European policy of partition of Africa. John Kasson, the U.S. delegate, introduced in a protocol to the Final Act of the conference the notion of 'modern international law' in relation to African problems. The European powers realized that they were compelled by the force of circumstances to carry out the partition of Africa in two stages: (1) the stage of bilateral treaties transferring territorial and other rights and (2) the stage of converting these bilateral arrangements into instruments of annexation of territory. African rulers had to play an active part at the first stage and the problem of their participation in negotiation and treaty making became essential.

Participation in treaty making required the free consent of the rulers. In this respect three conceptions can be distinguished in the field of international law. According to the classic concept of the Law of Nations the freedom of consent in treaty making was sacrosanct.[70] On the other hand, the positivist concept of consent to treaties admitted a measure of compulsion, exercised by one contracting party against the other which would not necessarily invalidate the treaty in question. 'Modern international law' as quoted by John Kasson, constitutes a reversion to the classic concept of consent. Lindley stated in relation to the positivist concept that 'a cession (which) was agreed to by the weaker party from fear of the stronger does not … render it of no effect in law'.[71] But he doubts whether such a rule, repugnant to morality and natural justice, can be applied to a situation of blatant inequality of chances.

John Kasson states in his declaration included in the Final Act of the Berlin Conference that 'Modern International Law steadily follows the road which leads to the recognition of the right of native races (African communities) to dispose

68 *Cooper v. Stuart* (1889) *AC*, Vol. 14, p. 286. This did not exclude the existence of private customary law among the aborigines.

69 See last para. of chapter VII. As to the American continent see Lindley, *op. cit.*, p. 27.

70 E. Vattel, *Droit des Gens*, Vol. II, ch. XII, para. 163, London, 1758.

71 Lindley, *op. cit.*, p. 174.

freely of themselves and of their hereditary soil'. Thus he requires the free consent of the African transferor of territory. The above declaration reflects the U.S. attitude to 'modern international law' as applied to the partition of Africa and it is important to recall that the U.S. did not ultimately ratify the Berlin Act of 1885. While the Berlin Conference did not expressly adopt Kasson's principles, it did not dare to reject them.[72] It is doubtful to what extent these principles affected European conduct in Africa but there seems to have been increasing awareness of the problem of freedom of consent and the presence of witnesses and interpreters in treaty negotiations was required as a safeguard of the validity of transactions. Even in treaties concluded by European colonial companies with minor African chiefs certain standard forms were respected guaranteeing the proper understanding of the text and its free acceptance by both contracting parties.

Hertslet quotes the various forms employed by the National African Company (later Royal Niger Company). The witnesses who participated in the conclusion of agreements declared in a standard form that the text had been 'duly and correctly explained' to the chiefs who 'fully understood it'. In another form the witnesses 'solemnly declared that the Kings and Chiefs ... have in our presence affixed their (marks) ... of their own free will and consent'.[73] The British East Africa Company (Association) applied forms of a similar pattern in its treaty negotiations (1887–1891). These treaties were concluded under the authority of the sultan of Zanzibar who had adhered to the Berlin Act of 1885.[74]

French treaty practice in Africa dates from the seventeenth century.[75] We read in the treaty concluded with the ruler of Commenda (1687): '*Tout le contenu du present acte nous ayant esté expliqué en langue portuguaise que nous declarons avoir parfaitement entendu, mot à mot ...*'.[76] This treaty which contained the cession of Aquitania on the Guinea coast to France, testifies to the care which was attached to the proper understanding of the text by the African ruler.

In the treaty with Laongo (Gabon) concluded nearly 200 years later (1883) the witnesses stated that they 'certify that the present treaty had been discussed (negotiated) freely with the King of Laongo, in the presence of all Chiefs of the country, that it was read and explained to them and that they agreed to it in perfect knowledge of the facts'.[77]

Interpreters used a different text such as: '*Attestation des Interprètes—Les Interprètes attestent que la présente declaration a été réellement traduite en langue Haoussa ... et que le Chef de Kaudi (Borgu) a apposé de sa main sousigné sur le présent acte ...*'.[78]

[72] *Ibid.*, p. 45. [73] Hertslet. *op. cit.*, Vol. I, pp. 137 ff. [74] *Ibid.*, p. 374.

[75] As to earlier treaties, see Rouard de Card, *op. cit.*

[76] 'The content of the present transactions has been explained to us in Portuguese language and we declare that we understood it perfectly, word by word'. Archives Coloniales, 3/407.

[77] 'Nous sousignés ... certifions que le présent traité a été discuté librement avec le Roi de Laongo, devant tous les Chefs du pays, qu'il leur a été lu, expliqué et commenté et qu'il a été consenti par eux en parfaite connaissance de cause'. Archives Coloniales 4/479, Gabon.

[78] Treaty with the King of Bouay (Dahomey) of 9 March 1895. Archives Coloniales 1/153. As to similar texts see Archives Coloniales 1/7, 2/209, 3/381 (Senegal).

Some of the best accounts of the procedure of treaty making have been left by Lord Lugard who concluded treaties in various parts of Africa (East and West).[79] He was faced with all the problems of treaty making between negotiators from different areas of civilization and legal tradition. The African treaty was a dual purpose instrument: it allowed the Europeans to obtain a foothold in a foreign continent and it enabled the Africans to establish indirectly a connexion with the universal Family of Nations. Lugard states that he found in African tradition an institution which embodies to some extent the principle '*pacta sunt servanda*'. He writes: 'When I learnt its significance, it seemed to me that I had found the nearest equivalent possible to our idea of a contract (treaty). This is the ceremony of blood brotherhood. It is held in Africa ... among the tribes as the most solemn and binding of contracts (treaties). The rite is performed in various ways, always with the utmost solemnity and empressement'. And further: 'Treaty making occupies a large place in most works of African travel, and since there are different methods of treaty making ... I am anxious to explain ... the proper procedure followed by responsible and *duly accredited diplomats*[80] in that continent'. Here follows a description of the procedure in detail.

Lugard pays special attention to treaty making at the court of Uganda.[81] He writes that the king and the chiefs 'thoroughly understand the nature of a written contract (treaty) and consider nothing definitely binding till it is written down. Most of them write. Every clause is discussed in all its bearings, sometimes for days; words are altered, and the foresight and discrimination which the natives show in forecasting the bearing in the future of every stipulation is as keen almost as would be that of Europeans; then the document is translated into their language (Kinganda) and read in silence and with intense attention before the assembled house'. After the treaties were signed, they were submitted for approval to HMG which testified to their *locus standi* in international law.

A detailed description of the ceremonial of treaty making appears in the treaty between Itou and Kiou (Casamance) concluded with French participation on 9 June 1853. It refers to the customs and religious traditions of the contracting parties and the ceremonial applied to give sanction to the agreement: '*Pour sanctionner la paix*'. During the ceremony the parties took oath in their name and in the name of their citizens and promised to keep perpetual peace: '*de maintenir entre eux une paix perpetuelle*'.[82]

Of special interest are the accounts of treaty making by Dr. Karl Peters the founder of the German colonies in East Africa.[83] He describes in detail his negotiations with

[79] F. D. Lugard, 'Treaty Making in Africa', *The Geographical Journal*, Vol. I, 1893, pp. 53–55, and *The Rise of our East African Empire*, Vol. II, Edinburgh and London, 1893, pp. 33, 579.

[80] Italics are mine.

[81] See also K. Ingham, *A History of East Africa*, London, 1963.

[82] Archives Coloniales 2/254 (French Congo). As to treaty making in French Africa see the works of H. Brunschwig, *L'Avènement de l'Afrique noire du XIXe siècle à nos jours*, London, 1963; *Mythes et Réalités de l'Imperialisme Colonial français* (1871–1914), London, 1960; and 'La négociation du traité Makoko', *Cahiers d'Études africaines*, 1965, p. 5.

[83] C. Peters, *Lebenserinnerungen*, Hamburg, 1918, p. 82 and *Die Gründung von Deutsch Ostafrika*, Berlin, 1906.

the sultan of Zanzibar and with the rulers on the mainland (Usagara, Nguru etc.). The treaties with the latter established '*Blutsbruderschaft*' (*pacte de sang*) and the ruler transferred to the German '*Blutsbruder*' sovereignty of the territory as well as ownership of the land.

The above accounts of treaty making reflect the efforts of the contracting parties to conclude agreements in an atmosphere of understanding and freedom of consent. These efforts may often have been frustrated by the differences between the parties. But while many village chiefs may not have fully grasped the meaning of agreements, the European negotiators did not necessarily excel in knowledge of international law or African politics and they often displayed deplorable ignorance of the circumstances in which they dealt with contracting parties belonging to a civilization so different from their own.

VI. Protectorates

The major part of treaties concluded by European Powers in Africa in the second half of the nineteenth century are treaties establishing protectorates. As stated above, these treaties reflect the procedure of partition of Africa in two phases *i.e.* the phase of co-existence of the European protector and the African protected country as an individual entity, and the ensuing separate phase of annexation of the latter by the former. A number of international lawyers maintained that the African protectorate was not a protectorate in the real sense of the word.[84] According to international law sovereignty in a protectorate is divided between the protector and the protected state in such a way that the protector exercises external sovereignty for the protected state, leaving to the latter a fair measure of internal sovereignty. This, it is maintained, is not the case in Africa where the protectorate became a camouflage of the imminent annexation of the protected territory by the protector. However evidence does not support entirely the above proposition.

Great Britain concluded numerous treaties of protection throughout the nineteenth century. They were all of the classic type, vesting external sovereignty in the Queen of Great Britain while leaving internal sovereignty to the African ruler or chief. When the ruler of Opobo asked the British government for an authoritative interpretation of the meaning of protectorate, Consul Hewitt, representing the British government in West Africa, gave a classic answer to the question. 'The Queen (of Great Britain) does not want to take your country or your markets but at the same time she is anxious that no other nation should take them; she undertakes to extend her gracious power and protection which will leave your country still under your government; she has no wish to disturb your rule'.[85]

[84] Oppenheim, *op. cit.* and Sabersky, *op. cit.*

[85] M. Crowder, *The Story of Nigeria*, London, 1962, p. 177 (letter of Consul Hewitt of 8 January 1884).

As mentioned above, the same view was expressed by one of the judges in *King v. Earl of Crewe ex parte Sekgome*[86] when he stated that 'The one common element in Protection is prohibition of all foreign relations except those permitted by the Protecting State'.

One of the characteristic features of African treaties of protection is the *negative* formulation of the external position of the ruler who submitted to European protection. The *negative* clause was one restricting external sovereignty in different ways such as by an undertaking of the ruler not to go to war, not to cede territory to other powers, not to enter into treaties with other powers or not to maintain relations with them without the consent of the protecting state. Thus in the treaty of protection between Great Britain and the King of Brekama of 1827 the king undertook not to resort to war without British consent.[87] On the other hand the British government accepted the principle of non-interference in the internal affairs of the kingdom. In the treaty of 1840 between the English East India Company, acting in Africa, and the Sultan of Tajourah, the latter engaged not to enter into treaties with any other Power which would prove detrimental or injurious to British interests. A more restrictive clause was inserted in the treaty of 1840 between the above company and the ruler (governor) of Zaila who undertook not to enter into any treaty with other European nations.[88] In 1841 the ruler of Cartabar undertook 'not to enter into any alliance, negotiation, or communication of any political nature whatever with any Power in the world without the knowledge and consent of the Queen of England'.[89] This clause forbids the ruler not only treaty relations with other European powers but with any power at all. The same formula later appears in the British–Zulu treaty of 1879 in which King Cetshwayo declares that 'he would not make any treaty or agreement with any Chief, people or government outside his territory without the consent and approval of the British Government'.[90]

The negative treaty was often combined with an undertaking on the part of the contracting ruler not to cede territory to foreign powers, a stipulation of importance in the 'scramble' for titles to African territory. This clause can be found *inter alia* in the British treaties concluded with the Jola country (1887) with the Almami of Umtong (1887), the King of Central Kiang (1887), the King of Jarra (1887), Prince Mansah Cetto of Batteling (1888), and in the treaties concluded between 1894 and 1901 leading to the establishment of the British protectorate of Gambia.[91] Here belong also the treaties of protection with rulers on the Gold Coast and in Nigeria.[92] In treaties concluded with hundreds of village chiefs certain uniform formulas were applied. Thus in treaties adopted by the (British) National African Company the rulers declared: 'We bind ourselves not to have any intercourse with any strangers or foreigners except through the said National African Company'. In a modified type of treaty the rulers undertook not to enter into treaties with other Powers and not to grant commercial rights to foreigners.

[86] *AC*, 1910, p. 588. [87] Hertslet, *op. cit.*, Vol. I, p. 11. Gambia.
[88] *Ibid.*, p. 408, Somaliland. [89] *Ibid.*, p. 13, Gambia. [90] *Ibid.*, p. 201.
[91] *Ibid.*, p. 19–20. [92] *Ibid.*, pp. 64–120.

The type of clause included in British treaties also appears in French treaties concluded in Africa, in particular the clause in which the contracting ruler undertakes not to cede territory to other European powers. Here belong for instance treaties with Malaguia of 17 April 1845, with *Bey* Sherbro of Samo of 3 April 1879, with the chief of Forrecarriah of 17 June 1877, with Chief Moré Sedan of Kaback of 21 April 1880, with Bélé Demba of 28 June 1880, with the King of Firdou of 3 November 1885 and other treaties.[93]

Guizot, French minister of foreign affairs, threw light on treaties of protection when he stated that sovereignty acquired by France in these treaties was *external* sovereignty; it could not mean interference in the internal sovereignty of the contracting African ruler.[94]

Similar negative clauses appear in treaties between Germany and South West African or East African rulers. The treaties concluded in South West Africa in 1884–1885 (*Schutzverträge*) are all treaties of protection and they leave to the contracting rulers (captains) a full measure of internal sovereignty which gave way to German control at a much later date in the 1890s. Among the South West African treaties are those with Joseph Fredericks of Bethany, Menasse of the Red Nation, Hermanus van Wyk of the Rehoboths and Maherero, paramount chief of the Hereros.[95] The rulers undertook in those treaties not to cede territory to any other nation and not to conclude agreements with other governments without German consent. While these treaties gave the Germans a limited right of interference in the internal affairs of the rulers, they also left to the latter certain rights of external sovereignty. Thus it was stipulated that the German emperor undertook to respect treaties and agreements concluded by the rulers earlier with other nations which constituted a far reaching recognition of their legal status in the international field.

To the extent to which treaties were concluded by colonial companies (incorporated in one or another European country) they required recognition by the sovereign of such country to acquire a *locus standi* in international law. The company (or explorer such as Dr. K. Peters in East Africa) acted at first as *negotiorum gestor*. The German emperor validated such treaties by issuing a '*Schutzbrief*' (instrument of protection). The situation was different from that created by the charter of the ordinary East India Company which had delegated sovereign powers and acted as '*mandatorius*' and not as '*negotiorum gestor*'.[96]

The colonial powers converted in the course of time the protectorates obtained by treaties into colonies. This development is strictly connected with the presumed plan of partition of the African continent by the European powers participating in

[93] Archives Coloniales 2/211, 218, 247 and *Annales Sénégalaises* pp. 475–6. The negative treaty clause can be found in the treaty between France and the King of Benito of 1875 (Archives Coloniales 4/467, Gabon) and in French treaties concluded in the region of Senegal and the Congo (Archives Coloniales 3/351–9).

[94] H. Brunschwig, 'French Exploration and Conquest in Tropical Africa, 1865–1890' in *Colonialism in Africa*, L. H. Gann and P. Duignan (eds.), Vol. I, Cambridge, 1969, p. 132.

[95] See Hesse, *op. cit.*, and G. F. de Martens, *Recueil des Principaux Traités*, Göttingen, 1791–1801. See also treaty with the King of Togo of 15 July 1884, (Martens, *op. cit.*)

[96] K. Büttner, *Die Anfänge der Deutschen Kolonialpolitik in Ostafrika*, Berlin, 1059, p. 50.

the Conference of Berlin (1884–1885). These powers gave each other *carte blanche* to convert a treaty relationship of protection of an African ruler into a relationship of annexation and absorption of territory. The only condition which the participating powers imposed on themselves was the duty of notification. According to Article 34 of the General Act of the Berlin Act any power which took possession of territory on the coast of the African continent (or later inland) or established a protectorate there, had to notify the other signatory powers.[97] The arrangements of the powers *inter se* meant that they considered the establishment of a protectorate as implying a right of annexation of territory. The question arose what was the effect of this multilateral arrangement on the bilateral treaties of protection to which a majority of African rulers were contracting parties and in which there was no question of annexation. It is suggested that the legal effect was nil, for *pacta tertiis nec nocent nec prosunt*. None of the treaties of protection authorized the European contracting party to absorb the protected state. The *carte blanche* arrangement had at most political significance; it was legally meaningless *vis-à-vis* African rulers. Intention of annexation was legally irrelevant. To quote one or two examples: The Italian government established in the treaty of 1889 a presumed protectorate over Ethiopia. It was stated in art. XVII of the treaty that 'His Majesty the King of Ethiopia consents to avail himself of the Italian Government for any negotiations which he may enter into with the other Powers or Governments'.[98] The Italian government interpreted art. XVII as authorizing it to exercise rights of external sovereignty over Ethiopia and notified the arrangement to the other signatories of the Berlin Act of 1885. The Emperor of Ethiopia who realized that Italy had the intention of annexing his country in the same way as other European powers annexed other protectorates, decided to resist Italian intentions. He rejected the idea that art. XVII created a protectorate at all and relied in this respect on the Amharic text of the treaty which in his view differed from the Italian text. In 1896 an Italian army invaded Ethiopia to enforce Italian claims but was wiped out in the battle of Adowa. The Ethiopian victory had spectacular consequences in international law. Ethiopia whose status had been considered ambiguous in the Family of Nations became at once a civilized country in the eyes of the powers and its membership in the Family of Nations was beyond question. What is important in the examination of the above events is the fact that intention of annexation had been entirely irrelevant from the legal point of view. Italy acted in breach of the treaty of 1889, and had the Italian army succeeded in defeating the Ethiopian army, Italy would have acquired Ethiopia by title of conquest.[99] The notion of 'colonial protectorate' connected with intention of annexation was a purely political device. Ortroy commenting on the Italian protectorate of Ethiopia called it a '*protectorat prétendu*'.[100]

[97] Article 35 of the Berlin Act (1885) required effective occupation of territory in Africa but did not extend to protectorates. Thus the African protectorate was not connected with transfer of internal sovereignty.

[98] Hertslet, *op. cit.*, Vol. I, p. 454.

[99] Examples of acquisition of African territory by conquest are Madagascar or Lobengula's kingdom (Matabeleland and Mashonaland).

[100] F. van Ortroy, *Conventions Internationales*, Brussels, 1898, p. 360.

Other examples of military or political resistance to European colonial protection or penetration are the North African States, two of which escaped annexation (Tunisia and Morocco). Tunisia accepted under French pressure the treaty of protection of 1881 and agreed to conclude no international act without French consent (art. VI). The ruler (*bey*) lost his active right of legation to the French Government but he could still exercise a passive right of legation and receive foreign envoys provided he would not conclude international agreements without French consent. The Ottoman Empire protested against French action on the ground that Tunisia had been a vassal State of the Ottoman Empire and had no legal capacity to renounce its sovereignty in favour of a third Power.[101] The French authorities had the intention to annex Tunisia but thanks to counteraction supported by the French *résident général* (Paul Cambon) Tunisia remained a Protectorate and kept its separate personality. Cambon considered Tunisia to be 'an old country with a high civilization of her own' not fit for absorption.[102] Thus Tunisia escaped the fate of Algeria which had earlier been converted into a *département* of France (1848).

Moroccan resistance to European penetration dates back to the battle of Alcasarquivir (1578) in which the sultan of Morocco wiped out the Portuguese army. To what extent the battles fought by Abd-el-Kader and Abd-el-Krim in the nineteenth century influenced North African history is uncertain. Morocco became a French protectorate in 1912 and remained a protectorate until the withdrawal of French control after World War II. Madagascar became a protectorate in 1885[103] and lost its independence in 1896.[104] France acquired the island by title of conquest. The British treaty of protection concluded with Zanzibar in 1890 guaranteed to the sultan and his successors the throne of Zanzibar (art. IV). Though the sultan lost his rights of external sovereignty, he acceded to the terms of the Berlin Act of 1885 which secured to him a high position on the African political scene.[105]

British overlordship over Lobengula, the ruler of Matabeleland and Mashonaland, constituted a presumed Protectorate, for in the treaty of 1888 he undertook not to part with any part of his territory without British consent (negative cession clause). Cecil Rhodes obtained from Lobengula mining concessions on behalf of the British South African Company which paved the way for British economic and political penetration. When the Portuguese made claims to Lobengula's territory he sent a mission to Great Britain to ask for assistance (1886). The British Government declared to the Portuguese that 'Lobengula was an independent King ... the

[101] Hertslet, *op. cit.*, Vol. III, p. 1187 and W. K. Eubank, *Paul Cambon*, Norman, 1960. Turkish suzerainty over Tunisia was nominal.

[102] Eubank, *op. cit.*, pp. 16–33.

[103] Hertslet, *op. cit.*, Vol. II, pp. 665, 670.

[104] French protectorates were also established in the treaty with the Almany of Fouta Djallan of 13 April 1896 (Archives Coloniales, 5/549–50). His empire was gradually dismembered and Foutan Central (part of the empire) made treaties with the French in 1883 and later (Archives Coloniales 3/360, Senegal). The Ahmedu of Segu submitted to French protection in 1887 (Rouard de Card, *op. cit.*, p. 132). The Almany Samory resisted French control to the end of the nineteenth century (Archives Coloniales 1/50, Sudan). As to Dahomey the kingdom of Porto Novo submitted to French protection in 1863 (Rouard de Card, *op. cit.*, p. 91). The Kingdom of Abomey was divided in two (Abomey and Allada) and both new states were under French protection (Archives Coloniales 1/112 and 5/570.)

[105] Hertslet, *op. cit.*, Vol. I, p. 308.

independent Ruler of Matabeleland and Mashonaland'. The judicial committee of the privy council considered *in re Southern Rhodesia* Lobengula's sovereignty as the starting point of the history of the country and held that 'after a fashion [his] was a regular government'.[106]

A protectorate was established in the treaty between Great Britain and the King of Buganda in 1895 and the king undertook not to conclude treaties with other European Powers without British consent.[107] According to art. XIV of the treaty 'the foreign relations of Uganda and its dependencies are hereby placed ... in the hands of Her Majesty's Representative'. It meant that internal sovereignty was still vested in the ruler though rights and duties of external sovereignty were exercised by the British Government.

Among treaties of protection concluded by Italy, the treaty with the Sultan of Migertini (Somaliland) of 1889 may be mentioned. The sultan declared in the treaty that he would 'not make treaties or contracts with any other Governments or persons'. He later defied the protectorate and in 1890 he declared his adherence to the General Act of the Brussels Conference (1890). He submitted again to Italian protection in 1901.[108]

This brief survey of treaties of protection shows that they transferred in principle only external sovereignty to the European protector. Restrictions on external sovereignty were imposed by negative clauses which could be either 'no treaty', 'no foreign relations', no 'cession of territory' or 'no war' clauses. The negative clause was evidence of the fact that the rulers had originally the power to make treaties, maintain foreign relations, cede territory or make war. What had to be legally limited must have legally existed and we must assume that these powers had been vested in a sovereign capable of exercising rights of external and internal sovereignty. As to the so called colonial protectorate, it must be considered a political concept. It never entered into the orbit of international law as a defined legal institution.

VII. Capitulations

As stated above, the capitulations regime has been quoted as evidence of the higher civilization of European Powers and lower civilizations of the Afro–Asian countries which had to tolerate foreign jurisdiction and law in their territory. The fallacy of this positivist conception has been discussed above. It had been ancient Asian tradition to allow foreign settlements to govern themselves by their own law. In the same way as in the East Indies, European settlements in Africa were allowed to exercise a measure of legal autonomy under the jurisdiction of the head of settlement (consul). Evidence of consular jurisdiction can be found in the North African states and

[106] *AC*, 1919, p. 211.

[107] Hertslet, *op. cit.*, Vol. I, p. 392. The Uganda Protectorate was followed by the establishment of the East Africa Protectorate. Ingham, *op. cit.*

[108] Hertslet, *op. cit.*, Vol. II, p. 1119.

the relevant treaties often gave reciprocal capitulatory rights to African residents in Europe. But in the nineteenth century capitulations degenerated into instruments of inequality which resulted from the *de facto* decline of the African state system. In this respect it is important to examine the treaty stipulations relating to mixed disputes which reflect the jurisdictional position. As in the East Indies, jurisdiction in mixed disputes (civil and criminal) could be assigned to mixed courts or the principle '*actor sequitur forum rei*' could be applied to them.[109] For instance the latter principle can be found in the British–Zanzibar treaty of 1886. The judicial authority of the nationality of the defendent (accused) assumed jurisdiction and applied the *lex fori*. In 1890 Zanzibar became a British protectorate and mixed disputes were assigned to mixed courts (art. XVI of the treaty of protection).[110] When the defendent (accused) was the subject of the sultan, the British consul would exercise jurisdiction in the case as the sultan's delegate but he was assisted by a Zanzibar *kadi*. This example shows how the decline of the external sovereignty of the ruler gradually affected his internal jurisdiction. A number of European powers enjoyed capitulatory privileges in Zanzibar but they were abrogated after 1890, the date of the establishment of the British protectorate.

In 1865 Great Britain made a treaty with Madagascar. Article XI of the treaty assigned mixed disputes to mixed courts. The same solution was adopted in the treaties concluded by France with Madagascar in 1868 and 1885.[111]

The principle '*actor sequitur forum rei*' can be found in the treaty of 1752 between the French East India Company and the Fantins. Art. XI of the treaty states: '*Nous promettons à la Compagnie d'ordonner à tous noir sujet de vivre respectueusement avec les français et en cas que quelqu'un y manquait il en sera fait briève et rigoureuse justice par les plaintes qui nous en seront faites; de punir les voleurs … à fin que la confidence puis-je s'établir … La Compagnie s'engageant de son côté à donner des ordrez pour que ses employés, soldats et ouvriers … ne fassent aucun tort ou insulte aux nègres. Pour des peines qui leur seront imposés suivant l'exigeance des cas, et conformes aux plaintes portées au Chef*'.[112] In later French treaties the mixed court solution prevailed such as in treaties with Somali chiefs (1884–1885) and the chiefs of the Comoros Islands (1886, 1892),[113] but where the power of the ruler declined to the level of submission, the French consul exercised jurisdiction in mixed disputes *e.g.* in the treaty with the king of Porto Novo of 1863.[114]

The mixed court solution was introduced in treaties concluded by the Germans in South West Africa in 1884 and 1885. Mixed disputes were under the jurisdiction of the German judicial officer acting jointly with a member of the ruler's council.[115]

[109] Disputes between European residents were in principle under the jurisdiction of the competent Consul.

[110] Hertslet, *op. cit.*, Vol. I, p. 301.

[111] *Ibid.*, Vol. II, pp. 665, 668.

[112] Archives Coloniales 3/408, Senegal. The caboceer (chief) of the Fantins was authorized to consider French complaints against his subjects.

[113] Rouard de Card, *op. cit.*, and *Les Traités de Protectorat conclus par la France en Afrique*, 1870–1895, Paris, 1897, ch. III.

[114] Archives Coloniales 1/76, Côte des Esclaves. The consul had to consult the king before taking a decision.

[115] Martens, *Recueil des Traités*, and Hesse, *op. cit.*

With the decline of the ruler's position his jurisdictional powers became more and more curtailed. According to the treaty between Great Britain and Buganda of 1893 (1895) jurisdiction in civil cases between subjects of Buganda were under the king's jurisdiction but subject to appeal to a British court. Criminal cases between subjects of Buganda were also under the king's jurisdiction but the British resident at the court of Buganda had a right of intervention.[116]

At the end of the nineteenth century the protectorate deteriorated into a political regime carrying the label of colonial protectorate, and capitulations lost their function of balancing African legal tradition and custom against the encroachment of European law. In hundreds of treaties made by heads of village communities with European agencies the problem of jurisdiction did not arise, since judicial power could not be considered divisible between the contracting parties. Village communities enjoying semi-sovereign status were able to convey a title to territory to the European newcomer but they were not prepared to deal with problems of foreigners belonging to a different civilization. Neither had they the capacity of survival in a Family of Nations in which they were unable to reach adequate standards of statehood or international legal personality. Sooner or later they were bound to submit to the inevitable process of centralization in order to create larger and viable entities within the Family of Nations. The present network of African states testifies to a collective rather than individual reversion of African countries to sovereignty.

VIII. The Legal Character of Treaties

Most treaties concluded by European powers with African communities, ruled by dynasties or quasi-dynasties, were real and not personal treaties. The rulers acted in their own name and in the name of their heirs and successors. Sometimes the European contracting party recognized the hereditary character of the African ruler. Thus in a number of French treaties it is expressly stated that power is according to local custom hereditary: '*le pouvoir est héréditaire*'.[117]

The formula of extending the binding force of treaties to the heirs and successors of the contracting ruler is clearly stated in the treaty of 1823 relating to the cession of the island of Lemain to Great Britain. The ruler declared: 'We bind and oblige ourselves, our heirs and successors, faithfully and truly to abide …'[118] A similar formula can be found in the treaty of 1820 relating to the transfer of the Banana Islands by Tim Manees of Onia to Great Britain, in the treaty of 1841 extending British protection to the king of Cartabar, in the British–Ethiopian treaty of 1849, in the treaty of 1850 between Great Britain and Dembar Sonko, king of Barra and in the treaty between the British South African Company and the king of Gazaland

116 Hertslet, *op. cit.*, Vol. I, p. 392.
117 Archives Coloniales 2/198, Rivières de Sud, and Archives Coloniales 3/597.
118 Hertslet, *op. cit.*, Vol. I, p. 7, Gambia.

(1890).[119] French and German treaties contain similar clauses, to mention only the treaties concluded with the Trarzas, Bracknas, the Congo rulers,[120] and the South West African treaties.[121]

It is maintained that African states were not states in the strict sense of the word and that rulers were not sovereigns. Consequently treaties were not considered as instruments of international law. Even if this view would be *per inconcessum* accepted, it would still be correct to say that the whole transfer of African territory to the European transferees was not effected in a legal vacuum. None of the territories were considered as *territorium nullius* and (with some exceptions) none were occupied unilaterally. The European powers insisted throughout the period of confrontation on the acquisition of legal titles in international law. What was transferred by treaties was sovereign rights, not rights of private property. Moreover, there were not only treaties of protection and cession of territory but also cases of 'retrocession' of territory by European powers to rulers (see above). For practical purposes it was irrelevant how the African title holding entity was classified in one or another doctrine of law or political science. What mattered was the effective transfer of sovereign rights by transferors to transferees in international law. The partition of Africa must be considered on the basis of facts and empirical rules, not of doctrines. The situation was *mutatis mutandis* the same as in the East Indies. It was different from that in the American continent[122] and in Australia.[123]

It is important that whenever African rulers transferred not sovereign rights but private rights to European agencies, the character of the 'private law' transaction was expressly stated in the relevant text. Thus the ruler of Combo passed in 1850 sovereign rights in certain territories to the queen of Great Britain and effected separately the conveyance of a 'fee simple' and property in certain lands which passed to the queen in 1840.[124] In a transaction concluded by the French with King Denis (Gabon) on 9 February 1842 the king transferred in article I sovereignty over territory and separately in article II effected the cession of a piece of land.[125] In 1855 General Faidherbe concluded on behalf of France a transaction with the chiefs of Khasso for the purchase of land and separately a treaty.[126] The same distinction between private and public law transactions can also be found in German sources.[127]

The judicial committee of the privy council dealt in *Ahmadu Tijani v. Secretary of Southern Nigeria*[128] with the cession of Lagos to Great Britain. It stated that this was a case of transfer of sovereignty and that 'a mere change of sovereignty is not to be presumed as meant to disturb the right of private owners ...'.

[119] *Ibid.* p. 28, Sierra Leone, p. 13, Gambia, Vol. II, p. 421, Vol. I, p. 14, Gambia, and p. 266.

[120] Archives Coloniales 3/422 and 1/11, Senegal, and *Annales Senegalaises*, pp. 397, 402, Archives Coloniales 5/626, Congo.

[121] Martens, *Recueil des Traités*, p. 404 ff.

[122] Lindley, *op. cit.*, pp. 27–31.

[123] *Cooper v. Stuart*, (1889) *AC*, Vol. XIV, p. 286.

[124] Hertslet, *op. cit.*, Vol. I, p. 16.

[125] Archives Coloniales 4/437.

[126] Archives Coloniales 4/576–7, Senegal.

[127] See the Lüderitz purchase referred to in the treaty with Fredericks of Bethany (above).

[128] *AC*, 1921, Vol. II, p. 399.

IX. Concluding Observations

It has been recalled that the African continent experienced European presence in the sixteenth, seventeenth and eighteenth centuries under the regime of the classic Law of Nations and then in the nineteenth century under the system of positivist international law. While the former was based on a universal law of nature which knew no discrimination on grounds of religion, race, colour or civilization, the latter ran parallel to colonialist policies. But even when the regime of the classic law gave way to positivist law, African countries were never treated as *territorium nullius* and thus the transfer of territory to the European powers was carried out not unilaterally but on a bilateral treaty basis. Partition took place in two distinct phases *i.e.* the transfer of legal titles to territory from the African transferor to the European transferee in which the ruler still played an active part and then the absorption of territory by annexation. Effective occupation by the Europeans came usually much later than the acquisition of legal title.

The ordinary protectorate established by European powers over African rulers, which in principle deprived the latter of external sovereignty only, degenerated in the partition period into the so called colonial protectorate. Its characteristic feature was protection combined with intention of annexation of territory. It has been emphasized that the reciprocal *carte blanche* arrangement of the European powers to the above effect could not have had any impact on the legal validity of treaties of protection concluded with African rulers, for *pacta tertiis nec nocent nec prosunt*. The colonial protectorate was at best a political device.

At the same time conversion of the institution of capitulations from an arrangement on a footing of equality (and often reciprocity) into an instrument of inequality indicated the gradual decline of the African countries in the course of the nineteenth century. It had been shown that capitulations or pre-capitulation arrangements were originally not the expression of different levels of civilization in different parts of the world (as claimed by the positivists) but reflected the personal law principle as applied to the customary treatment of foreign merchants in Asia or Africa.

The attempt to draw international law into the orbit of colonialism was ultimately not successful. The legacy of the classic law, though overshadowed by the progress of events in the nineteenth century, still exercised a measure of influence on the position of Afro–Asian countries. The intervention of John Kasson, the U.S. delegate at the conference in Berlin in 1884–1885, took place with reference to 'modern international law'. One of the commissions of the conference proclaimed an 'official guardianship' in relation to African countries which indicated the trend towards the adoption of the principle of the sacred trust of civilization, which became part and parcel of the Mandate system.[129]

[129] According to a Report of the Commission 'the Conference has thought proper to assume the role of *Official Guardian* ... the duties to aid (the people of Africa) to attain higher political and social status ... are unanimously recognized' (House of Repr. Ex. Documents, U.S.A., 1884–1885, Vol.

With the transfer of the last titles to territory at the end of the nineteenth century the partition of Africa was a *fait accompli*. The rulers had carried out their part as voluntary or involuntary transferors of titles and the whole continent merged into the sovereignty of the colonial powers. Their sovereignty had hardly a 'genuine link'[130] with the people of Africa who reverted to independence after a period of colonial rule lasting less than a century.

XXIX, No. 247,p. 83). Senate Report No. 393, p. 169 (*op. cit.*) refers to treaties concluded by European Powers with Congo chiefs and states that 'it can scarcely be denied that the native chiefs have the right to make treaties'.

[130] As to the concept of 'genuine link' in International Law, see the 'Nottebohm case', *International Court of Justice Reports*, 1955, p. 4.

20

THE ROLE OF TREATIES IN THE EUROPEAN–AFRICAN CONFRONTATION IN THE NINETEENTH CENTURY (1975)

I. Introduction*

When the Berlin Conference of 1885, which dealt on a wide scale with African problems, proceeded to the incorporation of its ultimate conclusion in a multilateral act, it confined the application of its two most important principles namely, that of notification and that of effective occupation, to the coasts of the African continent. Article 34 of the General Act states that:

> any Power which takes possession of territory on the *coasts* of the African Continent or establishes a Protectorate *there*, must notify the other signatory Powers.

Article 35 of the Act imposed on the contracting powers the obligation of establishing effective authority in the regions occupied by them on the *coasts* of the African continent. The British delegate at the conference had advocated the extension of these rules from coastal areas to the whole of Africa, but this proposal was rejected on the grounds that little was known of the interior of the African continent.[1] Thus the progress of the confrontation between the European powers and African rulers did not warrant, as late as 1885, the inclusion of the bulk of African territory in a multilateral legal instrument which purported to deal with the totality of outstanding African problems. We must therefore assume that the real and full scale confrontation took place not earlier than the last two decades of the nineteenth century. This assumption can be tested by a glance at the political maps of Africa in the early 1880s and at the end of the nineteenth century.

The first map shows the establishment of a few colonies or protectorates by European powers in the coastal or near coastal regions of Africa only. It is true that

* The author wishes to express his thanks to the Carnegie Endowment for International Peace for making in 1968 a grant to the Grotian Society which enabled him to carry out research into problems of international law relating to Afro–Asian countries.

[1] M. F. Lindley, *The Acquisition and Government of Backward Territory in International Law* (London, 1926), p. 145.

Algeria had already been absorbed into France and that some colonial administrations (British or French) existed in various parts of Africa, e.g., on the Gold Coast, in Gambia, Sierra Leone, Senegal, and Gabon. It is also true that the Portuguese had secured control of certain areas on the west and east coasts (a process dating from the sixteenth century) and that the Belgians, Germans, and Italians had already joined in the penetration of the African continent. But the interior of Africa was still under African rule and it was only in the late 1880s and during the last decade of the nineteenth century that the picture of the political map of Africa changed rapidly and radically, to show only a few independent or semi-independent African states.

A handbook written in 1872[2] for diplomats concerned with African problems shows among the remaining sovereign or semi-sovereign entities in Africa: Egypt (a tributary of Turkey but since 1882 under the *de facto* British occupation), the state of the Mahdi (which had conquered in the 1880s Khartoum and the Egyptian Sudan), Tripoli (a pashalik controlled by Turkey), Tunisia (a French protectorate), Morocco (an independent kingdom), Liberia (an independent republic), Dahomey (composed of two vassal states of France), the Fulani state of the Sultan of Sokoto (under British protection), the Sultans of the Central Sudan, such as Bornu and Kanem (in the British sphere of interest), the Sultanate of Zanzibar (under British protection), some semi-independent Somali chieftainships, and the empire of Ethiopia which had shaken off Italian protection. Among these states, only Egypt, Tunisia, Morocco, Liberia, and Ethiopia were to survive colonial domination as separate entities. The first three states continued as protectorates and only Liberia and Ethiopia remained entirely independent and thus eligible to join the League of Nations after World War I.

Historians called the period of sudden changes in the political map of Africa in the last two decades of the nineteenth century the period of 'the scramble for African territory', characterised, as it was, by a rapidity of transfer of power of dimensions unprecedented in the history of mankind. *Prima facie*, it might seem that such a kaleidoscopic change would be effected by the most rapid ways and means which international law had at its disposal for transfer of sovereignty, i.e., unilateral action followed by occupation or conquest. But this is far from being the case. The scramble for African territory was not only one for the land as such, but also a race for title deeds in the acquisition of which the European powers were to observe most of the rules and formalities of international negotiation and treaty making. The point was that the African continent could not, under any circumstances, have been considered *territorium nullius*.[3] It had for millennia been covered by a network of state organisations and empires of a great diversity which revealed at the same time some similarities and even traces of unity. The origins and the characteristic features of this network will be tentatively discussed below.

[2] Carl Kinsky, *Vade Mecum für Diplomatische Arbeit auf dem Afrikanischen Continent* (Vienna, 1897).

[3] As to rare cases of occupation of territory as *res nullius*, see the claim of the State of the Congo, in E. Rouard de Chard, *Les Territoires africaine et les conventions franco-anglaises* (Paris, 1901), chap. VI., p. 121.

The Europeans had had substantial contacts with North Africa since the days of the Roman Empire. Contacts with other parts of Africa followed in the wake of European efforts to capture the East Indian trade. These contacts were exclusively Portuguese throughout the sixteenth century and other Europeans followed only later in the seventeenth century. The Europeans, in their search for the merchandise of Asia, looked for harbours for their ships sailing to and from India and confined themselves to the coastal areas of Africa until the great explorers of the nineteenth century penetrated from the coast into the heart of Africa. However, exploration was not immediately followed by interstate activity. The pre-confrontation period of sporadic contacts prior to the nineteenth century was followed by an intensification of negotiations and mutual arrangements during the first seven or eight decades of the nineteenth century. The only colonial powers (apart from Portugal) which displayed any substantial interest in the African continent during this period were Great Britain and France. Then the Belgians, Germans, and Italians joined African power politics, and the race for title deeds and territory was fully in progress. It was in this period of confrontation that the bulk of treaty making took place. The international lawyer, in his attempt to analyse the treaties, is confronted with a number of difficult problems. In order to understand the extensive process of bargaining, he must fully explore its antecedents and its historical background. This will help him to comprehend its component legal elements and to appreciate the adequacy of rules of international law for state practices in Africa at the crucial period of confrontation.

The present inquiry will briefly discuss the origins and characteristic features of statehood in Africa and particularly the position at the time of the arrival of European agencies. The climate of opinion in which the first treaties were concluded will be examined and compared with the *sui generis* relationship between the contracting parties which later developed at the height of the confrontation. The rapidity of change resulted in some abnormal legal institutions, of which the 'colonial protectorate' is a typical example. The fallacy of its structure in international law deserves attention.

In the analysis of treaties a number of fundamental questions arise: the legal capacity of the contracting parties, particularly of the African rulers and chiefs; the freedom of consent in the particular African circumstances as emphasised at the Berlin Conference of 1885; and the form of treaties and the application of various treaty rules. Among the particular stipulations, those referring to the establishment of protectorates and to jurisdictional capitulations are singled out for special attention.

The role and the contribution of the European negotiator in this process of treaty making is reasonably ascertainable. But there may be some question about the African negotiator's contribution to the settlement of vital problems concerning his homeland. In this respect the following observations are relevant. While the leading African rulers must have welcomed their countries' chance of entry into the wider family of nations and the prospect of benefits to be derived from industrial progress, and while the temporary surrender of control of their external sovereignty was possibly instrumental in effecting such entry, the excessive interference of European powers with their internal sovereignty and their legal systems and traditions was not a constructive factor. The European newcomer was unfit to identify himself with a foreign continent and its people, whose civilisation and political institutions he could not immediately appreciate. However, international law is a mechanism which is not confined to the cooperation of states in conditions of perfect mutual understanding. Its purpose is to reconcile even opposing ideologies or civilisations in spite of each party's dogmatic insistence on certain principles. In such cases the task of international law is to provide a forum for coexistence and to reduce the barriers of prejudice. It has done so in the struggle between the Christian world and Islam in the past, and in the present-day contest between East and West. Treaties, diplomacy, and trade promote conditions of coexistence, and since, in the race for title deeds and territory, the European powers needed the cooperation of the African title holder,[4] they also had to accept some of his conditions and respect his personality and political and social tradition.

An important aspect of this inquiry is the examination of the nature of the African personality as revealed in the legal existence of sovereigns and the underlying political organisation of their communities, which had to face the first contact with Europe prior to the nineteenth century and which later bore the impact of the nineteenth century confrontation. Their tactics varied from case to case, but, on the whole, bilateral treaty making established a forum which provided the necessary barrier to unilateral action by extraneous powers. Although the positivist brand of international law which prevailed in the nineteenth century was less adequate in a confrontation than the classic law of nations which governed the earlier European–Asian confrontation, at least the situation was not one of a legal vacuum.

II. The Historical Background

General observations

Attention has been drawn to the division of European–African relations in the past into two or even three periods: the period of the main confrontation late in the second half of the nineteenth century, the pre-confrontation period covering three centuries of remote and sporadic contacts prior to the nineteenth century and the transition period between 1800 and 1880. This inquiry concentrates mainly on treaty making during the nineteenth century. However, one may precede this inquiry with a few introductory observations about the period during which the first links between European powers and African sovereigns were established and when relations gradually developed.

[4] What was transferred was territorial sovereignty and not a title in private law. If the transfer of such a title was actually negotiated, the expression 'fee simple' or other term of the law of real property was employed. See agreement of 1850 between Great Britain and the King of Combo (in Gambia), in E. Hertslet, *The Map of Africa by Treaty* (London, 1909), I: 16.

An interesting feature of the first contacts is connected with the fact that the Europeans who entered the African scene in the sixteenth century had the opportunity of coming face to face with the remnants of the great imperial state systems of Africa which were the product of earlier African history. Here, as a legal historian, one may seek to identify the rules of interstate conduct in force at the same period in another part of the world. In Asia, for example, particularly the East Indies, the rulers followed a code of interstate conduct which had first been conceived in a systematic way by Kautilya and embodied in the *Arthasastra*, a Hindu classic of the fourth century B.C. The Kautilyan tradition prevailed, subject to changes, for centuries in the Indian sub-continent and in further India: The European agencies which arrived there in the sixteenth century had to face Hindu or Islamic negotiators acting either on Hindu or Koranic tradition or on a combination of both.[5] In the light of this tradition the conduct of interstate relations in the East Indies was to some extent homogeneous and even predictable in its effects. The situation in Africa was different. The European agencies which had come into contact with African rulers since the sixteenth century had no way of exploring the rules of interstate conduct operative on 'the other side' other than through their purely practical experience in negotiations, treaty making and treaty implementation. This experience had to be gained by trial and error in various regions with different traditions. It was only in the course of time that Europeans came to better know the nature of the African political organisations.

Little is known about the processes and procedures observed and developed in European–African negotiations. It will be seen later that one of the rare accounts of such experience in the 1890s, which is of interest to international lawyers, is Captain (later Lord) Lugard's description of treaty making with various African chiefs and particularly with the king of Buganda. We have at our disposal the texts of hundreds of treaties which were the result of negotiations and of the bargaining process and which constitute the primary source for the international lawyer's inquiry. The texts of some of these treaties have been summarised in a general, usually cursory, manner by historians of the African continent, and thus the historian of international law has to study them clause by clause and draw his own conclusions from their reading.

Before an analysis of these treaties is attempted, reference may first be made to the early origins of the African state system, its internal organisation and its capacity of action in the interstate sphere. It is not necessary here to examine the history of the Roman presence in North Africa (Carthage) which at the time had little, if any, impact on the political situation of the sub-Saharan region. However, it should be pointed out that the more ancient Egyptian pattern of divine kingship and state organisation with its centre in Thebes (Luxor) exercised a definite influence on the Nubian state system in the south. The kingdom of Kush in this region (with its capital in Meroe) inherited some of the political institutions of the Egyptian monarchy

[5] 'Kautilyan Principles and the Law of Nations', in *British Year Book of International Law*. (1965–1966), p. 301 (p. 35 above).

which was already in decline in the first millennium B.C. The kingdom of Kush later came under the pressure of the empire of Axum (Ethiopia) which received the Christian faith in the middle of the fourth century A.D.[6]

It is remarkable that Hugo Grotius, 'the father of the law of nations,' in his '*De Jure Belli ac Pacis*' (Book I, Chapter 3, VIII, 9 and XVI, 3) classified Egypt and Ethiopia as monarchies governed by sovereigns with a highly centralised power. In this connection, he also draws a parallel between these African states and Persia (which had exercised a short-lived influence on Egypt[7] and stated in relation to Persia that '*Rex summo cum imperio erat*'. He then equated Egyptian and Ethiopian regal powers with that of Persia and again emphasised its '*summum imperium*'.

It so happened that the clash between Kush and Ethiopia produced significant results for the pattern of government in other parts of Africa. The royal family of Kush, after leaving its kingdom, continued to exercise its influence in the region between the Nile Valley and Lake Chad. In this way the Egyptian idea of kingship and state organisation was imposed on the local village organisation in the Sudan.[8] Its characteristic features were centralised power in a sovereign who governed through a powerful military and bureaucratic machinery, without establishing a feudal hierarchy. The idea of this type of statehood penetrated gradually through the region of the Sudan to the west coast of Africa. On the other hand, the Sudanese states traded as far to the south as Katanga and present-day Rhodesia and thus the combined Meroitic and Sudanese influence might have penetrated directly or indirectly to a vast number of African communities.

The second great influence on the development of statehood was felt in the African continent after the progress of Islam from Egypt to the borders of Spain and into the heart of the Iberian peninsula. The Muslim conquest of Spain in the eighth century brought a mixed Arab and African (Berber) presence into Europe. Islam also penetrated along the caravan routes across the Saharan desert to the south, where it met at first with vigorous resistance. One of the barriers to its expansion was the empire of Ghana.[9] Resistance gave way to entire or partial absorption of Islamic ideas and institutions which ultimately dominated a substantial part of Africa.[10]

Without pursuing in detail these brief references to the early pre-confrontation African state system, it may be emphasised that in spite of its diversity, it did reveal a measure of uniformity of political ideas.[11] The small village community based on

[6] R. Oliver, *The Dawn of African History*, (London, 1961); R. Oliver and J. D. Fage, *A Short History of Africa* (Harmondsworth, Middlesex, 1962), p. 39 ff.

[7] And perhaps even an influence on some East African countries such as Kilwa, see *Ibid.*, p. 51.

[8] *Ibid.*, p. 45. As to different views on the subjects, see Gann and Duignan, *Colonialism in Africa 1870-1960* (Cambridge, 1969).

[9] This state has nothing to do with the present state of Ghana.

[10] The Ghana Empire collapsed in the thirteenth century. Ibn Batuta who came to West Africa in the fourteenth century, found there the Mali Empire. This empire was conquered by the Songhai Empire with its capital in Gao. The latter declined in the sixteenth century and was destroyed by a Moroccan invasion in 1590. As to East Africa, the Empire of Mvenemetapa (Monomotapa) and the Swahili city states (Malindi, Mombasa, Mozambique) reached a high level of political organisation. Ibn Batuta visited Kilwa in the fourteenth century. Uganda and Zanzibar rose much later to significance.

[11] Oliver and Fage, *Short History*, p. 88 ff.

chieftaincy and governed by headmen was an entity which existed *mutatis mutandis* throughout the African continent. These village communities were often not the viable units which they came to be in the nineteenth century. Even if such units of tribal or quasi-tribal character were represented by independent chiefs who could sign agreements and maintain some external relations, they had sooner or later to join in a wider organisation which could be the repository of consolidated political power. Many of these units, often of a nomadic character, were united, prior to the arrival of the Europeans, by great political leaders who converted them into bigger territorial entities of a sovereign character. As previously shown, many of these entities came under the influence of the Sudanese pattern of statehood which may have drawn on the proto-pattern of Egyptian–Meroite kingship of a highly centralised character. Some of the states which followed this pattern, mainly in West Africa, achieved the level of empires such as Ghana, Mali, Songhai, and later the Fulanis. The Sudanese pattern combined here with the Islamic type of statehood which enriched it by a capacity for making war and peace according to an established code of conduct. The Islamic influence consolidated the power of the sovereign who governed with the help of scholars and grand officers of state (Viziers). The Europeans who entered the African scene in the sixteenth century must have come face to face with the Sudanese–Islamic state which survived into the nineteenth century.[12]

On the other hand, the states of the Guinea region constituted smaller and less autocratic units with more capacity for democratic institutions. To this category belong the Yoruba of Oyo, who drew on the Sudanese pattern but limited the powers of the king by an influential council and by the establishment of professional associations. Benin, Dahomey, and Ashanti followed different patterns. While Benin rose to a high level of cultural achievement, Dahomey remained a military dictatorship up to the days of confrontation with the French. On the other hand, the Ashantis worked out a compromise between centralisation and decentralisation by creating a confederation of chiefs in which the Golden Stool at Kumasi became the repository of sovereign power.

A characteristic feature of the first relations between this network of African states and European agencies was one of quality in mutual dealings, whether through informal understandings or formal agreements. The first Europeans to arrive on the west coast of Africa who were witness to the early African state formation were the Portuguese, circumnavigating Africa with a primary interest in capturing the East Indian trade. At first they had confined their contact with Africa to establishing a string of forts for the support of ships sailing to and from India. Until the nineteenth century, neither the Portuguese nor the Europeans who followed them on the route around Africa (the English, the Dutch, and the French) pursued any colonial policy or penetrated into the vast network of African states far behind the coastline. One cannot, therefore, speak about confrontation of any significance before the nineteenth century.

[12] The Fulani of the Niger, Nigeria and the North Cameroons were a nineteenth-century example.

But though there was no large-scale confrontation prior to the nineteenth century, diplomatic contacts with African courts led to the conclusion of treaties. The European–African relations which underlay these treaties are of considerable interest to historians of international law, if only for purposes of comparison. They were characterised by the complete absence of colonialism as understood in international law. The law applied by Europeans to these relations was the classic law of nations which was dominated by the natural law doctrine. The functional duality of this doctrine was the universality of the family of nations irrespective of race, creed, civilisation, or continent.[13] It was this law which the Europeans applied to their relations with the East Indies prior to the nineteenth century. The situation was basically different from that under the system of international law of the positivist period which governed the European–African confrontation in the nineteenth century, and which considered the European community of states as the inner club of the family of nations. This club assumed the discretionary power of admitting or rejecting Asian or African states; it also considered war and the application of force as legitimate means of settling power positions. No such discretion could be attributed to any power group in the universal family of nations prior to the nineteenth century. The correctness of this view can be tested by the nature of early treaty and diplomatic relations between the Portuguese and other European agencies on the one hand and African sovereigns on the other.

Early Portuguese treaties and diplomacy

One of the most significant contracts established by the Portuguese, in deviation from their early non-interference policy in the interior of Africa, was their relationship with the kingdom of Monomotapa (Mvenemetapa) which originated in the sixteenth century.[14] The ruler of Monomotapa who governed the Makaranga (Mashona) people was a priest-king surrounded by a court and aided by a hierarchy comprising the chancellor of the kingdom, military commanders, and other high officers. The provinces of the kingdom were governed by vassal rulers who formed its nobility. The type of structure prevailing in the Monomotapa state had its parallel in the structure of other kingdoms in Africa such as Uganda (Ankole), Ruanda, Burundi, the eastern Congo, and other states. Judice Biker included in his *Collecção de Tratados* (vol. I, 234) the text of a treaty between the Portuguese and Monomotapa (probably concluded in 1629). The following are the basic clauses of this treaty, translated from the Portuguese.

The first clause of the treaty established a suzerain–vassal relationship in favour of the king of Portugal. It follows from the text of the clause that the cessation of hostilities between the two contracting parties had resulted in negotiations for peace. The second clause guaranteed freedom of religion to Christians and it related

[13] Even the Dutch in the Cape Settlement established in 1652 knew nothing about racial discrimination. J. Hatch, *Africa Today and Tomorrow* (New York, 1960), p. 12.

[14] R. Oliver, *Dawn of African History*, p. 54.

to Monomotapa's Zimbahe.[15] The third clause referred to the establishment of diplomatic relations between the parties and to the privileges of the envoys. The fourth clause dealt with access of high Portuguese officers to Monomotapa's court. The subsequent clauses concerned jurisdictional (capitulatory) problems—particularly with respect to the authority of the captain of Massapa to decide civil and criminal cases—and with trading or mining concessions. It included, also, a provision stipulating the expulsion of 'all the Moors from (Monomotapa's) Kingdom', an obviously anti-Islamic discriminatory clause. The treaty was signed by Manuza, Emperor of Monomotapa.

It may be emphasised that there is no substantial difference between this treaty and the treaties concluded by the Portuguese in the East Indies, in accordance with basic notions of the classic law of nations of the seventeenth century. It was a bilateral instrument negotiated on a footing of equality. The stipulation of Portuguese suzerainty made insignificant inroads into the ruler's internal or even external sovereignty; and it may be assumed that Portuguese officers exercised jurisdiction in disputes of Portuguese nations *inter se* and in mixed disputes between the latter and the ruler's subjects. Vassalage must have been practically formal as the ruler kept his right of legation and the conduct of foreign relations. The treaty gave the Portuguese the benefit of a safety zone behind their coastal possessions. (Mozambique is mentioned in the text of the treaty.)

Of considerable significance also was the temporary intervention of the Portuguese in Ethiopia which saved the latter from Turkish aggression in the early sixteenth century. But Portuguese–Ethiopian relations soon came to an abrupt end, leaving Ethiopia to its next confrontation with Italy in the nineteenth century.[16]

Another sixteenth century Portuguese intervention in Africa took place in the kingdom of the Congo.[17] The Portuguese discovered the Congo River in 1482 and established treaty and diplomatic relations with the king of the Congo, who ruled over Bantu tribes. The king and part of his community received the Christian faith and ambassadors of the king (styled Dom Alfonso) visited Lisbon and Rome. The Portuguese treated him as an ally and the king of Portugal used to address him as the 'Most Powerful and Excellent King of the Congo' (1512). The Belgians, who established colonial rule in the Congo in the nineteenth century, found hardly any trace of the ancient kingdom.

[15] It may be mentioned that the ruins of Zimbabwe which are explored by archeologists, constitute one of the most remarkable examples of architecture of fortress dimensions (built by Bantu people). Their ruling caste was the Razwe who established the Monomotapa Empire. Zimbahe is not to be confused with Zimbabwe.

[16] Judice Biker, *Collecção de Tratados*, IV: 45–56, refers to letters written by Alfonso de Albuquerque, the Portuguese Governor of India to his King (1514). These letters deal with the Embassy from Prester John (Ethiopia) to India and with the possibilities of organising trade between the Persian Gulf and Massawa.

[17] R. Oliver, *Dawn of African History*, p. 125 and C. R. Boxer, *Portuguese Seaborne Empire* (New York, 1970). Vasco da Gama had been equipped with credentials addressed to the Zamorin of Calicut and to Prester John.

Early French treaties with North African states

Most of the African states on the Mediterranean coast (Egypt, Tripoli, Algeria, and Tunisia) came under Ottoman domination in the sixteenth century.[18] The Ottoman Empire converted them into pashaliks or vassal states, but the hereditary pashas emancipated themselves gradually from effective Turkish control, and thus the Sultan of Turkey remained the nominal suzerain of these states only. This relationship lasted into the nineteenth century, when Egypt came under British control, Algeria was absorbed by France, and Tunisia became a French protectorate; Tripoli came under Italian control in the early twentieth century, and Morocco remained independent until 1912 when the French extended their protection to them (a protection shared with Spain).

Among the treaties concluded between France and the regencies of Algeria, Tunisia, and Tripoli, two types of instruments can be distinguished, namely, treaties relating to commercial concessions and treaties of peace (which also contained commercial clauses).[19] In the first group of treaties, the African ruler granted recognition to European companies of merchants operating in these states. Trade privileges were exchanged, payment of debts was regulated, and the rules of the customs duties were laid down. Such treaties might also have contained stipulations concerning navigation, guarantees for the security of merchants and their premises, and the purchase of grain.

The second group of treaties was concerned with the settlement of political problems and questions of trade, and they contained clauses relating to: (1) the cessation of hostilities (mainly naval warfare); (2) the liberation of prisoners (including questions of ransom); (3) the restitution of prizes (connected with the practice of 'piracy');[20] (4) the privileges of consuls; (5) the protection of missionaries and freedom of religion; (6) problems of navigation; and (7) the duties connected with the law of neutrality. A number of treaties also contained capitulatory or jurisdictional clauses which are of particular interest to historians of international law.

At the time of the adoption of European–North African capitulation treaties, Tripoli, Tunisia, and Algeria were vassals of the Ottoman Empire (seventeenth and eighteenth centuries) and the Ottoman capitulations were formally extended to the North African states. But apart from such extension, these states made their own arrangements, particularly with France and some of them are remarkable for the principle of strict reciprocity which they observed. The positivists of the nineteenth century considered capitulations as evidence of inferior civilisation of Oriental countries which applied such capitulations. The argument runs in the direction of claiming the superiority of the European power whose subjects residing in an Oriental country were not subject to the jurisdiction of the territorial sovereign but to their own consular jurisdiction. This, it was argued, pointed to the inferiority of the civilisation of the contracting Oriental country which had to

[18] Not so Morocco, which resisted Ottoman as well as Portuguese aggression.

[19] E. Rouard de Card, *Traités de la France avec les pays de l'Afrique du Nord* (Paris, 1906), p. viii.

[20] See A. P. Rubin, 'Piracy' in *Grotian Society Papers* (1968).

tolerate limitations to its territorial sovereignty. The fallacy of this argumentation is obvious.[21] According to ancient Asian tradition the receiving sovereign would always allow a settlement of merchants to govern itself by its own law under its own jurisdiction. No inferiority or superiority of civilisation was involved in this sort of concession. The concessions owed their conversion into instruments of discrimination and inequality to the European concept of capitulations. Before this positivist development gathered momentum in the nineteenth century, Asian capitulation treaties sometimes granted jurisdictional privileges to Asian communities trading in Europe. An example is the Persian–Dutch treaty of 1631 which contained capitulations in favour of a Persian settlement in Amsterdam.[22] The same type of treaty *mutatis mutandis* was concluded by North African states (including Morocco) with France at the same period. Thus, for example, it was stipulated in Article IX of the French–Moroccan treaty of 24 September 1631[23] that if disputes arose between Moors (subjects of the Sultan of Morocco) residing in France, the Ambassador of Morocco in France would assume jurisdiction in such disputes. This stipulation corresponded to the concession granted to French residents in Morocco who were under French consular jurisdiction in such disputes. Article XII of the treaty stated that all judgements passed in mixed disputes (i.e., between Frenchmen and Moroccans) tried in Morocco would be carried out (if necessary) in France and the same applied to the execution of French decisions in mixed disputes in Moroccan territory.

The capitulation treaty of 17 May 1666 between France and Algeria[24] authorised the ruler of Algeria to send two representatives (agents) to Marseilles to hear complaints as to any breach of the treaty. A similar jurisdiction was stipulated for the French consul in Algeria. Article VI of the treaty, which contained the above provision, was not strictly speaking of a capitulatory nature; rather it testified to the acceptance of the principle of reciprocity between the contracting parties and it allowed the agents of Algeria in France to carry out functions of an extraterritorial nature, including the function of hearing complaints relating to jurisdictional competence conflicts.

The same type of stipulation can be found in the treaty of 3 June 1711 between France and Tunisia.[25] According to Article XXI of the treaty, the ruler (Bey or Dey) of Tunisia could send his representatives to Marseilles to hear claims in connection with the breach of the treaty.

As to the details of the jurisdictional provisions of the North African treaties, in the seventeenth and eighteenth century, Algeria conceded in the treaty of 23 April 1684 to French consuls jurisdiction in disputes between French residents in Algeria. Mixed disputes (between Frenchmen and Algerians) were to be settled

[21] 'The Afro-Asian World and the Law of Nations', *Recueil des Cours* I (1968), p. 189.

[22] *Ibid.*, p. 156.

[23] E. Rouard de Card, *Traités de la France*, p. 301. Morocco concluded treaties with Denmark (1757), England (1760), Sweden (1763), Venice (1765), Spain and France (1767), and the United States of America (1786).

[24] *Ibid.*, p. 26. [25] *Ibid.*, p. 163.

by the pasha's council. The concession consisted in the removal of such disputes from the jurisdiction of ordinary judges and their submission to the highest judicial authority (Article XVII).

The same position obtained in Tripoli in accord with the treaty of 22 June 1685 which conceded to the French consul jurisdiction in disputes between Frenchmen (Article XVIII). Mixed disputes went to the Council of the Dey which was to try them in the presence of the consul (Article XX). The position remained the same in the French–Tripoli treaties of 4 July 1720, 9 June 1729, and 18 June 1801.

Morocco conceded jurisdiction to the French ambassador or consul in Morocco in disputes between French Christians (but not Frenchmen professing other religions) (Article IX of the treaty of 3 September 1630).[26] Article XII of the same treaty gave the Moroccan judges jurisdiction in mixed disputes and the decision passed by them could be carried out in France, if necessary. According to the treaty of 29 January 1682, mixed disputes went to the ruler's council and the position remained the same in the French–Moroccan treaty of 28 August 1767 (Article XII).[27]

Tunisia conceded less to France than Algeria, Tripoli, or Morocco. According to the treaty of 25 November 1665 (Article XXII) disputes between French subjects in Tunisia went to the ruler not to the consul. But, as in the Algerian treaty, such disputes were removed from the jurisdiction of ordinary judges to the highest judicial authority. It was stipulated in the treaty concluded in the next year (17 May 1666) that if a Frenchman in Tunisia inflicted an injury on a Tunisian subject (Moor or Turk), he would be tried by Tunisian judges. It was, however, conceded that the French consul would be informed of the trial.

The Tunisian treaties with France in the eighteenth century contained a stipulation reserving mixed disputes to the Ruler's (Dey's) Council. Thus the treaty of 16 December 1710 (Article XVI), the treaty of 3 June 1711 (Article XVI), the treaty of 9 April 1742 (Article XVI), and the treaty of 24 June 1781 followed this pattern.[28] Article V of the latter treaty and Article VI of the treaty of June 1790 stated that disputes between agents of the French Company and Musulmans (Turks) should go to the Pasha's Court. The French consul had the right to appear in the proceedings.

Things changed in the nineteenth century, although not to a considerable extent. According to Article XIV of the Franco–Tunisian treaty of 15 November 1824, at first disputes between Frenchmen and Tunisian subjects were no longer reserved to the Pasha's Court, but submitted to a mixed court composed of French and Tunisian merchants. Whenever the votes of the judges were equally divided, the case was sent to the Dey for decision. However, the Dey took his decision in agreement with the French consul. Fifty-seven years later a French protectorate was established in Tunisia (1881) and, as will be seen later, a sharp controversy developed between, on the one hand, third powers claimingcontinuous consular jurisdiction for themselves in Tunisia, and, on the other hand, Paul Cambon (then

[26] *Ibid.*, p. 301. [27] *Ibid.*, pp. 315, 320. [28] *Ibid.*, pp. 153 ff.

French resident-general) who advocated the abolition of all consular jurisdiction as confusing and harmful to the interests of Tunisia and France.

III. African Treaties in the Nineteenth Century

Introductory observations

It has been stated that the nineteenth century history of African–European treaty relations could be divided into the immediate pre-confrontation period and the period of the confrontation proper in the last two decades of the century. However, a separate discussion of treaties in these two periods would not allow us to trace the peculiar line of development which runs through both. In principle, treaty making was the same in both periods, although at the end of the nineteenth century, it deteriorated into an operation accompanying the scramble for African territory conducted on a footing of inequality. However, the international lawyer is not concerned with a discussion of power politics as such, but rather with its manifestation in legal instruments. In this exercise, he must concentrate on the significance of treaties for the power struggle and emphasise the role of the law in the process of formalising power positions. The position is the same in the municipal field. While political, social, and economic relations inside a particular state are invariably dictated by a competition for power, the law provides the framework for the struggle. It remains one of its elements invested with the task of enforcement (which may be more or less effective). Interstate relations follow the same pattern, particularly in the case of an invasion of states from one continent into another, in conditions of a growing inequality of chances. If both sides to the struggle still resort to bilateral treaty making in preference to acting in a legal vacuum, both remain active participants to legal solutions which are considered preferable to an unorganised scramble for power.

With these considerations in mind, the discussion of nineteenth century African treaties must be subdivided into several sections such as those dealing with the legal capacity of the contracting parties in international law, their consent in the process of treaty making, the form of the treaties, and guarantees for their implementation. Among particular stipulations which dominate treaty texts are those relating to cession of territory, to the establishment of protectorates, to capitulations and jurisdictional solutions, boundaries, trade, maritime affairs, war, and diplomacy. The scope of this paper does not allow for a discussion of all of them, but protectorates and capitulations will deserve special attention in this study.

The legal capacity of African rulers

Examining the earliest Anglo–African treaties recorded by Hertslet we find a definition of the legal position of the ruler whenever he effected a cession of territory or other rights. Thus, for example, one of the rulers in the Gambia region, completing in 1823 the cession of the island of Lemain, stated in the preamble that '... all sovereignty of the said island at present lies in us and has been handed down to us by our ancestors'.[29] Also, in an earlier treaty of cession relating to the Tombo Island (1821),[30] the ruler referred to himself as 'commonly known by the style and title of Ba Mano, King and Principal Chief of the North Bulloms and districts of Loo Ma Samma' and declared that he possessed (together with the chiefs) 'all authority, absolute dominion and undisputed territorial right' in the island. In a cession made to Great Britain in 1826 by Bruney, King of Barra, of some of the areas of the Gambia River, it was stated that these areas 'have been held and possessed by the kings of Barra from time immemorial'.[31] In the same way, it was stated in the preamble of a treaty of cession of 1840 with Great Britain that '... all Sovereignty of the before specified territory is now vested in the said King of Combo and has descended to him from his ancestors'.[32]

The position in treaties concluded in the second half of the nineteenth century remained substantially the same. Thus, in the treaty with the ruler of Lagos in 1861, the latter was styled 'King in the usual African signification'.[33] The Congo Declaration of 1885, exchanged between the Belgian government and the International Association of the Congo, referred to treaties 'concluded with the legitimate Sovereigns in the basin of the Congo'.[34] In the treaty concluded between Great Britain and Ibadan (1893), the Alafin of Oyo was recognised as King of Yorubaland.[35]

In the general forms of treaties employed by African companies *vis-à-vis* rulers, cession of territory was effected 'with all sovereign rights'.[36] It may be emphasised that these were treaties with minor chiefs but their position as sovereign title holders of territory was never in doubt.

In the south of the African continent, Zululand was referred to in British government statements as 'Zulu Sovereignty'[37] and Lobengula was described by the Judicial Committee of the Privy Council as an independent king and the undisputed ruler of Matabeleland and Mashonaland ([1919] A. C. 211).

Apart from the emphasis on the sovereignty of rulers in treaties, there was also frequent reference to African law and custom which justified the particular action of a ruler. Thus, in 1850, the chief and the headman of Akropong (Gold Coast) swore fealty to her Britannic Majesty 'according to the fashion of their country'.[38] In 1861 and 1864 such allegiance was sworn to the Queen by the chiefs of Krepee and King Akinney of Accooafee, according to the custom of their country.[39] In the Delagoa Arbitration between Great Britain and Portugal it was argued that the chiefs who had made treaties with Great Britain had no power to make any treaties accord to the law and custom of Tembe.[40]

Here the question may be raised as to the extent to which notions of European and African territorial sovereignty ran on similar or dissimilar lines. Without engaging in considerations of a theoretical nature, it may be emphasised that in practice

[29] Hertslet, *op. cit.*, I:7. [30] *Ibid.*, p. 8. [31] *Ibid.* [32] *Ibid.*, 12.
[33] *Ibid.*, pp. 92–93. [34] Hertslet, *op. cit.*, II: 544. [35] Hertslet, *op. cit.*, I: 110.
[36] *Ibid.*, pp. 137 ff. [37] *Ibid.*, p. 203. [38] *Ibid.*, p. 64. [39] *Ibid.*
[40] Lindley, *Acquisition and Government*, p. 172.

sovereignty meant, from the European as well as African point of view, complete independence (internal and external). Sovereignty in Europe was at that time mostly vested in absolute emperors or semi-absolute monarchs whose sovereign rights were as much considered as derived from dynastic and divine origin as the sovereignty of African rulers. While the metaphysical or theological background of divinity and dynasty might have been different, both European and African rulers were in perfect agreement as to the nature of transactions concluded and as to the transfer of territorial sovereignty and title in international law.

As to the North African states on the Mediterranean coast, Bynkershoek *referred to them as 'civitates quae certam sedem atque ibi imperium habent'*,[41] a formula not dissimilar to that used by Grotius in relation to Egypt and Ethiopia.

Sir W. Scott (Later Lord Stowell) stated in the 'Habana' case[42] that the North African states (Barbary states) 'have long acquired the character of established governments with whom we have regular treaties acknowledging and confirming to them the relations of legal status'. The question might have arisen whether their dependence on the Ottoman Empire impaired their capacity of transacting external rights and obligations. As stated above, Ottoman suzerainty had been effective in the sixteenth century, but it declined in the seventeenth century and became nominal in the eighteenth (with the possible exception of Tripoli).[43]

The problem of the capacity of the rulers whose external sovereignty was limited by an overlord state arose not infrequently in African state practice. It was important for the transferee of a title obtained from an African ruler to make sure that the validity of the title would not be jeopardised by the opposing action of a possible suzerain of the transferor. The question was argued in several arbitration cases between Great Britain and Portugal. Thus in the Island of Bulama Arbitration of 1870[44] the British claimed to have obtained the title of cession of the island in 1792. But the chiefs who apparently ceded the territory to the British were in fact under earlier Portuguese overlordship and thus the title of cession was declared invalid. The arbitral award was given by Ulysses Grant, President of the United States.

In the Delagoa Arbitration of 1875[45] in which MacMahon, President of France, acted as arbitrator, the facts were similar. The British had obtained in 1823 treaties of cession of territory from chiefs in the Delagoa Bay who proved to be under Portuguese overlordship. The title of transfer was considered invalid, as the chiefs had no capacity of transferring territory. In the Barotse Arbitration case in which the king of Italy was arbitrator, a definition of overlord (paramount) and dependent rulers was attempted. The arbitrator stated as follows:

> A Paramount Ruler is he who exercises governmental authority according to [customary law], that is, by appointing the subordinate Chiefs, or by granting them investiture, by

[41] *Quaestionum Juris Publici, Libri Duo* I: 17.
[42] W. W. Bishop, *International Law, Cases and Materials* (New York, 1951), p. 211.
[43] Morocco had not been under Ottoman suzerainty and was until 1912 independent.
[44] Hertslet, *op. cit.*, III: 988. [45] *Ibid.*, p. 996.

deciding disputes between those chiefs, by deposing them where circumstances call for it and by obliging them to recognise him as their paramount Ruler.[46]

This is an important definition for international lawyers immunising the legal notion of chief and paramount chief against the vagaries of non-legal classification in some of the literature about Africa. The arbitrator drew his conclusions from the above definition and recognised the overlordship of Lewanika, the Barotse ruler, over zones near the Zambesi, rejecting his control over other regions or tribes.

Sometimes in treaties of cession of territory a special clause is found which guaranteed the legal capacity of the ruler to cede territorial rights by stating categorically that he was not dependent on any overlord ruler. Thus, in a treaty of 1888 between Great Britain and Igbessa, it was stated that 'The Kingdom of Igbessa … is perfectly independent and pays tribute to no other power', which excluded the existence of any vassalage or dependence.[47] The same formula can be found in other texts such as the declaration issued in 1888 by the chiefs of Ketu who stated that 'the Kingdom of Ketu is perfectly independent and pays tribute to no other power'.[48] This formula is repeated in 1888 in relation to the Ibu towns, the Kingdom of Ilaro, and the Kingdom of Ondo.[49]

The Sultan of Zanzibar who ruled over the islands of Zanzibar and Pemba had also widespread possessions on the 'Mrima' (the mainland) and claimed overlordship of its rulers. But the rulers on the mainland made frequent treaties with European powers conceding them territorial and other rights. This provoked the protests of the Sultan of Zanzibar and led to conflicts. Thus in an agreement between the ruler of Momero and the Germans (1884),[50] the conceding ruler stated that the Sultan of Zanzibar had no suzerainty or rights of protection on the mainland and he declared that he had never been dependent on the Sultan. The latter then notified the Emperor of Germany that certain territories on the mainland ceded to Germany were under his overlordship and that the ceding ruler had no legal capacity to effect the transfer of territorial rights. The same sort of conflict between Zanzibar and the Germans arose in the Kilimanjaro region.[51] The Germans in their defence upheld the legal capacity of the ceding rulers.[52]

When German action started in the interior of East Africa, the commander-in-chief of the Zanzibar army (General Mathews) obtained submission from some of the mainland rulers to the Sultan, particularly in the region of the Kilimanjaro. General Mathews hoisted the Sultan's flag at Kilima Kebomo, and the people of Taveta, Chagga, and other regions adhered to the Sultan. On the other hand the German East Africa Company extended its sway by treaty to a number of other rulers, e.g., the Sultan of Fungo.[53] The ascertainment of the capacity of a particular ruler to transfer rights to a prospective European protector often presented complicated problems.

[46] *Ibid.*, p. 1074. [47] Hertslet, *op. cit.*, I: 105. [48] *Ibid.*, p. 106.
[49] *Ibid.*, pp. 107–108. [50] Hertslet, *op. cit.*, II: 682–683. [51] *Ibid.*, p. 685.
[52] Lindley, *Acquisition and Government*, p. 118.
[53] *Accounts and Papers*, (1886), 47: 14, 38–41, 54.

Conflicts also arose between the British and the French. For instance, the latter questioned the treaty between the British and the Chief of Boussa, claiming that the latter was a vassal of the Chief of Nikki. Then a race developed to reach the suzerain and to obtain a treaty from him.[54] Other examples of conflicts over the legal capacity of rulers can be found in the British–Italian disputes in East Africa. When territory was obtained by the Italians from the Sultan of Roheita (1880–81), Great Britain argued that the territory was under the control of the Khedive of Egypt[55] and that the sultan had no legal capacity to transact external rights and obligations without Egyptian consent. When the French obtained treaties from chiefs in the northwestern part of Madagascar, the Malagasy ambassadors attacked these treaties which had been concluded with chiefs who were under the sovereignty of the Queen of Madagascar (1882) as they had no capacity of treaty making over the head of the Queen.[56]

When France declared a protectorate over Tunisia in 1881, the Sultan of Turkey protested, on the ground that Tunisia had been a vassal of the Ottoman Empire since the sixteenth century.[57] The Sultan denied to the Bey of Tunisia the capacity of submitting his state to the protection of a foreign power. But Turkey's suzerainty was no more factually effective than French protection was legally genuine. The first was in fact nominal only, the second was imposed by force. Nineteenth century international law was ready neither to lend support to the former nor to challenge the validity of the latter.

Statements relating to the capacity of African rulers and chiefs in treaties concluded with European agencies were frequently accompanied by references to the joint action of the ruler with his council, subordinate chiefs, or his people which were the expression of a democratic element in the organisation of some of the African states.[58] Thus, a declaration signed in 1788 by the king and chiefs of Sierra Leone for cession of territory to King George III of Great Britain stated that:

> Know all men by these presents that I, King Nambaner, Chief of Sierra Leone on the Grain Coast of Africa, by and with the consent of other Kings, Princes, Chiefs ... subscribing thereto....

In 1807 King Fizama and King Tom (Sierra Leone) effected a similar cession of territory with the consent of the headmen assembled. Similar formulas can be found in the treaty of 1821 between the King of North Bulloms and Great Britain, the treaty of 1824 between the same contracting parties, the treaty of 1825 between

[54] The British ultimately obtained the treaty, Lindley, *Acquisition and Government*, p. 170.

[55] *Ibid.* [56] *Ibid.* [57] Hertslet, *op. cit.*, III: 1185–1187.

[58] There are also occasional references to African nationhood such as to the Zulu nation (see treaty with Great Britain of 1893, Hertslet, I: 203) or to the Ashanti nation (see K. A. Busia, *The Position of the Chief in the Modern Political System of Ashanti* (London, 1951). In the treaty between the British South African Company and the King of Gazaland of 1890, the latter bound himself and the 'nation' (Hertslet I: 266). There are also frequent references to the subjects of African rulers as distinguished from foreigners. They are called 'native born subjects' which emphasizes the genuine link between Africans and their Rulers and communities, i.e., deep-rooted ties connected with the soil, tradition and common destiny.

King Sherbro and Great Britain, the treaty of 1826 between King Bruney of Barra (Gambia) and Great Britain, and the treaty of 1827 between the King of Brekama (Gambia) and Great Britain.[59] At a later date some of the territories ceded by rulers to Great Britain on the west coast of Africa were retroceded to the rulers and we find here in a treaty of 1872 the formula of retrocession to the king, the chiefs, and the people of Quiah.[60] It is quite clear from the formula that territory (land) had been jointly vested in the ruler and the community.

In the forms of treaties submitted by the National African Company (later Royal Niger Company) to various chiefs, the latter would effect the cession of territory by stating that 'We hereby approve and accept (the treaty) for ourselves and our people with their consent'. The emirs and chiefs of Boussa (Borgu) granted jurisdiction in their territories to the Royal Niger Company by acting in council assembled together with their tributaries.[61]

Lugard, in his account of treaty making in the Kingdom of Uganda, describes the Baraza (Durbar) of the Court of Uganda in which he carried out his diplomatic and treaty making functions.[62] Other treaty makers left similar accounts describing the Uganda Council of State (Lukiko) composed of three ministers, twenty sazas or county chiefs and sixty-six notables, all nominated by the Kabaka. The powers of the Lukiko were considerable extending to administrative and revenue problems and affairs of succession in the royal house.

In the same way descriptions of the federal structure of the Ashanti state show the presence of the democratic element in its constitution. Divisional chiefs were elected by elders and the people.[63] The head of the federation, the *Asantehene* at Kumasi, could not remove the chiefs, though the latter owed him allegiance. The system was not feudal for land was not held by the vassals *jure militari*, but belonged to the community. The chiefs were custodians of the land and individuals had only usufructuary rights.[64]

To conclude these observations relating to the legal capacity of African rulers (and the role of a ruler's council) in international law, attention may be drawn to one of the most controversial areas of Africa, i.e., southwest Africa, at present under South African domination.[65] The entry of this area through treaties with Germany

[59] Hertslet, *op. cit.*, I: 26. [60] *Ibid.*, p. 71. [61] *Ibid.*, p. 128.

[62] F. D. Lugard, *The Rise of an East African Empire* (Edinburgh and London, 1893), II: 23.

[63] R. Oliver, *Sir Henry Johnston and the Scramble for Africa* (London, 1964), p. 305.

[64] See *Amodu Tijani* v. *Secretary, Southern Provinces (Nigeria)* (1921) 2 A. C. 399 and Lindley, *Acquisition and Government*, p. 347. After the defeat of the Ashanti by Great Britain, the Federation ceased to exist but was restored in 1935. However, its whole structure changed under the influence of modern conditions. It became territorial (instead of its lineage character) and secularised which upset its traditional balance. K. A. Busia, *Position of the Chief.* See also D. Westerman, *The African Today and Tomorrow* (London, 1949) who describes the organisation of the Transkei Reserve, and its division into districts governed by headman and council. Above the divisional council was the general council (Bucega) composed of representatives from districts. This structure has been retained under British indirect rule. An interesting classification of rulers is attempted by M. Gluckman, *Ideas in Barotse Jurisprudence* (New Haven, 1965). See also W. E. F. Ward, *A History of the Gold Coast* (London, 1949), p. 95, and M. Crowder, *The Story of Nigeria* (London, 1962), p. 206.

[65] Which has been legally terminated by the United Nations. See J. Dugard, 62 *American Journal of International Law*, p. 78.

into the orbit of international law will be discussed below. It may, however, be recalled here that the existence of the legal capacity of southwest African rulers to enter into agreements with a European sovereign (Germany) had been categorically emphasised in German legal literature, particularly in the writings of Dr. Hermann Hesse.[66] Dr. Hesse refers to the principal southwest African rulers (called captains) who accepted German protection in the 1880s, and he attributes to them what he defines as 'Aktivlegitimation', i.e., the active capacity to confer rights in their territories to other sovereigns. The German agencies (companies) which were the transferees of these rights by treaty are defined as having 'Passivlegitimation', i.e., the capacity to receive the rights. Important consequences followed from the legal status of the contracting parties. Dr. Hesse underlines that the agreements concluded by them were transactions of public international law and not of private law. What was transferred was not ownership of the land but sovereignty. This decided once and for all the question of whether the contracting companies obtained the ownership of the land. Treaties of cession of territory did not affect private rights in the ceded territory though the new sovereign could, by exercise of legislative power in the territory, change the regime of private law and real property.

African companies

The basis of the legal capacity of companies operating in Africa was the charters granted to them by the appropriate national states in Europe. Charters conferred two categories of rights on companies, i.e., trading rights, other municipal rights, and delegated sovereign rights. It is the conferment of the latter which allowed a company to act in the international field, to conclude treaties, transact rights and obligations, acquire territory for its sovereign, maintain a military force, and carry out administrative functions in such territory. The exercise of rights of external sovereignty was under the strict control of the national government of the country which had granted the charter. Such control varied from country to country. English African companies were less restricted by government control than French or German companies. It was also characteristic that the European companies operating in Africa had not the full exercise of the active and passive right of legation. On the other hand, the European East India companies exercised such a right throughout the seventeenth and eighteenth centuries, a fact testifying to the high level of Asian diplomacy.

An early example of an African company established in Europe was the French company formed by Michel and Roland Frejus in 1665. Its name was Compagnie d'Albouzeme et du Bastion de France and its objective was trade in North Africa.[67] It may be emphasised that the company enjoyed the support of Colbert who had also been instrumental in the formation of the first French East India Company.

[66] H. Hesse, *Die Landfrage und die Frage der Rechtsgültigkeit der* [*Konzessionen in Südwestafrika*].

[67] It existed only until 1670. E. Rouard de Card, *Une compagnie française dans l'Empire du Maroc au XVII*^{e} *siècle* (Paris, 1908).

Among the early English companies was the Company of Merchants Trading to Africa from 1752 until 1821. A number of companies came into being in the second half of the nineteenth century, e.g., the English companies established on the pattern of the North Borneo Company (1881),[68] the Royal Niger Company (1886),[69] the British East Africa Company (1888), and the British South Africa Company (1889). Among other companies were the German Colonisation Society, the German South West Africa Company, the German East Africa Company, the Portuguese Mozambique Company, the Portuguese Nyasa Company, the International Association of the Congo, the Italian East Africa Company, the Italian Rubattino Company, and the Compagnie française de l'Afrique Equatoriale.[70]

While these companies derived their power from their own municipal law and while their territorial acquisitions were vested in the appropriate sovereign in Europe, they could also act on delegated powers granted to them by African rulers. Thus the Sultan of Zanzibar appointed the British East Africa Company his *wakil* or plenipotentiary which was reminiscent of the appointment by the Mogul emperor of the English East India Company as his *wakil* at the end of the eighteenth century.[71] In 1892 the Sultan of Zanzibar delegated similar powers to the Italian East Africa Company and the company administered some of the Sultan's territories on the mainland of Africa 'in the name of H. H. the Sultan and under his flag'.[72] Most of the African rulers recognised implicitly the 'Passivlegitimation' of the European companies, i.e., their legal capacity of receiving sovereign rights. However, sometimes such recognition was expressly stipulated in a treaty. Thus, the Sultan of Gandu declared in the treaty of 1894 with the Royal Niger Company that he recognised 'that the Company received their powers from the Queen of Great Britain and that they are H. M'.s representatives to me. I will not recognise any other white nation because the Company are my help'.[73]

Liberia

A separate case of a foreign company or association operating in Africa in the nineteenth century is that of the American societies which initiated the colonisation of Liberia.[74] In 1816, a committee was formed in Washington with the objective of restoring to the native soil in Africa those Africans who after the abolition of slavery obtained freedom. In 1822 a tract of land was acquired on the Pepper Coast of Upper Guinea. In 1828 the settlers started electing their own officers operating under the control of the governor of the Colonisation Society. In 1838 the colony was granted a charter and in 1847 followed the proclamation of independence of

[68] P. S. Reinsch, *Colonial Government* (London, 1902), p. 148.
[69] Originally the National African Company.
[70] Lindley, *Acquisition and Government*, p. 101 ff.
[71] R. Kemal, 'The Evolution of British Sovereignty in India,' *Indian Year Book of International Affairs*, (1957).
[72] Hertslet, *Map of Africa*, III: 1095.
[73] Hertslet, *op. cit.*, I: 155.
[74] Hertslet, *op. cit.*, III: 1130.

the Republic of Liberia, the first fully democratic state in Africa. The first European power to recognise Liberia was Great Britain which concluded a treaty with the former in 1847. Liberia's constitution dates from 1847 and it states in Article I Section 1 that 'All men are born equally free and independent'. According to Section 2 'all power is inherent in the people; all free Governments are instituted by their authority', a principle which did not apply in 1847 to most European monarchies. According to Article V Section 13:

> the great object of forming these colonies being to provide a home for dispersed and oppressed children of Africa, and to regenerate and enlighten this benighted continent, none but persons of colour shall be admitted to citizenship in this Republic.

This certainly implied the idea of *genuine link* in Liberian nationality.[75]

One of the primary tasks of early Liberian policy was to obtain recognition from the other great powers including the United States. France concluded a treaty with Liberia in 1852, but did not ratify it until 1857.[76] The Hansa towns ratified a treaty during the same year with Liberia. Prussia and Belgium recognised it without concluding treaties. The United States concluded a treaty in 1862. Though the U.S. government did not guarantee Liberia's independence, it frequently interposed its good offices to settle Liberian conflicts in the external field.

A second independent African state was established in 1854 under the name of the State of Maryland. It had the same origin as Liberia owing its formation to the settlement of free Negroes at Cape Palmas. Maryland concluded a treaty in 1857 with Liberia[77] which placed it in the family of nations. In Article VIII of the treaty, the exchange of consuls was stipulated and 'most favoured nation' treatment was made applicable to them. In January 1857 the two African republics concluded a treaty of alliance, of which one of its purposes was to provide Liberian assistance to Maryland to help the latter to settle its conflicts with tribes (Article I). Article II provided for cooperation between Liberian and Maryland armed forces and Article III settled questions of jurisdiction in relation to Liberian troops in Maryland territory. Article IV established a mixed Liberian–Maryland Commission for controlling the operations of the joint armed forces. Less than two months after the conclusion of this treaty, military operations were terminated and the two states concluded a new treaty (26 February 1857). The tribes 'place[d] themselves under the protection and exclusive jurisdiction of the government of the state of Maryland'.[78] Later in the year, Maryland was taken over by Liberia and annexed to its territory.

Freedom of consent and the form of treaties

The Berlin Conference of 1885 which was envisaged by the European powers as the multilateral framework of the European–African confrontation, witnessed certain conflicts of opinion relating to African treaty making. The unanimity of the

[75] See concluding observations below. [76] *State Papers*, 35: 1301, 46: 1092.
[77] *State Papers*, 46: 1132. [78] *State Papers*, 47: 582, 586.

powers at the conference was to some extent disturbed by the dissenting views of the American delegation. To understand the nature of these conflicts, it is useful to examine some of the details of the proceedings.

The U. S. government delegated to the conference its minister in Berlin, John Adam Kasson, who was assisted by two associate delegates, Colonel Henry S. Sanford and Henry M. Stanley, the famous African explorer. The conference concentrated at its meetings of 15 December 1884 and 5 January 1885 on the problems of acquisition of territory from African rulers and chiefs.[79] In the course of the discussion it was made clear that the normal media of acquisition of territory by European powers was bilateral treaties and not discovery or unilateral occupation. It was obvious that Africa was not *territorium nullius*, but a continent covered by a network of well-organised political entities governed by sovereign rulers or chiefs.

If transfer of territory was to be made by treaty of cession, it was also obvious that the free consent of the rulers to territorial changes was essential. But in this respect, there existed several conceptions in international law, namely, the classic rule of the law of nations according to which freedom of consent was sacrosanct,[80] the positivist concept according to which a measure of compulsion would not invalidate a treaty just as war remained a legitimate medium of settling international disputes, and modern international law, i.e., law which tended to revert to the classic concept. Mr. Lindley in his work on the acquisition of territory in extra-European areas states, in relation to the nineteenth century positivist concept, that 'a cession [which] was agreed to by the weaker State from fear of the stronger does not … render it of no effect in law'.[81] But he raises the question as to whether or not such a rule (repugnant to morality or natural justice) is applicable to situations of blatant inequality of chances. In this respect, Mr. Kasson, the American delegate, made the following declaration which he asked to be included in the Protocol of the Final Act of the Berlin Conference:[82]

(1) Modern International Law steadily follows the road which leads to the recognition of the right of native races (African communities) to dispose freely of themselves and of their hereditary soil. Conformably to this principle my Government would willingly support the more extended rule – one which should apply to the said occupation (of territory) in Africa, a principle looking to the voluntary consent of the natives of whose country possession is taken (by treaty) in all cases when they may not have provoked the act of aggression.

(2) I do not doubt the Conference is agreed upon the significance of the preamble. It only indicates the minimum of essential conditions to be fulfilled to justify a demand for the recognition of an occupation. It is always possible that an occupation may be made effective by acts of violence which are outside the principle of justice, of national and even of international right.

[79] *House of Representatives Executive Documents* (briefly Ex. Doc.).

[80] E. Vattel, *Droit des gens*, Book II, chap. XII, para. 163.

[81] Lindley, *Acquisition and Government*, p. 174.

[82] *Ex. Doc.*, p. 176 ff. and Hertslet, *Map of Africa*, I: vi.

The declaration is significant for treaty making in Africa and reflects also the American attitude to 'modern international law' and to the General Act of the Berlin Conference which ultimately was not ratified by the United States. It must be assumed that the principle of voluntary consent was at least tacitly accepted by the conference[83] and it remains to be shown to what extent it had been implemented in treaties prior to and after the conclusion of the Berlin Act.

Thus, in the agreement between Great Britain and the chiefs and headmen of the Congo River of 20 June 1854, the chiefs and headmen declared in Article VI that they understood the agreement and considered it binding.[84] In the treaty of protection between Italy and the Sultan of Migertini in East Africa (1889), the latter declared that we 'have of our own free will put to this Act our hand and seal'. Ibadan refused to sign a treaty which was not considered acceptable; but after assurance given by the British government that no interference with the country's freedom was intended, the agreement was accepted. The treaty recognised Alafin as King of Yorubaland.[85]

The European companies applied to treaties with minor African rulers certain standardised forms which contained guarantees for the understanding of the text and its free acceptance by both contracting parties. Thus, Hertslet quotes the various forms employed by the National African Company (later Royal Niger Company).[86] Special witnesses participated in the conclusion of agreements and declared that the contracting rulers or chiefs had validly entered into these agreements. The following is the form of the declaration:

> We, the undersigned are witnesses to the marks (i.e., signatures) of the [chiefs] and also vouch for their understanding what they have signed ... [We] do hereby declare that the foregoing agreement was duly and correctly explained to the [chiefs] and they fully understand it.

Then follow the signatures of the witnesses and contracting parties.

In another form the witnesses 'solemnly declare that the Kings and Chiefs... have in our presence affixed their [marks] ... of their own free will and consent'. This is followed by the declaration of the interpreter who states that he is 'well acquainted with the language' and that he 'truly and faithfully explained the above agreement to all the Chiefs present and that they understood its meaning'. Hundreds of treaties had been signed according to these forms.[87]

The British East Africa Company (Association) employed similar forms in the period of 1887–1891. The treaties following these forms were concluded under the authority of the Sultan of Zanzibar who had adhered to the Berlin Act of 1885 and observed all its principles.[88]

It has been stated above that the historian of international law lacks proper source material describing the actual process of treaty making observed by African rulers

[83] Lugard, *Rise of an East African Empire*, and 'Treaty Making in Africa' in *Geographical Journal*, January 1893.

[84] *State Papers*, 47: 540.

[85] M. Crowder, *Story of Nigeria*, p. 189.

[86] Hertslet, *Map of Africa*, I: 137 ff.

[87] A variety of seven forms was employed.

[88] Hertslet, *op. cit.*, I: 374.

and chiefs. However, an exceptional account of this process can be found in the writings of Lord Lugard.[89] He writes that throughout his career in Africa, he was faced with the vital question of how a meeting of minds could be effected between negotiators from two different continents, civilisations, and areas of legal tradition. A treaty was a dual purpose instrument, it allowed the Europeans to obtain a foothold in Africa and it enabled the African communities to join the universal family of nations.

Lugard states that in search of a pattern of treaty making, he found in Africa an institution which he considered parallel to the European idea of treaties as embodying the principle of *pacta sunt servanda*. He states that:

> When I learnt its significance, it seemed to me that I had found the nearest equivalent possible to our idea of a contract (treaty). This is the ceremony of blood brotherhood. It is held in Africa among... the tribes as the most solemn and binding of contracts (treaties). The rite is performed in various ways always with the utmost solemnity and empressement.

And further:

> Treaty making occupies a large place in most modern works of African travel, and since there are different methods of treaty making ... I am anxious to explain ... the proper procedure followed by responsible and duly accredited diplomats in that continent.

Lugard refers to the ruler's council or body of advisers, who must have been the chief's relatives or principal officers, who participated actively in the conclusion of treaties. The chief swore upon a sword (or other weapon) friendship with the European contracting party. Invocations were used, such as 'my country shall welcome you as a son of the soil'. The same ceremony was observed by the European negotiator and the latter's interpreter stood forward and repeated his pledge. Such pledges guaranteed to the African party non-interference in its affairs, responsibility of the principal European officer for offences committed by his subordinates, and assistance to be given in case of attack by an enemy (protection). On the other hand, the chief recognised the British company as his overlord (suzerain or protector). It was emphasized that the European agency had not come to deprive him of his land or to oust him from power. Other stipulations were added according to the circumstances of the case. After the completion of the ceremony the contracting parties rose as 'blood brothers'. Finally the various parts of the treaty were reduced to writing and signed.

The above type of treaty making with chiefs who were in principle not viable units for separate independent existence within the universal family of nations should be distinguished from treaties with kingdoms and states on a superior level. In this connexion, Lugard gives an account of his dealings with the Kingdom of Uganda in East Africa. He states that the king and his subordinate chiefs

> thoroughly understand the nature of a written contract (i.e., treaty) and consider nothing definitely binding till it is written down. Most of them write. Every clause is discussed in

[89] Lugard, *Rise of an East African Empire*, II: 33, 579.

all its bearings, sometimes for days; words are altered, and the foresight and discrimination which the natives show in forecasting the bearing in the future of every stipulation is as keen almost as would be that of Europeans; then the document is translated into their language (i.e., Kinganda) and read in silence and with intense attention before the assembled house.

Lugard also states that he 'read the treaty through sentence by sentence, putting it in simple English, and Duallo rendered it most admirably in Swahili - one or other of the Chiefs repeating it in Kinganda ... there were several questions asked - all most shrewd and intelligent, for those people are very clever ...'. After the treaties had been signed by the parties, they were submitted for approval to the British government which testifies to their international legal character.

The above description of the process of treaty making shows, first of all, that the principle of *pacta sunt servanda* was firmly in the minds of the contracting parties. The solemnities, the attitude to negotiation, insistence on a written text, all testify to the awareness of the binding nature of treaties.[90] Moreover, though the contracting parties may not have exactly understood each other's legal and political institutions, the natural elements of authority and of responsibility for action by authority on both sides, created the ordinary presumptions of treaty laws which are a sufficient basis of mutual understanding and legal validity in the field of interstate conduct.

As to the form and language of treaties, the award in the Lamu Arbitration case between the British East Africa Company and the German Witu Company states that

if no law prescribes any special form for conventions between independent States, it is nonetheless contrary to international usages to contract verbally engagements of that nature ...

The arbitrator emphasised the importance of the written and solemn form of treaties in African state practice.[91]

Treaties were either formulated in the language of the European contracting party and then translated or they were in two languages, i.e., European and African. Thus, for example, agreements between Italy and Ethiopia were in Italian and in Amharic. A conflict of far-reaching consequences developed out of the differences between the Italian and the Amharic texts of the treaty of 1889.[92] Article XIX of the treaty states that both texts were official. Article XVII (Italian text) included the consent of the Emperor of Ethiopia 'to avail himself of the Italian government for any negotiation which he may enter into with other Powers or Governments'. The Amharic text does not include the word 'consent' but states that the Emperor 'may use' the services of the Italian government. The Italian text was interpreted by Italy as a substantial limitation of the external sovereignty of Ethiopia, in fact as the establishment of an Italian protectorate over Ethiopia. The Emperor rejected this interpretation, maintaining that he 'may use' the services of the Italian government

[90] The binding effect of treaties was particularly emphasised in Islamic law. See C. H. Alexandrowicz, *Introduction to the History of the Law of Nations in the East Indies* (London, 1967), p. 177.

[91] Hertslet, *op. cit.*, III: 891. [92] *Ibid.*, I–III.

for negotiations with foreign powers, and that he was under no obligation to do so. The conflict resulted in war which ended with the defeat of Italy.

Treaties with Muslim rulers were nearly always in one of the European languages and in Arabic, as, for instance, the treaty between Italy and Sheikh Mohamed-ben-Abdullah (1905).[93] Sometimes memoranda were used to explain the meaning of certain terms in treaties. Thus, a memorandum exchanged between Great Britain and Italy (1905) interpreted the term 'tribe'. It was stated that

> It is understood that when the word 'tribe(s)' is used in the agreement … to describe the followers of Seyid Sheikh Mohamed-ben-Abdullah, this word is intended to denote any individual belonging to the Somali tribes who for the time being are with the Mullah.

This is an interpretation for legal purposes which may not coincide with the definition of 'tribe' adopted in other branches of knowledge.[94]

IV. General Observations Relating to Treaties

As to the means of securing the performance of African treaties, occupation of territory, oath, and hostages were occasionally used. The first was not necessarily stipulated in a formal way but as territory rapidly changed hands, sometimes only by transfer of possession, the latter served to secure the performance of treaty stipulations. Oath was used in several cases such as in the British–Gambia treaty of 1823, in which the parties 'call the Omnipotent God of Truth and Justice to witness'.[95] Hostages were given to secure the implementation of a peace treaty. Thus it was stated in the Convention of 1832 between Great Britain and the King of Barra that, on the conclusion of war (following upon breach of the treaty of 1826) the King of Barra was to deliver to the British in Bathurst hostages from the royal family of Barra.[96] Similarly, after the British–Ashanti war in 1827, two hostages from the Ashanti royal family were to be sent to the British.[97]

Some treaties contained stipulations relating to their implementation in municipal law. Thus, in the treaty of 1852 between Great Britain and the King of Kafir Bulloms, a clause was included stating that 'this treaty shall be forthwith proclaimed according to the usual and solemn country customs on like occasions and made law throughout the territory of the said kingdom'.[98] A similar clause can be found in the treaty between Great Britain and the King of Ma Bwetie (Kamba). It provided for the proclamation of the treaty 'immediately on its being concluded and signed, and be made law throughout the territories of the said Bey Farama' (the late king).[99]

[93] *Ibid.*, III: 1120.

[94] See Westermann, *The African*, pp. 72–82. The tribe is defined as the typical political unit (having cultural and political significance) in common territory under a common leader and subject to common customary law. Several tribes may unite under a Paramount Chief (often through conquest). See also Gluckman, *Ideas of Barotse Jurisprudence*.

[95] Hertslet, *op. cit.*, I: 7.

[96] *Ibid.*, p. 11.

[97] W. E. F. Ward, *History of the Gold Coast*, p. 179.

[98] Hertslet, *op. cit.*, I: 42.

[99] *Ibid.*

Two principles of treaty law which were of great importance to African treaty practice should be mentioned here, namely, *pacta tertiis nec nocent nec prosunt* and *rebus sic stantibus*. According to the first principle, a treaty which purports to impose an obligation on a third party without the latter's consent is to that extent null and void.[100] Thus when European powers made arrangements among themselves to convert a protectorate (established by a bilateral treaty between one of the European powers and an African state) into an instrument to annex the latter, such arrangement could not have been valid and could not have affected the treaty of protection which was outside the area of inter-European dealings. Moreover, if such inter-European arrangements were made (as envisaged behind the scenes of the Berlin Conference of 1885) they constituted a vital change of circumstances, from the African point of view, which is essential in the application of the principle of *rebus sic stantibus*. In most cases African states were not able to change the course of events and thus the European *fait accompli*, created in Africa, overshadowed the implementation of the two legal principles. There were, however, exceptions to the general course of events, e.g., the case of Ethiopia which had been bound in 1889 by a treaty of quasi-protection with Italy[101] but forced the latter to abandon the conversion of the treaty into an instrument of annexation. A new treaty between Italy and Ethiopia (1896)[102] did away with the stipulations of the treaty of 1889, taking account of the vital change of circumstances. Liberia had been on the brink of a similar development which menaced it with promises of protection but managed to escape European control thanks to United States support.[103] We shall revert to a discussion of these problems below.

It may be noted that most of the African treaties were real and not personal treaties. They were not only binding the contracting ruler but also his heirs and successors. Thus, in the treaty of 1823 relating to the cession of the island of Lemain to Great Britain, the ruler stated that 'We bind and oblige ourselves, our heirs and successors, faithfully and truly to abide …'.[104] The formula of the binding force of treaties on 'the heirs and successors' of the contracting sovereign can be found *inter alia* in the treaty of 1820 relating to the transfer of the Banana Islands by Tim Manees of Oma to Great Britain,[105] in the treaty of 1841 extending British protection to the King of Cartabar,[106] in the British–Ethiopian treaty of 1849,[107] in the treaty of 1850 between Great Britain and Dembar Sonko, King of Barra,[108] and in the treaty between the South Africa Company with the King of Gazaland (1890).[109]

It has sometimes been argued that African treaties were outside the pale of public international law and constituted only private law contracts for the acquisition of land. This view is not tenable in the light of African treaty practice which carefully distinguished between matters of public law and private law.[110] In this connection, it may be recalled that many African treaties contained stipulations to the effect

[100] Oppenheim-Lauterpacht, *International Law*, new edition, (London, 1953), I, para. 502.
[101] Hertslet, *op. cit.*, II: 454. [102] *Ibid.*, p. 458. [103] Hertslet, *op. cit.*, III: 1130.
[104] Hertslet, *op. cit.*, I: 7. [105] *Ibid.*, p. 28. [106] *Ibid.*, p. 13.
[107] Hertslet, *op. cit.*, II: 421. [108] Hertslet, *op. cit.*, I: 14. [109] *Ibid.*, p. 266.
[110] H. Hesse, *Landfrage und Frage.*

that transfer of sovereignty would not affect the private law rights of natives in territory transferred to a European agency. As examples of such treaties can be quoted *inter alia* the treaty with Bey Sherbro, ruler of Kafir Bulloms (1827), in which the British governor of Sierra Leone accepted the stipulated cession of territory and 'guarantee[d] to the Kafir family and to its inhabitants ... the continued and unmolested enjoyment of such lands and other property as they now possess'.[111] Also, it was stated in the treaty of cession of 1840 between Great Britain and the King of Combo that persons now in possession of property 'shall in no wise be disturbed in the enjoyment of the same by any provisions of this Convention'.[112] The charter of the National African Company (1886)[113] stated that acts of cession of territory to the company did not mean interference with native laws or private property. This formula appeared in the various forms of treaties.[114] Hundreds of these treaties were concluded during the period 1884–1892. They also guaranteed payment of compensation to those whose land was acquired by the company. The Judicial Committee of the Privy Council stated in the Nigerian case of *Amodu Tijani v. Secretary, Southern Provinces* ([1921] 2 A.C.299 that 'a mere change in Sovereignty is not to be presumed as meant to disturb rights of private owners'. The treaties relating to South-West Africa, in which an express distinction was made between public and private law matters will be discussed below. It is clear from all these treaties that they were not private law contracts transferring property but agreements in public international law which transferred the sovereignty over ceded territory.

The bulk of African treaties were bilateral contract treaties and not law making treaties (*traité-loi*). However, treaty making in Africa had its law making effects. Thus, stipulations relating to shipwreck[115] or the *droit d'aubaine* were instrumental in doing away with outdated rules of international customary law. This process had been earlier initiated in East Indian treaties. The same would apply to stipulations modifying the law relating to trade, navigation, and consular privileges.[116]

[111] Hertslet, *op. cit.*, I: 34. [112] *Ibid.*, p. 12. [113] *Ibid.*, p. 125.

[114] *Ibid.*, pp. 137 ff.

[115] Some of the treaties stipulated the transfer of maritime rights such as the treaty of 1820 transferring to Great Britain the sovereignty of the Banana Islands 'with all and every right and title to navigation, anchorage, waterage, fishing and other revenue and maritime claims in and over the harbours, bays, creeks ... around the said Islands'. The same formula can be found in other treaties such as the treaty of 1824 between Great Britain and King of North Bulloms, the treaty of 1825 and King Sherbro, the treaty of 1826 between Great Britain and the Chiefs of Soomba, the treaty of 1861 between Great Britain and Quiah, the treaty of 1877 between Great Britain and Samoo Bulloms, and other treaties (Hertslet, *op. cit.*, I: 27, 30, 31, 34, 42, 49). Grotius in his *Mare Liberum* (chap. VII) refers to customary maritime law in Africa according to which, the coastal communities acquired rights of navigation and fishing in adjacent maritime zones: *Accolae totius tractus 'Africani... partem maris quisque sibi proximam piscando and navigando perpetuo usurparunt* ...'. This is a significant contribution of African maritime practice to the development of International maritime law as witnessed by Grotius. The contribution is notable as at the time of the writing of *Mare Liberum* European maritime practice recognised neither the freedom of the high sea nor the rights of coastal states in maritime zones.

[116] As to the application of the most favoured nation clause in African treaties, see *Concluding Observations* below.

Some of the early treaties between France and North African states contain provisions formulated in an expressly law making way. An example of such a treaty is the Franco–Tripoli treaty of 1830[117] which stated in Article IV that 'any foreign ship shipwrecked at the coast of Tripoli will receive assistance of the Regency'. This provision related not only to French ships but also to '*tout batiment étranger*'. Moreover, if pillage of property occurred on the shipwrecked vessel, the Dey (ruler) of Tripoli was to make restitution to the consul of the nation concerned. According to Article VI of the treaty, all foreign subjects could trade freely with Tripolitan subjects. These provisions transcended the interests of the contracting parties and had a law making effect.

The question may be raised here as to the extent to which diplomatic activity supported African treaty making and treaty implementation. It may be pointed out that such activity was not the same as that which prevailed in Asia. It was perhaps one of the drawbacks of the African state system that it had not an adequately developed diplomatic machinery to support its entry into the family of nations on its own terms. It has already been stated above that some of the African courts achieved high standards of treaty negotiation. But they lacked an expert class of officers who could specialise in dealing with foreign affairs, particularly with treaty implementation. This, however, was a drawback not without significant exceptions. We have seen that the ancient Kingdom of Congo exchanged ambassadors with the Portuguese in the sixteenth century. So did other African courts at that period. But later, only a limited number of African sovereigns exercised the active and passive right of legation.[118] In this category were the North African states, Ethiopia, Liberia, Zanzibar, and Madagascar. Thus, Queen Elizabeth I of England sent in 1577 an ambassador to Morocco to negotiate a trade agreement.[119] According to the Franco–Moroccan treaty of 1630, the ambassador of France at the Moroccan court was guaranteed the same privileges which Moroccan ambassadors enjoyed in France (Article XIII).[120] According to Article XIX of the treaty of 1800 between the Dey of Algeria and France, the Dey had the right to appoint an ambassador in Paris, and in 1801 the Bey of Tripoli received a chargé d'affaires of the French Republic.[121] The Franco–Moroccan treaty of 1901 was concluded by the French government and the Moroccan ambassador in Paris.

Ethiopia stipulated diplomatic exchanges in treaties[122] e.g., in the treaties with Italy of 1883 (Shoa), 1889 (Article II), and 1896 (after the battle of Adowa).[123] As to Madagascar, Article IV of the British–Madagascar treaty of 1865 states that 'The Queen of Madagascar engages to receive a British Agent at her capital; and her

[117] E. Rouard de Card, *Traités de la France avec les pays de l'Afrique du Nord* (Paris, 1906), p. 301.

[118] If they exercised the right of legation, it was the passive rather than the active right of legation.

[119] N. Barbour, *Morocco* (London, 1965).

[120] E. Rouard de Card, *Traités de la France avec les pays de l'Afrique du Nord* (Paris, 1906), p. 301.

[121] *Ibid.*, p. 70. [122] Hertslet, *op. cit.*, II: 421 ff.

[123] In the interwar period Ethiopia received permanent legations from Germany, Belgium, France, Great Britain, and Italy. But it did not yet exercise the active right of legation on a wider scale. Hertslet, *op. cit.*, II: 423.

Britannic Majesty in like manner engages to receive at Mauritius or at London an Agent of the Queen of Madagascar'.[124]

According to Article II of the Franco–Madagascar treaty of 1868 each party had the right to appoint a resident political agent to the other party.[125] France established a protectorate over Madagascar in the treaty of 1885,[126] and according to Article II of the treaty, a French resident was to be at the court of Madagascar. The Sultan of Zanzibar received a diplomatic agent of Great Britain even after the establishment of the British protectorate by the treaty of 1890.[127] Liberia became an internationally recognised state after 1847 and maintained diplomatic relations with a number of powers.

Among other African powers which attempted the establishment of diplomatic relations with European states were the Ashantis, who received British diplomatic agents in Kumasi,[128] and Dahomey. Shaka Zulu tried to send a mission to London in 1828.[129] The ruler of Anobo sent a trade delegation to London to defend his commercial monopoly.[130] These examples do not extend to consular exchanges which were subject to separate arrangements and were stipulated in a number of African treaties.[131]

Treaties of protection and capitulations

It has been stated above that the entry of the African continent into the orbit of the family of nations was a process which called for the application of certain institutions of the law of nations. Two of these were the protectorate and the capitulations, in their original classic form. The European powers which were present in Africa had an opportunity to shelter and adjust the external sovereignty of those African states which were viable entities within the universal family of nations, without impairing their internal sovereignty or political and social traditions. According to Vattel (*Droit des Gens*, II, para 204) the convention by which a state places itself under the protection of another state is a treaty. But should the protecting state 'assume greater authority over the [protected] one than the treaty of protection of submission allows, the latter may consider the treaty as broken and provide for its safety according to its discretion' (Vattel I, chapter 16). This was a passage quoted by Edmund Burke in the trial of Warren Hastings (Governor-general of the English East India Company) in defence of the Raja of Benares (1786).[132] It has also been quoted by Lord Salisbury in the British–French conflict over the protectorate of Madagascar.[133]

124 Hertslet, *op. cit.*, II: 665. 125 *Ibid.*, p. 668. 126 *Ibid.*, p. 670.
127 K. Ingham, *History of East Africa* (New York, 1962), p. 241.
128 Hertslet, *op. cit.*, I: 77; W. E. F. Ward, *History of the Gold Coast*, p. 158.
129 Oliver and Fage, *Short History of Africa*, p. 158.
130 E. A. Ritter, *Shaka Zulu* (London, 1955), pp. 324–329.
131 R. Oliver, *Johnston and the Scramble for Africa*, p. 117.
132 Under some of these treaties Zanzibar consuls were to be sent to Europe, e.g. Austria.
133 *Recueil des cours*, p. 216.

When the European powers established themselves on the continent of Africa, the institutions of the classic law of nations had given way to nineteenth century international law of the positivist brand which had lost the functional qualities of the classic law, particularly the requirement of universality of the law, and its non-discriminatory application to all peoples on earth irrespective of race, creed, or civilisation. Hundreds of treaties of protection were concluded between European agencies and African rulers throughout the nineteenth century. At first they meant what they were intended to mean, namely, a limitation of external sovereignty of the rulers without affecting their rights of internal sovereignty. Thus Consul Hewitt (representing the British government in West Africa) wrote to the Ruler of Opobo in 1884 that

> The Queen (of Great Britain) does not want to take your country or your markets but at the same time she is anxious that no other nations should take them; she undertakes to extend her gracious power and *protection* which will leave your country still under your government; she has no wish to disturb your rule … [134]

This interpretation of protection just before the Berlin Conference of 1885 contains a clear distinction between external and internal sovereignty of the ruler, and provides for limitation of the first only so as to enable the protector to introduce the protected entity into the wider framework of the universal family of nations. But state practice after the Berlin Conference revealed a tendency to deform the original classic concept of the protectorate and to convert it into an instrument of colonialism. In fact, international lawyers of that period called the protectorate 'colonial protectorate' with a new connotation. Before examining its new meaning, however, a brief discussion of a few African treaties of protection and of the relevant clauses will be attempted here.

The characteristic feature of the texts of African treaties of protection is the *negative* formulation of the external position of the ruler who came under European control. Such formulation was a general feature of any treaty of protection, but it will be interesting to see how it was applied in African treaties. Thus the treaty of protection of 1827 between Great Britain and the King of Brekama stated that the king would *not* resort to war without British consent.[135] The British government accepted the principle of non-interference in the internal affairs of the kingdom. In 1837 Emir Abd-el-Kader (in conclusion of the war of 1833–1837) made a treaty with France in which he accepted the French *fait accompli* in Algeria, but was left with the government of Oran and some other territories. In Article XIII the Emir undertook *not* to cede coastal territories to any power without French consent.[136] In 1840 the English East India Company (acting in Africa) made a treaty with the Sultan of Tajourah in which he agreed *not* to enter into treaties with any other power which should prove detrimental or injurious to British interests, a formula which left the Sultan with somewhat limited possibilities for concluding treaties. In the

[134] *State Papers*, 89: 1089.
[135] Crowder, *Story of Nigeria*, p. 177. Italics are mine.
[136] Hertslet, *op. cit.*, I: 11.

same year the company made a treaty with the governor of Zaila who accepted the obligation *not* to enter into any treaties with other European nations,[137] a formula which still left the ruler with authority to make treaties with non-European nations. The same formula can be found in the treaty of 1847 between Great Britain and the chiefs of Rowallah.[138] In 1841, the Ruler of Cartabar undertook '*not* to enter into any alliance, negotiation or communication of any political nature whatever with any power in the world without the knowledge and consent of the Queen of England'.[139] This is a highly restrictive formula, but it does not eliminate entirely the ruler's external sovereignty for he could still act externally with the consent of the British government.

The same or similar formulas subject to certain variations can be found in treaties which were concluded in the second half of the nineteenth century. Thus, King Cetewayo of the Zulus, who after the termination of war with Great Britain was restored to the government of Zululand, declared in the treaty of 1879 that 'he would not make any treaty or agreement with any chief, people or government outside his territory without the consent and approval of the British Government …'.[140] In the same year a British protectorate was extended by treaty to the king and chiefs of Katanu in which the latter agreed '*not* to enter into negotiations with any foreign State except under the express permission of Her Majesty's Government'.[141] In 1881 France and the Bey of Tunisia concluded a treaty of protection and established a relationship which proved to be one of the most controversial in the field of the law of protection in Africa. According to Article VI of this treaty, the Bey of Tunisia agreed to conclude *no* international act without first coming to an understanding with France. The treaty deprived the Bey of his active right to legation as the French government would carry out for him all diplomatic activity; but the Bey could still exercise the passive right of legation and receive foreign envoys. As stated above, the establishment of the protectorate was followed by a protest of the Ottoman Empire which considered Tunisia a vassal of the empire and not legally authorised to submit to the protection of another power.[142] This protest was not effective. The attitude of France towards the administration of the protectorate became a complicated affair: some of the French government departments, as well as the French resident-general in Tunisia, Paul Cambon, were in favour of respecting the internal sovereignty of the Bey and his administration, while the French army and judiciary were for annexation of Tunisia.[143] Thus, Tunisia became a test case in a wider issue which affected Africa after the Berlin Conference of 1885. Paul Cambon appears here as one of the protagonists of the anti-annexation policy in relation to the advanced African protectorates, a policy which proved successful in the case of Tunisia. The Bey designated Cambon as the 'official intermediary in our relations with the representatives of friendly powers' and the resident-general, respecting the legal basis of the protectorate, carried out significant economic reforms in cooperation with

[137] Hertslet, *op. cit.*, II: 643. [138] Hertslet, *op. cit.*, I: 408. [139] *Ibid.*, p. 48.
[140] *Ibid.*, p. 13. [141] *Ibid.*, p. 201.
[142] *Ibid.*, p. 67; see also treaties with the chiefs of Sierra Leone and Nigeria, *Ibid.*, I.
[143] Hertslet, *op. cit.*, III: 1185.

the Bey's administration.[144] Tunisia never ceased to exist as a separate entity in the family of nations and obtained full independence after World War II.

Further cases of protectorate in areas which were at the higher level of African statehood were Madagascar, Zanzibar, Uganda, Egypt, Morocco, and Ethiopia.[145] A treaty of protection was signed between France and Madagascar in 1885.[146] According to Article I of the treaty, the French government 'will represent Madagascar in all its foreign relations'; but, according to Article XII, the Queen of Madagascar will continue 'to preside over the internal administration of the Madagascar Island'. This arrangement broke down in 1896. Unlike in the case of Tunisia, annexation policies got the upper hand and as Madagascar resisted the breach of the treaty of 1885 by France, war broke out which resulted in conquest and in the conclusion of a new treaty (1896).[147] This treaty deprived the Queen of external as well as internal sovereignty, though it left her royal status intact.

Zanzibar was an independent sultanate until 1890 when a treaty of protection with Great Britain came into force.[148] The Sultan lost his external sovereignty, but this did not affect his status as a signatory of the Berlin Act of 1885 which left him in the position of a leading sovereign in Africa. In 1895 the Uganda protectorate was established under which the King of Uganda acknowledged the control of the British East Africa Company.[149] According to the treaty of 1895, the King undertook *not* to make treaties with other European powers without British consent.[150] According to point XIV of the treaty, 'the foreign relations of Uganda and its dependencies are hereby placed ... in the hands of Her Majesty's Representative'. A shadow of external sovereignty of the ruler survived, but its administration belonged to Great Britain.

Egypt which had been a vassal state of the Ottoman Empire came under British *de facto* occupation in 1889.[151] The British protectorate established in 1914 brought Turkish suzerainty to an end. Egypt became an independent sovereign state in 1922 and later joined the League of Nations. Morocco became a French protectorate as late as 1912 under the treaty of Fez. It was also partly subject to Spanish control[152] but Abdel-el-Krim, the independence fighter, defeated the Spanish army at the battle of Mount Anual in 1921 and established the Republic of the Rif. This state came to an end in 1926.[153]

In none of the above cases was the colonial relationship the outcome of voluntary submission. Protectorates never meant more than a restriction of external sovereignty; and when the protecting European power attempted to interfere with internal sovereignty, the leading African states resisted and either collapsed or survived

[144] *Ibid.*, p. 1187.

[145] K. Eubank, *Paul Cambon: Master Diplomatist* (Mormon, Oklahoma, 1960).

[146] This is not an exhaustive enumeration and other African States may be added to this group of Protectorates such as for instance Basutoland (Chief Moshesh), Swaziland (see British–South African Agreement of 1894 referring to King Ungwane as Paramount Chief, article II); see also Lobengula's case.

[147] Hertslet, *op. cit.*, II: 670. [148] *Ibid.*, p. 673. [149] Hertslet, *op. cit.*, I: 308.

[150] *Ibid.*, p. 392. [151] *Ibid.* [152] Oliver and Fage, *Short History of Africa*, p. 185.

[153] Hertslet, *op. cit.*, III: 1149 ff. See also Franco–Spanish Declaration of 1904 and the Algeciras Conference (1906).

in one or another form. One of the African states which fully survived the trial of strength was Ethiopia. Italy, in the treaty of 1889, made an attempt to establish a protectorate over Ethiopia.[154] The Italian government interpreted Article XVII of the treaty as authorising it to assume external control over Ethiopia and notified the other European powers (signatories of the Berlin Act of 1885) of this arrangement. The Emperor resisted Italian interference and defeated the Italian army in the battle of Adowa (1896).[155] In the ensuing treaty of 1896 it was not Ethiopia which had to suffer restrictions but Italy which undertook not to cede certain territories in the neighbourhood of Ethiopia (Article V). Ortroy, commenting on the Italian protectorate over Ethiopia, describes it as a '*protectorat prétendu*'.[156]

Among other treaties of protection in Africa in the last two decades of the nineteenth century may be mentioned treaties with rulers of countries at a level of advanced statehood, and, separately, treaties with chiefs who were merely headmen of small communities. With respect to the latter, one may note the standardised forms of treaties used by some European agencies in Africa. In treaties adopted by the National African Company, for example, the rulers declared that[157]

> We bind ourselves *not* to have any intercourse with any strangers or foreigners except through the said National African Company and we give ... the company full power to exclude all other strangers or foreigners from territory at their discretion.

A type of treaty also appeared which stipulated the ruler's obligation *not* to enter into treaties with other powers or to grant commercial rights to foreigners. We see in these the employment of the negative formula for restricting the ruler's power in external affairs. In different treaties the negative formula was worded in different ways. It usually included the obligation not to cede territory and not to enter into treaties except with the consent of the protecting power, e.g., in treaties concluded by Great Britain with the Jolah country (1887), with the Almany of Umtong (1887), the King of Central Kiang (1887), the King of Jarra (1887), and Prince Mansah Cotto of Batteling (1888); and in the treaties concluded between 1894 and 1901 leading to the establishment of the British protectorate of Gambia.[158] Included in these are also the treaties of protectorate with rulers on the Gold Coast and in Nigeria.[159] French and German treaties of protection were concluded on the same line, e.g., the treaty between France and the Sultan of Gobad (1884), the treaty between France and the Sultan of Tajurah (1884), the treaty of France and the Sultan of Anjouan (1886), and the numerous treaties of protection concluded by the French in West Africa and in the Congo.[160]

A number of African military powers which were ready to fight for their independence managed to retain even external sovereignty for a limited period. Thus,

[154] R. Furneaux, *Abd-el Krim, Emir of the Rif* (London, 1967).
[155] Hertslet, *op. cit.*, I: 454. [156] *Ibid.*, p. 458.
[157] Ortroy, Conventions Internationales (Afrique) Bruxelles, 1898) p. 360.
[158] Hertslet, *op. cit.*, I: 137. [159] *Ibid.*, pp. 19–20.
[160] *Ibid.*, pp. 64–120; see treaty with King of Mahin (1885) and the Chiefs of Ketu (1888) (I: 100 ff); see also treaties with King of Gazaland (1890) and with Lobengula (1888).

for example, the Fulani ruler of Fouta Djallon (Guinea region) made treaties of protection with the French (1881, 1888) which did not impose any restrictions on the sovereignty of the ruler's confederation. In the same way, the French treaty of protection of 1887 with the Ahmedou of Segou (Sudan) imposed no restrictions on the ruler's sovereignty. Similarly the treaties obtained by France from the Emir of Samory (1887, 1889) imposed no restrictions on his sovereignty.[161]

There were other cases of protection which hung in the balance such as Lobengula's case. Lobengula, the ruler of the Matabele and the Mashona (Southern Rhodesia) concluded a treaty of protection with the British South Africa Company (1888) but resisted interference in his internal affairs and ultimately lost his country.[162] Southern Rhodesia's reversion to Lobengula's sovereignty would be a logical conclusion of the history of this part of Africa. One may also mention the case of the Sultan of Migertini (one of the Somali rulers) who, in a treaty with Italy (1889), declared that he would 'not make treaties or contracts with any other Governments or persons'. But the Sultan defied the protectorate in 1890 and declared his adherence to the General Act of Brussels (1890). However, he accepted Italian protection again in 1901.[163]

The German protectorates in southwest Africa deserve separate consideration, as they were established by a number of homogeneous treaties relating to the present-day region of Namibia, a former mandate under the League of Nations. They are to be found in G. F. de Marten's *Nouveau Recueil des Traités* (volume XI, 2nd Ser., 1887) and among them are the treaties concluded by Germany with the following southwest African rulers: Captain Joseph Fredricks of Bethany (1884), Chief Manasse of the Red Nation at Hoachana (1885), Captain Hermanus van Wyk of the Rehoboths (1885), and Maharero, the Paramount Chief of the Hereros (1885). The formula of limitation of external sovereignty used in these treaties put an obligation on the rulers *not* to cede territory to any other nation or its nations without German consent, and *not* to conclude agreements with other governments without such consent. One of the most characteristic stipulations in these treaties can be found in Article III of the treaty with Fredricks, Article II of the treaty with Manasse, Article II of the treaty with the Maharero. It was stipulated in these articles that the German emperor undertook to respect existing agreements and treaties between the contracting rulers and other nations. This was a significant recognition of some of the prerogatives of the rulers in the field of external affairs.[164] Reading these treaties, one is astonished that this region of Africa had been constituted into a Mandate C under the League of Nations.[165] The history of southwest Africa

[161] Hertslet, *op. cit.*, II: 642; *Annales sénégalaises de 1854 à 1885* (Paris, 1885).

[162] Hertslet, *op. cit.*, II: 628 ff. E. Rouard de Card, *Les Traités de protectorat conclus par la France en Afrique 1870-95* (Paris, 1897), p. 120ff.

[163] See the case of Southern Rhodesia in (1919) A. C. 211.

[164] Hertslet, *op. cit.*, II: 1119.

[165] Article 2 of the treaty with Joseph Fredericks, Article 3 of the treaty with Manasse, Article 3 of the treaty with Hermanus van Wyk, and Article 2 of the treaty with Maharero (see Martens pp. 464, 479, 480, and 482). Similar provisions can be found in the treaty of protection between Germany and the King of Togo (1884). See Martens, p. 461.

warranted a much higher classification of these states under the mandate system and their reversion to sovereignty today.

In course of time the African treaty of ordinary protection tended to degenerate into what was called 'the colonial protectorate'. The following were the characteristic features of this development as defined by nineteenth century and early twentieth century international lawyers.[166] The partition of Africa at and after the Berlin Conference of 1885 resulted in an understanding between the signatory powers of the Berlin Act according to which each obtained from the other *carte blanche* to convert its treaty relationship of protection *vis-à-vis* a contracting African State into a relationship of absorption and annexation. All that a European power had to do was to notify the other signatories in accordance with Article XXXIV of the Berlin Act.[167] Such a multilateral arrangement between the European powers could not have had any legal effect on any treaty of protection with an African ruler, for *pacta tertiis nec nocent nec prosunt*. No treaty of protection contained a stipulation allowing the European powers to annex the protected entity.[168] Hence, although the *carte blanche* arrangements together with the intention of annexation might have had political significance, they were legally meaningless *vis-à-vis* the contracting ruler or even illegal if a breach of treaty were envisaged (see Vattel, above). Intention of annexation was irrelevant in international law.

The 'colonial protectorate' remained a shadow of a legal institution which could neither take shape by intention nor by actual annexation. In the first case it was a political expectancy, in the second case there was no more room for any protectorate. It has been stated above that hundreds of small village communities awaited a process of centralisation to create viable units within the family of nations. But the colonial protectorate did not prove to be an instrument of reform or revitalisation of the African state system. Small units could have formed federations or unions on their own terms as in the case of the Ashanti Federation.[169] On the other hand, the larger states could have passed through a process of adaptation and, while the ruler's external sovereignty could have been guided towards membership in the family of nations, their internal sovereignty should have been respected as stipulated in the treaties.

The outcome of the power struggle in Africa varied from state to state. Ethiopia defeated its potential protector in 1896; Liberia was offered French protection in 1879 but escaped it thanks to United States support.[170] Some protectorates

[166] C. H. Alexandrowicz, 'New and Original States: The Issue of Reversion to Sovereignty,' *International Affairs* (July 1969) (chapter 27 below).

[167] J. Westlake, *Chapter on the Principles of International Law* (Cambridge, 1894), and *Collected Papers of Public International Law* (Cambridge, 1914), P. Fauchille, *Traité de droit international public* (Paris, 1922); W. E. Hall, *A Treatise of International Law* (Oxford, 1924).

[168] Hertslet, *op. cit.*, II: 484.

[169] In fact in certain treaties it was stipulated that annexation of territory would not follow such as in the treaty of 1887 between Italy and Menelik II, King of Shoa, Hertslet, *op. cit.*, I: 451.

[170] See also the Zulu State. Some of the Paramount Chiefs or Sultans had a number of vassal entities under their control *e.g.* the Sultan of Zanzibar or the King of Uganda (Lugard, *Rise of an East African Empire*, p. 480). The formation of Unions of Chiefs often took place through conquest.

survived as separate entities and some merged into European colonial administrations. Ultimately, colonial rule drew its own frontiers in the African continent and effected a process of centralisation or decentralisation on its own terms, irrespective of the political history of the continent or its ethnic division. This process influenced the boundaries of present-day African states which reverted to sovereignty without reviving the ancient political map of Africa.

Another legal institution in African treaties which deserves the attention of international lawyers is that of capitulations.[171] Capitulations originated from ancient Asian state practice according to which a ruler receiving a foreign community of merchants in his territory allowed them to pursue their own way of life and govern themselves by their own law under the jurisdiction of the head of the settlement. As stated above, the fact that the foreign community was not subject to territorial law was not considered as evidence of superior civilisation, and the fact that the receiving country renounced a measure of jurisdiction over foreigners was not considered as evidence of inferior civilisation. It is thanks to this ancient tradition that Europeans were able to embark, since the sixteenth century, upon their commercial career in the East Indies where they received concessions for the establishment of settlements and the privilege to govern themselves by their own law. In the course of time these concessions and privileges were embodied in bilateral treaties and became irrevocable, thus affecting the sovereignty of the territorial ruler. A similar development took place in Africa where we find capitulatory clauses in many of the treaties with African rulers. These capitulations varied from period to period. At first, they were negotiated on a footing of equality. But, in the nineteenth century, they degenerated into instruments of inequality and downgraded the status of the rulers.

The early French treaties with North African states and the jurisdictional clauses in these treaties have already been discussed above. The characteristic feature of these treaties was the stipulation of jurisdictional privileges for French subjects residing in North African states as well as for subjects of the latter residing in France. It may be recalled that in the seventeenth century, Moroccan ambassadors to France exercised jurisdiction over their subjects residing in France. During the same period, the rulers of Algeria and Tunisia were authorised by treaties to send their officers to Marseilles to hear claims in connection with the breach of these treaties. Though this did not mean the establishment of capitulatory privileges, African officers in France exercised, nevertheless, extraterritorial jurisdiction. If conflicts arose as to the exercise of jurisdiction over Algerians or Tunisians in France, the representatives of the rulers in Marseilles were authorised to hear claims and possibly to deal with competence conflicts.[172]

The nineteenth century capitulation treaties in Africa reflected gradual changes in the African state systems. Under those treaties, several jurisdictional solutions

[171] Hertslet, *op. cit.*, III: 1130.
[172] See Alexandrowicz, 'New and Original States,' (1969) (ch. 27 below).

were possible. Disputes (civil and criminal) between Europeans residing in African states belonged in principle to the jurisdiction of the European consul or other European officer; disputes between Europeans and subjects of the local ruler, the jurisdiction was entrusted to mixed courts. Alternatively, the principle *actor sequitur forum rei* was also adopted. Exceptionally, certain treaties, e.g., those concluded in North Africa reserved all jurisdiction to the local ruler to decide mixed cases in the highest court of the country, but always in the presence of the consul of the nationality of the European resident. In principle, European law, whatever the system, would be applied to Europeans, Islamic law to Muslims,[173] and indigenous African law to other Africans. These are the general principles usually found in treaties, though subject to certain deviations in special cases.

To quote a few examples of 'mixed dispute' solutions in treaties, the British–Zanzibar treaty of 1886 followed the principle *actor sequitur forum rei* and thus the judicial authority of the nationality of the defendant or the accused had jurisdiction. But when Zanzibar became a British protectorate in 1890, the treaty of protection assigned jurisdiction over mixed disputes, which had hitherto been vested in the Sultan, to mixed courts (Article XVI).[174] When the defendant or the accused was the Sultan's subject, the British consul assumed jurisdiction as the Sultan's delegate with the assistance of a *kadi* (judge) appointed by the Sultan. Here one could already see the inroads being made by the 'protection' agreements into the internal jurisdiction of a ruler. Other European powers had also concluded capitulation treaties with Zanzibar in the 1880s, but they were abrogated after the establishment of the British protectorate in 1890.[175]

The British–Madagascar treaty of 1875[176] assigned mixed disputes to mixed courts (Article XI). The same solution was adopted in the Franco–Madagascar treaty of 1868[177] and in the Franco–Madagascar treaty of protection of 1885. But when Madagascar's independence came to an end in 1896, the French judicial system was introduced.[178]

Ethiopia eliminated Italian protection in 1896 and thus adopted her own jurisdictional solutions. The French government obtained certain capitulatory privileges in 1908 in connexion with the construction of the railway lines from Addis Ababa to Djibuti by the French.[179]

It has been emphasised that the treaties of protection between Germany and southwest African rulers in the 1880s revealed a significant measure of independence for these rulers, which manifested itself *inter alia* in the interim establishment of mixed courts for the settlement of mixed disputes. According to the treaty of

[173] Hertslet, *op. cit.*, II. 3.

[174] Capitulations in Muslim countries are connected with the fact that non-Muslims residing in these countries are not governed by Islamic law. Thus foreigners had to rely on their own law and jurisdictional arrangements (see *Recueil des cours*, p. 183ff.).

[175] Hertslet, *op. cit.*, I: 301.

[176] See treaties with Germany (1883), Portugal (1883), France (1884), United States of America (1884), Italy (1885), and Austria (1887). The last treaty gave the Sultan of Zanzibar the right to appoint consuls in Austria (Article II). Hertslet, *op. cit.*, I: 315–324).

[177] Hertslet, *op. cit.*, II: 665. [178] *Ibid.*, p. 668. [179] *Ibid.*, p. 670.

1884 with Joseph Fredricks of Bethany, jurisdiction over such disputes was vested in a German judicial officer, acting with the assistance of a member of the Council of Bethany (Article X). Similar provisions can be found in the treaty of 1885 with Maharero (Article IV) and in the treaty of 1885 with Manasse, Chief of the Red Nation (Article V). The mixed court solution *inter alia* was adopted in the treaty of 1854 between Great Britain and the chiefs of the Congo River,[180] and in the French treaties concluded with Somali chiefs (1884–1885) and with the chiefs of the Comores Islands (1886, 1892).[181]

According to the British treaty of protection of 1893 (and also that of 1895) concluded with the King of Buganda, jurisdiction over Europeans was exercised normally by British officers, while disputes in civil cases between subjects of Uganda were under the King's jurisdiction and subject to appeal to a British court. Criminal cases between subjects of Uganda were also under the jurisdiction of the king, but subject to the possible interference of the British resident at the court of Uganda.[182] Though the Bey of Tunisia had a higher status in the category of protected sovereigns than African rulers under British protection, his judicial powers were severely cut by the introduction of the French judicial system after 1881.[183] This led to the abolition of all foreign capitulations which the French Resident-General, Paul Cambon, considered confusing and detrimental to French as well as Tunisian interests.[184] Cambon, as pointed out, proved to be an anti-annexationist and successfully defended the ruler's continued sovereignty.

As to the hundreds of village communities which made treaties with European agencies, usually treaties of transfer of territory, the question of capitulations did not arise in these treaties as judicial power was not divisible in these cases. All the communities were bound to undergo, sooner or later, a process of centralisation in order to form viable units within the family of nations. Reference may be made here to the arrangements which had to be effected by the states of Liberia and Maryland (independent African republics) with the tribes within their boundaries.

African treaties contain a variety of stipulations and we have seen that among such stipulations those referring to protection and capitulations occupy a prominent position. Cession of territory also dominates in the majority of treaties. Boundary problems were dealt with in arbitration as well as in treaties. The arbitration relating to the frontiers of the Barotse kingdom may be recalled.[185] Questions which were *sui generis* had to be settled in the Franco–Moroccan treaty of 1845 in which the contracting parties renounced the task of drawing territorial boundaries in the Sahara Desert[186], or in the Italian–Egyptian treaty of 1895 regulating the affairs of nomadic communities which defied precise frontier settlement.[187] In these cases

[180] Rouard de Card, *L'Ethiopie au point de vu du droit international* (Paris, 1928).

[181] *State Papers*, 47: 540.

[182] Rouard de Card, *Les Traités de protectorat conclus par la France en Afrique, 1870-95* (Paris, 1897), chap. III.

[183] Hertslet, *op. cit.*, III: 1185. [184] *Ibid.*, p. 1185.

[185] As to the judicial system which prevailed in Egypt (Islamic law, capitulations and Mixed Courts), see J. Y. Brinton, *The Mixed Courts of Egypt* (London, 1968).

[186] Hertslet, *op. cit.*, III: 1074. [187] *Ibid.*, p. 1146.

personal allegiance to a ruler provided a better basis for division of interests than territorial sovereignty.[188] Apart from their connexion with political issues, boundary problems often originated from technical or geographical difficulties peculiar to African conditions. Thus coastal possessions often had their frontiers open in the rear, and lack of correct territorial surveys, conflicting tribal claims, and unending disputes over titles made boundary disputes a complicated affair.[189] The difficulties still persist today as evidenced by the boundary disputes between African states such as those between Somalia and Ethiopia, Algeria and Morocco, Ghana and Togo, Ghana and Upper Volta, and Sudan and Chad.[190]

V. Conclusion

We have stated that European–African treaty making can be divided into three periods, namely, the pre-colonial period, the transition period, and the colonial period. The first period coincides with that of the classic law of nations which lasted until the end of the eighteenth century. The second period covers the first seven or eight decades of the nineteenth century though its real starting point was the Conference of Berlin in 1885.

During the first period European–African treaties reflected the classic concepts of the universal and non-discriminatory law of nations. Relations between European and African states were established on the basis of equality. This applied to Portuguese relations with some of the coastal states of Africa, and, particularly, to French relations with North African states. Treaties between France, on the one hand, and Morocco, Algeria, Tunisia, and Tripoli, on the other, contained stipulations which were equally beneficial to the contracting parties. A number of these treaties endowed envoys or agents of North African states in France with jurisdictional or capitulatory privileges.

The position gradually deteriorated in the nineteenth century. Great Britain and France expanded their network of treaty relations with African coastal states and, in the ensuing game of power politics, were later joined by Belgium, Germany, and Italy. The situation finally developed into a 'scramble for territory' in the whole African continent. The European powers were guided by the institutions of positivist international law of the nineteenth century, conceived for the purpose, such as the 'colonial protectorate' and capitulations on a footing of inequality. However, the African rulers and their governments constituted throughout the nineteenth century a barrier in the confrontation which did not allow the Europeans to apply unilateral treatment to the African continent. The barrier revealed active African

188 *Ibid.*, p. 1108.

189 On this point see Professor Clive Parry's observations during the Roundtable Conference on International Law Problems in Asia 1967, *Report publ.* (1969), pp. 106–107.

190 See Statement of British Foreign Secretary of 30th March 1872 and the list of Anglo-French Boundary Agreements (Hertslet, *op. cit.*, II: 750).

participation in events—a *sui generis* personality—which manifested itself in several ways.

First, the existence of sovereignty and of political organisation excluded the possibility of treating Africa as *territorium nullius*. Historical research points to two basic factors which helped to shape the institution of African sovereignty in the distant past,[191] i.e., ancient Egyptian influence which reached, via the kingdom of Kush, the Sudan and West Africa, and the Islamic influence which affected a great number of African states after its penetration from the Mediterranean, north to the south. Both factors led to centralisation of political and administrative power, to the consolidation of statehood, and to the establishment, often by conquest, of a number of empires and hereditary kingdoms. The ensuing cycles of centralisation and decentralisation of power never destroyed the village community which continued to be the pivot of tribal or quasi-tribal tradition and was only in the twentieth century caught in the cogs of a colonial administration from which there was no escape. Reversion to sovereignty after World War II produced a new political map of Africa composed of viable democratic entities.

The absence of *territorium nullius* in Africa made the European agencies resort to bilateral treaty making which started prior to the nineteenth century scramble for territory. In this process of treaty making African rulers were able to influence considerably the course of events. As the European agencies in Africa were engaged in a race for title deeds, effecting transfer of territorial rights, the ruler as title holder frequently influenced the details of treaty making or even the choice of the European contracting party.

Thus we have shown that the southwest African rulers negotiating with German agencies in the 1880s for the conclusion of treaties of protection, insisted on a stipulation in the treaties according to which Germany would respect previous treaties concluded by the rulers with third powers. This was an important concession in a treaty of protection, for it guaranteed temporarily a measure of external relationship between the rulers and third powers. The ruler's power in foreign affairs was to that extent maintained and this throws significant light on the treaty of protection of that period. Moreover, accounts of actual treaty negotiations such as Lord Lugard's account of treaty making with chiefs as well as with the court of Uganda show that some of the rulers had a significant impact on the formulation of treaties. In this respect, one of the most frequent stipulations was the provision which secured respect by the protecting agency of native law and property in the territory transferred by the ruler.

African rulers also influenced the choice of the European contracting party, particularly where a race for title deeds developed between competing European powers. The choice sometimes had far-reaching consequences for the present political map of Africa, Portugal claimed vast tracts of territory in the interior of Africa situated between her colonies of Angola and Mozambique. The Portuguese government obtained German and French support for the recognition of these claims but it met

[191] F. H. Hinsley, *Sovereignty* (London, 1966), p. 9ff.

with opposition from Great Britain and from a number of rulers who preferred British to Portuguese protection. This was particularly the case with Lewanika, the ruler of the Barotse. The attitude of the rulers was significant for this part of Africa, for if Portugal would have secured control over the whole region between Angola and Mozambique, the present political map of Africa might have been different.

African rulers also influenced the course of events by taking military action in defence of their independence and by obtaining favourable peace treaties. Some of the battles in African history had a decisive impact on world history. At the battle of Alcasarquivir of 1578, for example, the Sultan of Morocco wiped out a Portuguese army. Two years later Portugal lost her independence to Spain and reverted to sovereignty only in 1640. To what extent the nineteenth century African battles influenced the destiny of the continent is difficult to say. The Zulu won the battle of Isandlwana in 1817, the Ashanti the battle of Bousasa in 1824, the Mahdi conquered Kartoom and the Sudan in the 1880s, and the battles fought by Abd-el-Kader and Abd-el-Krim influenced North African history. But perhaps the most spectacular event in the history of war and treaty making in Africa was the defeat of the Italian army in Ethiopia in 1896 and the treaty concluded after the end of the war. The treaty of 1896 did away with the 1889 treaty of quasi-protection. It constituted a turning point in African history with a significance which was similar to the defeat of the Russian army by the Japanese in 1904. It proved that battles and treaties could be lost or won by Asians and Africans, and that vulnerability in the power struggle was not only the weakness of Asian and African states but of all states in the family of nations.[192]

The law of war in Africa was to some extent affected by the institution of *jihad*, based on Islamic law and tradition. *Jihad* turned treaties into temporary truce arrangements, eliminated neutrality, and submitted the laws of war to its own requirements (ransom, contraband, etc.). The nineteenth century witnessed several cases of *jihad* in Africa, the most prominent being the Fulani *jihad* as proclaimed by Usuman dan Fodio of Sokoto. *Jihad* was *inter alia* directed against the dissidents of Islamic faith in the Hausa states. *Jihad* was also proclaimed by Seku Ahmedou and Al-haji Umar of Fouta Djallan who broke up Seku's empire in 1862. Both rulers obtained treaties with France which recognised for some time their full sovereignty, internal and external. While the above cases of *jihad* were mainly connected with inter-Islamic conflicts, Mahdi *jihad*, in the Sudan, led to General Gordon's catastrophic end in 1885.[193]

In a gigantic operation of transfer of territorial rights relating to a whole continent, the safeguards of legality of transactions were important with respect to both the transferor and the relations between the transferees. There was an emphasis in the treaties on the legal capacity of the rulers, their free consent, and the form of treaty which was being concluded. The independence of rulers from would-be

[192] The partitions of Poland at the end of the eighteenth century were an example of scramble for territory in Europe.

[193] Hertslet, *op. cit.*, II: 617.

suzerains was frequently stipulated, and the councillors of the rulers, or their subordinate chiefs, were associated with the conclusion of treaties. The ruler's freedom of consent to treaties became the object of controversy at the Berlin Conference in 1885. It was thanks to United States insistence on observance of 'modern international law' (which followed the ideology of the classic law rather than that of the positivist school with its tolerance of war and of compulsion of the weaker contracting party) that increased safeguards were observed in numerous forms of treaty making in Africa (see declarations of witnesses or interpreters testifying to the regularity of the consent of the parties which have been noted already in this inquiry).

The Berlin Conference was also concerned with the controversy over the protectorates which were ultimately included in Article XXXIV of the Final Act (relating to notification) but excluded from the effective occupation clause in Article XXXV. It is difficult to see how the requirement of effective occupation could have been applied to protectorates. But most international lawyers of the positivist school (apparently relying on state practice) took a different view. They adopted an interpretation of the Berlin Act which was *contra legem* and declared themselves in favour of effective occupation in the case of protectorates. The logical consequence of the disregard of the express text of the Berlin Act was the appearance of the 'colonial protectorate', which defied the rules of the classic protectorate and replaced them by European control of African states with a view to their annexation. It has been shown that such an interpretation was beyond the pale of international law. It reduced protectorates to the level of political devices which had no legal significance. It has been argued that the positivist view originated from state practice. But this again may only be partially correct as some states refused to ratify the Berlin Act (U.S.A.) or to apply Article XXXV to protectorates, e.g., Spain.[194] Moreover, the case of Ethiopia proved conclusively that the colonial protectorate was meaningless whenever annexation was impossible.

Attention has been drawn to capitulations as reflecting the development of African treaties from one stage to another. In the pre-colonial period, North African states enjoyed the same capitulatory (jurisdictional) privileges in France as the latter enjoyed in North African states. The situation gradually changed in the nineteenth century, and capitulations tended to become onerous to African states until they were replaced by the judicial systems of the colonial powers which tolerated only to a limited extent the autonomous administration of African, including Islamic, law in relation to the local population.

Among other stipulations to be found in African treaties, the most favoured nation clause deserves attention. In the particular conditions of coexistence of African governments and European colonial administrations absurd situations were bound to arise. For example, it was stipulated in the British–Italian treaty of 1905[195] that British subjects as well as subjects of the Sultan of Zanzibar residing in Benadir territory (under Italian jurisdiction) shall enjoy most favoured nation

[194] See Lindley, *Acquisition and Government*, p. 149.
[195] Hertslet, *op. cit.*, III: 956–957.

treatment, as far as commercial and shipping affairs were concerned. Thus Africans who were subjects of the Sultan of Zanzibar were to receive better treatment in Benadir territory than Africans who were permanent inhabitants in the above territory under Italian control. The ensuing discrepancy in treatment required adjustment, and diplomatic action regarding the treaty of 1905 was taken. The Italian ambassador in London referred, in a note to the Foreign Office, to privileges which had been guaranteed by the treaty to the subjects of the Sultan of Zanzibar in Benadir territory and stated that 'if the proviso in question is to be held to apply equally to coloured persons (Zanzibaris), the Italian government might eventually find themselves bound to extend more favourable treatment to these latter than to their own subjects of the same category'.[196] Thus while the standard of most favoured nation treatment could have played a constructive role in reducing the application of discriminatory racial policies, it actually became a source of embarrassment with no prospect of improvement of race relations.

The discussion of the role of treaties in the European–African confrontation could be pursued beyond its third stage, i.e., to the stage of limitation of the internal sovereignty of African rulers by European powers aiming at the suppression of most of the attributes of separate statehood, but such discussion is beyond the scope of this inquiry. Suffice it to say that the acquisition of territory by colonial powers and the establishment of a thin layer of administration and control made the occupation of African states far less effective than required by the provisions of the Berlin Act of 1885. This was the position at the end of the nineteenth century and the beginning of the twentieth century. In many British and other colonial possessions indirect rule was introduced which left the ruler in the position of a quasi-official. His services were required to provide the link between the people and the colonial administrator. The latter, faced with the difficulty of identifying himself with communities of a different civilisation and political tradition, was not able to establish a genuine link with the country of his adopted nationality (See Nottebohm case[197]).

[196] Gann and Duignan, (*Colonialism in Africa*) state that 'the advocates of colonial expansion often had something of the outlook of real estate speculators gambling on a rise'.

[197] ICJ Reports 1955, 4.

21

THE ROLE OF GERMAN TREATY MAKING IN THE PARTITION OF AFRICA (1980)

I. Antecedents

European interest in the Continent of Africa dates back to the days of the Roman Empire. It was confined to the Mediterranean region which later came under the sway of Islam. When the Portuguese circumnavigated Africa at the end of the 15th century, they established stations on the coast of Africa, West and East, for their ships sailing to and from the East Indies. Other European powers joined the East Indian trade in the 17th century and followed the Portuguese maritime routes round Africa. They too established supply stations for their ships and came into contact with African Rulers with whom they opened trade relations. Still, inland penetration was on a minor scale. Even when the obsession for acquisition of African lands gathered momentum in the course of the 19th century, the scramble for territory was at first confined to coastal regions and the provisions of articles 34 and 35 of the Act of the Congress of Berlin of 1885 related only to coastal areas. The objective of the Congress was to bring some order into the chaos caused by the competition between European Colonial Powers and it was therefore agreed that all territorial acquisitions on the coast of the African Continent as well as the establishment of Protectorates over African countries should in each case be notified by the acting or contracting European power to all the other signatory States of the Act of Berlin (article 34). On the other hand article 35 stated that occupation (acquisition) of territory, equally confined to coastal regions, should be effective but article 35 did not apply to African Protectorates since occupation by a Protector State of the protected country would have been irreconcilable with the nature and concept of the Protectorate as such according to which the latter retains part of its sovereignty.[1]

The full scale extension of European penetration from coastal regions to the heart of Africa followed after 1885 and was to last for the next 15 years until the end of the century. It was during this period that Germany joined the scramble for African

[1] The view of some writers who applied the requirements of effective occupation to Protectorates runs contrary to the express provisions of article 35. See: *The Acquisition and Government of Backward Territory* by M. F. Lindley, 1926, pp. 148–9.

territory. However there was some earlier German action in Africa which dates back to the 17th century and this first deserves our attention.

Trade between Germany (Brandenburg) and Africa in the 17th century started with a treaty concluded on the 16th May, 1681 by Captain Blonk with Chiefs on the West coast (Pregette, Sophonge and Apany) who conceded to the Germans land for the erection of a trading station and fort situated between Axim and Cape de Tres Puntas on the Gold Coast.[2] Subsequently several African nobles arrived, viz Hamburg, in Berlin, where they were presented at the Court of the Grand Elector. In 1682 the Brandenburg Trading Company was established and the Grand Elector sent Captain Otto von der Groeben to the coast of Guinea.[3] Groeben in his account of his mission under the title 'Guineische Reisebeschribung' emphasised that the Guinea coast was open to foreign trade subject to agreement of the local communities.[4] He landed at Accada and obtained concessions first by oral and then by written agreement with the eight Chiefs of Anta and Fort Gross Friedrichsburg was founded. The agreements concluded by Groeben were bilateral, voluntary and non-discriminatory agreements and they were communicated to the local communities in the Portuguese language with which African negotiators were familiar at that period.[5] As to the countries surrounding the German settlements Groeben referred to the Kingdom of Ardres on the frontier of the Gold Coast and to the City of Benin, the Capital of an important kingdom of the same name.[6] Trade in ivory, pepper and other goods ensued but the experiment came to an end in 1721 when Gross Friedrichsburg was ceded to the Dutch. Captain von der Groeben died in 1782.

In connection with the above episode one or two observations are essential. First, the establishment of German trading stations had nothing to do with possibly wider German plans in the East Indies. Germany for one or another reason did not compete for a share in the lucrative East Indian trade. Had it done so, it would have come into competition with the Portuguese, the Dutch, the English and the French. Plans for a German Company trading in the East which would have relied on supply stations along the whole East and West Coast of Africa never led to the establishment of lasting commercial and colonial relations such as those developed by the great East India Companies, English Dutch and French. Both the Prussian East Indian Company of Emden and the Ostende Company[7] were abortive 18th century attempts to allow Germany to take a share in the profits of the East. Johannes Julius Surland gave expression to this unsatisfactory state of affairs in his monograph *Juris*

[2] *Deutschlands Kolonien* by Rochus Schmidt, 1894. p. X.

[3] *Histoire de la Colonisation Allemande* by Robert Cornevin, p. 9 seq.

[4] *Guineische Reisebeschreibumg* by O. Fr. von der Groeben, publ. 1913, pp. 53, 59, 64, 67, 75, 89.

[5] Among other Forts established by the Germans was Fort Arguin which was abandoned by the Brandenburg Company in 1713 and was later occupied by the Dutch and subsequently by the French. *The European–African Confrontation* by C. H. Alexandrowicz, 1973.

[6] *A Short History of Africa* by R. Oliver and J. D. Fage, 1966, pp. 105–6.

[7] *British Yearbook of International Law* 1961, pp. 508–9 (p. 171 above).

Germanorum Navigandi Indias Prima Fundamenta (1751). He refers to East Indian trade enjoyed by other European nations and complains: 'Solis germanis harum terrarum litora denegata fuerunt'.[8] At a later date J. J. Moser in his *First Basic Notions of the Present European Law of Nations* (1778) refers again to the share of the established colonial Powers in Asian and African trade and to their settlements and comptoirs and he emphasises that they should not monopolise overseas trade to the exclusion of other nations such as Germany, for (and this is of primary importance) trade was and is established 'on the basis of treaties concluded with Asian and African States' which are alone competent to exclude one or another European Power from overseas trade. Similar views were expressed by other German writers such as Pufendorf or Justi.[9] Dr. Karl Peters, the German explorer in East Africa in the 1880s, had this to say about Germany's colonial penetration: 'The German nation came out empty-handed in the partition of the earth as it progressed from the end of the 15th century up to our days. All the other nations of Europe have outside our part of the world settlements in which their language and way of life took firmly root and which are open to further development ... this fact so deplorable for our national pride means a considerable economic disadvantage for our people'.[10] As will be seen later, German colonial action in East Africa in the 1880s was due to the initiative of Dr. Peters. It was only then that Germany joined fully in overseas colonial penetration.

The second observation which is of significance to historians of international law, relates to the nature of the legal instruments which, as emphasised by J.J. Moser, were the basis of trade relations between European Powers and African Rulers prior to the 19th century, i.e. under the regime of the classic law of nations. The German agreements concluded with African Rulers in the 17th century were of the same pattern as those concluded at that period by the Portuguese, the French, the Dutch or the English. Perhaps the most remarkable example of a treaty concluded by a European Power with an African Sovereign in the 17th century was at Portuguese–Monomotapa treaty of 1629. It is recorded in J. Biker's collection of treaties[11] and it established suzerain–vassal relations between the King of Portugal and the Ruler of Monomotapa. The treaty follows the model of Portuguese treaties with East India Rulers in the 16th and 17th centuries. It deserves special attention, for this is the first treaty concluded with a powerful African State of the interior of East Africa. French treaty making in Africa in the 17th century was almost entirely confined to treaties with African sovereigns of the Mediterranean coast, but not exclusively. There were numerous French treaties concluded with Rulers on the West Coast[12] such as the

[8] And further: 'Nec tamen animum demittat ac de Indiarum commercii plane desperet moesta Germania'.

[9] *British Yearbook of International Law* 1968–9, p. 207 (p. 161 above). Pufendorf in his 'Introduction to the History of Asia, Africa and America' refers *inter alia* to Mauretania, Guinea, Sierra Leone and Benin. See: J. H. G. von Justi's work *Vergleichungen der europäischen mit den asiatischen und andern vermeintlich barbarischen Regierungen*, 1762.

[10] *K. Peters der Begründer von Deutsch-Ostafrika* by H. Böhme, 1939, p. 26.

[11] *Collecção de Tratados* I, 234.

[12] As to English treaties, see *The Map of Africa by Treaty* by E. Hertslet. As to French treaties, see Alexandrowicz *op. cit*, pp. 129–40.

King of Commendo (1687) the King of Solum (1686) and others.[13] Numerous French Companies operated at approximately the same time as the Brandenburg Company on the West coast of Africa and so did Dutch Companies which concluded during the 17th century treaties with African Rulers.[14] As stated above, the Dutch took over most of the Forts abandoned by the Brandenburg Company.

The fact that the above treaties, whether German, French or Portuguese, were subject to the regime of the classic law of nations, helped to shape relations between European and African sovereigns on the basis of equality and non-discrimination which was characteristic of the classic law as based on the natural law ideology. Anyhow it was unthinkable that European sovereigns could undermine in any way the authority of extra-European sovereigns since any sort of discrimination would have offended the idea of sovereignty in its universal context. Jean Bodin, its first formulator referred not only to European, but also to Asian and African sovereigns.[15] Thus trade agreements or alliances brought Asian as well as African State or quasi-State entities into the framework of inter-sovereign dealings. Asian and African Rulers were bearers of sovereign rights and the European Powers considered them potential contracting parties whenever they wished to establish commercial or other relations in their territories. If this is the case, one wonders at what point discrimination set in in the post-classic period when a shadow was cast by some politicians and international lawyers on the sovereignty and status of Afro-Asian Rulers and on the validity of treaties which they concluded in their desire to enter the wider Family of Nations and to seek association with the rest of the world. Their produce and merchandise were more and more in demand including spices, ivory, gold and a great variety of other goods which were believed to contribute to the

[13] The King of Commendo sent in 1672 Ambassadors to the French Court and he ceded subsequently Aquitania on the coast of Guinea to the King of France (1687). French Ambassadors acted in the negotiations leading to the conclusion of the treaty of 1765 with King Demel of Gorée by which the Madelaine Islands were ceded to the King of France. In 1787 the King of Ardres made a treaty of cession of territory to the French ('territoire d'Ardres au bord de la mer').

[14] Some of them were concluded by the General Chartered West India Company and directed against the Portuguese at Fort Elmina (1624) or they stipulated cession of territory on the Gold Coast (1657). The sovereignty of the acquired territory was vested in the States General of the Netherlands (V.W.I.S. 1162).

[15] *Les Six Livres de la Republique*, 1577, vol. VI, ch. II, p. 630. See also translation by Richard Knolles 'The Six Book of the Commonweale' 1606, I, VIII, pp. 114, 147–8. Bodin refers to the King of Morocco, the Negus of Ethiopia and 'the Kings of Tombut, of Guynéé, of Gaoga and other Kings who dwell more into the hart of Africa who know not the Caliphes command neither acknowledge any greater than themselves'. Treaties concluded in the 17th century testify to the equality of status of the contracting parties. In the treaty made in 1619 by Monsieur de Guise in the name of King Louis XIII with the Sovereign of Algiers the former called the latter: 'Mon très cher et parfait ami'. In 1631 a treaty between France and the Sovereign of Morocco gave the Moroccan Ambassador in France jurisdiction over disputes between African traders residing in France (article IX). A similar stipulation of a capitulatory nature was contained in the French–Algerian treaty of 1666 which allowed the African Sovereign to send envoys to Marseilles to hear complaints in cases of breach of the treaty (article VI). The same privilege was granted by France to the Ruler of Tripoli in the treaty of 1681 (article XXIII) and to the Ruler of Tunisia in the treaty of 1711 (article XXI). See: *Traités de la France avec les pays de l'Afrique du Nord* by E. Rouard de Card, 1906.

growth of European economy. Moreover in the wake of trade an exchange of ideas was bound to follow leading to a cross-fertilisation of civilisations. Again one wonders to what extent it had been expedient to write off the principle of the classic law of nations under which the continents of Asia and Africa had been of equal status with the continent of Europe and to abandon the conviction that treaties concluded from one continent to another had been meaningful legal transactions. It is only by comparison of 19th century colonial agreements with pre-19th century treaties that it becomes clear that the facts conditioning the actual relationship between Europe and the Afro–Asian world had hardly changed but that a doctrinal transformation had taken place which interrupted the continuity between pre-19th century dealings and 19th century transactions. This transformation tended to leave the Afro–Asian world at the mercy of unilateral European action. The view supporting and justifying such doctrinal change was not shared by all international lawyers, particularly by those who insisted on relying on facts irrespective of doctrine such as Lindley, Hesse and Büchner.[16] We shall revert to this point at a later stage.

German participation in the development of European–African relations under the regime of the classic law of nations had been of minor importance and confined to the West Coast of Africa for a period of about 40 years only. A new initiative was taken by Germany 160 years later in three regions, i.e. South West Africa, the West Coast of Africa (Togo and the Cameroons) and East Africa. On the eve of German action in the early 1880s only a small part of Africa was under European control. As mentioned above European possessions were mainly confined to coastal regions and effective inland rule had not yet been established on a major scale. But King Leopold II of Belgium had gone ahead with plans of forming an African International Association (1876) and these plans soon led to the foundation of European (Belgian) control over the Congo basin. Germany entered the African scene immediately afterwards and it is now maintained that this 'let loose the scramble' for territory which ultimately led to intensified European competition and to the partition of the whole continent.[17] Whether this view is justified by actual evidence is an open question; all that can be said is that Germany encountered only limited opposition on the part of other European Powers in her action in South-West Africa or in the Cameroons and in Togo. Moreover, Anglo–German competition in the East African region did not develop into an acute conflict but was amicably settled by treaty in 1890. Bismarck's policy relating to colonial acquisitions in Africa never allowed blind enthusiasm to get the better of his pioneering compatriots, whether they were colonial officers, traders, missionaries or other treaty makers.[18]

[16] See Lindley *op. cit.*; *Schutzverträge in Sudwestafrika* by Dr. H. Hesse, 1905; *Die Landfrage und die Frage der Rechtsgultigkeit der Konzessionen in Sudwestafrika* by the same author, 1906; *Aurora Colonialis* by Max Buchner, 1914. Hesse was critical of German treaty policy in Africa but his legal views were correct.

[17] Oliver and Fage *op. cit.* p. 185.

[18] *Bismarcks Kolonialpolitik* by Maximilian von Hagen, 1923.

II. Treaty Making 1884–1904

South-West Africa

The present enquiry is not concerned with German colonial history in Africa in its entirety but only with the history of treaty making and therefore no attempt will be made to discuss in detail the political or economic environment in which German action led to treaty negotiation. The resulting treaties represent the crucial point of confrontation between the European Powers and the African Communities at which the initial coexistence between the two was formally legalised within the framework of international law. They clearly reflect the main problems which required legal solution and the nature of the understanding which followed the bargaining between contracting parties belonging to different civilisations. South-West Africa was populated by pastoral and hunting communities of a heterogeneous character comprising the Namas (Hottentots) Hereros, and others who did not always see eye to eye as to the management of their internal or external affairs. German negotiators were able to take advantage of these differences, particularly of the deep seated conflict between the two most powerful Rulers (Captains) in South-West Africa: Hendrik Witbooi the leader of the Namas in the South, and Maharero, the Ruler of the Hereros in the North. Apart from this central conflict there were also other disputes between Captains such as those relating to the precarious settlement of frontiers and to dynastic succession. Among the German treaty makers Paster Büttner acting for G. Nachtigal, German Consul-General, was probably the most knowledgeable and skillful to exploit the conditions of local power politics.[19]

On the 1st May, 1883 the Bremen Company of Lüderitz signed through its representative in Angra Pequena a cession agreement with Captain Joseph Fredericks on Bethany (Bethanien). The agreement transferred to the firm Lüderitz the Gulf of Angra Pequena and the neighbouring land.[20] This was followed by a second agreement by the same contracting parties which transferred to the German firm the coast of the estuary of the Orange River. Both agreements are referred to in the subsequent treaty concluded on the 28th October, 1884 by Nachtigal, acting for the German Emperor, and Captain Fredericks.[21] This treaty is of fundamental interest to historians of international law and deserves detailed discussion.[22] Article 5 of the treaty states that 'H. M. the Emperor (of Germany) recognises the

[19] *Die Christliche Mission in Sudwestafrika* by H. Loth (In 'Studien zur Kolonialgeschichte' 1963). The author refers to Büttner's strategy of negotiation.

[20] The British had claimed Walfish Bay (Angra Pequena) in 1880 but later abandoned the claim. *L'Expansion Allemande Outre–Mer du XV siècle à nos jours* by H. Brunschwig, 1957.

[21] As to details about the life of Captain Fredricks, see: Reichskolonialamt (RKA) Bd 1, No. 2010, B1.24–5, as quoted in Loth *op. cit.*

[22] *Nouveau Recueil Général de Traités* by G. F. Martens (ctd. by F. Stoerk), vol. XI, 2nd ser., 1887, p. 464 seq.; Hesse *op. cit.*; *Geschichte der Deutschen Kolonial Gesellschaft für Sudwestafrika* by Dr. L. Sander, 1912, vol. II.

above cession of territory (comprised in the two previous agreements) and submits the territory to the protection of the German Reich and assumes sovereignty over it'. Dr. H. Hesse, in his commentary on the above transactions asks the question whether the German Company acquired by the above cession the property of the land or any other private law rights in it. The answer was of significance, for it affected directly the African sovereign who made the transfer as well as the German Reich which was the ultimate transferee of rights. Dr. Hesse, after an analysis of all the relevant elements of the transaction reached the conclusion that the Lüderitz Company had acquired territorial sovereignty (Gebietshoheit) subject to the recognition of the Reich. This recognition is stipulated in article 5 of the treaty in which the Company relinquished all sovereign rights to the Reich. Neither the treaty nor the two cession agreements were transactions of private law. If they were *per inconcessum*, there could have been only one municipal law governing the transaction and this was the *lex rei sitae*. The solution would have been absurd.[23] The point was that the company as provisional transferee acted as *negotiorum gestor* in a deal with a sovereign ruler (Captain Fredericks). The ultimate transferee was the Reich and only international law could be applicable to such a deal between sovereigns. Dr. Hesse emphasises that the Captain had what may be called 'Aktivlegitimation', i.e. legal capacity in international law to act as transferor of sovereign rights. On the other hand the company had 'Passivlegitimation' to receive the transfer of sovereign rights which it passed on, as *negotiorum gestor*, to the State of which it was a national (Germany). It may be underlined that this pattern of passing on sovereign rights, acquired by a company for its national State, was peculiar to German transactions in South-West Africa and in the Cameroons and Togoland on the West coast. A different method of transfer of sovereign rights was adopted in German transactions in East Africa where Dr. Karl Peters was the principal negotiator. Here too a private company (D.O.A.G.)[24] concluded treaties with independent Rulers for the transfer of sovereign rights and it acted as *negotiorum gestor*. But the Reich, the ultimate contracting party to deal with African sovereigns, validated the cession treaties by the issue of the Imperial 'Schutzbrief,' a legal instrument establishing German sovereignty and protection (Schutz) over the countries of the contracting Rulers. This legal mechanism will be discussed in more detail in the chapter on East Africa. The legal pattern applied in South-West Africa was different for here

[23] Hesse in his work on Treaties of Protection (*Schutzverträge*) p. 150, states that the notions of ownership peculiar to South-West African communities were different from those established in European law, Different legal and cultural traditions resulted in what Hesse describes as 'das Aufeinanderprallen zweier verschiedenen Kulturanschauungen'. In those circumstances the application of the *lex rei sitae* to European settlers was a difficult proposition. On the other hand, the law brought by settlers from Europe could not be easily fitted into the local property regime. The only way out was an understanding between Europeans and Africans in the frame-work of international law, i.e. by treaty and regulations issued under the treaty. The position was the same in East Africa. F. F. Miller in his *Deutschland—Zanzibar—Ostafrika* 1959 (p. 127) states that the land belonged to the community and was inalienable. Europeans could only acquire a joint ususfructus (Mitbenutzungsrecht).

[24] Deutsch-Ostafrikanische Gesellschaft.

sovereignty or protection was not established by the German Emperor's unilateral decree (Schutzbrief)[25] but within the framework of the bilateral treaty concluded with the African Ruler.[26] The consequences of these legal mechanisms were far-reaching. No colonial company could claim the ownership of land on the basis of cessions made by local Rulers.[27] This applied to occupied as well as non-occupied land. Occupied land meant cultivated land or land used in any other way. The transactions were transfers of sovereign rights governed by international law and not by any municipal law which was not fit to govern inter-sovereign relations.

Before proceeding further with the discussion of the treaty of 1884, attention may be drawn for comparative purposes to M.F. Lindley's classic work on 'The Acquisition and Government of Backward Territory in International Law' (1926) in which the author extends his discussion to the experience of all colonial Powers. Lindley, in the same way as Hesse, relies in the formulation of his views on the bare facts of 'the scramble for territory' and the details of treaties. It emerges from his assessment of these facts and details that there was in essence a 'scramble for *titles* to territory'. It was impossible for European Powers to ignore the existence of political organisation in Africa (and Asia), and to occupy territory unilaterally.[28] The presence of Rulers who were bearers of sovereign rights within communities occupying defined territory made it imperative for European Powers to act on the basis of bilateral instruments which respected the existing legal reality. Overseas territory was rarely *terra nullius* open to unilateral occupation.[29] No private rights were acquired on the basis of treaties (unless expressly stipulated) and either a Protectorate was established which left the rights of internal sovereignty in the local Ruler, or a complete cession of all sovereign rights took place. In the latter case the European transferee could of course exercise legislative powers and change the law relating to real property. It could also as sovereign declare all unoccupied land to be crown land (Kronland). But it always had to follow the mechanism of law which in the case of bilateral dealings between sovereigns attracted the application of the principles of the law of treaties.

[25] For a draft 'Schutzbrief' for German South-West Africa, see Bundesarchiv (Koblenz) R 101, I/1 (fol. 1–112) p. 10.

[26] The use of the term protection side by side with cession of sovereign rights may be misleading. It has to be remembered that South-West Africa was in the 1880s split into three parts: (1) the territory acquired by the Lüderitz agreements; (2) territory not ceded but under German protection; (3) territory of chiefs who neither ceded any rights nor submitted to protection. In territory of type (3) Germany may have claimed to have established a sphere of interest, a title of no legal significance *vis-à-vis* the Rulers; 'The changing legal status of boundaries in Africa' by Prof. Antony Allott, in *Foreign Relations of African States*, ed. by K. Ingram, 1973–4, pp. 117–20.

[27] Unless a private law cession was expressly incorporated into the body of the inter-Sovereign treaty. H. Loth quotes in Appendix 20 *op. cit.* a private law agreement recorded in R.K.A. 1207, Bl. 66 seq., concluded by the Rheinische Missionsgesellschaft with Chief Zacharias Zerana (10th November, 1897). The agreement was for purchase of land by the Missionary Society acting through Hugo Hahn.

[28] As to political organisation in Africa, see: *Züge aus der politischen organisation Afrikanischer Staaten und Völker* by G. Spannaus, 1929.

[29] Exceptions are Australia (see: Cooper v. Stuart, 1889, 14 A.C. 286) and parts of America, Lindley *op. cit.* p. 28.

It seemed advisable to make the above digression since a number of international lawyers in Germany and other European countries expressed views to the contrary on the subject of colonial acquisition without enquiring sufficiently into the details of the relevant transactions and the actual content of treaties. Thus Karl von Stengel in his treatise on German Protectorates[30] sees unilateral occupation as the usual title of acquisition of territory in Africa. He considers the territories in South-West Africa, the Cameroons, Togo and East Africa as 'völkerrechtlich herrenlos', i.e. deprived of adequate political organisation and he styles the treaties concluded with African Rulers treaties of submission (Unterwerfungsverträge) and in fact phantom treaties. He recognises only the Sultan of Zanzibar and Rulers of the same level as endowed with legal capacity in international law but he does not indicate the criteria which make him locate one Ruler within the edifice of the law and Family of Nations while relegating other Rulers to extra-mural status. This type of reasoning must be contrasted with the views of Hesse, Lindley and Büchner[31] and the convincing conclusions which they draw from a more exact study of the facts and details of treaty making in Africa.

The establishment of a Protectorate (Schutz) in article 1 of the treaty of 1884 invites the following observations. The article does not say anything beyond declaring the existence of protection, the German Emperor being the Protector and the African contracting party being the protected entity. As will be seen later, in East Africa the initial Protector in the 1880s was the D.O.A.G. acting through its representative Dr. Karl Peters or one or another of his assistants. A private company could not be the Protector in international law except as a short-lived *negotiorum gestor* and the situation as emphasised above had to be validated by the Emperor's 'Schutzbrief'. In South-West Africa and to some extent in the Cameroons and Togo where the Emperor acted through his Consul-General, his Consuls or Commissioners, protection was assumed within the body of the inter-sovereign treaty. According to existing notions of international law a Protectorate is conceived as an operation splitting sovereignty, external sovereignty being vested in the Protector and internal sovereignty remaining entirely or to a substantial degree in the protected entity. A treaty of Protection (Schutzvertrag) should therefore expressly indicate such a division of sovereignty to satisfy the above requirements of international law. In fact article 2 of the treaty of 1884 states that 'Captain Fredericks undertakes not to cede his territory or part of it to any other nation or its nationals without the consent of H.M. the German Emperor nor to conclude agreements with other Governments without the above consent'. This article contains what may be called the negative clause giving expression to the duty of the

[30] *Die Rechtsverhältnisse der Deutschen Schutzgebiete* by C. von Stengel, 1901; and by the same author *Die Deutschen Schutzgebiete*, 1889. See also: *Der Koloniale Inlands und Auslandsbegriff* by F. Sabersky, 1907 (and literature quoted by the author); *Die rechtliche Natur der Konzessionen und Schutzbriefe in den deutschen Schutzgebieten*, by K. Romberg, 1909; *Werden, Wandel und Gestaltung des Rechtes im Lichte der Völkerforschung* by R. Thurnwald, 1934; 'Völkerrechtliche Okkupation und deutsches Kolonialstaatsrecht' by R. Adam, in *Archiv für öffentliches Recht*, VI, 1891; *Verwaltungs und Gerichtsverfassung der deutschen Schutzgebiete* by H. Hoffmann, 1908.

[31] See: *Aurora Colonialis op. cit.*

protected Ruler not to exercise certain essential rights of external sovereignty. It was obvious that the Ruler must have possessed, prior to the conclusion of the treaty, rights of external sovereignty such as the right to cede territory or to conclude agreements; otherwise he would not have been able to renounce them. The presence of a negative clause in the treaty is therefore evidence of the legal status of the Ruler as a Sovereign in the meaning of international law and of the ensuing limitations of his external sovereignty. We are here faced with a real Protectorate and not a phantom protectorate as held by some international lawyers. Moreover, according to article 3, 'H.M. the German Emperor acknowledges the validity of existing commercial agreements and contracts previously concluded by other nations or their citizens (nationals) with the Ruler of Bethany …'. Thus the Protectorate as established by the treaty does not suppress the entire external sovereignty of the contracting Ruler. Article 3 reserves to the Ruler (Captain) the right of collection of revenues and the exercise of judicial power over his subjects. Respect for the internal sovereignty of the Ruler is reinforced by article 9 which imposes a duty on German nationals to respect the law of the country.[32] Though article 10 grants to them the privilege of their own capitulatory jurisdiction in disputes *inter se*, jurisdiction in mixed disputes between Germans and local subjects was assigned to mixed Courts composed of a German judicial officer and a member of the Ruler's Council, a far-reaching concession to the Ruler's independence.

It may be recalled that the granting of capitulations to Europeans residing in various Asian and African countries in the past had been interpreted by a number of international lawyers as proof of the higher civilisation of European countries and the lower civilisation of Afro–Asian countries which had to tolerate in their territory the application of foreign law and the exercise of foreign consular jurisdiction.[33] The consequences drawn from the above argument were significant, for the countries with a lower civilisation were considered as being outside the orbit of the family and law of nations. The fallacy of this sort of reasoning has been discussed elsewhere.[34] Reference may be made to the treaty of 1631 between France and Morocco which gave the Moroccan Ambassador in France jurisdiction over African traders residing in France and to a similar treaty concluded in the same year between Persia and the States-General of the Netherlands which approved the establishment of a Persian settlement in Amsterdam endowed with quasi-consular jurisdiction.[35] Capitulations had nothing to do with higher or lower civilisation.[33] They simply allowed a foreign community of traders to govern itself by its own law, an ancient tradition found in many parts of the world. The creation of mixed courts is not peculiar to the treaty between Germany and the Rulers of Bethany in 1884

[32] Article 9 also contains a most-favoured-nation clause in favour of German nationals and protected persons.

[33] Alexandrowicz *op. cit.* p. 83.

[34] 'The Partition of Africa by Treaty' by C. H. Alexandrowicz, in *Foreign Relations of African States* ed. by Professor K. Ingham, 1973–4 (ch. 19 above).

[35] Alexandrowicz *op. cit.* (*The European-African Confrontation*) p. 21.

but can be found in other South-West African treaties concluded by Germany and it testifies to the jurisdictional equality of the contracting parties.[36] A discussion of further South-West African treaties which followed the pattern of the Bethany treaty may now be attempted.

The most important treaties concluded by Germany in South-West Africa can be found in Martens's *Nouveau Recueil Général de Traités*.[37] Here belong apart from the Bethany treaty of 1884, the treaty of Hoachanas concluded with Captain Manasse of the Red Nation (2nd September, 1885), the treaty concluded with Captain Hermanus van Wyk, Chief of the Bastards of Rehoboth (15th September, 1885) and the treaty concluded with Maharero, the Paramount Chief of the Hereros (21st October, 1885)[38] Similarly to the Bethany treaty, each of the above treaties established a German Protectorate. The treaties contain the negative clause together with the German undertaking to respect agreements concluded by the Ruler with third parties in the past; they stipulate trading and mining rights for German citizens and contain a most-favoured-nation clause; and they establish a jurisdictional (capitulatory) regime providing for mixed Courts in mixed disputes. It may be underlined that the treaty with Captain Hermanus van Wyk states in article 4 that 'the citizens of Rehoboth reserve to themselves the liberty to fix conditions under which foreigners can reside in their territory', a significant legal stipulation testifying to the independence of the local community. While the treaty with Captain Fredericks was concluded by Nachtigal on behalf of the German Emperor, the treaties with Manasse and Hermanus van Wyk were concluded by C. G. Büttner as plenipotentiary of the Emperor. The treaty with Maharero was concluded by the Commissioner of the Reich, Dr. Heinrich Goering, acting jointly with Büttner.

Among further treaties which help to illustrate the trends of German policy in South-West Africa in the 20 years between 1884 and 1904 the following may be mentioned:[39] Treaties concluded with Piet Habib of Scheppmannsdorf (19th August, 1884), Ian Jonker Afrikaner (16th May, 1885), Cornelius Zwaartboi of Franzfontein (19th June, 1885), David Zwaartboi of Franzfontein (19th January, 1895), Ian Vixamab of Zessfontein (4th July, 1885), Jacobus Isaak of Bersaba (28th July, 1885), Dietrich Goliath of Bersaba (7th July, 1894), Manasse of Hoachanas (26th October, 1895), Hermanus van Wyk of Rehoboth (26th July, 1895) the Captains of Okahandya, Omaruru and Otymbingwe (30th November, 1894), Samuel Maharero of Okahandya (6th December, 1894), Manasse Tyiseseta

[36] However, article 8 states that disputes between Captain Fredricks and the Lüderitz Company 'will be the concern of the Imperial Government'.

[37] See Martens *op. cit.*

[38] The Herero treaty was supplemented by the Protocol of the 3rd November 1885 which contained the accession of the Chief of Omaruru and his Council to the above treaty. The treaty with Van Wyk was preceded by the agreement of 11th August, 1884 in which Dr. Höpfner acted for Nachtigal. See: Sander *op. cit.* II, 14. See also reference in the *Recueil* to treaties with Piet Habib, Ian Jonker and the Zwaartboois (1884–5). As to the position of Ian Jonker and Petrus Zwaartboois in international law ('Völkerrechtliche Stellung'), see letter of Lilienthal to 'Auswärtiges Amt' in Berlin of 15th July, 1885, in Bundesarchiv R 101, I/3, p. 5.

[39] See: List of treaties in Hesse *op. cit* (*Schutzverträge*) p. 171.

of Omaruru (3rd November, 30th November, 1894), William Christian of Bondelszwaart (21st August, 1890), the Bondelszwaarts (27th January, 1904), Ian Hendricks of Veldschoendragers (21st August, 1890), Hendrik Witbooi of Gibeon (15th September, 1894, 16th November, 1895), the Khausas Hottentots (3rd September, 1894, 4th February, 1895), Simon Cooper of Gochas (9th March, 1894) and Irlander of Rietfontein (27th July, 1894).[40] It follows from the above list of treaties compiled by H. Hesse that treaty making was intensive in the period of 1884–5 and then died out to be resumed in 1890 and subsequently in 1894–5. The first wave of treaty making in which the Consul-General and Büttner played a prominent role was followed by three separate periods, i.e. the term of office of Heinrich Goering, the Commissioner of the Reich from 1885 to 1890, the period of 1890 to 1894 in which C. von Francois was Commissioner and the Governorship of Leutwein from 1894 to 1904. Then followed the breakdown of the treaty regime of coexistence of the German Protector and the Captains which resulted in military action and the replacement of the South-West African Protectorates by German colonial rule.[41]

The period in which Goering represented the German Empire in South-West Africa was one of independent rule of the Captains which he, as Commissioner of the Reich, respected within the framework of the Protectorate. It has been emphasised that the two great Captains who were of primary importance in South-West African politics were Hendrik Witbooi of the Namaland[42] and Maharero, the Ruler of the Hereros.[43] As can be seen from Dr. Hesse's list of treaties, the former did not conclude a treaty of Protection with Germany before 1894. Curt von Francois who replaced Goering in 1890 and pursued a more active policy of Protection than his predecessor tried to convince Hendrik Witbooi to make peace with the Hereros and to accept German 'Schutz'. Witbooi answered that 'It would be unthinkable to ask an independent Sovereign who ruled his people, and had his own Government and administration of justice, to submit voluntarily to a foreign government … He did not wish to have a Protectorate'.[44]

[40] Hesse's list does not seem to be exhaustive. Hertslet *op. cit.* quotes an agreement concluded with the Bondelzwaarts in 1906. Most of the treaties listed by Hesse are treaties of protection (Schutzverträge). The treaties concluded with Ian Jonker (1885), Cornelius Zwaartbooi and Ian Uixamab (1885) are agreements of cession of territory to Lüderitz. After 1894 some treaties established not protection but sovereignty of the German Emperor (Oberhoheit) since co-existence tended to break down. To this category belong the treaties with Simon Cooper of the Gochas (1894), the Khauas (1894–5) and the Bondelzwaarts (1904). Among the treaties of protection some follow the pattern of the Bethany treaty such as the treaty with Jacob Isaak of Bersaba (1885) while other treaties deviated to some extent from the pattern. See: Hesse *op. cit.* (*Schutzverträge*) pp. 17, 46, 53, 60, 62, 101.

[41] Overseas territories in Africa were since 1890 the concern of the A.A., i.e. Auswärtiges Amt (Colonial Division). In 1907 the Reichskolonialamt (RKA) was established. See Hoffmann *op. cit* p. 12.

[42] As to details of Hendrik Witbooi's life, see his Diary: 'Das Tagebuch des Hottentoten Kapitäns Hendrik von Witbooi in Deutsch Südwestafrika aus den Jahren 1884–1894' in Bundesarchiv R 101 I/7, fol. 1.

[43] As to tribal organisation in South-West Afrca, see Hoffmann *op. cit.* p. 79.

[44] *Südwestafrika in der Deutschen Zeit* by Oskar Hintrager, 1956, p. 32–3. Francois acknowledged the principle of equality of power within the Protectorate. See: *Deutsch Südwestafrika* by C. von Francois, 1899, p. 19.

Among other Rulers who had refused treaties of Protection in the 1880s was William Christian of Bondelzwaart who wrote to Büttner on the 2nd July, 1885: 'As Paramount Chief of my land and my people I convoked after your departure my official Councillors and my people in the matter of your proposed treaty and I and my people consider it impossible to conclude a treaty with you acting in the name of H.M. the German Emperor'. Other Nama communities which refused to conclude treaties in the 1880s were the Veldschoendragers, the Franzmannschen and the Khauas. It is obvious that the Rulers enjoyed complete contractual freedom which was to last until the late 1890s.[45]

Though Maharero had concluded a treaty with Goering and Büttner in 1885, complications arose in the mutual relations between the contracting parties because of an earlier agreement concluded on the 9th September, 1885 by Paramount Chief Kamaherero with an Englishman R. Lewis. The 'Lewis' episode is an example of the initiative of a colonial trader who made an agreement with a Ruler by acting as a potential *negotiorum gestor* but his national State refused to back his initiative and to convert he agreement into a transaction in the meaning of international law. Kamaherero had given Lewis for a period of 20 years a mining concession which allowed him to make all the necessary installations, build roads and railways and even to recruit an armed force for his protection. But Kamaherero stipulated expressly that the concession was granted under the condition that Lewis or his successors will 'recognise at any time his authority (sovereignty) as Paramount Chief'. Moreover Lewis was under a duty to pay to Kamaherero twenty shillings and six pence for each ton of mineral ore mined by him with the exception of coal. It will be seen from this brief summary of the agreement that it was not governed by international law. Less than two months after its conclusion Maharero signed the treaty of Protection with Germany which was governed by international law. In order to explain the relationship between the Lewis agreement and the treaty, Goering's Chancellor in the Protectorate (Nels) wrote on the 24th April, 1886 to Bismarck to make it clear that the treaty had transferred to Germany the right to regulate 'public law' relations including mining rights.[46] When R. Lewis appeared at Maharero's court to vindicate his claims, Goering reported on the 8th November, 1888 to Bismarck that the Hereros had yielded to Lewis's demands and recognised his claims as based on the agreement of the 9th September, 1885.[47] To sort things out a meeting was arranged between the Hereros, Lewis and Goering.[48] Samuel Maharero then put the question to Goering whether a nation coming to foreign land can import its own law to which Goering replied that the problem was resolved by treaty which provided for shared jurisdiction.[49] Correspondence between Goering

[45] *Südwestafrika unter Deutscher Kolonialhehrschaft* by Horst Drechsler, 1966, p. 38. Drechsler gives an account of Büttner's negotiations with Wilhelm Christain, Chief of the Bondelzwaarts who refused to conclude a treaty with the German Commissioner (see Büttner's report to Bismark of the 28th June, 1885 in RKA No. 2152, B1.32).

[46] Bundesarchiv R. 101 I/3, p. 201.

[47] Bundesarchiv R. 101–5, p. 437.

[48] Bundesarchiv R. 101–5, p. 458 seq. (see Protocol of 30th October, 1888).

[49] Bundesarchiv R 101–5, p. 474.

and Lewis showed that the former insisted on the validity of the treaty of Protection conceded to Germany (letter of 5th November, 1888) while Lewis refused to recognise German authority in Herero country (letter of 6th November, 1888)[50] On the 15th November, 1888 Goering made it clear to Maharero that the treaty of Protection must be respected and cannot be abrogated unilaterally.[51] However, Goering faced with Maharero's hostile attitude had to withdraw to Walfish Bay.[52]

It is from this moment on that the German Commissioner in South-West Africa was assisted by a small military force[53] under the command of Captain C. von Francois who became Goering's successor as Commissioner.[54] The abortive adventure of Lewis who did not enjoy the support of the British Government came to an end in 1890 and Goering and Francois were able to report to Caprivi, Bismarck's successor, that Maharero had again recognised German Protection.[55] Here follows a characteristic turning point in the history of South-West Africa when Hendrik Witbooi made an appeal to Maharero to establish a common Herrero–Nama front against increasing German penetration.

Hendrik Witbooi, son of Moses Witbooi the Gibeon Chief, descended from what may be called the Orlam aristocracy in South-West Africa. He was educated by Christian missionaries and became the unifier of all Nama and Orlam tribes and head of the freedom fighters movement (Freiheitzkämpfer). Christian ideology played a great role in the development of this movement but it was slowed down by the traditional Nama–Herero controversies.[56] Maharero had sought German Protection in 1885 in the hope of cementing an anti-Nama alliance. Hendrik Witbooi refused to submit to German Protection and must have welcomed subsequent anti-German action taken by the Hereros in 1888 which led to the break-down of the regime of Protection. When Samuel Herero again recognised German Protection, Hendrik Witbooki sent a letter to Maharero dated Hornkranz 30th May, 1890 in which he offered him a forthright criticism of his policy. He wrote[57]: 'Damaraland belongs to the Herero nation only and constitutes an independent kingdom with its territory. On the other hand Namaqualand belongs to the Red nation only. The two are different kingdoms.... different peoples constitute different kingdoms and each Ruler governs his own people and territory. No other human being or sovereign may interfere with his rule or may tell him what to do or what not to do, for each King on this earth is the exclusive Representative of God and owes responsibility to God alone who is the King of all Kings and

[50] Bundesarchiv R 101–5, pp. 480, 482.

[51] Bundesarchiv R 101–5, p. 490, 553. The question arose whether Lewis had the support of the British Government. All evidence points to lack of such support. In a letter written to Bismark on the 23rd January, 1889 Hatzfeld observed that 'Lord Salisbury stated that the Foreign Office knew nothing about the Lewis affair'.

[52] Bundesarchiv R 101–5, p. 513.

[53] Nels, Goering's Deputy, reported to Chancellor Caprivi on the 3rd September, 1890 that 'the main functions of the Office of the Commissioner (Kommissariat) were negotiations with Chiefs, settlement of disputes between white people and between white people and natives, official correspondence, passing regulations, etc.'. See: Bundesarchiv R 101 I/5, p. 741.

[54] Bundesarchiv R 101 I/6, pp. 640–8.

[55] Bundesarchiv R 101 I/6, p. 720.

[56] Loth *op. cit.* (Die Christliche Mission in Südwestafrika), p. 105 (RKA, 2126, Bl.92–3)

[57] Bundesarchiv R 101 I/5, p. 723.

the Lord of all Lords ...' After this introduction of a theocratic nature Hendrik Witbooi addressed himself to Maharero personally and pointing to the latter's re-acceptance of the German Protectorate wrote: 'Dear Captain, You have now recognised another Government and you have delivered yourself into the hands of this Government in order to obtain from it Protection against all dangers, particularly against me in the war between us ... Dear Captain, do you really understand what you have done. Have you acted on the advice of others or did you rely on your own independent and enlightened judgment? ... You will deeply regret your decision to have transferred your land and its government to white people. In so far as the war between us is concerned, it is not as pernicious as you may think. We waged war on the basis of well defined premises and conditions and this war must result in peace as it is the will and decision of the Lord ... I am astonished that you have submitted to a foreign powerful Government. What is now your status as sovereign Captain? Are you still the Ruler of Damaraland and can you still call yourself such a Ruler after you accepted a Protector on whom you are dependent?'

In spite of Hendrik Witbooi's appeal no common Nama–Herero front was formed and Francois was able to attack in 1895 Witbooi's fortified position at Hornkrantz.[58] Francoi's successor, Governor Leutwein, concluded on the 15th September, 1894 a treaty with Witbooi which established German Protection. Paradoxically enough this treaty was similar to the treaties of the early 1880s. It is certainly a voluntary agreement and not one imposed on a defeated Ruler.[59] Article 6 stated as follows: 'Major Leutwein in reliance on his conviction that Captain Hendrik Witbooi would keep his word, leaves the latter in possession of his weapons and ammunition. The Captain guarantees that his men will not abuse the above concession. On the other hand Major Leutwein wishes to recuperate the German guns which came into possession of the Captain but he will not impose any duty on the Captain but at the latter's request he will simply expect him to do so. As soon as restitution is effected, the Captain will receive as compensation other guns or alternatively food whatever his wish'.[60] The German Emperor approved the treaty on the 15th November, 1895.

While Witbooi was able to resist German pressure for a few more years a number of other Chiefs had to submit in the 1890s to German treaties of Protection which were far from being voluntary on the part of the Chiefs. Dr. Hesse's list of treaties shows among them the treaties concluded with the Bondelzwaarts, the Khausas, Simon Cooper Chief of Franzfontein, Captain Vilander of Rietfontein, and other Chiefs. Some of these differ from the original treaties of Protection by establishing 'Oberherrschaft' (Sovereignty) instead of 'Schutzherrschaft' (Protection). They can be classified as 'Unterwerfungsverträge' (treaties of submission).[61] Nevertheless some of them contain the negative clause and accept mixed courts for mixed disputes which testified to their international legal character. The end of Leutwein's governorship witnessed the break-down of the traditional treaty policy heavily criticised by Hesse.[62] In 1904 General von Trotha replaced Leutwein to cope with the

[58] Francois had occupied Windhoek as *terra nullius* in spite of Herero protests.
[59] Drechsler *op. cit.* p. 89. [60] Drechsler *op. cit.* p. 89, (RKA 1487, B1.12-14).
[61] Drechsler *op. cit.* pp. 66–87. [62] Hesse *op. cit.* p. 40.

growing resistance of the Captains. The period of coexistence which had lasted for 20 years was at an end and as Drechsler puts it 'the last vestiges of international law thinking went overboard' as far as South-West Africa was concerned.[63]

Subsequent German colonial rule in South-West Africa lasted little more than 10 years, i.e. from the suppression of the rebellion by General Trotha to the outbreak of World War I. After the war South-West Africa became a Mandated Territory. The Mandatory Power (the Union of South Africa) did not submit South-West Africa to the Trusteeship regime after World War II. Under its present name of Namibia it remains the centre of an acute international controversy which was the concern of the International Court of Justice in several Advisory Opinions and in the case of *Ethiopia and Liberia* versus *the Union of South Africa*. (1966 *ICJ* Rep. 6.) The United Nations terminated the Mandate and appointed a Commissioner for Namibia to take over from the Union of South Africa but the latter refused to comply.[64]

Togo and the Cameroons

German treaty making on the West coast of Africa (Togo and the Cameroons) shows a similarity with treaties concluded in South-West Africa. First of all it was Nachtigal, the German envoy and principal treaty maker who took the initiative in both regions of West Africa, North and South. Moreover, the conditions of treaty making were to some extent the same though there were also significant differences. It is proposed to refer first to the similarities between treaties in both regions. Marten's *Nouveau Recueil* contains among the African treaties a treaty with Mlapa, King of Togo concluded by Nachtigal in Bogida on the 15th July, 1884,[65] i.e. three months earlier than the treaty with Captain Fredericks. Article 1 established a German Protectorate subject to the rights of third parties which were safeguarded. Article 2 contains the negative clause, particularly Mlapa undertook 'not to cede any part of his territory or rights of sovereignty to any foreign Power or person and not to conclude agreements with foreign powers without the consent of H.M. the German Emperor'. In article 4 the Emperor declared that he 'shall respect all previous commercial agreements concluded between King Mlapa and other parties….' Other articles refer to the rights of German traders in Togo, the operation of most-favoured-nation treatment, to customs duties and other matters. The similarity between this treaty and the South-West African treaties of Protection contained in the *Recueil* is obvious. There is only one important difference in that the Togo treaty does not include a jurisdictional (capitulatory) clause with the adoption of mixed courts. Copies of similar treaties relating to the Cameroons can be found in the documents of the Bundesarchiv in Koblenz. Thus the treaty of the 11th March, 1885 with King Amapatu of Mahin establishes a German Protectorate (article I). Article II contains the negative clause and in article III the German Emperor recognises

[63] Drechsler *op. cit.*, p. 178, 207.

[64] 'The Revocation of the Mandate for South–West Africa' by J. Dugard, 62, *American Journal of International Law* 78 (1968); *Völkerrecht* by I, Seidl-Hohenveldern, 1969 pp. 30, 142.

[65] *See also* Bundesarchiv R 101 I/1, fol. 1.

agreements concluded by the contracting King with other Powers. Article IV contains a transaction of private law, i.e. a purchase contract of land which was ceded to a German trader from Hamburg (G. L. Gaiser). The cession of land was effected jointly with the transfer of sovereign rights over the territory. Further articles refer to taxes, customs duties and other matters. There is no jurisdictional clause in the treaty. It is signed by Nachtigal, King Amapatu, three Chiefs and witnesses.[66]

While the Lüderitz Company monopolised trade and partly treaty making in South–West Africa, in Togo and the Cameroons it was the Woermann Company from Hamburg which acted side by side with German Consular Officers and created a *sui generis* pattern of treaties.[67] Reference may be made to the treaty with King Dido of the 11th July, 1884 in which the King conveyed to the German Company his 'rights of sovereignty, legislation and administration' under the following conditions: (1) Respect for the rights of any third parties; (2) Respect for friendship and commercial treaties made by the King previously with other foreign governments which are still in force and (3) the land now cultivated or occupied by the local people and the habitations and towns which are built there shall be the property of the present owners and their successors. Further stipulations uphold the right of the Ruler to 'Coumie' (the levying of taxes) and they guarantee respect for local law and traditions. In the negotiations the legal capacity of the King and the Chiefs was emphasised and acknowledged by the German Consul, Emil Schulze: 'Gegen deren Verfügungsfähigkeit kein Bedenken obwaltet'. The same type of treaty was concluded on the 12th July, 1884 with King Bell and King Aqua in the Cameroons and on the 15th July, 1884 with twelve Chiefs who were under King Bell's jurisdiction.[68] The contracting Company appears in all these treaties as *negotiorum gestor* accepting the transfer of sovereign rights to be ultimately vested in the German Emperor. The element of protection is not emphasised in these treaties and thus the negative clause restricting the Ruler's external sovereignty is not employed.

Yet in another type of treaty the Consul-General appears as principal contracting party on behalf of Germany without participation of the Woermann Company. Nachtigal concluded these treaties in January, 1885 with five Kings in the Cameroons, particularly King Kumbo of Vanda, King Ekume of Bunje, King Njeka of Benga, King Debundje of Botako and King Madiba of Bono. The Kings acted in their name and on behalf of their successors: 'Für sich und seine Nachkommen'. These are brief texts establishing what is called 'Schutzherrlichkeit', Emperor Wilhelm I extending his protection to the contracting kingdoms (article 1). It is therefore quite logical that article 2 attracted the negative clause, i.e. the undertaking of the protected Kings not to conclude treaties with other Powers without the consent of the German Emperor as Protector. There are no other stipulations, neither those respecting existing treaties nor jurisdictional clauses nor stipulations regulating matters of revenue

[66] Bundesarchiv Erw. No. 340/I, p. 26. Bundesarchiv R 101 I/1, fol. 1. As to further treaties of this type, *see* Büchner *op cit.* p. 58.

[67] Bundesarchiv R 1901 I/1, fol. 1.

[68] Büchner *op cit.* pp. 68–70.

or land tenure.[69] A similar treaty was concluded on the 25th February, 1885 by Nachtigal with the King of Pundu.[70]

It will be seen from the above that German treaty policy on the West coast of Africa oscillated between concluding treaties of Protection and treaties of cession with transfer of sovereign rights. In most cases a clear choice was made either for Protection or for cession which no doubt depended on the attitude of the Ruler and the existing balance of power. However, in a number of treaties a stipulation can be found establishing expressly Protection (Schutz) but providing at the same time for the possible conversion of the Protectorate into full sovereignty of the Protector. In this respect it would be interesting to examine the treaty concluded by H. Zoeller as Nachtigal's representative with King Mosassi and the Chiefs of Mopanza (7th January, 1885).[71] Apart from the principal contracting parties two German traders, Knut Knutson and Georg Walden who had acquired private property in the territory of Mopanza, were associated with the conclusion of the treaty. Article 1 stipulated the transfer by the King to the German Emperor of 'all and every right of sovereignty'. Similarly the two traders transferred in the treaty 'any right of sovereignty or similar to sovereignty' which they had acquired by buying the territory of Mopanza (*negotiorum gestio*). However, article 2 makes it clear that the full transfer of sovereignty was in a way suspended and that the treaty was primarily a treaty of Protection with all legal consequences flowing therefrom. These consequences are stated in the negative clause forbidding the Ruler to make treaties with foreign Powers. Article 3 reveals the ultimate policy of Germany in relation to the above Protectorate, for it states that 'In case that H.M. the German Emperor or his authorised Official should consider it convenient to replace the Protectorate established by the second Article of this treaty by the exercise of the right of sovereignty such as legislation, jurisdiction, etc., no further treaty or agreement shall be necessary for this purpose'. The treaty is a combination of cession and protection and it explains the difference between protection and sovereignty in article 4 which emphasises that 'for so long as the Protection is not replaced by the full exercise of rights of sovereignty', internal sovereignty remains temporarily in the Ruler.

Another transaction in the same category is the treaty with King Bwea and the Chiefs of 1885 concluded by H. Zoeller as Representative of the Consul-General.[72] This too is a treaty combining cession of sovereign rights with Protection (articles 1 and 2) which is convertible into full sovereignty on behalf of the German Protector

[69] Bundesarchiv R 101 I/1, fol. 1.

[70] Büchner *op cit.* p. 237. Büchner's *Aurora Colonialis* contains a number of further treaties which follow one or another pattern mentioned above, e.g. the treaty with King Leva of the 16th January, 1885, the treaty with Koto of the 17th January, 1885 and the treaty with the Chiefs of Mudeal and Hukunda (p. 237). In the negotiations with King Ikuelle of Muinko doubts arose as to whether the King was not a vassal of the King of Pundu (Souveränitätszweifel). *See* Büchner *op. cit.* p. 265. Rochus Schmidt refers to a case of limited legal capacity in the case of the Sultan of Tibati (Cameroons) who declared in treaty negotiations that he submitted to the Emir of Yola as his overlord. Schmidt *op. cit.* p. 122.

[71] *Als Jurnalist und Forscher in Deutschlands grosser Kolonialzeit* by H. Zoeller, 1930. Bundesarchiv R 101 I/1, fol. 1 p. 44.

[72] Zoeller *op cit.* pp. 198–9.

(article 3). But as long as conversion is not resorted to, the King and the Chiefs of Bwea could exercise rights of internal sovereignty (article 4). Article 4 also contains the negative clause. In view of the existence of this type of legal instrument in which the component elements of sovereignty and Protection and the difference between the two were clearly defined in the body of the text, it is not possible to share the opinion of those international lawyers who classify African Protectorates as phantom ('colonial') Protectorates.[73] The analysis of the texts of treaties of Protection testifies to the recognition by Germany (and other European Powers) of real sovereignty in African Rulers and to sovereignty sharing within the traditional institution of Protection as known to international law.[74] As long as a Protectorate was legally in force, the Ruler had internal sovereignty. He renounced at first only the exercise of rights of external sovereignty in the negative clause. Whenever he lost, at a later stage, his internal sovereignty, the Protectorate was formally terminated. Thus the African Protectorate was not a phantom institution but a legal reality. The fact that it was sometimes formally convertible into full sovereignty to be vested in the Protecting European Power was the expression of a historical process in the course of which the whole African Continent was bound to go through the filter of colonialism to re-emerge after an interval of 50 years or so as a network of democratic States.[75]

It has been underlined that the legal position in relation to South-West Africa had been clearly stated by Dr. H. Hesse in his classic work on Protectorates.[76] We shall see that in relation to East Africa, the writings of Dr. K. Peters, the principal treaty maker, will provide an authentic analysis. As far as Togo and the Camermons are concerned an authentic record of treaty making is contained in Dr. Max Büchner's '*Aurora Colonialis*'. Dr. Buchner became in 1885 Imperial Commissioner in the Cameroons and Nachtigal entrusted him with the task of concluding treaties for the enlargement of the German Protectorate.

Büchner offers an account of his treaty expeditions and after reviewing some of the treaties obtained he puts the crucial question:[77] What is the binding force of

[73] *See:* Stengel *op. cit.;* Sabersky *op. cit.;* and *Die Rechtsstellung des Kaisers in den Deutschen Schutzgebieten* by K. Munstermann, 1911; *Die Rechtslage der Deutschen Kolonien* by Karl von Rekowsky, 1939; *L'Afrique en droit international* by R. Yakemtchouk, 1971; and the article on 'Okkupation' in *Deutsches Kolonial-Lexikon* ed. by H. Schnee, II, 673.

[74] Alexandrowicz *op. cit.* p. 30 seq.

[75] The Congress of Berlin of 1884–5 revealed the reality of Protectorates in Africa in article 35 of the Final Act in which protection was excluded from the requirement of effective occupation and not identified with the assumption of sovereignty. It was only behind the scene of the Congress that the European Powers gave each other *carte blanche* to absorb African territory but this was an informal inter-European arrangement which was legally meaningless *vis-à-vis* African Rulers. As to present day developments in the network of African States, see: 'Major policy shifts in the Organisation of African Unity, 1963–1973' by Dr. Z. Cervenka (in *Foreign Relations of African States* ed. by K. Ingham, 1973–4).

[76] Hesse *op. cit.* (Landfrage) pp. 1, 85, 88, 93, 96, 97, 98, 106; Hesse *op. cit.* (*Schutzverträge*) p. 5 seq.

[77] Buchner refers to his negotiations with Bala Demba, Ruler at the mouth of the river Dubreka; the Ruler of Little Popo; Mlapa, King of Togo (see above); the Chiefs of Lome who signed a treaty on the lines of the Togo treaty of 1884; Kings Dido, Bell and Aqua; the Chiefs of Backundu who signed a treaty in 1884; King Leva (see above); King Ikuelle of Muinko and others. Büchner *op. cit.* pp. 32, 42, 55, 56, 68, 70, 147, 237, 263, 332.

the treaties concluded in Africa and what is their validity in international law? In an attempt to answer this question he refers to the protracted controversies in legal literature and the school of thought according to which African States were not really States and agreements made by them were therefore outside the pale of international law. Büchner does not engage in a critical examination of this view but simply asks the further question: What is the alternative solution if acquisition of territory was not by title of cession, i.e. by a valid bilateral transaction between Germany and the Rulers? The answer he gives is that 'Even the most courageous Professor would prefer to make treaties than to resort to war in order to acquire territory' (unilaterally by conquest). He adds that 'all over the world there was reliance on treaties since the employment of brutal force proved to be a failure. Here in Africa treaties are not underestimated. The Africans have respect for the written text. Whenever they express their consent in writing, they believe they have resorted to the exercise of a sacred power'. Then follows this remarkable statement by Büchner: 'Die Neger stehen doch viel hoher als von den Weissen meistens geglaubt wird, und die Weissen selten so höch, wie sie gerne ven sich meinen', a view in which more foresight was revealed as to the destiny of Africa and as to its still unknown history then many international lawyers were prepared to admit.[78]

Before concluding the chapter on treaty making in Togo and the Cameroons, a few observations may be offered on the extension of the German Protectorate to wider inland areas. This was achieved by a number of treaty expeditions undertaken by L. Wolf, Gruner, Carnap, Schwartz, Prittwitz, Kund, Tappenbeck, Morgan, Zintgraff and others (1885–1897).[79] In certain regions there was resistance of the people to treaties negotiated by their Rulers such as in Douala (later French Cameroons).[80] The presence of German warships under Admiral Knorr on the West coast of Africa strengthened the position of Chiefs *vis-à-vis* the people and facilitated treaty making. One of the difficulties was that the land was considered to be the collective property of the tribes which feared European penetration.[81]

Another difficulty in the progress of German action in Togo and the Cameroons was the competition with the English and the French. The English had established a 'Court of Equity' in the Cameroons which settled disputes between Europeans and local people and between Kings and Chiefs.[82] In spite of the establishment of this type of jurisdiction, no British Protectorate was proclaimed. On the other hand the Woermann Company opened trade and the way to further official German action. Consul Hewitt acting on behalf of the British Government came too late to counteract effectively.[83] The German *fait accompli* was definitely established in 1885 and

[78] Büchner *op. cit.* p. 332. [79] Cornevin *op. cit.* p. 52.

[80] Bala Demba refused Nachtigal's proposal for German protection. Büchner *op. cit.* pp. 30–2.

[81] See: 'Kamerun unter Deutscher Kolonialherrschaft,' Collection of Studies ed. by H. Stoeker, 1966, pp. 66–7; 'Die Deutsche Annexion' by H. P. Jaeck, in the above collection, p. 64 (reference to RKA 4202, 4204, 4447).

[82] Schmidt *op. cit.* II, pp. 53, 60, 177.

[83] Büchner came into conflict with British agents trying to conclude treaties with Chiefs. An agreement was signed by the Chiefs of Momanga with the British agents of the Victoria colony (25th January, 1885), Büchner *op. cit*, p. 280. Togoland belonged partly to the Ewes, a community greatly admired for their agricultural skill. See: *Togo—eine Musterkolonie?* by M. Nussbaum, 1962, p. 52. The

German treaty making had legalised the position. In comparison with South-West Africa the period of co-existence foreseen by the treaties was much shorter and absorption came much earlier. As stated above, this was effected by treaties of cession and by short-lived treaties of Protection which were frequently convertible into instruments of absorption.

East Africa

As stated earlier, the pioneering German treaty maker in East Africa was Dr. Karl Peters. There is no doubt that he was highly aware of the importance of obtaining titles to territory in order to lay the foundations of a German colonial realm in this part of the world. It has already been emphasised that his treaty policy was different from that applied in West Africa (South and North) by Nachtigal and his team. While the latter was the envoy (Consul-General) of the Reich in West Africa and while the participation of German firms such as Lüderitz and Woermann was of an auxiliary nature only, Peters did not enter the African scene as an official of the Imperial Government. He took action in the name of a private corporation, the 'Gesellschaft fur Deutsche Kolonisation' (later 'Deutsch-Ostafrikanische Gesellschaft'—D.O.A.G.)'[84] which was constantly in search of funds and which acting as *negotiorum gestor* in the conclusion of treaties had to find an appropriate legal formula and instrument to validate *ex post* the acquisition of title to sovereignty for the German Reich. The means of achieving such validation of legal titles in international law was the 'Schutzbrief',[85] i.e. the Emperor's, decree by which the Reich took over the sovereign rights which had been provisionally vested by the Rulers in Peters as the Principal Representative of the colonial corporation. The history of the 'Schutzbrief', granted or refused, revealed the limited sympathy which Bismarck could generate in his mind for the ambitious plans of Peters with his dream of a new African Empire. At first Peters managed to obtain the approval of his Government for the acquisition of territories on the 'Mrima' (the mainland of East Africa) but as he penetrated further, mainly into the sphere of interest of the Sultan of Zanzibar on the 'Mrima,' he came into conflict with the British Government which stood behind the Sultan as his Protector.[86] The realisation of

author refers to the treaty of protection with Samme, Ruler of Gamme (p. 22). In Togoland the Chiefs of Little Popo had issued a declaration (1882) complaining about the danger of English annexation of territory and asking for German 'Schutz'. The declaration was signed by the King of Little Popo and his subordinate Chiefs. There was also French penetration in the region but Germany kept Togoland including Little Popo and Porto Seguro (1885).

[84] D.O.A.G. was founded on the 28th March, 1884.

[85] A 'Schutzbrief' had been issued by the Emperor to the German New Guinea Company. Lindley *op. cit.* p. 103. The question may be asked whether the 'Schutzbrief' was the approximate equivalent of a Royal Charter granted to a colonial company. Even if there was a similarity between the two, the difference was that the German Company acted as *negotiorum gestor* while the colonial companies established by Royal Charter (such as the East India Companies) acted usually on delegated sovereign powers. Lindley *op. cit.* p. 91.

[86] In distinction to the Mrima, the Islands of Zanzibar and Pemba were under the undisputed sovereignty of the Sultan.

his plans was bound to depend on the outcome of the wider issue of Anglo-German relations.

One of the first transactions concluded by Peters was the treaty with Sultan Muinin Sagara, Lord of Usagara (4th December, 1884).[87] The Ruler was defined in the treaty as 'sole and absolute Lord of Usagara' ('alleiniger und absoluter Herr'), a definition found in most treaties to assert the African transferor's legal capacity to convey a valid title. The Ruler submitted in the treaty to the protection of the German contracting party, the 'Gesellschaft für Deutsche Kolonisation' as represented by Peters. The treaty contains the cession of private and public rights over Usagara to the German transferee. The first were given for the purpose of private law exploitation of Usagara ('privatrechtliche Ausnützung von ganz Usagara'). The second cession was one of rights which according to German 'Staatsrecht' (public law) constitute sovereignty ('Oberhoheit'). The latter extended *inter alia* to rights of mining, exploitation of rivers and forests, the right to impose customs duties and taxes, to run a German judicial and territorial administration and to maintain troops. Peters guaranteed to the Sultan his private property and promised in the name of the contracting corporation to protect his country against Zanzibar slave hunters. The treaty was concluded in legally binding form and in the presence of translators and witnesses. Similar treaties were concluded with the Rulers of Nguru, Useguha, Ukami and others (November and December 1884).[88]

Attention should be drawn to the inclusion in some of the above and later treaties of the clause relating to 'Blutbruderschaft', i.e. the blood pact or blood bond. Thus it is stated in the Nguru treaty of the 23rd November 1884 that Peters concluded with contracting Ruler (Mafungu, Sultan of Nguru) a customary blood pact.[89] It is obvious that he must have submitted to local law and the question arises what is the meaning of this peculiar African tradition.[90] Historical and ethnological investigations show that Chiefs would at the termination of hostilities or at the conclusion of an agreement make an incision in their skin and press these incisions against each other thus becoming 'blood brothers'.[91] The ritual was often performed to mark the conclusion of an alliance or the resumption of trade. H. Tegnaeus emphasises that

[87] *Das Deutsch-Ostafrikanische Schutzgebiet* by Dr. K. Peters, 1895, pp, 420–44; *Lebenserinnerungen* by the same author, 1918, pp. 77–165. Peters entered East African territory from Zanzibar on the 12th November, 1884 and made 12 treaties with 10 Chiefs. Müller *op. cit.* p. 122 seq.

[88] Among the treaties concluded by Peters on the same pattern in 1884, was the treaty with the Sultan of Kimala, dated Mangubube in Usagara, the 27th November, 1884. It was stipulated in this treaty that the transfer of sovereign rights to the contracting German company should not prejudice the rights of Sultan Muinin Sagara. Peters concluded at the same time in the same region (Usagara) a treaty with Sultan Kamuende observing the legal treaty forms prevailing in Usagara, and a treaty with the Sultan of Msovero (29th November, 1884). The latter acted in his name and for his own people: 'Für sein ganzes Volk'. Again, a cession of rights was effected subject to the sovereign rights of Muinin Sagara. The contracting Sultan declared that he was independent of the Sultan of Zanzibar. See also treaties with the Sultan of Mongungo of North Msovero, with Lady Mbumi of the Sultanate of Mkondogna of the 2nd December 1884, and with Masanjo, the eldest son of Muinin Sagara and Lord of Sima of the 6th December, 1884. Peters *op. cit.*

[89] Peters concluded with the Sultan of Nguru a second treaty (24th November, 1884) in which the latter expressed the desire to establish closer relations with his blood brother (Peters) recognising him as 'Ausschlieslicher Oberherr'. See: *Das Deutsch—Ostafrikanische Schtzgebiet* by K. Peters, 1895, p. 422.

[90] It might also be accompanied by the tradition of drinking 'Blutbruderschaft'.

[91] See: *Blood-Brothers* by H. Tegnaeus, 1952, p. 54 seq.

the exchange of blood had only magical or symbolic significance for kinship within the tribe and was not based on blood relationship but on social connection.[92] Be that as it may, the interpretation by various writers does not point to the real significance of the ceremony which (in my view) is the assertion of the principle '*Pacta sunt servanda*'. What it meant was the guarantee of keeping the promise given in the agreement to renounce hostilities, to keep the peace, or to carry out other duties. It is important to emphasise that this principle appears in various parts of the world as guarantee for carrying out contractual obligations. This is so, *mutatis mutandis* in European, Islamic, Hindu and African law.[93] It is not maintained here that the existence of such a corroborating ritual points to the development of a systematic regional international law in Africa as it appeared in Europe but it amounts to the formulation of a fundamental principle within a code of inter-sovereign conduct. It allows us to assume that African Rulers observed customary rules in their mutual relations.[94] A more sophisticated code of conduct of this type existed in Ancient India. Kautilya, in the fourth century B.C. collected the rules of inter-sovereign conduct in his classic 'Arthasastra' written in Sanskrit.[95]

After concluding the first 12 treaties Peters sought in Berlin to obtain the 'Schutzbrief' of the Emperor in order to invest the transfer of sovereignty with real meaning in international law. The Emperor signed the relevant decree on the 27th February, 1884[96] and he referred in it expressly to the treaties by which sovereignty over the territories had been transferred by the Rulers to the German colonial Corporation acting as *negotiorum gestor*. This territory was now submitted to Imperial sovereignty and protection. The Emperor then entrusted the Corporation with exercise of all rights resulting from the treaties: 'Ausübung aller aus den Uns vorgelegten Verträgen fliessenden Rechte'.

Peters states that the treaties extended to an area equal to that of South Germany. It covered territories on the mainland of Africa (Mrima) opposite the island of Zanzibar and provoked a controversy with the Sultan of Zanzibar[97] who protested to the Imperial Government about German interference in an area over which he claimed suzerainty. To strengthen the German position, Peters opened negotiations with the Plenipotentiary of the Sultan on the mainland (Salim bin Hamid) who issued on the 26th November, 1884 a declaration (Mvomero declaration)[98] in which he stated that the Sultan had neither sovereignty nor Protector's rights on the mainland of East Africa and that the contracting Rulers had been absolutely independent without any restriction to their legal capacity. Peters argued in support that the Sultan of Zanzibar regularly imposed on goods coming from the interior of East Africa customs duties which proved that he treated the Rulers of the mainland as independent sovereigns.[99] Ultimately the Sultan was convinced to recognise

[92] Tegnaeus *op. cit.* p. 159.

[93] 'Le Principe Pacta Servanda' by M. Sibert, in *Indian Year Book of International Affairs*, 1956.

[94] The Chief was the Representative of the community in external affairs. He decided about war and peace. See: *Ostafrika* by B. Ankermann, 1929, p. 18.

[95] *British Yearbook of International Law* 1965, p. 301 (p. 35 above).

[96] Peters *op. cit.* p. 74 (Lebenserinnerungen) [97] Peters *op. cit.* p. 80.

[98] Hertslet *op. cit.* II, 681–2. [99] Müller *op. cit.* p. 134 seq.

German Protection and Overlordship over Usagara, Nguru, Useguha, Ukami and the territory of Witu[100] which was now exercised by D.O.A.G.

The history of treaty making in East Africa in its second phase shows the conclusion of a series of treaties by members of Dr. Peters's team. Here belong in the first instance the treaties made by Dr. Karl Jühlke during 1885. One of the earliest was the treaty with the Sultan of Quafungo concluded on the 16th May, 1885 for an unlimited period of time: 'Für ewige Zeiten'. The Ruler ceded to the D.O.A.G. represented by Jühlke all his sovereign rights, sovereignty being understood according to European ideas: 'Europäische Vorstellungen'. Para 3 of the treaty explained the consequence of the cession which gave the corporation the right of legislation and administration, particularly the right of exploitation of the land, rivers and mines and the right to bring settlers to the land. The Sultan and his people remained only in possession of the land occupied by them and cultivated for their own needs. As to the form of the treaty, African tradition was observed and it was signed in the presence of witnesses and translators. There was no reference to the establishment of a Protectorate. Similar treaties were concluded by Jühlke with Sultan Muin Hadji Abaho on the 17th May, 1885; with Sultan Suakuhu-bin Kimvero on the 25th May, 1885; with Sultan Madafa on the 8th June, 1885; with Sultan Mandara on the 19th June, 1885; with Sultan Galassoni on the 21st June, 1885; with Sultan Hamabomo on the 3rd July, 1885; and with Sultan Muango on the 30th July 1885. Some of the treaties emphasise the sovereign rights of the Rulers and their legal capacity to cede territory and in the last four treaties the contracting German corporation promised the Rulers protection against their enemies. However, no negative clause is included in the treaties and thus the use of the term Protection (Schutz) cannot mean here the establishment of a Protectorate in the strict sense of the word. These were treaties of cession subject to preservation of certain rights on behalf of the Rulers and their people.[101]

Among further treaties accompanying the extension of German rule in East Africa was the treaty concluded on the 6th September, 1885 by Hörnecke with the Grand Sultan of the Somali tribes. This treaty is similar to the Jühlke treaties.[102] Treaties were also concluded by Anderten with Makkaro, Lord of Wanjika (1886) and by Lucas with Mbaruk of the dynasty of Masaru to which belonged the sultanates of Mombasa and Melinde.[103]

It would be beyond the scope of this enquiry to cover in its entirety the vast treaty material relating to East Africa.[104] No such attempt was made in relation to South-West Africa, Togo and the Cameroons. The discussion was limited to an examination of pattern treaties. It is however important to discuss the treaties made by Peters with the Sultan of Zanzibar and the Ruler of Uganda and to refer

[100] The treaty of protection with the Sultan of Witu was concluded in 1885 by the Brothers Denhardt. *Das Deutsche Kolonialreich* by G. Wegener, 1937, p. 47.

[101] Peters: *Gesammelte Schriften* 1943 Vol. II, *Lebenserinnerungen* p. 126.

[102] Peters *op. cit.* p. 125. [103] Peters *op. cit.* p. 127.

[104] Müller *op. cit.* p. 228 contains the following list of acquisitions of D.O.A.G.:

(1) Usagara expedition I, Peters, Jühlke, Pfeil, Otto.
(2) Usagara expedition II, Schmidt and Moris (development of Sima station)
(3) Tana expedition, Hoernecke, March 1885, failed.

briefly to the last phase of treaty making in East Africa which marked the end of Dr. Peters's influence on German policy and the consolidation of the position by a final demarcation of German and British interests. Reference has been made earlier to the protest of the Sultan of Zanzibar against German acquisition on the Mrima which the Sultan considered as being under his suzerainty (27th April, 1884). Bismarck stated in reply to the protest that the acquisitions were made by treaties with independent Princes. The emphasis on their independence points to the acceptance of their status in international law, particularly as bearers of sovereign rights which they had the capacity to cede to other legal entities in international law in Bismarck's words: 'Die Unabhangigkeit dieser Fürsten kann keinem Zweifel unterliegen' and he states further that the Sultan of Zanzibar cannot show any legal title to the territories in question. On the other hand the sovereign rights acquired from the Rulers by the German corporation are now exercised under the control of the German Imperial Government. Sir John Kirk who guided Zanzibar policy, made on the 14th August, 1884 a declaration to the effect that the Sultan now recognised the German Protectorates over Usgara, Nguru, Useguha, Ukami and the territory of Witu.

Three years later the Sultan was ready to make further concessions and he signed an agreement with Peters on the 30th July, 1887.[105] However this was not a transfer of sovereign rights but only a cession of administrative rights on the coast from Umbo to the Rovuma. The D.O.A.G. as transferee was to exercise these rights

(4) Nyanza expedition, Major Déviviére, April 1885, failed.
(5) Kilimandjaro expedition, Jühlke, May 1885, acquisition of Usambara, Bondei, Pare, Arusha, Djoga, Kahe and Ugeno.
(6) Chutu expedition, Pfeil, June, 1885, acquisition of Chutu.
(7) Usaramo expedition, Schmidt, September 1885, acquisition of Usaramo.
(8) Nyanza expedition II, Pfeil, November, 1885, acquisition of Ubena, Maconde, Mohenje, Gindo.
(9) Somali expedition I, Hoernecke etc., September 1885, acquisition of Somali coast from Bender Gasen Warscheich.
(10) Comores expedition I, Schulz, October 1885, failed
(11) Kilimandjaro expedition II, Hoernecke etc., December 1885, Foundation of Korogwe, station in Usambara.
(12) Sabaki expedition, Aderten, January, 1886, acquisition of Girijama, Nuikaland Gallaland and Ukamba
(13) Gasi expedition, Lucas etc., January 1886, treaty of Gasi.
(14) Somali expedition II, Pfeil, January 1886, foundation of Halula station.
(15) Comores expedition II, Schmidt, May 1886, ratification of private purchase agreement.
(16) Somali expedition III, Jühlke, August 1886, acquisition of estuary of Wabushi.
(17) Expeditions in the Protectorates, Schmidt, autumn 1886.
(18) Somali expedition IV, Pfeil.

Müller *op. cit.* maintains that there was rarely effective occupation. The DOAG had at first a 'Phantombesitz' until the government stepped in. Müller's monograph contains a number of documents from the German Zentralarchiv in Potsdam. No. 31 is a defence by Clemens Denhardt of the rights of the Sultan of Swaheleland, 9th November, 1886.

[105] Peters *op. cit* p. 82 describes his negotiations with the Sultan of Zanzibar. But he states that the German Government was not pleased with his action because of the 'Kolonialehe' with England. It led ultimately to the resignation of Peters from D.O.A.G.

in the name of the Sultan and under his flag and sovereignty (article I). In article 2 the Sultan authorised the D.O.A.G. to nominate in his name Commissioners and Administrators for the territory in question. The D.O.A.G. was also authorised to conclude agreements in the Sultan's name and to appoint Judges with the exception of Khadis whom the Sultan would appoint himself. Articles 3 and 4 gave the D.O.A.G. the right to engage in trade, acquire property and levy customs duties. The Sultan stipulated that all these rights must be exercised by the D.O.A.G. in accordance with treaties which he had concluded with other States. Articles 5 to 7 related to the foundation of German forts and mining rights and to the right of note issue. All these rights were according to article 8 granted for 50 years.[106]

Dr. Peters was in Berlin in 1887–88. His treaty with Zanzibar was accepted by the German Government but he had by now lost the confidence of the Government.[107] The frontiers of German East Africa were now less determined by the intensity of the drive for acquiring titles to territory and the corresponding resistance to such drives than by the need of sorting out problems which arose from the inter-European scramble for titles whether they were followed by effective occupation or not.[108] However a last attempt made by Peters to obtain new treaties and to enlarge the frontiers of German control in East Africa deserves attention. The occasion was the Emin Pasha episode in which Peters played a significant role. Emin Pasha, one of General Gordon's recruits[109] had been the Governor of the Equatorial Province under the control of the Anglo–Egyptian Government. When the latter abandoned the Province in 1886, Emin Pasha found himself in a precarious position in a territory which became *terra nullius* according to international law. At that point Peters went to East Africa at the head of a rescue expedition with the intention of saving Emin Pasha and acquiring the Province for Germany. On the way he made a treaty with the Galla Sultanate (16th October, 1888) in which the Gallas recognised Peters as their Overlord: 'Die Gallay erkennen Dr. Peters unbedingt als ihren Herrn an….'[110]. The treaty also stipulated on behalf of Peters land and trade concessions. On the 8th January, 1890 Peters obtained a treaty from the Rulers (Elders) of Waquafi who recognised him as their Overlord and asked him to extend German Protection to Baringoland. In this treaty Peters declared his readiness to associate Emin Pasha with the transaction. On the 1st February, 1890 followed the treaty with Sultan Sakwa which made Peters Overlord of Kawirondo. The reality of those and other arrangements depended in the last instance on the co-operation of Emin Pasha who at first accepted Peters's plan in Mpuapua (20th June, 1891) and issued an act declaring the Equatorial Province as being under his control and open to the German Emperor's protection. Thus a new *negotiorum gestio* was initiated and Peters planned to establish a German Protectorate with Emin Pasha's Province as its nucleus and stretching to the East to the frontiers of Witu on the Indian Ocean.

[106] Article 9 refers to customs duties and rights in territorial waters and article 10 to the guarantee of dividends.

[107] Peters *op. cit.* pp. 163–231.

[108] Oliver and Fage *op. cit.* p. 189 seq.

[109] *History of East Africa* by K. Ingham, 1963, p. 120

[110] Peters *op. cit.* pp. 255–6.

Uganda and Lake Victoria would have been included in this realm.[111] However when Emin Pasha left his Province with Stanley, Dr. Peter's plans came to an end.

During the Emin Pasha expedition, Peters concluded a treaty with King Mwanga (Kabaka of Buganda) on the 28th February, 1890.[112] In this treaty the King accepted the provisions of the Act of the Berlin Congress of 1885 in so far as they were relevant to Uganda and its tributaries. He opened all his lands to German subjects and other Europeans, a provision transcending the scope of the treaty giving rights to subjects of other European Powers which were not parties to the treaty. He further guaranteed to German subjects and other Europeans full freedom of commerce and movement, and freedom to settle in Buganda and in the tributary lands. This was followed by a reciprocal stipulation giving subjects of the King the same freedoms in the territories under the sovereignty of the German Emperor: 'Koenig Mwanga tritt in Freundschaft mit Sr. Majestät dem Kaiser von Deutschland und erhält Freiheit des Handels. Freizügigkeit und freies Ansiedlungsrecht für seine Untertanen in allen Gebieten Sr. Majestät des Kaisers von Deutschland'. Peters stated that this treaty could have been later converted into a Protectorate. As stated above, the German Government did not follow up Dr. Peters's ambitious plans and in the subsequent agreement with Great Britain Germany kept the original acquisitions but without extension of German rule to Zanzibar, Witu or Uganda.[113]

The two treaties (with Zanzibar and Uganda) invite certain observations. They are remarkable for their conclusion on a basis of perfect reciprocity. All the other treaties, whether obtained in South-West Africa, Togo, the Cameroons or East Africa, were treaties of cession of sovereign rights or treaties of Protection. In the first case they established a State within the State, i.e. the German contracting entity acquired territory within an African country in which it exercised legislative, administrative and judicial powers. In many cases the Ruler was left only with personal jurisdiction over his people and with rights for himself and his people in the residue of the land not taken over by the transferee. Moreover, the German Government exercised rights of external sovereignty for the Ruler. In the case of a Protectorate the Ruler continued to exercise rights of internal sovereignty and sometimes a measure of rights of external sovereignty which in principle was vested in the Protector. It has been shown that in South-West Africa a protracted period of co-existence of German and indigenous rule lasted until the turn of the century when the process of absorption of African countries set in. This period of co-existence was much shorter in Togo and the Cameroons. In East Africa Peter's treaty policy enabled the D.O.A.G. to acquire from Rulers a plenitude of rights subject to the issue of the 'Schutzbrief'. The latter vested all rights in the Government which delegated (re-transferred) the exercise of powers to the D.O.A.G. Thus whenever occupation of land by German settlers became effective, the process of absorption was much more imminent than on the West coast of Africa. The first wave of treaty

[111] Peters *op. cit.* p. 268. [112] Peters *op. cit.* p. 259.

[113] Peters *op. cit.* p. 260 seq. See also 'Foreign Relations of the Kingdoms of Western Uganda' by K. Ingham, in *Foreign Relations of African States., op.cit.*

making resulted in recognition of the German *fait accompli* by other European Powers and in the second phase it was extended to the wider areas of the Mrima. The further attempt to get hold of the more powerful East African Kingdoms such as Zanzibar or Uganda proved a failure. Italy experienced such a failure in Ethiopia when it tried to make its Protectorate over Emperor Menelik II effective and when its invasion army lost the battle of Adowa in 1896. German progress was arrested by the inherent obstacles which Dr. Peters and his team had to face. He was not backed by his Government which avoided any open confrontation with Great Britain. Even if he had secured its support, his methods of treaty making and his strategy of dealing with African Rulers would have failed him in the confrontation with the more powerful State entities such as Zanzibar or Uganda.

The Zanzibar dynasty had transferred its headquarters from Oman in the Persian Gulf to East Africa in 1840 where it established a State of considerable political and economic significance'.[114] The treaties concluded by the Sultan with Germany and other European Powers testify to the legal status which he and his country enjoyed in the Family and Law of Nations in the 19th century. He acceded to the Act of the Congress of Berlin of 1885 which included him in one of the most important multilateral transactions of international law. The treaty of 1887 which Peters obtained from the Sultan, gave the D.O.A.G. rights in certain mainland regions (outside the islands of Zanzibar and Pembe) but these rights had to be exercised in the name of the Sultan and under his sovereignty. Thus the D.O.A.G. had no rights of Protection or rights based on cession of sovereignty but it found itself in the restricted position of administrator under the Sultan's overlordship, whatever the degree of control which he could actually exercise. The same observations must apply to the case of Uganda. The Kabaka made no concessions in the nature of protection or cession of sovereignty to Germany. All that the treaty with Peters stipulated was reciprocal freedom of trading in each other's territories. Moreover, the Kabaka declared his adherence to the stipulations of the Berlin Act. International lawyers of the 19th century, faced with this type of treaty, could not have had any doubt about the status of the African Ruler concerned. Oliver and Fage in their History of Africa[115] make certain comparative observations which may be of interest to international lawyers. Discussing the status of Emperor Menelik of Ethiopia[116] they say that it was comparable [117] with that of the Ruler of Buganda, the Kabarega of Bunyoro or the Msiri of Katanga. If so, an international level or category can be defined which must include those Rulers who satisfy certain criteria of legal status indicated by the status of the Rulers of Ethiopia, Zanzibar, Uganda (Buganda) and others. Were these criteria satisfied by the Queen of Madagascar, the Asantahene of the Ashantis, or by Shaka Zulu? There is little doubt that the Rulers of Morocco and Tunisia satisfied these requirements but the question arises where does the dividing line between status in international law and lack of status run?[118] International lawyers such as

[114] Ingham *op. cit.* pp. 26, 72.
[115] Oliver and Fage *op. cit.* p. 179.
[116] The Emperor grew out of Menelik of Shoa; Oliver and Fage *op. cit.* p. 179.
[117] i.e. his status as a scrambler for Africa, Oliver and Fage *op. cit.* p. 179.
[118] The test cannot be participation in the scramble for territory.

Hesse or Lindley relied on the 'Aktivlegitimation' of the African Ruler who as head of the political organisation must have been presumed to be bearer of sovereign rights. If this argument is rejected, the treaties concluded by Germany (and other European Powers) with the Rulers are driven out of the category of valid bilateral instruments and the partition of Africa is reduced to a unilateral operation dividing a whole continent in disregard of history, civilisation and political organisation which cannot be denied to the African people in the past.

III. The Partition of Africa and International Law

The progress of treaty making which allowed the Reich to take a share in the partition of Africa has been discussed in three parts, i.e. in relation to South-West Africa, Togo and the Cameroons and East Africa. Some of the similarities and differences between German treaty policy in the three regions have been examined on the basis of the textual analysis of treaties and the circumstances surrounding their conclusion. This analysis threw light on the status of African Rulers in 19th century international law, on the legal character of the treaties as bilateral instruments and on their role in the partition of Africa. Reference was made to the views of writers who carried out a detailed independent study of African treaties such as Hese, Büchner[119] and Lindley. Their writings enabled us to see the scramble for African territory in its proper perspective: As a scramble for *titles* to territory. The acquisition of titles in South-West Africa initiated a period of co-existence between the Rulers and the German Protector which lasted about 20 years until co-existence failed for reasons outside the treaty regime and until the process of absorption set in. The take-over came earlier in Togo and the Cameroons accompanied by a special type of treaty which carried the seeds of absorption and combined Protection and assumption of sovereignty, the former being often automatically convertible into the latter. East Africa was the scene of a different development mainly conditioned by the individuality of the principal treaty maker (Dr. Peters) which was different from that of G. Nachtigal, the German Envoy in West Africa, South and North. Dr. Peters's impetus in acting as *negotiorum gestor* and trying to validate his treaties of submission by the Emperor's Schutzbrief was gradually slowed down by counteraction of the Government of the Reich and by Bismarck's caution and reluctance to provoke an open British–German confrontation.

A summary examination of some of the characteristic features of the provisions of treaties under discussion shows that in most of them the legal capacity of the Ruler was either emphasised in a positive or a negative way. The ruler was described as 'Uneingeschrankter Herrscher' or as 'Alleiniger Souveran'. On the other hand his full capacity to act in international law was sometimes defined by stating in a negative way his non-dependence on a possible or alleged overlord,

[119] Büchner in his *Aurora Colonialis* p. 332 states that 'negroes were on a higher level than we think they are, and the white people are rarely on a level as high as they think they are' (transl. of text quoted above).

e.g. the independence of the 'Mrima' Rulers from the Sultan of Zanzibar.[120] The theoretical speculation of so many international lawyers as to whether African Rulers were real sovereigns or whether the communities over which they ruled were State entities contributed little to the understanding of the political scene or the partition of Africa. It is more important to ascertain what the Rulers had to offer as entry ticket into the Family of Nations. The Rulers were in fact bearers of sovereign rights which were capable of being transferred to entities capable of acquiring them.[121] In this respect Hesse gives a definite answer attributing to African Rulers 'Aktivlegitimation' and to the authorised German colonial corporations 'Passivlegitimation'. Büchner hails treaties as an alternative to conquest and Adam writes that 'One must recognise the personality in international law (of African Rulers) to the extent to which they are capable through international treaties to transfer sovereignty over their territory'.[122]

International lawyers were confronted with the heterogeneity of the political map of Africa on which Chiefs figured as village Chiefs, provincial Chiefs, paramount Chiefs, Sultans or Kings of superior status. But wherever political organisation existed, primitive or advanced, the territory in question could not be considered '*terra nullius*'. It could not be acquired by unilateral occupation but only by bilateral transaction.[123] African history, like the history of other continents, is one of alternating unification of smaller entities into larger viable units or one of disintegration of Empires. Hundreds of village or provincial Chiefs were doomed to be absorbed by more powerful unifiers, whether African or colonial. The entry of Africa into the Family of Nations required the re-groupment of the continent into viable entities. The present day network of African Republics with their policy of '*quieta non movere*' ('*uti possidetis*')[124] testifies to the historical necessity of transforming the continent of Africa and the preparation of its commodities for independent existence in a modern world. Whether the actual partition of Africa was the happiest solution is another question. The solution would have been a happier one if the principle of the sacred trust of civilisation could have been fully respected and followed in its moral as well as its legal meaning. In fact the Berlin Conference of 1884–85 convened by Bismarck proclaimed through one of its committees the assumption of *official guardianship* by the European colonial Powers over African communities. This was certainly a legal declaration and it was passed unopposed. The Committee stated in its report that 'It is the future of Africa which is here at issue'.[125]

The question may also be asked whether the treaties under discussion were voluntary or imposed on the contracting Rulers. John Kasson, the U.S. envoy at the Berlin Conference, concerned himself deeply with this question and so did, at a

[120] Goering in a letter to Hendrik Witbooi (21st November, 1885) denied him the status of an independent Chief. Thus according to traditional Nama law he could not wage war (Bundesarchiv R 101 I/3). Witbooi defined his own status in a letter to Maharero (see above).

[121] As to the inalienability of land or territory in African law, see above (Müller *op. cit.* p. 127).

[122] Adam *op.cit.*

[123] An exception may be the occupation of Windhoek by Major Francois, see above.

[124] 'African State Practice' by V. Mayakrishnan in *Indian Year Book of International Affairs* 1965.

[125] Alexandrowicz *op. cit.* p. 115.

later stage, a number of writers such as Lindley,[126] Hesse or Büchner. The study of the available material suggests caution against any generalisation and each case must be judged on its own merits. H. Loth in his work on the Christian Mission in South-West Africa states 'that the examination of the system of treaty making proves that it is a scientifically untenable simplification to maintain that ignorance on the part of the Chiefs was responsible for their readiness to conclude treaties of protection'. And further: 'Even if the contracting Chiefs were *a priori* not quite aware of the consequences of their action, they cannot be considered as acting out of ignorance of the circumstances'.[127] The author based his view on a careful study of treaties, particularly those concluded in South-West Africa. The present enquiry showed that nearly everywhere treaties were signed in the presence of witnesses and translators.[128] However, there must have been numerous cases of imposition of treaties which Rulers, particularly village Chiefs, had to accept whether they understood all the stipulations or not.[129] Reference has been made to the treaty concluded by Major Leutwein with Hendrick Witbooi after the defeat of the latter in 1893 which in spite of all was considered by Drechsler a voluntary treaty. The active and conscious participation of Rulers in the conclusion of many treaties is evident by resort to 'Blutbruderschaft', an African legal institution expressing the principle '*pacta sunt servanda*'. The blood pact clause appears particularly in East African treaties. The Rulers influenced the formation of treaties also in other ways. Clauses were included in treaties to the effect that the property of the land which was occupied or cultivated by the Ruler and his community would remain with the latter. It is important to remember that the prevailing regime of real property was capable of being transferred by the colonial power only in case of transfer of sovereignty but not in case of the establishment of a Protectorate which left the exercise of rights of internal sovereignty to the Ruler. In this connection reference may be made to the proceedings in the case of Southern Rhodesia (1919 AC 211) before the Privy Council in which counsel for the native community pleaded that all rights acquired by the colonial Power must be held in trust for that community.

Most of the treaties were real not personal treaties, i.e. concluded in the name of the Rulers and their heirs and successors which testified to the existence of dynastic continuity. Stipulations contained in the treaties related *inter alia* to trade, residence of foreigners, most-favoured-nation treatment and jurisdictional matters. The privilege of consular or quasi-consular jurisdiction was granted to German settlers while the Ruler kept personal jurisdiction over his own subjects.[130] In mixed

[126] Lindley *op. cit.* p. 174.

[127] Loth *op. cit.* p. 111 ('Die Untersuchung des Systems der Vertragabschlüsse beweist dass es eine wissentschaftlich unhaltbare Vereinfachung ist wenn für die Bereitschaft der Häuptlinge Schutzverträge abzuschliessen ihre Unwissenheit verantwortlich gemacht wird'. And further: 'Wenn sich auch die vertragschliessenden Häuptlinge über alle Folgen ihres Schrittes von vornherein nicht klar waren, so handelten sie dennoch keinesfalls aus Unwissenheit').

[128] Treaties with Islamic Rulers were often in two texts (Arabic and European). The treaty with Uganda was in Kiganda and French.

[129] Lindley *op. cit.* p. 173.

[130] Even when the Ruler had lost the exercise of his rights of territorial sovereignty, he was still left with the exercise of personal jurisdiction over his subjects. The colonial Power, not having as Sovereign

disputes the 'mixed court' solution was adopted in South-West African treaties of the period of co-existence.[131] Emphasis has been placed on the provisions relating to the establishment of Protectorates, particularly to clauses according to which the protected Ruler undertook not to exercise rights of external sovereignty such as concluding agreements with other Powers or ceding sovereign rights to them. The protected Ruler kept of course a substantial measure of rights of internal sovereignty. The view of some international lawyers that the African Protectorate was a phantom institution is not supported by evidence. The African Protectorate was a legal reality although it constituted a transitory phase leading sooner or later to absorption.[132]

This enquiry started with a comparison of pre-19th century African treaties with treaties concluded subsequently. Attention has been drawn to the undisputed legal character of African treaties concluded under the regime of the classic law of nations which according to its natural law premises was a universal and non-discriminatory law operating irrespective of civilisation, religion, race or continent. Germany participated in the 17th and beginning of the 18th century, to a limited extent in this early process of treaty making when the Brandenburg Company established a number of forts or stations on the west coast of Africa. So did other European Powers such as Portugal, England, France or the Netherlands. The process of making treaties in Africa continued into the 19th century on the same lines but a number of international lawyers relegated the later treaties to an inferior level not because the facts of treaty making were different but because of doctrinal change. The view of these lawyers may have reflected a new climate of opinion but they are not supported by State practice in Africa. The partition of the African continent came in two distinct phases, i.e. the conclusion of valid treaties initiating a longer or shorter period of co-existence between the European and Rulers and subsequent absorption. Attention has been drawn to protracted co-existence in South-West Africa under German protection, to a mixture of protection and sovereignty in Togo and the Cameroons, and to the situation in East Africa where absorption followed soon after the conclusion of treaties.[133] The great kingdoms in this region (Zanzibar, Uganda) escaped the acquisitive plans of Dr. Peters. The latter's initiative was anyhow not backed by the Government of the Reich.

a genuine link with a foreign community belonging to a different civilisation, had to use the Ruler as an intermediary. In English colonial possession the indirect rule was applied (*the Dual Mandate* by F. D. Lugard). In some German possessions Residents (Residenturen) were appointed, e.g. in Ruanda and Urundi.

131 Europeans in South-West Africa had in many instances to submit to the jurisdiction of the Rulers. See: *Elf Jahre Gouverneur in Deutsch Südwestafrika* by Theodor Leutwein, 1906, pp. 243–4. In mixed disputes the principle '*actor sequitur forum rei*' was applicable. The national court of the defendant (accused) assumed jurisdiction Hoffmann *op. cit.* pp. 57–9.

132 Subject to exceptions such as in the case of Ethiopia, Morocco or Tunisia.

133 The situation is summed up in a Memoire presented by Bismarck to the Reichstag under the title 'Denkschrift über die Deutschen Schutzgebiete', dated the 2nd December, 1885. See: Martens *op. cit.* Vol. XI, p. 48.

The partition of Africa opened, after its absorption, a comparatively short period of colonial rule which constitutes only an episode in African history as a whole. Historians of the 19th century faced with the entry of the Afro–Asian world into the Family of Nations at first divided nations into those which make history (geschichtsbildende) and those which lack history (geschichtslose), a classification sometimes styled as the 'Ranksche Irrlehre'.[134] Whatever its merits or demerits, Ranke's theory had a far-reaching influence on the history of the law of nations, for nations without history were considered as uncivilised and as such they could not be independent members of the Family of Nations in the past.[135] This shut the Afro–Asian world out of the orbit of the law of nations and made it appear only now (for the first time) in the Family of Nations. However, when this theory was born in the 19th century, the history of the Afro–Asian world was still largely unknown. Now that it is progressively explored and written, showing the greatness of certain extra-European civilisations, including political organisation and legal institutions, are we to carry on with the outdated axioms of historians of international law still basing the *universal* international law, valid for all continents, on nothing but Western history? An analysis of this question would be beyond the scope of this enquiry but the latter may contain a measure of factual material which could contribute to a possible answer.

[134] Stoecker *op. cit.* p. 100 speaks about 'die Ranksche Irrlehre von der vorgeblichen Geschichtslosigkeit der Afrikanischen Völker'. See also *Geschichte und Geschichtsbild Afrikas* 1960, in 'Beiträge der Arbeitstagung für neuere und neueste Geschichte Afrikas', April 1959.

[135] 'Probleme der Geschichte Afrikas' by K. Büttner, *Wissenschaftliche Zeitschrift der Universität Leipzig,* Gesellschafts und Sprachwissenschaftliche Reihe, 14 Jahrgang, 1965, p. 701; 'Fragen der Genesis und Bedeutung der vorimperialistischen Kolonialsysteme' by Walter Markow, in *Wissenschaftliche Zeitschrift op.cit.*, 4 Jahrgang, 154/5, p. 58; *Afrika, Geschichte und Gegenwart* by Hans Murakovsky, 1961, p, 7.

22

THE JURIDICAL EXPRESSION OF THE SACRED TRUST OF CIVILIZATION (1971)

I.

On July 18, 1966, the International Court of Justice delivered its judgment in the second phase of the *South West Africa Cases* (*Ethiopia* v. *South Africa* and *Liberia* v. *South Africa*).[1] The votes of the judges were equally divided, but by the President's casting vote the Court decided to reject the claims of the Empire of Ethiopia and the Republic of Liberia. It came to the conclusion that the Applicants could not be considered to have established any legal right or interest appertaining to them in the subject matter of the claims against the mandatory Power (South Africa) and that, accordingly, it had to decline to give effect to them. It is not intended in this brief inquiry to recall all the legal problems and arguments raised in the proceedings or to discuss the details of the judgment. Attention may, however, be drawn to one particular aspect of the cases, *i.e.*, the possibility of deriving from the principle of the sacred trust of civilization a legal right or interest in the conduct of the Mandate, with special reference to the Mandate for South West Africa. The Court drew a distinction between the 'conduct' and the 'special interest' provisions of the various instruments of the Mandate, and it asked the question whether a Mandatory (South Africa) had any direct obligation towards the other Members of the League of Nations individually (*e.g.* Ethiopia and Liberia) as regards the carrying out of the 'conduct' provisions of the Mandate for South West Africa. The judgment states as follows:

> ... [T]he Court must examine what is perhaps the most important contention of a general character that has been advanced ... namely the contention by which it is sought to derive a legal right or interest in the conduct of the mandate from the simple existence, or principle, of the 'sacred trust'....[2]

The Court then proceeded to examine the meaning of this principle:

[1] *South West Africa Cases*, Second Phase, [1966] I.C.J. Rep. 6; 61 A.J.I.L. 116 (1967).
[2] *South West Africa Cases*, *loc. cit.* note 1 above, at 34.

The sacred trust, it is said, is a 'sacred trust of civilization'. Hence all civilized nations have an interest in seeing that it is carried out. An interest, no doubt;—but in order that this interest may take on a specifically legal character, the sacred trust itself must be or become something more than a moral or humanitarian ideal....

The Court had stated earlier that:

Humanitarian considerations may constitute the inspirational basis for rules of law, just as, for instance, the preambular parts of the United Nations Charter constitute the moral and political basis for the specific legal provisions thereafter set out. Such considerations do not, however, in themselves amount to rules of law. All States are interested— have an interest— in such matters. But the existence of an 'interest' does not of itself entail that this interest is specifically juridical in character.

Thus (the Court proceeded) the sacred trust of civilization, in order to generate legal rights and obligations, must be given 'juridical expression and be clothed in legal form'. It is in this connection that the Court made its most important pronouncement, for it said that 'In the present case the principle of the sacred trust has as its *sole juridical expression*[3] the mandates system'. Thus the *locus standi* of the Applicants in the case must depend on the legal analysis of the various instruments of the Mandate. The Court also made it clear that 'the principle of the sacred trust has no residual juridical content which could, so far as any particular mandate is concerned operate *per se* to give rise to legal rights and obligations outside the system as a whole' and justify the existence of a justiciable legal interest in the violation of the Mandate by the Mandatory Power (South Africa).

In a case in which the votes of the judges are equally divided, the precarious balance of adjudication makes the opinions of the dissenting judges deserving of particular attention. Judge Forster, in his dissenting opinion, had this to say:

... [T]his same Court, which gave the three ... Advisory Opinions in 1950,[4] 1955 and 1956 and which in 1962 delivered a judgment upholding its jurisdiction to adjudicate upon the merits of the dispute, this Court now declares the claim to be inadmissible and rejects it on the ground that Ethiopia and Liberia have no legal interest in the action.

This passes my understanding.[5]

A number of dissenting judges, including Judge Jessup (p. 324), Judge Koretsky (p. 245), and Judge Padilla Nervo (p. 453), made particular reference to the principle of the sacred trust of civilization. Judge Tanaka (p. 265) referred to the historical aspects of the principle and stated:

The idea that it belongs to the noble obligation of conquering powers to treat indigenous peoples of conquered territories and to promote their well-being has existed for many hundred years, at least since the era of Vitoria....

[3] Emphasis supplied.

[4] Lord McNair in his separate opinion in the *South West Africa Case* of 1950 described mandates as valid *in rem* and thus permanent and capable of surviving the disappearance of the League of Nations. International Status of South West Africa, [1950] I.C.J. Rep. 128, at 156–157.

[5] *Ibid.* at 478.

Without tracing the antecedents of the mandate (and trusteeship) system to the period of the classic writers, which in itself would be a tempting proposition,[6] we may recall some of the fundamental details of the European–African confrontation in the nineteenth century, particularly the hundreds of *bilateral* treaties, by which European Powers assumed the protection of African countries or acquired their territory, and the general *multilateral* arrangement made by the Powers at the Berlin Conference of 1884–1885. As the American approach to African problems at this Conference differed to some extent from that of the European Powers, it would be particularly interesting to examine some of the details of United States participation in the Berlin proceedings. Such an examination may perhaps allow us to detect the existence of the principle of the sacred trust of civilization in nineteenth-century international law, and to discuss critically the restrictive view expressed by the International Court of Justice to the effect that the mandate system is the *sole juridical expression* of the principle.

II.

At the time of convening the Berlin Conference, the European–African confrontation had gradually gathered momentum, and a number of European Powers had already entered the African scene and established treaty relations with African Rulers and Chiefs. It has to be remembered that the African Continent then presented and now presents to the international lawyer a highly heterogeneous picture. The political organization of African states on the Mediterranean coast had to its credit a more ancient tradition than the remainder of African countries. Again, while the countries on the East African coast followed to some extent the pattern of Islamic states surrounding the Indian Ocean (particularly Zanzibar), the states and Chieftainships of West, Central and South Africa followed different patterns. But, however heterogeneous the political map of Africa might have been, African territory could not, any more than Asian territory, be treated as *terra nullius* by the European newcomer. Hence the need for negotiations with Rulers and Chiefs, which either led to the conclusion of treaties of protection or treaties of cession, or treaties of friendship and commerce. The purpose of the Berlin Conference was to sort out the ensuing conflicts and problems, particularly in the Congo Basin, and to establish a measure of uniformity in the policies of European Powers aiming at inter-European co-operation in Africa. It must also be emphasized that, though African Rulers were not represented at the Berlin Conference,[7] their rôle in the over-all African settlement was not entirely passive, for all European Powers pursued a consistent policy of reliance on treaties with Rulers and not on unilateral action

[6] See, for instance, H. R. Wagner, *The Life and Writings of Bartolomé de las Casas* (1967); Wright, *Mandates Under the League of Nations* 2–23 (1930).

[7] Zanzibar acceded later to the Berlin Act of 1885. Turkey, being the suzerain of a number of African dependencies, participated throughout in the Conference. See 29 H. R. Exec. Docs. (1884–1885), No. 247 (48th Cong., 2nd Sess.), p. 179 (hereinafter cited as J3. R. Exec. Doc.).

by unilateral occupation of territory. The proceedings of the Berlin Conference showed clearly that the above treaties were considered as real treaties in the meaning of international law. Particularly as to treaties concluded between Germany and South West African Rulers, there is evidence in German legal literature that the treaties were classified as instruments of international law transferring sovereignty over South West African territory from the Rulers to the German Empire.[8]

A discussion of the various types of African treaties has been attempted elsewhere[9] and does not call for repetition. Suffice it to say that among these treaties the treaty of protection was one of the leading instruments for introducing the African communities into the orbit of the law of nations. European Powers undertook in each case to secure to the African communities the benefits of European civilization without impairing their national and cultural identity. The principle of the sacred trust of civilization was implied in them; and when, at a later date, the nature of these treaties was discussed at the Berlin Conference, the existence of such a trust for the protection of the African communities was expressly acknowledged. It is with these considerations in mind that some of the relevant proceedings of the Conference and United States participation in them may be recalled.

III.

On October 11, 1884, the German Government, through its Minister in Washington, made propositions to the United States Government for the latter's participation in the future Berlin Conference, which had three main objectives: (1) liberty of trade in the Basin and in the Delta of the Congo; (2) application to the Congo and the Niger of the principles adopted by the Congress of Vienna of 1815 relating to freedom of navigation upon international rivers; and (3) definition of the formalities to be observed in order that any new occupation of territory upon the African coasts should be deemed to be effective. It is the third point which deserves attention. This principle extended to the African coasts in general and not merely to the Basin of the Congo. The term occupation, as the proceedings show, was not used in the meaning of unilateral occupation but as occupation in consequence of the acquisition from Rulers of titles to territory.[10]

Following the German invitation, Mr. John Adam Kasson, United States Minister in Berlin,[11] reported to the Secretary of State, Frederick T. Frelinghuysen,

[8] See particularly the writings of Dr. Herman Hesse: *Schutzverträge* (1905), relating to South West African treaties of protection; and *Rechtsgültigkeit der Konzessionen* (1906), relating to the legal validity of concessions.

[9] Alexandrowicz, 'The Afro-Asian World and the Law of Nations,' 123 Hague Academy, *Recueil des Cours* 117–124 (1968, I).

[10] H. R. Exec. Doc., *op. cit.* note 7 above, at 1–179.

[11] John Adam Kasson (1822–1910) had become, on President Lincoln's election, Assistant Postmaster General, in which position he was instrumental in convening the World Postal Congress in Paris in 1863. He was elected to Congress in 1862 but later entered the diplomatic profession. In 1877 he was appointed U. S. Minister to Vienna, and in 1884 to Berlin. See 10 Dictionary of American Biography 260–261 (1933).

that the third German proposition relating to the acquisition of African territory was 'restrictive and conservative of the rights of the native tribes [Rulers] against foreign encroachments'. Mr. Kasson was subsequently appointed United States Delegate to the Berlin Conference[12] and he was to act with the assistance of two associate Delegates, Col. Henry S. Sanford, and Henry M. Stanley, the famous African explorer. In his address to the Conference on November 19, 1884, Mr. Kasson referred to Mr. Stanley as '[a]n American citizen, who was qualified by courage, perseverance, and itelligence [*sic*], and by a remarkable intrepidity and aptitude in exploration'. He then added that

> [i]t was the earnest desire of the United States that these [African] discoveries should be utilized for the *civilization* of the native races and for the abolition of the slave trade.[13]

And further: 'An International Association of Americans and Europeans was formed under high and philanthropic European patronage [the King of the Belgians] to give reality to such a purpose. They obtained concessions and jurisdiction throughout the Basin of the Congo from the native *sovereignties* which were the sole authorities existing there and exercising dominion over the soil or the people ...'. At the meetings of the Conference on December 15, 1884, and January 5, 1885, the question of acquisition of territory from African Rulers or Chiefs was further pursued, and it was stated that 'the older assumption of rights by original discovery, apart from actual settlements is practically abandoned'.[14] Neither was occupation by original title a feasible proposition, as the concept of *terra nullius* was not applicable to a politically organized continent.

The establishment of the principle of the sacred trust of civilization is strictly connected with the transfer by the African communities of their territory, their sovereignty and their destiny to the European Powers, which, through the relevant transactions, assumed the rôle of guardians of these communities. Senate Report No. 393 (48th Congress, 1st Session),[15] referring to the work of the African International Association, stated as follows:

> ... [I]ts agents have made nearly one hundred treaties with the chiefs of the different tribes in the Congo country. In each of these treaties there are valuable commercial agreements and regulations touching law and order, and certain delegations of limited powers, all of which are intended for the better government of the country.
>
> The powers are not ceded to a new and usurping sovereignty seeking to destroy existing Governments, but are delegated to a common agent for common welfare [trust]. In the language of the first treaty, concluded at Vivi June 13, 1880, and which is the plan after

[12] The reason for U. S. participation in the Berlin Conference was, apart from its interest in freedom of trade in Africa, its intimate connection with the Republic of Liberia, established thanks to the initiative of American colonization societies which settled free American Negroes on the West Coast of Africa. This colony of settlers under U. S. protection achieved independent statehood in 1847. See Mr. Kasson's reference to Liberia, in Exec. Doc., *op. cit.* note 7 above, at 14–18. In 1862 the United States concluded a treaty with Liberia. See 1 Malloy, *Treaties, Conventions, International Acts, Protocols and Agreements between the United States and Other Powers, 1776–1909*, p. 1050 (1910).

[13] H. R. Exec. Doc., *op. cit.* note 7 above, at 7. Emphasis supplied.

[14] *Ibid.* at 10.

[15] *Ibid.* at 167.

which nearly one hundred subsequent treaties have been modelled—'the aforesaid chiefs of the district of Vivi recognize that it is highly desirable that the *comité d'études* of the Congo [the predecessor of the Association] should create and develop in their states establishments calculated to foster commerce and trade, and to assure to the country and its inhabitants the advantages [of civilization] which are the consequence thereof.

'With this object in view they cede and abandon, in full property ... to the *comité d'etudes*, the territory comprised within the following limits....'[16]

The report further refers to the numerous treaties concluded by Great Britain[17] and France with African Rulers, and it concludes that 'it can scarcely be denied that the native chiefs have the right to make [these] treaties'.[18] The massive transfer of territorial sovereignty to the European Powers created, in the words of the French delegate to the Berlin Conference, 'the necessity to manage as much as possible the acquired rights and the legitimate interests of the indigenous chiefs'.[19] In this connection Mr. Kasson asked 'if it would be agreed to affirm explicitly the intentions of the Conference to respect, in a general manner, the rights of the indigenous Chiefs ... limited by these acts'.

A review of documents in the principal collections of African treaties (among which E. Hertslet's collection is the most systematic) would reveal that the transfer of sovereign rights or titles by the African Rulers to the protecting European Powers was either expressly[20] or implicitly connected with the duty of civilization, *i.e.*, the task of the transferee to assist African communities in achieving a higher level of civilization before they re-entered the family of nations as equal sovereign entities. It may be recalled that prior to the Berlin Conference a Committee of the British House of Commons had in 1865 made a statement to the effect that

all further extension of territory or assumption of government, of new treaties offering any protection to native tribes, would be inexpedient; and that the object of our policy should be to encourage in the natives the exercise of those qualities which may render it possible for us more and more to transfer to them the administration of all the governments with a view to our ultimate withdrawal ...[21]

[16] In 1884 the International Association of the Congo issued a declaration relating to the acquisition of territories from 'the legitimate sovereigns in the Basin of the Congo'. The U. S. Secretary of State recognized the flag of the Association in the same year. 1 Malloy, *op. cit.* note 12 above, at p. 327; 3 A.J.I.L. Supp. 5 (1909).

[17] The British Ambassador at the Berlin Conference, Sir Edward Mallet, declared at its session on Nov. 15, 1884, that 'the welfare of the natives is not to be neglected'. It must be remembered that they 'are not represented at this Conference and that, nevertheless, the decisions of this body will be of the gravest importance to them'. H. R. Exec. Doc., *op. cit.* note 7 above, at 34.

[18] *Ibid.* at 169. [19] *Ibid.* at 157.

[20] 1 Hertslet, *The Map of Africa by Treaty* 49, 103, 345 (3d ed., 1909). See, for instance, the Treaty of 1877 between Great Britain and King Samoo Bullom for the promotion of 'commerce and civilization' and the Treaty of 1885 between Great Britain and the King of Malin which was 'to promote to his subjects the advantages of civilization'. The Charter of the Imperial British East Africa Company of 1888 stated trade and good government and the advancement of civilization to be among the objectives of the Company. The General Act of the Conference of Berlin relates to trade and civilization. 2 Hertslet at 468.

[21] 3 Hertslet, cited above, at 780.

A report submitted by a commission of the Berlin Conference, charged to examine the project of the Declaration concerning liberty of commerce in the Basin of the Congo and its affluents refers in Article VI[22] to the indigenous populations

> who, in the present state of affairs, are scarcely qualified to defend their own interests' and states that 'the Conference has thought proper to assume the role of *official guardian* … [T]he duty to aid them to attain higher political and social status, the obligation to instruct and initiate them into the advantages of civilization are unanimously recognized … No dissent manifested itself, nor could manifest itself, in this respect in the Commission.[23]

This multilateral statement on guardianship, made within the framework of the transactions of the Conference, must be considered as declaratory of the consensus of opinion of all civilized states. The Commission added these weighty words at the end of the statement: 'It is the future of Africa which is here at issue'.

The question may be asked whether it is possible, in view of the hundreds of *bilateral* treaties by which the African communities sought the protection of European Powers and in view of the *multilateral* statement of Powers united in a world conference, to assume that the principle of the sacred trust of civilization which found its expression in these nineteenth-century legal instruments nevertheless existed in a legal vacuum. Should the answer to this question be in the negative, it would not be possible to persist in the conviction that the mandates system is the sole *juridical expression* of the above principle. Its pre-mandatory legal reality is worthy of the attention of international lawyers.

IV.

The General Act of the Berlin Conference contained two important principles in Articles 34 and 35. Article 34 laid down the principle of notification to the contracting Powers of any future taking of possession of any territory on the coasts of Africa. Article 35 embodied the principle of effective occupation of territory. While the principle of notification was extended to protectorates, the principle of effective occupation was not to be applied to them.[24] The protectorate as such was not defined in the two articles, and thus *prima facie* it must be assumed that reference had been made to the classic protectorate, which excludes the occupation of dependent territory and which implies no more than the transfer of the exercise of external sovereignty from the protected entity to the protector.[25] But in practice the African protectorate started degenerating into an instrument of annexation of territory, irrespective of the legitimate rights of the contracting Rulers or Chiefs.[26] It was for this reason, *inter alia*, that the United States did not ultimately ratify the

22 H. R. Exec. Doc., *op. cit.* note 7 above, at 83.

23 Emphasis supplied.

24 2 Hertslet, *op. cit.* note 20, at 484–485; see also 3 A.J.I.L. Supp. 24 (1909).

25 As to the views of certain writers to the contrary, see Hague Academy, *Recueil des Cours*, *op. cit.* note 9 above, at 194.

26 *Ibid.* at 193.

final Act of the Berlin Conference. In this connection Mr. Kasson committed two observations to the protocol of the Final Act:

1. *Modern international law* steadily follows the road which leads to the recognition of the right of native races to dispose freely of themselves and of their hereditary soil. Conformably to this principle, my Government would willingly support a more extended rule—one which should apply to the said occupations in Africa—a principle looking at the voluntary consent of the natives, of whose country possession is taken in all cases where they may not have provoked the act of aggression.
2. I do not doubt the Conference is agreed upon the significance of the preamble. It only indicates the *minimum* of essential conditions to be fulfilled to justify a demand for the recognition of an occupation. It is always possible that an occupation may be made 'effective' by acts of violence, which are outside of the principles of justice, of national and even of international right. Consequently, it ought to be well understood that it is reserved to the signatory powers respectively to appreciate all other conditions—of right as well as of fact—which must be complied with before an occupation can be recognized as valid.[27]

It is suggested that, among the other conditions, the capacity and readiness of the European Powers to fulfill their rôle as international trustees of civilization for the protection of African communities were essential. The proceedings of the Berlin Conference bear ample witness to a general awareness of the connection between transfer of sovereignty, whether through treaties of protection, treaties of cession or through conquest,[28] and the establishment of a trust of civilization in favour of the communities which became the concern of the Powers, assuming the rôle of collective guardianship, with the ultimate aim of reversion to sovereignty—a political and legal state of affairs which has been almost universally realized in the last ten or twenty years.

Among the non-European Powers which ratified the Berlin Act was the Ottoman Empire, which reserved at the Conference its rights in its African dependencies. The Sultan of Zanzibar acceded to the Berlin Act in 1886. The General Act of the Brussels Conference of 1890 counted among its non-European signatories Persia, Turkey and Zanzibar. Ethiopia and Liberia acceded to the Act in 1890 and 1892 respectively.[29] Though the Brussels Act was primarily concerned with the slave trade, it was in essence a continuation of the proceedings of the Berlin Conference which had been declaratory of the principle of the sacred trust of civilization.[30]

[27] H. R. Exec. Doc., *op. cit.* note 7 above, at 177. Emphasis supplied.

[28] *E.g.*, Southern Rhodesia under King Lobengula, or Madagascar. Hague Academy, *Recueil des Cours, op. cit.* note 9 above, at 195.

[29] 2 Hertslet, *op. cit.* note 20 above, at 488. See also 3 *American Journal of International Law* Supp. 29 (1909).

[30] M. F. Lindley, *The Acquisition and Government of Backward Territories in International Law* 333 (1926).

Ethiopia and Liberia appear here as contracting parties and active participants in its development as a legal principle at the pre-mandatory stage—a circumstance which would justify or at least support their *locus standi* in the *South West Africa Cases*. The abrogation of the Berlin and Brussels Acts between the Powers which ratified the Convention of St. Germain-en-Laye of 1919 did not mean any change in the legal rights and duties of these Powers. Their commitments towards the African communities as trustees of civilization were in substance re-enacted by Article 11 of the Convention of 1919. In fact the latter extended the provisions of Article VI of the Berlin Act, which had been conceived in a spirit of international *guardianship*, to all the African territories belonging to the Powers concerned. Article 11 stated that 'the Signatory Powers exercising sovereign rights or authority in African territories will continue to watch over the preservation of the native populations and to supervise the improvement of the conditions of their moral and material well-being' with the ultimate aim of self-government.[31]

The formulation of the mandate system within the framework of the League of Nations reflects the efforts of President Wilson to give full and unexceptional expression to the principle of trust. Paradoxically enough, General Smuts, who had inspired the adoption of the idea of a sacred trust of civilization within the mandate system, fought at the Peace Conference in 1919 for the annexation of South West Africa by the Union of South Africa.[32] President Wilson's reaction was that 'he could not return to America with the world parcelled out by the great powers'. He said that 'the fundamental idea would be that the world was acting as trustee through a mandatory'.[33]

The League of Nations mandatory system applied only to certain African, Pacific and Asian territories which were taken over from Germany and the Ottoman Empire after World War I. But the principle of trust of civilization was not confined to these territories within the mandate system. It applied also to other colonial territories which, prior to World War I or later, had come under the sway of the Powers.

[31] Lindley, *ibid.* at 334.

[32] The British Labour Party supported President Wilson's policy. See W. R. Louis, 'The South-West African Origins of the Sacred Trust 1914–19,' 66 *African Affairs* 20–39 (1967).

[33] See Louis, cited above, at 35, and *South West Africa Cases*, 4 I.C.J. Pleadings, Oral Arguments, Documents 235 (1966). The Applicants in the *South West Africa case* introduced 'the organized international community' theory in the proceedings. This meant that the enforcement of the sacred trust became the responsibility of the organized international community, a concept distinct from that of the League of Nations. 5 I.C.J. Pleadings, etc. 36–37 (1966). While it is true to say that the international community, *i.e.*, the family of nations, is different from the League of Nations, it is not the former but the Conferences of Berlin (1885) and of Brussels (1890) which, prior to the mandate system, gave legal expression to the sacred trust of civilization. Through the Acts of these Conferences the contracting parties assumed the rôle of guardians of African communities from which they had acquired territory on the basis of bilateral treaties. Ethiopia and Liberia became contracting parties to the Brussels Act and thus acquired a legal interest in the conduct of the guardianship, of which the mandate system was a further legal expression. Ethiopia and Liberia did not refer in their pleadings to the official guardianship proclaimed at the Berlin Conference or to the consequences of their accession to the Brussels Act. But this did not justify the categorical statement of the Court that the mandate system is the sole juridical expression of the sacred trust of civilization and that the latter has no 'residual juridical content'.

Under Article 23(b) of the League of Nations Covenant, the Members of the League '... (b) undertake to secure just treatment of the native inhabitants of territories under their control; ...' Thus the British Government declared expressly in 1923 that in the administration of Kenya the interests of the African population must be paramount, as the latter are the beneficiaries of the sacred trust of civilization exercised on their behalf.[34] The same argument applies to all territories in Africa, the Pacific or Asia in which a trust relationship had been established long before the days of the League of Nations. As witnessed at the Berlin Conference of 1885, this trust relationship must be deemed to be of a juridical character with all corresponding rights and duties attaching to the participating Powers. Moreover, Liberia and Ethiopia had, prior to the mandate system, joined as contracting parties to the Brussels Act of 1890 which, even if not directly relevant to the case, cannot be dismissed as a vital link in the chain of legal development.[35]

The Institute of International Law at its Cambridge meeting in 1931 made the remarkable statement that '[t]he communities under mandate are subjects of international law. They have a patrimony distinct from that of the mandatory State; they possess a national status, and they may acquire rights or be held to their obligations'.[36] The collapse of the sovereignty of the colonial Powers over these communities marked the end of the era of trust relationships, which had existed legally since the nineteenth century, and the independence of most of the African countries. As such, they were able in a reorganized form to re-enter the family of nations and regain the territories ceded to the Powers in the past.

The General Assembly has now terminated the Mandate for South West Africa. Though such termination is not a right provided for in Article 22 of the Covenant of the League of Nations or the relevant Mandate Agreement, it may be considered as implied in the sacred trust of civilization.[37] Whatever the legal character of this important step taken by the United Nations, it creates a situation which is awkward from the political as well as legal point of view. When the General Assembly at its 21st Session in 1966 considered the draft resolution introduced by 54 African and Asian states condemning the administration of the mandated territory of South West Africa by the Republic of South Africa and proposing its termination and

[34] Lindley, *op. cit.* note 30 above, at 335.

[35] S. F. Bemis, *Diplomatic History of the United States* 576 (4th ed., 1955), states that the principle of trust, as envisaged by the Berlin Conference of 1885, carries the 'germ of the idea of international mandate'. Art. 6 of the Berlin Act states that 'All the Powers exercising sovereign rights or influence in the aforesaid territories *bind* themselves to watch over the preservation of the native tribes, and to care for the improvement of the conditions of their moral and material well-being ...'. The Brussels Act of 1890 refers to 'assuring to that vast continent the benefits of peace and civilisation ...'. The author of a League of Nations publication on the mandate system, which was referred to in the proceedings before the I.C.J., states that while the Brussels Act created legal obligations as to the slave trade and other matters, there are no legal obligations in the Berlin Act, a view not reconcilable with the term 'bind' in the Berlin Act. See 4 I.C.J. Pleadings, etc., *op. cit.* note 33, at 233, citing League of Nations, The Mandates System; Origins—Principles—Application 9, 10 (League of Nations Pub. 1945, VI.A. 1.).

[36] See 26 *American Journal of International Law* 91, 6 (1932), and J. G. Starke, *Introduction to International Law* 164 (1967).

[37] John Dugard, 'The Revocation of the Mandate for South West Africa', 62 *American Journal of International Law* 78–97 (1968).

take-over by the United Nations, most Members expressed disappointment in the ruling of the International Court of Justice of 1966.[38]

The purpose of the above observations has not been to deal with this disappointment from the political point of view. It has rather been to point to the fact that the majority judges failed to explore the historical background of the sacred trust of civilization, which might have tipped the precarious balance of the votes in a different direction. Even if it is admitted that the jurisdiction of the Court was confined to the consideration of the case from the point of view of the mandate system only, the statement of the Court relating to 'the sole juridical expression of the sacred trust of civilization' is highly doubtful if not untenable in international law.[39]

[38] See, *e.g.*, the remarks of the representatives of Ghana, Iraq, Ceylon, and the United Arab Republic, General Assembly, 21st Sess., 1419th Meeting, U. N. Doc. A/PV. 1419 (1966). See also General Assembly Resolutions 2498 (XXIV), Oct. 31, 1969, 2517 and 2518 (XXIV), Dec. 1, 1969, General Assembly, 24th Sess., Official Records, Supp. No. 30, at 65 and 68, U. N. Doc. A/7630 (1970), in which the General Assembly, relying on earlier Security Council resolutions, condemned the Government of South Africa for its refusal to withdraw its administration from Namibia (South West Africa).

[39] See R. Higgins, 'The International Court and South West Africa: The Implications of the Judgment,' 42 *International Affairs* 573 (1966).

PART IV

THE RECOGNITION OF NEW STATES IN INTERNATIONAL LAW

23

EMPIRICAL AND DOCTRINAL POSITIVISM IN INTERNATIONAL LAW (1974–75)

The reader of post-war German literature on Afro–Asian history (including the history of the Law of Nations) must be astonished to find in so many publications a concerted attack[1] on the nineteenth-century German historian Leopold Ranke. The attack aims at Ranke's classification of nations into those which made history (*Geschichtsbildende Völker*) and those which lack history (*Geschichtslose Völker*). The classification is of vital interest to the New States, most of which are supposed to be *geschichtslos*. Some of them have already publicly protested, to mention only India and Ceylon. The question arose in the Indo–Portuguese dispute over the right of passage to the enclaves of Dadra and Nagar Aveli before the International Court of Justice and found particular expression in Judge Moreno Quintana's dissenting opinion in which he contended that India is not a New State but has reverted to sovereignty.[2] As to Ceylon, its representative in the General Assembly (Sixth Committee) objected expressly in 1968 and 1969 to the classification of Ceylon as a New State. Ceylon, he said, cannot be considered *geschichtslos*. It existed as an independent State for centuries with the exception only of the colonial interlude lasting less than 150 years.[3]

Among the critics of Leopold Ranke, Kurt Büttner[4] deserves special mention. He discusses Ranke's impact on nineteenth-century international lawyers who considered the Afro–Asian countries as deprived of any State organization and being *völkerrechtlich herrenlos*, i.e. in a legal vacuum. During the same year in which Büttner published his work (1959) a Conference on African history held in Leipzig stated that 'one of the most pernicious theories used by the defenders of colonialism is based on the view that the world is composed of nations which made history and

[1] Such as in the publications by Kurt Büttner, Thea Büttner, Heinrich Loth, Hans Murakovsky and others (quoted below in detail).

[2] *I.C.J. Reports*, 1960, p. 6.

[3] See C. H. Alexandrowicz, 'New and Original States', in *International Affairs*, vol. 45, no. 3 (1969), p. 465 (p. 390 below).

[4] Kurt Büttner, *Die Anfänge der deutschen Kolonialpolitik in Ost Afrika* (*eine kritische Untersuchung an Hand unveröffentlichen Quellen*), Berlin (1959).

of nations which lack history, the Afro-Asian countries being classified as lacking history'.[5] History or lack of history conditioned their present-day status.

Büttner returned to his attack on Ranke in 1965 when he published his *Problems of the History of Africa*.[6] He asks the vital question what is the objective criterion at the basis of Ranke's ideology which would justify his classification of nations. Ranke, he says, conceived the idea of two great areas of culture (*Kulturkreise*), the area of cultured nations and the area of primitive nations (*Kultur-* and *Naturvölker*). The search for such an objective criterion is bound to remain futile. In this respect Büttner refers to the African Empires of the past such as the Empire of Ghana (ninth to eleventh centuries), the Empire of Mali (thirteenth to fifteenth centuries) and the Empire of Monomotapa with which the Portuguese made a treaty in 1629. At that period the African State organization (hitherto so rich in history) started declining, and it declined more and more with the increasing pressure of European colonial expansion. Büttner states that historical research has shown that until the sixteenth century the advanced countries of Africa were not behind other continents. There were no racially conditioned causes of backwardness in Africa. Stagnation set in or coincided with the advent of the Europeans. The same convincing arguments have been brought forward by Van Leur in respect of Asia.[7]

Another writer (Thea Büttner) concerned herself with the time-table of development of civilizations in various parts of the world.[8] Continents had different time-tables of social and economic growth, and their political structures and status in the Family of Nations grew accordingly. Feudalism came to an end earlier in Europe than in Asia or Africa, but that hardly justifies the view that the two continents were backward in the past. Neither does it explain the classification of nations into those which made history and those which lack history, for this must lead to a distortion of the universal history of the Family and Law of Nations. Moreover, the classification was invented when little was known of Afro–Asian history. In spite of hundreds of treaties concluded between European and Afro–Asian countries prior to the nineteenth century, the history of the latter has been systematically explored in the twentieth century only. Thus arose the fallacy of classifying non-European nations as lacking history: they were considered as *geschichtslos* because their history was unknown, not because it was lacking.

Another German writer, Heinrich Loth,[9] in his *Colonial History* (1963) refers to Treitschke's views on the capacity of extra-European nations to make history.

[5] *Geschichte und Geschichtsbild Afrikas* (1960), p. 222 (*Beiträge der Arbeitstagung für neuere und neueste Geschichte Afrikas, 17–18 April 1959, Leipzig*).

[6] Kurt Büttner, 'Probleme der Geschichte Afrikas', *Wissenschaftliche Zeitschrift der Universität in Leipzig, Gesellschafts und sprachenwissenschaftliche Reihe*, 14 Jg. (1965), H. 1, pp. 701, 710.

[7] J. C. Van Leur, *Indonesian Trade and Society* (1960) (published in Bandung for the Royal Tropical Institute, Amsterdam).

[8] Thea Büttner, 'Zu Fragen des Standortes der historischen und ethnologischen Literatur zur Geschichte Afrikas in der vorkolonialen Zeit', *Wissenschaftliche Zeitschrift der Universität in Leipzig* (as above, n. 6), Jg. 14 (1965).

[9] Heinrich Loth, *Studien zur Kolonialgeschichte und Geschichte der nationalen und kolonialen Befreiungsbewegung* (*die christliche Mission in S. W. Afrika*) (1963), pp. 7, 96, 102, 111, Appendix 11, 17.

Treitschke speaks about the legal institutions which 'our philosophers conceived for the world' and further of the European school of legal thought which 'originated from the depths of the German spirit ... and conceived the juridical life of nations as an eternal process of development'.[10] No objective criterion of classification of nations was capable of emerging out of this sort of irrational inspiration.

Loth concerns himself with the treaties concluded between European powers and African Rulers and rejects the presumption (not justified by generally valid evidence) that 'the readiness of Rulers to conclude treaties of protection ... can be ascribed to their ignorance'. M. F. Lindley[11] made a careful inquiry into the problem and warned international lawyers of the danger of generalizations. It is also of great interest to read in the work of Loth the correspondence between African Rulers *inter se* (e.g. between those in Namibia) which shows a perfect awareness of the imminent loss of sovereignty which German colonial penetration was likely to bring about.[12] The conviction of European writers as to the absence of Statehood in Africa and Asia is hardly justified if it is realized that no European power wished to acquire territory by conquest or unilateral occupation but by negotiation with the legitimate bearers of sovereign rights from whom territory could be acquired bilaterally by title of cession.

Another writer, Hans Murakovsky, describes in his *Africa, Past and Present*[13] the contemporary research of German writers as showing 'the end of the great fallacy of any inherent superiority of Europe'. He states that 'the culture of mankind cannot be ascribed to any single group'. The realization of this fact 'emerges out of the mist of conflicting European nationalisms which raged against each other for so long'. Murakovsky points out that unknown Africa is well known today and its history has joined the stream of world history. Can it really be considered *geschichtslos*?

In an attempt to define 'world history' Ranke fell into the *pars pro toto* fallacy of identifying European history with world history. To international lawyers the correction of this fallacy is essential, for the New States, many of which had maintained treaty and diplomatic relations with European powers prior to the nineteenth century, are now concerned with their position in the Family of Nations in which past and present are equally relevant to defining status.[14]

The concept of the *European* Law of Nations emerged only in the second half of the eighteenth century. It did not really exist before, simply because there was no consistent Concert of Europe in the nineteenth-century meaning. The only concentration of political power in Europe had been in the Holy Roman Empire which covered only part of Europe, excluding France, England, Scotland and East Europe. Spain had been connected with it for a while through a common dynasty (the Habsburgs) and Italy remained the playground of the conflicting interests of

[10] Loth, op. cit., p. 7.

[11] M. F. Lindley, *The Acquisition and Government of Backward Territory in International Law* (1926).

[12] Loth, op. cit., Appendix, Documents, Reichskolonialamt (RKA), No. 17.

[13] Hans Murakovsky, *Afrika, Geschichte und Gegenwart*, Vienna (1961), pp. 7, 39, 66.

[14] Büttner, 'Probleme der Geschichte Afrikas' (above, n. 6), p. 703, and Leopold von Ranke, *Weltgeschichte*, vol. 1 (1880), p. 18 (as quoted by Büttner).

the Powers. There was no reason for conceiving a European Law of Nations. The Law of Nations was inherently a universal concept, conditioned by its affiliation with the law of nature and by the highly important and world-wide relations on a footing of equality between the European Powers and the East Indian and North African Rulers joining in a great trade adventure. The treaties and documents of diplomatic and commercial relations emerging from European and extra-European State practice piled up in the course of the sixteenth, seventeenth and eighteenth centuries and were gradually sorted out by the late eighteenth-century positivists, among whom C. F. de Martens was the most systematic one. It was the period of transit of the Law of Nations from the natural law ideology to positivism, and it would have been logical if the positivists had proceeded in an empirical way, taking the whole material as a basis for extracting rules of international law. For positivism is an empirical concept relying on State practice. It contrasted itself with the doctrinal approach to the law which was characteristic of the law of nature.

G. F. de Martens quotes among treaties in his *Précis du droit des gens*[15] at least eighty treaties concluded with Afro–Asian countries. He collected more of these treaties in his *Recueil* and *Cours diplomatique*.[16] Some of these treaties provided for capitulations on behalf of Asian or African traders in Europe. Why have these treaties not been accepted as reliable historical source material on the same level as inter-European treaties from which rules of international law could be drawn? Ompteda in his *Literature of the Law of Nations*[17] had already been puzzled by the non-extension of positivist international law from Europe to other continents which through treaties and diplomatic and commercial relations had close connections with European powers. The concept of universality of international law declined with the decline of the natural law doctrine, but why has it been impossible to build universality into the positivist reality of international law? The reason seems to be that positivism, in its endeavour to be empirical and in its determination to do away with doctrinal international law (based on the law of nature and nations) became itself doctrinal, adopting as much of the factual historical material as it wished to, and rejecting the remainder. The rejection of extra-European source material was instrumental in building up a new *European* (pseudo-universal) international law. This was hardly an empirical exercise. It was doctrinally eurocentric and bound to falsify history. The problem is of concern to international lawyers who deal with the entry of the New States or the so-called New States into the Family of Nations.

The question has been asked what is the attitude of the New States to existing international law as they find it at their entry into the orbit of international law. One view is that they are born into it and have little choice. This view is obviously not confirmed by actual (empirical) State practice of our days.[18] In fact, the New

[15] G. F. de Martens, *Compendium of the Law of Nations* (translated by William Cobbett), London (June 1802), List of Treaties, pp. 357–454.

[16] G. F. de Martens, *Recueil des traités* (1791, 1817), and *Cours diplomatique* (1801) by the same author.

[17] D. H. L. Ompteda, *Literatur des gesammten sowohl natürlichen wie positiven Völkerrechts* (1785).

[18] R. P. Anand, *New States and International Law* (1972).

States do not accept certain principles of international law in the making of which they had no share in the nineteenth century. On the other hand, if it is true to say that many of the New States have an identity with States in the classic past such as India, Ceylon, Madagascar, Algeria and other States, they cannot be considered as *geschichtslos*. They had a presence in the pre-colonial Family of Nations and must be considered as participants in law-making in the classic period. To that extent they are bound to accept the traditional structure of international law and some of its fundamental principles. While they now exercise the choice of accepting or rejecting certain rules of *jus dispositivum*, they have not rejected the idea of *jus cogens*, which they are ready to acknowledge as a peremptory law from which no derogation is permitted.[19]

Whatever the ultimate outcome of the present transformation of international law caused by the appearance or reappearance of the Afro–Asian States, it is important not to apply to such transformation doctrinal positivism. Positivism is by its nature empirical and should respect and follow the facts of international life without any *a priori* discrimination. The error committed by Ranke and his followers of identifying Western history with universal history and of classifying nations into those who make history and those who lack history should be avoided. The pride of nations in their history must be mutually respected. It will certainly take the sting of bitterness out of the colonial controversy, which is no more than an ordinary chapter of power politics.

[19] H. Bokor-Szegö, *New States and International Law* (1970).

24

THE THEORY OF RECOGNITION *IN FIERI* (1958)

I.

THE historian of international law who attempts an inquiry into the law of recognition of States and governments in its formative stage, particularly into eighteenth-century sources, is bound to consult the first historical survey of the literature of the law of nations by D. H. L. Ompteda, published in 1785.[1] Ompteda, a half-naturalist half-positivist who conceives the law of nations on the traditional basis of the law of nature subject to modifications brought about in the intercourse between nations by their express, tacit or presumed consent, refers to problems of recognition under the general heading of the fundamental right of nations to freedom and independence. In the absence of any precise and formulated theory, recognition had not found a separate place in the works of the classic writers whether of the naturalist or early positivist period, and this is the reason why Ompteda observes that nothing special has been written on the subject. All the essays mentioned by him as being directly or indirectly relevant to problems of recognition of new States or rulers are, with the exception of a short essay by F. C. Moser, written by comparatively unknown authors. Among them Justi and Steck are perhaps the most active participants in the first attempts at formulating a theory of recognition.[2] The purpose of this paper is to draw the attention of historians of international law to these early attempts, and particularly to the direct influence of Justi and Steck on Martens and Klueber, and through them on Henry Wheaton and some of the early nineteenth-century writers.

Justi's essay appeared in his historical and juridical studies published in Frankfurt in 1760; its rather lengthy title is: 'Discussion of the question whether the protests of third monarchs against the election of a person to the throne of an elective monarchy are justifiable in the law of nature and the law of nations'.[3] The problem of

[1] *Litteratur des gesammten sowohl natürlichen als positiven Völkerrechts* (1785), p. 484.

[2] Ompteda, op. cit., quotes also F. A. Kunhold's *Diss. de Statu Naturali Rerum Publicarum* (1723); and F. C. Moser's essay on the 'Rights of a Sovereign, etc'. (*Kleine Schriften*, pp. 287–347).

[3] See Johann Heinrich Gottlieb von Justi, *Historische und Juristische Schriften* (1760), pp. 185–99. It is interesting to note that Justi was a British Royal Counsellor of Mines (*Königlicher Grossbritannischer Bergrath*).

recognition arose here in connexion with the position of elective rulers within the family of nations. While the legitimate rights of succession of hereditary monarchs were generally accepted in the international field, the election of a ruler in an elective monarchy not infrequently presented complicated problems because of the external influence exercised by foreign rulers on the elections. For instance, Justi quotes the opposition of certain German princes to the election of the Austrian dynasty to the throne of the German emperors.

Before going into Justi's argumentation we may state that the problem which he puts before us is one of recognition of the new head of a State. At that time the ordinary ruler represented generally the supreme executive power of the State in so far as his ministers were responsible to him and not to the representatives of the people assembled in a legislature, and the problem was therefore in essence one of recognition of governments.

Justi asks the question: What is the validity in the law of nations of protests of rulers who oppose the election of an undesirable Prince in another State, one, for instance, who is not likely to observe the sanctity of treaties? To answer this question he enters first into considerations of a political nature and comes to the conclusion that power politics played by rulers in relation to an elective monarchy may involve the latter in endless complications and chaos as demonstrated by the example of Poland (an elective monarchy) in the eighteenth century.[4] To avoid such arbitrary action on the part of foreign powers, an elective ruler must, according to Justi, be treated on the same footing as an hereditary ruler. If his people consider him worthy of election to the throne of their country and useful to their welfare, they endow him automatically with the same rights which an hereditary ruler enjoys according to traditional principles of legitimism. They need not look to the policy of other States, as their welfare is the supreme consideration. Thus Justi lays down the general rule that the succession to the throne of an elective monarchy (as in an hereditary monarchy) is not capable of being validly challenged by other States. In Justi's view an elective monarch cannot concede to other rulers the *right to recognition* as this would mean intervention and result in submission which would stultify the fundamental right of States to equality guaranteed by the law of nature and nations. The elimination of recognition is further justified by the following considerations: a country may have its internal State secrets which explain the choice of its elective ruler in conformity with its interests. These secrets cannot be made known to other States which cannot set themselves up as judges of government succession in foreign countries. Moreover, *sovereignty* is during the interregnum vested in the whole State as such and the latter is under no duty to tolerate an interference from outside just as a reigning ruler could not accept it according to the law of nations.

Exceptions to this rule serve only to confirm its essential validity. It might seem that such an exception is afforded by the right of the German Emperor to exclude a

[4] Justi illustrates this point in a somewhat Machiavellian way by saying that 'our enemy may become the friend of our neighbour' and our friend 'may become the enemy of a third neighbour' all competing for influence on the election of a monarch.

cardinal from the election of the Pope and so to influence the result of the election. However, this right is a relic of old times and cannot, according to Justi, support a commendable principle.[5]

Another exception may occur in the case where a ruler assumes a higher rank or title than he actually enjoys. In principle he may, according to Justi, receive a higher rank or title from his own subjects but if he tends to derive it from third powers he must secure their recognition. In particular Justi observes that the assumption of a higher rank may entail changes concerning status and ceremonial which cannot be imposed on third powers but must be recognized by them. On the other hand, if an elective ruler derives his rank legitimately from his predecessors in power, it is bound to be recognized by other States as its denial would amount to a violation of the law of nations. In case of such denial of status the elective ruler, in the absence of a supreme international agency which could settle inter-State disputes, may take counteraction and either assert his rights by exercising military pressure, or, if this should prejudice the welfare of his subjects, he may proceed to reprisals. Thus he may retaliate against non-recognition by mutual non-recognition. 'Who would deny to a lawfully elected ruler', says Justi, 'the right not to recognize the Kings of France and Spain as such if they denied him recognition of his position which he obtained by an indisputable election? The Law of Nations would fully approve of such action'.

The following observations may be offered to Justi's argumentation:

(1) In his attempt at analysing the problem of recognition of rulers, Justi is faced with the traditional principles of dynastic legitimism which in his view fully apply to the succession of hereditary rulers. Sovereignty in an hereditary monarchy is derived and perfected from within and vests in the Sovereign. As his legal status does not depend on foreign powers, the problem of recognition does not in principle arise.

(2) As to elective rulers, Justi divides his reasoning into two parts: he states first the general rule and then enumerates exceptions to it. He makes it clear that during the period of an interregnum before the election of a new monarch by the people, *sovereignty* is in the whole State. Thus, if through the will of the people the State elects a new ruler, he derives his position, similarly to an hereditary ruler, from within and becomes the sovereign in the full sense of the word. As Justi equates elective with hereditary sovereigns, third powers have no power of recognition. Acts of recognition or non-recognition of elective rulers which occur in State practice cannot make or unmake the new Head of the State and its government, as the law of nations relies on the *fait accompli* created in the internal law of the country concerned. Foreign powers have no right to interfere with the succession in an elective monarchy as this would result in submission of the latter and offend the principle of equality of States.

[5] But see the protest of the Austrian Emperor against the election of Cardinal Rampolla at the Conclave in 1903.

(3) Thus according to Justi the elective ruler enjoys in the same way as an hereditary ruler the right to oppose intervention of foreign powers except when he is guilty of revolt, breach of peace or violation of treaties.

(4) While the problem of recognition does not in principle arise in the above case, it gains importance in the case of assumption of a higher rank or title by an elective ruler. Though Justi's remarks in this respect refer to situations which would not occur today, they nevertheless throw light on a *sui generis* conception of recognition which has general significance. Justi observes that recognition is unnecessary when the ruler *derives* his rank or title from his own people. In that case its legitimation takes place from within, without need of external approval (*Einwilligung*). But if he *derives* his rank or title from other powers, then recognition is necessary to perfect his status.[6]

On the other hand, if an elected ruler *derives* his rank or title legitimately from his predecessors in power, non-recognition would be a violation of the law of nations. Justi's views in this respect are revealing: he says that in the absence of an international authority which could consider complaints against a State wrongdoer, the elective ruler himself may proceed to the enforcement of his right. If he considers the use of arms inconsistent with the welfare of his subjects, he may apply reprisals, for instance by mutual non-recognition, and Justi makes it clear that a ruler whose rights are offended could fight back with the help of non-recognition even against such powerful kings as those of France and Spain.

It follows from the foregoing that there are two main aspects of the problem of recognition to which Justi seems particularly to pay attention, first, what may be called its derivative aspect, and second, its tortious aspect. The classic doctrine of legitimacy relating to hereditary monarchies is no doubt at the basis of his reasoning. As the legal status of the ruler is derived and perfected from within and as internal legality determines external legality in the law of nations, foreign powers cannot by recognition confer on a ruler rights which are not capable of being derived from their action. The extension of this doctrine from hereditary to elective rulers whose position is based on popular sovereignty is a significant factor in Justi's essay.

Where, however, a particular rank or title of the elective ruler is derived from without, i.e. from the actual concession of foreign powers, its recognition is exceptionally conceded. Whether conceded or not, the term 'recognition' as used by Justi in the above cases signifies approval (*Einwilligung*) which is tantamount to a constructive or constitutive act.

On the other hand, Justi refers to acts of recognition in actual State practice in another meaning also, that of acceptance by third powers of the *fait accompli* established within a particular State. In fact foreign powers are said to be under the duty to 'recognize' elective rulers, the duty lying in the acknowledgement of situations of fact and in the respect for the significance and the consequences which the law

[6] See also Christian Wolff, *Jus Gentium in Methodo Scientifica Pertractatum* (*The Classics of International Law*, ed. by J. B. Scott), pp. 125–6.

of nations ascribes to them.[7] The term 'recognition' means here an act declaratory in nature. But, as was later brought into relief by Steck, foreign powers need not acknowledge situations of fact by express recognition but should simply accord proper treatment to new sovereigns by the maintenance of intercourse. The use of *Erkennung* (recognition) in two different meanings may lend itself to misleading interpretation but this can be safely avoided if the derivative aspect of sovereign rights and the intrinsic nature of acts of recognition as emphasized by Justi are kept in mind.

The tortious aspect of the problem is according to Justi intimately connected with the above considerations. For if one ruler takes action against the succession of a ruler in another State, he assumes an unauthorized power by interfering in what is legally constituted beyond his reach. This is intervention which offends the natural equality of States and amounts to a delictual act. As such it entitles the aggrieved party to take counteraction and even to apply mutual non-recognition which, though in itself illegal, is applicable by way of reprisal.

In conclusion Justi states that he considered the whole matter on the basis of the law of nations and nature and not from the point of view of what he calls State prudence (*Staatsklugheit*). As to the latter he observes that though it must be derived from the law of nations, it relies also on other sources, obviously connected with political expediency (see below). Justi makes it clear that he formulated his arguments without reference to other writers. His essay is no doubt one of the first original efforts to sort out problems of recognition in a fairly systematic way.

II.

Whereas Justi is concerned with the problem of recognition of a ruler (government), Johann Christian Wilhelm von Steck, a German professor of law well known in the eighteenth century, concentrates on the problem of recognition of States. He opens his essay on 'The Recognition of Independence of a Nation and a State' (published in 1783 in his collection of essays on various political and legal matters[8]), with the consideration of the case of the rebellion of a nation, province or colony against the mother State. Such rebellion, assumes Steck, may take place because of tyrannical treatment, breach of treaties, violation of principles, privileges and liberties, or refusal of protection. The whole process of emancipation of the new State is envisaged by Steck in several stages. The first is the formal and solemn declaration of independence from the mother State. Such a declaration, Steck proceeds, was

[7] See also Johann Jacob Moser, who, referring to newly elected sovereigns, speaks about the duty of their recognition by other powers (*Beyträge zu dem neuesten Europäischen Völkerrecht in Fridenszeiten* (1778), vol. i, p. 329). But he also makes it clear that succession of sovereigns is the internal affair of the State concerned and all that foreign powers should do is not to make difficulties in its recognition which would amount to intervention (*Grundsätze des jetzt üblichen Europäischen Völkerrechts in Fridenszeiten* (1763), ch. v).

[8] von Steck, *Versuche über verschiedene Materien politischer und rechtlicher Kenntnisse* (1783).

made by the Netherlands in 1581 when the King of Spain was declared deprived of his overlordship (*Oberherrschaft*) and the people of the Netherlands declared themselves free and sovereign.[9]

Another example quoted by Steck is that of the Tartars of Crimea who repudiated obedience to Turkey in 1772 and declared themselves an independent State no longer subordinated to their previous overlord. In this respect Steck quotes Moser who gives more details concerning the case.[10] The discontinuance of the Turkish–Crimean relationship was connected with the simultaneous conclusion of a treaty between the Crimean Tartars and the Russian Empire in 1772 in which the former sought the protection of the latter. The hereditary ruler of Crimea, Sagib-Giray, announced at the same time 'that he regained his ancient liberty and independence and that Crimea had become a State independent of foreign powers'. He 'expressed the hope that the Sublime Porte will accept it and leave Crimea in the enjoyment of her rights which belong to her by the law of Nature and ancient privileges of the Tartars'.[11]

Finally, the third and most important case quoted by Steck is the Declaration of Independence of North America in 1776.

The declaration of independence is only the first stage. Steck observes that by itself it is not a sufficient title to independence, at least no longer than it is asserted and possessed. In the second stage the mother State should be induced (peacefully) or compelled (by arms) to renounce its sovereignty, to accept the separation and thus to recognize the independence of the new State.[12] Here the example of Switzerland serves as an illustration. The independence of the Helvetian Republic, though *de facto* enjoyed by its people for a long time, was recognized by the German Reich only in the Peace Treaty of Westphalia after the Imperial decrees of 6 and 14 May 1647 had been issued.[13]

Steck discusses then the case of the Netherlands in its second stage. The independence of the Netherlands was recognized by the King of Spain and the House of Austria in the armistice treaty of 9 April 1609 and afterwards confirmed in the Peace Treaty of Münster between the Spanish Crown and the United Netherlands of 30 January 1648 (Article 2).[14]

[9] Steck quotes also the declaration made by the Netherlands in 1579 in the Union of Utrecht.

[10] Moser, *Versuch des neuesten Europäischen Völkerrechts* (1778), vol. vii, pp. 126–7.

[11] In connexion with recognition of new States Moser (op. cit.) discusses three cases: (1) that of Corsica which claimed unsuccessfully independence from France, (2) that of Crimea, and (3) that of the U.S.A. As to the latter Moser observes that third powers were more or less neutral *vis-à-vis* the North American colonies but he mentions a notice of Congress at Philadelphia of 10 December 1776 relating to the assistance received from foreign powers.

[12] In this respect Steck relies on Vattel's *Droit des Gens* (Part I, Book 1, ch. xvii).

[13] Steck quotes Moser's *Gerettete Souveränität der Eidgenossenschaft* (1731).

[14] According to Steck it was stipulated in Article 53 that the Spanish Crown would receive an assurance from the Emperor and the Reich that they would maintain neutrality, good neighbourhood and amity. This declaration was also issued by the Emperor and the Reich and though it did not contain an express recognition of independence of the Netherlands, it was tacitly implied in it.

As to Crimea, Turkey had to recognize the independence of the former in the Peace Treaty of Kainardgi in 1774 concluded with Russia. Only religious dependence and the rights of the Sultan as the Caliph were preserved.

As to the United States, Steck notes that Great Britain after her frustrated efforts to restore the position in the American colonies had to renounce her sovereignty and to recognize them as a free, sovereign and independent State.

After having discussed the relationship between the new State and the mother State, Steck proceeds to the third and most important problem, that of the relationship between the new State and third powers. In this respect Steck observes that once the mother State recognized the new State, the latter 'does not require the recognition of third powers' ('so bedarf es der Erkennung anderer Mächte nicht weiter'). They must then treat it as a free and sovereign people and it is not in their discretion to concede or to refuse these qualities as they did not have any overlordship over them. If the over-lordship of the mother State comes to an end, other nations have no right to force the new State back into submission which would obviously amount to intervention in its affairs. 'In the eyes of all other [States] it is thanks to the natural equality of nations free and independent'. Here Steck draws his conclusion by quoting the example of Spain and her recognition policy towards the U.S.A. and says: 'It would be preposterous to believe that Spain, after England has liberated the USA from all submission, would make difficulties to recognise them as an independent State'. But Steck emphasizes that 'it would be equally absurd to expect all other powers to *recognise* the USA expressly as an independent State. They must rather regard them and treat them now as such and they cannot refuse to meet them in the above capacity, to receive their envoys and treat them as those of a free State'.

On the other hand, third powers cannot, according to Steck, recognize a new State before the mother State has renounced its sovereignty even if the rebelling people disclaimed their obedience, separated themselves and asserted their freedom with arms. Such recognition would amount to unfriendly intervention. In this respect Steck quotes the example of the premature recognition of the United States by France[15] and expresses his own view in the following words: 'One can hardly think of a more serious offence than that of declaring a people which abandons its mother State and tears itself away from it as absolved of its obligations and of recognising such a people free and independent'; and further: 'Such declaration and recognition by a third power has merely an effect in relation to the latter but cannot affect the sovereignty of the mother State from which a defaulting people separates itself, *provided the mother State can assert its real sovereignty.* The people recognised as

[15] Steck quotes the French-American Treaty of Commerce concluded on 6 February 1778 which meant recognition of the unified English colonies in North America as an independent State. At the same time an alliance was entered into by the two powers. The King of France then notified the English Court of the above arrangement. Great Britain, which in the Peace Treaty of 1773 (Article I) had received a promise from the French Crown that the latter would not assist (directly or secretly) any nation against her, considered the above arrangements as unfriendly acts and a breach of peace (see Steck, op. cit.).

independent by a third power draw no further benefits from such recognition than appropriate treatment by the recognising power which will send and receive envoys, conduct negotiations, enter into alliances and give full assistance to the new entity'. However, Steck adds that 'if the mother State succeeds in restoring the position and in submitting the rebelling State to obedience, the recognition of third powers would not afford a basis for independence'.

The following conclusions may be drawn from these statements:

(1) Steck, like Justi, belongs, subject to reservations, to the legitimist school and considers the release of a new State by the mother State as essential for its sovereignty and independence.[16] Such sovereignty is in principle derived from within, i.e. from the declaration and assumption of independence and its recognition by the legitimate Sovereign, the mother State.

(2) The position of third powers in relation to the new State is therefore different before and after its recognition by the mother State. Once the latter recognized the new State, there is nothing that third powers can add substantially to its legal status in the law of nations. Though Steck eliminates recognition (*Erkennung*) by third powers in the meaning of a constitutive act, he says at the same time that third powers should recognize (*erkennen*) the released State in another meaning, i.e. by the establishment of diplomatic, treaty and other relations. Referring to the United States of America after their release by Great Britain, he emphasizes that it would be absurd to expect their express recognition by third powers. The latter must simply regard and treat them as sovereign and independent. Steck does not indicate whether the establishment of intercourse amounts to recognition *per facta concludentia*, but if it did so it would certainly mean acknowledgement declaratory in nature.However, third powers might deny 'recognition,' i.e. due treatment to a new State, though the latter had lawfully gained its independence. Steck quotes in this respect the recognition policy of Spain towards the United States, and observes that their non-recognition by Spain would be improper (*ungereimt*). Though he does not say that he would classify it as delictual (tortious), it seems that he regards it as such. Such denial of right would amount in his view to forcing the new State into submission to the former Sovereign (mother State) and violate the natural equality of nations.[17]

(3) Steck is more emphatic as to the tortious aspect of premature recognition of a new State by third powers which he considers as intervention in the affairs of the mother State. The term 'premature' refers in principle to the period after declaration and assertion of independence by a new State but before its recognition by the mother State. The new State 'prematurely' recognized by third powers draws no further benefit from such recognition than

[16] Steck does not quote Justi in his essay but he is familiar with his writings. See *Abhandlungen aus dem Deutschen Staats- und Lehrrecht* (1757), p. 150.

[17] See also Puffendorf, *De Jure Naturae et Gentium Libri Octo*, Book VIII, ch. 4, p. 18; and Wolff, *Jus Gentium*, para. 348 (*The Classics of International Law*).

provisional establishment of intercourse. Should the mother State succeed in re-establishing its sway over the new State, the latter must be considered as non-existent in the law of nations. The question remains what is the legal position of a new State if the mother State is ultimately out of the picture but still denies its recognition. Steck gives no definite answer to this question but one or two of his dicta as quoted above seem to indicate that the period of 'prematureness' of recognition would die a natural death. More light is thrown on this question by later writers such as Martens and Klueber.

Though the term *Erkennung* or *erkennen* is not used consistently by Steck, there is little doubt that what he eliminates as not conceded by the law of nations is recognition as a constructive act. On the other hand, recognition as a declaratory act is superfluous. Acknowledgement of facts by third powers takes place normally by the establishment of intercourse and treaty making. As in Justi solutions are determined by the peculiar eighteenth-century blend of the naturalist and positivist doctrines.

III.

The influence of Steck as an active participant in the formulation of problems of recognition was not confined to his immediate contemporaries but extended to a number of prominent lawyers of the late eighteenth and early nineteenth centuries, to mention only Martens and Klueber. Moreover, it extended indirectly through Klueber to Henry Wheaton and the editors of the posthumous editions of his *Elements of International Law* and thus it is reflected in some of the treatises of the most eminent publicists in the field of international law.

Martens, discussing the case when a nation, or part of it, wishes to drive the Sovereign from the throne, or when part of it endeavours to declare itself independent, distinguishes two points for the consideration of foreign powers: (1) the conduct to be observed towards the old or new Sovereign or towards the people who, after having revolted, declare themselves independent, and (2) the assistance to be given to either party.[18]

With regard to the first point, Martens observes that 'a foreign nation, not under any obligation to interfere, does not appear to violate its perfect obligations nor to deviate from the principles of neutrality if, in adhering to the possession[19] (without examining into its legality) it treats as Sovereign him who is actually on the throne and as an independent nation people who have declared and still maintain themselves independent'.

[18] Martens, *A Compendium of the Law of Nations* (1789) (transl. by Cobbett, 1802), p. 18 et seq.

[19] Grotius, writing about a usurper in power, states that if he 'is in *possession* the acts of government which he performs may have a binding force arising not from a right possessed by him for no such right exists, but from the fact that one to whom the sovereignty actually belongs ... would prefer that measures promulgated by him should meanwhile have the force of law, in order to avoid utter confusion which would result from the subversion of laws and suppression of the Courts' (*De Jure Belli ac Pacis*, Book I, ch. 4, para. 15).

Martens quotes Steck in support of his statement, and in fact he follows predominantly his reasoning except for a rather more emphatic repudiation of legitimism in its rigid form. The behaviour of third powers towards a new State is, according to Martens, determined by two considerations: (1) the declaration of independence of the people who separated themselves from the mother State, and (2) the *de facto* maintenance of independence. If these two conditions are fulfilled, third powers will have to accept the situation of fact as conclusive for the determination of its legality in the law of nations, and will have to treat the new State as sovereign and independent. As to the treatment of a new Sovereign (government), Martens, similarly to Justi, refers specially to elective Kingdoms and observes that the right to elect the Sovereign belongs to the people. Foreign princes may make recommendations 'but they have no right to interfere authoritatively …'. In support Justi's essay is quoted. Martens quotes Poland as an example of an elective monarchy and emphasizes that the interference of foreign powers in the elections of Polish kings has no foundation in the law of nations.

Turning to the second point, i.e. the assistance given by third powers to either of the conflicting parties, Martens writes:

> When once obedience has been formally refused and the refusing party has entered into the possession of the independence demanded, the dispute becomes the same as those which happen between independent States; consequently any foreign prince has a right to lend assistance to the party who he believes has justice on his side, whether he be obliged so to do by treaty, or not; provided, however, that he has not promised to observe a strict neutrality. But, as to espouse an unjust cause is unlawful, and as it is impossible that the opinion of the two parties should not differ with respect to the justice of their cause, it is also impossible that those against whom succours are directed should not consider such a step as a departure from neutrality and as an injury.

Bringing the tortious aspect of the problem at this stage (assistance) into the picture, Martens states that the party aggrieved, whether mother State or previous Sovereign, has two alternatives. It may either 'dissemble or at most complain of the injury' or it may 'seek retaliation'. Martens adds that 'the conduct that Great Britain observed, particularly towards France, Spain and the Pope after the revolution of 1688, and that which she observed towards several other powers after the colonies of North America declared themselves independent, may serve to illustrate this subject'.

Finally, if the aggrieved party admits defeat, i.e. the mother State acknowledges the independence of the new State or a sovereign renounces his throne, third powers have no more alternative but to accept the situation. They have no right to oppose the revolution and Martens adds significantly: '*Nor is the acknowledgment of its validity necessary*'. In support of this statement Steck is quoted as the only authority on the subject.

Thus Martens follows in principle the views of Justi and Steck.[20] But while Justi admits recognition as a constructive act exceptionally in the case of the rank or title

[20] It is interesting to note that Martens, op. cit., quotes several essays of Justi and Steck on various subjects. See pp. 19, 58, 59, 126, 129, 130, 154, 156, 171, 235, 284, 285, 311, 345, 347, 350 and 351. These frequent quotations testify to the importance of both writers at that period.

of a ruler derived from the recognizant, Steck and Martens seem not to admit any situation in which such an act could be exercised by third powers. Recognition as a constructive act is not conceded and as a declaratory act it is in principle superfluous. The legitimation of a new State or Sovereign takes place from within and third powers are bound to act in accordance with facts which determine at the same time the position in internal (municipal) law as well as in the law of nations.

It may be interesting to note that Martens exercised a considerable influence on Robert Ward, one of the earliest historians of the law of nations. Ward is *inter alia* concerned with the assumption of a higher rank or title by a sovereign, a problem discussed previously by Justi. He refers to the conversion of the Duchy of Prussia into a kingdom and states that when in 1701 the Elector of Brandenburg assumed the royal title of King of Prussia, 'the Emperor was prevailed upon to acknowledge him first and the rest of the Princes of Europe were induced to follow his example'. Relying on Martens who followed in this respect Justi's views, Ward underlines that the royal title was not *conferred* by the Emperor but simply acknowledged by him.[21]

IV.

The position of third powers in relation to new States is similarly formulated by Jean Louis Klueber, though subject to some deviations from the views expressed by earlier writers.[22] Klueber states that 'Sovereignty is acquired by a State either at its foundation or at the time when it legitimately rids itself of dependence in which it found itself previously.[23] To be valid, it needs no recognition or guarantee by any foreign power provided that its possession is not imperfect. However, it may be *prudent*[24] to have it recognised expressly or tacitly and to obtain the guarantee of one or more

[21] Ward, *An Enquiry into the Foundation and History of the Law of Nations in Europe* (1795), pp. 410–14.

Ward also discusses generally the Republican form of government and states that it is in no way inferior to monarchies: 'The sovereignty of every State must be somewhere lodged ... it matters little, with respect to foreign nations, whether it is possessed by one man, or by many, by hereditary descent or by election'. Discarding principles of hereditary legitimism, Ward turns to the case of a rebelling State and says that its sovereignty must depend on the success of the rebellion. In his discussion of treaties, he refers to the emergence of the Helvetian Republic (Switzerland) in the fourteenth century as an independent State and writes: 'It was through the operation of these treaties (by which the Union of Cantons came to be formed) that the *Swiss Peasantry* erected themselves into independent States; and that from treaties which were afterwards made with them by other powers, their Sovereignty came ultimately to be *acknowledged*'. Ward follows here the views of Steck who had drawn attention to the existence of Swiss independence long before its formal stabilization at the Peace Treaty of Westphalia (see Ward, op. cit., pp. 276, 445).

The formation of a republic had also been discussed by Justi in his essay 'Ob die Nachfolger in der Regierung oder die Erben die Schulden eines verstorbenen Reichs-Fürsten zu bezahlen gehalten sind' (*Historische und Juristische Schriften*, p. 129). See also J. W. Textor, *Synopsis of the Law of Nations* (1680), ch. 10, 'Of Republics and their Legal Institution' (*The Classics of International Law*, ed. by J. B. Scott, 1916).

[22] Klueber, *Droit des Gens Modernes de l'Europe* (1831).

[23] Here Klueber relies also on Moser's view that the question whether people may form a new State depends, according to the law of nations, on whether the old sovereign was able or willing to protect them (see Moser's *Versuch des neuesten Europäischen Völkerrechts* (1778), vol. vii, p. 126 et seq.).

[24] See *Staatsklugheit* in Justi.

third powers'. Klueber quotes Steck and Moser in support and draws our attention to numerous examples from State practice. He writes: 'We find examples (of express recognition) in the peace treaty of Munster concluded between Spain and the United Provinces of the Netherlands in 1648, in the peace treaty of Kainardgi of the 10–21 July 1774 (art. 3) and the treaty of Paris of 1783 (art. 1)'. The following further examples of express recognition are drawn from the Napoleonic period:

The recognition of the Kingdom of Westphalia by Russia in the peace treaty of Tilsit, 1807 (arts. 18–20) and by Prussia in the treaty of Tilsit (arts. 6–9); the recognition of the Rhine Confederation by Prussia in the same treaty (art. 4); the recognition of the new Kings of Naples and Holland by Russia and Prussia in the same treaty (arts. 14 and 3); the recognition of the Kingdom and Sovereignty of Bavaria and Wirtemberg as also of Emperor Napoleon as King of Italy by Austria in the treaty of Pressbourg, 1805 (arts. 5, 7, 14). Austria and France recognised the independence of the Helvetian and Batavian Republics in the same treaty (art. 18). In the peace treaty of Vienna, 1809 (art. 15) Austria recognised all changes which had taken place or would take place in Spain, Portugal and Italy. The final act of the Congress of Vienna contains several examples of express recognition in relation to the Kingdoms of Hanover, the Netherlands, and the two Sicilies and Switzerland in arts. 26, 65, 74 and 104.

As to tacit recognition Klueber quotes: 'The peace treaty of Munster of 1648 (art. 53). See also the final Act of the Congress of Vienna (arts. 1, 6, 17, 53, 65 et seq., 98, 99, 101 and 103)'.[25]

It is characteristic that these examples which Klueber quotes in support of the view that recognition, though unnecessary for the validity of the legal status of a new State in the law of nations, may be nevertheless granted by third powers as a matter of *prudence*—are drawn from the Napoleonic period as well as from earlier State practice such as the Treaty of Munster or the Treaty of Kainardgi. Klueber defines prudence as 'convenance de la politique' in inter-State relations. It is obvious that he does not conceive recognition as a constructive or constitutive act, whether in relation to the past or to his own period, but views it as a declaratory act dictated by the requirements of political expediency. In distinction to Justi and Steck, Klueber does not limit the normal role of third powers to due *treatment* accorded to new States or sovereigns in accordance with their lawful rights but finds it also advisable that they should give formal expression to it.[26]

[25] As to guarantees Klueber quotes: 'The treaty of alliance between France and Switzerland of 1777 (art. 4). The Treaty concluded in 1778 between France and the United States of America (art. 11). Guarantee of integrity of the States of the Rhine Confederation promised by Russia in the Treaty of Tilsit of 1807 (art. 25). Reciprocal guarantees of the States concerned in the treaty concluded by France with Bavaria, Wirtemberg and the Elector of Baden (reference to Klueber's *Staatsrecht des Rheinbundes*, para. 135). France guaranteed the integrity of the possessions of the House of Austria in the Treaty of Peace of Pressbourg 1805 (art. 17) and in the Treaty of Vienna, 1809 (art. 14)'. Finally, Klueber quotes further examples by reference to the Acts of the Congress of Vienna.

[26] Klueber restates his views once more in relation to the position of new sovereigns. He writes: 'The Sovereign, that is to say the reigning person who represents the State, partakes in the independence of the latter. It is for this reason that the legality of this dignity, as far as foreign nations are concerned, does not depend at all on the inauguration of the coronation or on the recognition by foreign States …' though it is the usage in Europe (which is not obligatory) to notify foreign powers of the accession of a sovereign to the throne (Klueber, op. cit., p. 80, paras. 48–49).

As to the tortious aspect of recognition, Klueber distinguishes between the recognition of interim possession and the recognition of definite independence of a people rebelling unlawfully or of a usurper. While the first does not violate the rights of the mother State or the lawful sovereign, the second is in his view an outrage against them and continues to be so as long as they have not renounced their rights or are *presumed* to have done so.[27] This presumption is a significant step forward. For while in Steck's essay the period of prematureness suffers from indefiniteness, it is in Klueber's view possible to presume that it has come to an end in a particular case if the mother State has definitely lost its sway over the rebelling people. In that case the presumption seems as good as irrebuttable and it would then be a matter of prudence for foreign powers to recognize the new State and acknowledge its legal position.

Before proceeding to a discussion of Wheaton's views on which Klueber exercised a direct influence, one more writer deserves attention, i.e. Friedrich Saalfeld.[28] The importance of his opinion lies *inter alia* in a joint discussion of sovereignty and recognition. He observes that 'in order to consider the sovereignty of a State as complete in the Law of Nations, there is no need for its recognition by foreign powers; though the latter may appear useful, the de facto existence of sovereignty is sufficient'. Referring further to the problem of legitimacy, Saalfeld states that the way in which sovereignty was acquired by a State has no influence on its recognition by third powers as 'thanks to the perfect independence of States a foreign power is not authorised to judge the legality or illegality of what happens in another State but has to take only facts into consideration. Anyhow recognition of sovereignty given by a third State does not put any restraint on the possible action of the State which intends to question such sovereignty'. In support Saalfeld quotes Martens and Klueber.

Saalfeld repeats the same arguments when he discusses the position of a State which emerged out of a revolution. As to the position of the State which opposes the sovereignty of the new State (mother State), Saalfeld examines the circumstances in which recognition by third States would amount to an offence (*Beleidigung*). In principle such recognition is not yet an offence in itself but the State which feels itself injured does not lose the right to question the sovereignty of the new State. All depends on the fact whether the latter is ultimately established. Saalfeld observes that 'sovereignty is not decisively established if the previous Sovereign still has a footing in the country concerned, if he behaves there as an independent Sovereign, in other words if he still possesses fortified positions and maintains an army in the field'. The period of prematureness is here fairly well defined and affords sufficient guidance for third powers in their relationship to the revolutionary entity.

However, Saalfeld referring to a new instance of State practice, particularly to the Greek revolution, warns the reader of a revival of legitimism accompanied by new principles of intervention. According to these principles armed intervention

[27] Klueber, op. cit., vol. i, para. 23.
[28] Saalfeld, *Handbuch des positiven Völkerrechts* (1833), pp. 26, 63.

by third powers in the revolutionary area is admissible if an uprising originated not from the ruler but from the people, if the results of the revolution are condemnable, if the changes are a bad example for the subjects of the intervening State and if the changes constitute a breach of universal peace. Saalfeld observes that, if recognition is judged by the above standards, one has to look not only at facts but also at their 'legitimacy'.

These observations reflect the tentative revival of the conception of legitimism as propounded by the 'Holy Alliance' school of thought after the Napoleonic wars. Authority of inquiring into the legitimacy of changes in the Family of Nations, whether resulting in the creation of new States or governments, appears here as a discretionary power which would enable the existing States to judge new situations by legitimist tests and to approve or disapprove of them irrespective of the compelling force of facts. This is constitutivism with a vengeance, a solution totally different from that proposed by the early positivist writers for the adjustment of political changes. To appreciate the significance of legal developments at this point a brief recapitulation of the views of these writers seems essential.

We have seen that Justi rejected the interference of foreign powers in elective monarchies by equating elective with hereditary rulers. During an interregnum sovereignty, according to him, is vested in the whole State and the problem of change of the Head of State (government) is the internal problem of its people or its lawful representatives. Recognition does not appear as a medium of legitimating changes from the international point of view.

Steck emphasized, *mutatis mutandis*, the same view in relation to the recognition of new States and reached the conclusion that while third powers should not recognize prematurely, they need not expressly recognize new States after the period of prematureness is over. The legitimist doctrine found here its expression in the preservation of the traditional rights of the mother State. However, these rights were not said to be preserved at any price, and third powers were allowed to establish intercourse with a new revolutionary State even before its release by the mother State, if possession was effectively asserted. Martens and Klueber followed the same conception and the latter introduced a convenient presumption of termination of prematureness. In all these cases the problem of recognition was formulated in a manner to show that the disturbance of the static legal order, which had prevailed in the past during the period of dynastic legitimism, was not allowed to prevent the reconciliation of new political changes with the tentative principles of a flexible and potentially progressive law. For this purpose a kind of basically revised 'legitimism' extending to all independent nations, irrespective of their form of government, was introduced by a number of writers. It aimed at re-establishing in each particular case the disturbed legal order on new equalitarian conditions without the loss of the principle which made it coherent in the past. Thus the orthodox dogma of immutability of the *inter-dynastic* set up in Europe was gradually abandoned and the creation of a new *international* legal order was tentatively proposed to serve the relations between nations and not dynastic interests. Once immutability ceased to be a taboo, and popular sovereignty started to be an equally compelling fountain of law, new States or heads of States (governments) were capable of deriving their legal status from within this legal source. As the law of nations accepted their legal position side by side with the old European powers whose sovereignty dated back to the pre-Bodin period, there was no immediate need of a doctrine authorizing foreign powers to recognize new States or sovereigns in a constructive manner. Recognition continued to perform its traditional function of acknowledgement of facts accompanied by respect for the consequences which the law of nations attached to them, and it was not necessary for the validity of such acknowledgement to be given by an express act. On the other hand, recognition, in so far as it presented itself as a possible weapon for slowing down modern developments, was not allowed to enter the theoretical framework of the law of nations and this no doubt explains the extreme caution with which its first systematic formulation was attempted.

The writers of the early period of eighteenth-century positivism, whenever faced with the eventuality of recognition as a medium of fitting the new political reality into the law, on the whole rejected such a solution, choosing a solution more consistent with the natural law tradition. Even if the law of nations was conceived as based on the consent of States, this anti-naturalist trend was not yet allowed to extend to the field of recognition. Even Klueber who gives recognition a more prominent place in his treatise, treats it as a matter of prudence, an act which could be hardly considered constructive in nature. Moreover, he extends this interpretation retrospectively to such cases in the distant past as, for instance, the legitimation of the Netherlands. Saalfeld follows the same line of reasoning; but he draws our attention to the 'Holy Alliance' conception of legitimism which proposed a different solution, one of preservation of the political balance of power created at the Congress of Vienna by combating revolutionary changes with the help of intervention and discretionary denial of recognition. This solution, which he mentions with reference to the Greek revolution, was to authorize the existing powers to examine the legitimacy of a revolutionary change from without. As we have seen, Saalfeld rejects it as inconsistent with the generally accepted conception of sovereignty.

V.

It is with these considerations in mind that Henry Wheaton's views on recognition may be briefly examined. Wheaton's treatise on international law has already appeared in its fifteenth edition (thirteen of them posthumous) and it is therefore significant as a work of remarkable continuity.[29] It is also important for the examination of the historical aspect of recognition as Wheaton, in his attempt to

[29] The first great systematic works on international law originating from the common law world were written by James Kent and Henry Wheaton. However, Kent's work (started in 1826) was a general Commentary of Law, part of which only was devoted to international law. The problem of recognition is discussed by Kent with reference to revolutionary changes in Europe and America. The principle of defactoism is emphasized in a significant statement: 'Rebellion until it has succeeded is treason; when it is successful it becomes independence; and thus the only real test of independence is final success'. Kent, *Commentary on International Law* (ed. by J. T. Abdy, 1878), p. 88.

formulate the problem of recognition, refers to Klueber who relied on a number of eighteenth-century writers.

The reader of treatises of international law of the nineteenth and twentieth centuries must be struck by the fact that many of their authors referring to Wheaton's views on recognition, confine themselves to quotations from his posthumous editions. There is rarely any reference to the first edition of his *Elements of International Law* which, however, is the most illustrative for the theory of recognition in its early formative stage.

Discussing the problem of sovereignty, Wheaton writes in his first edition: 'Sovereignty is acquired by a State either at the origin of the civil Society of which it consists or when it separates itself lawfully from the community of which it previously formed a part and on which it was dependent'. Here Wheaton quotes Klueber in support.[30]

However, he deviates from Klueber's views when he refers to the formation of a new State by revolutionary change: 'If the revolution in a State be effected by a province or colony shaking off its sovereignty, so long as the independence of the new State is not *acknowledged* by other powers, it may seem doubtful, in an international point of view, whether its sovereignty can be considered as complete however it may be regarded by its own government and citizens'. Though Wheaton suggests here a constitutive theory of recognition, his views on the subject are not yet definite and this follows also from other statements made in the first edition of his treatise.

In a passage on the independence of the Spanish American Republics, he refers to their recognition by the United States and Great Britain 'whilst the parent country (Spain) still continues to withhold her assent' and observes that this example of 'acknowledgment of independence ... concurs to illustrate the general understanding of nations that where a revolted province or colony has declared and shown its ability to maintain its independence, the recognition of its sovereignty by other foreign States is a question of policy and *prudence* only'.[31] This is entirely Klueber's language and the passage by itself might convey the *prima facie* impression that Klueber is not alien to his views.

In another passage Wheaton refers to the independence of Switzerland and the Netherlands who 'so long levied war, concluded peace, contracted alliances and performed every act of sovereignty before their independence was finally acknowledged—that of the first by the German Empire and that of the latter by Spain'. These examples, Wheaton believes—'go far to show the general sense of mankind on this subject'. The general sense of mankind—similarly to prudence—reveals itself through the establishment of intercourse by third powers with new States before their formal release by the mother State.

Finally, Wheaton turns to the problem of American independence in his *Elements of International Law* as well as in his *Histoire des Progrès du Droit des Gens en Europe*

[30] Wheaton, *Elements of International Law* (1836), p. 91 et seq., para. 15.
[31] Wheaton, op. cit.

published in 1841.[32] In the latter he refers to the treaties concluded by France with the United States before their recognition by Great Britain and explains the way in which the French Court tried to justify its policy. In particular, French action in relation to the United States was based on the fact that 'they were in possession of independence when the treaties of alliance and commerce were concluded on 6 February 1778 and that according to undisputed principles of public law this fact was sufficient for the (French) King to enter the above treaties without examining the *legality* of their independence'.[33]

Thus in the light of arguments brought forward in both his treatises Wheaton seems confronted with two solutions relating to recognition: one based on legitimist doctrine, the other on principles of defactoism. He rejects the first together with the corresponding theory of recognition of an interventionist type. Referring to the alliance of Russia, Austria, Prussia, Great Britain and France (the latter since the Congress of Aix-la-Chapelle, 1818) he writes:

> This union was intended to form a perpetual system of intervention among European States, adopted to prevent any such change in the internal forms of their respective governments as might endanger the existence of the monarchical institutions which had been re-established under the legitimate dynasties of their respective reigning houses. The general right of interference was sometimes defined so as to be applicable to every case of popular revolution, where the change in the form of government did not proceed from the voluntary concession of the reigning Sovereign.

It extended also to every revolutionary movement which these powers considered dangerous to 'the social order of Europe'. Wheaton refers here with approval to the policy of the British government which considered the alliance only as one for the liberation of Europe from the military dominance of France. It did not contemplate further intervention: 'It never was ... intended as a union for the government of the world, or for the superintendence of the internal affairs of other States'.[34]

The second solution which presented itself logically to Wheaton was the defactoist one as propounded by the writers whom he quotes and whose terminology he adopts. This solution had been followed in American State practice since Jefferson—to recall his well-known statement that 'it accords with our principles to acknowledge any government to be rightful which is formed by the will of the nation substantially declared'. This statement gives expression to the doctrine of defactoism in its purest form and it was no doubt applied by

[32] p. 395 et seq.

[33] Wheaton adds that it had not been the task of the French Court to examine whether the United States had or had not the right to throw off English sovereignty; whether their independence was legal or not. Neither the law of nations, nor treaties, nor morality, nor politics imposed on the King of France a duty to be the guardian of the allegiance of English subjects to their Sovereign. It was enough that the colonies formed by their population and territory a considerable nation, established their independence, not only by a solemn declaration but also by asserting it against English efforts.

[34] Wheaton, op. cit., pp. 114–17.

the United States to the South American Republics in the early decades of the nineteenth century.[35]

However, Wheaton seems to lean towards a third solution when he expresses his doubt whether sovereignty of a new State can be completed without recognition by third powers. This solution reverts to constitutivism though divorced from principles of legitimism. Wheaton gives full expression to this theory in his third edition of *Elements of International Law* published in Leipzig where he writes that while *de facto* independence of a State is sufficient to establish *internal* sovereignty, its *external* sovereignty 'may require *recognition* of other States in order to render it perfect and complete'.[36] The matter is no more one of doubt as it was in the first edition. Wheaton now splits sovereignty into internal and external. The *de facto* independence of a State no longer determines its external position in the law of nations but is confined in its consequences to the internal sphere. As the external sovereignty of a State is not *derived* from within, it calls for action from without which must be taken by the existing Member States of the Family of Nations. Wheaton considers their recognition as essential for the participation of a new State in all the advantages of the Society of Nations. It is recognition (not acknowledgement) which renders the sovereignty of a new State perfect and complete.

Without going into the reasons which made Wheaton adopt this new solution, it may not be irrelevant to recall what the editor of one of the posthumous editions of his treatise observes in this respect. He draws attention to the fact that it was after the publication of the first two editions that the influence of Bentham, Savigny, Heffter and, above all, of Hegel made itself strongly felt in the sphere of legal doctrine.[37] Hegel derives the legal existence of a new State from the will of the existing powers.[38] Their consent is not only at the basis of international law as such, it also determines membership in the Family of Nations.[39] This constituted a deviation from the views of the earlier positivists who did not envisage an extension of the theory of consent of States to the field of recognition of States and governments. The sovereignty of a new State or the legal position of the Head of State or government was in their view totally determined from within with full validity in the external sphere. The Hegelian school combined positivism with constitutivism and abandoned the pure defactoist basis of sovereignty and recognition. Wheaton, seemingly under the impact of these trends, abandons the conception of

[35] Goebel Jr., *The Recognition Policy of the United States* (in *Studies in History, Economics and Public Law* (1915), vol. lxvi).

[36] Wheaton, *Elements of International Law* (1848) (repeated in Dana's ed., 1866, Part I, paras. 20–27).

[37] Wheaton, *Elements of International Law* (ed. by Wilson, *The Classics of International Law*, p. 14*a*).

[38] Hegel, *Werke* (1854), vol. viii, part iii, para. 331. See also Sir Hersch Lauterpacht, *Recognition in International Law* (1948), p. 38.

[39] Nussbaum, *A Concise History of the Law of Nations* (1954), p. 237, observes: 'Hegel opens the door to intervention by arguing that a State cannot be indifferent to what is going on internally in another State (more precisely, such internal developments may justify denial of recognition to that State)'. See also the general observations made by Goebel Jr., op. cit.

homogeneous sovereignty, divides it into internal and external and makes the latter dependent on the consent of States.

However, this division does not seem to eliminate entirely the defactoist tradition. Though external sovereignty is no more self-constitutive within a new State but depends on recognition by foreign powers, its internal sovereignty is still a matter of factual formation and not of legitimacy which, in Wheaton's view, is not the concern of the recognizing powers.

VI.

The purpose of this inquiry is not to engage in a discussion of further developments in the nineteenth and twentieth centuries. Our considerations were confined to the early historical aspect of recognition and their purpose was to draw the attention of historians of international law to the first monographic attempts in this field. It has been shown that the need for sorting out State practice in the field of recognition and for ascertaining certain principles presented itself during the period of the gradual decline of dynastic legitimism. With the occurrence of frequent changes in membership of the Family of Nations and with the appearance of new forms of government and the corresponding conflicts between new State and mother State or between Sovereign and Sovereign (government), third powers started looking for legal guidance and recognition came to claim a separate chapter in treatises of international law which it did not enjoy in the works of the great classic writers of the late naturalist and earlier positivist period. It is at this turning-point that the first monographs on the subject appear. With legitimism struggling for its preservation in Europe, several solutions presented themselves in a tentative way. We have drawn attention to what Justi and Steck proposed in their essays. Martens studied both of them and thus their views were reflected in one of the most outstanding treatises of the law of nations. The Napoleonic period had much to add to the volume of State practice in the field of recognition. Napoleon obtained recognition from the dynastic powers on the continent of Europe for his policy of creating new States and Sovereigns and we find in Klueber a writer facing squarely the lessons of the period. Klueber, relying on Steck, still follows the defactoist principle though he introduces an element of 'convenance de la politique' and advocates the stabilization of political situations by express or tacit recognition, unlike his predecessors who considered the establishment of intercourse as a sufficient medium for normalizing the relations of the existing powers with new States or governments. Wheaton is not only faced with the pre- and immediate post-Napoleonic material but examines also the policy of Great Britain and the United States applied to the Spanish–South American conflict. Like his predecessors he is anti-legitimist but he is also reluctant to follow the defactoist doctrine in its entirety. After the publication of the first edition of his *Elements of International Law* Wheaton, influenced by Hegelian ideology, is faced with a new possible solution. In his third edition he adheres to this new solution and adopts a constitutive theory of recognition.

Our attention has also been drawn to the tortious aspect of recognition. The most important problem in this respect is that of prematureness of recognition of a new State or Sovereign (government) in violation of the rights of the mother State or the previous Sovereign. The term 'prematureness' in relation to a new State meant in conditions of legitimism the period preceding its recognition by the mother State. Steck tears himself away from this conception of prematureness but not without difficulty. Anyhow, he admits intercourse between a rebel State and third powers dictated by the circumstances of each particular case. In the view of later writers such as Martens and Klueber the period of prematureness is significantly shortened and third powers do not run the risk of committing a delict by acknowledging the independence of a new State if the mother State has lost its grip over the former, even prior to the recognition of the new State by the mother State. This tortious aspect of recognition remains part and parcel of our notions of international law whether in relation to premature recognition of States or governments and it testifies to the potentialities of the legal character of recognition.

There was, however, another and perhaps more significant aspect of the delictual character of recognition emphasized by eighteenth-century writers, i.e. that arising out of unlawful denial of recognition of new States or Heads of States by foreign powers. Justi speaking about denial to an elective ruler of recognition of his title or rank derived not from foreign powers but from his predecessors in power, considers such non-recognition as a delict which entitles the injured ruler to proceed to mutual non-recognition by way of reprisals. Moser speaks about the duty of recognition of a new elective ruler in terms similar to those in Justi's essay. But, as already pointed out, it is important to remember that in the view of the early positivist writers the duty of recognition of new States or rulers (governments) by foreign powers lies in the acknowledgement of situations of fact and the respect for the significance and for the consequences which the law ascribes to them. In this sense their writings contain no doubt the rudiments of a legal theory of recognition. Steck, discussing the recognition policy of Spain in relation to the United States of America at the close of the eighteenth century, goes so far as to say that non-recognition would amount to forcing the new State into submission to the former mother State and violates the natural right of States to equality. This peculiar tortious aspect of recognition loses some of its original significance in the treatises of early nineteenth-century writers. A discussion of the legal theory of recognition and its possible co-existence with the constitutive theory in subsequent literature and State practice would be beyond the scope of our considerations.[40] Equally outside their scope is the discussion of other aspects of recognition such as recognition of belligerency or the distinction between *de facto* and *de jure* recognition as revealed in Canning's recognition policy in South America.[41]

A better understanding of the early formative stage of the theory of recognition called for a survey of the views of the first comparatively unknown monographers

[40] For a discussion of this problem see Lauterpacht, op. cit.
[41] Temperley, *The Foreign Policy of Canning* (1925), p. 143.

on the subject, whose impact on the writers of the generally known treatises should not escape the attention of historians of international law. Without having exhausted the list of the former or the latter, an attempt has been made to examine the different solutions which suggested themselves in the period of great political and ideological changes. Whether the theory of recognition has since outgrown its formative stage if viewed in a wider perspective may still seem doubtful. State practice and the divergent views of writers present up to our day a confusing picture out of which no satisfactory measure of common opinion seems capable of emerging. In a way the theory of recognition seems still to be *in fieri.*

25

THE QUASI-JUDICIAL FUNCTION IN RECOGNITION OF STATES AND GOVERNMENTS (1952)

For several generations past international lawyers have discussed the problem whether recognition of states, governments and belligerency is a matter of law or of policy. They have been unable to reach uniform conclusions. Some of them, like Professor Lauterpacht in his book on recognition, have advocated the view that there is a right to recognition and a duty to recognize.[1] This attempt has proved unsuccessful and has not been supported by the majority of writers. The legal theory of recognition is of great value *de lege ferenda*, but it is definitely not backed by the actual practice of states. The case of recognition of the revolutionary government of China showed an unexpected diversity of views all over the world. Had the East alone granted recognition to the regime of Mao Tse-Tung, and the West unanimously refused to accord it, it would have proved that the West at least, has a uniform conception of recognition. However, diversity prevailed not only between East and West, but also between the main Powers in the West. Diversity of practice and views shows that the political theory of recognition has not grown to the level of a legal theory. But in spite of different views on the nature of recognition, international lawyers were able to agree on the nature of the discretion exercised by states in the process of recognition. There is no doubt that this discretion, though it is political, is neither absolute nor arbitrary. States considering the according or refusal of recognition have, without exception, examined certain facts which are essential for their final decisions. The examination of these facts amounts to a fact-finding inquiry in which states perform a *sui generis* function. The juristic formulation of this function seems of primary importance, the more so that it may throw more light on the whole process of recognition and be helpful in clarifying the confusion which has accompanied the prolonged discussion on the subject.

Professor Hans Kelsen has drawn our attention to the fact that recognition is connected with a process of cognizance or cognition which has the same character as the establishment of a legally relevant fact by a court.[2] He unfortunately identified

[1] H. Lauterpacht, *Recognition in International Law* (1948).

[2] Hans Kelsen, 'Recognition in International Law', *American Journal of International Law*, Vol. 35 (1941), p. 605 *et seq*.

cognition with recognition, though the first always precedes the second in time, and constitutes a separate stage in the process of recognition as a whole. In the stage of cognition, recognizing states do not perform judicial functions *sensu stricto*, neither formally nor in substance. First of all it is the executive and not the judicial authority of the recognizing state which is competent to deal with the matter and it does not act as a court but as an administrative authority. However, administrative authorities in many parts of the world may be under a duty to act in a quasi-judicial capacity before they reach decisions as a matter of policy, and the judiciary may be called upon to control the quasi-judicial function. This is in many cases the practice adopted by the English legal system and by countries which have based their law on the above system. The interconnection between law and policy in the national field and the legal structure of this interconnection are not irrelevant for international lawyers who try to define the complex process of recognition in which law and policy mutually depend upon each other. A better understanding of recognition as a whole depends to a great extent on a thorough analysis of the process of cognition and its relationship to decisions which follow the above process. As the practice of states does not entitle us to consider recognition as an act of law but as an act of policy only, we have to look for the legal element in cognition without confusing it with recognition, otherwise we are forced to consider recognition as entirely outside the field of law, which would be even more absurd than to consider recognition as an act of law. Many writers confining themselves to two alternatives, *i.e.*, the legal or political conception of recognition, had to adopt extreme views and have maneuvered themselves into a cul-de-sac from which withdrawal back to reality seems desirable. It is of interest to examine whether the legal element in recognition can be identified with the quasi-judicial function, and whether the latter is performed by the recognizing state in the same way as it is exercised by administrative authorities in the national field. Such an examination first calls for a brief analysis of the above function as such.[3]

The exercise of power by an administrative authority often involves a process which is partly executive and partly judicial. We may call the judicial element quasi-judicial, and thus the whole power quasi-judicial. An administrative officer may have to perform a fact-finding inquiry before he reaches his final decision and therefore the exercise of discretion is preceded by a *sui generis* process. But although the officer acts in much the same way as a judge in the above inquiry, he does not apply a rule of law to the facts, but finally exercises his discretion and judgement as a matter of policy. Discretion is connected with a choice between two or more courses of action. A judge does not exercise his discretion, except in certain branches of law such as criminal law; he applies a rule of law to the facts of the case. An administrator has two or more courses of action and his choice is not a matter of law. Under the English legal system his decision cannot be questioned in a court of law on the ground that he made the wrong choice. As an administrative officer he is first of all

[3] E. C. S. Wade and G. G. Philips, *Constitutional Law* (1950), p. 280 *et seq.*; W. W. Willoughby, *The Constitutional Law of the United States* (1929), p. 1655 *et seq.*

politically and not judicially responsible. The body called upon to criticize his decisions is Parliament. Under a presidential regime such as in the United States he is responsible to the head of the executive branch of the government. But although an administrative officer is, through his Minister or Head of Department, politically responsible, his decisions are not in every respect free from judicial control. Under common law he has rarely absolute or arbitrary discretionary powers, and though the court cannot re-examine his decisions in substance, it can question them on certain other well-established grounds. It can prevent an administrator from exceeding his statutory power whenever he acts *ultra vires*, and it can prevent him from exercising his discretion wrongfully. The *ultra vires* rule does not call for an explanation. More interesting to the international lawyer who looks for an analogy between the national and international sphere, is the case of wrongful exercise of discretion. An administrative decision may be challenged in court whenever the executive officer is guilty of abuse of power. This is the position under most legal systems based on English law as well as under the law of the United States. French administrative law has termed the above abuse of power '*détournement de pouvoir*'.[4]

Thus when an administrative officer exercises his powers for an improper purpose, when he takes into account irrelevant considerations or overlooks relevant considerations, when he infringes the rules of natural justice or whenever he acts *mala fide*, the court will intervene and examine the case. Whenever an administrative officer is under a duty to hold a fact-finding inquiry to which a party is entitled to submit relevant material, he has to observe certain rules which govern the quasi-judicial process of cognition. For instance, in the United Kingdom, area traffic commissioners or a transport tribunal perform functions which are neither entirely administrative nor judicial. The powers of these bodies are quasi-judicial in respect of the procedure which has to be observed before administrative decisions are reached by them. In the United States the courts have an even wider power of control over administrative decisions, and they can in certain instances declare a law unconstitutional and inapplicable to the case and can examine whether the administrator has made a correct finding of facts and drawn the right conclusions therefrom.[5]

We may ask ourselves whether the decision of an executive relating to the recognition of foreign states or governments falls within the category of subjects in which the decision is one of policy, but where in the fact-finding inquiry preceding the decision certain legal rules should be observed. There is no doubt that the declaration of a government in the matter of recognition is conclusive and binding upon courts in English as well as in United States law. The courts have to draw the necessary conclusions from official statements issued by government departments concerned with foreign affairs, and no judicial control of cognition is possible. However this is the position in municipal law only.[6] States which are recognized

[4] M. Waline, *Manuel de Droit Administratif* (1935).

[5] As to the substantial evidence rule, see Bernard Schwarz, *Law and the Executive in Britain, a Comparative Study* (1949), p. 277 *et seq.*

[6] P. C. Jessup, 'Has the Supreme Court Abdicated One of Its Functions?' *American Journal of International Law*, Vol. 40 (1946), p. 168 *et seq.*

members of the family of nations are bound by international law and the question arises: What are the consequences, if any, in the international sphere, of disregarding the rules of international law governing the process of cognition? These rules are connected with the quasi-judicial function performed by states in the course of a fact-finding inquiry.[7] A brief analysis of these rules seems essential in order to answer the above question.

Whenever a new state or government appears in the international sphere, it will as a rule become a candidate or applicant for recognition. It will, by unilateral request, approach other Powers who become, individually, the judges of the case.[8] In dealing with such a request they must examine the facts of the case. It serves no useful purpose to speculate as to whether such an examination aims at a *declaration* of facts, or at recognition of a *constitutive* character. The facts must be proved by evidence in the course of the inquiry. The examining Powers have to ascertain whether an applicant state has a government which has established its jurisdiction over people in a certain territory. This means that the fact-finding inquiry cannot ignore the objective tests of statehood. It is impossible to recognize legally a state which does not exist *de facto*. It is equally impossible to recognize the government of an existing state unless such a government has come into existence. In other words, a fact-finding inquiry cannot be performed in a vacuum, the more so that such *vacua* cannot be presumed to exist in the international field.[9] In our present state of affairs territory inhabited by people is always covered by some national jurisdiction, and *de facto* authorities which exercise such jurisdiction cannot be ignored from the international point of view.[10] Though in the absence of recognition there may be no state or government in the eyes of international law, there is always some body aiming at recognition which must be considered at least temporarily as endowed with quasi-statehood or quasi-governmental capacity. Such applicant state or government submits itself to a fact-finding inquiry, and an examination of facts takes place in which relevant considerations have to be taken into account and irrelevant considerations ignored irrespective of final decisions.

The Powers which consider the question of granting or refusing recognition have to examine all the facts relevant to the purpose of the inquiry and have to act *bona fide*. The close interconnection between the basic indicia of statehood is of utmost importance in the process of the inquiry. As a government must prove that it has established effective jurisdiction over people in a certain territory, express or implied acceptance of this jurisdiction by the people is essential. The *political* existence of an applicant state or government is essential for the success of its application in the *legal* sphere. To some degree it must have internal sovereignty

[7] H. Lauterpacht, 'Recognition of States in International Law', *Yale Law Journal*, Vol. 53 (1943/4), p. 407.

[8] *Ibid.*, p. 437.

[9] P. M. Brown, 'The Effects of Recognition', *American Journal of International Law*, Vol. 36 (1942), p. 107.

[10] The case of the Tinoco Concessions, in L. C. Green, *International Law Through the Cases* (1951), p. 103 *et seq.*; also *American Journal of International Law*, Vol. 18 (1924), p. 147.

to be able to become externally sovereign. The governments of the existing Powers are called upon to judge the circumstances of each case. The practice of states since the time of Jefferson has proved that apart from objective tests of effective possession of authority established by candidate states or governments, there are subjective tests which render the process of the fact-finding inquiry more precarious. The representative character of a government may be considered an objective test, but should the existing Powers desire to test the lawfulness of democratic elections announced and initiated by a candidate government, they may approach the borderline of intervention and go beyond the limits of the inquiry.[11] Willingness to fulfill international obligations seems to be a subjective test, though the recognizing Powers have in many instances insisted on its inclusion in the process of cognition. The fact-finding inquiry in its entirety has not taken a uniform shape. Certain tests applied by Powers have varied from case to case, but there is no risk in saying that the basic objective tests relating to statehood and governmental capacity have never been ignored. In fact it would be difficult to imagine how any Power could consider its final decision of recognition without having first full cognizance of the existence of a suitable candidate state or government.

The differences which appeared between Powers at various times as to tests which are either subjective or have a flavour of subjectiveness cannot be overlooked by the international lawyer. The constant changes in Latin American Republics made the United States Government cautious in granting recognition to new revolutionary administrations.[12] The insistence of President Wilson on the truly democratic character of a government as a test of recognition left a significant mark on the institution of recognition as such. Willingness to fulfill international obligations became a further important element in inquiries. The practice of the United States deviated, in the period preceding the first World War, from Jefferson's view that effectiveness is the only decisive test. The recognition of the Soviet Government after the first World War became the great test case in the history of recognition. Whereas Great Britain recognized the Soviet Government *de facto* in 1921, the United States conducted their fact-finding inquiry for years and recognition followed as late as 1933. But there is no reason to see any essential difference in the process of cognition as applied by Great Britain and by the United States. Though evidence was weighed differently here and there, and though the speed of the inquiry was not the same, cognizance of basic facts took place in the same way. The United States Government took the view that a new government in the above circumstances can be considered permanent only after some length of time. A prolonged process of cognition resulting in *tardy* recognition helps to ascertain whether people under a new government have acquiesced in the new rule and whether the new government gives a guarantee, by conduct and not by words only, that it has capacity and willingness to fulfill its international obligations.[13] In other words, in a cautious

[11] C. C. Hyde, *International Law* (1947), Vol. I, p. 182. [12] *Ibid.*, p. 165 *et seq.*

[13] Edwin Borchard, 'Recognition and Non-Recognition', *American Journal of International Law*, Vol. 36 (1942), p. 110.

process of cognition the subjective tests are better merged into the objective test of effectiveness. This writer cannot see what other difference is shown by American and British practice in the case. Both Powers have acted on the basic assumption that facts cannot be ignored and if convincing evidence of facts is secured, recognition is granted, sooner or later.

The same situation seems to be arising in the case of recognition of the present revolutionary government of China, in which India has followed British practice, and other Powers, France among them, have followed that of the United States. It is difficult to assume that any Power ignores the objective test of effectiveness in the present case. However, the United States Government is still conducting its fact-finding inquiry, whereas other Powers have concluded theirs and granted recognition. To consider the withholding of recognition as an act of politics or power politics, does not mean that the legal basis of the inquiry is ignored. To assume its abandonment would mean the sanctioning of a legal vacuum which cannot be presumed to exist. On the other hand, the fact that an inquiry to test the conduct of the new government and the record of its leaders, is prolonged for years, does not deprive it of its real significance. All it means is that sufficient time is taken to consider the evidence conclusive.[14]

It is not unreasonable to consider the entirety of existing Powers as a partnership in which many co-ordinated functions are performed. The principal Powers, being the decisive element in the partnership, may act with more or less unanimity, or there may be deeper differences of opinion between them.[15] Whenever one of them disregards universally accepted tests in the conduct of a fact-finding inquiry preceding recognition, other members of the partnership may disapprove deviations from basic rules.[16] There is no likelihood of the whole partnership going against the reality of facts. This tendency to base international law on facts is independent of power politics which are concerned with shaping facts. In the process of shaping facts some balance always follows unbalance when international law is called upon to perform the function of the law of power.[17] Unbalance is not synonymous with war, or even with 'cold war'. Any important difference of opinion in a vital matter is a *sui generis* unbalance which is followed sooner or later by some settlement. When facts again become static the law gives legal sanctity to the balance achieved. Thus, if there is a vital difference of opinion in the matter of recognition of a particular state or government, fact-finding inquiries may be performed speedily by those who consider the facts settled, but they may be performed with caution by those who consider the *de facto* position as still open. As long as facts cannot be judged with some unanimity, decisions seem to be premature. Those who accord to candidate

[14] C. G. Fenwick, 'The Recognition of New Governments Instituted by Force,' *American Journal of International Law*, Vol. 38 (1944), p. 448 *et seq.*

[15] C. H. Alexandrowicz, 'Israel *in Fieri*', *International Law Quarterly*, July, 1951 (ch. 26 below).

[16] In the case of recognition of the Tinoco regime in Costa Rica the State Department announced to three Central American states that it would disapprove the recognition of General Tinoco by any of them. See C. C. Hyde, *op. cit.*, p. 168.

[17] G. Schwarzenberger, *Power Politics* (1951), p. 203 *et seq.*

states or governments premature recognition may commit a tort against another state or government whose rights are violated. They may also anticipate events while such events are relevant facts in the inquiry itself. There is always an element of risk in recognizing a state or government which may not survive events: the risk of taking part in the shaping of events instead of allowing them to take shape before they can be inquired into in a legal way. To judge facts in the international field calls for caution and the Powers should act as cautious judges. If one Power grants speedy recognition, another Power may become in its own inquiry the judge of an inquiry previously concluded. If the partnership of Powers mutually controls the examination of facts, a more objective decision is likely to result from the inquiries as a whole. In exceptional cases states have granted collective recognition such as in the case of the recognition of Bulgaria, Montenegro, Serbia, and Rumania at the Berlin Congress in 1878. In the majority of cases the powers were mutually the judges of the quasi-judicial function performed separately by each of them. In spite of differences of opinion they have always in the long run reached unanimous conclusions. No candidate state or government has ultimately remained on the international scene by a majority of votes. It has either disappeared or secured unanimous recognition.

The history of recognition shows various types of candidate states and governments which appeared on the international scene. Individuals seeking power who had hardly grown above the level of adventure tried to secure an international status.[18] The attempt of Sydney Burt to form, in 1871, an independent government in the Fiji Islands, and Hardy Hicky's efforts to establish a state on an island several hundred miles off the coast of Brazil, never resulted in recognition by the family of nations, who welcomes serious newcomers but not adventurers. Manchoukuo was never considered an independent state, and all *ad hoc* created states and governments formed by Hitler never rose above the status of puppet formations. On the other hand, the international position of the Holy See which has for centuries enjoyed universal recognition, was never questioned, even during the period between 1871 and 1929 when it was deprived of territory. We may say with confidence that whenever new states or governments were able to state a case before the existing Powers as the judges of facts, the dignity of the judicial function, which we termed quasi-judicial, compelled them sooner or later to live up to a high standard in their world political decisions. A *coup d'état* initiated by an adventurer was always distinguished from a revolution, which has deeper roots in social and economic changes. Newcomers to the international scene, convinced of the righteousness of their cause, may become impatient when the old Powers proceed cautiously in their inquiry into revolutionary facts and events. To prevent existing governments from exercising their discretion in an arbitrary manner, some higher control of executive power is needed, at least in the same degree as it is applied in the national field. The Powers exercising a quasi-judicial function apply rules of international law and are agents of an international order. Instead of aiming at the impossible and

[18] Lauterpacht, *loc. cit.*, p. 431.

considering recognition as an act of law, international lawyers should first define the rules of the quasi-judicial process of cognition which are supported by the actual practice of states.

A cautious appreciation of facts relating to recognition is often connected with another essential issue, that of representation and membership rights of the candidate government in the comprehensive international organization. In the case of the admission of a new state, the United Nations, following the League of Nations' tradition, considers statements of fact from the applicant state and conducts a fact-finding inquiry preceding the eventual admission to the Organization.[19] Whereas admission is a political act, the inquiry is, here also, of a quasi-judicial nature. The following are the tests of admission which are applied in the process of cognition: The candidate community must be, according to Article 4 of the United Nations Charter, a state; it must be peace-loving, accept the obligations of the Charter, and must, in the judgement of the organization be able and willing to carry out these obligations. It is of importance to note that a candidate state becomes a quasi-party to the inquiry. The same must apply to a candidate government which seeks the right of representation of an existing state in the Organization. Apart from subjective tests, statehood and governmental capacity are objective tests of admission to the United Nations in the same way as in individual cases of recognition. No state or government has a right to admission to membership in the United Nations, but if a fact-finding inquiry is held following an application, legally defined tests must be applied. There is a duty to inquire into relevant facts and a right to have them examined in good faith. In other words, the United Nations acts in the same way as an administrator acts in the national field whenever he performs a quasi-judicial function before giving his decision as a matter of policy.

The International Court of Justice, at the request of the General Assembly, has recently given an advisory opinion on the question whether a Member of the United Nations which is called upon, in virtue of Article 4 of the Charter, to pronounce itself by vote on the admission of a state to membership in the United Nations, is juridically entitled to make its consent to the admission dependent on conditions not expressly provided by paragraph 1 of the said article. The Court gave a negative answer to the above question.[20] If we rightly understand the above opinion it means that Members of the United Nations who are the judges in cases of admission to membership do not exercise absolute or arbitrary discretion. Though their decision, expressed by vote, cannot be legally questioned, they can act only on the basis of relevant considerations, and cannot arbitrarily introduce into the case irrelevant elements not included in Article 4 of the Charter. This pronouncement of the International Court is significant and applies, *mutatis mutandis*, to the field of recognition also, though there is no written charter of conditions of recognition.

[19] Hans Kelsen, *The Law of the United Nations* (1950), p. 66 *et seq.*

[20] I.C.J. Reports, 1948, p. 57; *American Journal of International Law*, Vol. 42 (1948), p. 927; Kelsen, *op. cit.*, pp. 72–73.

The question arises: Can an international body perform the same function in the international field as courts perform under English and American law whenever they exercise judicial control of administrative power? Without attempting to suggest such a body by name, we may say that if it were an international tribunal it could be approached by an application for a kind of prerogative writ or order and exercise judicial control over the process of cognition, without substituting its discretion for the discretion of the body or Power which admits a candidate state or government to participation in international rights and duties. If it is not a court, it would have to examine the process of cognition at least in a quasi-judicial way, that is to say, it would exercise quasi-judicial control of administrative power. Such a solution would be possible if the extreme views of the legal and political theory of recognition were avoided. The analogy between admission to the United Nations and recognition has been stressed to show the nature of the fact-finding inquiry as distinct from final decisions.

In the present state of affairs the International Court of Justice would not treat refusal of recognition by a Power to a new state or government as a breach of duty. To insist on the assumption of such jurisdiction by the International Court would be crying for the ideal. However, international lawyers, by defining the quasi-judicial function performed by Powers in the process of cognition, could prepare the ground for the International Court to assume, in future, judicial control of the fact-finding inquiry in the same way as municipal courts exercise it under the English and American legal systems. Many obstacles of a technical nature would have to be overcome before such a courageous step could be taken. One of the main problems would be to ascertain whether a candidate state or government in the case of refusal of recognition, could be considered a member of the judicial community of nations and whether it could apply to the International Court for a judgment or order in the nature of *certiorari* and act as a party to the proceedings.[21] This seems to be a matter for considerable doubt, but it is less impossible than to ask the International Court to consider refusal of recognition as an international tort. Unrecognized communities are treated in many respects as if they were subjects of international law, and unrecognized governments are often considered as endowed with quasi-governmental capacity.[22] If the International Court would, at its initiative or at the initiative of Powers interested in a particular case, examine fact-finding inquiries which resulted in refusal of recognition, the existing rules relating to these inquiries would take uniform legal shape. Cases of premature or tardy recognition could then be reduced to a minimum and recognition as a political act could be made more or less independent of the game of power politics, a step essential for the consolidation of the international society.

[21] As to membership in the judicial community see Kelsen's *Law of the United Nations*, p. 489 *et seq.* As to the capacity of non-recognized states to act in the international field, particularly to participate in the activities of the United Nations, see Kelsen *op. cit.*, pp. 79, 226–227.

[22] P. M. Brown, 'The Recognition of Israel', *American Journal of International Law*, Vol. 42 (1948), p. 624.

26

ISRAEL *IN FIERI* (1951)

In International Law States may establish Sovereignty over a certain territory by the acquisition of an original or derivative title. In the first case their title is independent of any previous title; if they acquire territory by occupation, they enter an international legal vacuum. In the second case Sovereignty is transferred from one State to another State by cession and the subsequent title depends on the validity of the previous title. There may, however, be the case of a State whose title is not derived from that of another State, but who cannot be considered an original occupier of the territory. For instance, one State may renounce its title to a certain territory, but before a succeeding State assumes Sovereignty over it there may be an interregnum which does not immediately fit into the classic conceptions of International Law. The Mandate of Palestine following upon the disintegration of the Turkish Empire is an example. The above question may seem to be of theoretical significance only, but has also certain practical consequences. The answer suggested may help to explain the birth of the State of Israel as an International Person and some of its rights and duties as a new member of the Family of Nations. A short analysis of all relevant facts beginning with the end of the First World War is essential to our examination.[1]

There is no doubt that when under the Treaty of Lausanne, 1923, the Turkish Empire was divested of Sovereignty over Palestine, no legal vacuum appeared, as Sovereignty was transferred to the Principal Allied Powers. The text of the Treaty is less clear here than the Treaty of Versailles where Sovereignty over German overseas possessions is specifically transferred to the Principal Allied Powers (Article 119). But as these Powers proceeded in both cases to the establishment of Mandates, they may safely be considered holders of the titles to all former German and Turkish territories over which they established *joint Sovereignty*. The description of this state of affairs as joint Sovereignty, and not as con-dominium or co-imperium seems appropriate, as it corresponds best to the fact of joint acquisition. In subsequent legal transactions the Principal Allied Powers acted as joint holders of this supreme title, conferring on other States minor titles connected with the Mandates. It is true that Sovereignty was not transferred to a legal person, but the existence of a

[1] Quincy Wright, *Mandates under the League of Nations*, 1930; Norman Bentwich, *The Mandates System*, 1930; G. Schwarzenberger, *Das Völkerbunds-Mandat für Palästina*, 1929; J. C. Hales, *The Creation and Application of the Mandate System* (25 Transactions of the Grotius Society, 1939).

partnership of Powers, acting through a Supreme Council, was enough to preclude a legal vacuum.

The right to allocate Mandates was vested by Article 118 of the Treaty of Versailles in the Principal Allied (and Associated) Powers. Mr. Hymans in his report on Mandates suggested the following procedure to the Council of the League of Nations:[2] the 'pentarchy' would assign particular Mandates to particular States and notify the Council that these States had become Mandatory Powers. The Council would take formal notice of the consequent status of the Mandatory Powers, which was quite distinct from what it would have been had they, as individual countries, acquired derivative titles to enemy territory by acts of cession. The Council of the League adopted Mr. Hymans' report and requested the Principal Allied Powers to allocate Mandates; to inform it of the frontiers of the mandated territories; and to communicate to it proposed terms and conditions of the Mandates. It follows that neither the League of Nations nor the Mandatory Powers acquired Sovereignty. But what happened after the dissolution of the Supreme Council of the Principal Allied Powers? In dealing with the aftermath of war, they had acted as a *partnership* of Powers. Upon the disappearance of the Supreme Council they ceased to act jointly as a partnership, though they did not transfer to any other authority Sovereignty over the mandated territories. Supervision and control of the administration of the Mandates remained, however, with the League of Nations, though the existence of Mandates was not dependent on the existence of the League itself.[3]

The Mandate of Palestine states clearly that the Principal Allied Powers had entrusted the Mandatory Power with the administration (minor title) of the mandated territory and had agreed that the latter should be responsible for putting into effect the Balfour Declaration concerning the establishment in Palestine of a national home for the Jewish people. The function of the League was to define the limits of authority, control and administration and this the League did in the various provisions of the Mandate; inter alia, a Jewish agency was created to co-operate with the Mandatory Power. The Mandatory Power acquired the right of internal administration and of control of the foreign relations of Palestine, but it could neither alienate nor lease any of its territory, this being an attribute of Sovereignty (Article 5).

By Article 22 of the Covenant of the League of Nations the national communities in the class of mandated territories were recognised as potentially independent nations, over which the Mandatory had to exercise a temporary tutelage as a sacred trust of civilisation. We may dismiss at once the theory of some international lawyers that Sovereignty was vested in these communities.[4] All that our generally accepted rules of International Law entitle us to assume is the existence of a community; only when it became possessed of a defined territory and an established government, could it be recognised as a new International Person. The conception

[2] J. C. Hales, *op. cit.*, p. 125.

[3] See opinion of International Court of Justice on Status of South-West Africa.

[4] Stoyanowsky, *La théorie générale des mandats internationaux*, 1925.

of trust was often mis-translated and misunderstood. If we attempt to apply the English institution of trust, we must look for the holder of the nominal title (trustee) and for the beneficiaries. The nominal title of Sovereignty was vested in the Principal Allied Powers who did not confer directly any rights upon the beneficiaries (the communities). Thus the Mandatory Powers could only be regarded as trustees of the right of administration, as this was the only right vested in them.

One of the Principal Allied Powers, the U.S.A., not being a member of the League of Nations, entered in December, 1925, into a special agreement with the Mandatory Power in Palestine. The rights of U.S. nationals were secured in the agreement, and the Mandatory Power undertook to send to the U.S. Government copies of its reports to the League. The other Principal Powers were members of the League.[5]

The link between the League and the 'pentarchy' did not, however, affect the distinction between the supreme title and the minor title and did not alter the fact that their holders were different. The dissolution of the League did not affect the existence of the Mandate as such, but only its supervision, as is confirmed by the opinion of the International Court of Justice upon the status of South-West Africa.[6]

The above opinion is essential for understanding the interrelationship between the Mandatory Administration and the State of Israel. The Court expressed the unanimous opinion that Mandates survived the League and that Sovereignty was never vested in the Mandatories. No Mandatory Power was capable therefore of transferring the supreme title. It is true that the Principal Allied Powers, the holders of Sovereignty, ceased to act, but lack of action could not result in a legal vacuum. The Mandates of class 'A' were according to Article 22 of the Covenant to undergo a speedy evolution towards the establishment of new States. It is noteworthy that the Resolution of November, 1947, of the General Assembly of the United Nations, which provided for the establishment of Jewish and Arab States, made a clear distinction between the independence of the new State and its membership of the United Nations. Independence, in other words Sovereignty, is a matter of membership of the Family of Nations, of which the Principal Powers are members. This inner circle of the Family of Nations, which had assumed the shape of a partnership after the First World War, is not now the same as it was before, but this seems irrelevant, as the Principal Powers of the Family of Nations are a partnership with changing membership. Their recognition is always essential for a new State to join the Family. Thus there is no reason to exclude *continuity* of Sovereignty in the case of Israel. Without continuity we would have to accept the alternative, of acquisition of territory by Israel by an original title, which is impossible in the absence of any *terra nullius*. There remains, however, the difficulty that no actual cession took place and that therefore Israel's title cannot be derivative. We must therefore consider its legal status as *sui generis*: there was first a transfer of Sovereignty by the Turkish

[5] Norman Bentwich, *op cit.*; Dr. G. Weiss, *Die Entstehung des Staates Israel, Zeitschrift für ausländisches öffentliches Recht und Völkerrecht*, February, 1950.

[6] *I. C. J. Reports*, 1950, p. 128.

Empire to the Principal Powers as joint Sovereigns. It is this multipartite arrangement that made possible the *release* of Sovereignty to the State of Israel as the final transferee. The conception, favoured by some, of 'revival' of Sovereignty after the recognition of Israel seems harmless, as long as it does not imply that Sovereignty was previously 'in abeyance' so that a legal vacuum must be assumed.[7] The latter would destroy continuity, a solution acceptable neither by the Family of Nations nor by the new State whose present rights and duties should as far as possible be linked with the past.

The part played by the U. N. at the request of the Mandatory Power in the last stages of the formation of Israel was important. According to the opinion of the majority of judges of the International Court upon South-West Africa, the U. N. is entitled to exercise certain rights of supervision over the Mandatory Power, though it is not the legal successor to the League. We have seen that this function has nothing to do with the location of Sovereignty. The November Resolution of the General Assembly sought to establish the Statehood of Israel in two stages.[8] It provided for a transitional period between the dates of the Resolution and of the acquisition of independence, that is, recognition of Israel by the Family of Nations with the Principal Powers at the centre. It defined the territory of the Jewish State, the Arab State and the City of Jerusalem. In the first stage of the transitional period the Mandatory Power was to turn over the administration of Palestine to the U. N. Special Committee (U.N.S.C.O.P.), which would have established Provisional Councils of government for the future States. In the second stage, after the termination of the Mandate, the Provisional Councils would have received from the Committee full responsibility for administration though still acting under its supervision and control. Independence would then follow (not later than October, 1948) and the new State 'in esse' apply to the U. N. for membership. In this way continuity of administration would have been secured.

But whereas continuity of Sovereignty was not interrupted, continuity of administration broke down. The Mandatory Power decided to terminate the Mandate on May 15, 1948, and to withdraw from the territory. It did not, however, hand over the administration to the Provisional Councils to be established by U.N.S.C.O.P. or to any other authority. The Statehood of Israel was declared to take effect upon the termination of the Mandate.[9] It was gradually recognised by the main Powers and other countries (*de jure* or *de facto*) and applied for membership of the U. N. which was granted by Resolution of the General Assembly of May 11, 1949. The Israeli Government has on different occasions declared that it is not a successor of the Mandatory Power in respect of its rights and duties in what was formerly Palestine. We shall return to this point later.

The State of Israel established effective control first over the area assigned to it under the November Resolution and later over territory lying outside that area. In

[7] *I. C. J. Reports*, 1950, p. 150 (separate opinions).

[8] *U. N. Background Paper No.* 47 (1949); *U. N. Resolution*, Gen. Assembly 181 (II).

[9] N. Feinberg and J. Stoyanowsky, 'Israel's Declaration of Independence' (*Jewish Yearbook of International Law*, 1949).

the first case Sovereignty was established and administration introduced in accordance with the assignment of the territory by the United Nations, though the procedure prescribed was disregarded. In the second case, that is, in the Negev area and certain other districts, effective control was established, but the question arises whether and how Sovereignty was here acquired. There is no doubt that Sovereignty followed the acts of annexation by reason of the acquiescence of the Family of Nations, but it may be argued that it was title by occupation, since the United Nations had assigned the areas in question to another State. Is the taking of possession by force of the additional areas acquisition of an original title? It is doubtful: the Arab State did not appear at all. We have also seen that until the appropriate International Person appeared in the territory of Palestine to assume Sovereignty, the latter was still vested in the joint Sovereigns acting now through the U. N. Thus where no legal vacuum and no *terra nullius* can be assumed, no occupation could take place. Interruption in the continuity of the minor title could not affect the supreme title; we cannot argue from developments in the sphere of administration in favour of similar developments in the sphere of Sovereignty. We have seen above that no cession took place, but this does not exclude the derivative character of the supreme title, which may be understood by reference to the special status of the joint Sovereigns acting through international organs.

What then are the international rights and duties of Israel in the light of the above examination?[10] We cannot answer this question in detail as this would lead to a special analysis beyond our present purpose. But it is, first of all, clear that the Israeli Government is not a successor to the Mandatory Power. Part C of the November Resolution (Declaration) provided for continuity of certain rights and duties, but it was never made effective. Under Part C the Provisional Government was to have made, before independence, a declaration assuming the rights and obligations of all international agreements which had been extended to the Mandated Territory of Palestine. In particular paragraph 3a of Part C made provision for the future of commercial concessions granted before November, 1947. These concessions were to remain valid according to their terms, unless modified by agreement between the concession holder and the State. Part E of the Resolution provided that movable assets of the Mandatory Power would be assigned to the new State(s). Immovable assets would belong to the State on whose territory they were situated.

In the absence of succession to rights and duties by agreement between the State of Israel and the Mandatory Power we have to turn to general rules of International Law. First of all we must exclude general succession; but certain rights and duties may devolve upon the new State where one International Person follows another in the possession of territory (subrogation). There is, of course, no succession of political rights and duties. As Israel is not a party to previous commercial and other treaties, conventions and agreements, there is no succession to the Mandatory Power in

[10] Dr. E. H. Feilchenfeld, *Public Debts and State Succession*, 1931; J. W. Garner, 'Questions of State Succession' (*British Yearbook of International Law*, 1938); Francis B. Sayre, 'Change of Sovereignty and Private Ownership of Land' (12 *American Journal of International Law*, 1918).

this respect. But local rights and duties connected with the land (*jura in rem*) devolve upon the succeeding State and so do fiscal property and debts. Further, while public law changes automatically with a change of Sovereignty, private law remains unchanged unless the new Sovereign decides otherwise. There may be also mixed relations based on public and private law, for instance, certain types of concessions. According to press reports[11] concerning the Dead Sea concession on which the Israeli potash industry is based, the State of Israel did not consider itself bound by the concession which was granted by the Mandatory Power to a British company. Such a concession, apart from being an act of public law, contains also some elements of private law such as the lease of the concessionary land. There is no doubt that the concession holder can be deprived of his concession under Israeli public law, but he is entitled to damages for damnum emergens and lucrum cessans. The responsibility of the Sovereign rests on a breach of International Customary Law and if he disregards the rights of the concession holder he is liable as for an international tort. Thus in spite of no continuity of rights and duties based on a transfer of administration, there is continuity of rights and duties connected with the continuity of Sovereignty, and based on well-established principles of International Law, such as the maintenance of private rights, and the permanence of burdens running with the land. Their basis is International Customary Law, including notions of quasi-contract, unjust enrichment and equity.

Thus we must conclude our considerations by assuming continuity of Sovereignty, that is to say a continuous transfer of the supreme title to the territory. We can see no interruption of this continuity, though the link in the interim period between the withdrawal of the Turkish Empire and the assumption of Sovereignty by Israel is sui generis. There was no continuity in the minor title of administration. However, at the time of withdrawal of the Mandatory Power the new Sovereign was already at hand. Continuity of rights and duties is provided by general principles of International Law, the breach of which would make the State of Israel a tortfeasor. Thus the case of Israel can in its main aspects be fitted into our system of International Law.

[11] *E.g.*, *Neue Zürcher Zeitung*, 7/12 1949, No. 336.

27

NEW AND ORIGINAL STATES

THE ISSUE OF REVERSION TO SOVEREIGNTY (1969)

I.

DURING the discussion in the Sixth Committee of the UN General Assembly of the Report of the International Law Commission on Succession of States and Governments in respect of Treaties, in October 1968,[1] the Representative of Ceylon questioned the use of the term 'New State' as distinguished from 'old State' or 'original State'. He emphasised that the term 'new' could not properly be applied in the case of an ancient State, such as Ceylon, which had lost its sovereignty to a colonial Power and then gained political independence in the 20th century. In his view such a 'new' State should rather be termed 'original' State. He stated that principles of international law should have a sound historical basis. Thus not only the immediate pre-independence phase of a country's past but also the period of independence prior to colonial rule might be relevant in determining the principles applicable in respect of State succession.

If it is correct to say that Ceylon and States in a similar position are not new States but that they already existed in the past, it is also correct to assume that they reverted to sovereignty and that they are not newcomers to the Family of Nations. It must also be assumed that they reverted to the same Family of Nations from which they had been eliminated. The Family of Nations is obviously a continuous community of States subject to fluctuations of membership and to changes caused by the disappearance and appearance of member States. The question may arise whether it was possible for Asian (or African) States to have legally existed in the past. Are they capable of being classified within the category of 'original' States? Two answers are possible to this question, one given by the positivist writers of international law of the 19th century and early 20th century,[2] and the other given by the classic writers of the Law of Nations, or by the non-positivist school of thought.[3]

[1] A/C 6/SR 1036 (discussion of the Report on Succession of States and Governments in respect of Treaties by Sir Humphrey Waldock, Special Rapporteur).

[2] *Das Völkerrecht* by Franz von Liszt (1921), p. 3; *The Principles of International Law* by T. J. Lawrence (1923), p. 82; *International Law* by Oppenheim, Vol. I, paras. 26–27.

[3] *Le Droit International Codifié* by M. Bluntschli (1870), p. 17.

According to the positivist view the Family of Nations originated in Europe only. It was exclusively within this continent that the Law of Nations grew through relations between States which adopted the Christian civilisation. One of the important consequences which resulted from the formation of the Christian community of countries in Europe was its consolidation into a founder club of 'original' States which assumed the power of admission of other States, either within the area of the same civilisation or outside it. For centuries no extra-European State was admitted by the club.[4]

The first States outside Europe (formed by European settlers) to be admitted to the Family of Nations were the Christian States of North and South America. Then followed Christian States with a non-European population such as Liberia and Haiti. It was only in 1856 that the first non-Christian Power (Turkey) was admitted to the Family of Nations. Though this was formally an admission to the Concert of Europe, it was in essence conferment of membership in the Family of Nations.[5] But, according to the positivist view, the status of the Ottoman Empire in the Family of Nations remained ambiguous because of the inferiority of its civilisation. Evidence of inferior civilisation is (according to this view) to be found in the existence of the régime of capitulations. The latter allowed European residents in Turkey, and in other Oriental countries to govern themselves by their own law, and they were under the jurisdiction of their own consuls, a state of affairs which pointed to the inferiority of the judicial system of the particular Oriental country. The fallacy of this type of reasoning will be discussed below.

After Turkey, some other Asian States were said to be admitted to the Family of Nations, such as Siam, Persia or China, but their status was still ambiguous because of the considerations of civilisation. Other non-European Powers, which had earlier disappeared from the political map of the world, were considered as never having legally existed. In this category, for instance, would belong the Mogul Empire and the Maratha State in India, the Kingdoms of Ceylon and Burma and other entities. Only after the First World War did religion and civilisation cease to be tests of membership of the Family of Nations.

The first, and most important, gap in the above theory of the development of the Family and Law of Nations is revealed by the fact that the positivists never asked what the pre-19th-century Family of Nations thought about itself and about the problem of membership. Even if it is conceded that positivism is the expression of a state of affairs prevailing in 19th-century Europe, there is no reason blindly to assume that the position was the same prior to the 19th century. Positivism committed the error of projecting its own ideology backwards into the past without taking

[4] There existed a school of thought which considered Rulers outside the Christian world as not endowed with sovereignty and which banned all alliances or treaties between Christian Sovereigns and non-Christian Rulers. Among the early canon lawyers Hostiensis was its main exponent, but it gave way to the teachings of St. Thomas Aquinas who did not consider sovereignty a matter of *jus divinum* and admitted the existence of non-Christian sovereigns. The two views clashed at the Council of Constance (1414–18) which leaned towards the doctrine of St. Thomas.

[5] *Le Droit des Gens* by Sir Travers Twiss (1887), p. 83.

into consideration the ideology of the classic writers and State practice reflected in the works of these writers. Moreover, the positivists adopted the constitutive theory of recognition according to which a new State acquired international personality only through recognition by the existing States. This enabled the existing States (*i.e.*, original States) to exercise a considerable measure of discretion in conferring international personality on the new States, and in admitting them to the Family of Nations. No such constitutive theory of recognition existed in the pre-positivist world. In fact, the classic writers never formulated any coherent theory of recognition. If acts of recognition of States or Governments (Sovereigns) occurred in State practice, they were considered as declaratory of the existence of the recognised entity. All they meant was that the recognising entity was ready to open diplomatic, commercial and other relations with the recognised or admitted entity.[6]

The positivist writers failed no doubt to appreciate the significance of the pre-19th-century doctrine of the evolution of the Family and Law of Nations. Their tendency to project the present into the past had been sharply criticised by J. C. Van Leur, the Dutch historian, who insisted on an objective evaluation of Asian history.[7] Van Leur particularly exposed the fallacy of assuming that the gap created between Europe and Asia by the industrial revolution of the 19th century had existed in the past. His research in Asian history showed that some of the East Indian Powers dealt with the European Powers up to the end of the 18th century on a footing of equality.

The fallacy of projecting the present into the past was recently exposed by the International Court of Justice in the Indo-Portuguese dispute over the right of passage of the Portuguese through Indian territory.[8] The Court was concerned with the interpretation of the treaty of 1779 concluded between the Portuguese and the Maratha State. In this treaty the Marathas had transferred to the Portuguese the enclaves of Dadra and Nagar Aveli, in South-West India, giving them both a feudal title (but not sovereignty) over the enclaves and access to them through Maratha territory (without conceding a *right* of access). It was maintained in the proceedings that the above treaty could not be considered a treaty in international law as it did not comply with the legal requirements of our treaty law. The Court refused to apply to the treaty of 1779 our present-day notions of international law and insisted on the evaluation of its form and contents according to 18th-century law, including the recognised legal traditions prevailing in the Indian sub-continent at that time, *e.g.*, the institution of *jagir* or *saranjam*, which constituted the feudal title granted to the Portuguese. The absence of Portuguese sovereignty over the enclaves implied the absence of a legal right of passage through Maratha territory in the 18th century. The Court stated that it did not consider it necessary to deal with objections raised to the form of the treaty or to the procedure of its conclusion. The judges declared that 'the validity of a treaty concluded as long ago as the last quarter of

[6] *Introduction to the History of the Law of Nations in the East Indies* by C. H. Alexandrowicz (1967), p. 9. (Hereafter referred to as *Introduction*.)

[7] *Indonesian Trade and Society* by J. C. Van Leur (1955).

[8] ICJ Reports (1960) 6.

the eighteenth century ... should not be judged upon the basis of (legal) practices and procedures which have since developed only gradually'. The Court rejected an interpretation of the treaty by *ex post facto* law.

One of the judges, Moreno Quintana, stated that the exchange of treaty documents between the Marathas and the Portuguese 'was no doubt the expression of common agreement creating mutual rights and obligations between *two legal persons* recognised as such in their international relationships ... the instrument is a treaty in the wide sense given to this word by international jurisprudence and doctrine'.

If the logic of judicial pronouncement is allowed to speak, we must reach the conclusion that the Maratha State was endowed with international personality in the 18th-century Family of Nations, and that, if this was so, other States in a similar position, such as the Mogul Empire or the Kingdoms of Ceylon and Burma or the Indonesian States, were not in a legal vacuum but had participated since the 16th century in that universal community of the Law of Nations which received its first formulation by the classic writers of the 16th and 17th centuries, spreading from Europe to the East Indies and to parts of Africa.

Among the classic writers Hugo Grotius and Seraphim de Freitas deserve particular attention because they concentrated in some of their writings entirely on the legal aspects of the East Indian trade.[9] The Portuguese were the first to capture the benefits of the Asian spice trade in the 16th century, and when Portuguese rule in the Indian Ocean tended to monopolise trade and navigation, it was challenged by the Dutch, who gradually reduced the Portuguese position to minor dimensions. Grotius, in his work on the *Freedom of the Sea* (1608), speaks, in the first instance, about the Dutch–Portuguese struggle and the legal position of East Indian Sovereigns who allied themselves with some of the European Powers. It is through the study of these alliances and treaties of a commercial and political character, and of the diplomatic missions dealing with their conclusion and implementation, that the position of East Indian Sovereigns in the pre-19th-century Family of Nations can be properly assessed. Grotius has no hesitation in calling their sovereign status in the Law of Nations by its proper name.

Seventeen years after the publication of Grotius's work, Seraphim de Freitas brought out his remarkable treatise under the title *De Justo imperio Lusitanorum Asiatico* (1625). This is a reply to Grotius's defence of Dutch rights in the East Indies. Freitas rejects the Grotian principle of liberty of navigation and trade to the extent to which it offends the sovereignty of the country on which such trade and navigation tends to be imposed by an aggressive Power. But, by doing so, he defends the independent position of the East Indian Sovereigns, though he claims a right for Portugal as a Christian Power to attack Islam in its hinterland in Asia. Be that as it may, Freitas agrees with Grotius that the East Indian world entered the community of the Law of Nations through treaty-making, alliances and other transactions.

[9] The first classic writer to discuss East Indian Trade was Jean Bodin, see *Les Six Livres de la Republique* (1577), L. VI, c. ii, 630.

For both writers, as well as for the classic writers who followed them (to mention only Wolff and Vattel), the Law of Nations is a universal and non-discriminatory system of law. It could not have been otherwise, as the classic law was based on the natural law concept, apart from drawing its operable rules from State practice. Quite irrespective of the philosophical background of the naturalist doctrine, the latter had certain functional qualities which accompanied the history of natural law through all its phases, whether the theological period (Vitoria, Suarez), the Grotian period or the 18th-century period of enlightenment (Vattel). The universality of the Family of Nations, the multi-ideological character of the Law of Nations (its attitude towards ideological struggles such as the Christian–Islamic or the Catholic–Protestant conflicts), its non-discriminatory approach to civilisation, religion or race, declaratorism in respect of recognition as well as the doctrine of *bellum justum* were all functional qualities peculiar to the 'natural law' system within the classic law of nations. They tended to be swept away in the 19th century by positivism, which would not tolerate any of the elements of naturalism, and their elimination contributed to a system of international law which accepted colonial expansion and the institution of war as a mode of settlement of international conflicts, a state of affairs opposed only later by the League Covenant and the UN Charter.

The important link between Europe and Asia which brought about the establishment of treaty and diplomatic relations was the East Indian trade which flourished during the period of the development of the Law of Nations in Europe.[10] A study of these treaties and relations shows that certain Asian traditional institutions influenced the growth of our Law of Nations. A detailed discussion of this influence would be beyond the scope of this inquiry,[11] but it may be emphasised that the gathering momentum of European–East Indian treaty relations certainly precipitated the process of secularisation of our Law of Nations.[12] Moreover, the institution of capitulations deserves our attention. Positivist writers quoted them as evidence of the inferior civilisation of Eastern countries. But, in fact, their origin is to be sought in an ancient Asian tradition according to which a community of traders settling in a foreign country was normally allowed to govern itself by its own law and enjoyed a measure of autonomy under the control of its own heads of a *quasi*-consular character.[13] These arrangements, which preceded the capitulation treaties, were never derogatory to the sovereignty of the Ruler receiving the foreign community. They were the expression of high standards of treatment of foreigners. In course of time they degenerated into irrevocable arrangements giving the nationals of a European country residing in the East a privileged status at the expense of the Eastern Sovereign. But they cannot be considered evidence of the inferiority of

[10] These considerations do not apply to China and Japan which joined the Family of Nations in the 19th century.

[11] The influence revealed itself *inter alia* in the principles of freedom of the sea, the law of shipwreck, *droit d'aubaine, temperamenta belli, etc.*

[12] The strongest influence in this respect originated from the classic Hindu tradition according to which the political (secular) function of the Ruler was separated from the religious function reserved to the priestly (brahmin) caste (*Homo Hierarchicus* by L. Dumont 1967).

[13] 'Inter-State Relations in Asia' by K. A. N. Sastri, *Indian Year Book of International Affairs*, 1953.

one civilisation or the superiority of another and they could not affect admission to the Family of Nations. On the contrary, there are examples of capitulation treaties in favour of Asian settlers in Europe. For instance, the Persian–Dutch treaty of 1631 accorded capitulatory privileges to Persian settlers in Amsterdam.[14]

Enough has been said in the limits of this brief inquiry to show that pre-19th-century State practice, as revealed in treaties and diplomatic transactions, as well in the views of the classic writers, favoured the existence of a Family of Nations which was not limited to the European continent but extended to a great part of Asia, including the States surrounding the Indian Ocean, though excluding China and Japan which, prior to the 19th century, remained in isolation and did not participate at that period in the evolution of our system of international law.[15]

In the light of the above observations it seems possible to agree with the claim of the Government of Ceylon that Ceylon is not in the category of new States, but is one of the original States of the Family of Nations which reverted to sovereignty after the Second World War. The same would apply to other States in the East Indies, such as Burma, the Republic of India or Indonesia. In fact, Judge Moreno Quintana expressed the view, in his Opinion in the Indo–Portuguese dispute, that India reverted to the sovereignty of the Maratha State. This problem will be considered later. There are also a number of Asian States, such as Persia and Siam, which never lost their sovereignty, but which, according to the positivist view, were admitted to the Family of Nations in the early 20th century. This view seems untenable if it is realised that Persia and Siam were linked with a number of European Powers by treaty and diplomatic relations in the 17th and 18th centuries. In fact, Persia appears in that context even earlier, as an ally of the Holy Roman Empire in the struggle against the Ottoman Empire. Siam had intensive diplomatic exchanges with France in the 17th century, and these led to the conclusion of a number of treaties. It is difficult to imagine that Persia and Siam, which were members of the pre-19th-century Family of Nations, ceased to be original members in the 19th century and had to be re-admitted in the early 20th century. A State can hardly drop out of the Family of Nations because of ideological change in the structure of the Law of Nations. If these States were part and parcel of the universal Family of Nations, according to the principles of the classic law (backed by State practice), they could not be eliminated from it by positivist ideology alone. The proposition is too absurd to deserve being upheld, and it seems advisable to rewrite some of our history of the Law of Nations to make it consistent with the reality of the pre-19th-century Family of Nations.[16]

While part of the continent of Asia must be considered as having entered the Family of Nations prior to the 19th century, most of the countries of the African continent joined the Family of Nations, in one way or another, in the course of

[14] *Introduction*, p. 119

[15] Treaties which testify to early European–East Indian co-operation can be found in the Collections of Treaties by Judice Biker *(Collecção de Tratados)*, Heeres *(Corpus Diplomaticum Neerlando-Indicum)*, Aitchison, Hertslet, etc.

[16] *Introduction*, p. 235.

the 19th century, mostly after the Congress of Berlin in 1885. But the European–African confrontation was different from the earlier European–East Indian confrontation. In the East Indies trade was at its centre; in Africa it was predominantly acquisition of territory by the European Powers. Nevertheless, the position as to titles to territory was similar in both continents. Territory has rarely been treated as *terra nullius*, and thus, with some exceptions, it was not acquired by the European Powers by discovery or by occupation of empty land[17] but rather by title of cession, as expressed in bilateral agreements between a European Power and a non-European Ruler. In rare cases conquest was instrumental in the transfer of land. Thus, territory taken over from an Asian or African entity appears normally in treaties as having been transferred by a Sovereign to a Sovereign (sometimes a delegated one).[18]

One of the essential differences between the European–East Indian confrontation and the European–African confrontation was the absence of diplomacy in the process of negotiations in Africa. While in the East Indies both sides exercised the active and passive right of legation mainly for concluding and supervising the implementation of treaties, African Rulers were rarely able to live up to the level of diplomatic bargaining in the proper sense of the word. With a few exceptions (Ethiopia, Zanzibar or the North African States) the vast majority of African Chieftains were not capable of relations with European entities on a footing of equality, and thus the entry of the African continent tended to be effected by unequal agreement or through the instrumentality of the 'colonial protectorate'.[19]

The latter, which appeared mainly after the Congress of Berlin in 1885, meant in principle the establishment of an ordinary protectorate over an African Ruler, normally by agreement. But in fact the European protector received *carte blanche* from the other contracting parties to the Berlin Act to deal with the protected entity, and he usually aimed at the annexation of the protected territory.[20] Without going into the details of this complex institution, which hardly fits into the normal structure of international law, it must be stated that while the European–East Indian confrontation contributed to the development of our Law of Nations, which proved adequate to serve the purposes of the confrontation and particularly the purposes of world trade, the 19th-century system of international law proved generally inadequate to serve the purposes of the European–African confrontation, which deteriorated into the 'scramble for Africa' and into the partition of the continent, irrespective of the ethnological and social traditions of the African communities.[21] The African State entities which emerged after the Second World War from this chaotic political and economic set-up hardly have a claim to identity with the vast number of States and Chieftainships which had disappeared in the melting pot of colonial absorption.

[17] Unlike in Australia, see *Cooper v. Stuart* (1889) 14 App.Cas. 296.

[18] *The Map of Africa by Treaty* by E. Hertslet (1909). The exercise of sovereign powers was often delegated to the East India Companies or to the African Companies.

[19] *The Acquisition and Government of Backward Territory* by M. F. Lindley (1926).

[20] *Chapters on the Principles of International Law* by John Westlake (1894), p. 179; *International Law* by T. Baty (1909), p. 304; *International Law* by C. C. Hyde (1927), Vol. I, para. 25; *Cours de Droit International* by D. Anzilotti (1929), pp. 234–235.

[21] Hertslet, *op. cit.*

Thus, unlike the case of countries in the East Indies, there is generally no room for a claim to their classification as original States. Most of the African State entities are new States in the present-day meaning of the word, and reversion to sovereignty has no application.[22]

II.

An attempt has been made to explore in brief outline the historical premises of 'reversion to sovereignty' as claimed by Ceylon or other States which consider themselves original rather than new States.[23] Two versions or formulations of reversion are possible in international law. The first was propounded by Judge Moreno Quintana in his Opinion above mentioned.[24] He referred to the fact that the Marathas transferred only a feudal title, and not sovereignty, over the enclaves to the Portuguese who, therefore, did not acquire a right of passage through Maratha territory. Thus, no international servitude was established. However, the majority of judges came to the conclusion that the British Administration which took over Maratha territory in 1817 recognised Portuguese sovereignty over the enclaves and their right of passage through British (later Indian) territory. Judge Moreno Quintana, disagreeing with the majority of the judges, stated that 'the British do not seem to have renounced the exercise of the powers of the territorial sovereign any more than the Marathas did'. In fact the British Government made no statement to this effect in the proceedings. Thus, in Judge Moreno Quintana's view, the Portuguese could not claim more against the British than they possessed under Maratha rule prior to 1817, and when the Republic of India succeeded to the British Administration, the Portuguese could not claim against India more than they possessed under the rule of the Marathas (and the British). Judge Moreno Quintana stated: 'India made no fundamental change in the established system.... We must not forget that India, as the territorial successor, was not acquiring the territory for the first time, but was recovering an independence (sovereignty) lost long since. Its legal position at once *reverted* to what it had been more than a hundred years before, as though British occupation had made no difference'.

The above Moreno Quintana concept of reversion to sovereignty could be summarised in the following way: There is a legal presumption that a State which lost its sovereignty but reverted to it (before the dust of history had settled), recovers a full and unencumbered sovereignty. The interpretation of rights and obligations connected with such sovereignty would therefore be in favour of the reverting State. Particularly in the case of the intervention of a colonial Power in the independence of a State, the presumption can never be in favour of the former. Judge Moreno Quintana stated that 'to support the Portuguese claims in this case, which

[22] However, different considerations would apply to the African States on the Mediterranean coast (below).

[23] *Introduction*, p. 240.

[24] ICJ Reports (1960) 6.

implies survival of the colonial system without categorical and conclusive proof, is to fly in the face of the UN Charter'.[25] The whole concept is, according to Moreno Quintana, a *procedural* one. It does not deprive the intervening colonial Power of its right to do anything that a Sovereign can do in territory under his sovereignty, though there is a presumption that the State, reverting to its lost sovereignty, reverts to the same quantum and degree of sovereignty which it lost at the time of elimination from the Family of Nations. If the intervening colonial Power wishes to rely on changes effected through the exercise of its (external and internal) sovereign powers, it must produce 'categorical and conclusive' proof. The *onus probandi* is on it, and failure to produce such proof would allow the State reverting to sovereignty to insist on its rights, *i.e.*, on revival of unencumbered and unmodified sovereignty. In the particular case, Judge Moreno Quintana declared that the Portuguese failed to produce evidence showing that the British Administration gave them sovereignty over the enclaves and that they acquired a right of passage through British (later Indian) territory. In the absence of such evidence, India (reverting to the sovereignty of the Marathas) regained, in the learned judge's view, its territory unencumbered by a right of passage on behalf of the Portuguese.

The question may be asked whether, and how, does reversion to sovereignty affect State succession. In fact, in case of such reversion there are two instances of State succession, one from the disappearing sovereign to the intervening colonial Power(s) and the second from the latter to the former. Why then bother about reversion to sovereignty as a separate institution of international law if it is identical with two (or more) cases of State succession? The answer is that reversion to sovereignty in the Moreno Quintana interpretation is a sort of indirect self-succession, and creates a special presumption in favour of the reverting State which ordinary State succession would not create. As reversion is of a procedural character, it does not essentially affect the course of State succession. As has been stated, reversion to sovereignty in the above interpretation does not affect the acts of the colonial Power resulting from the legitimate exercise of its rights of sovereignty in the intervening period.

However, the above is not the only possible interpretation. Dr. Ian Brownlie, interpreting reversion in a different way, states that 'when a transfer of sovereignty occurs, and the successor is generally recognised as recovering a previous state of independence, that successor is not bound by territorial grants or recognition of territorial changes by the previous holder. The State now restored reverts to the legal position prior to its loss of independence'.[26] The author refers to Judge Moreno Quintana's Opinion, but his interpretation seems to differ from that of the learned judge, who confines reversion to procedural dimensions. Anyhow, reversion to sovereignty, if interpreted in a trans-procedural way, would affect the normal course of the principles of State succession.

[25] Thus the learned judge seems to support his presumption by the anti-colonial provisions of the UN Charter and possibly ensuing UN practice.

[26] *Principles of Public International Law* by I. Brownlie (1966), p. 152.

III.

In the search for precedents in the field of reversion to sovereignty which could help to explain some of the differences in its interpretation, it is only logical to look to the case of Poland which lost its sovereignty, first at the time of the partitions at the end of the 18th century, and, later, at the time of the breakdown of the Kingdom of Poland created at the Congress of Vienna in 1815. It has never been maintained that Poland was a victim of colonialism. But there is scant difference between her case and that of colonial territories. Both can be explained by power politics, of which colonialism is only a different expression. Poland reverted to sovereignty after the First World War when a dereliction of its former territories by the U.S.S.R., Germany and the Austro-Hungarian Empire followed. The Preamble to the special treaty between Poland and the Allied Powers (Versailles 1919) speaks about the restoration of the Polish Nation to independence.[27] The Polish Supreme Court considered this problem in a number of cases, but it applied not reversion to sovereignty but the *jus postliminii* in order to justify the claims of the parties concerned.

Jus postliminii is an institution of Roman law taken over by the Law of Nations.[28] It originally meant that a Roman citizen, detained or enslaved in a foreign hostile country, regained, on his return to Roman territory, all rights by a process of restoration and reverted to his former status. In international law the institution of *postliminium* came to mean that territory, property and individuals which, during the period of a war, were under enemy control or occupation return after the withdrawal of the enemy (or reconquest or a peace treaty or *levée en masse*) to the control (jurisdiction) of their legal sovereign. The effect of *postliminium* in international law is the revival of a former condition of things. But it has to be remembered that the institution of *postliminium* applies only to cases in which the enemy (belligerent) occupies territory without acquiring a right of sovereignty over it. After the enemy's withdrawal the Sovereign returns to the exercise of his rights, and is again responsible to third States for events in the recovered territory. Meanwhile the enemy as the occupying Power, but not as sovereign, may have performed certain acts in the territory which are valid in international law or other acts which are invalid. Collection of taxes would be a valid exercise of control, but sale of immovable State property would be invalid as not allowed to a non-sovereign. However, if the occupied territory is formally ceded by the Sovereign to the occupying Power, the latter becomes the successor-sovereign, and if the previous Sovereign later regains the territory, there is no *postliminium* but reversion to sovereignty. The fundamental difference between the two institutions is the sovereign character of the intervening Power in one case (reversion) and the non-sovereign position of the occupying Power in the other (*postliminium*). In the latter there is no State succession at all, but a complete

[27] *The Problem of State Succession with respect to Treaties* by R. W. G. De Muralt (1954).
[28] Oppenheim, *op. cit.*, Vol. II, para. 279 (p. 481).

return of the Sovereign to the exercise of his rights (and not to sovereignty which was never lost).[29]

The Polish Supreme Court was faced with claims of successors of Polish citizens who had been independence fighters in the 19th century and who were captured by the Russians and exiled to Siberia. Their estates were confiscated and given to Russian citizens for a nominal sum, or retained by the Russian Government occupying Poland. The claims were brought for recovery of the estates, either against the successors of the Russian owners or against the Polish Treasury as the successor to the Russian Treasury holding the estates. The Court assumed that, as the fight for independence had continued, Russia never became the sovereign in Poland. The post-partition period in Poland was considered by the judges to have been a *de facto* condition, and the acts of the Russian Government against the independence of Poland were held to be invalid. Confiscation of property of the predecessors of the claimants was also held to be invalid, and the Court restored it to the plaintiffs.[30] Thus the Court applied the *jus postliminii* to these cases. The concept of reversion to sovereignty was inapplicable as the present Polish State was considered a continuation of pre-partition Poland. The most important among the cases in which successors of Russian owners were sued is *Kulakowski* v. *Szumkowski*.[31] Among the cases brought against the Polish Treasury as the successor to the Russian Government are *A.G.* v. *Serewicz* and *Uszycka* v. *Polish Treasury*.[32]

The Polish Supreme Court failed to rely in these cases on the essential texts of the classic writers which could have supported its decisions from the point of view of international law. Nearly all the classic writers discussed the institution of *postliminium*. Grotius speaks in his *De Jure Belli ac Pacis* (Book III, Chapter IX) about *quasi-postliminium* in the Law of Nations as distinguished from the Roman institution. Pufendorf states in his *Law of Nations* (Book VIII, Chapter VI) that 'a whole nation when it has ... shaken off an enemy's yoke, without doubt recovers its liberty and ancient State'. G. F. de Martens deals with *postliminium* in his *Compendium of the Law of Nations* (translated by W. Cobbett (1802), (p. 299) and Vattel in his *Droit des Gens* (Book III, Chapter XIV). Vattel states in para. 213 that when a nation (State) has been entirely subdued, the question may arise whether a revolution can entitle it to the right of *postliminium*. If a conquered people (State) have not acquiesced in their new subjection, and have only ceased to resist from inability, such people are not subdued but defeated and oppressed. If delivered from oppression 'they doubtless return to their former situation'. It is only in case of voluntary submission to the conqueror that a people become subjects of the new Sovereign. Then the former State is destroyed. 'All its relations, all its alliances are extinguished'. Vattel quotes, as an example of revival of a State, Portugal which was

[29] *Traité de droit international public* by P. Fauchille (1921), Vol. II, para. 1710.

[30] However, the court admitted that *bona fide* purchasers of the property would enjoy legal protection.

[31] *Annual Digest* (*A.D.*), 1927–28, case 375.

[32] *A.D.*, 1923–24, case 25, and *A.D.*, 1929–30, case 289.

seized by Phillip II of Spain under the pretence of a hereditary right, but in reality by force (1580), and re-established 60 years later.[33]

IV.

It may be stated, in conclusion of this brief inquiry, that the opposition of the Government of Ceylon to its classification as a 'new State' seems justified from the historical point of view. An analysis of relations between European Powers and Asian (African) States allows us to assume that some of the latter were original members of the Family of Nations though most of them had lost their independence. It must therefore be conceded that on regaining independence they reverted to sovereignty rather than joined the Family of Nations as newcomers. As stated above, the Moreno Quintana interpretation of reversion to sovereignty assigns to this new institution of international law a procedural meaning only. It does not affect the normal course of the law of State succession, as the intervening colonial Power had full sovereignty up to the moment of reversion. However, the reverting State can rely on a presumption of reversion to the same quantum and measure of sovereignty as that which it had to abandon at the moment of elimination from the Family of Nations in the past. The onus of proof that there are changes in sovereignty (*e.g.*, its encumbrance by a right of passage) is on the colonial Power, which must provide categorical and conclusive evidence to that effect. Judge Moreno Quintana found that such evidence had not been produced by Portugal in the Indo–Portuguese dispute, but his Opinion was (on this point) a dissenting one only. Moreover, if reversion to sovereignty is accepted as generating a presumption in favour of the reverting State, the latter must be identical with the State which disappeared from the Family of Nations in the past. This is a doubtful proposition as far as the identity of the Republic of India with the Maratha State is concerned.[34] However, there are cases in which such identity is obvious, to mention only Ceylon, Madagascar or Poland.[35]

[33] For other examples of *postliminium* see *A Treatise on International Law* by A. P. Higgins (1924), pp, 580–581 (referring to the republic of Genoa). The period of the Second World War may also have witnessed cases of *postliminium* after the collapse of the Nazi régime, *e.g.*, in the case of Austria. See decision of the Austrian Supreme Court in *Jordan* v. *Austrian Republic* (1947), *A.D.*, 1947, case 15. It was stated in the Arbitration concerning 'Gold looted by Germany from Rome in 1943' (*International Law Reports* 1953, p. 465) that *postliminium* in international law is 'founded on the Roman concept of *postliminium* whose significance is widened so that this term now means an invalidation of all acts contrary to the law of nations, performed in time of war by the occupant, and a revival, when the occupation is ended, of all legal relations illegitimately modified by the occupant in war, in their former conditions….'

[34] Unless it is maintained that the Maratha State for some period controlled the Mogul Empire. (See R. Kemal in *Indian Year Book of International Affairs*, 1957, p. 143.)

[35] Among the North African States, Algeria would be a case of reversion to sovereignty but not Morocco and Tunisia which in the 19th century shifted from submission to Ottoman overlordship to the position of French Protectorates. Some of their treaties with third powers tended to be upheld, *e.g.*, the British–Moroccan Convention of Commerce and Navigation of 1856 remained valid, and in 1957 was modified by mutual agreement of the contracting parties (abrogation of article 7). See *HMSO Treaty Series* No. 38 (1957) Cmnd. 144.

Finally, it must be emphasised that a State reverting to sovereignty must be presumed to revert, not only to the measure of sovereignty which it lost in the past, but also to the régime of the Law of Nations (with the ensuing rights and obligations) which it was forced to abandon at the time of its elimination from the community of the Law of Nations. It was stated above that most of the East Indian States were closely connected with the European Powers through treaties and diplomatic relations. This implied acceptance of the system of the Law of Nations in force at the time of the conclusion of the relevant transactions, and such acceptance must be presumed to revive with reversion to sovereignty. Anyhow, reverting (as well as new) States must be presumed to be bound by norms of international law which can be classified as *jus cogens*.[36] The International Law Commission gave its support to the existence of such a *jus cogens* (see article 37 of the draft articles of the law of treaties). It considered 'a treaty void if it conflicts with a peremptory norm of general international law from which no derogation is permitted and which can be modified only by a subsequent norm of general international law having the same character'.[37] The International Law Commission gave no examples of such peremptory norms, but they can be partly found in customary law and in universal treaties.

Though *jus cogens* does not consist of immutable rules, they are *mutatis mutandis* of a similar character to rules of natural law of a functional character which must be considered as inherent in the system of international law in force at a particular period. The elimination of such rules from the system would frustrate its functioning. It has been stated above that among those norms the principles of universality of the Law of Nations and of non-discrimination on grounds of religion, civilisation or race are most important. To this category would also belong the rules prohibiting aggressive war (the former principle of *bellum justum*), genocide, slave trade, piracy and other crimes against humanity (condemned by the Nuremberg trials). Dr. Ian Brownlie also includes in this category the principle of self-determination,[38] and he states that the operation of this principle 'as a part of the *jus cogens* may support a doctrine of reversion'. Thus, rights of way granted by a colonial Power may not be consistent with recovery of full sovereignty by the reverting State. In this respect the learned author seems to go further than Judge Moreno Quintana who, as stated above, allows to the reverting State reliance on a presumption of recovery of full sovereignty (procedural right) without denying to the colonial Power the right to bring evidence to the contrary and to uphold all changes effected by it as the former legitimate Sovereign in the territory.

[36] I. Brownlie, *op. cit.*, p. 417.

[37] Report of the International Law Commission A/6309; 'The New States and International Law' by H. Boker-Szegö (*Questions of International Law*, 1968); 'International Jus Cogens?' by G. Schwarzenberger (*Texas Law Review*, March 1965).

[38] I. Brownlie, *op. cit.*, pp. 79, 417, 482–485. See UN General Assembly A/6230, June 27, 1966, p. 204.

It was shown that the case of Poland, which *prima facie* provided a precedent of reversion to sovereignty, was not helpful in the clarification of its legal contents, as Polish judicial authority relied not on a reversion but on the *jus postliminii*. Whether this view is justified by State practice as applied by the Powers to the case of Poland between the partitions and her revival in 1918, must be open to doubt.[39]

[39] See Oppenheim, *op. cit.*, Vol. II, para. 279, and De Muralt, *op. cit.*, p. 105.

28

THE NEW STATES AND INTERNATIONAL LAW (1974)

One of the more spectacular phenomena of our age is the rise of the number of member states of the Family of Nations, from 51 at the San Francisco Conference to about 140 at present. It is possible to speak about a 'state explosion' and the question arises, what are the consequences of this significant development? Political scientists, economists and historians have joined to give an answer, and it would also be interesting to analyse the issue from the angle of international law. To examine all the legal problems resulting from the entry of the New States (mainly the Afro–Asian countries) into the Family of Nations would be beyond the scope of this brief inquiry. It will only be possible to take a short-cut through these problems and draw attention to those which most urgently require a legal solution.

Among international lawyers who concern themselves with the position of New States in international law, two schools of thought are discernible: the orthodox and the revisionist. The orthodox view is that New States have no choice as to the law which shall apply to them since they are born into the existing international order and must accept its tenets.[1] As will be seen below, this view applies mainly to international customary law, for as to the multilateral conventions which have codified international law (such as the Geneva Conventions on the Law of the Sea of 1958, the Vienna Convention on Diplomatic Relations of 1961, the Vienna Convention on Consular Relations of 1963 or the Vienna Convention on the Law of Treaties of 1969) it is open to the New States to accede or not to accede to them, though in the case of non-accession the question remains whether they will accept or reject the underlying customary law which was codified in these conventions.

The orthodox view, however, that New States are faced with the *fait accompli* of the existing international legal order and must accept its principles as they find them is open to serious doubt since the practice of the New States does not supply sufficient evidence of such a *fait accompli*. In this respect, it is interesting to look on the one hand at examples of legal rules which tend to be rejected by the New States and on the other hand at rules which they wish to have included in the existing body of international law.

[1] See: *The New Nations in International Law and Diplomacy*, ed. W. V. O'Brien (London, 1965).

Turning first to the latter, it may be emphasised that the Founding Fathers of the United Nations adopted in the framework of the Charter certain principles relating to the birth and dissolution of states. These principles have been widely relied on by the New States. Though vital consequences flow from the appearance or disappearance of a state, international law in the past did not (since the end of the eighteenth century) submit the fact of birth or of dissolution of a state to international legal regulation. Both events were considered to be brought about in the sphere of political facts and thus the disappearance of independent Poland at the end of the eighteenth century was generally accepted by the Great Powers, though some historians of international law have called it an international crime. But the Charter of the United Nations adopts a different approach to the birth and dissolution of States, for according to Article 2 (4) 'all Members shall refrain in their international relations from the threat or use of force against the territorial integrity or political independence of any State....' Thus cases of the extinction of states which would be justifiable under international law are now somewhat limited.

On the other hand, a community may have a claim to forming a New State on the basis of the principle of self-determination which is incorporated in Articles 1 and 55 of the United Nations Charter. The history of the principle of self-determination would show that it existed as a *lex imperfecta* in natural law, giving a politically organised community the right to a presence on the political map of the world. In this respect examples of state practice in the more distant past could be found in the claims of republics such as Switzerland or the Netherlands to international legal status in the midst of European monarchies ruled by the principle of dynastic legitimism.[2] The USA relied on the same right at the end of the eighteenth century. The nineteenth century witnessed an eclipse of the principle (perhaps with the exception of the claims of the Balkan states) but it revived after the First World War and more decisively after the Second. A number of General Assembly resolutions give expression to the inalienable right of self-determination, and the overwhelming majority of the member states of the United Nations have invoked it in support of the creation of New States in territories which had been or still are under colonial domination.[3]

Some New States have claimed more than a right to legal existence in the Family of Nations. They invoke the principle of reversion to sovereignty.[4] Thus in 1968 and 1969 the representative of Ceylon in the Sixth Committee of the General Assembly of the United Nations protested against the classification of Ceylon as a New State (as distinct from an original state). He argued that Ceylon existed as an

[2] C. H. Alexandrowicz, 'The Theory of Recognition *in Fieri*', *British Yearbook of International Law* 1958 (chapter 24 above).

[3] See General Assembly Resolutions 637/A (VII); 742 (VIII); 1514 (XV); 1654 (XVI); 1810 (XVII); 1904 (XVIII); 2131 (XX); 2189 (XXI). Between 1957 and 1960 nine communities under the Trusteeship system gained independence leaving only two Trusteeship territories in existence (New Guinea and the Pacific Islands). See also reference of the General Assembly Resolution of December 1973 to the inalienable right of self-determination.

[4] See: C. H. Alexandrowicz, 'New and Original States,' in *International Affairs*, Vol. 45, No. 3, 1969, p. 465 (page 390 above).

independent kingdom prior to the nineteenth century and should be classified as an original state in the Family of Nations. In fact Ceylon and a number of other Afro–Asian countries maintained diplomatic relations and made treaties, under the classic law of nations, with several European Powers or with other Afro–Asian countries. The problem of reversion to sovereignty has been raised (in relation to India) in the Indo–Portuguese dispute before the International Court of Justice. Its legal consequences have been discussed elsewhere.[5] What may be emphasised here is that the New States have invoked (often unwittingly) certain legal rights which had been part and parcel of the classic law of nations, while displaying a negative attitude towards nineteenth-century international law. This is quite understandable, since nineteenth-century international law was Eurocentric and suppressed certain principles of the classic law such as the principle of universality of the law of nations, non-discrimination on grounds of civilisation, religion, race or colour, and the principle of *bellum justum*. State practice reveals a paradoxical development in the present attitude of New States to international law. It shows that they tend to demand a revision of the Eurocentric international law of the nineteenth century, in the formation of which they were not allowed to participate and which survived until the middle of the present century. On the other hand, they accept certain principles of the classic law of nations which were based on natural law doctrine such as the principles mentioned above, now revived in a different shape within the framework of the United Nations.[6]

Among the existing principles of international law which the New States refused to accept or which they accepted with far-reaching reservations, the legal principles relating to economic relations deserve primary attention. For example, some of the existing international law as generated in the nineteenth century offends the right of economic self-determination of New States. The General Assembly gave expression to this right in its Resolution 1803 (XVII) of December 14, 1962. It refers to the inherent right of countries to sovereignty over their national wealth and economic resources. (In this field the Latin American countries proved to be the forerunners of New States in their endeavour to defend their economic rights.) As a result, New States are frequently driven to the adoption of programmes of nationalisation, usually in the framework of national economic planning. Foreign investors or concession holders, dissatisfied with the compensation or the treatment which they receive in the case of expropriation of their property, could in the past rely on minimum standards of international law. Thus whatever the treatment which a developing country (new or old) gave to its nationals, foreign investors were entitled to certain minimum standards which were usually higher than standards of national treatment. They could insist on the payment of full or just compensation and invoke the assistance of their national state, usually a major financial power. In reply the New (and Latin American) States insisted on the application of the

[5] *Ibid.*

[6] For a correct appreciation of the subject, see R. P. Anand, *The New States and International Law*, (Delhi, 1972).

principle of territorial jurisdiction, which in their view should take precedence over the principle of personal jurisdiction under which the national state of the investor takes up the claim of its citizen against the expropriating state. The issue of territorial *versus* personal jurisdiction dates back to the first formulation of the 'Calvo doctrine' in the nineteenth century, which shows that the Latin American world was leading the way in anticipation of the problems of the New States. A number of Central and South American governments insisted that foreign investors should not invoke the support of their home state (seeking international adjudication) but defend their rights solely in accordance with the territorial municipal law of the developing country in which the investment was made (Calvo clause). The weakness of the 'Calvo doctrine' lies in the fact that a foreign investor may indeed undertake to follow a certain line of behaviour, but he cannot impose on his own national state the obligation not to take up the case of its own national. Whatever the differences of opinion, the trend towards revision of nineteenth-century international law relating to the treatment of foreigners found its expression in state practice and in General Assembly Resolution 1803 (XVII), which limits the right of foreign-national investors to appropriate compensation, as distinct from the traditional concept of full, adequate, prompt or effective compensation. This type of General Assembly resolution is the expression of an *opinio juris communis* of the member states of the Family of Nations. It compels foreign investors hit by nationalisation decrees issued in developing (new) states to fall back on national treatment without resort to minimum standards which have lost much of their former legal validity.

Another field in which some of the traditional nineteenth-century principles of international law are under revisionist pressure from the New States is the law of state succession. A discussion of the relevant problems would require a detailed survey of the tottering edifice of the law of state succession which would be beyond the scope of this inquiry.[7] Suffice it to say that most of the New States had to sign 'Devolution Agreements' with Metropolitan Powers which granted them independence. Some of the New States, contracting parties to these agreements, denounced them as unequal treaties. The resolutions of the Conference of the International Law Association in Buenos Aires in 1968 testify to the precarious situation of the international law of succession. Even the traditional principle of succession to rights and obligations which 'run with the land' such as international servitudes ceased to command general respect.

There are also other branches of international law in which the New States insist on revision, such as the law of the sea. The present Law of the Sea Conferences will no doubt reveal some of the official proposals of the New States.

In connection with these revisionist trends, the more general question may be asked: What is the attitude of the New States to international customary law as such? In attempting to answer this question it must be emphasised that

[7] See D. P. O'Connell, *The Law of State Succession* (Cambridge, 1956). See also Ingrid Delupis, *International Law and the Independent State* (Epping, 1974). The author denies automatic devolution and considers the possibility of withdrawal of New States from devolution agreements on the basis of *rebus sic stantibus* or the theory of continuous consent.

nineteenth-century international law, which is the main target of revision, was the outcome of a law-making process within a Family of Nations of a highly homogeneous character. The New States were colonies, and their peoples had no voice in the *fora* of nations. They were governed from one or another Metropolitan Centre which alone exercised rights of sovereignty. Thus approximately 30 states following the same social and economic ideology (though divided by power politics) were instrumental in generating international usages which by a common *opinio juris* were converted into principles of international customary law. The *opinio juris* was revealed by the consent of the majority of states, the presumption being that in a homogeneous set-up the express voice of the majority was good enough to generate the law. The situation changed after the First World War. Power politics ceased to be played within a Family of Nations in which states had similar social and economic structures. The USSR, following Marxist ideology, removed itself from the area of homogeneous law-making. After the Second World War more Marxist Powers appeared, and then came the 'state explosion' which brought the Afro–Asian world into the orbit of international law. The Family of Nations became highly heterogeneous, if only because of the differing mechanisms of economic and social relations. The West stuck to the pattern of a free competitive economy corrected by a system of framework planning. In the international field this found expression in the creation of a number of co-ordinating agencies which are in charge of planning one or another sector of economic or social activity. The Marxist countries rely on central economic (total) planning which requires different legal media. Moreover, the New States as well as other developing countries follow the tenets of development planning which represents a compromise solution. These three groups of states voice their ideologies and strategies within UNCTAD (United Nations Conference on Trade and Development), which is an organ of the UN General Assembly.

In these circumstances the generation of rules of international customary law can no longer follow the procedure of nineteenth-century law-making. It is impossible to presume that such rules could be created by a majority of states. Such is the present day heterogeneity of the Family of Nations that the voice of the majority cannot be representative of the totality of member states since their social and economic structures have ceased to be uniform and neither warrant the former legal presumptions nor sustain the old methods of 'weighted' international law-making in which the leading Powers had a decisive voice. The New States did not participate in nineteenth-century international law-making, and their proposals for transformation of the law—e.g. for enlarging territorial waters or for economic maritime zones reaching far out into the high seas—were until recently ignored. But the pressure for revision makes itself felt at present.[8]

The question may be asked whether the New States are bound to accept the *jus cogens* as they find it after their entry into the Family of Nations. *Jus cogens* has

[8] It may be interesting to recall that a classic writer, E. Vattel, in his *Droit des Gens* (I, XXIII, 287) anticipated the progress of the law by referring to the pearl fisheries of some of the East Indian Rulers which were in fact rights on the continental shelf far exceeding the customary limits of territorial waters.

been defined in the Vienna Convention on the Law of Treaties (1969) as the body of peremptory rules from which no derogation is permitted. A Hungarian writer, Hanna Bokor-Szegö, states that 'the solution of the problems of *jus cogens* presents no difficulty to the followers of the natural law conception, because they differentiate from the outset between legal norms existing independently of the will of states and norms deriving from the states' express or implied will. The latter according to that conception cannot be at variance with natural law'.[9] The International Law Commission drafting the Vienna Convention on the Law of Treaties did not equate *jus cogens* with natural law but in fact natural law can be conceived as having certain functional (as distinguished from doctrinal) qualities.[10] Thus the principles of the classic law of nations enshrining the requirement of universality of the law and its non-discriminatory application irrespective of civilisation, religion, race or colour, are principles without which no international law serving the purposes of mankind is practically conceivable. These principles, after having been suspended during the nineteenth-century interval, have been re-incorporated in present-day international law and are in the nature of peremptory rules from which no derogation is possible. So are other rules such as the rule of self-determination or the rule against aggressive war which is reminiscent of the doctrine of *bellum justum*. These and other rules of *jus cogens* must be accepted by the New States, and there is a consensus of opinion on this point to which even Communist writers have adhered. If this is so, the capacity of law revision of the New States in the field of customary law must be considered as limited to the realm of *jus dispositivum* as distinguished from *jus cogens*.[11]

The further question arises, when should a New State make it known to other member states of the Family of Nations that it accepts or rejects a particular rule of customary law? It would be logical to suggest that the right time is when the New State is recognised by the existing Powers. However, a state seeking recognition is hardly in a position to demand a change of the law, and the better view would therefore be that the right time is when the New State is admitted to the United Nations, where as a member it can participate in the passing of resolutions and recommendations affecting the existing body of international law. Moreover, the fact of signing the charter of the United Nations imposes a duty on the New States of accepting all rules of *jus dispositivum* and *jus cogens* which are embodied in the Charter.[12]

In conclusion, attention may be drawn to UNCTAD's initiative of adopting a Charter of Economic Rights and Duties of States. The UNCTAD Drafting Committee proposed a structure for the Charter in two parts with a Preamble.[13] The Preamble emphasises the urgent need of adapting the precarious international legal order to the new events and concepts in international economic relations. Chapter I would contain the Fundamentals, and Chapter II the Detailed Provisions. The

[9] H. Bokor-Szegö, *New States and International Law* (Budapest, 1970), p. 66.

[10] Alexandrowicz, 'New and Original States,' (ch. 27 above).

[11] Soviet legal theory tends to define *jus cogens* as imperative voluntary law, a *contradictum in adjecto*, resulting from the rejection by Soviet writers of natural law (see H. Bokor-Szegö, *op. cit.*).

[12] See Bokor-Szegö, *op. cit.*

[13] UNCTAD, T.D./B/AC 12/3, Mar. 18, 1974.

Committee agreed to include a text relating to the strengthening of the economic independence of developing countries, but no agreement was reached on a clause concerning the promotion of collective economic security.

The chapter on Fundamentals contains *inter alia* the principles of equality of states, non-aggression, non-intervention, self-determination, peaceful settlement of disputes and respect for human rights. The chapter on the Detailed Provisions is headed by the principle containing the right of each state to choose its own economic and social structure. It embodies among other things, the principle of the sovereignty of each state over its wealth and economic resources (see the General Assembly Resolution of December 14, 1962), the right to dispose of the marine resources within the limits of extended national jurisdiction, the application of the concept of *res communis* to the seabed and ocean floor, and the right of each state to nationalisation of property in the course of development planning, including foreign property. No agreement was reached on the formula of compensation for such property taken. Some states participating in the drafting of the Charter insisted on the sole jurisdiction of municipal courts of the expropriating state to settle compensation and other claims, and one proposal stated that 'no state whose nationals invest in a foreign country shall demand privileged treatment for them nor present claims on their behalf', a proposal which would mean a limitation of the right of the national state to take up the case of its nationals and the abolition or restriction of minimum standards of international law. While the latter proposal seems to be supported by extensive state practice,[14] the former is inherently unacceptable as stifling an inalienable right of the sovereign state. The Draft Charter also adopted the vital principle of non-reciprocity in economic relations between the industrial Powers and developing countries. This principle has already been promoted by UNCTAD and accepted by the Contracting Parties to GATT (Part IV). It means that exceptions would be made from most-favoured-nation treatment in favour of developing countries. It will be seen from the above observations that the Charter, if adopted in one or another form,[15] would give expression to the revisionist policy of the New States in the economic field and in related sectors of international law which require transformation.[16]

[14] See J. Fawcett in *British Yearbook of International Law* 1950, p. 355.

[15] The acceptance of the Charter is now being considered by the UNCTAD Conference which started in Mexico in June 1974.

[16] The question whether the New States are bound to accept the General principles of Law (the third main source of international law) has not been discussed above. Sir Hersch Lauterpacht's weighty dictum that the General Principles 'sound the death knell of positivism' may be recalled. International lawyers in the New States can hardly be enthusiastic about the type of positivism which was running on parallel lines with colonialism in the nineteenth century. Moreover, the influence of certain fundamental principles of Hindu and Islamic law on the General Principles of Law at present may be considered. They played also a significant role in the past when many Afro–Asian countries maintained diplomatic relations with European Powers and made treaties with them. These countries contributed no doubt to the secularisation of the law of nations prior to the nineteenth century and to the strengthening of certain General Principles, to mention only the principle *pacta sunt servanda*. They can confidently defy the Eurocentric classification of nations into those which made history and those which lack history (Anand, *op. cit.*).

29

THE CHARTER OF ECONOMIC RIGHTS AND DUTIES OF STATES (1975)

The Charter of Economic Rights and Duties of States which has recently been adopted by the General Assembly of the United Nations is a triumph of numbers over weight. First initiated by the United Nations Conference on Trade and Development (UNCTAD), an organ of the General Assembly, the draft charter was the object of prolonged wrangling and bargaining between the great number of developing countries with limited economic power and the few powerful industrial countries, until a compromise solution, full of generalisations, was reached. But generalisations apart, there are in the Charter a few detailed provisions which are of great interest to international lawyers and economists. In fact the Charter constitutes a hidden turning point in the history of international law which marks the progress of the family of nations from a homogeneous society of States, as it still was at the San Francisco Conference of 1945, to a highly heterogeneous society which requires certain adjustments in the rules of international law. The heterogeneity of the new society found for the first time its precise institutional expression in the creation and structure of UNCTAD which is composed of three groups: the advanced industrial powers, the socialist countries and the developing countries whose numbers overshadow the forum of UNCTAD. Originally called the group of the 77, they now number more than 100. The economic heterogeneity is at the same time a political and a legal one, for the group of the 77 is mainly composed of the so-called New States while the others are the original member States of the family of nations.

The formal adoption of the Charter took place on December 12, 1974, not in the form of a multilateral treaty creating rights and obligations of States, but as a unilaterally issued code of behaviour which is in the nature of a General Assembly recommendation. It consists of a preamble and four chapters, the most important of which is Chapter I relating to the fundamentals of international economic relations, and Chapter II on the detailed economic rights and duties of States. The first contains general principles such as the sovereignty and equality of States and other principles the adoption of which presented few difficulties to the members of UNCTAD. On the other hand the provisions of Chapter II, particularly article 2, were the subject of hard bargaining in which the negotiating States had to face some of the most controversial problems of international law in the economic field. The outcome of the bargaining marked the eclipse of certain principles of international law which had been precariously evolved in the past but are no longer reconcilable with the reality of present day world economy and politics. The first casualty in the process of bargaining was the principle of minimum standards of international law which can be summed up in the following way: A State may treat its own citizens by the municipal (national) standards of its own making but there is a limit to the treatment of foreigners who are under the protection of international law. Thus, if for instance, a State (usually a developing State) expropriates the property of foreigners and does not pay just, or at least adequate compensation, the national State of the foreign investor (usually an industrial State) can take up the latter's case at the international level and take the State of residence of the foreigner to an international forum. In other words it was understood that the treatment of the foreigner must not fall below minimum standards of international law, down to the level of lower standards of municipal law. The conflict is one between the jurisdiction of the territorial State in which foreigners make investments and the State which exercises personal jurisdiction over its citizen-investors. The former will invariably insist on having disputes relating to investment settled in its own legal fora according to its own municipal law. On the other hand the latter will insist that there is a point (after the exhaustion of local remedies in the territorial State) at which a dispute over the treatment of the foreigner, for instance, for payment of compensation, must be dealt with on the inter-State level according to principles of international law.

The records of the proceedings of the Drafting Group of the Charter show the intensity of this legal–ideological split. What is the compromise ultimately reached? Article 2 of Chapter II states that each State has a right to deal with foreign investment within its national jurisdiction according to its own municipal law and it 'shall not be compelled to grant preferential treatment to foreign investment'. Thus the principle of traditional international law relating to minimum standards goes overboard. The territorial State has of course the right to nationalise or expropriate foreign property and it must according to the Charter pay *appropriate* compensation (whatever that may mean), but controversies over such compensation shall be settled in the courts of the expropriating State under its law. All that Article 2 concedes is that the States, parties to an issue, can agree on another mode of settlement and this could include the application of international law under international jurisdiction. In this way the only concession to the requirements of traditional international law is subject to the agreement of the expropriating State. Similarly the activities of trans-national corporations are subject to the principles of the relevant territorial municipal law.

The records of the final proceedings for the adoption of the Charter show that 120 States were determined to discard certain principles of the old international customary law prevailing in this field. They voted for the adoption of the Charter in its present form with six votes against and with 10 abstentions. The group of 16 comprised the industrial powers including all the E.E.C. countries, and the U.S.A. In voting against the adoption of the Charter the present Government of the U.K. saw eye to eye with its predecessor on this historical document.

The process of discarding certain principles of international law which the old homogeneous family of nations tried to preserve has set in. The pressure of legal change is bound to come from the new (developing) States which have come into existence only since World War II and which did not actively participate in international law making in the 19th century or later. The economic and political weight of the industrial powers (the old States) will be under the pressure of numbers. International law is the outcome of the consent of States as expressed in treaties or in State practice (international customary law). Since all member States of the United Nations are legally equal no traditional principle of international customary law can be ultimately forced on the new States without their consent. They are in an overwhelming majority, enjoying the support of the Socialist countries and the industrial powers are bound to face the reality of legal change. How this will affect the prospects of international investment is an open question, but UNCTAD research has shown that international investment and aid received by the developing countries has done little to narrow down the ever widening economic gap between them and the industrial powers.

Bibliography of the Writings of C. H. Alexandrowicz

[*included in this volume]

1927

Karol Aleksandrowicz, *Konsens małżeński w nowym kodeksie prawa kanonicznego i w dawnem prawie kanonicznem* (Włocławek, 1927).

Karol Aleksandrowicz, 'Błąd, przymus i bojaźń przy zawieraniu małżeństw według nowego i dawnego prawa kościelnego', *Ateneum Kapłańskie*, 19 (1927), 468–81.

1931

Karol Aleksandrowicz, *Zezwolenie na małżeństwo w prawie kanonicznem i w prawie polskiem* (Włocławek, 1931).[1]

1931–32

Karol Aleksandrowicz (ed.), *Żywe Słowo Księdza Oraczewskiego: tygodniowe pytania i odpowiedzi o sprawach bieżącego życia* (Warsaw, 1931–32).

1933

Carolus Alexandrowicz, *De primis vinculi matrimonii in judicio episcoporum cracoviensium defensoribus (saec. XVIII)* (Rome, 1933).

1934

Karol Aleksandrowicz, *Brachium saeculare według obecnie obowiązujących i dawniejszych konkordatów* (Kraków, 1934).

Karol Aleksandrowicz, *Małżeństwa domniemane w prawie kanonicznym* (Kraków, 1934).

1943

Karol Aleksandrowicz, *Prawo małżeńskie* (London, 1943).

1944

Karol Aleksandrowicz, *Prawo osobowe, według kodeksu cywilnego b. Królestwa Polskiego (przy uwzględnieniu prawa cywilnego francuskiego)* (London, 1944).

1945

'Marriage Law in Poland: A Problem of Comparative Law', in *Studies in Polish and Comparative Law: A Symposium of Twelve Articles* (London, 1945), pp. 156–67.

This bibliography does not include Alexandrowicz's unsigned case-notes from the *International Law Reports* and elsewhere, his numerous book reviews, or posthumous reprintings of his work.

[1] Rptd. from *Ateneum Kapłańskie*, 27 (1931), 434–51.

1947

'The Economic Recovery of Poland', *World Affairs*, 1 (1947), 163–70.

1948

'The European Economic Institutions', *The Year Book of World Affairs*, 2 (1948), 162–96.
'The Havana Charter', *World Affairs*, 2 (1948), 398–409.

1949

'The Economic Commission for Europe', *World Affairs*, 3 (1949), 43–54.

1950

'Comecon: The Soviet Retort to the Marshall Plan', *World Affairs*, 4 (1950), 35–47.
'The Study of International Economics', *The Year Book of World Affairs*, 4 (1950), 213–33.

1951

*'Israel *in Fieri*', *International Law Quarterly*, 4 (1951), 423–30.
'International Trade and Tariffs at Torquay', *World Affairs*, 5 (1951), 211–21.
'The Supreme Court of India as a Habeas Corpus Bench', *Journal of the Madras University. Section A. Humanities*, 22 (1951), 71–81.

1952–61

(ed.) *The Indian Year Book of International Affairs* (Madras, 1952–61).

1952

International Economic Organisations (London, 1952).
'American Influence in Indian Constitution Making', *Journal of the Madras University. Section A. Humanities*, 23 (1952), 78–87.
'Foreign Investment Laws and Regulations of the Countries of Asia and the Far East', *International and Comparative Law Quarterly*, 1 (1952), 29–39.
'Indian and General Investment Trust, Ltd. *v.* Sri Ramachandra Mardaraja Deo, Raja of Khalikote', *International and Comparative Law Quarterly*, 1 (1952), 565–68.
'International Law in India', *International and Comparative Law Quarterly*, 1 (1952), 289–300.
*'The Quasi-Judicial Function in Recognition of States and Governments', *American Journal of International Law*, 46 (1952), 631–40.
'Vertical and Horizontal Divisions of the International Society', *The Indian Year Book of International Affairs*, 1 (1952), 88–96.

1953

'Chinese Suzerainty over Tibet', *Journal of the Madras University. Section A. Humanities*, 24 (1953), 1–17.
'Common Law Prerogative Writs in India', *The Indian Year Book of International Affairs*, 2 (1953), 199–213.
'India and the Tibetan Tragedy', *Foreign Affairs*, 31, 3 (April 1953), 495–500.
'The Indian Constitution', *The Year Book of World Affairs*, 7 (1953), 258–82.

1954

'Delegation of Legislative Power in India', *American Journal of Comparative Law*, 3 (1954), 72–79.

*'Grotius and India', *The Indian Year Book of International Affairs*, 3 (1954), 357–67.

*'Is India a Federation?', *International and Comparative Law Quarterly*, 3 (1954), 393–403.

'The Indian Committee of Comparative Law', *International and Comparative Law Quarterly*, 3 (1954), 101–102.

'The Kashmir Deadlock', *Political Quarterly*, 25 (1954), 236–45.

*'The Legal Position of Tibet', *American Journal of International Law*, 48 (1954), 265–74.

1955

*'Mogul Sovereignty and the Law of Nations', *The Indian Year Book of International Affairs*, 4 (1955), 316–24.[2]

1956

'American Influence on Constitutional Interpretation in India', *American Journal of Comparative Law*, 5 (1956), 98–105.

'Le Cachemire: aspect juridique du conflit Indo-Pakistanais', *Österreichische Zeitschrift für Öffentliches Recht*, 7 (1956), 296–308.

'Comment on the "Legal Position of Tibet"', *The Indian Year Book of International Affairs*, 5 (1956), 172–74.

*'The Continuity of the Sovereign Status of China in International Law', *The Indian Year Book of International Affairs*, 5 (1956), 84–94.

'India's Himalayan Dependencies', *The Year Book of World Affairs*, 10 (1956), 128–43.

*' "Jus Gentium" and the Law of Nature in Asia', *The Aryan Path*, 27 (1956), 13–19.

1957

Constitutional Developments in India (Bombay, 1957).

'Department of International and Constitutional Law', *Journal of the Madras University. Section A. Humanities*, 28 (1957), 361–62.

*'The Discriminatory Clause in South Asian Treaties in the Seventeenth and Eighteenth Centuries', *The Indian Year Book of International Affairs*, 6 (1957), 126–42.[3]

'L'influence française sur la Constitution de l'Inde', *The Indian Year Book of International Affairs*, 6 (1957), 376–85.

1958

(ed.) *A Bibliography of Indian Law* (Madras, 1958).

'India Before and After Reorganisation', *The Year Book of World Affairs*, 12 (1958), 133–55.

*'A Persian–Dutch Treaty in the Seventeenth Century', *The Indian Year Book of International Affairs*, 7 (1958), 201–206.

*'The Theory of Recognition *in Fieri*', *British Year Book of International Law*, 34 (1958), 176–98.

'The Voting Procedure in the Security Council', *Justitia* (Hyderabad), 4 (1958), 21–25.

[2] Rptd. in *Studies in Law: An Anthology of Essays in Municipal and International Law. Patna Law College Golden Jubilee Commemoration Volume* (Bombay, 1961), pp. 115–26.

[3] Rptd. in Joginder Singh Bains, ed., *Studies in Political Science* (Bombay, 1961), pp. 91–109.

1959

'Föderalismus in Indien', *Schweizer Monatshefte*, 39 (1959), 754–64.
*'Freitas *Versus* Grotius', *British Year Book of International Law*, 35 (1959), 162–82.

1960

'The Secular State in India and in the United States', *Journal of the Indian Law Institute*, 2 (1960), 273–96.
'Treaty and Diplomatic Relations between European and South Asian Powers in the Seventeenth and Eighteenth Centuries', *Recueil des Cours*, 100 (1960), 203–320.

1961

*'Doctrinal Aspects of the Universality of the Law of Nations', *British Year Book of International Law*, 37 (1961), 506–15.
'Personal Liberty and Preventive Detention', *Journal of the Indian Law Institute*, 3 (1961), 445–58.
*'A Treatise by J. H. G. Justi on Asian Government', *The Indian Year Book of International Affairs*, 9–10 (1960–61), 136–42.

1962

World Economic Agencies: Law and Practice (London, 1962).
'The Contribution of the U.P.U., I.T.U. and I.L.O. to the Development of Principles of International Law', in *Volkenrechtelijke opstellen, aangeboden aan Professor Dr. Gesina H. J. van der Molen, gewoon hoogleraar in het volkenrecht en de leer der internationale betrekkingen aan de Vrije Universiteit, ter gelegenheid van haar zeventigste verjaardag door vrienden, collegae en oud-leerlingen* (Kampen, 1962), pp. 12–27.
'The Secretary-General of the United Nations', *International and Comparative Law Quarterly*, 11 (1962), 1109–30.[4]

1963

*'Paulus Vladimiri and the Development of the Doctrine of the Coexistence of Christian and Non-Christian Countries', *British Year Book of International Law*, 39 (1963), 441–48.
*'Some Problems in the History of the Law of Nations in Asia', *The Indian Year Book of International Affairs*, 12 (1963), 3–11.
'The Soviet Conception of International Law and the Doctrine of Positivism', Australian Society of Legal Philosophy (12 December 1963), in ASLP, [Proceedings and Papers] (Sydney, 1960–75), ASLP 18a.

1964

(ed.) *Studies in the History of the Law of Nations (Grotian Society Papers), The Indian Year Book of International Affairs*, 13, pt. II (1964).
*'G. F. de Martens on Asian Treaty Practice', *The Indian Year Book of International Affairs*, 13, pt. II (1964), 59–77.
*'Le Droit des Nations aux Indes Orientales: Aux XVIe, XVIIe, XVIIIe siècles', *Annales. Histoire, Sciences Sociales*, 19 (1964), 869–84, 1066–84.

[4] Rptd. in Richard A. Falk and Saul H. Mendlovitz, eds., *The Strategy of World Order*, 4 vols. (New York, 1966), III, pp. 304–25.

'International Law in the Municipal Sphere According to Australian Decisions', *International and Comparative Law Quarterly*, 13 (1964), 78–95.
'La liberté religieuse dans la Constitution de l'Inde', *Revue internationale de droit comparé*, 16 (1964), 319–30.

1965

'Australia and G.A.T.T.', in D. P. O'Connell, ed., *International Law in Australia* (London, 1965), pp. 87–114.

1966

'The Convention on Facilitation of International Maritime Traffic and International Technical Regulation (A Comparative Study)', *International and Comparative Law Quarterly*, 15 (1966), 621–60.
*'Kautilyan Principles and the Law of Nations', *British Year Book of International Law*, 41 (1965–66), 301–20.

1967

An Introduction to the History of the Law of Nations in the East Indies (16th, 17th and 18th Centuries) (Oxford, 1967).
'The Grotian Society', *American Journal of International Law*, 61 (1967), 1058.

1968

'The Afro-Asian World and the Law of Nations', *Recueil des Cours*, 123 (1968), 121–210.
'Introduction', in Gesina H. J. van der Molen, ed., *Alberico Gentili and the Development of International Law: His Life, Work and Times*, 2nd revised edn. (Leiden, 1968), pp. vii–ix.
'Legal Education', in Humayun Kabir, ed., *The Teaching of Social Sciences in India, 1947–67* (Delhi, 1968), pp. 191–200.

1969

'Colloquium on the History of the Law of Nations', *International and Comparative Law Quarterly*, 18 (1969), 482.
*'New and Original States: The Issue of Reversion to Sovereignty', *International Affairs*, 45 (1969), 465–80.
*'Puffendorf–Crull and the Afro–Asian World', *British Year Book of International Law*, 43 (1968–69), 205–208.

1970

(ed.) *Grotian Society Papers 1968: Studies in the History of the Law of Nations* (The Hague, 1970).
*'Le rôle des traités dans les relations entre les puissances européennes et les souverains africains (Aspects historiques)', *Revue internationale du droit comparé*, 22 (1970), 703–709.

1971

The Law of Global Communications (New York, 1971).
*'The Juridical Expression of the Sacred Trust of Civilization', *American Journal of International Law*, 65 (1971), 149–55.

1972

(ed.) *Grotian Society Papers 1972: Studies in the History of the Law of Nations* (The Hague, 1972).

1973

The European-African Confrontation: A Study in Treaty Making (Leiden, 1973).

The Law-Making Functions of the Specialised Agencies of the United Nations (Sydney, 1973).

'The Dichotomy in Control of Legal Education (Academic and Professional)', in S. K. Agrawala, ed., *Legal Education in India: Problems and Perspectives* (Bombay, 1973), pp. 48A–51.

1974

*'The New States and International Law', *Millennium*, 3 (1974), 226–33.

*'The Partition of Africa by Treaty', in Kenneth Ingham, ed., *Foreign Relations of African States: Proceedings of the Twentyfifth Symposium of the Colston Research Society Held in the University of Bristol, April 4th to 7th, 1973* (London, 1974), pp. 129–57.

'Les pays afro-asiatiques et le droit des nations: le problème du retour à la souveraineté', *Comptes rendus trimestriels des séances de l'Académie des sciences d'outre-mer*, 34 (1974), 629–37.

1975

*'The Charter of Economic Rights and Duties of States', *Millennium*, 4 (1975), 72–74.

*'Empirical and Doctrinal Positivism in International Law', *British Year Book of International Law*, 47 (1974–75), 286–89.

'Paralysis Symptoms of the Treaty of Rome of 1958', *Co-Existence*, 12 (1975), 13–19.

*'The Role of Treaties in the European-African Confrontation in the Nineteenth Century', in A. K. Mensah-Brown, ed., *African International Legal History* (New York, 1975), pp. 27–68, 191–99.

1980

*'The Role of German Treaty Making in the Partition of Africa', *The Indian Year Book of International Affairs*, 18, pt. II (1980), 161–203.

Index

The manufacturer's authorised representative in the EU for product safety is Oxford University Press España S.A. of El Parque Empresarial San Fernando de Henares, Avenida de Castilla, 2 - 28830 Madrid (www.oup.es/en or product.safety@oup.com). OUP España S.A. also acts as importer into Spain of products made by the manufacturer.
Printed and bound by CPI Group (UK) Ltd, Croydon, CR0 4YY
14/09/2026
02216284-0008